Emotional Development

Emotional Development:

Recent Research Advances

Edited by

Jacqueline Nadel
Directeur de recherche
UMR 7593 CNRS-Paris 6
Hôpital de la Salpêtrière
Paris, France
and

Darwin Muir
Professor Emeritus
Department of Psychology
Queen's University
Kingston, Ontario, Canada

OXFORD
UNIVERSITY PRESS

This book has been printed digitally and produced in a standard specification
in order to ensure its continuing availability

OXFORD
UNIVERSITY PRESS

Great Clarendon Street, Oxford OX2 6DP

Oxford University Press is a department of the University of Oxford.
It furthers the University's objective of excellence in research, scholarship,
and education by publishing worldwide in

Oxford New York

Auckland   Cape Town Dar es Salaam Hong Kong   Karachi
Kuala Lumpur Madrid Melbourne Mexico City   Nairobi
New Delhi Shanghai Taipei Toronto
With offices in
Argentina Austria Brazil Chile Czech Republic France Greece
Guatemala Hungary Italy Japan South Korea Poland Portugal
Singapore Switzerland Thailand Turkey Ukraine Vietnam

Oxford is a registered trade mark of Oxford University Press
in the UK and in certain other countries

Published in the United States
by Oxford University Press Inc., New York

ISBN 978-0-19-852884-5

Acknowledgements

We gratefully aknowledge the financial support for the symposium from the French Ministry of Research, Cognitique Program. The symposium took place in Paris, at the Hospital La Salpêtrière, in the famous Amphitheatre Charcot.

Contents

Contributors

Kim A. Bard
Centre for the Study of Emotion
Department of Psychology
University of Portsmouth
Portsmouth, UK

Philippe Brun
Université de Rouen
Laboratoire PSY.CO
Mont-Saint-Aignan, France

Lola Cañamero
Dept of Computer Science
University of Hertfordshire
Hatfield, UK

David Cohen
Service de Psychopathologie de l'Enfant
   et de l'Adolescent
Hôpital de la Salpêtrière
Paris, France

George Downing
Hôpital de la Salpêtrière
Paris, France

Stéphanie Dubal
CNRS UMR 7593
Hôpital de la Salpêtrière
Paris, France

Tiffany Field
Touch Research Institutes
Department of Pediatrics
University of Miami School of Medicine
Miami FL, USA

Martine Flament
University of Ottawa Institute of Mental
   Health Research
Royal Ottawa Hospital

Ottawa, Ontario
Canada

Philippe Gaussier
Neurocybernetics Team
CNRS UMR 8051
University of Cergy-Pontoise
Cergy-Pontoise, France

Christine Hains
Department of Psychology
Queen's University
Kingston, Ontario
Canada

Sylvia Hains
Department of Psychology
Queen's University
Kingston, Ontario
Canada

Roland Jouvent
CNRS UMR 7593
Hôpital de la Salpêtrière
Paris, France

Theano Kokkinaki
Department of Psychology
University of Crete
Rethymnon
Crete, Greece

Giannis Kugiumutzakis
Department of Philosophy and
   Social Studies
University of Crete
Rethymnon
Crete, Greece

Linda LaGasse
Infant Development Center
Women and Infants' Hospital
Providence RI, USA

Kang Lee
Dept of Psychology
Queen's University
Kingston, Ontario
Canada

Barry Lester
Infant Development Center
Women and Infants' Hospital
Providence RI, USA

Katherine A. Loveland
Center for Human Development
Research
University of Texas Medical School
Houston TX, USA

Maria Makrodimitraki
Department of Philosophy and
Social Studies
University of Crete
Rethymnon
Crete, Greece

Darwin Muir
Department of Psychology
Queen's University
Kingston, Ontario
Canada

Jacqueline Nadel
UMR 7593
CNRS-Paris 6
Hôpital de la Salpêtrière
Paris, France

Harriet Oster
McGhee Division

School of Continuing and
Professional Studies
New York University
New York NY, USA

Jaak Panksepp
J. P. Scott Center For Neuroscience,
Mind, and Behavior
Department of Psychology
Bowling Green State University
Bowling Green OH, USA
and Department of Psychology
Centre for the Study of Emotions
University of Portsmouth
Portsmouth, UK

Vasudevi Reddy
Centre for the Study of Emotion
Department of Psychology
University of Portsmouth
Portsmouth, UK

Amy Salisbury
Infant Development Center
Women and Infants' Hospital
Providence RI, USA

Benoist Schaal
CNRS UMR 5170
University of Bourgogne
Dijon, France

Marcia Smith-Pasqualini
Department of Psychology
Centre for Neuropsychology and
Cognitive Neuroscience
University of Kansas Medical Center
Kansas City KS, USA

Robert Soussignan
CNRS UMR 7593
Hôpital de la Salpêtrière
Paris, France

Hélène Tremblay
Université de Rouen
Laboratoire PSY.CO
Mont-Saint-Aignan, France

Colwyn Trevarthen
Department of Psychology
University of Edinburgh
Edinburgh, UK

Edward Tronick
Child Development Unit
Harvard Medical School
Boston MA, USA

Elena Vitalaki
Department of Philosophy and
    Social Studies
University of Crete
Rethymnon
Crete, Greece

Penelope Yanni
Infant Development Center
Women and Infants' Hospital
Providence RI, USA

Editors' Introduction

Jacqueline Nadel and Darwin Muir

Several books published by Oxford University Press already have documented the recent burst of interest in emotional processes. The unique contribution of the proposed volume is to present the latest *developmental* perspective on human emotions by specialists from such diverse areas including neuroscience, robotics, psychopathology, and prenatal development. These experts who use different methodologies and updated technology present a converging story about the development of emotional processes.

It took us 120 years to follow Darwin's seminal insight on the importance of emotion for evolution and development, and to alter the traditional view that: (1) emotions simply reflect underlying physiological states that needed to be controlled (held constant) in experimental work on cognition and social development; and (2) abnormal emotional regulation by individuals classified as 'emotionally disturbed' simply blocks cognitive and social development with devastating results. The primary lesson we learned from the Darwinian perspective that was revisited about 25 years ago is that the importance of emotion increases with the complexity of the species. Far from being an impediment, emotional processes play a key role in adaptation. Our ability to recognize and respond to the emotional signals of others shapes our attention and disposition; this ability allows us to choose, according to our hedonic preferences, between several solutions that are equally available. Our own emotional displays give others a look inside us. Once we develop that insight about how much information we offer when we express ourselves, we start to disguise our emotional signals in order to present the public view that we would like others to believe about what we feel (see Scherer *et al.*, 2001, OUP). Before mastering this key to our individuality, we begin life by sharing our emotional brain neurochemistry with our mother. According to whether or not this neurochemistry is optimal, we are more or less likely to experience stress with its cascade of effects on cognition, socialization, and metacognition. In this book, based on recent research advances in the study of emotions in typical and clinical populations, leading specialists in the field of emotional development discuss the factors that optimize emotional development, on one hand, and result in various psychopathologies, on the other.

General description of the contents for each section

In Section I, readers will receive an update on issues concerning neural bases and evolution of emotional development, and a review of the latest work on the ontogeny of emotional reactions. We include several chapters on the emotional reactions of fetuses and newborns. The emergence and refinement of emotional responses and personality characteristics during the first few years of life are discussed, with emphasis on both the perception of emotional signals and the emergence of Theory of Mind processing in human infancy. This section ends with chapters outlining the latest technical advances in computer technology related to the study of emotional development (e.g. interactions with virtual adults, building an emotional robot).

In Section II, comparative studies of typical and impaired emotional development are covered. Seven chapters will cover clinical applications in the study of infants and children with disorders of emotional regulation and affect, including maternal/childhood depression, autism, obsessive-compulsive disorders, and anhedonia. The effects of early emotional dysfunction on social and cognitive development will be discussed.

Finally, the options and data presented in the book are discussed and an overview is presented.

The challenge for each of our contributors was to write a chapter that provides the readers with a description of the most recent research and theory in their fields of expertise, plus a preview of where their field is heading. A unique aspect of this collection is the relatively equal space given to research on both average and clinical populations. Increasing scientific attention on the role of emotions in human development has led to major interdisciplinary advances. The intention is to appeal to a very broad audience of scientists who need to be informed about the latest advances in the study of emotional development.

Section I. Psychobiological approaches and evolutionary perspectives

A major feature of this section is the emphasis on an evolutionary perspective by many of the contributors, and a general agreement that emotional processes are central motivators designed to organize cognition and action.

Neural basis of emotions and evolutionary perspectives

Jaak Panksepp and Marcia Smith-Pasqualini point out that humans begin to navigate the complexities of the world, and to learn about the values and contingencies of the environment at birth. They review brain imaging studies and recent advances in understanding basic emotional systems of the mammalian brain, and implications for understanding the nature of affective feelings in humans.

A discussion of the evolutionary perspective is provided in the next two chapters. Kim Bard studies the reactions of newborn chimpanzees during their interactions with human adults. She has discovered that newborn chimpanzees respond emotionally in a similar manner to newborn humans. They express interest and joy (smiling) during positive engagements, and anger and fear when humans violate their 'social expectations'. Colwyn Trevarthen introduces the argument that emotions are proactive in the human mind. He suggests that the evolution of the social functions of emotions and of inter-subjective behaviours in infancy lead to cultural learning and language acquisition.

Ontogeny

The ontogeny of emotional development is complex and begins prior to birth. Amy Salisbury, Penelope Yanni, Linda Lagasse, and Barry Lester introduce this section by demonstrating, with ultrasound techniques, that fetuses react to emotional events. Furthermore, they suggest that the physiological and psychological state of fetuses experiencing persistent stress via their mothers may be modified when their mothers receive appropriate prenatal medication.

The basic question about the level of organization and differentiation of emotional systems early in life is considered in the next three chapters. Robert Soussignan and Benoît Schaal describe the early plasticity of emotional responses, showing, for instance, that immediately after birth, human newborns display various facial expressions to positive and negative stimuli that may be related to fetal exposure to these stimuli. Giannis Kugiumutzakis, Theano Kokkinaki, Maria Makrodimitraki, and Elena Vitalaki present evidence of strong emotional reactions during imitative inter-actions between newborns and adults. They emphasize the need for naturalistic studies of spontaneous imitation to comprehend the emotional components of imitation that until now have been largely neglected. This sub-section is concluded by Vasudevi Reddy who provides new evidence of early self-awareness and its influence on the development of emotions often thought to be secondary emotions, such as shyness. She reports that both shyness and showing off may be present as early as 2 months of age.

New technology

New technologies are covered in the last two chapters of this first section. Darwin Muir, Kang Lee, Christine Hains, and Sylvia Hains introduce two new software programmes for studying emotional development. They describe a free program on the Internet for frame-by-frame coding of videotapes of the emotional expressions of both infants and adults during face-to-face interactions. They also have produced a 'virtual adult' that is effective in engaging infants as young as 3 months of age in face-to-face interactions. Manipulations of the computer display demonstrate how sensitive young infants are to various perturbations in adult facial and vocal expressions.

Lola Cañamero and Philippe Gaussier introduce affective computing. They adopt a bottom-up approach in their attempt to build autonomous robotic systems, which are animal-like automata, called 'animats'. This work is of interest not only for robotics, but also for developmental psychology. Cañamero and Gaussier discuss the importance of emotional components to a system that faces several simultaneous problems. They conclude that emotions can be considered as a second-order controller, monitoring the system's activity, and providing interfaces between a robot and other agents in the environment.

Section II. Comparative approaches: typical and impaired emotional development

If emotions are organizers for development itself, as most of us claim, emotional impairments should have disastrous effects on social, as well as on cognitive development. Unfortunately, little is known to-date about mediating processes or processes that are specific to emotions. The field of developmental psychopathology offers a rich source of information concerning the effect of abnormal emotional development on perceptual, cognitive, and social epigenesis. Harriet Oster uses her Baby FACS system to show that infant facial expressions are universal biologically-based adaptations. Her coding system highlights the developmental differences in facial emotional expressions produced by infants with atypical facial morphology, compared with typical populations.

Although emotion regulation is critical in initiating, motivating and organizing adaptive behaviour, and preventing stress, researchers have just begun the work of describing the processes of emotion regulation in infancy and childhood. The study of maternal depression is one of the more promising bases for such descriptions. Tiffany Field shows that maternal depression has a negative effect on infant behaviour and physiology, even during the prenatal period. Field proposes that the negative effects result from both the prenatal exposure to an imbalanced physiological and hormonal environment and the postnatal exposure to an emotionally unavailable mother who is unable to provide the infant with adequate stimulation and arousal modulation. She thus highlights the importance of considering dyadic states.

Edward Tronick introduces his new model of infant–mother interaction—the 'Dyadic States of Consciousness' (DSC)—following, in part, from his Still-Face procedure. According to his DSC hypothesis, Tronick predicts that infants who interact with depressed parents will seek out sad states of consciousness if that is the only way they can achieve DSC. Tronick's focus on dyadic states has important theoretical and methodological implications and leads us to the argument for a two-body psychology, which emphasizes the importance of the use of an interactive context to study emotional development and regulation.

The use of a two-body psychology is shared by many of the contributors in Section I, and all the contributors in Section II. Within the two-body framework, Hélène Tremblay, Philippe Brun and Jacqueline Nadel describe the links between emotion and the evolving self-other system. They stress the importance of situated studies of emotion besides studies of emotion knowledge in children with typical and impaired development.

Katherine Loveland also emphasizes the importance of the context in the study of emotional regulation. Using a Gibsonian framework (ecological psychology), she presents an interactive view of the autistic spectrum disorder as a discordant relationship between a person and his/her environment throughout development. She argues that a model of brain dysfunction in autism must include not only those structures and systems that subserve social cognition and emotion recognition, but also those that subserve the regulation of behaviour in response to a changing social environment.

It has been proposed that some regulatory processes are aimed at establishing specific emotional states, whereas others have emotion-cognition and emotion-action links. Martine Flament and David Cohen address this issue by examining psychological, biochemical and neurological models of obsessive-compulsive disorders in children.

Another disease model that focuses on the link between positive emotions and cognition is anhedonia (the inability to experience pleasure). Stéphanie Dubal and Roland Jouvent review the literature on anhedonia and discuss their research, which demonstrates a relationship between anhedonia and attention deficits. Their work on emotional impairments in late adolescence illustrates the link between emotional development research and the work on the relationships between emotion and cognition in adults covered by many other OUP books.

In the final chapter, George Downing discusses novel targets, tools, ideas, research designs, and frameworks that emerged from the 16 chapters on typical and impaired emotional development.

Section I

Psychobiological approaches and evolutionary perspectives

Neural bases of emotions and evolutionary perspectives

Chapter 1

The search for the fundamental brain/mind sources of affective experience

Jaak Panksepp and Marcia Smith-Pasqualini

Introduction

Among the greatest mysteries of the mind is the fundamental nature of affective experiences—the various feelings that accompany the arousal of emotional processes. However, the remarkable fact that subjective experience does exist in a physiochemical world is no longer impenetrable. Modern neuroscience, in conjunction with human psychological and animal behavioural studies, affords new and substantive ways to untangle this 'world-knot'. Although the basic affective processes of the brain are not readily visible to the tools of science, they can be theoretically inferred from behavioural neuroscience studies in other animals and subsequently empirically evaluated in humans, as long as common neurological currencies can be specified for both types of studies. Here, we will develop the idea that such a currency can be found among the evolved neuroanatomies and neurochemistries of mammalian brains. Indeed, if we can first define the basic emotional tools with which all mammalian brains are endowed, we can then come to better appreciate how interacting emotional-cognitive complexities emerge along specific developmental landscapes, and lead to the emotional strengths and weaknesses that govern, to some extent, our children's psychological qualities (Panksepp, 2001).

We subscribe to the position that affective states, the many distinct ways we feel our lives, constitute organic 'centres of gravity' around which our more informationally-based cognitive apparatus revolves. When we are hungry, thirsty, or cold, our cognitions begin to focus obsessively on how such disturbing (i.e. negatively valenced) feelings can be alleviated. When we are angry with someone, our mind is filled with retributive thoughts. When we are scared or lonely, we think of ways to alleviate the angst. When nurturant feelings well up inside us, caring thoughts and actions seem to easily follow. When we feel joyous, loving, or lusty, our minds open up to new social possibilities. There are natural categories of affective processes, some related to anticipation of events in the world, some linked to sensing the world, some related to actions in the world, and some related to post-consummatory reactions. Here, we will focus largely on exemplars of the third category, which constitute the emotional affects.

Although some investigators suggest that there is no need to discriminate emotional from cognitive processes (Lane and Nadel, 2000), we see such distinctions as fundamental for making sense of many brain functions. This controversy may be fuelled primarily by semantic issues. We use the term *emotion* as the larger umbrella category that includes behavioural, autonomic, cognitive, and affective aspects. Emotional systems allow organisms to generate adaptive instinctual behaviours during various life-challenging situations. However, it is the valenced feeling aspect of emotions—the *affect*—that is often thought to be the defining feature of emotions. If affect were taken away, mental processes would no longer be emotional, except in formalistic academic ways.

Affect arises substantially from ancient neural systems that can be discriminated from recently emerged neocortico-cognitive functions, especially if we envision cognitive information to be largely about the perception and evaluation of factual information about the many 'differences' of the world. From the perspective that an enormous number of cognitive deliberations accompany affective experiences, however, the areas of the brain that elaborate cognitive/affective interactions are bound to be widespread, which may explain why so many higher brain areas are aroused in response to so many types of emotional stimuli and tasks (Phan *et al.*, 2002). We must also remember that brain imaging technologies are commonly insensitive to detecting changes in comparatively small, densely packed regions of the brainstem, especially if opponent processes are closely situated anatomically.

Affective states are not mere information-processing consequences of rapidly firing neuronal circuits, but large-scale brain–mind dynamics that typically operate by longer-term influences on the neuro-symbolic, virtual body representations within the brain that control and regulate the autonomic and somatic tone of the actual body. At present, there is a tendency for many to seek the nature of feelings in the projections of bodily information into the higher neocortical fields that mediate perceptual/cognitive consciousness (e.g. Damasio, 2003; LeDoux, 1996; Rolls, 1999), as opposed to the instinctual emotional action systems that are concentrated subcortically (Panksepp, 1998a). In our estimation, that type of sensory-centric focus creates more problems than it solves, at least for emotional feelings (Panksepp, 2000a, 2003a), albeit not as much for the sensory affects such as taste, which have also been used as a basis for theorizing about the nature of emotions (Rolls, 1999). Those views typically ignore an enormous amount of troublesome evidence, suggesting a sub-neocortical locus of control for emotional affects (e.g. Panksepp, 1998a). Although much of modern brain imaging in humans shows the importance of neocortical processes in many aspects of emotional information processing in the brain and can even highlight brain loci that may control human feelings such as sympathy (Decety and Chaminade, 2003), the likelihood that those higher systems are essential for affective feelings is getting more and more remote (Adolphs *et al.*, 2003; Damasio *et al.*, 2000; Panksepp, 2003a), and there is no credible evidence that the feelings could emerge without essential subcortical arousals (Damasio *et al.*, 2000).

As feeling states, affects are by definition conscious, even though other aspects of emotions often are not. In human studies that provide subliminally-presented stimuli and claim that the emotions elicited are unconscious, the key issue for us is whether the stimuli provoked any affective changes, regardless of whether other aspects of an emotional reaction occurred. Affects are also not the same as the ultra-short emotional reflexes and fixed-action patterns (e.g. startle) that many behaviourally- and cognitively-orientated researchers investigate in their studies of fear conditioning, and the perception of emotional stimuli. Such reflexes may well be unconscious, without a feeling tone, except perhaps during the period of arousal after the reflexive response has already subsided (LeDoux, 1996; Rolls, 1999). Yet few of these studies ever attempt to evaluate changes in affective tone (typically called 'mood'), which often fluctuates slowly, to a time that is more metabolic/biochemical, rather than synaptically projectile.

Even though the concept of affect commonly causes conceptual consternation for neuroscientists, it is a rather straightforward phenomenological concept, with complex neural underpinnings. Affect is the here and now feeling state that serves an adaptive role in keeping organisms in a certain kind of action readiness. For instance, when one is away from home, the desire to be home increases (presumably as a mild separation anxiety emerges), and the satisfaction one feels on returning is often intense. However, if one has been home for a while, the desire to explore and visit other places increases, perhaps as the felt satisfaction of being home diminishes. The problem is that scientists have difficulty envisioning how an insubstantial entity, such as affect, can have causal consequences on a substantial entity, i.e. the body. That dualistic dilemma is only a problem if one cannot fathom how basic psychological processes might be embodied aspects of brain dynamics. In our embodied view of mind, affective experiences are one property of complex brain systems in action. For a more resolved view of affect, we include a provisional definition, adapted from Panksepp (2004a), as an appendix to this chapter.

Until recently, the nature of our emotional feelings has remained resistant to anything but a superficial phenomenological analysis. Modern brain imaging has now given us abundant cerebral correlates that are almost impossible to dissect at a causal level, except perhaps through the use of modern psychopharmaceuticals and the occasional instances of deep-brain stimulation performed during neurosurgery (e.g. Bejjani et al., 1999). More recently, surface cortical stimulation of the intact human brain has been achieved with transcranial magnetic stimulation (TMS), which takes advantage of Faraday's law of induction (Pascual-Leone et al., 2000; Stewart et al., 2001; Schutter et al., 2004). These are all relatively coarse approaches that provide only estimates of the brain regions where the detailed properties of the underlying neural systems need to be revealed.

An evolutionary view of emotional feelings

An emerging evolutionary view, asserting that we share many basic emotional operating systems and resulting affective feeling states with other animals (Panksepp, 1998a,

2003c; Panksepp and Panksepp, 2000), has opened up the possibility that we may finally understand the sources of many of our own feelings by studying the relevant brain substrates in other mammals. If modern molecular biology has taught us anything of profound general significance, it is that we are really not that different from other animals in the biological realm, even in most brain matters. This is especially true below the neocortex, but not in our expansive cerebral mantle—wherein lies the essential neural repository for our unparalleled human capacity to think about the nature of our world and our existence in the living order. Of course, it does seem likely that other animals live in a limited 'time-window', where their psychological abilities are restricted to the very recent past, the present, and immediate future (Clayton *et al.*, 2003), but this does not disqualify them from experiencing a sophisticated here-and-now affective consciousness, which also facilitates their anticipation of future events. Despite the vast interpretive difficulties in linking mind to brain functions (Uttal, 2002), the project is doable, as long as we focus our empirical efforts first upon the problems that can be currently solved (Bechtel, 2002). We would argue that, while understanding the neural nature of the basic affects is possible, its solution requires an organic as opposed to an informational stance (Panksepp, 2003a).

We are great fans of Descartes' third rule of science, which basically says that to make scientific progress we must try to simplify complexity, only gradually aspiring for more and more detailed knowledge. As most mind scientists these days, we too are foes of his dualism, which hindered a substantive neuroscientific study of subjectivity throughout the past century. Now that an ever increasing number of scholars are willing to acknowledge that there is no insubstantial 'spirit stuff' aside from that arising from the neurobiological dynamics of the brain-mind interacting with the world, it is becoming ever clearer that, in order to understand the evolutionary underpinnings of the human mind, we must come to terms with the evolved nature of affective processes—ancient forms of consciousness, ranging from the experience of pain to playful joy, that we still share with many other animals (Panksepp, 1998a; Solms and Turnbull, 2002).

Such ancient, affective qualities of consciousness may be the foundation for more recent cognitive developments. If the core affects do have essential neuroanatomical (probably largely subcortical) and neurochemical (largely neuropeptidergic) codes, the cerebral sources of our feelings may, in fact, be much easier to understand than our thoughts, since many can be detailed in animal models. The higher, cognitive variants of consciousness, many of which are unique to the expansive human cortico-cognitive apparatus, probably have no distinct neurochemical codes, and their neuroanatomies may be more variable because they are manifested through many plastic and relatively homogeneous, 'random access' information based memory fields of the neocortex (Clayton *et al.*, 2003).

The critical role of epigenetic emergence in cognitive functions is much greater than in affective ones. Just consider the fact that young children who lose the use of their left-hemisphere language areas have little difficulty in using the other side of their brains to establish communicative competence. Likewise, as one loses use of one's sensory system (e.g. even by temporary blinding), other sensory systems begin to utilize the now unused cortical space for their own ends. It will be most interesting to see if any comparable re-representation occurs in the core emotional systems concentrated in sub-cortical regions of the brain, but we suspect that such effects would be much smaller. On the other hand, use-dependent plasticity, whereby emotional systems get stronger or weaker in both neuroanatomical and neurochemical terms, is likely, as will be highlighted later.

The genetically ingrained emotional systems of the mammalian brain are an excellent place to begin to decipher the neural nature of affective consciousness. At present, the systems have been identified largely through studies that successfully evoked emotional behaviours with localized electrical stimulation of subcortical circuits of the brain. Those behavioural effects are remarkably similar across species, including humans (Heath, 1996; Panksepp, 1985), and all behavioural indicators (e.g. learned approach and avoidance) suggest that coherently orchestrated emotional behavioural and physiological arousals are accompanied by internally experienced affective states. We assume these primitive psychological states are direct aspects of the material dynamics of certain ancient organic systems of the mammalian brain and they are there to encode survival values in a way that can interface with the flexibility provided by learning. In short, there are basic emotional systems in the brain and their activities are essential for the experience of emotional affects (a general neurally-based definition of an emotional operating system is provided in Fig. 1.1).

Since these emotional operating systems (and brain trigger-spots) are surely only part, albeit an essential part, of cerebral emotional processing, we have here designated them in capitalized vernacular terms, a convention introduced by Panksepp (1998a). These include systems for:

- generalized investigative, approach, reward-SEEKING;
- FEAR;
- RAGE;
- male and female LUST;
- maternal CARE;
- separation anxiety or PANIC;
- rough-and-tumble PLAY.

The details concerning these systems have recently been summarized comprehensively (Panksepp, 1998a) and synoptically (Panksepp, 2000b). There are surely many other affective systems (e.g. the pleasures and displeasures of sensation—see Appendix), but the seven systems listed are the only ones we can presently defend as being neurobiologically innate *emotional* circuits and a categorization of major

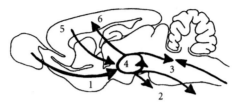

Fig. 1.1 This schematic summarizes the various neural interactions that are characteristics of all core emotional systems of the brain: (1) various sensory stimuli can unconditionally access emotional systems; (2) emotional systems can generate instinctual motor outputs, as well as (3) modulate sensory inputs. (4) Emotional systems have positive feed-back components, which can sustain emotional arousal after precipitating events have passed; (5) these systems can be modulated by cognitive inputs and (6) modify and channel cognitive activities. Also the important criterion that emotional systems create affective states is not included, but it is assumed that arousal of whole trajectory of the distinct executive circuits for each of the basic emotion is essential for getting emotional feelings elaborated within the brain, perhaps by interacting with other brain circuits for self-representation as appear to exist in the central regions of the midbrain, such as the Periaqueductal Gray, that interact with frontal cortical systems that regulate emotional output. [Reprinted from fig. 3.3 of *Affective Neuroscience* (Panksepp, 1998a) with permission of Oxford University Press.]

and minor psychiatric disorder can easily be overlaid on this scheme (see Table. 1). Perhaps social DOMINANCE will soon emerge as another system, but for now one can envision dominance emerging epigenetically from other systems, including FEAR and RAGE, and especially those that mediate rough-and-tumble PLAY earlier in development. We can also envision how many socially-constructed feelings might be created from basic affective processes interacting with sophisticated information-processing tissues such as the human neo-cortex. The simplest premise, and a reasonable working hypothesis, is that all of these derivative affective states also operate through the auspices of such instinctual action programmes of the brain.

Many of the other social sentiments that we humans experience, from jealousy to shame, from pride to arrogance, presumably arise developmentally through social learning—reflecting, we believe, the many ways that various basic emotional systems blend with each other and interact with cognitive life structures. Although such a blending view is neither a generally accepted nor a popular perspective, no better solution has yet been advanced. One alternative is that there are unique affect-related epistemological engravings in neocortical expansions of our species, as some module-entranced evolutionary psychologists assume. This solution is certainly possible, but it requires a grand assumption with no solid psychobiological grounding (Panksepp and Panksepp, 2000; Panksepp *et al.*, 2002c).

To really understand feelings, we need to develop a deeper respect for the subtlety and power of organic processes in the generation of mind. Now that we know that many genetic transcriptions can be environmentally influenced, the old nature-nurture debate has become a less relevant and contentious battleground, and the willingness to

Table 1.1 Postulated relationships between basic emotional systems, common emotional processes, and major psychiatric disorders. The last two columns provide hypotheses of the major relationships. Obviously, multiple emotional influences contribute to each of the emergent emotions (e.g. jealousy is also tinged by separation distress and anger) and all the emotional disorders have multiple determinants. Plus and minus signs after each indicate major types of affective valence that each system can presumably generate (adapted from Panksepp, 2000c)

Basic emotional system (Panksepp, 1982, 1998a, 2000b)	Emergent emotions	Related emotional disorders
SEEKING (+ and −)	Interest Frustration Craving	Obsessive-compulsive Paranoid schizophrenia Addictive personalities
RAGE (− and +)	Anger Irritability Contempt and hatred	Aggression Psychopathic tendencies Personality disorders
FEAR (−)	Simple anxiety Worry Psychic trauma	Generalized anxiety disorders Phobias PTSD variants
PANIC (−)	Separation distress Sadness Guilt/shame Shyness Embarrassment	Panic attacks Pathological grief Depression Agoraphobia Social phobias, autism
PLAY (+)	Joy and glee Happy playfulness	Mania ADHD
LUST (+ and −)	Erotic feelings Jealousy	Fetishes Sexual addictions
CARE (+)	Nurturance Love Attraction	Dependency disorders Autistic aloofness Attachment disorders
The **SELF**—a substrate for core consciousness and the generation of emotional feelings. (see Panksepp, 1998b)		Multiple personality disorders?

Capitalizations are used to designate the various emotional systems to highlight the fact that these are instantiated as distinct neural entities, rather than simply psychological concepts. The essential neural components constitute command influences that coordinate the basic behavioural, physiological and psychological aspects of each emotional response.

pursue research programmes along conjoint lines has dramatically increased (Meaney, 2001). At our present intellectual juncture, few would deny that nature and nurture are completely interpenetrant. Since the basic genetically ingrained emotional systems were designed to respond to life challenges, neuroscientists should not ignore the epigenetic brain-mind complexities that emerge when creatures encounter real world challenges. The plasticity of all brain systems is remarkable and the emotional state-control systems are no exception to that rule (for review, see Panksepp, 2001). Equally importantly, we should not deny a substantive evolutionary role for our underlying animalian nature, even though it can be refined, repressed, or distorted through many cognitive and cultural developments.

We humans do possess the rudiments of a nature (i.e. archetypal evolutionary 'memories') that few evolutionary psychologists or humanists have yet acknowledged. Evolution has provided neuronal frameworks for various ancestral affective/emotional urges and competencies that constitute some of the basic mental tools we need for existence. These systems need to be understood neuroscientifically in order to clarify the ground of our being, which is so important to conceptualize clearly in developmental and psychotherapeutic contexts. This emotional ground of being constitutes the foundation of our capacity for subjective affective experiences and allows us to elaborate our lives effectively through learning. We must come to terms with such ancient 'gifts' to understand how lives flower or get stunted through iterative experiences in the world. Thus, our basic premise is that the common denominator for healthy emotional development and for all successful psychiatric therapies (both biologic and interpersonal) is facilitation of affect regulation.

What emerges most during development is the higher capacity to regulate emotional states and to construct more complex behavioural strategies to cope with emotionally challenging events. Every emotion, if it remains unexpressed, has the potential to go underground and persist as an unresolved tension that can become an undesired force within the nervous system—a persistent feeling tendency in subjective experience. Although cognitive repressions can reduce and distort the felt intensity of emotions, it is within the education of our animal emotions that the greatest happiness might be achieved. We assume that a rich emotional intelligence will emerge more readily if infants and children are allowed to express their feelings fairly freely, and if feelings are more explicitly recognized and respected in the mental economy of their lives.

If we are ever really going to understand affect as a key psycho-neural process and characterize the fundamental role of affect in emotional development, we need credible epistemological strategies. We are pretty much in the same position as molecular biologists several decades ago—they could not have made the dramatic progress of the past three decades without first investing in relevant model systems (e.g. fruit flies and bacteria) that allowed them to develop the essential tools and concepts to move to the human level (Brookes, 2001; Panksepp et al., 2002c). Basic neuroscientists are often depicted as mere 'rat-runners', but many of us do the animal work because we are convinced that deep evolutionary points of view must under-gird even our more subtle socio-psychological inquiries (Panksepp and Panksepp, 2000).

Accordingly, one aim of affective neuroscience is to study basic affective processes in as many species as possible, in order to identify the most universal principles. Laboratory rats are excellent model species to work out certain issues (e.g. the fundamental nature of play), but for others they are not (e.g. laboratory rats are vestigial when it comes to separation distress). When Panksepp's laboratory initiated work on separation-distress systems of the brain, the initial species studied were dogs, guinea-pigs, birds, cats, and humans, but rats were neglected because they are not an optimal species for such studies (Panksepp, 1998a). Unfortunately, that lesson has barely been heard by neo-neuro-behaviourists, who continue to find great flaws with such animal emotion research (e.g. Blumberg and Sokoloff, 2001, with rebuttal: Panksepp, 2003b).

Indeed, ontological disagreements concerning the fundamental nature of mental life remain prominent on the intellectual landscape, not only in the humanities and social sciences, but also the neuro- and mind-sciences. Those of us who believe basic affective values lie at the foundation of brain/mind evolution remain in the minority, while those who would view animate life 'below' the human level as being essentially zombie-like and, hence, with no experiential value structures, continue to prevail. We might remember that only a few hundred years ago, many in America believed that their black slaves did not have human feelings. We should also recall that the radically mechanistic behaviourists did not professionally 'die' *en masse* following the success of the 'cognitive revolution'. Rather, a great number entered neuroscience a quarter of a century ago, which, being radically positivistic at the epistemological level, but fairly open to diverse ontological views, was a reasonably welcome home for behavioral viewpoints that had little tolerance for mental constructs.

The economics of neuroscience thus remains wedded to the assumption that the biologies of brain mechanisms are as intrinsically valueless as the external and objective physical world. For instance, most amygadalo-centric fear researchers remain stubbornly unwilling to discuss the potential affective experiences of the animals they study in remarkably stressful situations. They claim that the agnostic view is the only scientifically credible option, which reduces the willingness of new generations of investigators to tackle the affective psychobiological underbelly of human nature. This also effectively serves to encourage an ever-increasing rift between the humanities and brain sciences, and perhaps various forms of social intolerance around the world.

The 'affective neuroscience' approach

An alternative to the 'zombie' view is the 'affective neuroscience' approach (Panksepp, 1982, 1998a), which is premised on the ontological position that affective/emotional processes—emotional values—were built into brain evolution a very long time ago, and that we will not understand the sources of animal behaviour nor the sources of human emotional feelings until we fathom how affect emerges from brain processes (Panksepp, 2000a,b, 2003a). A further assumption of this view is that our more recent human cognitive abilities (which may, in fact, elaborate less intrinsic affective-value stuff), remain securely tethered to our neuro-affective ground of being even though the tethering is comparatively loose when no strong emotions or motivations prevail in the mental apparatus. Indeed, when the cortico-cognitive apparatus is disconnected from affective systems, as with frontal lobe damage, human decision-making abilities become severely compromised (Damasio, 1996). Presumably, this is because cognitive ideas that are dissociated from emotional feelings are relatively impotent. It might ironically be noted that recent evidence indicates that humans with selective amygdala damage appear to exhibit little measurable change in their day-to-day affective experiences (Anderson and Phelps, 2002).

Because of evidence like this, together with the abundant evidence for subcortical emotional systems in animals, we advocate the position that affective consciousness was originally an ancient subcortical function of the brain (Panksepp, 2003a). Investigators who have sought to image internal affective states with the most appropriate technologies (e.g. PET as opposed to fMRI scans) have found anatomies that dramatically corroborate the lessons learned from the animal work (Damasio *et al.*, 2000). In suggesting a sub-neocortical role for emotional affects, we do not deny that many paleocortical limbic areas (e.g. insula, claustrum, anterior cingulate cortex) are important for elaborating human emotions and that other affects, such as taste qualities, may have orbitofrontal, neocortical representations (e.g. Rolls, 1999), but we do suggest that our understanding of the neurochemical specificities for emotional processes will be advanced most by studying the subcortical emotional command systems (Panksepp and Harro, 2004). When *all* the evidence is considered, it becomes clear that the essential locus of control for the generation of affective feelings first emerged in subcortical regions of the brain and expanded into limbic areas, such as insula, anterior cingulate, and orbitomedial frontal cortical areas.

Panksepp's (1982, 1998a) scientific inquiry into the foundations of human emotions has been largely devoted to discovering the common affective themes that permeate human and animal lives. To illustrate this approach, we will briefly highlight two lines of clinically-relevant research into the nature of grief and sadness (i.e. separation distress systems) and social joy (play and laughter systems).

For instance, consider the case of a newborn baby chicken. If left alone, it cries pitifully for hours. However, if held gently in human hands, it shows a wonderful comfort response (Fig. 1.2). It rapidly closes its eyes, lowers its head and falls asleep. Part of this comfort response is mediated by endogenous opioids released in the brain (Panksepp, Bean, Bishop, Vilberg, and Sahley, 1980a), an idea that was based on the discovery in the mid-1970s that endogenous opioids were among the most powerful ways to alleviate separation distress in a variety of species (Panksepp *et al.*, 1980b). Across the years, only the oxytocin family of molecules has superceded the power of opioids to inhibit behavioural measures of separation anxiety in animal models. However, not only are little birds' behaviours comforted by social contact, but we are willing to assume that such baby birds are probably also experiencing a positive affect, most certainly the alleviation of distress. These positive affective states, mediated by opioids and oxytocin among many other neurochemistries, are crucial for social bonding to emerge, and disorders of social bonding (such as autistic symptoms) may occur

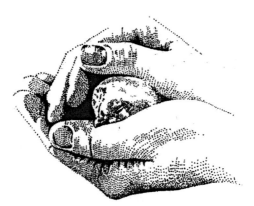

Fig. 1.2 When held gently in human hands, newborn chicks exhibit a comfort response consisting of the cessation of vocalizations and eye closure. These effects are attenuated by the opiate receptor blocking agent naloxone, indicating internal opioids help mediate the comfort response. [Reprinted from fig. 14.9 of *Affective Neuroscience* (Panksepp, 1998a) with permission of Oxford University Press.]

when these neurochemistries are excessive or deficient (Panksepp *et al.*, 1991; Nelson and Panksepp, 1998).

We may never understand such subjective aspects of mind in any absolute sense (no suitable 'mind-scope' may ever be developed to monitor subjective experience directly), but our ontological/theoretical position promptly leads to new predictions at the human level: opioid stimulants should alleviate human grief, while opiate antagonists should exacerbate such feelings. With regard to their endogenous systems, people with exquisite social sensitivity may exhibit abundant opioid release to socially positive interactions, while those who are less socially inclined may exhibit little release. Similar predictions can now be made for many other neuropeptide systems that have been revealed in the brain (Panksepp and Harro, 2004). In other words, the scientific results culled from animal models can be evaluated in human causal studies, as long as testable manipulations, such as pharmacological/neurochemical ones, are available to evaluate new predictions about human emotional feeling states (Panksepp, 1998a, 1999, 2000a,b). In this way, theoretical schemes concerning the nature of affects developed through animal affective neuroscience can be evaluated (and potentially disconfirmed) by appropriately designed human studies that carefully monitor subjective experiences and behavioural changes in various situations.

Emotional systems and childhood disorders

Early childhood autism is a psychiatric disorder that has been linked to an empirical analysis of separation distress and social bonding processes (Panksepp and Sahley, 1987). Although this neurodevelopmental disorder has strong genetic components that lead to demonstrable changes in brain organization (e.g. cerebellar and limbic abnormalities), hope remains that neurochemical interventions can provide some symptomatic relief. Many of the symptoms of the autism triad, namely reduced socialization, deficient communicative intent and various compulsive behaviours can be simulated in animals by facilitating opioid neurotransmission (Panksepp and Sahley, 1987). This finding led to the hypothesis that some of the symptoms might be ameliorated with opiate receptor antagonists such as naltrexone. Although some benefits have been seen in about 40% of the children, especially if caretakers respond positively to social changes (Panksepp *et al.*, 1991), the magnitude of the effects is rarely spectacular. This medication only works optimally in the context of psycho-social supports, which highlights ways of thinking that are needed to develop new generations of emotion-specific neuropeptide modulatory agents. In certain high-functioning autistic children, the beneficial effects of low doses of naltrexone (~0.25 mg/kg) are sufficient to make family life more easy and pleasant. The one social behaviour that is promoted by low doses of opioids, namely rough-and-tumble play, is also the one social behaviour that can be indicative of an autistic spectrum disorder, if it is the only social activity a child seeks to engage in. Opiate antagonists consistently reduce this behavioural urge, and generally reduce troublesome over-activity and sometimes self-destructive urges as well.

Let us now consider the case of social joy. Panksepp *et al.* (1984), initiated the study of how playful urges arise in the nervous system. Again, the brain areas that seem to be decisive for generating this psychobiological urge are subcortically situated (Panksepp *et al.*, 1994; Gordon *et al.*, 2002). Since one category of drugs that is especially effective in reducing playfulness is the class of psychostimulants that are routinely prescribed for children diagnosed with Attention Deficit Hyperactivity Disorder (ADHD), it seemed obvious to consider the possibility that many ADHD symptoms actually reflected playfulness and that the medicines may be so effective in part because they reduce such behaviours in classroom settings. This idea also forces us to consider what types of beneficial effects for brain development might be advanced by allowing abundant *natural* play during childhood and whether administration of play-reducing psychostimulants might reduce such benefits (Panksepp, 1998b). Although there is considerable animal data to warrant further consideration of such ideas (Panksepp, Burgdorf, Gordon, and Turner, 2002a, 2003), it is also possible that psychostimulants may actually produce long-term benefits for certain aspects of brain development (Castellanos and Tannock, 2002). However, we simply do not know, and recent neurochemical data suggesting that psychostimulants given to young rats can permanently stunt the development of brain dopamine systems (Moll *et al.*, 2001) should be of considerable concern, especially since such findings could suggest earlier onset of Parkinsonian symptoms in organisms with such brain deficits.

Hopefully, these examples help clarify why it is so important to take cross-species translations seriously. Most of the relevant neurobiological studies needed to decode the nature of affective processes simply cannot be done in humans. Using such lines of evidence from relevant animal models, however, we may be able to evaluate well-targeted neurochemical hypotheses in our own species. Some still believe that animal research will not be informative about human emotions, but evolutionary thinking strongly suggests they are wrong. Others have doubts whether it is ethically appropriate to pursue this kind of animal research, and if other animals do in fact have affective feelings, it is surely an ethical compromise that should encourage us to have the utmost respect for the animals we study. Some of us choose to make the compromises, for if we are ever going to have a science of affective experience that can inform human emotional development and the affective underpinnings of psychiatric disorders, we will need to study the shared neural foundations of human and animal nature. The neuroscience revolution has provided compelling reasons to believe that many general principles of affective life apply to all mammals (Panksepp, 1998a). Ever increasingly, this knowledge demands our sensitive attention to help assure that the life-values of other animals are not marginalized (as they are in concentration-camp type 'factory farms' that are ever more abundant on the agricultural scene, especially in the United States).

Unless we are willing to probe these emotional state-control systems in some detail, we will falter in our quest to understand what emotions and their affects really are. If, however, we learn to judiciously blend the neural knowledge that can be derived from animal models with our understanding of human feelings, then we can create a thriving intellectual enterprise that converges on issues of ultimate and shared concern. The most pressing issue is whether we can generate credible neuropsychological ideas of how affective states are actually created within the brain. In our estimation, a solution to this problem will have to seriously consider the deep organic nature of core emotional systems of the brain and the fundamental ways in which a primal sense of self becomes manifest through neuronal activities. A proposal advanced by Panksepp (1998a,b), complemented by ideas advanced by Damasio (1999), is that the very foundation of 'the self' is concentrated at the core of the brain—in those medial mesencephalic (midbrain) and diencephalic (thalamic and hypothalamic) tissues where a diversity of basic emotional and motivational circuits converge to generate an array of instinctual survival-promoting behaviours, as well as gut-level affective experiences (Panksepp, 1993; 1998a,b,c).

In this view, the core of primitive emotional bodily self-representation was first laid down in evolution within periaqueductal gray (PAG) of the midbrain. This essential substratum that permitted the emergence of many other mental activities in brain evolution (Holstege, Bandler, and Saper, 1996), may contain the organic competence to sustain a primordial form of immediate bodily awareness—the first glimmer of affective consciousness in mind/brain evolution. Glucose metabolic studies of human infant brain activities indicate that the first few weeks of life are accompanied by more relative arousal in such brainstem regions than other areas of the brain (Chugani, 1996). Although there is a massive complexity of neural systems in these regions of the brain (Holstege et al., 1996), one aspect of the function is to generate intrinsic bodily dynamics that are immediately recognizable as characteristic of instinctual emotional behaviours. When these core structures of the brain are damaged, the capacity for consciousness is severely compromised (Schiff and Plum, 2000; Watt and Pincus, 2003). These systems may be essential for boot-strapping the rest of the brain/mind into psychological growth-promoting interactions with the environment during development.

Certainly, this is the brain area where a great deal of instinctual bodily coherence is produced for many distinct emotional processes. This is where a small amount of brain damage is capable of compromising consciousness more than damage of this size anywhere else in the brain. This brain area also has some of the richest and most widespread connections with other areas of the brain. For semantic convenience and to highlight the potential importance of this primitive neural complex at the center of the midbrain, Panksepp designated it as the SELF—a Simple Ego-type Life Form—capitalized to highlight that it refers to a specific brain system)—a neuro-symbolic homunculus, grounded in action urges, from which a variety of core emotional 'states of being' could emerge. This brain system, built around emotional motor/action coordinates, is conceived to be *essential* for any concept of a foundational self, which in turn is essential for the organism to mature into a fully functioning organism. To the best of our knowledge, without the PAG, nothing resembling normal mental life is possible.

Within this view, it is highly unlikely that any 'brain in a vat' could ever sustain consciousness for long, for effective actions in the world—the capacity of many brain areas working cooperatively within environments that afford various actions—is probably essential for the maintenance of mental activity. Briefly, for the idea is more fully developed elsewhere (Panksepp, 1998a,c), we would emphasize that the PAG of the brain could not achieve much on its own. This brain system probably allows many other brain areas to develop affective potentials. We think that all animals, from men to mice, experience their lives in affective terms. We all base many of our life decisions on how world events and our actions within the world make us feel.

If this is a fundamentally correct view of how our brain/minds operate, then we have to come to terms with how central an understanding of affect is for knowing how minds develop and operate in the world. Affects help code the survival value of worldly objects and the survival consequences of acting in the world. In recognizing the intrinsic and important role of affect in the governance of human affairs, we can also come to better appreciate why many of our values are relatively invisible and non-materialistic, since they reflect certain ancient and often long-term neurodynamic potentials of the brain. These can only be indirectly monitored through the behaviouristic study of actions, including linguistic outputs. However, these values are projected onto worldly items and events in ways that allow our perceptions of material objects and living subjects to become valued or devalued, depending on our associated feelings.

In summary, an understanding of the neurobiological nature of affect has enormous consequences for how we understand and live our lives, from the impulsive emotional actions of individuals to the construction of our social institutions. We stand at the very beginning of substantive inquiries into how such brain systems help create the human spirit. For instance, only recently has brain imaging highlighted how certain ancient slowly acting touch systems of the human brain may mediate the positive effects of pleasant touch (e.g. cuddling) by arousing limbic cortical areas of the insula (Olausson *et al.*, 2002).

In the remainder of this chapter, we will briefly highlight two emerging and converging lines of research that promise to further our understanding of how affective systems develop: behavioural genetics and use-dependent plasticity.

Developments in behavioural genetics have proceeded in recent years at a phenomenal rate. Remarkable changes in behaviour have been reported in model systems, particularly the mouse, due to genetic manipulations. Because of the high genetic conservation within all mammalian species, the mouse provides a useful model system for identifying and describing inherited influences on emotional systems (Skuse, 2000). At present, there are literally hundreds if not thousands of 'designer mice' with intriguing behavioural changes, many of which are only beginning to be detailed.

Despite these considerable advances in genetic research, we have little understanding of how genetic variation leads to variation in brain structure or function in humans (Skuse, 2000). Furthermore, the use of genetic manipulation techniques to understand or control our own emotional heritage is severely limited by both practical and ethical constraints. Even with these limitations, however, we believe that these lines of inquiry will ultimately reveal significant new solutions to the affective puzzle.

We can look again to ADHD, for examples of how techniques of behavioural genetics might be exploited. One difficulty in studying the genetic basis of psychiatric disorders is the notorious unreliability of many diagnostic categories, including ADHD (Panksepp, 2004a). In fact, we would argue that the diagnosis of ADHD is largely a social construct, with limited data supporting its status as a coherent syndrome with a predictable course. An additional problem is that we know little about possible genotypic profiles that might underlie the expression of symptoms associated with ADHD (Peterson and Panksepp, 2004). We do know, however, that on average the brains of children with ADHD tend to show about a 5% reduction in the right frontal lobe (Castellanos *et al.*, 2002). We could use these measures of frontal lobe size to identify 'endophenotypes', those children whose right frontal lobes are more dramatically reduced (say 10% smaller than average), as probands for genetic analyses (Castellanos and Tannock, 2002). Alternatively, we could identify endophenotypes on the basis of behaviour. For example, impulsivity is considered to be one of the most prominent and consistent characteristics displayed by children diagnosed with ADHD (Peterson and Panksepp, 2004). Independent of diagnoses, therefore, we could choose as probands those children who score most highly on measures of impulsivity.

If we are to believe the data suggesting that many ADHD symptoms actually reflect playfulness in humans and other mammals, still more research strategies emerge. While studying the PLAY systems of the brain in rats, a vocal activity (50 kHz chirps) was discovered that seems to be especially abundant during social play, and we subsequently found that we could increase this vocalization dramatically by simply tickling the animals (Panksepp and Burgdorf, 1999, 2000). We now entertain the radical idea that this vocal activity, which seems to be an indicator of social joy, may be a type of primitive laughter. We have many reasons to believe that it could be used as a simple indicator variable to help decode the nature of one of the most affectively positive emotional responses of the mammalian brain (Knutson et al., 2002; Panksepp et al., 2002b). Since this response can be amplified within four generations of selective breeding (Panksepp et al., 2001), we hold out the possibility that we might be able to track down the genes that are critical for establishing such joy patterns within the nervous system (Panksepp et al., 2002c), genes that may be relevant for development of ADHD as well.

These issues relate to the broader scientific question of how we might best understand changes in emotional systems as a function of early emotional experiences. At this point, it is fairly certain that the psychological well-being of an adult is critically dependent on many childhood experiences that may go back as far as the peri-natal period. Research investigating how cognition-emotion interactions modify feelings, as well as thoughts is a growth area in human neuropsychology (a project that relies on the ability to decode experiences through the medium of language), as is exploration of the nature of use-dependent plasticity in the basic emotional systems in animal brains (a project that can only be effectively pursued in carefully selected animal models).

So, can we make organisms chronically angrier by excessive early thwarting? Can we make organisms more fearful by an abundance of early threats? Can we make them more curious, more loving, more sad with those respective experiences? Although the basic organizational structure of the mammalian brain is strongly constrained by genetic factors, there is an emerging recognition that the fine details, which can have profound long-term psychosocial consequences, are highly responsive to environmental influences (Merzenich et al., 1996). We, along with many other developmentalists, believe that certain positive early emotional experiences promote optimism, resilience, and mental health, while certain negative ones do the reverse (Atkinson and Zuker, 1997; Ryff and Singer, 1998). There is remarkably little evidence, however, about how the neural substrates and the psychobehavioural manifestations of specific emotional systems change as a function of developmental experiences, especially in humans. So far, the most compelling findings come from animal kindling studies, where the permeability of affective systems to incoming stimuli can be increased by electrically stimulating specific emotional circuits, as will be described in the next section.

Developmentally, the basic emotional systems may be like dynamic system attractors that get larger, more complex and more sophisticated as they pull various cognitive-informational structures into their spheres of influence. As a general principle, the larger the sphere of influence of the positive emotions, the more likely is the child to become a productive and happy member of society. The more he or she is influenced by negative emotions, the more the paths toward unhappiness are paved. There is every reason to believe that such systems are molded during early development by various life experiences. The number of growth factors and neuronal guidance molecules that have been found in the brain, most of which are probably responsive to environmental stimulation, is enormous (Finkbeiner, 1996; Strittmatter, 1995). The evidence for a key role for brain glutamate transmission in such dynamic plasticities is impressive (Constantine-Patton, 1998; Anwyl, 1999). Thus, the ability of early emotional experiences, perhaps even mild negative ones, to have important positive consequences on children's brains and lives, remains a tantalizing possibility. Unfortunately, the amount of incisive behavioural neuroscience work that has practical consequences for molding developmental processes remains modest, but some of the existing data provides important consideration for the ways the emotional systems of our children may be changed by early emotional experiences.

There are a large number of characteristics about emotion-cognition interactions to be considered from an affective neuroscience perspective. First, although many believe that there cannot be any emotional responses without preceding attributions, if one simply stays at that level of analysis one is faced by the dilemma that 'low energy' attributions can provoke 'high energy' emotional responses. How can this be achieved if the emotional urges and responses are not evolutionarily prepared states of the nervous system? Secondly, aroused emotions tend to have predictable psychological consequences, including shifts in attention, perceptual focusing and various cognitive encodings (e.g. state-dependent memories and thoughts). Finally, emotional systems can become chronically changed because of life experiences, because all of the underlying neural systems exhibit use-dependent plasticities. It is especially within an understanding of such long-term changes in emotional responsivity that some important clues to understanding the etiology of psychiatric disorders may lie.

Six of the core emotional systems revealed by affective neuroscience

Let us now briefly consider six of the core emotional systems revealed by affective neuroscience with respect to how the underlying substrates may be molded by emotional experiences, potentially yielding psychiatrically significant shifts in the vigor of the underlying emotional systems (e.g. Table 1.1). Most of the evidence comes from animal models, where mental contents are very difficult if not impossible to analyse scientifically, but we would suggest that when these types of brain changes occur in humans, there will be demonstrable changes in the flow of both cognitive and affective contents in the mental apparatus. A better understanding of these semi-permanent brain/mind changes may help us to design and promote better child-rearing practices.

FEAR

The study of the classical conditioning of fear (i.e. the development of unconscious trigger points to the FEAR circuitry), has been extensively studied (see Panksepp, 2004b, for recent overview). These trigger spots may help explain the development of specific phobias, but such classical conditioning models are not as important for understanding the chronic changes that can occur in FEAR systems to provoke chronic anxiety. For this, the kindling models are very useful, whereby one electrically stimulates the FEAR system briefly each day for about a week until an epileptogenic sensitization has emerged (Panksepp, 2004b). Once the FEAR system has been sensitized, animals exhibit a chronic facilitation of anxious tendencies (Adamec and Young, 2000). Although no one has found ways to reverse this type of sensitization once it has developed, a few neurochemical manipulations (e.g. choleocystokinin receptor antagonism), have been effective in providing prophylaxis for its emergence during traumatic episodes (Adamec and Young, 2000). If such manoeuvers were implemented in humans during traumatic experiences, perhaps the emergence of chronic anxieties such as those that characterize post-traumatic stress disorders (PTSD) could be aborted. In general, we would expect that these types of FEAR experiences can create excessively anxious children.

RAGE

For some perplexing reason, the study of the details of anger systems in the brain, and the analysis of how this system learns has diminished to a trickle during the past 30 years. However, we already do know much about the anatomy and neurochemistry of the systems (Panksepp, 1998a) and everyone realizes that one of the major environmental triggers of anger is frustrative non-reward. The cognitive consequences of anger are obsessive thoughts of retribution and revenge for perceived slights, offences, or other abuses of one's sense of freedom and dignity. Especially important for psychiatrically significant forms of irritability are the changes in aggressive temperament that can be achieved by stimulating the RAGE system in a manner similar to that just described for the FEAR system. Animals with kindling of such systems exhibit a very 'short fuse' and are likely to attack to minimal provocations/attributions. Presumably, repeated anger experiences can promote chronic states of irritability in children.

PANIC (separation distress)

During grief, the mind obsessively returns to mental images of the lost loved one and to ways the loss of the attachment bonds might have been averted. There has been little work on the use-dependent plasticity of this system, but it is bound to be as profound for subsequent temperamental tendencies as the changes in the other emotional systems. It is reasonably well established that early social loss has long-term consequences, which facilitate a depressive outlook on life (Panksepp, 2001), and social loss has long been considered to be a major factor that contributes to susceptibility to clinically significant depression (Panksepp et al., 2002).

CARE

Nurturant maternal urges—tender loving care, in the vernacular—can be sensitized by exposure of older animals to infants (Panksepp, 1998a). Rat mothers exhibit a distinct type of care, ano-genital licking, which has recently been shown to have life-long positive effects on the offspring. The positive effects include widespread benefits for the nervous system: the offspring are more inquisitive, courageous and less likely to be severely influenced by stress (Meaney, 2001). These benefits become permanent habits, the benefits of which are then passed on transgenerationally in non-genetic ways.

PLAY

The cognitive relationships with rough-and-tumble PLAY systems have been even less well mapped than with the other emotions, but it is likely that this type of emotional engagement helps solidify social habits that can promote a better understanding of what one can and cannot do in social situations. While captivated by playful energies, one's mind tends to go quite naturally to new associations that have the potential for sustaining and amplifying the fun. Perhaps these short-term changes can help widen behavioural options for organisms in many types of future emotional encounters. The possibility that play can have long term therapeutic effects for various childhood disorders, especially attention-hyperactivity problems, has already been addressed (Panksepp *et al.*, 2002a, 2003). Current evidence suggests that play may not only facilitate the programming of social circuits, but may also provide tonic effects on neuronal growth factors (Gordon *et al.*, 2003). These effects may, in turn, facilitate frontal lobe maturation, and thereby enhance executive psychological functions that promote more thoughtful engagements with the world and other lives (Panksepp, 2001).

SEEKING—wanting-expectancy

The pursuit of every resource requires the energization of this general purpose system for desires and appetitive engagements with the various fruits of the environment. A great deal of work has been conducted on how this system participates in learning, leading to a variety of terminologies that often detracts from communicative clarity. However, most viewpoints are converging on the idea that the system is essential for appetitive eagerness, regardless of the reward that is being pursued (Panksepp and Moskal, 2004). This system sensitizes when animals are periodically exposed to psychostimulants that activate it, such as amphetamines and cocaine (Kalivas and Nakamura, 1999; Robinson and Berridge, 2003) and sensitized animals then exhibit a general elevation of pursuit strength for a variety of incentives (Nocjar and Panksepp, 2002). It is to be expected that a psychostimulant-sensitized brain would tend to exhibit different types of thought patterns than 'normal', but at present, there is little psychoethological work on that issue.

The scientific analysis of how the 'mental apparatus' is modified by chronic changes in the arousability of brain emotional systems remains in its infancy. To do this properly, new psychological approaches such as 'psycho-ethology' need to be implemented that permit the analysis of fluctuating psychological contents of the mental apparatus under various conditions (Panksepp, 1999). In general, we tend to side with the view that a much greater amount of the overall interactive equation will be solved by focusing on how basic emotional arousals modify the cognitive apparatus than in the way cognitive attributions provoke emotions. In other words, once an emotional episode is triggered, the resulting ruminations take off in a self-organizing orbit that is substantially stronger, longer-lasting and more influential within the mental apparatus than the initial attributions that may have instigated the episode (see Parkinson, 1995, for a fuller development of this interactive cascade). As noted earlier, one general principle may be emerging from this work: negative emotions (e.g. FEAR, RAGE, PANIC) probably narrow decision-making, leading to an obsessive rumination on fairly narrow cognitive concerns. On the other hand, positive emotions (e.g. CARE, PLAY, SEEKING, and LUST) tend to broaden decision making processes, allowing one to recruit new ideas into an ever widening network of associations.

Some investigators believe that neuroscience data will eventually clarify how such negative and positive paths can be strengthened through early influences (Lopez *et al.*, 1999), but that will require a new era of integrative behavioural brain research. It remains a reasonable hope that devoted application of enlightened social interventions can help teach an increasing number of caretakers new and effective emotional skills and perspectives that can optimize infant development—consistent attitudes of warmth, nurturance, vigorous playfulness, along with a better recognition of how rhythmic-melodic interactions and positive growth challenges may allow brain systems to flourish (Malloch, 1999/2000; Beebe *et al.*, 2000). This approach should yield new insights on how we might promote mental health and vibrant lives by the way we rear our children from the earliest days onward.

To achieve this goal, we will need to translate basic science issues into forms that are digestible by the people who need such information as guides for better living, child rearing and education. One recent project in this realm is a guidebook for parental emotional education that is based on our current understanding of the basic emotional systems (Sunderland, 2005). The recognition that an understanding of our core emotional nature can have positive societal consequences will become more widely appreciated as we recognize that even though mind functions are critically dependent on brain functions, the mental apparatus is fully embodied—being closely connected to various bodily functions, as well as to the qualities of the external world. Emotional education must promote the harmonious blending of these disparate sources of influence on our emotional lives, so that the borderlands between the biological, psychological, and sociological become replete with rich commerce as opposed to unthoughtful antagonism.

Appendix

A *definition of affect* (from Panksepp, 2004c):

> Affect is typically considered to reflect the feelings associated with emotional processes, which are related in presently unknown ways to the other major components—expressive, autonomic, and cognitive. Affective experience has been among the most difficult aspects of mind to understand

scientifically, since it is so thoroughly subjective. Its importance in human economic, political and social affairs has long been subsumed under the concept of *utility*—the recognition that societies must aspire to the greatest good (and the least suffering) for the greatest number. As Jeremy Bentham (1789, *Introduction to the Principles of Morals and Legislation*) famously said: 'Utility is . . . that property in any object, whereby it tends to produce benefit, advantage, pleasure, good, or happiness . . . or . . . to prevent the happening of mischief, pain, evil, or unhappiness'. Experienced affect is the neural currency for such cost-benefit 'calculations' in the economy of the brain. When linked to specific perceptions, affective feelings typically signal the survival utility of objects.

There are, of course, an enormous number of affects, and it is by no means certain how any are instantiated within the brain. Although emotional feelings often appear related to objects of the world (since brains project feelings onto sensory/perceptual processes), affects are actually elaborated by specific brain systems. To the best of our knowledge, the critical systems are concentrated in ancient brain areas also found in many other animals.

Conceptually, affects may be divided into those that reflect bodily needs and disturbances— the hungers, thirst, and various other pains and pleasures of the world—while others are more closely related to instinctual actions—the expressive emotional urges of the mind. To understand the former, a guiding principle is that objects of the world that support survival are generally experienced as delightful and pleasant, while those incompatible with survival, are experienced as aversive and unpleasant. The 'sensory-linked affects' are typically studied as perceptual experiences of the brain; for instance, the taste of chocolate or the disgust engendered by the smell of feces. Such valenced experiences—the varieties of goodness and badness—are mediated by specific brain circuits that course upward through brainstem, thalamus and hypothalamus to ancient limbic cortical areas of the brain. For instance, people with *insular* cortical damage are deficient in experiencing negative feelings such as pain, disgust, and coldness. Yet other cortical areas (e.g. orbito-frontal cortex) help distinguish many sensory pleasures.

The other major category of affective experience is more closely linked to emotional systems that allow organisms generate adaptive instinctual behaviours during various life-challenging situations. Thus, all mammals have brain systems for i) seeking resources, ii) becoming angry if access to resources are thwarted, iii) becoming scared when one's bodily well-being is threatened, iv) various sexual desires that are somewhat different in males and females, v) urges to exhibit loving and attentive care toward one's offspring, vi) feelings of panic and distress when one has lost contact with loved ones, and vii) the boisterous joyousness of rough and tumble playfulness. Each is manifested through characteristic action patterns that reflect the dynamics of the associated feelings. All other mammals may experience such basic feelings because of brain systems they share with humans. For instance, other mammals are attracted to the drugs that humans commonly overuse and abuse, and they dislike similar drug-induced experiences. Of course, there are many socially-derived feelings as various basic emotions are thwarted and blended in real-life situations (yielding frustrations and feelings such as shame, jealousy, guilt, embarrassment, many of which may be uniquely human).

The vast human capacity to think and to symbolize experience in language and culture has added subtle layers of complexity to our feelings, especially our aesthetic experiences. As scientists categorize the diverse affective dimensions of life, many are tempted to simplify emotional complexities into holistic schemes (e.g. *positive* and *negative* affects) that may partly reflect our linguistic capacity to over-simplify. But there may also be super-ordinate brain systems for such global feelings.

Although humans have many special feelings ranging from awe to zoophobia, scientific understanding of the evolved nature of feelings is best obtained through the study of ancient brain systems we share with other animals. Recent evidence indicates these systems do have chemical codes, such as the neuropeptides, which help conduct specific neuro-affective tunes.

Most of these substances, which barely cross blood-brain barriers, must be placed directly into animals' brains. However, as related medicinal agents are developed, we can anticipate the emergence of new and selective psychiatric drugs to control troublesome or excessive human feelings. For millennia, human-kind had only one such drug, opium, which could alleviate physical pain as well as the painful grief arising from social loss.

So what, in a deep neural sense, are emotional feelings? They reflect the various types of neurodynamics that establish characteristic, mentally experienced 'forces' that regulate and reflect action readiness within the nervous system—the pounding force of anger, the shivery feelings of fear, the caress of love, the urgent thrusting of sexuality, the painful pangs of grief, the exuberance of joy, and the persistent 'nosy' poking about of organisms seeking resources. Moods and many psychiatric disorders may reflect the long-term balance of the various positive and negative affective systems.

And how do the material events of the brain get converted into the mystery of subjective experience? No one is certain, but some have suggested that the core of our being is organized around neuro-symbolic motor-action coordinates of the brain. The various basic neurodynamics of such a core 'self', evident in the instinctual action dynamics of each animal, may be critical for the transformation of brain activities into emotional experiences. If this is the case, then certain affective values were built in at the very core of mammalian brain evolution, thereby providing a solid grounding for mental life. This view of brain-mind organization, not widely accepted by certain schools of materialist (e.g. behaviourist) thought, has the potential to contribute to a more admirable scientific image of life than was evident during the 20th century.

References

Adamec, R. E. and Young, B. (2000). Neuroplasticity in specific limbic system circuits may mediate specific kindling induced changes in animal affect-implications for understanding anxiety associated with epilepsy. *Neuroscience Biobehavioural Reviews*, **24**, 705–23.

Adolphs, R., Tranel, D., and Damasio, A. R. (2003). Dissociable neural systems for recognizing emotions. *Brain and Cognition*, **52**, 61–9.

Anderson, A. K. and Phelps, E. A. (2002). Is the human amygdala critical for the subjective experience of emotions? Evidence of intact dispositional affect in patients with amygdala lesions. *Journal of Cognitive Neuroscience*, **14**, 709–20.

Anwyl, R. (1999). Metabotropic glutamate receptors: electrophysiological properties and role in plasticity. *Brain Research Reviews*, **29**, 83–120.

Atkinson, L. and Zucker, K. J. (ed.) (1997). *Attachment and psychopathology*. New York, NY: Guilford Press.

Bechtel, W. (2002). Decomposing the mind-brain: a long term pursuit. *Brain and Mind*, **3**, 229–42.

Beebe, B., Jaffe, J., Lachmann, F., *et al.* (2000). Systems models in development and psychoanalysis: the case of vocal rhythm coordination and attachment. *Infant Mental Health Journal*, **21**, 99–122.

Bejjani, B. P., Damier, P., Arnulf, I., *et al.* (1999). Brief report: transient acute depression induced by high-frequency deep-brain stimulation. *New England Journal of Medicine*, **340**, 1476–80.

Blumberg, M. S. and Sokoloff, G. (2001). Do infant rats cry? *Psychological Review*, **108**, 83–95.

Brookes, M. (2001). *Fly: the unsung hero of 20th century science*. New York, NY: Harper Collins.

Castellanos, F. X. and Tannock, R. (2002). Neuroscience of attention-deficit/hyperactivity disorder: the search for endophenotypes. *Nature Reviews Neuroscience*, **3**, 617–28.

Castellanos, F. X., Lee, P. P., Wharp, W., *et al.* (2002). Developmental trajectories of brain volume abnormalities in children and adolescents with attention-deficit/hyperactivity disorder. *Journal of the American Medical Association*, **9**, 1740–8.

Chugani, H. T. (1996). Neuroimaging of developmental nonlinearity and developmental pathologies. In *Developmental neuroimaging: mapping the development of brain and behaviour* (ed. R. W. Thatcher, G. Reid Lyon, J. Rumsey *et al.*), pp. 187–95. San Diego, CA: Academic Press.

Clayton, N. S., Bussey, T. J., and Dickinson, A. (2003). Can animals recall the past and plan for the future? *Nature Reviews Neuroscience*, **4(8)**, 685–91.

Constantine-Patton, M. (1998). Activity-dependent synaptogenesis. In *Advancing research on developmental plasticity* (ed. D. M. Hann, L. C. Huffman, I. I. Lederhendler *et al.*), pp. 21–33. Washington, DC: National Institute of Mental Health.

Damasio, A. R. (1996). *Descartes' error*. London: Papermac.

Damasio, A. R. (1999). *The feeling of what happens: body and emotion in the making of consciousness*. New York, NY: Harcourt Brace.

Damasio, A. R. (2003). *Looking for Spinoza*, Orlando, FL: Harcourt.

Damasio, A. R., Grabowski, T. J., Bechara, A., *et al.* (2000). Subcortical and cortical brain activity during the feeling of self-generated emotions. *Nature Neuroscience*, **3**, 1049–56.

Decety, J. and Chaminade, T. (2003). Neural correlates of feeling sympathy. *Neuropsychologia*, **41**, 127–38.

Finkbeiner, S. (1996). Neurotrophins and the synanpse. *Neuroscientist*, **2**, 139–42.

Gordon, N. S., Kollack-Walker, S., Akil, H., *et al.* (2002). Expression of c-fos gene activation during rough and tumble play in juvenile rats. *Brain Research Bulletin*, **57**, 651–9.

Gordon, N. S., Burke, S., Akil, H., *et al.* (2003). Socially induced brain fertilization: play promotes brain derived neurotrophic factor expression. *Neuroscience Letters* **341**, 17–20.

Gunnar, M. R. (1994). Psychoendocrine studies of temperament and stress in early childhood: Expanding current models. In *Temperament: individual differences at the interface of biology and behaviour* (ed. J. E. Bates and T. D. Wachs), pp. 175–98. Washington, DC: American Psychological Association.

Heath, R. G. (1996). *Exploring the mind-brain relationship*. Moran Printing Inc.: Baton Rouge, LA.

Holstege, G., Bandler, R., and Saper, C. B. (1996). The emotional motor system. *Progress in Brain Research*, **107**, 3–6.

Holt, R. (1980). *Freud Reappraised*. New York: Guilford Press.

Kalivas, P. W. and Nakamura, M. (1999). Neural systems for behavioural activation and reward. *Current Opinion in Neurobiology*, **9**, 223–7.

Knutson, B., Burgdorf, J., and Panksepp, J. (2002). Ultrasonic vocalizations as indices of affective states in rat. *Psychological Bulletin*, **128**, 961–77.

Lane, R. D. and Nadel, L. (ed.) (2000). *Cognitive neuroscience of emotion*. New York, NY: Oxford University Press.

LeDoux, J. (1996). *The emotional brain. The mysterious underpinnings of emotional life*. New York, NY: Simon and Schuster.

Lopez, J. F., Akil, H., and Watson, S. (1999). Role of biological and psychological factors in early development and their impact on adult life: neural circuits mediating stress. *Biological Psychiatry*, **46**, 1461–71.

Malloch, S. N. (1999/2000). Mothers and infants and communicative musicality. *Musicae Scientas* 1999/2000 (Special Issue), 29–57.

Meaney, M. J. (2001). Maternal care, gene expression, and the transmission of individual differences in stress reactivity across generations. *Annual Review of Neuroscience*, **24**, 1161–92.

Merzenich, M. M., Jenkins, W. M., Honston, P., *et al.* (1996). Temporal processing deficits of language-learning impaired children ameliorated by training. *Science*, **271**, 77–81.

Moll, G. H., Hause, S., Ruther, E., *et al.* (2001). Early methylphenidate administration to young rats causes a persistent reduction in the density of striatal dopamine transporters. *Journal of Child and Adolescent Psychopharmacology*, **11**, 15–24.

Nelson, E. E. and Panksepp, J. (1998). Brain substrates of infant-mother attachment: contributions of opioids, oxytocin, and norepinephrine. *Neuroscience and Biobehavioural Reviews*, **22**, 437–52.

Nocjar, C. and Panksepp, J. (2002). Chronic intermittent amphetamine pretreatment enhances future appetitive behaviour for drug- and natural-reward: interaction with environmental variables. *Behavioural Brain Research*, **128**, 189–203.

Olausson, H., Lamarre, Y., Backlund, H., *et al.* (2002). Unmyelinated tactile afferents signal touch and project to insular cortex. *Nature Neuroscience*, **5**, 900–4.

Panksepp, J. (1982). Toward a general psychobiological theory of emotions. *Behavioural and Brain Sciences*, **5**, 407–67.

Panksepp, J. (1985). Mood changes. In *Handbook of clinical neurology. Vol. 1(45): Clinical neuropsychology* (ed. P. J. Vinken, G. W. Bruyn, and H. L. Klawans), pp. 271–85. Amsterdam: Elsevier Science Publishers.

Panksepp, J. (1993). Neurochemical control of moods and emotions: amino acids to neuropeptides. In *The handbook of emotions* (ed. M. Lewis and J. Haviland), pp. 87–107. New York, NY: Guilford Press.

Panksepp, J. (1998a). *Affective neuroscience: the foundations of human and animal emotions.* New York, NY: Oxford University Press.

Panksepp, J. (1998b). Attention deficit disorders, psychostimulants, and intolerance of childhood playfulness: a tragedy in the making? *Current Directions in Psychological Sciences*, **7**, 91–8.

Panksepp, J. (1998c) The periconscious substrates of consciousness: affective states and the evolutionary origins of the SELF. *Journal of Consciousness Studies*, **5**, 566–82.

Panksepp, J. (1999). Emotions as viewed by psychoanalysis and neuroscience: an exercise in consilience, and accompanying commentaries. *NeuroPsychoanalysis*, **1**, 15–89.

Panksepp, J. (2000a). Affective consciousness and the instinctual motor system: The neural sources of sadness and joy. In *The caldron of consciousness, motivation, affect and self-organization*, Advances in Consciousness Research, Vol. **16** (ed. R. Ellis and N. Newton), pp. 27–54. Amsterdam: John Benjamins Pub. Co.

Panksepp, J. (2000b). Emotions as natural kinds within the mammalian brain. In *The handbook of emotions*, 2nd edn (ed. M. Lewis and J. Haviland), pp. 137–56. New York, NY: Guilford Press.

Panksepp, J. (2000c). The neuro-evolutionary cusp between emotions and cognitions. *Consciousness and Emotion*, **1**, 15–54.

Panksepp, J. (2001). The long-term psychobiological consequences of infant emotions: prescriptions for the 21st century. *Infant Mental Health Journal*, **22**, 132–73.

Panksepp, J. (2003a). At the interface of affective, behavioural and cognitive neurosciences. Decoding the emotional feelings of the brain. *Brain and Cognition*, **52**, 4–14.

Panksepp, J. (2003b). Can anthropomorphic analyses of 'separation cries' in other animals inform us about the emotional nature of social loss in humans? *Psychological Reviews*, **110**, 376–88.

Panksepp, J. (ed.) (2004a). *Textbook of biological psychiatry.* Hoboken, NJ: Wiley.

Panksepp, J. (2004b). The emerging neuroscience of fear and anxiety: therapeutic practice and clinical implications. In *Textbook of biological psychiatry* (ed. J. Panksepp), pp. 489–519. Hoboken, NJ: Wiley.

Panksepp, J. (2004c). Affect. In *Concise Corsini Encyclopedia of Psychology and Behavioural Science* (ed. W. E. Craighead and C. B. Nemeroff), pp. 22–3. Hoboken, NJ: Wiley.

Panksepp, J. and Burgdorf, J. (1999). Laughing rats? Playful tickling arouses high frequency ultrasonic chirping in young rodents. In *Toward a science of consciousness III* (ed. S. Hameroff, D. Chalmers, and A. Kazniak), pp. 124–36. Cambridge, MA: MIT Press.

Panksepp, J. and Burgdorf, J. (2000). 50 k-Hz chirping (laughter?) in response to conditioned and unconditioned tickle-induced reward in rats: effects of social housing and genetic variables. *Behavioural Brain Research*, **115**, 25–38.

Panksepp, J. and Harro, J. (2003). The future of neuropeptides in biological psychiatry and emotional psychopharmacology: goals and strategies. In *Textbook of biological psychiatry* (ed. J. Panksepp), pp. 627–59. Hoboken, NJ: Wiley.

Panksepp, J. and Moskal, J. (2004). Dopamine, pleasure and appetitive eagerness: an emotional systems overview of the trans-hypothalamic 'reward' system in the genesis of addictive urges. In *Cognitive and affective neuroscience of psychopathology* (ed. D. Barch) (in press). Oxford: Oxford University Press.

Panksepp, J. and Panksepp, J. B. (2000). The seven sins of evolutionary psychology, *Evolution and Cognition*, **6**, 108–31.

Panksepp, J. and Sahley, T. (1987). Possible brain opioid involvement in disrupted social intent and language development of autism. In *Neurobiological issues in autism* (ed. E. Schopler and G. Mesibov), pp. 357–82. New York, NY: Plenum Press.

Panksepp, J., Bean, N. J., Bishop, P., *et al.* (1980a). Opioid blockade and social comfort in chicks. *Pharmacology Biochemistry and Behaviour*, **13**, 673–83.

Panksepp, J., Herman, B. H., Vilberg, T., *et al.* (1980b). Endogenous opioids and social behaviour. *Neuroscience and Biobehavioural Reviews*, **4**, 473–87.

Panksepp, J., Siviy, S., and Normansell, L. (1984). The psychobiology of play: theoretical and methodological perspectives. *Neuroscience and Biobehavioural Reviews*, **8**, 465–92.

Panksepp, J., Lensing, P., Leboyer, M., *et al.* (1991). Naltrexone and other potential new pharmacological treatments of autism. *Brain Dysfunction*, **4**, 281–300.

Panksepp, J., Newman, J. D., and Insel, T. R. (1992). Critical conceptual issues in the analysis of separation-distress systems of the brain. In *International review of studies on emotion*, Vol. **2** (ed. K. T. Strongman), pp. 51–72. Chichester: John Wiley and Sons.

Panksepp, J., Normansell, L., Cox, J., *et al.* (1994). Effects of neonatal decortication on the social play of juvenile rats. *Physiology and Behaviour*, **56**, 429–43.

Panksepp, J., Burgdorf, J., and Gordon, N. (2001). Toward a genetics of joy: breeding rats for 'laughter'. In *Emotion, Qualia, and Consciousness* (ed. A. Kazniak), pp. 124–36 . Singapore: World Scientific.

Panksepp, J., Burgdorf, J., Gordon, N., *et al.* (2002a). Treatment of ADHD with methylphenidate may sensitize brain substrates of desire. Implications for changes in drug abuse potential from an animal model. *Consciousness and Emotion*, **3**, 7–19.

Panksepp, J., Knutson, B., and Burgdorf, J. (2002b). The role of brain emotional systems in addictions: a neuro-evolutionary perspective and new 'self-report' animal model. *Addiction*, **97**, 459–69.

Panksepp, J., Moskal, J., Panksepp, J. B., *et al.* (2002c). Comparative approaches in evolutionary psychology: molecular neuroscience meets the mind. *Neuroendocrinology Letters*, **23 (Suppl. 4)**, 105–15.

Panksepp, J., Burgdorf, J., Turner, C., *et al.* (2003). Modeling ADHD-type arousal with unilateral frontal cortex damage in rats and beneficial effects of play therapy. *Brain and Cognition*, **52**, 97–105.

Parkinson, B. (1995). *Ideas and realities of emotion.* London: Routledge.

Pascual-Leone, A., Walsh, V., and Rothwell, J. (2000) Transcranial magnetic stimulation in cognitive neuroscience: virtual lesion, chronometry, and functional connectivity. *Current Opinion in Neurobiology,* **10**, 232–7.

Peterson, B. and Panksepp, J. (2004). The biological basis of childhood neuropsychiatric disorders. In *Textbook of biological psychiatry* (ed. J. Panksepp), pp. 393–436. Hoboken, NJ: Wiley.

Phan, K. L., Wager, T., Taylor, S. F., *et al.* (2002). Functional neuroanatomy of emotion: a meta-analysis of emotion activation studies in PET and fMRI. *Neuroimage,* **16**, 331–48.

Robinson T. E. and Berridge, K. C. (2003). Addiction. *Annual Review of Psychology,* **I 54**, 25–53.

Rolls, E. T. (1999). *The brain and emotion.* Oxford: Oxford University Press.

Ryff, C. D. and Singer, B. (1998). The contours of positive human health. *Psychological Inquiry,* **9**, 1–28.

Schiff, N. D. and Plum, F. (2000). The role of arousal and 'gating' systems in the neurology of impaired consciousness. *Journal of Clinical Neurophysiology,* **17**, 438–52.

Schutter, D. J. L. G., van Honk, J., and Panksepp, J. (2004). Introducing repetitive transcranial magnetic stimulation (rTMS) and its property of causal interference in investigating brain-function relationships. *Synthese* (in press).

Skuse, D. H. (2000). Behavioural neuroscience and child pathology: Insights from model systems. *Journal of Child Psychology and Psychiatry,* **41(1)**, 3–31.

Solms, M. and Turnbull, O. (2002). *The brain and the inner world: an introduction to the neuroscience of subjective experience.* New York, NY: Other Press.

Stewart, L. M., Ellison, A., Walsh, V., *et al.* (2001). The role of transcranial magnetic stimulation (TMS) in studies of vision, attention and cognition, *Acta Psychologica,* **107**, 275–91.

Strittmatter, S. M. (1995). Neuronal guidance molecules: inhibitory and soluble factors. *Neuroscientist,* **1**, 255–8.

Sunderland, M. (2005). Your child's emotional brain—why it's vital you know. (in press)

Uttal, W. R. (2002). Precis of the new phrenology: the limits of localizaing cognitive processes in the brain. *Brain and Mind,* **3**, 221–8.

Watt, D. and Pincus, D. (2004). The neural substrates of consciousness. In *Textbook of biological psychiatry* (ed. J. Panksepp), pp. 75–110. Hoboken, NJ: Wiley.

Chapter 2

Emotions in chimpanzee infants: the value of a comparative developmental approach to understand the evolutionary bases of emotion

Kim A. Bard

A comparative perspective is necessary for developmental psychology (Chevalier-Skolnikoff, 1976; Bullowa, 1979; Nugent et al., 1989; Rogoff and Morelli, 1989; Custance and Bard, 1994; Tomasello, 1999; Want and Harris, 2002; Keller et al., 2004; Tomonaga et al., in press). In order to fully understand developmental processes in humans, particularly for claims of unique human propensities, we must actively compare human developmental processes to those in other animals. In this regard, non-human primates are good candidates. I chose to study developmental processes in chimpanzees, to better understand species-specific characteristics not only of the chimpanzee, but also in humans. If we wish to make claims about specific links of early propensities to later developmental milestones, for instance, neonatal imitation of mouth movements as precursors for speech, then we need to know that neonatal imitation of mouth movements does not occur in other primates that do not develop speech. Clearly, humans have many species unique characteristics, like speech, but it is only by comparing early development across primate species that we discover those characteristics that are uniquely human.

In this chapter, I will discuss the evidence that chimpanzees share with humans many early behaviours (Jacobsen et al., 1932; Yerkes and Tomilin, 1935; Yerkes and Yerkes, 1936; Yerkes and Nissen, 1939; Hayes and Hayes, 1952; van Lawick-Goodall, 1968; Plooij, 1979; Chevalier-Skolnikoff, 1982; Hallock et al., 1989a; Bard et al., 1992, 1995, 2003; Tomasello et al., 1993; Bard, 1994b, 2003/2004; Custance et al., 1995; Myowa, 1996; Russell et al., 1997; Whiten, 2000; Matsuzawa, 2001; Tomonaga et al., 2002). I will present summaries of several studies that demonstrate the flexibility in the behavioural repertoire of chimpanzees. The flexibility is illustrated as responsiveness to different social environments. Moreover, these studies illustrate the similarities between chimpanzees and humans that are especially apparent during the early postnatal period of life. One of the main points I wish to make throughout this chapter, is that the process of development is epigenetic, that is, the interaction of environmental and endogenous factors is apparent already in the first days of life. It is the interaction of individual characteristics and environmental regularities that results in most aspects of behaviour, including emotional behaviour, even in the first 30 days of life, and even in chimpanzees. There is not a single developmental pathway for chimpanzees or for humans (Greenfield et al., 2003). For each individual, whether human or chimpanzee, the environment in which they live has a great impact. The flexibility built in by evolution allows for individuals to develop differently in interaction with environmental conditions, which include both social and non-social factors (Bruner, 1972; Kagan, 2003). 'The point is that epigenesis begins at conception, not birth' (Chisholm, 1989, p. 353).

It is the emotional system, I believe, that is the most responsive to environmental contingencies and which begins to develop very early in life. Human infants, by 8 weeks of age, exhibit physiological arousal patterns to human face-to-face interactions that are a demonstrable product of early rearing and a result of prenatal environmental effects (Bard et al., 2000), and as early as 4 months, prefer their mother's imperfect interactional contingencies as opposed to 'perfect' contingencies of a trained examiner (Bigelow, 1998). There is a paucity of research in emotions in non-human primates (but see Parr et al., 1998; Preston and de Waal, 2002), albeit that many studies have been done on the vocalizations and facial movements used in communication (see Seyfarth and Cheney, 2003, for a review).

I will weave together the results from four chimpanzee studies, on neonatal imitation [at 7– 11 days of age: (Bard, 2004)], on mutual gaze [across the first 3 months of life (Bard et al., 2003), on early emotional development in the first month of life (Bard, 1998, 2000, 2003)], and on early neurobehavioural integrity in the first month of life (Bard et al., 1992, 2001) in comparison with the information that we know about these capabilities in human infants. I will highlight similarities and differences, in order to allow for better understanding of early human and early great ape development, especially the interplay between genes and experience.

Neonatal Behavioural Assessment Scale (NBAS)

The assessment of the behaviour of the human newborn has advanced over the past three decades, in part due to new ways of looking at the newborn, and in part with new discoveries of the abilities of newborns (Kugiumutzakis, 1985; Maratos, 1985; Meltzoff and Moore, 1989; Nugent et al., 1989; Brazelton and Nugent, 1995; Nadel and Butterworth, 1999; Trevarthen and Aitken, 2001). These new views have been based on observations of single behaviours (such as burst-pause sucking), tests of processes (such as instrumental learning of head turns), and descriptions of single aspects of behaviour (such as behavioural states of sleeping, alert, and crying). One of the most widely used assessments, the Neonatal Behavioural Assessment Scale measures neurobehavioural integrity, in other words functioning organizational systems of the newborn (Sameroff, 1978; Brazelton and Nugent, 1995). These systems are indexed behaviourally, and are both observed and actively manipulated. This 25-minute assessment includes the full range of functioning systems, from social engagement to inborn reflexes. Here, we will present new comparative data on five behavioural clusters (Lester, 1984).

NBAS clusters

If we translate the NBAS terms into the everyday equivalents:

- ORIENTATION concerns the infants' attention to the social world and object-filled world;
- MOTOR concerns the muscular tone and amount of active movement of the infant;
- RANGE concerns the emotional arousal and arousability of infants;
- REGULATION concerns the coping of infants, measuring how well they use their own resources (hand-to-mouth, self-quieting), or resources provided by the examiner (cuddliness, consolability) to maintain a quiet behavioural state;
- ANS STABILITY measures signs of stress in the autonomic nervous system, reflecting 'homeostatic adjustments of the nervous system' (Lester, 1984, p. 89).

My first question relates to whether there are distinct differences in the neonatal neurobehavioural integrity of one group of humans (infants born in middle to upper-middle class, two-parent families in the Eastern USA) compared with four groups of chimpanzees (three groups raised in nursery conditions by human caregivers, and one group raised by their biological mothers). In other words, are there any aspects of neonatal neurobehaviour in which species differences are clearly apparent?

We would expect to find that the human group is different from the chimpanzee groups and this would provide good evidence that genetic factors evident in the first 30 days of life predominate over environmental similarities. However, if the human group was found to be similar to one (or more) of the chimpanzees, but different from other chimpanzee groups, then we might be able to make some suggestions about the effect of particular aspects of the early environment on neonatal behaviour and their influence on neonatal neurobehavioural integrity. I can think of two ways that the chimpanzee and human groups might be distributed—first along an aspect of exposure to humans, with the human group having the most human exposure, and among the chimpanzee groups, the RC nursery and then ST nursery groups having the most human contact. The SW has the least human contact, as even when humans provide food their expressive faces are hidden from view and touch is minimalized with the use of gloves, boots, and coats. Clearly, the most extreme group along the dimension of exposure to humans would be the mother-raised chimpanzee group, as they have only distal visual contact with humans.

A third way that the groups might be distributed is along the lines of the extent of cradling contact with a caregiver (disregarding the species of the caregiver), with mother-raised chimpanzees having 100% cradling contact in the first month of life, human infants having lots of cradling contact, but in the US middle class culture of Providence RI, much less than 100% contact. The RC chimpanzees had 4 hours per day of additional cradling contact, compared with the ST nursery chimpanzee infants, but both these groups had long periods of cradling contact with warm caregivers multiple times a day. The SW nursery chimpanzee group had the least cradling contact with caregivers. So, we will look for these three patterns of neurobehavioural integrity in the results: species differences, differences explainable by exposure to humans, and differences explainable by amount of cradling contact.

Human—Eastern USA

The human group consisted of 42 healthy full-term newborns from Providence RI, US born primarily to Caucasian, middle- to upper-class SES two-parent families (see Bard et al., 1992; Lester et al., 1989, for further details).

There are four groups of chimpanzee newborns, two nursery-raised groups from Yerkes (Bard et al., 2001), one nursery-raised from SFBR (San Antonio TX), and one mother-raised group (from New Mexico TX: Hallock et al., 1989).

Standard nursery—Yerkes (ST)

This group of 21 nursery-raised chimpanzees were placed in incubators (for no more than the first 30 days of life) when initially placed in the nursery. Their contact with humans consisted of being held in the lap when given milk from bottles, initially on a 2-hour schedule and then on a 4-hour schedule, with diaper changes and health checks surrounding these scheduled contacts. Caregivers wore white lab coats and washed with soap before contacting the babies. Some sat on rocking chairs during contact, whereas most fed the ST chimpanzees while sitting in straight back chairs.

Responsive Care nursery—Yerkes (RC)

This group of 17 nursery-raised chimpanzees were placed in incubators when initially placed in the nursery (and when not in contact with caregivers). Their contact with humans except for 4 hours each day (5 days per week) was identical to the ST infants. For 4 hours per day, Monday to Friday, however, these infants remained in 100% cradling contact with a human caregiver, and feeding, cleaning, and playing were 'on-demand'. RC caregivers were encouraged to be physically active, walking around the Yerkes nursery and Great Ape Wing. RC caregivers encouraged the infants to develop motoric competence in supporting their own weight, and provided chimpanzee species-typical vestibular/kinaesthetic stimulation. They were also encouraged to be socially active: social interactions included spending some time in interaction with older chimpanzees in the nursery and viewing (but not interacting with) adult chimpanzees on the GAW, and interacting with humans, talking to a variety of researchers and staff, and encouraging the development of appropriate chimpanzee species-typical social responses (vocalizations, gestures, and emotional expressions).

Southwest Foundation for Biomedical Research nursery (SW)

This group of nine nursery-raised chimpanzees were also in incubators for some days when placed in the nursery. Their contact with humans was on a schedule, initially every 2 hours, and then every 4 hours. However, contact was limited in at least two ways. Caregivers always wore gloves covering their hands, bio-safety hair nets covering their hair, and bio-safety face masks covering their nose and mouth to prevent the spread of infectious diseases. Secondly, the time spent with each infant was more limited at SW than even ST at Yerkes, as often infants were returned to the incubator immediately after feeding or given a bottle propped, rather than being held until sleeping as often happened at Yerkes.

Mother-raised

The final chimpanzee group includes seven infants that were raised by their chimpanzee mothers, and only removed temporarily from her care for the purposes of running the NBAS tests (details reported in Hallock *et al.*, 1989). So, except for the time that the infant was being tested by the human examiner, the infants experienced 100% cradling contact with their biological chimpanzee mothers, for 24 hours a day, for each of their first 30 days of life. Chimpanzee mothers, even in the first 30 days of life, engage in lots of interaction with their babies (see Bard, 1994, for more details; see Bard, 2002, for details of parenting in chimpanzees in comparison with other primates).

Hypotheses and explanations of NBAS results

So, we will look for three patterns in the results of neonatal neurobehavioural integrity: species differences (where the human group is distinctly different from all groups of chimpanzees), differences explainable by exposure to humans (where the pattern is Human > RC = ST > SW > mother chimpanzee), and differences explainable by amount of cradling contact (where the pattern is mother chimpanzee > human > RC > ST > SW). Repeated measures ANOVAs were conducted on each NBAS Cluster. Planned contrast comparisons were conducted to test whether the human group was significantly different from each of the other groups. When a significant interaction of group and age was found, then planned group contrasts were conducted at each age separately (sometimes increasing the sample size of available subjects).

This first thing to note from viewing Figs. 2.1–2.5, is that in all the Cluster scores, the human group was indistinguishable from at least one of the chimpanzee groups. Thus, differences in neurobehavioural integrity cannot be explained solely with reference to species. In other words, during the neonatal period, the behavioural competencies and underlying neurobehavioural integrity of humans and chimpanzees are not distinctly different.

In ORIENTATION (Fig. 2.1), a significant age effect, significant group effect, and significant age by group interaction, $F(4,79) = 9.02$, $p < 0.001$, eta2 = 0.31, required

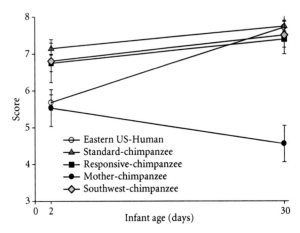

Fig. 2.1 Neonatal performance on the ORIENTATION cluster of the NBAS.

Table 2.1 Are human newborns distinctively different from chimpanzee newborns?

	Humans different from which chimpanzee groups?					
	Nursery reared			Mother raised	Pattern	Explanation
	RC	ST	SW			
ORIENTATION						
Day 2	**	***	*	ns	Nursery > Human = Mother	Physical contact
Day 30	ns	ns	ns	***	Nursery = Human > Mother	Exposure to humans
MOTOR	**	***	ns	+	Nursery > Human > Mother	Physical contact
RANGE	***	**	ns	ns	Human = Mother > RC = ST	Physical contact
REGULATION	**	***	ns	***	Nursery > Human > Mother	Physical contact
ANS STABILITY						
Day 2	**	***	ns	***	Mother > ST = RC > SW = Human	Exposure to humans
Day 30	ns	ns	*	***	Mother = SW > ST = RC = Human	Exposure to humans
Smiles						
Day 2	ns	ns	ns	ns	Chimpanzee = human	No differences
Day 30	*	ns	+	*	RC = ST > Human > Mother = SW	Exposure to humans
Rapidity of Build-up						
	**	**	**	ns	Mother = Human > ST = RC = SW	Physical contact

ns p > 0.1; +0.1 > p > 0.05; *p < 0.05; **p < 0.01; ***p < 0.001.

consideration of significant group differences on Day 2, $F(4,87) = 7.08$, $p < 0.001$, eta2 $= 0.25$, separately from Day 30, $F(4,83) = 17.01$, $p < 0.001$, eta2 $= 0.45$. As clearly evident in this figure, on Day 2, the human group was similar to the mother-raised chimpanzees (planned simple contrast $= -0.15$, ns), but different from each of the nursery-raised chimpanzee groups (planned simple contrast, versus ST $= 1.46$, $p < 0.001$, versus RC $= 1.07$, $p < 0.002$, versus SW $= 1.12$, $p < 0.05$). On Day 30, the human group was similar to all groups of nursery-raised chimpanzees (planned contrasts all ns) but significantly different from the mother-raised chimpanzee group (planned contrast $= 3.16$, $p < 0.001$). Thus, we can conclude that ORIENTATION appears to be influenced by exposure to humans, with the effect minimal at Day 2, but maximal at Day 30, with the human group and nursery chimpanzees indistinguishable from each other, but distinct from the mother-raised chimpanzees (Table 2.1).

In the MOTOR cluster (Fig. 2.2), there was significant improvement from Day 2 to Day 30, significant group effect, $F(4, 78)v = 7.62$, $p < 0.001$, eta2 $= 0.28$, but no age by group interaction. Planned simple contrasts revealed that the human group was almost distinguishable from mother-raised chimpanzees (-0.356, $p = 0.074$), but significantly different from two nursery groups (ST $= 0.57$, $p < 0.001$, RC $= 0.41$, $p < 0.01$). Note that the human group is intermediate, with more mature MOTOR performance than the mother-raised chimpanzee group and less mature MOTOR performance compared with the nursery-raised chimpanzees. The ordering of the groups falls nicely into the order predicted by an explanation of extent of cradling contact. Note here that the infants with the most cradling contact have the lowest MOTOR performance scores, that nursery-reared chimpanzees, with the least cradling contact have the most rapidly developing MOTOR systems within the first 30 days of life.

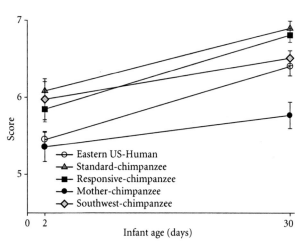

Fig. 2.2 Neonatal performance on the MOTOR cluster of the NBAS.

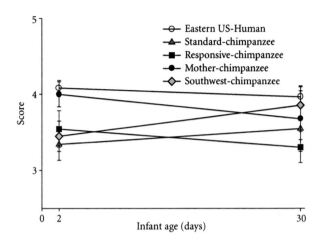

Fig. 2.3 Neonatal performance on the RANGE cluster of the NBAS.

More apparently relevant to emotion than the previous clusters, are the NBAS clusters of RANGE and REGULATION. RANGE, or general arousal and arousability, did not differ by age, but the groups differed significantly, $F(4, 78) = 4.25$, $p < 0.01$, eta2 $= 0.18$ (Fig. 2.3). Planned contrast revealed that the human group differed from the 2 nursery groups of chimpanzees (ST $= 0.54$, $p < 0.01$; RC $= 0.60$, $p < 0.001$), but did not differ from the mother-raised chimpanzees or from SW nursery-raised chimpanzees. In this cluster, the human group and mother-raised chimpanzee group were the most aroused groups, and the Yerkes nursery-raised groups were the least aroused groups. So, in terms of RANGE of state or general arousal during the NBAS examination, it appears extent of cradling contact is a major influence.

STATE REGULATION, a measure of early coping, differed among the groups, $F(4, 77) = 13.23$, $p < 0.001$, eta2 $= 0.41$, but the age by group interaction was not significant. Planned contrasts revealed that the human group differed from the Yerkes nursery-raised chimpanzee groups (ST $= 1.34$, $p < 0.001$; RC $= 0.80$, $p < 0.01$), but not from the SW group. Moreover, the human group differed from the mother-raised chimpanzee group (-1.32, $p < 0.001$). It is clear in Fig. 2.4, that the nursery chimpanzee groups are the most highly regulated and the mother-raised chimpanzee group is the least highly regulated (comparisons with Bonferroni correction revealed that the mother-raised group significantly differs from all other groups with t values all significant, p values < 0.014). Note that the human group, although significantly different from each chimpanzee group, is moderated well regulated, with intermediate REGULATION values. This is the pattern predicted by the extent of cradling contact.

Finally, ANS STABILITY, an index of stress in the autonomic nervous system, differed by group, $F(4, 78) = 7.73$, $p < 0.001$, eta2 $= 0.28$, but not by age (Fig. 2.5). A significant group by age interaction, $F(4, 78) = 3.31$, $p < 0.05$, eta2 $= 0.15$, however, necessitated consideration of the significant group differences on Day 2, $F(4, 86) = 6.99$, $p < 0.001$, eta2 $= 0.25$ separately from the significant group differences on Day 30,

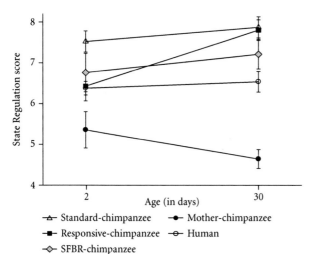

Fig. 2.4 Neonatal performance on the REGULATION cluster of the NBAS.

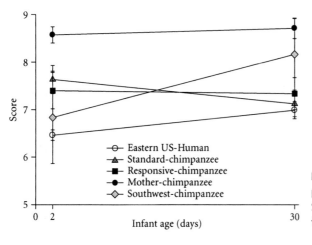

Fig. 2.5 Neonatal performance on the ANS STABILITY cluster of the NBAS.

$F(4, 83) = 3.82$, $p < 0.01$, eta2 $= 0.16$. On Day 2, the human group was significantly different from the Yerkes nursery chimpanzee groups (ST $= 1.17$, $p < 0.001$; RC $= 0.94$, $p < 0.01$), and from the mother-raised chimpanzee group (2.11, $p < 0.001$), but did not differ from the SW nursery group. On Day 30, the human group was not different from the Yerkes nursery groups, but was significantly different from the mother-raised chimpanzee group (1.72, $p < 0.001$) and was significantly different from the SW nursery group (1.17, $p < 0.05$).

To illustrate more concretely these patterns of NBAS results and their relation to emotional development, let us consider two individual items, number of smiles and rapidity of build-up. Rapidity of build-up is in the RANGE cluster and is defined as the point in the examination when the infant first cries. Since the examination is structured

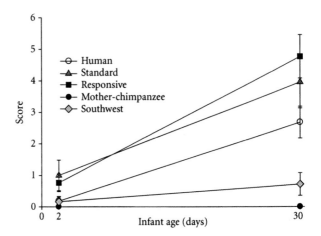

Fig. 2.6 Neonatal performance on the NBAS item, Smiles.

from least to most intrusive and the infant is presumed to move from a sleeping state at the start of the examination to a crying one at the end, this item measures how well the infant maintains control over his or her behavioural state in response to the increasingly intrusive stimulation of the examination (Brazelton and Nugent, 1995, p. 48). The lowest scores are given to the infant who maintains a calm state throughout the examination and never cries, whereas the highest scores are given to the infant who never is quiet and begins to cry at the very start of the examination. Smiling is simply the number of smiles observed, without rigid determination of whether the observed facial expression is a grimace, or an appropriate response to social stimuli. Brazelton argues that whatever it 'really' is, this facial expression is what the human mother reinforces as a precursor to a social smile (Brazelton and Nugent, 1984, p. 52).

First consider the number of social smiles (Fig. 2.6), for which the repeated measures ANOVA revealed significant group differences, $F(4, 62) = 6.61, p < 0.001$, eta2 $=$ 0.30, significant age differences, and a significant interaction between group and age, $F(4, 62) = 2.79, p < 0.05$, eta2 $= 0.15$. On Day 2, there were no group differences in number of smiles observed, $F(4, 71) = 1.72, p = 0.16$, eta2 $= 0.09$, although the planned contrasts revealed that the human group differed significantly from ST nursery chimpanzees ($0.82, p < 0.05$) who exhibited the most smiles. On Day 30, there was a significant group difference $F(4, 77) = 5.32, p < 0.001$, eta2 $= 0.22$, with planned contrasts revealing that the human group differed from RC ($2.09, p < 0.02$), and from the mother-raised chimpanzee groups ($-2.68, p < 0.03$). On day 30, the human newborns were observed to smile 2.7 times on average, whereas the RC chimpanzees smiled 4.8 times, and mother-raised chimpanzees were not observed to smile at all. So, it is clear just by comparing the nursery group with the mother raised group of chimpanzees that there is environmental interaction in this item. With responsive stimulation from human caregivers, the number of smiles given by the infants increases in the first 30 days of life, but that without responsive stimulation by humans there are very

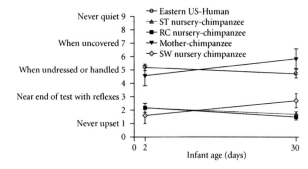

Never quiet 9

8

When uncovered 7

6

When undressed or handled 5

4

Near end of test with reflexes 3

2

Never upset 1

0

0 2   30

Infant age (days)

-◦- Eastern US-Human
-▲- ST nursery-chimpanzee
-■- RC nursery-chimpanzee
-▼- Mother-chimpanzee
-◊- SW nursery chimpanzee

Fig. 2.7 Neonatal performance on the NBAS item, Rapidity of Build-up.

few or no social smiles. That it is responsive interaction, not just interaction with people is verified by comparison of the nursery groups. The largest differences are found between the Yerkes nursery groups and the SW group. Recall that at the nursery at SW, the face of the human caregiver was not visible to the chimpanzee infant with the exception of the NBAS tests. The number of smiles in the human group is intermediate between the Yerkes chimpanzees, and the mother-raised chimpanzees, revealing the interaction of species with environment as a result of exposure to interactive humans. The change from Days 2 to 30 is further support by the fact that, with repeated days of exposure to human partners, there is greater influence.

In the item of rapidity of build-up (Fig. 2.7), there is a significant group difference, $F(4, 76) = 33.46, p < 0.001$, eta2 $= 0.64$, that appears explainable by extent of cradling contact. The human group is not significantly different from the mother-raised chimpanzees, but the human group is significantly different from all of the nursery chimpanzees (ST $= -3.03, p < 0.001$, RC $= -3.10, p < 0.001$, SW $= -2.60, p < 0.001$). The nursery reared chimpanzees, on average, were rarely upset during the course of the 20–25-minute NBAS examination. If they became fussy or cried, it was very close to the end of the examination, in response to the last reflex item, elicitation of the Moro reflex, which involves a loss of support to the head and neck. In contrast, the mother-raised chimpanzees and the human group became upset much earlier in the examination, when their body was handled for the first time, within the first 10 minutes. Handling consisted of either removing the clothes, or moving the infants arms and legs to assess passive tone. Thus, this group difference pattern in the item Rapidity of Build-up can be explained by cradling contact, rather than species differences or interactive exposure to humans. It is interesting that the effects of cradling contact are apparent already at 2 days of age and do not change across the first 30 days.

Summary of NBAS

A comparison of neonatal behaviour as assessed in the NBAS examination reveals no species differences, but rather we found effects attributable either to exposure to humans (ORIENTATION—Day 30; ANS STABILITY—Days 2 and 30; Smiles—Day 30) or to the extent of cradling contact (MOTOR; RANGE—arousability: REGULATION-coping: Rapidity of Build-up). Exposure to humans in these cases really refers to exposure to Western parenting values (e.g. Keller *et al.*, in press), with an emphasis on face-to-face interaction and a relative decrease in physical contact. So, to have cultural values influencing attention to the social world and object-filled world (i.e. ORIENTATION) is really not surprising. What is remarkable, however, is that the influence is evident within the first 30 days of life, in infants that are born able to be responsive to social interaction. In ORIENTATION, the human group is indistinguishable from the nursery-reared chimpanzees (who were surrounded by many objects), but the groups exposed to human nursery environments are distinct from the mother-raised chimpanzees. This effect is seen clearly in the item 'number of smiles'. The smiles observed in the human group are intermediate between the Yerkes chimpanzees and the mother-raised chimpanzees, revealing the interaction of species with environment as a result of exposure to interactive humans. The change from Days 2 to 30 is further support that with repeated days of interactive exposure to human partners, there is greater influence. That the humans need to be interactive is highlighted by the difference between the Yerkes nursery environments, and the SW environment where the people wore protective masks, gloves, and spent little time with each infant.

It is possible that something different might account for the influence of exposure to humans on ANS STABILITY, which measures homeostasis in the autonomic nervous system (Lester, 1984, p. 89). Consideration of each item of this cluster (startles, tremors, and change in skin colour) reveals that:

- For startles, at 30 days of age, there is not a pattern of group difference at 30 days of age consistent with exposure to humans
- For tremors, there was a pattern of group differences among the chimpanzees that was consistent with exposure to humans, however humans were intermediate between Yerkes nursery and mother-raised chimpanzees. Humans exhibited tremors while sleeping (scoring 2 on the average) significantly different from the Yerkes groups who exhibited tremors after startles (scoring 3 on the average). Humans were also significantly different from mother-raised chimpanzees, who did not exhibit any tremors (scoring 1 on the average). Clearly, human infants had more exposure to humans than did nursery chimpanzees, and so we can not conclude that the pattern holds for the item of tremors
- Changes in skin colour were not recorded for the chimpanzees, as it is difficult to observe in any dark skinned baby.

In determining the cluster score, only two items were averaged for the chimpanzees, whereas three items were averaged for the humans. Integrating the data presented in this chapter, with published data from two human groups, the Efe and the Navajo, is revealing. The Efe, with continuous cradling contact, exhibited the highest levels of startles, showing 3 startles on average (Tronick and Winn, 1992), and the Navajo infants exhibited the same as the US infants (Chisholm, 1989). Thus, at Day 2, the human groups might be distinct from all the chimpanzee groups. Tremors were observed more than three times in States 5 or 6 in the Efe, compared with less than once in States 5 or 6 in the Navajo. However, both of these groups exhibited more tremors than the nursery chimpanzees, whereas the Eastern US infants exhibited fewer tremors. Clearly, this pattern also does not fit into the expected pattern in which exposure to humans is a likely environmental explanation.

The second pattern of group differences reflected cradling contact. The amount of cradling contact, as opposed to simply physical contact accounts for group differences in MOTOR performance, the muscular tone and amount of active movement in infants. Note here that the infants with the *most* cradling contact (i.e. mother chimpanzees and then Eastern US humans) have the lowest MOTOR performance scores, and the infants with the *least* cradling contact (i.e. nursery-reared chimpanzees) have the most rapidly developing MOTOR systems within the first 30 days of life. Although there are clear differences in motor maturation among human groups with different cultural values in motor skills (e.g. Keller *et al.*, 2004), it is likely that this effect of cradling contact on motor development does not have a great long-term influence on the attainment of motor milestones, which appears to have a strong genetic component.

The amount of cradling contact also influences infant neurobehavioural integrity in the two clusters that relate most directly to emotionality: RANGE, which concerns the emotional arousal and arousability of infants, and REGULATION, which concerns the coping of infants, how well they can use resources to maintain an alert behavioural state. However, the patterns are slightly different. In RANGE, human infants appear the most aroused, with the highest scores (Fig. 2.5). Statistically, the humans scores are indistinguishable from the lower scores of the mother-raised chimpanzees, but the nursery chimpanzees have the lowest scores. The human group is not distinct, and because the group that they are most similar to is the mother-raised chimpanzees, the pattern is explainable by extent of cradling contact. If we look at one item of this cluster, Peak of Excitement—the most aroused state of the infant during the examination—the US human group and the mother-raised chimpanzees reach a crying state from which it is difficult to console, whereas the nursery chimpanzees may reach a crying state, but only once and they self console. The Efe infants, with 100% cradling contact, and the Navajo infants, daily on the cradleboard, are intermediate between the US human infants and the nursery chimpanzees at 2 days of age. However, by 10 days of age, the Efe are peaking at the US human levels and the Navajo are indistinguishable from the low excitement peak of the nursery chimpanzees. In this case, it seems clear that the extent of cradling, as opposed to the vestibular and kinesthetic stimulation that accompanies being carried, is the mechanism that may explain these group differences. The hypothesis is that caregivers act in ways to modulate the infant's state, by providing soothing comfort or opportunities to nurse upon which the infant appropriately relies. The NBAS is designed to assess the infant, in part, on its own. When the infant is manipulated (aroused) and arousability is measured, infants who have had the most responsive caregivers are the most aroused, whereas those who have not, are the least aroused.

In REGULATION, the humans are intermediate, with better coping scores than the mother-raised chimpanzees, but significantly worse coping scores than the nursery chimpanzees. It is illustrative to look at an individual item with the REGULATION cluster in order to give a concrete behavioural example. Thus, this group difference pattern in the item Rapidity of Build-up can be explained by cradling contact, rather than species differences or interactive exposure to humans. It is interesting that the effects of cradling contact are apparent already at 2 days of age, and do not change across the first 30 days. Interestingly, comparision of data from traditional Navajo, who carry their infants in cradleboards, illustrating the rapid effect of environment on neonatal behaviour. Comparison of the Navajo infants with the Efe infants (Tronick and Winn, 1992) help to illustrate the distinction between physical contact (with vesitbular and kinaesthetic stimulation) and cradling contact that is socially interactive (Chisholm, 1989). At 2 days of age, the values of the Navajo infants are intermediate between the chimpanzee groups, getting upset near the end of the test with the assessment of gross body reflexes. By 7 days of age, however, the Navajo infants' values are within the range of the nursery-chimpanzees, getting upset at the very end of the examination, with the elicitation of the Moro. These infants were less arousable, more able to control their arousal compared with Eastern US human infants. Comparison with NBAS data from the Efe (an African tribe with a nomadic lifestyle and close to 100% cradling contact with their infants), confirm the pattern explainable by extent of cradling contact, as their values are slightly higher than the human group from Eastern US, first getting upset between elicitation of reflexes in the feet and handling, moving of the arms and legs (Tronick and Winn, 1992). So, it does appear that neonatal arousability, as measured by performance on this NBAS item, is explainable by cradling contact, and not just physical contact.

Neonatal imitation

Newborn chimpanzees match facial and vocal actions that were modelled by humans (Bard and Russell, 1999; Bard, 2004). An ethological approach was adopted with a full behavioural description being considered as the important first step, while addressing the question of function (Miklosi, 1999). In this study, the functional aspects of imitation were probed by using two test paradigms, differing in the extent to which they simulate a social interaction. Two procedures were used to assess imitation in newborn chimpanzees: one paralleled that of Meltzoff and Moore (1989), which was standardized, rigid, and time-based, whereas the other paradigm, adapted from Kugiumutzakis (1999) was both communicative and interactive. If newborn chimpanzees exhibited more imitation in a context of social interaction then imitation might be suggested to serve a communicative function, as proposed for human newborns (Kugiumutzakis, 1999; Trevarthen and Aitken, 2001). In contrast, if more imitation is found in the context of structured noninteractive presentations of a model then the function served might be a more general learning process, e.g. associative sequence learning (Heyes, 2001) or active intermodal processing (Meltzoff and Moore, 1977).

In the structured paradigm, neonatal chimpanzees imitated mouth opening (MO). In other words, 7–15 day-old chimpanzees exhibited more MO when MO was modeled by an adult human than when tongue protrusions (TP) were modeled. Moreover, the rate of MO by chimpanzee infants given a MO model was significantly elevated over a baseline rate. In the structured paradigm, infant chimpanzees did not imitate TP. In the communicative paradigm, infant actions corresponded to the three modelled actions significantly more often than expected by chance. In the communicative paradigm, all newborn chimpanzees matched MO (100%), 60% matched tongue protrusion, 50% matched the clicking sound of a tongue click, and 50% matched the series of three actions involved in the tongue click (TC) model.

Two tentative conclusions emerge. Newborn chimpanzees exhibit imitation of facial actions including some sound production, and performance appears to be better in an interactive compared with a structured paradigm. Newborn chimpanzees matched significantly more responses in the communicative paradigm (with an average of 2.2 matching responses) than in the structured paradigm (with an average of 1 matched response), $t(4) = 6.00$, $p < 0.01$; however, there were many variables that differed between the two test paradigms including the potential number of models that could be imitated. This would suggest that imitation serves a communicative function for chimpanzees, as it does for humans (Kugiumutzakis, 1999).

The evidence for neonatal imitation is based on a very small sample. The early reports of imitation in human newborns were based similarly on very small sample sizes, e.g. six infants (Meltzoff and Moore, 1977) and 12 infants (Maratos, 1985). Further study is clearly needed. Yet these findings of neonatal imitation with even a small number of chimpanzees are important to highlight a capacity within the species. It is possible that the neonatal imitation by chimpanzees is part of an innate capacity to engage in intersubjectivity, providing a new focus on socially-based communicative actions. It is possible that the propensity to exhibit MO in chimpanzees is linked to the muscular morphology of the chimpanzee smile (e.g. relaxed open mouth 'playface'; van Lawick-Goodall, 1968), as even in newborns, the chimpanzee smile consists of an open mouth (e.g. Bard et al., 1992). Note, however, that TP in humans is not linked with positive affect, but rather with sustained alert attention (e.g. Anisfeld, 1996). Primary intersubjectivity may be the foundation for imitation, in both chimpanzee and human infants, providing a mechanism to explain flexibility and responsiveness to the social environment. Thus, we are encouraged to study imitation within a social emotional communicative framework (e.g. Nadel, 2002).

Intuitive parenting support of mutual gaze in chimpanzees

In humans, eye contact occurs during interactions when infants and their caregivers are *en face*. This eye contact is called mutual gaze and has variously been linked with many uniquely human functions. Mutual gaze is said to elicit social smiles (Robson, 1967), to be at the foundation of emotional attachment, and to set the occasion for communicative exchanges (Bullowa, 1979; Trevarthen and Aitken, 2001). It is clear that the human infant is an active partner in these interactions. Newborn human infants are sensitive to and prefer to look at a face that is gazing at them (Farroni *et al.*, 2002). The infant is enmeshed in an active, although not necessarily verbalized, socialization process. There is variability across human cultures in the enculturation of gaze patterns. In many human cultures, mutual gaze between mothers and infants is actively nurtured (Bullowa, 1979), in other human cultures, in contrast, mutual gaze occurs rarely. Thus, there are clear differences in mutual gaze patterns across human cultures (Bullowa, 1979; Ochs and Schieffelin, 1984; Keller *et al.*, 1988).

It is widely assumed that only humans exhibit mutual gaze (Hobson, 2002) and that, among non-human primates, eye contact occurs only in agnostic contexts. There is much to be learned about the social functions and understanding of eye gaze from a comparative developmental evolutionary approach (Parker and Gibson, 1990; Emery, 2000) Mutual gaze was reported to occur between mother and infant chimpanzees at the Yerkes Center (Bard, 1994a) and in the wild (van Lawick-Goodall, 1968). In these settings, it appears that mutual gaze was not encouraged by chimpanzee mothers, but rather that communicative interactions were nurtured through tactile means (van Lawick-Goodall, 1968; Bard, 2002).

It is likely that caregivers across cultures encourage different eye gaze patterns, as they encourage other forms of communication, through unconscious, intuitive parenting behaviours (Bullowa, 1979; Ochs and Schieffelin, 1984; Papousek and Papousek, 1987; Keller *et al.*, 1988; Trevarthen and Aitken, 2001). Intuitive parenting processes appear to have an evolutionary foundation, as chimpanzee mothers are reported to encourage and support their infants in developing social, communicative, and motor competencies (Bard, 1994a, 2002).

There appear to be differences in the eye gaze patterns of adult chimpanzees in different settings. For example, in the wild, adult chimpanzees do not engage in long sustained eye gaze with other chimpanzees (van Lawick-Goodall, 1968). Yet in some laboratory settings (e.g. in language training settings), chimpanzees do engage in long periods of sustained eye gaze with adult social partners (human researchers, for instance). Yet, the functions served by these differences and the mechanisms by which they came to be, have not been documented. Although it has not been explicitly investigated, chimpanzees raised by humans engage in eye gaze with caregiving adults rather more easily and for longer durations than do chimpanzees reared by their own mothers, even in the captive setting (personal experience). These eye gaze patterns are well established by 3 months of age. Sustained eye gaze with adult caregivers (humans) was evident in 3-month old chimpanzees raised in the Yerkes nursery (Fig. 2.8), whereas 3-month-olds infant raised by their biological mothers at the Yerkes Field Station did not engage in sustained eye gaze with their mothers (see fig. 11.7 in Bard, 1998).

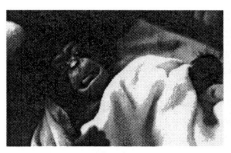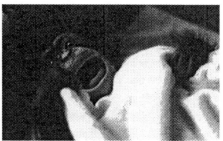

Fig. 2.8 The eye gaze pattern of a 3-month chimpanzee infant, raised in daily interaction with human caregivers, is directed to the social partner with long sustained duration during play.

The pattern of mutual gaze found in chimpanzees appears to be supported by maternal intuitive parenting behaviours, an enculturation process similarly identified for human infants. Investigations of the evolutionary foundations of culture have, to date, focused on cognitively complex phenomenon, such as tool use (Whiten *et al.*, 1999; de Waal, 2001). Studies of more fundamental social behaviours (i.e. basic gestures or early communicative behaviours), which clearly show differences across human cultures, might be more profitably utilized in primate studies of culture. Early communication, evident during play and gestural development is nurtured through primarily tactile means in many non-human primates (van Lawick-Goodall, 1968; Plooij, 1979) and also in some human cultures (Sorenson, 1979; Stack, 2001). Recently, we conducted a study comparing mother-infant mutual gaze in chimpanzees living in two different eye gaze 'cultures' (Bard *et al.*, 2003).

Regardless of how it came to be that adults at Yerkes and at PRI came to engage in different patterns of eye gaze, the specific aim of this study was to investigate the ways in which chimpanzee mothers engaged with their newborn infants with regard to developing eye gaze patterns and intuitive parenting behaviours. By using an approach that combines a developmental perspective (describing changes in mutual gaze in the first 3 months of life) with comparative data (documenting mutual gaze and intuitive parenting behaviours across different groups and across species), we can obtain a combined perspectives that may disentangle necessary and sufficient conditions in the social functions of eye gaze, and allow us to explore developmental prerequisites and consequences of mutual gaze.

The specific aims of this study are to compare the development of mutual gaze in chimpanzee mother-infants pairs across two different settings, and to describe those intuitive parenting behaviours linked with mutual gaze. Observations of eight mothers with their infants at Yerkes and three mothers with their infants at PRI were videotaped and microanalysed. Three hours of observation were used for each mother-infant pair, 1 hour when the infant was between 2 and 4 weeks of age (1 month), 1 hour when the infant was between 6 and 8 weeks of age (2 months), and 1 hour when the infant was between 10 and 12 weeks of age (3 months) (for further details see Bard, 1994a; Bard *et al.*, 2003).

Maternal gaze was classified in one of three mutually exclusive and exhaustive categories (at the infant's body, at the infant's face, or not looking at the infant). Mutual gaze was recorded when the infant looked at the mother's face during the times when the mother was looking at the infants' face. The *interactive context* was classified into one of 12 mutually exclusive and exhaustive categories of maternal behaviours (see Bard, 1994a). Interactive context classified those maternal behaviours that nurtured the development of infants' social, communicative, and motor skills (i.e. intuitive parenting behaviours; Papousek and Papousek, 1987; Bard, 1994a).

The initial report of mutual gaze in mother-raised chimpanzees (Bard, 1994a) compared mutual gaze in chimpanzees with full and inadequate maternal competence. The search was for ways to classify maternal competence via intuitive parenting behaviours. I found that chimpanzees with good maternal skills engaged in approximately 10 instances of mutual gaze in an hour with their 1-, 2-, and 3-month-old infants. Chimpanzee mothers with insufficient maternal skills engaged in fewer instances of mutual gaze with their infants: eight instances of mutual gaze with 1-month-olds, and two instances with 2-month-olds. These mothers also spent less time looking at their 2-month-old infant's face or their 2-month-old infant's body, less time nurturing motor development through exercise, and less time playing with their infants.

Mothers with inadequate competence placed their infants on the floor, out of physical contact, an average of 33% of the time when infants were 2 months old, in contrast to those with good maternal competence who never placed with infant out of physical contact at any time during the 3-monthly observation hours. At Yerkes, placing infants out of contact was a definite sign of inadequate maternal care (Bard, 1994a), typically requiring placement of these infants into nursery care. All infants of marginal mothers were placed in the nursery by the time they were 3 months of age. So, mothers with insufficient maternal competence presented a pattern of lower amount of cradling, exercising, playing, and lower amounts of mutual gaze.

PRI mothers, in contrast, appeared to be acting in ways to foster development in their infants even though they did place their infants out of physical contact. There was a significant group difference in cradling (Fig. 2.9), as well as the group difference in eye gaze. At PRI, mothers cradled their 3-month-old infants about 40% of the time and gazed at them over 25 times in an hour, whereas at Yerkes, mothers cradled their 3-month-old babies over 70% of the time and gazed at them only 11 times in an hour.

Using observations of chimpanzees with good maternal competence from Yerkes and the PRI mothers, we found a significant and inverse relation between cradling and rate of mutual gaze (Bard *et al.*, 2003). This is curious because it is not intuitive. Good mothers who cradled their infants less, engaged in more mutual gazing with them. Other indices that confirmed that the PRI mothers had good maternal competence included the equivalent amount of play when infants were 3 months old (13% of the time), and the fact that PRI and Yerkes mothers soothed, caressed and safeguarded their 3-month-old infants equally often (PRI 8% compared with 3% for the good

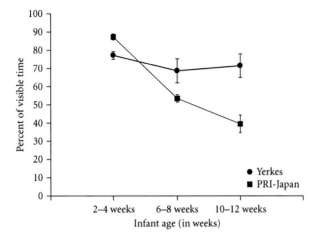

Fig. 2.9 Percentage of time competent chimpanzee mothers at a facility in Japan (Primate Research Institute) and in USA (Yerkes) spend cradling their infants in the first 3 months.

mothers at Yerkes). Confirming the impression that the PRI mothers were nurturing motor development, was the finding that PRI mothers spent more time exercising their 3-month-old infants (mean 33.1%, SD = 16.2) than did the good mothers at Yerkes (mean 6.5%, SD = 8.4, $F(1, 8)$ = 12.49, $p < 0.01$, eta2 = 0.61).

We were interested in specifying the maternal interactive behaviours (Papousek and Papousek, 1987; Bard, 1994a) that support mutual gaze. Clearly, the group difference in mutual gaze was not a function of how much mothers looked at their infants. Rather, it appeared that there were differences in the actions of the mother or infant during the times when mothers were looking at their infants' faces. It appeared that mothers at PRI were actively encouraging mutual gaze by tilting or holding up the infant's chin with her finger while looking into her infants eyes (see fig. 2 in Bard et al., 2003). Intuitive parenting mechanisms might explain the development of both visual and tactile communication occurring, and moreover, occurring in culture-specific ways without conscious awareness. Early communication in some cultures and in most non-human primates relies heavily on the tactile mode (physical contact), rather than the visual mode (Sorenson, 1979; Stack, 2001; Bard, 2002).

This study confirmed that mutual gaze, the developmentally earliest eye gaze pattern, occurs between mother and infant chimpanzees. There are many commonalties between chimpanzees and humans, which are especially notable in early social communicative interactions, such as the rich mother-infant communicative system (van Lawick-Goodall, 1968; Plooij, 1979; Matsuzawa, 2001; Bard, 2002). It is clear that early social communicative exchanges in chimpanzees and in humans can include mutual gaze, and the rate can be comparable, e.g. 17 an hour in chimpanzees compared with 18–20 an hour reported in Canadians (Ling and Ling, 1974). Developmental theories that link eye gaze to more advanced social cognitive functions, including understanding of others as intentional beings (Tomasello, 1999), need to be reconsidered.

Considering the extent of mutual gaze found in the chimpanzees and comparing it with published data on eye gaze from human mother-infant pairs living in Canada, and Italy we can conclude that:

- mutual gaze in the first 3 months of life is not unique to the human species;
- chimpanzees exhibit inter-group variation in the rate of mutual gaze;
- the variation in rate of mutual gaze is significant and inversely related to extent of physical cradling.

We concluded that mutual engagement between caregivers and infants is supported through multiple modalities. Again, by bringing in a cross cultural perspective, we see that there is substantial variation among humans in different cultures, both in mutual gaze and in the extent of physical cradling (Sorenson, 1979; Ochs and Schieffelin, 1984; Papousek and Papousek, 1987; Rogoff and Morelli, 1989). Moreover, cross-cultural comparisons suggest that mutual gaze and physical contact might be inversely related (Keller et al., 2004).

There was a significant difference in mutual gaze in chimpanzees between the two captive settings. Group-specific differences in mutual gaze were learned by infants through interactions with their chimpanzee mothers, providing evidence for cultural variation in chimpanzees. The enculturation process of intuitive parenting behaviour in chimpanzees appears strikingly similar to the process used by humans (Papousek and Papousek, 1987; Keller et al., 1988; de Waal, 2001; Trevarthen and Aitken, 2001; Lavelli and Fogel, 2002). Recent investigations of the evolutionary foundations of culture have focused on relatively complex cognitive phenomena, such as tool use (Whiten et al., 1999; Matsuzawa, 2001), rather than more basic social behaviours, i.e. communicative gestures (except Nakamura, 2002). Human cultures clearly differ in communicative gestures (Bullowa, 1979; Sorenson, 1979; de Waal, 2001).

Reduced face-to-face interactions, and reduced amounts of mutual gaze are reported in some human cultures that have increased physical contact with infants, compared with Western norms (Sorenson, 1979; Ochs and Schieffelin, 1984; Keller et al., 1988). In an experimental study of human mother-infant pairs (Lavelli and Fogel, 2002), mutual gaze increased when 2- and 3-month-old infants were placed out-of-contact compared with being held by their mothers. One implication is that we should re-think the assumption that mutual gaze causes intense bonding (Robson, 1967). Rather, it appears that mutual gaze is a consequence of breaks in physical contact. Mutual gaze may function to repair and restore engagement. When physical contact is broken, the modality for mutual engagement changes from primarily tactile to more predominantly visual, setting the stage for the development of mutual gaze. Intuitive parenting mechanisms might explain the development of both visual and tactile communication occurring, and moreover, occurring in culture-specific ways without conscious awareness. Early communication in some cultures and in most non-human primates relies heavily on the tactile mode (physical contact), rather than the visual mode (Sorenson, 1979; Stack, 2001; Bard, 2002).

This change in perspective allows for an integration of the human, cross-cultural, and non-human primate data with regard to mutual gaze.

Early eye gaze patterns may provide a foundation for later understanding of eye gaze, in chimpanzees as in humans (Tomasello, 1999). In humans, the social functions of eye gaze develop beyond those evident in the dyad (i.e. primary intersubjectivity; Trevarthen and Aitken, 2001), to those that involve a triad of the infant, social partner, and object (i.e. joint attention). Differences in mutual gaze might relate to later differences in social communicative behaviours, such as in intentional communication, joint visual attention, understanding the visual perspective of others, and, indeed, mental state attribution (i.e. theory of mind). Moreover, mother–infant chimpanzees in Japan exhibited higher rates of mutual gaze than did mother–infant chimpanzees in a US center, providing evidence that chimpanzee infants are learning group-specific patterns through interaction with their mothers (demonstrating that infant chimpanzees, like humans, are responsive to social rules of their social group, i.e. intersubjectivity; Bard, 1998). We eagerly await future studies that will chart the developmental consequences of these cultural variations in mutual gaze in chimpanzees.

'Basic' emotions

Chimpanzee infants, like human infants, exhibit some emotional expressions in the first days of life, and additional expressions develop over the first months of life (Bard, 1998). Very young chimpanzees give positive vocal greetings and smiles in response to familiar faces and voices, and even express anger. The chimpanzee emotional system, just like the human emotional system, develops in interaction with the social environment, as evident in the differential number of smiles, and different levels of crying during the first weeks of life (Bard, 2000, 2003).

Emotional expressions were recorded as they occurred during the Brazelton Neonatal Behavioural Assessment Scale (NBAS; Bard et al., 1992). NBAS assessments were conducted every other day from 2 or 3 days after birth through 42 days of age. Twenty-one chimpanzees were raised in a Standard Care (ST) nursery in which the philosophy was that social, emotional, and communicative needs of young chimpanzees would be met by being raised with same-aged peers, but that humans were necessary to provide for health needs. Sixteen chimpanzees were raised in the Responsive Care nursery (RC) with a different philosophy, specifically that specially trained humans would meet the infant's emotional, social and health needs, especially enhancing the development of chimpanzee species-typical communication. For each individual, the facial and vocal expressions were noted. Summaries were made of the number of individuals and age of onset for each expression (see Table 2.2). Fussing and crying were evident in the first or second NBAS test (by 4 and 5 days of age, respectively). Every infant chimpanzee also exhibited relaxed social smiles (by 11 days of age on average, i.e. 'play face'). The majority of infant chimpanzees vocalized greetings

Table 2.2 Vocal and facial emotional expressions in young chimpanzees: age of onset (number of individuals; after Bard, 1998)

Joy	Anger	Distress
Smile 11 days (37)	Mad face* 21 days (17)	Fuss 3.5 days (37)
Greeting* 7 days (29)	Threat bark 36 days (12)	Cry 5 days (37)
Laughter 37 days (30)	Alarm call 19 days (8)	Cry face 14 days (29)
		Pout 17 days (37)

Note: * indicates a rearing group difference (see text for details).

(by 7 days of age) and effort grunts (by 14 days of age). Most of the infant chimpanzee also laughed (by 37 days of age), mostly in response to tickles in the neck, stomach, or groin. The rearing environment did not affect either the number of individuals or the timing of these emotional responses.

However, anger did vary as a function of rearing. Only a few Standard Care infants (14% of ST) compared with the majority of Responsive Care infants (88% of RC), which is a significant difference: $\chi^2(1) = 19.3$, $p < 0.01$). Rearing also influenced the number of individual who expressed greetings (67% of ST versus 94% of RC vocalized greetings, $\chi^2(1) = 3.931$, $p < 0.05$, Fischer's exact $p = 0.053$ to correct for small expected frequencies). I believe that this is a reflection of the generally improved social, communicative, and emotional health of the RC infants.

Discussion

The chimpanzee emotional system appears to develop in interaction with the emotional responsiveness of social partners. There were significant differences in some realms of emotional expression as a function of rearing environment. It appears that a more responsive rearing environment results in a more positively expressive infant, and less fussy infant (Bard, 2000), effects that are evident even within the first weeks of life. Minimally, the study suggests that early emotional interactions are important in the development of emotional expression.

Primary intersubjectivity develops through social and emotional communicative exchanges. It appears that newborn humans and newborn chimpanzees share an innate predisposition for primary intersubjectivity, as they are indistinguishable in many aspect of neurobehavioural integrity, they share flexibility in interpersonal interactions with mutual gaze, show an equal capacity for neonatal imitation of sounds and facial actions, especially with more matching in an interactive context than a rigidly structured one and express emotions in similar contexts. The socialization context has an extraordinary influence on human and chimpanzee behavioural development.

Primary intersubjectivity is responsivity to social interaction, found in human and chimpanzee infants, most often in face-to-face interactions. The flexibility in infant behaviour in interaction with parenting styles allows for the nurturing of early communicative patterns in humans (Papousek and Papousek, 1987; Keller *et al.*, 1988; Trevarthen and Aitken, 2001) and chimpanzees (Bard, 1994a, 1996, 1998, 2002). Primary intersubjectivity develops through social and emotional exchanges, and is thought to occur as a result of the infants' ability to adapt their own purposeful acts to the subjectivity of others (Trevarthen, 1979) and provides the foundation for the secondary intersubjectivity (Trevarthen and Hubley, 1978). Secondary intersubjectivity is when an infant can coordinate attention and action on an object, with the attention and action with a social partner. Chimpanzees engage in at least two different forms of secondary intersubjectivity, intentional communication and social referencing (Leavens *et al.*, 1996; Russell *et al.*, 1997; Menzel, 1999), providing further support that chimpanzees have primary intersubjectivity.

Future directions

There are tremendous opportunities for future research in emotions in non-human primates. 'Hot' new topics include empathy (Preston and de Waal, 2002), links of facial with vocal expressions of affect (Ghazanfar and Logothetis, 2003), a consideration of emotion without cognition (e.g. Panksepp, 1998), consideration of 'positive' emotions in animals (see chapter 1 by Panksepp and Smith-Pasqualini), and reconsideration of 'nasty' emotions (e.g. special issue of *Emotion Researcher: Official Newsletter of the International Society of Researchers in Emotion*, 2002). There is renewed interest in topics, such as personality, cooperation, 'moral emotions', and love, that captured the interest of early comparative psychologists (Bingham, 1927; Crawford, 1935; Foley, 1935; Kohts, 1935; McCulloch, 1937; McCulloch and Haslerud, 1939; Yerkes, 1939; Hebb, 1945, 1946a,b; Falk, 1958; Harlow, 1958; Forman and Kochanska, 2001).

The causes and consequences of individual differences in emotional reactions has been of interest and recent research has explored the biological bases of emotional reactions (Fairbanks, 2001). The evolutionary bases of specific emotions among primates would be an important area of study (that is beyond the common mammalian roots, and beyond the consideration of only fear). For example, de Waal explored the evolutionary underpinnings of empathy (i.e. peacemaking: de Waal, 1989) and the moral emotions (de Waal, 1996). Pioneering research by Parr and colleagues brings together their interest in emotions with technological advances in computer testing (Parr *et al.*, 1998). Chimpanzees understand the emotional meaning of non-social events by matching then with a photograph of the emotionally appropriate species-typical face: 'match-to-meaning' (Parr, 2001). It is clear that there is much that we still do not know, or are unwilling to conjecture: 'the degree to which non-human primates have a concept of emotion . . . is yet to be demonstrated' (p. 9).

We are studying emotions in chimpanzees, in part, by developing a chimpanzee facial action coding system (chimp FACS), in the spirit of the human FACS (Ekman and Friesen, 1978). The initial task was to compare underlying musculature of the chimpanzee and human face, in order to make predictions about facial movements (Waller *et al.*, 2003). The studies that follow will utilize the proven methodology of Ekman, to distinguish between similar looking facial expressions that might perform different communicative functions. For example, the human smile containing a cheek raise, is said to be different from one without a cheek raise (e.g. 'felt' smile versus 'false' smiles; Ekman and Friesen, 1982). We have determined that some chimpanzee facial expressions contain the cheek raise movement (although without the fat deposits in the face, chimpanzees do not have much of a 'cheek'). It remains a question, however, whether the chimpanzee expressions with and without a cheek raise movement are expressing different emotion, communicate different information, or are simply naturally occurring variation without predictable emotional, social, or communicative meaning (Russell *et al.*, 2003).

There is an additionally exciting area of research in human and non-human primates that is demonstrating long-term effects of early emotional events, especially powerfully aversive events that occur early in life.

Acknowledgements

The research presented in this chapter was supported financially in part, by NIH Grants RR-00165 (to the Yerkes Center), RR-03951 (to B. Swenson), RR-01658 (to K. A. Bard), HD-21013 (to D. Fragazy), HD-07105 (to K. A. Bard), and NICHD Intramural Research Program (to S. J. Suomi), by the British Council (to K. A. Bard), grant-in-aid of scientific research from the Ministry of Education, Culture, Sports, Science and Technology (to PRI, Kyoto University, Japan), the Nuffield Foundation (Undergraduate Bursary to J. Quinn and P. Morris), and the Leverhulme Trust (to K. A. Bard). The Yerkes Regional Primate Research Center of Emory University is fully accredited by the American Association of Laboratory Animal Care. Grateful appreciation is extended to Kelly McDonald, Carolyn Fort, Josh Schneider, and Kathy Gardner for their general support to the research program. The collaboration of Dr Linda Brent, Dr Dorothy Fragaszy, Kelly McDonald, and Erica Yeager for the study of neonatal imitation is particularly appreciated. I thank my colleagues Masako Myowa-Yamokoshi, Masaki Tomonaga, Masayuki Tanaka, Alan Costall and Tetsuro Matsuzawa, for their collaboration in the mutual gaze study, where essential assistance was provided (1) with the Yerkes chimpanzees and data, by Kathy Gardner, Kelly McDonald, Josh Schneider, Jayne Sylvester, Claudia Herdieckerhoff, Dana Padgett, Ben Jones, Carolyn Fort, and Lindsay Cohen, and (2) with the PRI chimpanzees and data, by Yuu Mizuno, Jayne Sylvester, and the Language and Intelligence section. Grateful appreciation is extended to Dorothy Fragaszy, Vicky Roberts, Vasudevi Reddy, Kathleen Platzman, Roger Bakeman, and especially Hanus and Mechthild Papousek for the mutual gaze study.

For the NBAS study, I am grateful to Research Assistants, especially, Ms Carolyn Fort, Ms Kathy Gardner, Mr Josh Schneider, and Ms Kelly McDonald, to the assistance provided by Dr Mary Schneider, by the staff of the Great Ape Nursery and Veterinary Staff of the Yerkes Center, and numerous students of Emory University, Oxford College, and Georgia State University. Dr Worobey graciously provided the standard deviations from the Hallock *et al.* (1989) paper reporting NBAS performance of chimpanzees. Dr David Leavens offered many constructive comments on each of the studies reported here.

References

Anisfeld, M. (1996). Only tongue protrusion modeling is matched by neonates. *Developmental Review*, **16**, 149–61.

Bard, K. A. (1994a). Evolutionary roots of intuitive parenting: maternal competence in chimpanzees. *Early Development and Parenting*, **3**, 19–28.

Bard, K. A. (1994b). Very early social learning: the effect of neonatal environment on chimpanzees' social responsiveness. In *Current primatology: Vol III: social development, learning, and behaviour* (ed. J. Roeder, B. Thierry, J. R. Anderson, *et al.*), pp. 339–46. Strasbourg: Universite Louis Pasteur.

Bard, K. A. (1996). *Responsive care: a behavioral intervention program for nursery-reared chimpanzees.* Tuscon, AZ: Jane Goodall Insititute.

Bard, K. A. (1998). Social-experiential contributions to imitation and emotion in chimpanzees. In *Intersubjective communication and emotion in early ontogeny: a source book* (ed. S. Braten), pp. 208–27. Cambridge: Cambridge University Press.

Bard, K. A. (2000). Crying in infant primates: insights into the development of crying in chimpanzees. In *Crying as a sign, a sympton, and a signal: developmental and clinical aspects of early crying behaviour* (ed. R. Barr, B. Hopkins, and J. Green), pp. 157–75. London: MacKeith Press.

Bard, K. A. (2002). Primate parenting. In *Handbook of Parenting, Vol. 2: Biology and ecology of parenting*, 2nd edn (ed. M. Bornstein), pp. 99–140. Mahwah, NJ: L. Erlbaum.

Bard, K. A. (2003). Development of emotions in young chimpanzees (*Pan troglodytes*). *Annals of the New York Academy of Sciences*, **1000**, 88–90.

Bard, K. A. (2004). Neonatal imitation in chimpanzees (*Pan troglodytes*). Unpublished manuscript.

Bard, K. A. and Russell, C. L. (1999). Evolutionary foundations of imitation: Social, cognitive, and developmental aspects of imitative processes in non-human primates. In *Imitation in infancy: Progress and prospects of current research* (ed. J. Nadel and G. Butterworth), pp. 89–123. Cambridge, UK: Cambridge University Press.

Bard, K. A., Platzman, K. A., Lester, B. M., *et al.* (1992). Orientation to social and nonsocial stimuli in neonatal chimpanzees and humans. *Infant Behaviour and Development*, **15**, 43–56.

Bard, K. A., Fragaszy, D., and Visalberghi, E. (1995). Acquisition and comprehension of a tool-using behaviour by young chimpanzees: effects of age and modeling. *International Journal of Comparative Psychology*, **8**, 47–68.

Bard, K. A., Coles, C., Platzman, K. A., *et al.* (2000). The effects of prenatal drug exposure, term status, and caregiving on arousal and arousal modulation in 8-week-old infants. *Developmental Psychobiology*, **36**, 194–212.

Bard, K. A., Platzman, K. A., Lester, B. M., *et al.* (2001). Developpement neurobiologique et emotions chez les nouveau-nes chimpanzes et humains (Neurobehavioural integrity and emotions in chimpanzee and human neonates). *Enfance*, **3**, 226–35.

Bard, K. A., Myowa-Yamakoshi, M., Tomonaga, M., *et al.* (2003). Cultural variation in the mutual gaze of chimpanzees (*Pan troglodytes*). Unpublished manuscript.

Bigelow, A. (1998). Infants' sensitivity to familiar imperfect contingencies in social interaction. *Infant Behaviour and Development*, **21**, 149–62.

Bingham, H. C. (1927). Parental play of chimpanzees. *Journal of Mammalogy*, **8**, 77–89.

Brazelton, T. B. and Nugent, J. K. (1995). *Neonatal behavioural assessment scale*, 3rd edn. London: Mac Keith Press.

Bruner, J. (1972). Nature and uses of immaturity. *American Psychologist*, **27**, 687–708.

Bullowa, M. (1979). Introduction: prelinguistic communication: a field for scientific study. In *Before speech: the beginnings of interpersonal communication* (ed. M. Bullowa), pp. 1–62. New York, NY: Cambridge University Press.

Chevalier-Skolnikoff, S. (1976). The ontogeny of primate intelligence and its implications for communicative potential: a preliminary report. *Annals of the New York Academy of Sciences*, **280**, 173–211.

Chevalier-Skolnikoff, S. (1982). A cognitive analysis of facial behaviour in Old World monkeys, apes, and human beings. In *Primate communication* (ed. C. Snowden, C. H. Brown, and M. R. Peterson), pp. 303–68. New York, NY: Cambridge University Press.

Chisholm, J. (1989). Biology, culture, and the development of temperament: a Navajo example. In *The cultural context of infancy* (ed. J. K. Nugent, B. M. Lester, and T. B. Brazelton), pp. 341–64. New Jersey: Ablex.

Crawford, M. P. (1935). Cooperative behaviour in chimpanzee. *Psychological Bulletin*, **32**, 714.

Custance, D. and Bard, K. A. (1994). The comparative and developmental study of self-recognition and imitation: the importance of social factors. In *Self-awareness in animals and humans: developmental perspectives* (ed. S. T. Parker, K. R. Gibson, and M. Boccia), pp. 207–26. New York, NY: Cambridge University Press.

Custance, D. M., Whiten, A., and Bard, K. A. (1995). Can young chimpanzees (*Pan troglodytes*) imitate arbitrary actions? Hayes and Hayes (1952) revisited. *Behaviour*, **132(11–12)**, 837–59.

de Waal, F. X. (1989). *Peacemaking among primates*. Cambridge: Cambridge University Press.

de Waal, F. X. (1996). *Good natured: the origina of right an dworng in humans and other animals*. Cambridge: Cambridge University Press.

de Waal, F. X. (2001). *The ape and the sushi master: cultural reflections by a primatologist*. London: Allen Lane/Penguin Press.

Ekman, P. and Friesen, W. (1978). *Facial action coding system: a technique for the measurement of facial movement*. Palo Alto: Consulting Psychologists.

Ekman, P. and Friesen, W. (1982). Felt, false, and miserable smiles. *Journal of Nonverbal Behaviour*, **6**, 238–52.

Emery, N. J. (2000). The eyes have it: the neuroethology, function and evolution of social gaze. *Neuroscience and Biobehavioural Reviews*, **24**, 581–604.

Fairbanks, L. (2001). Individual differences in response to a stranger: social impulsivity as a dimension of temperament in vervet monkeys (*Cercopithecus aethiops sabaues*). *Journal of Comparative Psychology*, **115**, 22–8.

Falk, J. L. (1958). The grooming behaviour of the chimpanzee as a reinforcer. *Journal of the Experimental Analysis of Behaviour*, **1**, 83–5.

Farroni, T., Csibra, G., Simion, F., *et al.* (2002). Eye contact detection in humans from birth. *Proceedings of the National Academy of Sciences of the United States of America*, **99**, 9602–5.

Fischer, A. and Cornelius, R. (ed.) (2002). Nasty emotions. *Emotion Researcher (Official Newsletter of the International Society for Research on Emotion)*. **16**, 1–16.

Foley, J. P. (1935). Judgment of facial expression of emotion in the chimpanzee. *Journal of Social Psychology*, **6**, 31–67.

Forman, D. R. and Kochanska, G. (2001). Viewing imitation as child responsiveness: a link between teaching and discipline domains of socialization. *Developmental Psychology*, **37(2)**, 198–206.

Ghazanfar, A. A. and Logothetis, N. K. (2003). Facial expressions linked to monkey calls. *Nature*, **423**, 937–8.

Greenfield, P. M., Keller, H., Fuligni, A., *et al.* (2003). Cultural pathways through universal development. *Annual Review of Psychology*, **54**, 461–90.

Hallock, M. B., Worobey, J., and Self, P. (1989). Behavioural development in chimpanzees (*Pan troglodytes*) and human newborns across the first month of life. *International Journal of Behavioural Development*, **12**, 527–40.

Harlow, H. (1958). The nature of love. *American Psychologist*, **13**, 673–85.

Hayes, K. J. and Hayes, C. (1952). Imitation in a home-raised chimpanzee. *Journal of Comparative and Physiological Psychology*, **45**, 450–9.

Hebb, D. O. (1945). The forms and conditions of chimpanzee anger. *Bulletin of the Canadian Psychological Association*, **5**, 32–5.

Hebb, D. O. (1946a). Emotion in man and animal: an analysis of the intuitive processes of recognition. *Psychological Review*, **53**, 88–106.

Hebb, D. O. (1946b). The objective description of temperament. *American Psychologist*, **1**, 275–6.

Heyes, C. (2001). Causes and consequences of imitation. *Trends in Cognitive Sciences*, **6**, 253–61.

Hobson, P. (2002). *The cradle of thought: exploring the origins of thinking*. London: Macmillan.

Jacobsen, C. F., Jacobsen, M. M., and Yoshioka, J. G. (1932). Development of an infant chimpanzee during her first year. *Comparative Psychology Monographs*, **9**, 94.

Kagan, J. (2003). Biology, context, and developmental inquiry. *Annual Review of Psychology*, **54**, 1–23.

Keller, H., Scholmerich, A., and Eibl-Eiblesfeldt, I. (1988). Communication patterns in adult-infant interactions in western and non-western cultures. *Journal of Cross-Cultural Psychology*, **19**, 427–45.

Keller, H., Lohaus, A., Kuensemueller, P., *et al.* (2004) The bio-culture of parenting: evidence from five cultural communities. *Parenting*, **4(1)**, 25–50.

Kohts, N. (1935). *Infant ape and human child (instincts, emotions, play, habits)*. Moscow: Publisher unknown.

Kugiumutzakis, G. (1985). *The origin, development, and function of the early infant imitation*. Unpublished PhD Dissertation, University of Uppsala, Uppsala.

Kugiumutzakis, G. (1999). Genesis and development of early infant mimesis to facial and vocal models. In *Imitation in infancy* (ed. J. Nadel and G. Butterworth), pp. 36–59. Cambridge: Cambridge University Press.

Lavelli, M. and Fogel, A. (2002). Developmental changes in mother-infant face-to-face communication. *Developmental Psychology*, **38**, 288–305.

Leavens, D. A., Hopkins, W. D., and Bard, K. A. (1996). Indexical and referential pointing in chimpanzees (*Pan troglodytes*). *Journal of Comparative Psychology*, **110(4)**, 346–53.

Lester, B. M. (1984). Data analysis and prediction. In *Neonatal Behavioural Assessment Scale* (ed. T. B. Brazelton), 2nd edn, pp. 85–96. London: Spastics International Medical Publications.

Lester, B. M., Anderson, L. T., Boukydis, C. F. Z., *et al.* (1989). Early detection of infants at risk for later handicap through acoustic cry analysis. In *Research in infant assessment* (ed. N. Paul). New York: March of Dimes Birth Defect Foundation.

Ling, D. and Ling, A. (1974). Communication development in the first three years of life. *Journal of Speech and Hearing Research*, **17**, 146–159.

Maratos, O. (1985). Trends in the development of imitation in early infancy. In *Regressions in mental development: basic phenomena and theories* (ed. T. G. Bever), pp. 81–101. Hillsdale, NJ: L. Erlbaum.

Matsuzawa, T. (2001). *Primate origins of human cognition and behaviour.* Tokyo: Springer-Verlag.

McCulloch, T. L. (1937). The use of the 'comfort' drive as motivation in visual discrimination by the infant chimpanzee. *Psychological Bulletin*, **34**, 540–1.

McCulloch, T. L. and Haslerud, G. M. (1939). Affective responses of an infant chimpanzee reared in isolation from its kind. *Journal of Comparative Psychology*, **28**, 437–45.

Meltzoff, A. and Moore, M. K. (1977). Imitation of facial and manual gestures by human neonates. *Science*, **198**, 75–8.

Meltzoff, A. and Moore, M. K. (1989). Imitation in newborn infants: exploring the range of gestures imitated and the underlying mechanisms. *Developmental Psychology*, **25**, 954–62.

Menzel, C. (1999). Unprompted recall and reporting of hidden objects by a chimpanzee (*Pan troglodytes*) after extended delays. *Journal of Comparative Psychology*, **113**, 426–34.

Miklosi, A. (1999). The ethological analysis of imitation. *Biological Review*, **74**, 347–74.

Myowa, M. (1996). Imitation of facial gestures by an infant chimpanzee. *Primates*, **37**, 207–13.

Nadel, J. (2002). Imitation and imitation recognition: functional use in preverbal infants and nonverbal children with autism. In *The imitative mind: development, evolution, and brain bases* (ed. A. Meltzoff and W. Prinz), pp. 42–62. Cambridge: Cambridge University Press.

Nadel, J. and Butterworth, G. (1999). *Imitation in infancy.* Cambridge: Cambridge University Press.

Nakamura, M. (2002). Grooming-hand-clasp in Mahale M Group chimpanzees: implications for culture in social behaviours. In *Behavioural diversity in chimpanzees and bonobos* (ed. C. Boesch, G. Hohmann, and L. F. Marchant), pp. 71–83. Cambridge: Cambridge University Press.

Nugent, J. K., Lester, B. M., and Brazelton, T. B. (1989). *The cultural context of infancy.* New Jersey: Ablex.

Ochs, E. and Schieffelin, B. B. (1984). Language acquistion and socialization: three developmental stories and their implications. In *Culture theory* (ed. R. Shweder and R. LeVine), pp. 276–320. Cambridge: Cambridge University Press.

Panksepp, J. (1998). *Affective neuroscience: the foundations of human and animal emotions.* Oxford: Oxford University Press.

Papousek, H. and Papousek, M. (1987). Intuitive parenting: a dialectic counterpart to the infant's integrative competence. In *Handbook of infant development*, 2nd edn (ed. J. Osofsky), pp. 669–720. New York, NY: Wiley.

Parker, S. T. and Gibson, K. R. (1990). *'Language' and intelligence in monkeys and apes: comparative developmental perspectives.* New York, NY: Cambridge University Press.

Parr, L. A. (2001). Cognitive and physiological markers of emotional awareness in chimpanzees (*Pan toglodytes*). *Animal Cognition*, **4**, 223–9.

Parr, L. A., Hopkins, W. D., and de Waal, F. X. (1998). The perception of facial expressions in chimpanzees (*Pan troglodytes*). *Evolution of Communication*, **2**, 1–23.

Plooij, F. (1979). How wild chimpanzee babies trigger the onset of mother-infant play—and what the mother makes of it. In *Before speech: the beginning of interpersonal communication* (ed. M. Bullowa), pp. 223–43. New York, NY: Cambridge University Press.

Preston, S. D. and de Waal, F. X. (2002). Empathy: its ultimate and proximate bases. *Behavioural and Brain Sciences*, **25**(1), 1–71.

Robson, K. (1967). The role of eye-to-eye contact in maternal-infant attachment. *Journal of Child Psycholgy and Psychiatry*, **8**, 13–25.

Rogoff, B. and Morelli, G. (1989). Perspectives on children's development from cultural psychology. *American Psychologist*, **44**, 343–8.

Russell, C. L., Bard, K. A., and Adamson, L. B. (1997). Social referencing by young chimpanzees (Pan troglodytes). *Journal of Comparative Psychology*, **111(2)**, 185–91.

Russell, J. A., Bachorowski, J., and Fernandez-Dols, J.-M. (2003). Facial and vocal expressions of emotion. *Annual Review of Psychology*, **54**, 329–49.

Sameroff, A. (1978). Organization and stability of newborn behaviour: a commentary on the Brazelton Neonatal Behavioral Assessment Scale. *Monographs of the Society for Research in Child Development*, **43**.

Seyfarth, R. M. and Cheney, D. L. (2003). Signalers and receivers in animal communication. *Annual Review of Psychology*, **54**, 145–73.

Sorenson, E. R. (1979). Early tactile communication and the patterns of human organization: a New Guinea case study. In *Before speech: the beginning of interpersonal communication* (ed. M. Bullowa), pp. 289–305. New York, NY: Cambridge University Press.

Stack, D. M. (2001). The salience of touch and physical contact during infancy: unraveling some of the mysteries of the somesthetic sense. In *Blackwell handbook of infant development* (ed. G. Bremner and A. Fogel), pp. 351–78. Oxford: Blackwell.

Tomasello, M. (1999). *The cultural origins of human cognition*. Cambridge: Harvard University Press.

Tomasello, M., Savage-Rumbaugh, E. S., and Kruger, A. (1993). Imitative learning of actions on objects by children, chimpanzees, and enculturated chimpanzees. *Child Development*, **64**, 1688–705.

Tomonaga, M., Okamoto, S., Myowa-Yamakoshi, M., *et al.* (2002). *Recognition of face and gaze in infant chimpanzees (Pan troglodytes)*. Paper presented at the Second international symposium on comparative cognitive science, 'Social transmission of knowledge', Inyuma, Japan.

Tomonaga, M., Myowa-Yamakoshi, M., Mizuno, Y., *et al.* (in press). Development of social cognition in infant chimpanzees (*Pan troglodytes*): face recognition, smiling, mutual gaze, gaze following, and the lack of triadic interactions. *Japanese Psychological Research*.

Trevarthen, C. (1979). Communication and cooperation in early infancy: a descriptive of primary intersubjectivity. In *Before speech: the beginnings of interpersonal communication* (ed. M. Bullowa), pp. 321–47. New York: Cambridge University Press.

Trevarthen, C. and Hubley, P. (1978). Secondary intersubjectivity: confidence, confiding, and acts of meaning in the first year of life. In *Action, gesture, symbol: the emergence of language* (ed. A. Lock), pp. 183–229. New York, NY: Academic Press.

Trevarthen, C. and Aitken, K. J. (2001). Infant intersubjectivity: research, theory, and clinical applications. *Journal of Child Psychology and Psychiatry*, **42**, 3–48.

Tronick, E. Z. and Winn, S. A. (1992). The neurobehavioural organization of Efe (Pygmy) infants. *Developmental and Behavioural Pediatrics*, **13**, 421–4.

van Lawick-Goodall, J. (1968). The behaviour of free-living chimpanzees of the Gombe Stream Nature reserve. *Animal Behaviour Monographs*, **1**, 161–311.

Waller, B., Vick, S., Parr, L. A., *et al.* (2003). Comparative facial musculature of *Pan troglodytes* and *Homo sapiens*—How similar are the tools of facial communication? *American Journal of Physical Anthropology* (revised and resubmitted).

Want, S. C. and Harris, P. L. (2002). How do children ape: Applying concepts from the study of non-human primates to the developmental study of 'imitation' in children. *Developmental Science*, **5**, 1–41.

Whiten, A. (2000). Primate culture and social learning. *Cognitive Science*, **24(3)**, 477–508.

Whiten, A., Goodall, J., McGrew, W. C., *et al.* (1999). Cultures in chimpanzees. *Nature*, **399**, 682–5.

Yerkes, R. M. (1939). Presidential address: the life history and personality of the chimpanzee. *American Naturalist*, **73**, 97–112.

Yerkes, R. M. and Nissen, H. W. (1939). Prelinguistic sign behaviour in chimpanzee. *Science*, **89**, 585–7.

Yerkes, R. M. and Tomilin, M. I. (1935). Mother infant relations in chimpanzee. *Journal of Comparative Psychology*, **20**, 321–59.

Yerkes, R. M. and Yerkes, A. W. (1936). Nature and conditions of avoidance (fear) response in chimpanzee. *Journal of Comparative Psychology*, **21**, 53–66.

Chapter 3

Action and emotion in development of cultural intelligence: why infants have feelings like ours

Colwyn Trevarthen

Introduction: emotions are innate, and they regulate agency and social sympathy

A valid psychology of emotions is concerned with motives

Emotions seem the least understood mind function, perhaps because they are part of the cause of consciousness and remote from rational explanations that reflect experience. This chapter assumes that the activity of emotions is clear in infants, who search for experience with less reflection.

I believe that the prevailing 'models' of emotion lack real life validity because they fail to consider how emotions are essentially part of the *generation of motor activity*, for which emotional evaluations are essential (Averill, 1980; Frijda, 1986; Ekman and Davidson, 1994; Schulkin *et al.*, 2003). Emotions have been treated as protective *reactions*, not vital and optimistic *causes* of experience. This, I judge, is largely a consequence of reductive assumptions about how behaviours are generated and guided, and the application of the experimental method to test reactions of passive subjects or to assess verbal reports of experience.

A more coherent account can be given if emotions are taken to start inside the mind, with intentions to act in specific ways (Trevarthen, 1993, 1997, 2001a,b). Emotions are inseparable from *motives*—processes of prospective or ' future-sensitive' vitality that move the body and that regulate the acting self as a coherent open dynamic system (Bertalanffy, 1968; Zei Pollermann, 2002). The communication of emotions between intending human Selves, which has driven the development of more elaborate emotions characteristic of humans, depends on *intersubjective sympathy* between individuals, a sympathy active in human brains that detects and identifies with the prospective control of the movements that prepare for and implement others' intentions (Smith, 1759; Lewis and Granic, 2000; Blakemore and Decety, 2001; Bierhoff, 2002; Decety and Chaminade, 2003).

At the end of his famous book on *The expressions of emotions in man and animals*, Charles Darwin (1872/1998) concluded that a mother's emotions guide the child by assisting purposes toward good effects:

> They serve as the first means of communication between the mother and her infant; she smiles
> approval, and thus encourages her child on the right path, or frowns disapproval.

I take this to mean Darwin thought that human emotions evolved to transmit and receive the 'good sense' of an active and intelligent life in the community.

I find that cognitive neuroscience theories of emotion do not give sufficient attention to what purposeful communal intelligence entails. A first step is to relate emotions and their sympathetic communication to the production and regulation of movements—that is, to the motives that coordinate movements. Then we have to explain how motives may be communicated.

How persons communicate the values of motives to make common sense

A biological account that links emotions to the prospective control of motor activity must address the intrinsic rhythms and modulations of energy in body movement (Trevarthen, 1999). It will also relate emotions to the autonomic regulations of energy and metabolism in body state (MacLean, 1990; Porges, 2003), and to the output of neural systems that formulate anticipations of experience, in acting, thinking, and communication—neural systems that purposefully 'take up' information for perception of expected goals.

Emotions are the expectant internal evaluators that anticipate the realization of our projects, experiences and relationships in society. They guide us into ways of consciously perceiving the same 'common sense' world, and knowing how to live in it together. Emotional illness is pathology of common sense (Stanghellini, 2001). In contrast, our cognitions define goal objects 'after the fact'. They retain models and maps of reality based on what we have experienced, and in that role are 'corrective' and 'retentive' (Lazarus, 1991). Cognitions cannot, alone, initiate what moves us to be interested, nor can they balance internal state of the body against what is expected to come from outgoing action (Damasio, 1999; Freeman, 2000). In the social realm, it is not cognitions that estimate in advance who are the persons we should trust.

The emotional life of infants

Observation of a contented and wakeful infant receiving the attentions of an affectionate parent finds displays of emotion that can only function in engaging the other's interest and in stimulating future interpersonal communication. Why does a newborn baby orientate expectantly to the face of a person if not to discover and share expressions of such feelings of 'interest', 'anxiety' and 'joy' that relate to their contact? Why are games and baby songs enjoyed so much by a 5-month-old, and with such skilful anticipatory timing? What causes an infant to display rage or sad withdrawal in a relationship that is not working as expected, and why does a contented infant's mind sometimes hide behind a silent mask of inwardness, apparently inventing thoughts? Such questions lead us to consider the developmental advantages of emotions that guide the seeking of reflections, memories and the trans-generational invention of ideas in sympathetic company, in what Peter Hobson calls the 'cradle of thought' (Hobson, 2002).

Clinical research and the experience of psychotherapists prove how important are the affections of early attachments, and especially those pleasurable states that support a loving protective association between a mother and an infant (Stern, 1993, 2000; Schore, 1994, 2003). Sensitive parental care is shown to be important for the fostering of a creative and resilient emotional life and personality. Attachment Theory (Bowlby, 1958) attributes the behaviours of infant and caregiver to innate biological capacities, and assumes that adaptive development of the infant's emotional system 'expects' this human environmental support for physical and emotional well-being.

John Bowlby describes the sensitive mother as also supplying her child with a 'secure base' for exploration. But discovery of meaning is not something the child wants to do on his or her own, by going away from company. Meaning is made by emotions that may turn to and address others, to share the fun of discovering and doing. Children's emotions are adapted to draw ('educate') them into the life of others, and thence into a cultural community. They establish, evaluate and reinforce the companionships, by which the knowledge and tasks of the community are built and learned in collaborative social activity (Trevarthen, 2001a, 2004).

Intentions of animals: vital self-regulation in the active pursuit of experience

Emotions as manners of moving, and of responding to movements

The biology of animal action focuses on how prospective motor images, or the impulses of agency and embodied commitment, are generated and regulated by an animal's brain in fluid continuity, rather than on how environmental information is processed and stored, chunk-by-chunk or bit-by-bit. It views the primary function of the mind as the production of action (Sperry, 1952). Consciousness, as Donald (2001) has pointed out, is not made up of momentary cognitive responses to unitary forms or events. It has purposeful executive coherence. It seeks discovery in motivated sequences of action (Lashley, 1951). This the phenomenologists knew (Merlean-Ponty, 1962; Stern, 2004).

Emotions are part of this animal vitality—of actions to maintain bodily well-being and of conscious agency in experiencing the world, including the social world of other agents (MacLean, 1990). Expressive movements manifest how healthy, strong and alert animal bodies are, what events are moving them, and how movements are being planned to achieve particular ends. Emotions evaluate the experience of an integrated conscious subject finding things: navigating through places for exploration and adventure, choosing objects to use them, noting which may offer benefit or bring danger (Panksepp, 1998, 2000b; Porges, 2003). Actions and emotions determine what the subject will remember and what will be ignored or forgotten (Tulving, 2002; Trevarthen, 2003b).

When an animal moves, a 'coherent dynamic, body-related self-state' must be adjusted to present and future conditions in such a way that the *energy* to be expended or assimilated is accounted for (Panksepp, 1998a; Damasio, 1999). Every animal displays emotion in the *way* it moves—its power, rate, and reactions to sensed consequences. Emotions describe the coherence or organization of the motor images or plans, and how their energy economy is regulated (Scherer, 1986; Zei Pollermann, 2002). The 'manner' of coordination and regulation of movement and of its physiological cost *is* emotion, and social communication depends on detection of emotions in movement. There is an evolutionary progression to more effective ways of collaborating socially by movements that regulate approaches and contacts between individuals (Porges, 2003).

Play communicates motives of discovery, contest, joy and affiliation

Many animals play, apparently 'wasting' energy (Bekoff and Byers, 1998). Juvenile birds and mammals of species that grow up in complex societies where adaptive skills develop slowly, play long and hard. They move expressively, with stereotyped motor posturing or exaggerated kinds of locomoting, with movements of 'sensory accessory motor organs' (ears, face and jaws), or of other body appendages, such as tails, that show quick shifts of interest and pleasure, and by vocal calls that signal vigorous delight or mock startle, aggression and flight (Scherer, 1986). Play regulates the seeking of peaceful or intimate and affectionate collaboration with social partners, fighting others for advantage, avoiding threats and attack, chasing prey, fleeing predators, freezing movement to escape detection or steady attention. Meta-communicative emotional signals also regulate antagonistic encounters between rival individuals or groups, as they do the interspecies attack and flight behaviours of many kinds of predator and prey. They enable sharing of feelings about the environment and what it offers (Marler *et al.*, 1992; Merker, 2000).

Playful affectionate and aesthetic feelings of humans appear to have evolved by elaboration of both 'experience seeking' and 'attachment regulating' motives and emotions of sub-cultural but highly sociable species (Trevarthen, 1995; Dissanayake, 2000; Panksepp, 2000 and this volume; Panksepp and Burgdorf, 2003).

The intrinsic timing of animal movement and of emotions

As the animal body moves with agency and prospective control, every act is motivated with intrinsic rhythm and intensity in the 'vitality' (Stern, 1993, 1999) or 'sentic forms' (Clynes, 1980) of emotions. To comprehend this control we need a theory of 'time in the mind' (Pöppel, 1994; Pöppel and Wittmann, 1999). The timing of animal actions is intrinsic—it depends on the rate and intensity of physical and chemical processes passing through the neural assemblies of the brain.

I believe it makes sense to classify emotions initially in terms of the time course of the intended action that they serve (Pöppel and Wittmann, 1999; Trevarthen, 1999).

This conclusion accords well with phenomenological conceptions of mental processes (Merleau Ponty, 1962; Michotte, 1962; Husserl, 1964) and with the theory of open self-regulating dynamic systems (Bertalanffy, 1968). Movements are formulated in the following broad time bands:

- The fastest changes of emotion, and momentary shifts of thought, correspond with units in skeleto-muscular action and orientations of special-sense awareness measuring a few hundred milliseconds—possibly guided by senses, but faster than conscious monitoring.

- Emotions that communicate distinct states of interest and purpose in body movements, showing differing qualities of pleasure, anxiety, etc., apply their evaluations in the period of the continuously monitored conscious and intentional time, the 'psychological present', over 2–6 seconds (Stern, 2004).

- 'Narrative' cycles of emotional fluctuation, driven more 'viscerally' by spontaneous cycles of autonomic arousal, and expectations of vitality and fatigue lead to an experience of a new adventure that starts, then gains in confidence and vigour, reaches a climax, and relaxes back to a relative quiet. Narrative cycles last 30 seconds to a minute or two.

With experience and knowledge, this third 'emotional narrative' range sets the time for 'executive planning' of complex sequences and variations of movement, and for 'problem solving' in thought. Executive planning acquires greatly extended scope in memory (Tulving, 2002; Trevarthen, 2003b). Long-term recollections require categorization of experiences and are aided in their retention, as in their communication, by symbolic representations, and symbols draw their power of reference and function most meaningfully in stories (Turner, 1996). These are principles that apply in some degree, at least at a pre-symbolic level, to all active and intelligent creatures, not just to humans, but humans can give a verbal account of them, perform them as drama or music, and write them as texts or musical scores.

The approach that identifies regularities and hierarchies in the temporal change of affective states of animals, from 'instant' emotional reactions to lasting 'moods' and 'roles' or 'characters' is strongly supported by analysis of patterns of communication in sound. Animal vocalizations engage individuals in collaborative action and awareness, linking their self-regulatory states (Scherer, 1986; Zei Pollermann, 2002). Communication of emotions by sound production to serve the needs of a social community has led to the evolution of human emotive musicality (Merker, 2000; Krumhansl, 2000; Panksepp and Bernatzky, 2002).

Emotional autonomics: maintaining the energy economy of animal movement inside the body

Brains carry anatomical 'somatotopic' maps of the whole configuration of the body, separately laying out neural systems for the sensory surface and special receptors, for the muscles and skeletal frame, and for the internal organs (Trevarthen, 1985). A common chemical code of 'neurospecificity' determines the equivalence and coherent functioning of the different parts in the embryo when the nerve circuits are first laid down (Sperry, 1963). Moving the body by coordinated muscle action requires an anticipatory spatio-temporal configuration of neural activity or 'motor image' (Jeannerod, 1994). Motor images in the CNS are accompanied or preceded by autonomic activity— changes in heart activity and respiration, for example. An animal moves with different levels of excitement or 'arousal', within a changing estimation of the physiological cost or benefit of moving. This leads to a fundamental operational distinction between energy expending and energy conserving actions (Fig. 3.1).

Adventurous actions explore and discover; they seek information, or take hold of objects and use them. They may make advances to enter into the action and awareness of other subjects. All cost metabolic energy, the amount depending on the power and duration of activity, on what mass of muscles is active and for how long. Hess (1954) called these *ergotropic* activities.

Other actions, which Hess labelled *trophotropic*, or nurture seeking, take advantage of comfortable and 'healthy' situations—warmth, sleep, fresh air to breathe, pure food and water. These correspond, respectively, to the contrasting regulatory activities of the sympathetic and parasympathetic components of the autonomic nervous system (Berntson *et al.*, 2003). Trophotropic actions also desire intimate affectionate contact with other individuals to gain energy and restore vital functions with their aid (Schore, 2003).

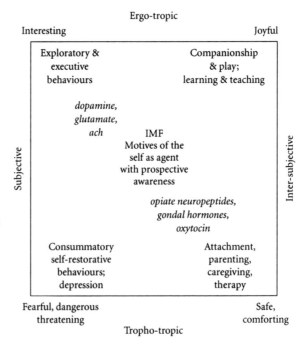

Fig. 3.1 A map of the 'Field of Emotions', representing how the active agency of the subject is balanced against self-protecting and restorative states, and how individual subjective behaviours are transformed into collaborative agency by sympathetic motives of intersubjectivity.

The prospective estimation and control of that energy cost (the 'ergic/trophic' equilibrium) is expressed as emotions, and this is one dimension on which emotions may be plotted. The other dimension of emotions regulates the balance between 'subjective' or self-related action toward objects in the world taken as non-animate, and 'intersubjective' communication with other sentient animate beings. The collective action of animals in societies requires expression in both dimensions (Fig. 3.1), and this requirement has driven the evolution of emotions into the intricate aesthetic and moral forms that humans experience and show from early childhood. We experience cycles of energy in moving and the emotive qualities of movement when we hear music (Trevarthen, 1999).

The emotional brain and its tools for communication

The neural regulation of reciprocal sympathy in actions

'Motor images' in the brain may be inferred, on the outside, from biomechanical analysis of the forces in movements (Bernstein, 1967). Outbursts of neuronal activity that precede movement and perception, inside the brain, may be detected by electro-physiological recording or neuro-imaging. The form and dynamics of 'motives' (Trevarthen, 1997), 'motor images' (Jeannerod, 1994), or psychomotor 'tau' functions (Lee, 1998) can also be 'read' by another voluntary agent directly, by sympathetic neural response to messages conveyed in movements. Human observers, including infants, detect the effort or rhythmic grace of another person moving, sensing their comfort or pain, and any sensory modality may serve this detection (Trevarthen, 1986a).

When animals interact socially, their emotions are picked up, and elaborated or 'negotiated' in the inter-subjective space between them (Aitken and Trevarthen, 1997). Intersubjective volition requires representations of other subjects as equivalent in their motives and emotions to the self, and at the same time awareness that those others are separate from the self is preserved (Decety and Somerville, 2003). The recently discovered 'mirror neurons' (Rizzolatti *et al.*, 2001), better conceived as 'sympathy neurons', have opened the way to a radical re-conception of the social brain as an organ for sympathetic engagement between motives in physically separate moving bodies. Functional brain imaging is beginning to explore the neural anatomy of those emotions that enable us to share the quality and vitality of consciousness that comes to life in our separate bodies as they move and respond to one another. (Blakemore and Decety, 2001; Adolphs, 2003; Decety and Chaminade, 2003).

Single brain structures, for example the amygdala or anterior cingulate, however important they may be as nodal structures in larger circuits, cannot be expected to be dedicated to any one emotional or social process (Rolls, 1999; Le Doux, 2000; Wicker *et al.*, 2003). Understanding how they function in the communication of emotion requires consideration of the brainstem centres that control motor expressions of emotion. Panksepp (1998, this volume) reviews the evidence for widespread mechanisms in the vertebrate brain that define the 'foundations of human and animal emotions'.

The unique anatomy of human expression

Humans have the most complex expressive motor structures in the highly communicative primate group, and the limbic and cortico-bulbar systems of emotional expression in the brain are most elaborate in humans (MacLean, 1990; Holstege *et al.*, 1996; Porges, 2003). Facial, vocal, and manual expressions show many features unique to humans. Only human eyes have white scleras that, in a horizontally oval gap between lids equipped with conspicuous lashes, make displacements of gaze clearly visible acts of communication (Kobayashi and Kohshima, 2001). The human face carries new muscles that move the cheeks and mouth to signal changes in pleasure or displeasure and disgust, acceptance or rejection, curiosity and wonder, determination and animation, or depression, as well as for mediating emotional modulation of vocal sounds.

The human breathing and vocal apparatus is transformed with the evolution of upright standing and bipedal walking, giving rise to a capacity for driving a sustained flow of air through the vocal cords at controlled pressure by movements of the stomach, diaphragm, and chest, as in speech and song. Adjustments of larynx, jaws, and tongue manipulate the resonance of the sound carrying system in intricate patterns with infinite productivity, and this has changed the human mind (Lieberman, 1991). The vocal cords mediate an exceptional range of pitch variation, as well as contributing to an impressive modulation of power and spectral quality in the sound (Scherer, 1986). This is the source of the moving narratives of emotion carried in the rhythmic phrases of music (Krumhansl, 2000).

Lastly, human hands can express every sort of motivation, thought and feeling: giving touch comfort and security to the self or an other; signalling direction and precise aim of interest, acceptance or rejection of experience, the confidence and energy of intentions, aggressive or defensive impulses, and the hesitant or confident planning of sequences of actions that combine intentions and select different goals (Trevarthen, 1986b; McNeill, 1992; Goldin-Meadow and McNeill, 1999). Human hand movements also convey learned conventions of affection, greeting, defiance, appeasement and denial. They make permanent messages in writing and create pictures and symbolic representations of objects or ideas.

Conversation uses all expressive movements, as well as posturing of the whole body, to convey intentions and cognitions (Trevarthen, 2003a). In the deaf, hand gestures may take over the functions of language (Goldin-Meadow and McNeill, 1999). All expressions are active in infants, coordinated in the cyclic displays of intentions, communicative impulses and emotions (Trevarthen, 1984, 1990). Their equivalence in the unschooled expression of motives proves expressions are animated by a core brain mechanism that modulates actions of the whole body.

Growth of the human emotional brain

Developments in the meso-limbic cortices of the temporal and frontal lobes in infants and toddlers expand functions of autonomic self-regulation, emotions in communication, and motives for action (Schore, 1994; Trevarthen, 2001b; Trevarthen and Aitken, 2003). The neocortical circuits mature in reciprocal, dynamic involvement with the prenatally formed Intrinsic Motive Formation (IMF), which integrates elaborate subcortical systems with the limbic cortex (Trevarthen and Aitken, 1994). The basic innate affective neurosystem of the brainstem is elaborated, not superseded.

An emotional attachment to the mother's voice forms *in utero*, before a baby's visual awareness undergoes rapid development after birth. The brain of the 2-month old maps out a both coherent self and sympathetic equivalence of motive states with others. Cortical face-representing parts resonate with the experience of the face of another and, remarkably, prospective regions for facial articulation of speech and for auditory monitoring of the speech of self or other are already defined, 2 years before language (Tzourio-Mazoyer *et al.*, 2002). Conversation with language grows within this innate formation of functional neural systems of intersubjectivity (Trevarthen, 2003a)

A mother's compassionate, unthinking engagement with her infant affects the physiology of the baby and becomes a vital factor assisting the auto-regulation of the rapidly developing infant brain (Schore, 2003). Left-right asymmetries in the infants' hand gestures and face expressions prove that the emotional systems of the two sides of the brain are organized in complementary ways to regulate intimate human engagement when the circuits of the cerebral cortex are rudimentary (Trevarthen, 1986b, 2001b). Receptive emotional functions controlling the interpersonal context for exchange of messages, as well as self-nurturant trophotropic states protective of the body that may be more noradrenergic or seratonergic, are stronger in the right brain, which matures first (Davidson and Fox, 1982; Schore, 1994, 2003; Tucker *et al.*, 2000). More active, outgoing ergotropic orientation to the environment, which is dopaminergic, is stronger in the later developing left brain.

Young mammals receive essential protection from stress and distress from affectionate parental care (Hofer, 1990; Schore, 1994; Carter *et al.*, 1997). If nurturing parental attention is not forthcoming, a defensive withdrawal may protect the organism from irreparable harm (Porges, 2003), but only for a time. In the end an affectionate attachment relationship is essential for survival. Human infants are born highly dependent on sympathetic parental responses. Identifying features of the mother are picked up quickly after birth, and other individuals who offer care and sympathetic company are also soon recognized. Their love is required not only for the physiological support and protection of the baby, but also for the normal maturation of motives for exploration and learning, and self-confident negotiation of contacts with the physical and social worlds (Stern, 2000; Porges, 2003; Schore, 2003).

Infants' sympathetic emotions seek to share meaning by negotiating interests and affections

Darwin (1872/1998) did not limit his classification of emotions to a short list of discrete 'basic' responses (fear, anger, surprise, sadness, joy, disgust and perhaps contempt). He included intersubjective or moral qualities of motivation, such as 'love', 'tenderness', 'sulkiness', 'hatred', 'contempt', 'guilt', 'pride', 'shame' among those he attribu- ted to the behaviours of animals and children that he called emotional expressions. His other terms denote different states of the subject's bodily feeling or reaction to objects ('suffering', 'anxiety', 'grief', 'despair', 'joy', 'anger', 'fear', 'disgust'), or states of experiencing and thinking ('meditation', 'determination', 'patience', 'surprise').

Modern naturalistic research uses frame-by-frame microanalysis of films and videos and high fidelity sound recordings to describe dynamic expressions of emotion in infants: when they are communicating and playing games or performing cooperative tasks with their mothers; when they are confronted with a stranger; when they are exploring the immediate environment; and when they are seeking, following, reaching for and manipulating or mouthing objects. An object's potential usefulness or signific- ance must be defined by certain criteria of 'naïve physics' relating to the properties of things and their motions (Spelke, 1998), and these criteria will depend on the infant's innate motives for moving (von Hofsten, 2001).

The emotions associated with infants' investigative motives open the way for com- munication and collaboration. Records of the emotional interactions between an infant and other persons when the infant is attending to an object show that objects are often 'animated' by the adult, to interest, amuse or tease the baby. The emotions they share arise from the infant subject's interest in objects or events, and in the affections between the infant and the person who accepts to play. Rich description of the actions and interactions in infant–adult engagements has gained us insight into the contribu- tion made by the intelligence and feelings of the infant to the development of instruct- ive relationships with 'older and wiser' persons (Trevarthen and Aitken, 2001).

'Periods of rapid change' and 'difficult transitions' in the development of human emotions before language

Before 3 years of age, when most children have mastered language, there are periods when the body and behaviour of the child transform, bringing in new interests, activit- ies and thinking, changing the ways communication is used (Fig. 3.2). At least six important transformations in behaviour and the emergence of new ways of learning are recognized in the first 2 years (Heimann, 2003). These have immediate effects on communication with the caregiver, and on cognitive growth. They elaborate the inher- ent sociability of emotions and extend their range. Emotional adjustments affecting relationships precede each new phase of development (Plooij, 2003; Trevarthen and Aitken, 2003), and these correlate with changes in the immune system and susceptibility of a baby to illness (Plooij et al., 2003).

The newborn in maternal protection

The neonate has special sensory readiness to detect and recognize the mother's affec- tionate presence and the support, comfort and nourishment she provides. Increased

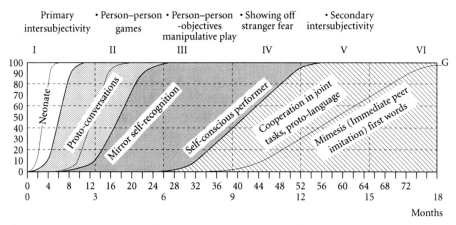

Fig. 3.2 Stages in the growth of socio-emotional behaviours of infants, with Periods of Rapid Change indicated by curves that summarize longitudinal data on percentage of attainment of age-related abilities (see Trevarthen and Aitken, 2003, for the sources of data).

mass and inertia of the body in air, and a new freedom to move the limbs away from the body, require new muscle strength and new proprio-senses. Developments of eyes and visual brain facilitate adaptation to the environment of light. Facial, vocal and manual expressions signal changing interest, pleasure or displeasure, and others' expressions can be imitated. The need for sleep reduces, increasing the infant's capacity to seek experience of things outside the body.

First conversations

After the first month, the baby is often awake for hours at a time, and can orientate to, track, or focus on attractive events. Developments between 4 and 6 weeks also transform the link between an affectionate mother's searching for communication and the baby's interest in emotional exchanges 'just for fun'. This is when the protoconversations of primary intersubjectivity begin.

Exploring surroundings and playing games

At 4 months, motor control is becoming more versatile. The baby looks, reaches and manipulates more effectively, and often turns attention away from the mother when she seeks to 'chat', to explore a wider space of experience, and to manipulate objects. In response, the mother becomes more animated, assertive, and challenging in her efforts to attract communication—more playful. She attracts her infant in person–person games: rhythmic body play, chanting, and by singing baby songs (Trevarthen and Hubley, 1978; Trevarthen, 1999). Teasing and joking routines grow with the infant's sense of humour (Sroufe and Waters, 1976; Reddy, 2003). The baby is also attracted to the image of his or her face in a mirror—a peculiar sort of 'playless' company that is studied thoughtfully, or used to experiment with expressions and mannerisms.

Expressions of amusement seem to appreciate that 'mocking' the image of the self can make a 'joke' (Reddy, 2003).

Self-awareness and manipulating objects

By 7 or 8 months the baby is intently exploring objects with hands and mouth, and, as person–person–object games flourish, the social life of the family is enriched by the baby's delight in 'showing off' for company, or for the mirror (Reddy, 2003; Trevarthen and Hubley, 1978; Trevarthen, 1990). This is the time a baby may become seriously unhappy if approached by a stranger, indicating how important are the special relationships that have developed in play with family and other well-known 'friends' (Sroufe, 1977; Trevarthen, 1986b, 1990, 2002). The baby may exhibit clever sociability with same age companions, needing no adult help to solicit contact and communicate (Selby and Bradley, 2003).

Cooperative understanding

A major change at 9–10 months marks the transition from the period of games to secondary intersubjectivity or cooperative 'person person object awareness' (Trevarthen and Hubley, 1978). Now the baby is eager to imitate conventional gestures, ways of acting and ways of using objects (Trevarthen and Aitken, 2003). Memory for the meaning of things is strong and cultural learning of 'acts of meaning', expressed in 'protolanguage', begins (Halliday, 1975). There are few words, but the 1-year-olds readiness for learning how to communicate by speech and gesture is clearly evident (Bruner, 1983; Tomasello, 1988; Trevarthen, 1990, 1994, 2003a, 2004).

Imaginative play with meanings and roles

In the second year, developments lead the baby from infancy to language and a period of rich mimetic imagination and fantasy play with family and peers (Nadel and Pezé, 1993; Nadel et al., 1999b). A time of awkward dependency, comparable with the anxious time around 7 months, has been found in the second half of the second year (Kagan, 1982), and this appears linked to the start of rapid word learning and the beginning of new developments in the left hemisphere of the brain (Trevarthen, 2003a).

At each age-related change, intrinsic regulations of ergotropic and trophotropic motives in the brain release advances in awareness, learning and motor skill (Trevarthen and Aitken, 2003). Companions of the baby are lead by their sympathetic appreciation of what moves the child, and what feelings are expressed, to change their behaviour. The child is grows and learns within a responsive intersubjective environment (Papousek and Papousek, 1987; Fogel, 1993; Stern, 1993, 2000; Lewis and Granic, 2000; Pantoia et al., 2001). The effects of weakness or discontinuity in this support prove the importance of shared dynamic emotions for the advances in the child's abilities and understanding, and for the growth of a self-confident and confiding personality (Murray and Cooper, 1997; Gratier, 1999; Robb, 1999; Schore, 2003).

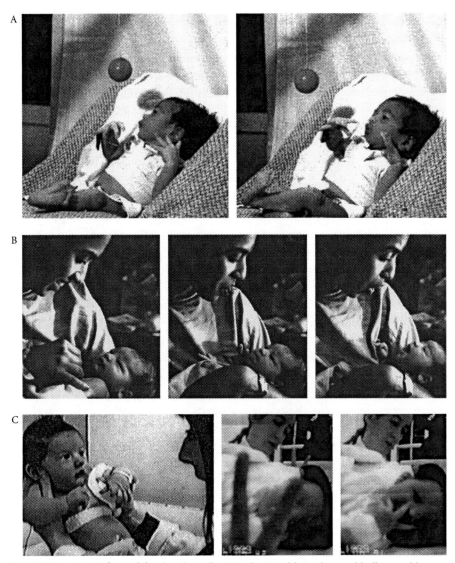

Fig. 3.3 Newborn infants. (A) A boy in India, 20 minutes old, tracks a red ball moved by a nurse. (B) Shamini at about 30 minutes after birth: her mother greets her with a smile, then she imitates 'tongue protrusion' and 'mouth opening'. (C) Tests of a newborn baby's initiative in imitation. The band round the infant's chest records heart rate. He imitates when Emese Nagy (whose face is seen in a mirror) holds up two fingers. Heart rate recordings show he does so intentionally, and with interest in getting a response for his effort (Nagy and Molnár, 2003). (Photos A and B by Kevin Bundell.)

Learning how to communicate and who to communicate with

Emotions associated with the three different orientations of the body to experiences—to the self, toward a communicative person, and to inspect a thing outside the body—suggest that the newborn infant's mind already has different intentional forms of consciousness appropriate for these different uses (Trevarthen, 1993), see Fig. 3.9.

The abilities of newborns to imitate many forms of expressive movement (Fig. 3.3) prove they are ready to engage with other persons' motives and interact in communication (Kugiumutzakis, 1998). At the time of imitating or just before, the infant's heart accelerates significantly, indicating active intention. When the infant is acting to invite or 'provoke' the adult to imitate, there is an anticipatory heart rate deceleration, indicating a receptive focusing of attention. A newborn baby seeks communication with intentional preparation of complementary conscious states—imitating is intentional and provocating is attentive (Nagy and Molnár, 2003).

Any adult who enters into intimate sympathetic relationship with a newborn infant has to depend first on emotional responses and behaviours that are unconsciously controlled and cannot be learned. The similarities that appear in the intonation, timing, pitch and rhythms of vocalizations to very young babies in different cultures are evidence both for the universal needs of the newborn, and for *intuitive parenting* motivation to meet these needs (Papousek and Papousek, 1987; Fernald, 1992). The emotional 'codes' in infant and adult, and their affective expressions fit one another as sympathetic complements.

Extensive analyses of the protoconversations with two-month-olds (Fig. 3.4) has proved that humans are born with a dual representation of self and other that permits them to enter into immediate relation with one another's emotions in 'dialogic closure' (Bråten, 1988, 1992). The rudiments of such a capacity may be evident immediately after birth, even in a 2-month-premature infant (Trevarthen, 1993; Malloch, 1999). Voices of parents talking to young infants in different languages have regular rhythms and patterns of prosody or musical form and quality. The infant is attending to and giving responses to the 'attuned' affectivity of the adult who is strongly moved by affectionate concern for the infant. The infant is perceived as a person who is expressing interests and feelings, 'thinking' and wanting to 'talk' about thoughts (Fig. 3.4).

Feelings of contact, and of loss of contact

The emotions in protoconversations have been tested by introducing interruptions and delays to well-patterned positive interactions, and watching how the infants respond (Tronick *et al.*, 1978; Murray and Trevarthen, 1985). The range of sympathetic expressions is illustrated by photographs of images taken from a Double Television (DTV) intercommunication experiment where a mother eventually gained her 8-week-old daughter's attention and joined in a lively 'chat' with her (Trevarthen, 1993; Fig. 3.5). At first, the infant was frightened by a loud, high-pitched sound in the

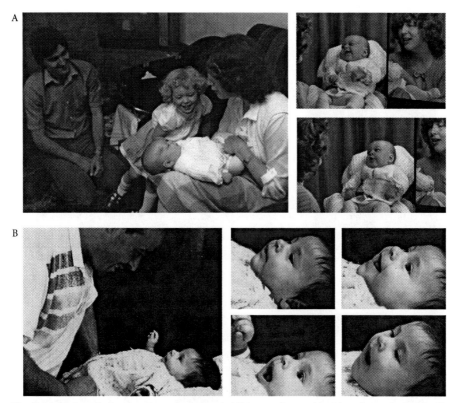

Fig. 3.4 Infants enjoying 'protoconversations'. (A) Laura, 3 months old, at home in Scotland is attentive to her mother's talking. Her 3-year-old sister wants to join in and father watches proudly from the side. At 6 weeks, in the University of Edinburgh Laura smiles and coos at her mother, whose reactions can be seen in a mirror. (Photos by Penelope and John Hubley and Colwyn Trevarthen.) (B) Hande, 11 weeks old, is Turkish, photographed in Holland with her father. She watches her father's face, smiles, moves hand, mouth and tongue with a serious face as if talking, and looks away while she 'thinks'. (Photos from a video by Saskia van Rees of the "Body Language Foundation". www.stichtinglichaamstaal.nl.)

loudspeaker carrying the mother's voice, and her pout evoked an instantaneous horror expression from the mother who said, "Oh! I do not want to see a pouty face." They then made eye contact, and this triggered a big smile from the mother and initiated a well-paced exchange. After 1 minute 30 seconds the baby was happy. At this point, one minute of the mother's most joyful chat was replayed to the baby. This unresponsive and non-contingent behaviour made the infant puzzled, and within 30 seconds caused her to withdraw, and make gestures, vocalizations, and face expressions of distress.

'Still Face' and 'DTV Replay' tests prove that 2-month-olds have expectancies for sensitive reciprocal engagement of affectionate and expressive states, and a need to coordinate cycles of interest and pleasure with the Other (Murray and Trevarthen, 1985; Nadel *et al.*, 1999a). That the baby is expecting shared timing and a supportive

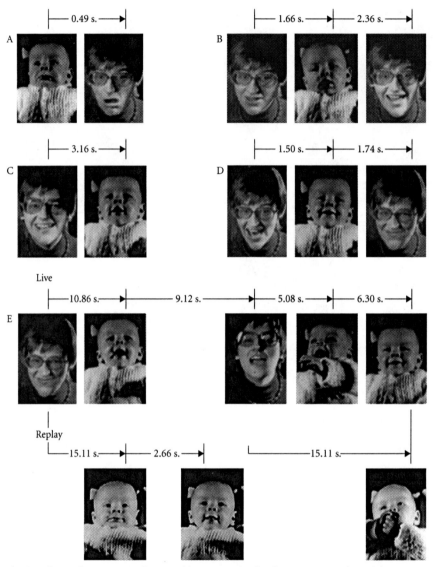

Fig. 3.5 Photos from an experiment with communication between a mother and an 8-week-old girl by Double Television. They coordinate their expressions sympathetically in 'live' communication, but the infant shows distress when the contingency of the mother's behaviour is lost in 'replay' (see text).

quality of response from the adult is proved by expressions of disappointment or frustration when responses fail.

Vitality affects and narratives of adventure: 'communicative musicality' and the mind time of emotions

Play with infants 3 or 4 months old (Fig. 3.6) has timing and expressive modulations that invite description in terms used for the arts of music or dance (Stern, 1993,

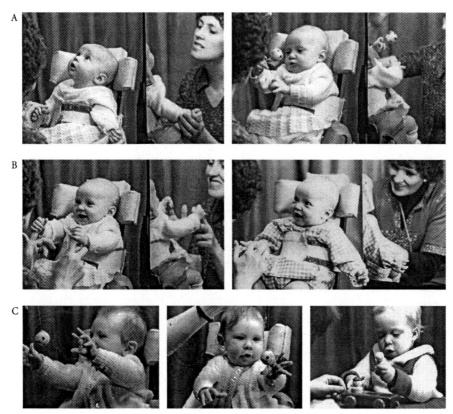

Fig. 3.6 Infants gain new interests. Scottish subjects photographed in the University of Edinburgh. (A) Leanne, at 4 months, is explores the room, and her mother asks, 'What do you see?' She tries to grasp a ping-pong ball on a thread, presented by her mother. (B) Four-month-old Leanne enjoys a singing, hand-bouncing game with her mother, and at 5 months waits for the surprise ending (a tickle under her arm) of the baby song, 'Round and round the garden, like a teddy bear', which she knows well. (C) Infants over 6 months old enjoy chasing and handling objects, and parents offer games and toys. Notice how 'expectant' their mouths are. (Photos by Colwyn Trevarthen.)

1999, 2000). Stern describes the 'relational' emotions that sustain this play as 'vitality affects', and he emphasizes the 'affect attunement' of the game. Beebe and colleagues have made statistical analyses of the Coordinated Interpersonal Timing in mother–infant communication, applying techniques of 'conversational analysis' to show the synchronizations, pauses, and turn-taking of natural interactions similar to those between adults. The dynamic quality of interaction between a mother and a young baby can be predictive of the emotional attachment relationship between them many months later (Jaffe *et al.*, 2001).

Musical acoustic techniques applied to protoconversations show how a mother speaking to her infant produces musically organized utterances with a regular beat, phrasing and systematic development of excitement in longer 'narrative' cycles, and the infant may respond in a precisely coordinated manner (Malloch, 1999; Trevarthen and Malloch, 2002). Acoustic analysis also shows how a depressed mother fails to give communication that has the rhythmic expressive features of 'musicality' (Robb, 1999), and the method has been used to demonstrate effects on the emotional presence of a mother who has had to emigrate from her home country to a foreign land, and lost the feeling of 'belonging' (Gratier, 1999). A mother's loneliness, linked to a felling of loss of support from her own mother, makes it difficult for her to respond sensitively and happily to her baby's efforts to communicate.

The theory of Communicative Musicality (Malloch, 1999) proposes that basic expressive forms and preferences for particular patterns of expressive movement and vocal sound can be described by analysis in terms of poetic, musical, gestural and dramatic expression. The compelling ways shared creations in the temporal arts; of poetry, music, dance or theatre, are responded to emotionally and remembered proves the relationship of motives for moving in rhythmic expressive ways to the development of communal understanding by the 'thinking', story-telling mind (Turner, 1996; Trevarthen, 1999, 2002; Dissanayake, 2000: Krumhansl, 2000).

Relational emotions, between persons, including pride, jealousy, shame, resentment, rage, and the lasting evaluations and empathy of admiration, love, hate, contempt that we can develop in regard to particular individuals—have their foundations in dynamic reactions of even young infants to the feel of 'being present' with another (Stern, 1993, 2000; Bråten, 1998). They contribute to the building of relationships of affectionate attachment, trust and companionship, and to defence against abuse, mistrust and disregard, and they appear to be fundamental to human consciousness of meaning (Barnes, 2000; Trevarthen, 2002) (see Figs. 3.7 and 3.8).

Sociability beyond parental care

Research has focused on emotions in infant–adult dyads. Nevertheless, there is evidence that infants can communicate with peers. Infants and toddlers join in constructive emotional exchanges in groups (Nadel and Pezé, 1993; Nash and Hay, 2003; Selby and Bradley, 2003).

Research by Fiamenghi (Fiamenghi, 1997; Trevarthen et al., 1999) demonstrated that pairs of infants 5–9 months old, seated facing each other in pushchairs, outside view of their mothers, use reciprocal imitation of gestures, postures, facial expressions, vocalizations, and feet movements to establish contact and communicate. Fiamenghi used a mirror box containing a camera to demonstrate that engagement with a self-image has features indicating that the baby perceives that a reflection cannot 'play the game'. He found sex differences, boys 'showing off' more to the mirror, while girls showed a wider range of social expressions. Both boys and girls made self-exploring movements, while watching the mirror, indicating that they detect that the 'other baby' is actually their own self.

Selby and Bradley (2003) sat trios of babies between 6 and 10 months of age on their own in their pushchairs at equal distances from one another in a triangle. Complex

Fig. 3.7 Emma, 6 months old, in Scotland, is proud to know 'Clap-a-clap-a-handies', a traditional baby song. She sits on her father's knee at home and responds gleefully when her mother invites her to perform for the photographer. In the university, she shows how her mother taught her, and watches her reflection in the camera window as she imitates. She is too young to understand what her mother means when she asks her to put the wooden doll in the truck. (Photos by Penelope and John Hubley and Colwyn Trevarthen.)

and subtle expressive behaviours and exchanges established mini dramas between the interactants, demonstrating a far greater capacity for sociable encounters than has been expected for infants under one year.

Discovering the values of objects and rituals shared: first companionship in 'art, knowledge and skills'

After 4 months, infants explore their surroundings, turning head and eyes to look about and reaching to handle objects with emotional investment of curiosity and pleasure in discovery (Fig. 3.6). These moves are signalled to companions in expressions of interest, surprise, wonder, and of pleasure or fear and irritation. The infant is aware of the person they are turning away from to pursue self-centred interests and is

Fig. 3.8 Basilie, 12 months old, cooperates in a task and knows about useful objects. She understands when her mother asks her to, 'Put the doll in the truck', and looks pleased as her mother congratulates her. On her mother's knee at the University, she asked for *The National Geographical* magazine, recognizing its yellow colour, takes the book and starts 'reading it', looking at the pictures. At home with her mother, she shares the post. (Photos by Penelope and John Hubley and Colwyn Trevarthen.)

receptive to any 'presentation' of objects by others. The natural response of a playmate is to create routines of dramatic play and to tease. Games with infants exercise sympathetic mirroring and imitation of the motives of agency, i.e. of intentions, attentions and feelings. Infants at 6 months show subtle transitions of interest and disinterest, determination and doubt, amusement and irritation, surprise and confident recognition (Trevarthen, 1986b, 1990), and they begin to laugh (Sroufe and Waters, 1976). They habituate quickly to dull repeating events, seeking new experiences. They learn to value the reappearance of events that bring pleasures, or to fear and withdraw from those that signal recurrence of unpleasant experience.

Their exploring and rapid habituation make infants beyond 4 months ideal subjects in laboratory experiments on discriminative recognition, categorization, 'intentional stance', and deferred imitation. The infants are sensitive to dynamic parameters in artificial displays (Watson, 1972; Gergely and Watson, 1999). They are detecting 'animacy' and can predict the intentional aim of persons' movements represented in dynamic visual displays (Legerstee, 1992). This kind of 'intention sensitivity', with selective response to mobiles that show 'contingent re-activity', leads some researchers to deny infants 'real' awareness of other persons as separate subjects. I see it as further evidence, albeit artificially obtained, for innate inter-subjectivity. In natural circumstances, infant's investigative intelligence and sense of humour facilitate pleasurable communication with real persons.

The early-developed signs of interest in human purposes recall the pioneering experiments of Michotte (1962) who, using simple visual displays with dynamic properties, proved that subjects have internal criteria for identifying vital, psychologically-motivated phenomena. In experiments to analyse how movies carry messages of human action in changing patterns of light, Michotte charted the dimensions of change that evoke particular emotions, and found critical values that all observers share. The parameters he identified correspond with the 'sentic forms' Manfred Clynes (1980) has found as carriers of emotion in music.

Infants are sensitive to the invariants in human action and expression discovered by Michotte and by Clynes, and these sensibilities are exploited in psychologists' experiments as by parents in game routines. Body action games and songs played with infants (Figs. 3.6 and 3.7) employ narrative sequences to capture the infant's interest and generate shared amusement, and to modulate the infant's excitement and enjoyment or to calm (Rock *et al.*, 1999; Trevarthen, 1999). Joking and teasing, involving mutual interest and prediction, is a sure sign of a secure and loving relationship. Fun in games is infectious and it makes friendships, as it does for young animals (Panksepp and Burgdorf, 2003). Unsympathetic game play with an infant provokes distress and even violent protest. Nakano (Nakano and Kanaya, 1993) has studied the subtle variations in 'fun' with infants and identified a shared motivation for 'tricky' situations, which he calls 'incident affinity'. This essential foundation for negotiating complex intentions and cooperative awareness is motivated on both sides, from the infant and from the parent.

Reflecting and thinking to oneself: taking 'time off' from sociability to explore the flow of ideas in a recollected world

Margaret Donaldson, in *Human minds* (Donaldson, 1992), proposes that the development of 'recall memory' increases a child's conscious imagining by steps. She describes the changes as a journey through 'point', 'line', 'elaborated' and 'transcendent' modes of awareness and purposefulness. She offers the challenging proposal that there is a parallel development of emotional intelligence through comparable stages. She points out that it is difficult to know if a young baby can recall—he or she may be just acting with 'recognition' of immediately familiar events or objects. However, there are signs of imaginative reconstruction of past events in infants before a year of age (e.g. Halliday, 1975), and this is essential preparation for 'telling' experiences and judgements with others.

Introspective states of withdrawal from present activity into imagination and memory, which are essential features of intelligent consciousness (Donald, 2001), do seem to occur in very young infants (Fig. 3.4). By 3 or 4 months a baby may be stubbornly drawn into 'thinking' states that resist others' temptations to communicate (Fig. 3.6). All parents who have sought to play with a baby will recognize these withdrawals. I believe the ways inner and outer experience are managed, and shared are vital and necessary factors in the sharing of games. The social withdrawal may often be a paradoxical communicative signal, a ploy to state a measure of independence or even defiance. The infant's avoidances are often comical and infants may smile as they avoid contact. I would relate this to Vasu Reddy's discoveries of smiling 'coyness' when a 3-month-old is held by their mother up to a mirror, and to her explorations of incidents in which infants apparently act deliberately as show-offs or 'clowns' (Reddy, 2003).

Peter Hobson in *The cradle of thought* (Hobson, 2002) gives the sharing of reflective states, which he illustrates with a painting of the virgin and child in meditative mood, a key role in the nurturing of thinking. It allows the minds of companions to be together while wandering through their separate recollected experience and purposes.

Development of a social identity, and 'self-awareness': conscious predictive control of the evaluation of self by others

The well-charted crisis of self-consciousness of the 7-month-old, who is bold and exuberant with persons who are familiar and loved (Fig. 3.7), but timid or fearful with a stranger (Sroufe, 1977), relates to an important forthcoming development in the intersubjectivity of play that takes place about 9 months after birth (Trevarthen and Hubley, 1978). Then infants become both able and willing to attend to, and comment about, purposeful actions they or others direct toward environmental goals (Fig. 3.8). They start to comply with instructions, as well as imitating manners of behaving (Meltzoff, 1995; Hobson, 2002). Their gestures and expressions carry evidence of self-conscious mental states, such as 'showing off' or 'acting a part' (Trevarthen, 1990; Reddy, 2003). For the first time the baby systematically combines vocalization and gestures of 'protolanguage' to communicate wishes, feelings, purposes, or experiences to their partners (Halliday, 1975). This bridge between attending and commenting, between interest and the pleasure of company, is crucial for the child's entry into the world of meanings and the words or other symbols that may 'encode' them (Trevarthen, 1994).

A state of sympathetic participation with others in social life by 'mutual attention' (Reddy, 2003) is fundamental to any collaborative awareness and convergence of interests and purposes or 'joint attention' between persons (Tomasello, 1988). The motives that initiate cultural learning in infants are essentially intersubjective, in the sense that they require sympathy of feelings between the child and companions, not just identification of the diexis or aim of consciousness to a selected object of interest. The child has shown awareness of the orientation and shifts in direction of interest of a partner in communication many months before prompt 'joint attention' behaviours become common around 9 months. What does change is the motives of the child for sharing the interest and value of another persons' exploratory or manipulative intelligence (Trevarthen, 1980, 1987, 1994, 1998, 2001a). It is an advance in person-person-object awareness founded on intimate awareness of the other as a particular, trusted friend (Fig. 3.9).

'Complex basic emotions' can be seen in the first year (Draghi-Lorenz *et al.*, 2001; Reddy, 2003). Observations of spontaneous expressions of infants in familiar circumstances, or with strangers, show that 'self-other awareness' is regulated in the first 6 months by explicit relational states of 'pride', 'shame', jealousy and 'mistrust' (Fig. 3.7).

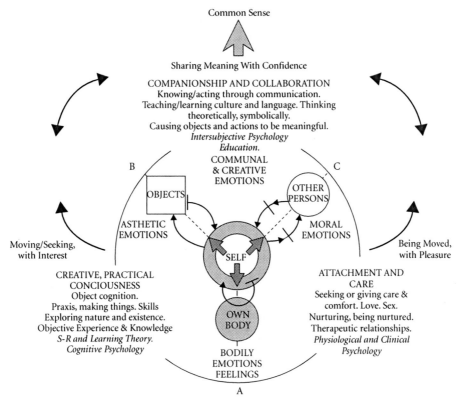

Fig. 3.9 The cycle of interactions and communication that generates 'common sense'. An infant's 'self' is engaged in controlled relations with the infant's body (A), with physical objects (B), and with other persons (C). These different realms of action and awareness are coordinated by emotions of interest and pleasure, and combine in the creation of meaning through sympathetic communication in companionship.

Expressions of delight, pleased satisfaction, surprise, irritation, or grief to displacements of gaze to or away from other person's eyes regulate the infant's communication with peers, in family triads and with strangers. Self-consciousness and showing off with the mirror or with strangers, and with peers, prove that young infants use complex emotions to regulate the dynamic balance of interest and initiative with others. They help infants and their partners to share meanings that have been invented together, and the infants mark their identity as 'knowers' (Trevarthen, 1990, 2002).

Cultural learning: the development of thinking about things with sense of other persons' interests and feelings (Fig. 3.9)

An ability to acquire cultural skills and conventional or symbolic forms of acting shows itself in rich displays of mimetic play when a toddler can speak very few, if any, words (Nadel *et al.*, 1999b). It is at this stage that adventure creating and story-making 'fantasy' play takes off, soon to be given the added power that talking gives (Nelson, 1996). The toddler is a generator of metaphorical ideas and an infectious playmate for invention of blended meanings.

Intersubjective awareness, conversational exchanges and narrative imagination (mimesis and metaphor) have a unique complexity and efficacy in humans (Turner, 1996; Donald, 2001). Human toddlers and older children observe, learn, and re-enact social mannerisms, ethical principles and cognitive interests, as well as investigative problem-solving behaviour. Before they walk, they represent to themselves elaborate technical and artistic routines in imaginative play, referring to objects goals that are remote in time and space, many of which the community has invested with value and meaning over generations (Trevarthen and Logotheti, 1987). All these purposes are assisted by self-other-conscious emotions (Reddy, 2003) and the enjoyment of intentionally supportive teaching behaviours that more experienced partners offer the child (Bruner, 1996; Rogoff *et al.*, 2003). They are enriched by language, which fixes words to the actions and objects of cooperative understanding, and to the feelings and qualities of acting and experiencing. In the first stages of language learning, imitation, immediate and deferred, plays a key role (Tomasello, 1999). Emotions of relating (of affection and mistrust, pride and shame) are crucial in the negotiation of purposes and interests in symbolic activity and language (Trevarthen, 1994).

References

Adolphs, R. (2003). Investigating the cognitive neuroscience of social behavior. *Neuropsychologia*, **41**, 119–26.

Aitken, K. J. and Trevarthen, C. (1997). Self-other organization in human psychological development. *Development and Psychopathology*, **9**, 651–75.

Averill, J. (1980). A constructivist view of emotion. In *Emotion theory research and experience* (ed. R. Plutchik and H. Kellerman), Vol. 1, pp. 305–40. Academic Press: New York.

Barnes, B. (2000). *Understanding agency: social theory and responsible action.* Beverley Hills: Sage.

Bernstein, N. (1967). *Coordination and regulation of movements.* New York: Pergamon.

Bekoff, M. and Byers, J. A. (1998). *Animal play: evolutionary, comparative and ecological approaches.* New York: Cambridge University Press.

Berntson, G. G., Sarter, M., and Cacioppo, J. T. (2003). Autonomic nervous system. In *Encyclopedia of cognitive science* (Editor in Chief Lynn Nadel) Article **406**, Vol. **1**, pp. 301–8. Oxford: Nature Publishing Group, Macmillan Publishers Ltd.

Bertalanffy, von L. (1968). *General system theory.* New York: George Brazilier.

Bierhoff, H-W. (2002). *Prosocial behaviour.* Hove: Psychology Press/New York: Taylor and Francis.

Blakemore, S-J. and Decety, J. (2001). From the perception of action to the understanding of intention. *Nature Reviews Neuroscience*, **2**, 561–7.

Bowlby, J. (1958). The nature of the child's tie to his mother. *International Journal of Psychoanalysis*, **39**, 1–23.

Bråten, S. (1988). Dialogic mind: The infant and adult in protoconversation. In *Nature, cognition and system.* (ed. M. Cavallo), pp. 187–205. Dordrecht: Kluwer Academic Publications.

Bråten, S. (1992). The virtual other in infants' minds and social feelings. In *The dialogical alternative* (Festschrift for Ragnar Rommetveit). (ed A. H. Wold), pp. 77–97. Oslo/Oxford: Scandanavian University Press/Oxford University Press.

Bråten, S. (1998). Intersubjective communion and understanding: development and perturbation. In *Intersubjective communication and emotion in early ontogeny* (ed. S. Bråten), pp. 372–82. Cambridge: Cambridge University Press.

Bruner, J. S. (1983). *Child's talk. Learning to use language.* New York: Norton.

Bruner, J. S. (1996). *The culture of education.* Cambridge, MA: Harvard University Press.

Carter, C. S., Lederhendler, I. I., and Kirkpatrick, B. (ed.) (1997). The integrative neurobiology of affiliation. *Annals of the New York Academy of Sciences*, **807**.

Clynes, M. (1980). The communication of emotion: theory of sentics. In *Emotion: theory, research and experience, Vol. 1: Theories of emotion* (ed. R. Plutchik and H. Kellerman). New York: Academic Press.

Damasio, A. R. (1999). *The feeling of what happens: body, emotion and the making of consciousness.* London: Heinemann.

Darwin, C. (1872/1998). *The expression of the emotions in man and animals*, 3rd edn. New York: Oxford University Press.

Davidson, R. J. and Fox, N. A. (1982). Asymmetric brain activity discriminates between positive and negative affective stimuli in human infants. *Science*, **218**, 1235–7.

Decety, J. and Chaminade, T. (2003). Neural correlates of feeling sympathy. *Neuropsychologia*, **41**, 127–38.

Dissanayake, E. (2000). *Art and intimacy: how the arts began.* Seattle: University of Washington Press.

Donald, M. (2001). *A mind so rare: the evolution of human consciousness.* New York, NY: Norton.

Donaldson, M. (1992). *Human minds: an exploration.* London: Allen Lane/Penguin Books.

Draghi-Lorenz, R., Reddy, V., and Costall, A. (2001). Rethinking the development of 'non-basic' emotions: a critical review of existing theories. *Developmental Review*, **21**(3), 263–304.

Ekman, P. and Davidson, R. J. (ed.) (1994). *The nature of emotion. Fundamental questions.* New York: Oxford University Press.

Fernald, A. (1992). Meaningful melodies in mothers' speech to infants. In *Nonverbal vocal communication: comparative and developmental aspects* (ed. H. Papousek, U. Jürgens, and M. Papousek), pp. 262–82. Cambridge: Cambridge University Press/Paris: Editions de la Maison des Sciences de l'Homme.

Fiamenghi, G. A. (1997). Intersubjectivity and infant-infant interaction: imitation as a way of making contact. *Annual Report, Research and Clinical Center for Child Development*, **19**, 15–21.

Fogel, A. (1993). *Developing through relationships.* Chicago: University of Chicago Press.

Freeman, W. J. (2000). Emotion is essential to all intentional behaviors. In *Emotion, development, and self-organisation: dynamic systems approaches to emotional development* (ed. M. Turner and I. Granic), pp. 209–35. Cambridge: Cambridge University Press.

Frijda, N. H. (1986). *The emotions.* Cambridge: Cambridge University Press.

Gergely, G. and Watson, J. (1999). Early social development: contingency perception and the social bio-feedback model. In *Early social cognition: understanding others in the first months of life* (ed. P. Rochat), pp. 101–36. Mahwah. NJ: Erlbaum.

Goldin-Meadow, S. and McNeill, D. (1999). The role of gesture and mimetic representation in making language. In *The descent of mind: psychological perspectives on hominid evolution* (ed. M. C. Corballis and E. G. Lea), pp. 155–72. Oxford: Oxford University Press.

Gratier, M. (1999). Expressions of belonging: the effect of acculturation on the rhythm and harmony of mother-infant vocal interaction. In *Rhythms, musical narrative, and the origins of human communication*, Musicae Scientiae, Special Issue, 1999–2000 (ed. I. Deliège), pp. 93–122. Liège: European Society for the Cognitive Sciences of Music.

Halliday, M. A. K. (1975). *Learning how to mean: explorations in the development of language.* London: Edward Arnold.

Heimann, M. (ed.) (2003). *Regression periods in human infancy,*. Mahwah, NJ: Erlbaum.

Hess, W. R. (1954). *Diencephalon: autonomic and extrapyramidal functions*. Orlando, FL: Grune and Stratton.

Hobson, P. (2002). *The cradle of thought: exploring the origins of thinking*. London: Macmillan.

Hofer, M. A. (1990). Early symbiotic processes: hard evidence from a soft place. In *Pleasure beyond the pleasure principle* (ed. R. A. Glick and S. Bone), pp. 55–78. New Haven, CT: Yale University Press.

Holstege, G., Bandler, R., and Saper, C. B. (ed.) (1996). *The emotional motor system*, Progress in Brain Research Volume 107. Amsterdam: Elsevier.

Husserl, E. (1964). *Phenomenology of internal time-consciousness*. (J. S. Churchill Trans.) Bloomington: Indiana University Press. The Hague.

Jaffe, J., Beebe, B., Felstein, S., Crown, C., *et al.* (2001). *Rhythms of dialogue in infancy: coordinated timing and social development*, Society of Child Development Monographs, Serial No. 265, Vol. **66(2)**. Oxford: Blackwell.

Jeannerod, M. (1994). The representing brain: neural correlates of motor intention and imagery. *Behavioral and Brain Sciences*, **17**, 187–245.

Kagan, J. (1982). The emergence of self. *Journal of Child Psychology and Psychiatry*, **23**, 363–81.

Kobayashi, H. and Kohshima, S. (2001). Evolution of the human eye as a device for communication. In *Primate origins of human cognition and behavior* (ed. T. Matsuzawa), pp. 383–401. Tokyo: Springer Verlag.

Krumhansl, C. L. (2000). Music and affect: empirical and theoretical contributions from experimental psychology. In *Musicology and sister disciplines: past, present, future* (ed. D. Greer), pp. 88–99. Oxford: Oxford University Press.

Kugiumutzakis, G. (1998). Neonatal imitation in the intersubjective companion space. In *Intersubjective Communication and Emotion in Early Ontogeny* (ed. S. Bråten), pp. 63–88. Cambridge: Cambridge University Press.

Lashley, K. S. (1951). The problems of serial order in behavior. In: *Cerebral mechanisms in behavior* (ed. L. A. Jeffress), pp. 112–36. New York: Wiley.

Lazarus, R. S. (1991). *Emotion and adaptation*. New York, NY: Oxford University Press.

LeDoux, J. E. (2000). Emotion circuits in the brain. *Annual Review of Neuroscience*, **23**, 155–84.

Lee, D. N. (1998). Guiding movement by coupling taus. *Ecological Psychology*, **10(3–4)**, 221–50.

Legerstee, M. (1992). A review of the animate-inanimate distinction in infancy: implications for models of social and cognitive knowing. *Early Development and Parenting*, **1**, 59–67.

Lewis, M. (1995). Self-conscious emotions. *American Psychologist*, **63**, 68–78.

Lewis, M. D. and Granic, I. (2000). Introduction: a new approach to the study of emotional development. In *Emotion, development, and self-organization: dynamic systems approaches to emotional development* (ed. M. D. Lewis and I. Granik), pp. 1–12. Cambridge: Cambridge University Press.

Lieberman, P. (1991). *Uniquely human: the evolution of speech, thought and selfless behaviour*. Cambridge, MA: Harvard University Press.

MacLean, P. (1990). *The triune brain in evolution*. New York: Plenum Press.

Malloch, S. (1999). Mother and infants and communicative musicality. In: *Rhythms, musical narrative, and the origins of human communication*, Musicae Scientiae, Special Issue, 1999–2000, (ed. I. Deliège), pp. 29–57. Liège, Belgium: European Society for the Cognitive Sciences of Music.

Marler, P., Evans, C. S., and Hauser, M. C. (1992). Animal signals: motivational, referential or both? In *Nonverbal vocal communication: comparative and developmental aspects* (ed. H. Papousek, U. Jurgens, and M. Papousek), pp. 66–86. Cambridge: Cambridge University Press/ Paris: Editions de la Maison des Sciences de l'Homme.

McNeill, D. (1992). *Hand and mind: What gestures reveal about thought.* Chicago: University of Chicago Press.

Meltzoff, A. N. (1995). Understanding the intentions of others: re-enactment of intended acts by 18-month-old children. *Developmental Psychology*, **31**, 838–50.

Merker, B. (2000). Synchronous chorusing and human origins. In *The origins of music* (ed. N. L. Wallin, B. Merker, and S. Brown), pp. (315–28). Cambridge, MA: MIT Press.

Merleau-Ponty, M. (1962). *Phenomenology of perception.* London: Routledge and Kegan Paul.

Michotte, A. (1962). *Causalité, Permanence et Réalité Phénomenales.* Louvain: Publications Universitaires.

Murray, L. and Cooper, P. J. (ed.) (1997). *Postpartum depression and child development.* New York: Guilford Press.

Murray, L. and Trevarthen, C. (1985). Emotional regulation of interactions between two-month-olds and their mothers. In *Social perception in infants* (ed. T. Field and N. Fox), pp. 177–97. Norwood, NJ: Ablex.

Nadel, J. and Pezé, A. (1993). What makes immediate imitation communicative in toddlers and autistic children? In J. Nadel and L. Camaioni (ed.) *New perspectives in early communicative development.* (pp. 139–156) London: Routledge.

Nadel, J., Carchon, I., Kervella, C., *et al.* (1999). Expectancies for social contingency in 2-month-olds. *Developmental Science*, **2**, 164–73.

Nadel, J., Guérini, C., Pezé, A., *et al.* (1999). The evolving nature of imitation as a format for communication. In *Imitation in infancy* (ed. J. Nadel and G. Butterworth), pp. 209–34. Cambridge: Cambridge University Press.

Nagy, E. and Molnár, P. (2003). *Homo imitans* or *Homo provocans*? Human imprinting model of neonatal imitation. *Infant Behaviour and Development*, **27**, 54–63.

Nakano, S. and Kanaya, Y. (1993). The effects of mothers' teasing: do Japanese infants read their mothers' play intention in teasing? *Early Development and Parenting*, **2**, 7–17.

Nash, A. and Hay, D. F. (2003). Social relations in infancy: origins and evidence. *Human Development*, **46**, 222–32.

Nelson, K. (1996). *Language in cognitive development: emergence of the mediated mind.* New York, NY: Cambridge University Press.

Panksepp, J. (1998). *Affective neuroscience: the foundations of human and animal emotions.* New York, NY: Oxford University Press.

Panksepp, J. (2000). Affective consciousness and the instinctual motor system, The neural sources of sadness and joy. *The caldron of consciousness, motivation, affect and self-organization*, Advances in Consciousness Research, Vol **16** (ed. R. Ellis and N. Newton) , pp. 27–54. Amsterdam: John Benjamins Pub. Co.

Panksepp, J. and Bernatzky, G. (2002). Emotional sounds and the brain: the neuro-affective foundations of musical appreciation. *Behavioural Processes*, **60**, 133–55.

Panksepp, J. and Burgdorf, J. (2003). 'Laughing' rats and the evolutionary antecedents of human joy? *Physiology and Behavior*, **79**, 533–47.

Pantoja, A. P. F., Nelson-Goens, C., and Fogel, A. (2001). A dynamical systems approach to the study of early emotional development in the context of mother-infant communication. In A. F. Kalverboer and A. Gramsbergen (ed.), *Handbook on brain and behavior in human development* (pp. 901–920). Dordrecht, The Netherlands: Kluwer Academic Publishers.

Papousek, H. and Papousek, M. (1987). Intuitive parenting: a dialectic counterpart to the infant's integrative competence. In *Handbook of infant development*, 2nd edn (ed. J. D. Osofsky), pp. 669–720. New York, NY: Wiley.

Plooij, F. X. (2003). The trilogy of mind. In *Regression periods in human infancy* (ed. M. Heimann), pp. 185–205. Mahwah, NJ: Erlbaum.

Plooij, F. X., van de Rijt-Plooij, H. H. C., van der Stelt, J. M., *et al.* (2003). Illness peaks during infancy and regression periods. In *Regression Periods in Human Infancy* (ed. M. Heimann), pp. 81–95. Mahwah, NJ: Erlbaum.

Pöppel, E. (1994). Temporal mechanisms in perception. *International Review of Neurobiology*, **37**, 185–202.

Pöppel, E. and Wittmann, M. (1999). Time in the mind. In *The MIT encyclopedia of the cognitive sciences* (ed. R. Wilson and F. Keil), pp. 836–7. Cambridge, MA: MIT Press.

Porges, S. W. (2003). The polyvagal theory: phylogenetic contributions to social behavior. *Physiology and Behavior*, **79**, 503–13.

Reddy, V. (2003). On being the object of attention: implications for self–other consciousness. *TRENDS in Cognitive Sciences*, **7(9)**, 397–402.

Rizzolatti, G., Fogassi, L., and Gallese, V. (2001). Neurophysiological mechanisms underlying the understanding and imitation of action. *Nature Reviews Neuroscience*, **2**, 661–70.

Robb, L. (1999). Emotional musicality in mother-infant vocal affect, and an acoustic study of postnatal depression. In *Rhythms, musical narrative, and the origins of human communication*, Musicae Scientiae, Special Issue, 1999–2000, pp. 123–51. Liøge: European Society for the Cognitive Sciences of Music.

Rock, A. M. L., Trainor, L. J., and Addison, T. L. (1999). Distinctive messages in infant-directed lullabies and play songs. *Developmental Psychology*, **35**, 527–34.

Rogoff, B., Paradise, R., Arauz, R. M., *et al.* (2003). Firsthand learning through intent participation. *Annual Review of Psychology*, **54**, 175–203.

Rolls, E. T. (1999). *The brain and emotion*. Oxford: Oxford University Press.

Rothbart, M. K. (1994). What develops in emotional development? Emotional development: changes in reactivity and self-regulation. In *The nature of emotions* (ed. P. Ekman and J. Davidson), pp. (369–72). Oxford: Oxford University Press.

Scherer, K. R. (1986). Vocal affect expression: a review and a model for future research. *Psychological Bulletin*, **99**, 143–65.

Schore, A. N. (1994). *Affect regulation and the origin of the self: the neurobiology of emotional development*. Hillsdale, NJ: Erlbaum.

Schore, A. N. (2003). *Affect regulation and disorders of the self*. New York: Norton.

Schulkin, J., Thompson, B. L., and Rosen, J. B. (2003). Demythologising the emotions: adaptation, cognition, and visceral representations of emotion in the nervous system. *Brain and Cognition*, **52**, 15–23.

Selby, J. M. and Bradley, B. S. (2003). Infants in groups: a paradigm for study of early social experience. *Human Development*, **46**, 197–221.

Smith, A. (1759). *Theory of moral sentiments*. Edinburgh (Modern edition, ed. D. D. Raphael and A. L. Macfie, Oxford: Clarendon, 1976. Reprint, Indianapolis: Liberty Fund, 1984).

Spelke, E. S. (1998). Nativism, empiricism, and the origins of knowledge. Infant *Behavior and Development*, **21**, 181–200.

Sperry, R. W. (1952). Neurology and the mind-brain problem. *American Scientist*, **40**, 291–312.

Sperry, R. W. (1963). Chemoaffinity in the orderly growth of nerve fiber patterns and connections *Proceedings of the National Academy of Sciences, USA*, **50**, 703–10.

Sroufe, L. A. (1977). Wariness of strangers and the study of infant development. *Child Development*, **48**, 731–46.

Sroufe, L. A. (1996). *Emotional development: the organisation of emotional life in the early years.* New York, NY: Cambridge University Press.

Sroufe, L. A. and Waters, E. (1976). The ontogenesis of smiling and laughter: a perspective on the organization of development in infancy. *Psychological Reviews,* **83,** 173–89.

Stanghellini , G. (2001). Psychopathology of common sense. In *Philosophy, psychiatry, and psychology,* Vol. **8(2/3),** June/September 2001. Special Issue: *On understanding and explaining schizophrenia* (Guest ed. Ch. Hoerl), pp. 201–18 (with a commentary by L. A. Sass).

Stern, D. N. (1993). The role of feelings for an interpersonal self. In *The perceived self: ecological and interpersonal sources of self-knowledge* (ed. U. Neisser), pp. 205–15. New York, NY: Cambridge University Press.

Stern, D. N. (1999). Vitality contours: the temporal contour of feelings as a basic unit for constructing the infant's social experience. In *Early social cognition: understanding others in the first months of life* (ed. P. Rochat), pp. 67–90. Mahwah, NJ: Erlbaum.

Stern, D. N. (2000). *The interpersonal world of the infant: a view from psychoanalysis and development psychology,* 2nd edn. New York, NY: Basic Books.

Stern, D. N. (2004). *The present moment: in psychotherapy and everyday life.* New York: Norton.

Tomasello, M. (1988). The role of joint attentional processes in early language development. *Language Sciences,* **10,** 69–88.

Tomasello, M. (1999). *The cultural origins of human cognition.* Cambridge, MA: Harvard University Press.

Trevarthen, C. (1980). The foundations of intersubjectivity: development of interpersonal and cooperative understanding of infants. In: *The social foundations of language and thought: essays in honor of J. S. Bruner* (ed. D. Olson), pp. 316–42. New York, NY: W. W. Norton.

Trevarthen, C. (1984). Emotions in infancy: regulators of contacts and relationships with persons. In *Approaches to emotion* (ed. K. Scherer and P. Ekman), pp. 129–57. Hillsdale, NJ: Erlbaum.

Trevarthen, C. (1985). Neuroembryology and the development of perceptual mechanisms. In *Human growth,* 2nd edn (ed. F. Falkner and J. M. Tanner), pp. 301–83. New York, NY: Plenum.

Trevarthen, C. (1986a). Development of intersubjective motor control in infants. In *Motor Development in children: aspects of coordination and control* (ed. M. G. Wade and H. T. A. Whiting), pp. 209–61. Dordrecht: Martinus Nijhof.

Trevarthen, C. (1986b). Form, significance and psychological potential of hand gestures of infants. In *The biological foundation of gestures: motor and semiotic aspects* (ed. J-L. Nespoulous, P. Perron, and A. R. Lecours), pp. 149–202. Hillsdale, NJ: Erlbaum.

Trevarthen, C. (1987). Sharing makes sense: Intersubjectivity and the making of an infant's meaning. In R. Steele and T. Threadgold (ed.), *Language topics: essays in honour of Michael Halliday,* Vol. 1 (pp. 177–199). Amsterdam and Philadelphia: John Benjamins.

Trevarthen, C. (1990). Signs before speech. In: *The semiotic web, 1989* (ed. T. A. Sebeok and J. Umiker-Sebeok), pp. 689–755. Berlin: Mouton de Gruyter.

Trevarthen, C. (1993). The function of emotions in early infant communication and development. In *New perspectives in early communicative development* (ed. J. Nadel and L. Camaioni), pp. 48–81. London: Routledge.

Trevarthen, C. (1994). Infant semiosis. In *Origins of semiosis* (ed. W. Noth), pp. 219–52. Berlin: Mouton de Gruyter.

Trevarthen, C. (1995). Mother and baby—seeing artfully eye to eye. In *The artful eye* (ed. R. Gregory, J. Harris, D. Rose, *et al.*), pp. 157–200. Oxford: Oxford University Press.

Trevarthen, C. (1997). The nature of motives for human consciousness. *Psychology: Journal of the Hellenic Psychological Society* (Special Issue: *The Place of Psychology in Contemporary Sciences*, Part 2. Guest editor, T. Velli), **4(3)**, 187–221.

Trevarthen, C. (1998). The concept and foundations of infant intersubjectivity. In *Intersubjective communication and emotion in early ontogeny* (ed. S. Bråten), pp. 15–46. Cambridge: Cambridge University Press.

Trevarthen, C. (1999). Musicality and the intrinsic motive pulse: evidence from human psychobiology and infant communication. In *Rhythms, Musical Narrative, and the Origins of Human Communication*, Musicae Scientiae, Special Issue, 1999–2000, pp. 157–213. European Society for the Cognitive Sciences of Music, Liège.

Trevarthen, C. (2001a) Intrinsic motives for companionship in understanding: their origin, development and significance for infant mental health. *Infant Mental Health Journal*, **22(1–2)**, 95–131.

Trevarthen, C. (2001b). The neurobiology of early communication: Intersubjective regulations in human brain development. In: *Handbook on brain and behavior in human development* (ed. A. F. Kalverboer and A. Gramsbergen) , pp. 841–82. Dordrecht: Kluwer.

Trevarthen, C. (2002). Origins of musical identity: evidence from infancy for musical social awareness. In *Musical identities* (ed. R. MacDonald, D. J. Hargreaves, and D. Miell), pp. 21–38. Oxford: Oxford University Press.

Trevarthen, C. (2003a). Language development: mechanisms in the brain. In: *Encyclopedia of Neuroscience* (ed. G. Adelman and B. H. Smith), 3rd edn, with CD-ROM. Amsterdam: Elsevier Science.

Trevarthen, C. (2003b). Memory as motor activity: the brain making time, going places and finding objectives in company. In *Frühe Kommunikation und autobiographisches Gedächtnis. BIOS: Zeitschrift für Biographieforschung, Oral History und Lebensverlaufsanalysen*, **2**, 213–40.

Trevarthen, C. (2004). How infants learn how to mean. In *A learning zone of one's own*, SONY Future of Learning Series (ed. M. Tokoro and L. Steels), (in press). Amsterdam: IOS Press.

Trevarthen, C. and Aitken K. J. (1994). Brain development, infant communication, and empathy disorders: Intrinsic factors in child mental health. *Development and Psychopathology*, **6**, 599–635.

Trevarthen, C. and Aitken, K. J. (2001). Infant intersubjectivity: research, theory, and clinical applications. *Annual Research Review. Journal of Child Psychology and Psychiatry and Allied Disciplines*, **42(1)**, 3–48.

Trevarthen, C. and Aitken, K. J. (2003). Regulation of brain development and age-related changes in infants' motives: the developmental function of 'regressive' periods. In *Regression periods in human infancy* (ed. M. Heimann), pp. 107–84. Mahwah, NJ: Erlbaum.

Trevarthen, C. and Hubley, P. (1978). Secondary intersubjectivity: confidence, confiding and acts of meaning in the first year. In: *Action, gesture and symbol: the emergence of language* (ed. A. Lock), pp. 183–229. London: Academic Press.

Trevarthen, C. and Logotheti, K. (1987). First symbols and the nature of human knowledge. In *Symbolisme et connaissance (Symbolism and knowledge)*, Cahier No. 8, Jean Piaget Archives Fondation (ed. J. Montangero, A. Tryphon, and S. Dionnet), pp. 65–92. Geneva: Jean Piaget Archives Fondation.

Trevarthen, C. and Malloch, S. (2002). Musicality and music before three: human vitality and invention shared with pride. *Zero to Three*, **23(1)**, 10–18.

Trevarthen, C., Kokkinaki, T., and Fiamenghi, G. A. Jr (1999). What infants' imitations communicate: with mothers, with fathers and with peers. In *Imitation in Infancy* (ed. J. Nadel and G. Butterworth), pp. 127–85. Cambridge: Cambridge University Press.

Tronick, E. Z., Als, H., Adamson, L., Wise, S., and Brazelton, T. B. (1978). The infant's response to entrapment between contradictory messages in face-to-face interaction. *Journal of the American Academy of Child Psychiatry*, **17**, 1–13.

Tucker, D. M., Derryberry, D., and Luu, P. (2000). Anatomy and physiology of human emotion. In *Neuropsychology of emotion* (ed. J. C. Borod), pp. 56–79. New York: Oxford University Press.

Tulving, E. (2002). Episodic memory from mind to brain. *Annual Review of Psychology*, **53**, 1–25.

Turner, F. (1991). *Beauty: the value of values*. Charlottesville: University Press of Virginia.

Turner, M. (1996). *The literary mind: the origins of thought and language*. New York: Oxford University Press.

Tzourio-Mazoyer, N., De Schonen, S., *et al.* (2002). Neural correlates of woman face processing by 2-month-old infants. *NeuroImage*, **15**, 454–61.

Von Hofsten, C. (2001). On the early development of action, perception, and cognition. In F. Lacerda, C. von Hofsten, and M. Heimann (ed.), *Emerging cognitive abilities in early infancy* (pp. 73–89). Mahwah, NJ: Erlbaum.

Watson, J. S. (1972). Smiling, cooing and the game. *Merrill-Palmer Quarterly*, **18**, 323–39.

Wicker, B., Perrett, D. I., Baron-Cohen, S. *et al.* (2003). Being the target of another's emotion: a PET study. *Neuropsychologia*, **41**, 139–46.

Zei Pollermann, B. (2002). A place for prosody in a unified model of cognition and emotion. In: *Proceedings of Speech Prosody 2002*, Universitié de Aix-en-Provence, France.

Ontogeny

Chapter 4

Maternal–fetal psychobiology: a very early look at emotional development

Amy Salisbury, Penelope Yanni, Linda Lagasse, and Barry Lester

Emotional development begins long before the newborn takes in the first breath of air. It is commonly believed that maternal emotions affect the fetus and may influence emotional development. However, surprisingly little is known about the impact of maternal emotions on the fetus, especially in humans. The purpose of this chapter is to explore how maternal emotions during pregnancy, particularly those that are thought to be negative emotions, affect fetal behavioural development. We will focus on depression and anxiety as these disturbances are very common in women and may play a significant role in shaping emotional development in the infant.

The relationship between maternal depression and anxiety and fetal development is just beginning to be explored. We begin the chapter by reviewing the epidemiology of depression and anxiety in women to demonstrate the significant impact of these disorders on women of child-bearing age. We then review fetal and newborn effects that have been described. This is followed by a discussion of physiological mechanisms by which depression and anxiety can affect the fetus. Depression and anxiety are inherently tied to stress and its physiological underpinnings, and we review the available literature on this relationship. Next we turn to our own work on developing methods to measure fetal neurobehaviour and present some preliminary findings supporting the sensitivity of these methods. We conclude with a discussion of conceptual and methodological issues that need to be addressed for future directions in this field.

Epidemiology of depression and anxiety in women

Mood and anxiety disorders are the most common psychiatric illnesses and affect nearly twice as many women as men. These disorders often begin during the child-bearing years, presenting unique considerations and complications for women. Major Depressive Disorder (MDD) in women occurs at a rate of 7.4–25%, with the highest amounts occurring in lower socioeconomic samples (O'Hara *et al.*, 1984; Wisner *et al.*, 1995; Josefsson *et al.*, 2001). Anxiety Disorders occur in 5–8% of women. Ten to 20%

of women with MDD have co-morbid panic disorders, and 30–40% have co-morbid Generalized Anxiety Disorder (GAD; Kendler *et al.*, 1992b; Stuart *et al.*, 1998). MDD is also a common clinical outcome in those with a chronic anxiety disorder. The prevalence of these disorders remains the same during pregnancy, however it is more likely that a woman will have her first episode during pregnancy and is more likely to go untreated (Gotlib, *et al.*, 1989; O'Hara *et al.*, 1984; Sundstrom *et al.*, 2001). Untreated depression and/or anxiety expose the fetus to the biological and behavioural manifestations of the illness.

Fetal exposure to maternal depression and anxiety

The fetus is directly and indirectly exposed to the mother's illness through the placenta and the intrauterine environment (Sandman *et al.*, 1994). The placenta is not a barrier. Hormones, neurotransmitters, and peptides that are often altered in depression and anxiety are shared with the fetus through the umbilical cord and placenta (Blackburn, 2003). As we will discuss in the next section, the stress response associated with these disorders may increase fetal exposure to excessive levels of glucocorticoids, products of the stress response that are widely believed to be responsible for an altered set point for physiological, metabolic, and behavioural responses. (Welberg and Seckl, 2001; Matthews, 2002).

Deleterious behaviours and destructive symptoms common during episodes of depression and anxiety can have adverse effects on the fetus (Zuckerman *et al.*, 1989). Drug abuse (including alcohol and nicotine) may expose the fetus to teratogens that may have direct effects on the fetus, as well as decrease fetal-placental functioning (McAnarney and Stevens-Simon, 1990; Chrousos *et al.*, 1998). Poor appetite often leads to inadequate nutrition for both the mother and the fetus, and has been shown to have a negative effect on infant birthweight (Steer *et al.*, 1992).

Inadequate sleep with accompanying alterations in circadian (sleep-wake cycles) and ultradian (rapid-eye-movement (REM) and non-REM sleep alternation) rhythms is a hallmark symptom in both mood and anxiety disorders and may also be a source of significant, yet understudied, influence on fetal development. For those with depression, there is frequently decreased rapid-eye-movement (REM) latency, increased REM density, increased awakenings and decreased total sleep time, along with phase advances in daily rhythms of REM, cortisol, and body temperature (Riemann *et al.*, 2001). In individuals with anxiety disorders there is often increased REM latency, decreased slow-wave sleep, and extended sleep onset (Fuller *et al.*, 1997; Papadimitriou *et al.*, 1988). The brain regions and neurotransmitters central to the promotion and inhibition of circadian and ultradian rhythms are also involved in the pathophysiology of both depression and anxiety, in particular the neurotransmitters and neuronal pathways within the limbic system, amygdala, and hypothalamus. The suprachiasmatic nucleus (SCN) of the hypothalamus is responsible for the generation and entrainment of circadian and ultradian rhythms. The fetal SCN develops in utero, but is not functioning until late in gestation, leaving fetal rhythms to run according to maternal circadian and ultradian rhythms (Reppert *et al.*, 1987; Kennaway *et al.*, 1996; Kennaway, 2000; Rivkees and Hao, 2000). It is reasonable to consider that early exposure to altered rhythms and the underlying pathophysiology may influence circadian and ultradian rhythm development in the child (Kennaway, 2002). This may add another source of vulnerability to the development of emotional well-being. The relationship of altered SCN development to later emotional development has yet to be explored.

To fully understand the effect of maternal physical and emotional state on fetal development it is important to also examine fetal factors that may have an impact on the mother. The fetus has its own sensory experience of intra- and extra-uterine stimuli and can respond to sound, vibration, and vestibular changes as well as taste and smell amniotic fluid components (Timor-Tritsch, 1986; Smotherman and Robinson, 1988; Kisilevsky and Muir, 1991; Kiuchi *et al.*, 2000; Lecanuet *et al.*, 2000; El-Haddad *et al.*, 2002). Fetal responsiveness to sensory experiences in the form of movement or heightened activity can be perceived by the mother, and incorporated into her perceptions of the fetus' personality and temperament (Rubin, 1972, 1975; Leifer, 1977; Josten, 1982). The perceptions and interpretations by the mother underlie the development of maternal–fetal attachment, which can be influenced by mood and anxiety during the pregnancy. Maternal–fetal attachment is significant for the role it plays in promoting a woman's drive or desire to care for herself for the benefit of the fetus (Gaffney, 1986; Fowles, 1988; Grace, 1989; Lindgren, 2001; Shieh and Kravitz, 2002; Salisbury *et al.*, 2003).

Infant outcomes related to maternal depression and anxiety

The first forays into the relationship between maternal mental illness and child development involved extensive work on postpartum depression and child outcomes. Strong relationships were found between maternal depression and decreased quality of mother–child interaction (Lovejoy *et al.*, 2000), altered maternal responsiveness (Field, 1984, 1998) and increased child behaviour and mood disorders (Beardslee *et al.*, 1983; Beck, 1995; Harnish *et al.*, 1995; Biederman *et al.*, 2001).

Prospective studies confirm that women most vulnerable to postpartum depression are those that had previously been diagnosed with depression (Atkinson and Rickel, 1984; O'Hara *et al.*, 1990; O'Hara *et al.*, 1991). In fact, antenatal depression has stood out as the single most predictive factor for postpartum depression (Gotlib *et al.*, 1989; DaCosta *et al.*, 2000). The child is then exposed to the illness in utero and may continue to experience the effects of depressed maternal mood and interactions postnatally.

Limited data are available demonstrating the relationship between antenatal maternal depression and infant outcomes. The data thus far support the hypothesis that there are effects of fetal exposure to maternal depression (see Table 4.1 for summary). Infants of mothers with MDD during pregnancy have had less optimal neurobehavioural scores

Table 4.1 Summary of findings in human and animal studies in response to prenatal stress, anxiety or depression

Fetal behaviour and physiology	Infant behaviour and physiology
Increased activity	Increased HPA output
Increased responsivity to stress	Altered NT levels (DA, NE, 5-HT)
Delayed response to stress	Younger gestational age
Fewer movements in active sleep	Lower birth weight
Increased quiet sleep	Decreased adaptive behaviours Immature neuromotor development Decreased immunity Sleep difficulties More negative emotionality

DA = dopamine; NE = norepinephrine; 5-HT = serotonin.

at birth (Jones *et al.*, 1998) and 1 month (Salisbury *et al.*, 2002), cried excessively, and were more difficult to soothe (Zuckerman *et al.*, 1990). Armstrong *et al.* (1998) found increased sleep problems in children who were exposed *in utero* to maternal depression. Infants of depressed mothers were reported to be less developmentally mature than infants of non-depressed mothers (Field *et al.*, 2002). The mechanisms associated with these findings are unknown. It is possible that the effects are secondary to birth outcomes such as lower birth weight and gestational age. A recent study of over 1000 African-American women found that women with high depressive symptoms during pregnancy delivered their infants earlier in gestation and the infants had lower birthweights than women with low depressive symptoms (Orr *et al.*, 2002). As we will discuss, there are many potential confounding and contributing factors to consider in this research.

The possible relationship between anxiety disorders during pregnancy and infant-child outcomes is not well understood; only a few studies have explored anxiety symptoms per se and infant outcomes. In one study, women rated their anxious symptoms during pregnancy using the Speilberger State-Trait Anxiety Inventory (STAI; Spielberger, 1983). Infants born to women scoring high on the STAI were found to have decreased motor maturity, decreased vagal tone, decreased physical growth, and increased quiet sleep compared to infants of low scoring mothers (Field *et al.*, 2003). Similar findings were reported by Groome *et al.* (1995) in a study of fetal behaviour; fetuses of women with high trait anxiety scores spent significantly more time in quiet sleep and had fewer movements in active sleep. A longitudinal study found that high maternal anxiety scores during pregnancy significantly predicted behavioural and emotional problems for the children at the age of 4. The correlation was significant even after controlling for antenatal and postnatal depressive symptoms (O'Connor *et al.*, 2002).

Effects of prenatal stress on fetal and infant neurobehavioural development

Although little research data exists on the effects of depression and anxiety *per se* on the developing fetus, animal research has provided a wealth of information on the effects of prenatal stress on the neurobiological development of the organism. Stress, particularly chronic or persistent stress, may be a key predisposing factor in the development of mood and anxiety disorders. In fact, when exposed to persistent stress, rodents and primates begin to display the emotional and physiological disruptions that are common during depression and anxiety.

The findings to date on fetal and neonatal outcomes associated with fetal exposure to maternal stress have been largely consistent with those found in the limited studies on fetuses exposed to depression or anxiety (see Table 4.1). Prenatally stressed individuals are often described as having a higher amount of anxiety, fear-related behaviour and hyperemotional states (Davis, 1992; Takahashi *et al.*, 1992; Gray and Bingaman, 1996; Williams *et al.*, 1998). Prenatally stressed animals consistently display exaggerated neuroendocrine and behavioural responses to stress (Weinstock *et al.*, 1992; Henry *et al.*, 1994; Vallee *et al.*, 1997). Non-human primates prenatally exposed to stress show altered behavioural responses to maternal separation after birth, including decreased adaptive behaviours, immature neuromotor behaviours, and increased inattention (Schneider, 1992a,b; Schneider and Coe, 1993). In both animal and human studies, prenatal stress is usually associated with lower infant birth weight and younger gestational age at birth (Wadhwa, 1993;Sandman *et al.*, 1997; Rini *et al.*, 1999; Schneider *et al.*, 1999). In an acute stress model, pregnant women with high anxiety scores exposed to a cognitive task had lower elevations in blood pressure than non-anxious women and their fetuses had greater FHR increases following the task (Monk *et al.*, 2000, 2003).

The fetus may experience stress directly via sound, light, or vibration. More commonly, however, the pregnant mother is exposed directly to the stressor with fetal experience assumed to be secondary to maternal physiological changes. The mechanisms of the physiological responses to stress in the nervous system as well as in the uterus and placenta are currently being studied in many different species.

Biologic determinants of fetal exposure to maternal stress, depression and anxiety in utero

Figure 4.1 depicts the proposed mechanisms for the relationship between stress, depression and anxiety and how maternal physiological and behavioural manifestations may affect fetal development. The human body reacts to stressors that threaten homeostasis by activating a coordinated and complex repertoire of physiological and behavioural responses, including the 'fight or flight' response described by Walter Cannon in the early 1900s. The *adaptive* stress response is crucial for the dynamic

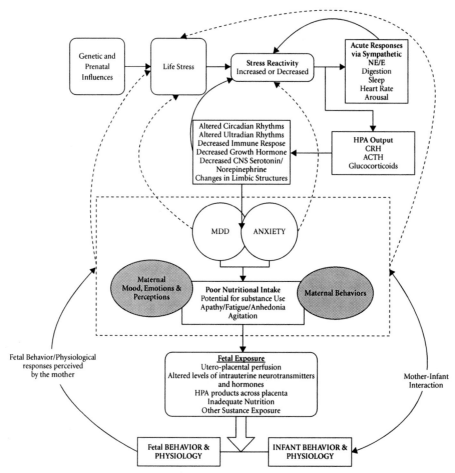

Fig. 4.1 Model of the potential relationship between stress, emotions, and fetal exposure.

equilibrium and the survival of the individual. As reviewed by Stratakis and Chrousos (1995) and O'Connor *et al.* (2000), the central components of the stress system are the corticotrophin-releasing hormone (CRH), CRH neurons, arginine-vasopressin (AVP) neurons of the hypothalamus, and the catecholaminergic neurons of the medulla and pons, in particular the locus ceruleus. The peripheral limbs of the stress system are the hypothalamic-pituitary-adrenal (HPA) axis and the efferent sympathetic/adrenomedullary system. Control of the stress response takes place at extra-hypothalamic sites including the hippocampus and the amygdala, which are components of the limbic system responsible for behavioural integration, mood and arousal (Jacobson and Sapolsky, 1991; Herman and Cullinan, 1997; Feldman *et al.*, 1998). Along with many other connections, the hippocampus and amygdala receive sensory input from the cerebral cortices and project to the hypothalamus (Heimer, 1983). They are themselves sites of CRH production and CRH receptors and likely play an important role in the integration of stress signals, resulting in behavioural and neuroendocrine responses (Brunson *et al.*, 2001).

Under non-stressful conditions, CRH and AVP are released in a pulsatile manner with a circadian rhythm of higher secretion in the morning and lower at night. Disruptions of other circadian factors, such as light and sleep, and exposure to stress alter the circadian rhythm of CRH and AVP release. During stress CRH and AVP are released from the hypothalamus and stimulate ACTH release from the pituitary. CRH and AVP are synergistic in their release of ACTH, however AVP cannot release ACTH independently. It has recently been found that CRH may, in fact, belong to a family of peptides, with CRH receptor agonists consistently mimicking and CRH receptor antagonists lessening the functional consequences of stressor exposure in animal models (Smagin *et al.*, 2001). There are two known CRH receptors both located in the brain and periphery (Coste *et al.*, 2001). Amongst other locations, CRH-1 receptors are found in the pituitary and are probably the primary CRH receptor in the activation of the HPA axis. CRH type 1 receptor knockout mice were shown to have an impaired stress response (Smith *et al.*, 1998). CRH-2 receptors are located mainly in the peripheral vasculature and the heart and may play a role in recovery processes, as evidenced by CRH type 2 knock out mice being hypersensitive to stress (Coste *et al.*, 2000).

ACTH is the key stimulator of glucocorticoid release from the adrenal cortex. Glucocorticoids (cortisol in humans, corticosterone in rodents) increase blood pressure, blood volume, glucose and amino acids and are the final effectors of the HPA axis. They provide negative feedback on the hypothalamic synthesis of CRH and directly on pituitary ACTH.

The sympathetic division of the autonomic nervous system (ANS) responds rapidly to stress. It innervates the smooth muscle cells of the vasculature, the heart, skeletal muscles, kidney, gut and many other organs. In addition to the primary preganglionic neurotransmitter acetylcholine and postganglionic neurotransmitter norepinephrine (NE), the ANS also contains neurons expressing a variety of neuropeptides including neuropeptide Y, somatostatin, enkephalin, and neurotensin. In addition, the sympathetic system also has a humoral component consisting of epinephrine and norepinephrine released from the adrenal medulla. The sympathetic system acts globally in the 'fight or flight' response, decreasing neurovegetative functions, such as digestion and sleep, and increasing gluconeogenesis, heart rate, and arousal. NE also activates the amygdala, the principal brain locus for fear-related behaviours, and enhances the long-term storage of aversely charged emotional experiences, an adaptive function for learning to protect oneself.

The stress system interacts with several endocrine functions. The reproductive axis is inhibited at many levels by various components of the stress system (Torpy, 1998). CRH production inhibits the secretion of gonadotropin releasing hormone (GNRH), which in turn inhibits the release of follicle stimulating hormone, leutinizing hormone, and resulting ovarian products (oestradiol, oestrogen, progesterone). Oestradiol feeds-back into the hypothalamus to regulate CRH levels. Glucocorticoids inhibit GNRH neurons, which causes sex-steroid target tissues to be resistant to these hormones. During the normal course of pregnancy there is a gradual increase in the levels of glucocorticoids, ACTH, beta-endorphin (βE), and CRH (Liu and Rebar, 1998).The stress-endocrine system may be particularly vulnerable during pregnancy to the effects of stress on the HPA axis and the resulting cascade of responses. The degree of susceptibility is likely to be gestational age dependent. Evidence for this relationship comes from studies showing a link between younger gestational age at birth and prenatal stress (Lobel et al., 1992; Sandman et al., 1997; Wadhwa et al., 1998; Rini et al., 1999). This outcome may be due to a precocious elevation of CRH, which plays a major role in the timing of labor and delivery and is related to the risk of preterm delivery (Wadhwa et al., 1993; Sandman et al., 1997; Rini et al., 1999).

The effects of stress on the growth axis may also account for lower birth weight in infants exposed to prenatal stress (Stratakis et al., 1995; O'Connor et al., 2000). While acute stress has been shown to stimulate GH levels; prolonged stress results in the suppression of growth hormone (GH) via CRH-induced elevations in somatostatin levels and inhibition of target tissue response to insulin-like growth factor-1 (IGF-1) (Stratakis et al., 1996). Decreased GH secretion is a characteristic finding in 'psychosocial dwarfism', which is the decreased growth and short stature that can occur in children subject to emotional deprivation or psychological abuse. Decreased growth has been thought to be independent of food intake in these children (Stratakis et al., 1995).

The stress system also suppresses thyroid axis function with inhibited TSH production and secretion and inhibition of the conversion of T4 to T3. In animal models, chronic, stress-induced hypercortisolism also induces insulin-resistance, osteoporosis, and truncal obesity (Stratakis et al., 1995). Stress inhibits gastric emptying and increases colonic motility via CRH and the sympathetic nervous system, possibly involving the secretion of vasoactive intestinal peptide. Glucocorticoids in concert with the sympathetic nervous system inhibit many components of the immune response including virtually all inflammatory cells. Amongst other mechanisms, this occurs via inhibition of the production of the cytokines TNF alpha, IL-1, IL-2, and IL-6, inhibition of leukotrienes, and lympholysis (O'Connor et al., 2000).

In addition to affecting endocrine and immunologic function, stress has been shown to alter brain structure and function and is thought to contribute to mood and anxiety disorders via persistent changes in the HPA axis and other mechanisms. Early life stress can result in long-term HPA axis dysfunction. For example, Coplan et al. (1998) demonstrated that cerebro-spinal fluid CRH was persistently elevated in macaques nursed during early infancy by mothers undergoing stressful conditions. These animals were also found to have abnormal cortisol and immune responses to social stress (Smith et al., 2002) and elevated levels of somatostatin, and serotonin and dopamine metabolites (Coplan et al., 1998). Others have shown increased corticosterone and ACTH responses to stress in adult rats subjected to maternal deprivation in infancy as well as altered CRH mRNA and receptor levels (Ladd *et al.*, 1996; Plotsky and Meaney, 1993). Similarly, women with histories of childhood abuse displayed increased pituitary-adrenal and autonomic responses to stress compared to age-matched controls. This included a several-fold increase in ACTH levels in response to stress, which was particularly robust in women with current major depressive disorder (Heim *et al.*, 2000).

PTSD clearly is a mental illness caused by stressful life experiences, often early life stress and trauma, that have resulted in persistent neuropsychological changes. Supra-suppression of cortisol following low dose dexamethasone test (which provides a measure of HPA axis negative feedback sensitivity) in chronic PTSD has been replicated in several studies (Yehuda *et al.*, 1993; Grossman *et al.*, 2003). The number of glucocorticoid receptors (measured on lymphocytes) also appears to be decreased.

It has been suggested that elevated cortisol may result in neuronal damage (Sapolsky, 1996). In animal models, stress has been shown to inhibit neurogenesis in the hippocampus (Gould *et al.*, 1998) and, indeed, early-life administration of CRH has been found to cause long-term progressive hippocampal cell loss and dysfunction (Brunson *et al.*, 2001). Stress can also affect the production of neurotrophins (Post *et al.*, 1995), which could also result in altered brain structure. Interestingly, several studies have shown decreased hippocampal volumes in individuals with PTSD (Bremner *et al.*, 1995; Gurvits *et al.*, 1996; Stein *et al.*, 1997) and functional neuroimaging studies have demonstrated multiple region specific alterations in brain function, for example, decreased function in the hippocampus and increased function in the amgdala in patients with PTSD (reviewed by Bremner, 2003).

Stressful life events have also been linked to vulnerability to psychiatric disorders other than PTSD, for example, both increased depression and anxiety are observed in women who have been victims of childhood abuse (McCauley *et al.*, 1997) and loss of a parent has been shown to increase the risk of MDD and GAD (Kendler *et al.*, 1992a). Interestingly, it has recently been shown that allelic differences in the serotonin transporter gene conferred vulnerability to developing MDD in individuals following life stressors (Caspi *et al.*, 2003). It has also been noted that melancholic MDD looks like a hyperactive stress response with increased arousal, loss of appetite and libido and atypical depression may represent a hypoarousal state, with increased appetite and fatigue. There is evidence to support the influence of CRH overproduction in depression (Gold *et al.*, 1995) and a blunted ACTH response to CRH administration (Heim *et al.*, 2001). Similar to PTSD, individuals with MDD have been found to have smaller hippocampi (Frodl *et al.*, 2002).

Panic disorder and GAD are often comorbid with MDD and PTSD; however, CRH levels have not been found to be elevated in either of these disorders (Jolkkonen *et al.*, 1993; Fossey *et al.*, 1996). Panic disorder patients have been found to have higher cortisol levels and MHPG (3-methoxy-4-hydroxyphenylglycol, a norepinephrine metabolite) than individuals with PTSD and controls (Marshall *et al.*, 2002). Yohimbine, an α_2 receptor antagonist produced panic attacks in patients with a history of panic attacks at a vastly increased rate than controls (Gurguis *et al.*, 1997). Yohimbine administration to individuals with GAD gave similar results to normal controls (Charney *et al.*, 1989; Cameron *et al.*, 1990). This data suggests a hyperresponsive norepinephrine system in Panic disorder, but not GAD or PTSD. Finally decreased benzodiazepine receptor binding was found in individuals with PTSD and Panic disorder (Bremner *et al.*, 2000a,b).

If stress can have such profound long-term effects on an individual, one would expect that a fetus undergoing rapid brain development and neurogenesis, exposed to the same endocrine mediators would be subject to altered brain development and responses to stress. The fetal HPA system is particularly susceptible to early life events. Stress to the mother during pregnancy alters HPA axis output in the offspring, includ- ing increases in β-endorphin, ACTH and concentrations of plasma corticosterone (Sandman *et al.*, 1994). Other changes in offspring exposed to prenatal stress include impaired cellular immunity and neurotransmitter alterations (Mastorakos *et al.*, 1995). Prenatal stress has been linked to changes in norepinephrine, dopamine, and serotonin concentrations as well as the density of receptors for these neurotransmitters (Schneider *et al.*, 1998). This includes brain systems and the hypothalamic structures involved in behaviour. Prenatal stress reduces serotonin, norepinephrine and dopamine levels and turnover in the adult brain (Takahashi *et al.*, 1992; Hayashi *et al.*, 1998). It also increases hippocampal acetylcholine release in response to stress. The brain changes are described as 'permanent' or 'programmed' because of the life-long changes that prenatal stress induces (Seckl, 1998, 2001; Welberg *et al.*, 2001). However, other research suggests that stress-induced changes in brain structure and behaviour can be reversed with enrichment or other enhancements (Chapillon *et al.*, 2002).

In human research, the environment plays a significant role in the effects of prenatal exposure on the fetus. Wadhwa *et al.* (1996) found that neuroendocrine changes dur- ing pregnancy were significantly related to prenatal psychosocial stress, social support, and personality variables. A combination of the maternal psychosocial and socio- demographic factors during pregnancy were significantly related to levels of ACTH, cor- tisol, and βE. In the animal literature, a variety of manipulations during pregnancy in experimental animal models, including restraint stress and fear responses have been shown to evoke a rise in plasma ACTH and cortisol in dams and non-human primates (Weinstock *et al.*, 1992; Clarke *et al.*, 1994; Henry *et al.*, 1994; Vallee *et al.*, 1997; Weinstein *et al.*, 1997). In a recent study by Sandman *et al.*, human fetuses of mothers with highly elevated CRH were found to be non-responsive to repeated presentations of a vibroacoustic simulus (Sandman *et al.*, 1997).

The findings outlined here demonstrate how prenatal exposure to maternal stress, depression and/or anxiety may predispose the child to long-term physiological changes that may influence emotional and behavioural development. The evidence points to a need to study the prenatal period and the potential role of the maternal–fetal system in contributing to vulnerability in the child. Due to this vulnerability, fetal 'exposure' to the altered psychobiological environment of maternal mental illness may be a potential factor in the growing list of contributors and/or mediators of child psychopathology. Identifying these factors is more critical than ever to understand; the prevalence of childhood psychopathology is substantial and continues to rise every year. The most recent estimates by the National Institutes of Mental Health Multi-Site Epidemiologic Surveys of Mental Disorders in Child and Adolescent Populations (MECA) suggest that 1 in 10 (20%) of children in the USA are diagnosed with a psychiatric illness every year (Lahey *et al.*, 1996; Shaffer *et al.*, 1996). Only one in five of those children receives treatment. Depression occurs in 3–8% of children and adolescents, while 13% of children are diagnosed with an anxiety disorder. By 2020, a 50% increase is expected in the prevalence rate of mental disorders in children (Saraceno, 2002).

Methods to measure infant and fetal neurobehavioural development

Studying the fetus enables us to look at potential effects during the time of exposure, before the influence of other variables that appear to be more salient in the newborn period, such as the stress of the labor and delivery process, sex differences, and potential effects of other drugs given during labor and delivery or immediately after birth. There are obvious limitations to studying human fetal behaviour, such as access to observe and measure fetal variables without imposing a source of stress or risk to the fetus or mother. Recent technological advances have made safe, relatively unobtrusive measurement of the fetus possible. Ultrasound techniques monitor fetal behaviours and activity across gestation and doppler technology monitors and records fetal heart rate (FHR). The combination of a FHR monitor and an actogram has enabled the simultaneous measurement of FHR and fetal activity, which aids in the determination of fetal behavioural state. FHR, fetal motor activity, and fetal state are reflections of CNS functioning; measurement of these variables may provide important data on the effects of maternal physiology on the developing fetus [see DiPietro (2001) for review].

To gain an understanding of the maternal–fetal system in response to the psychobiological and physiological alterations in depression and anxiety our research program is examining the relationships between maternal mental health, maternal–fetal attachment, circadian and ultradian rhythms, and fetal and infant neurobehavioural development.

Fetal and infant neurobehaviour reflects Central Nervous System (CNS) functioning, the measure of which can provide us with data about obvious effects of exposure as well as subtle effects that may otherwise go unnoticed. As we have seen in the cocaine exposure literature, subtle effects during early development are not trivial, but may be indicative of vulnerability that when combined with other factors may influence later development (LaGasse *et al.*, 1999). Neurobehaviour is a construct originally introduced over 30 years ago by Brazelton (Brazelton, 1978) and other infant behaviour scientists (Wolff, 1959, 1965, 1967; Prechtl, 1969; Thoman *et al.*, 1976) as a means of observing and assessing neurological integrity. In the newborn, examining reflexes, motor activity and tone, responsivity, attention, and habituation in the context of behavioural state operationally define neurobehaviour.

Infant neurobehaviour in response to intra-uterine exposure is measured in our program using the NICU Network Neurobehavioural Scale (NNNS; Lester and Tronick, 2004). The NNNS was developed as part of the neurodevelopmental battery for the Maternal Lifestyles Study (MLS) under the direction of Barry Lester. The MLS Project is a large multi-site longitudinal study of the sequelae of intrauterine drug exposure, conducted in the NICHD-directed Neonatal Research Network at four sites (Lester, 1998). The NNNS examines the neurobehavioural organization, reflexes, motor development, active and passive tone, as well as signs of stress and withdrawal of drug-exposed infants. It was developed to provide a comprehensive assessment of both neurological integrity and behavioural function, as well as to document the range of withdrawal and stress behaviour likely to be observed in a study of high risk infants including substance-exposed infants. Traditionally, scales that measure neonatal abstinence such as the Neonatal Abstinence Score (Finnegan et al., 1975) are treated separately from neurological and behavioural evaluation, even though there is some overlap in what is assessed. A stress/abstinence scale was incorporated into the neurobehavioural scale by recording signs of stress and withdrawal observed during the neurobehavioural examination. Thus, in addition to utilizing the behavioural items developed by Brazelton (1973), the NNNS provides a neurological examination and a separate stress/abstinence scale. The NNNS is applicable to term, normal healthy infants, preterm infants, and infants at-risk due to factors, such as prenatal substance exposure, maternal psychiatric disorders or prenatal stress.

Fetal neurobehaviour is an extension of the original construct of infant neurobehaviour in that similar behaviours can be observed and measured using obstetrical ultrasound and fetal heart rate monitoring. Fetal neurobehaviour is comprised of four domains: fetal heart rate, motor activity, behavioural state, and responsiveness to extrauterine stimuli (DiPietro, 2001). Assessment of these domains across gestational age provides critical information about CNS development (Nijhuis, 1986; Prechtl and Einspieler, 1997; DiPietro et al., 2002). Baseline FHR and FHR variability indicate maturity of the peripheral nervous system (sympathetic and parasympathetic nervous systems), central nervous system and overall fetal well being. FHR response to an external stimulus is also a reflection of CNS maturity and is often assessed in fetal observations.

In early pregnancy fetal movements appear to be random and uncoordinated, with no discernible pattern. As pregnancy advances, these movements become increasingly sophisticated and integrated. In studies of fetuses between 32 and 40 weeks gestation, the temporal association of different types of somatic movements, eye movements, and heart rate patterns suggest distinct recurring patterns (Nijhuis et al., 1982, 1999). These patterns are analogous to four of the six states that are well documented in the newborn and have been designated as fetal states, 1F–4F, each with a specific heart rate pattern. The use of ultrasound technology enables visualization of the fetus to observe specific fetal action patterns, motor activity, quality and amplitude of movements, and eye movements. For a thorough review of fetal behavioural development, fetal observation methods and methodological considerations please see Lecanuet *et al.* (1995) and DiPietro (2001).

Methods in our laboratory included the use of real-time ultrasound (Toshiba diagnostic ultrasound machine model SSA-340A with a 3.75-MHz transducer) to examine fetal movement and specific behaviours. Fetuses were observed and recorded by holding the transducer (3.75 MHz) to obtain a longitudinal view of the fetal face, trunk and upper limbs. The recordings were conducted for 20 minutes: 10 minutes of baseline recording, followed by a single 3-second Vibroacoustic Stimulus (VAS; TOCO ultrasonic transducer B5600) applied to the maternal abdomen, and 10 minutes of post-VAS recording. The videotape is then copied and dubbed with a SMPTE time code, which has a resolution up to a 30th of a second, onto one of two audio channels of the ultrasound recording. The SMPTE dub was then coded for fetal behaviours using a computer-based behavioural coding system: the Action, Analysis, Coding, and Training (AACT) Program.

The AACT program allowed for frame by frame analysis of movements and behaviours to measure the variables of mean duration and overall amount of fetal head, limb, and trunk movement (see Fig. 4.2). Each 10-second epoch that included movement

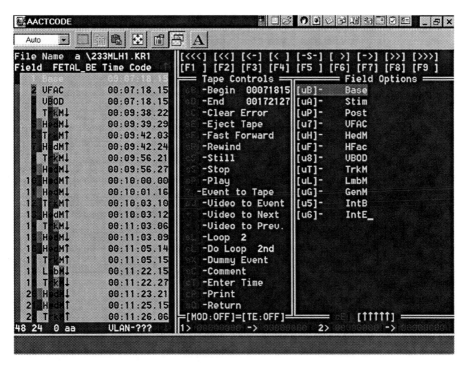

Fig. 4.2 Example of a screen depicting the AACT behaviour coding system.

Table 4.2 Fetal behaviour coding definitions

Rest–activity cycle*	Definition
Quiescence	Inactivity interrupted only by a single burst of gross motor activity, such as a startle, without a change to a more active pattern of movement. Mouthing may be present
Activity	More than one burst of gross body movement or more than two large isolated limb movements in the 15 seconds epoch
Indeterminate	Features of both quiescence and activity so that is could not be determined which predominated the epoch
Unscorable	Use for any epoch in which the fetus is not visible at all
Behaviour**	Definition
Hand-to-face	The hand touching any part of the face or mouth. Can occur alone or as part of a general movement—code separately
Startle	A quick, generalized movement, initiated in limbs (flexion or extension) and sometimes spreading to neck and trunk
Tremor	Small rhythmic movement of an extremity (1 or more)
Climb wall	Climbing motion involving upper and lower extremities against the uterine wall
Void	Relative change in bladder size before and after void
Hyperflexion	Flexion of the trunk and maintenance of this position for greater than 1 second
Back arch	Extension of the trunk and maintenance in this position for greater than 1 second
Stretch	A slow, forceful extension of the back, retroflexion of the head, and external rotation and elevation of the arms
Breathing movements	Movement of the diaphragm with inward movement of the thorax and outward movement of the abdomen
Suck	Rhythmical bursts of regular jaw opening and closing at a rate of about one per second
Yawn	Prolonged wide opening of the jaws followed by quick closure
Swallow	Jaw opening and closing with displacements of the tongue and/or larynx. Swallowing often follows sucking behaviours
Mouthing	Jaw opening may be slow or quick, can occur once, in repetition or may be rhythmic
Hiccup	Consists of a jerky contraction of the diaphragm. Hiccups are usually repetitive but may occur as a single event

* Definitions adapted from M. Pillai (1990).

** Definitions adapted form de Vries *et al.* (1982).

was also scored for the quality of the movements present (smooth versus jerky). Behavioural patterns indicative of stress or self-regulation/adaptation are scored for presence or absence during each 10-second epoch: hand to face, startle, tremor, climb wall, void, hyperflexion, back arch, stretch, breathing, suck, swallow, yawn, mouth, and hiccup (see Table 4.2). Inter-rater reliability ranged from 77 to 83% agreement. Fetal heart rate (FHR) was recorded in beats per minute (bpm) on a Corometrics Fetal Heart Monitor 145 (model 0145AAL).

Preliminary findings

Responsiveness to a single vibroacoustic stimulus

In an attempt to stimulate a cardio-acceleratory response in cases of a non-reactive stress test (NST), obstetricians have introduced a vibroacoustic stimulus (VAS), which uses a commercially available vibratory and acoustic stimulus applied to the maternal abdomen, and is used as a clinical assessment of fetal well being (Smith *et al.*, 1986). The use of a vibroacoustic stimulus to measure fetal reactivity has been consistently shown to differentiate between healthy and at-risk fetuses (Smith *et al.*, 1988; Kisilevsky *et al.*, 1990; Gingras and O'Donnell, 1998; Sandman *et al.*, 1999). However, there has been some controversy over the safety of this device in the past few years. Most of the concern focuses on the delivery of sound stimuli greater than 82 dB to the fetal ear and prolonged FHR accelerations after repeated VAS presentations (Kisilevsky, 1990; Visser and Mulder, 1993; Kisilevsky, 1995). There have been no published reports on damage to the fetal ear from VAS presentation in utero (Kisilevsky, 1995), and excessive FHR reactivity or signs of excessive fetal stress were found in fetuses with baseline tachycardia or other FHR patterns indicating suspect health status of the fetus (Visser and Mulder, 1993). The cumulative evidence suggests that vibroacoustic stimulation of the fetus is clinically safe (Smith, 1995).

Baseline fetal motor activity has been shown to decrease with advancing GA (Gagnon, 1995). Fetal response (increased movement and or heart rate) to a VAS has been found to occur by 27 weeks GA (Kisilevsky *et al.*, 1992) with increasing responsiveness over age. Previous studies used multiple VAS presentations and non-stimulus control trials to determine responsiveness. Because we wanted to use only one VAS presentation in our in our at-risk cohorts, we first wanted to determine if fetuses would respond similarly to those in the previous studies.

Fetal behaviour was observed in 133 mother-fetus dyads from a healthy, community sample using a Toshiba Ultrasound (model 146) with a 3.75 Mhz transducer for 20 minutes. During the first quiescent period (no movement for at least 1 minute) after the first 10 minutes of recording, a single vibroacoustic stimulus (VAS) was delivered to the fetus via the maternal abdomen for 3 seconds. An additional 10 minutes of fetal behaviour was recorded following the VAS. Due to the short duration of the observations a no-stimulus control trial was not included in the design. Rather, the VAS was

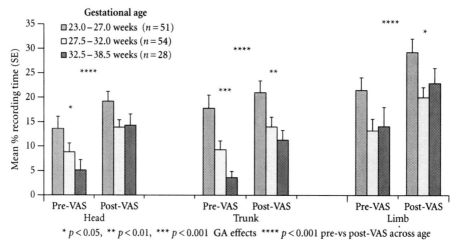

$* p < 0.05$, $** p < 0.01$, $*** p < 0.001$ GA effects $**** p < 0.001$ pre-vs post-VAS across age

Fig. 4.3 Fetal movements before and after VAS at three gestational ages.

delivered to the mothers' outstretched arms (away from the maternal abdomen) prior to the observation to get them accustom to the feel and the sound.

Three gestational age groups were formed from the total sample: 23–27 weeks ($n = 51$), 27.5–32 weeks ($n = 54$), and 32.5–38.5 weeks ($n = 28$). The groups were analysed using repeated measures ANOVA procedures for pre and post VAS behaviours. Figure 4.3 shows the results for each of the three groups. Fetuses spent significantly less time moving their heads and trunks with advancing gestational age, but did not differ with advancing gestational age in how much time they spent moving their limbs in the baseline period. Fetuses at all ages spent more time moving head, trunk and limbs after the VAS than before the VAS. The results indicate that although fetuses move less with advancing gestational age, they continue to demonstrate a significant behavioural response to a single VAS presentation. This is consistent with other studies using multiple VAS presentations that reported increased behavioural response to the VAS with increasing GA (see Kisilevsky, 1995).

Fetal heart rate responses to maternal depressed mood

The relationship of maternal mood to fetal heart rate and fetal heart rate reactivity to vibroacoustic stimulation (VAS) was examined in a pilot study of pregnant women with untreated depressed mood (Allister *et al.*, 2001). Subjects consisted of twenty 32–36-week pregnant women divided into depressed mood ($n = 10$) and non-depressed mood ($n = 10$) groups based on the Beck Depression Inventory (BDI; Beck *et al.*, 1961). Subjects were attached to a fetal heart monitor and 10 minutes of baseline fetal heart rate was recorded. A VAS was presented in a quiescent state approximating state 1F and 10 additional minutes of fetal heart rate was recorded. FHR was recorded in beats per minute (bpm). Mean FHR was computed every 10 seconds and averaged in five 2-minute periods for the 10 minutes immediately preceding the presentation of

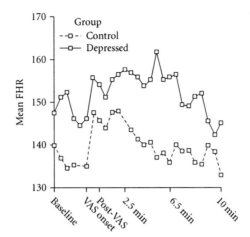

Fig. 4.4 Estimated marginal means of FHR.

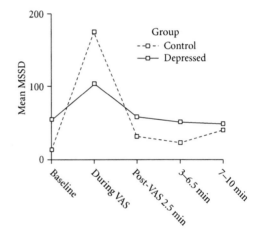

Fig. 4.5 Estimated marginal means of MSSD.

the VAS, constituting the pre-stimulus or baseline period. FHR was also obtained at 1- and 5-second periods during the presentation of the VAS. The post-stimulus period included the mean FHR immediately following presentation of the VAS, computed every 10 seconds and averaged in 30-second periods.

FHR variability was computed as the mean squared successive difference (MSSD) (Varni *et al.*, 1971; Heslegrave *et al.*, 1979) for each 2-minute period during baseline and for each 20-second period post-stimulus. Shorter post-stimulus (30 seconds) than baseline (2-minute) periods were selected to determine the potential time course of heart rate reactivity to the VAS. To measure the changes in heart rate reactivity during and following the presentation of VAS, FHR difference scores were computed at baseline, during the presentation of the VAS, and post-stimulus.

Figure 4.4 shows the mean FHR of the depressed and the control group across the baseline, the presentation of the stimulus, and the post-stimulus periods. Fetuses of depressed mothers had an elevated baseline fetal heart rate and a 3.5-fold delay in return to baseline fetal heart rate after VAS presentation. Fetuses in the control group reacted with greater accelerations in heart rate than those in the depressed group, indicating quicker and greater responsivity to the environment. Figure 4. 5 presents the MSSD (heart rate variability) at baseline, during VAS, and for selected time periods post-VAS presentation. Overall, there was a significant change in FHR variability for both groups. The depressed group showed lower FHR variability during the VAS presentation, which combined with the FHR data, suggests a delayed, weaker, but longer reaction to external stimulus.

Fetuses of mothers with elevated mood symptoms display differential rest-activity cycles in response to a VAS

In this pilot study, we monitored 35 mother-fetal dyads according to the protocol described previously. In addition, we asked each mother to fill out the BDI (Beck *et al.*, 1961) and the Speilberger State-Trait Anxiety Inventory (STAI; Spielberger, 1983) prior to ultrasound examination. All fetuses were 25–30 weeks GA. We analysed fetal behaviours in mothers with high depressed mood (BDI > 15) and mothers with low depressed mood (BDI < 7). None of the women were taking antidepressant medications. Mothers in the high depressed mood group also had significantly higher state and trait anxiety scores. Fetuses of depressed mothers showed a trend of spending less time in active periods and more time in quiet periods at baseline. Fetuses of depressed mothers responded to the VAS by increasing their time in active periods while fetuses of non-depressed mothers did not exhibit changes in rest-active periods in response to the VAS (see Fig. 4.6). Lower amounts of activity at baseline and increased active periods following a mild stress are consistent with previous studies examining maternal anxiety and fetal behaviour (Groome *et al.*, 1995) and maternal depression and infant behaviour (Jones *et al.*, 1998). The mechanism, significance, and long-term sequelae of these effects are unknown and in great need of further study.

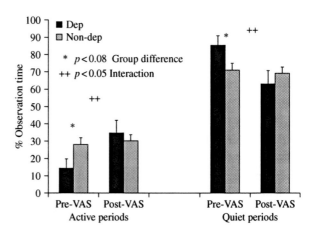

Fig. 4.6 Rest–activity cycles in fetuses of mothers with high and low depressed moods.

Methodological issues

There were limitations to our original methods that we needed to address before undertaking further study. First, the recoding period was too short to accurately assess the full potential of baseline behaviours. We also wanted to include measures of fetal behavioural state at later gestational ages and needed to have at least 40–50 minutes of recording to adequately measure state (Pillai *et al.*, 1992). In our original studies, 10 minutes post-VAS observation was long enough to observe reactivity, but not always long enough to observe a full recovery. Therefore, we revised our methods to include a 10-minute baseline FHR assessment, followed by 40-minutes of baseline ultrasound behaviour observation in conjunction with FHR and a 20-minute post-VAS observation period.

We incorporated the use of actocardiography, a highly accurate and reliable method for monitoring fetal heart rate, FHR variability, and fetal activity (Toitu MT325, HAH Medical). The actocardiograph is used simultaneously with the ultrasound machine, with specific procedures to avoid interference of the two ultrasound signals. We use the methods described by Merialdi *et al.* (1999) for manual scoring of the actocardiograph strips. Figure 4.7 displays an example of an actocardiograph strip at 26 weeks and 36 weeks gestational age.

The study of fetal behaviour involves careful consideration and control of factors that may influence fetal behaviour outside of the maternal condition being studied. These factors include, but are not limited to, maternal caffeine and other substance use, time of the last meal, time of day of the recording, and comfort of the recording conditions (Pillai and James, 1990; Pillai *et al.*, 1992; Devoe *et al.*, 1993; Lecanuet *et al.*, 1995; Mulder *et al.*, 1998).

To study the effects of maternal depression and anxiety on fetal and infant behaviour requires stringent criteria for group determination and consideration of the unique methodological issues in this research. First, it is important to distinguish between depressed mood and major depression as a diagnosis. The same is true for the symptoms of anxiety and a specific anxiety disorder. The timing of the disorder, severity of symptoms, and co-morbidity are critical measures for examining the question of fetal and infant outcomes related to maternal mental health, particularly when trying to determine possible mechanisms for these effects. Different diagnoses and symptoms may correspond to separate brain areas or neurotransmitter systems, necessitating research to become more focused on specific symptoms and symptom profiles.

Other critical and potentially confounding factors include the quality of the care-giving environment before and after birth (social support for the mother, as well as the infant), substance use (including smoking), socio-economic status, maternal nutrition, genetics, family history, method of feeding the infant, treatment methods, and medication for the psychiatric disorder.

One of the most effective treatments for MDD and anxiety disorders is antidepressant medication. This poses a difficult problem during pregnancy, as both the disorders

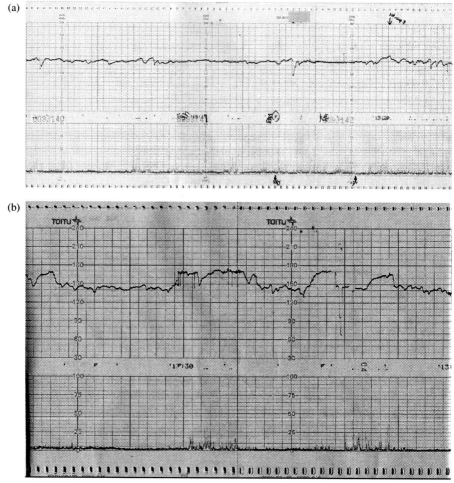

Fig. 4.7 (a) FHR (top line) and actogram (bottom line) at 26 weeks gestational age (GA). There are some accelerations and decelerations present, not always in response to movement. On this strip the VAS was delivered (marked on strip in ink) and was followed by a FHR deceleration with a slightly delayed change in the FHR and movement pattern. (b) FHR and actogram at 36 weeks GA. This strip shows FHR accelerations (prolonged in the first episode) in response to moderate amplitude movements.

and the treatment may be harmful to the fetus. Physicians are sometimes reluctant to prescribe antidepressant medications during pregnancy for this reason, often with detriment to the mothers' health. Recent data support the use of antidepressant medications during pregnancy and more often than not, women with MDD are offered medication treatment during pregnancy.

The current first-line choice of clinicians for somatic therapies during pregnancy is serotonin-selective reuptake inhibitors (SSRIs) due to their lower side-effect profiles and relatively low-risk to the fetus (Altshuler *et al.*, 2001; Swinkels and de Jonghe, 1995).

According to the data published to date, there is little evidence that SSRI medications increase the risk of intrauterine fetal death, physical malformations, or cause any significant growth impairments (Altshuler *et al.*, 1996; Wisner *et al.*, 2000). However, evidence of the acute effects on the neonate or neonatal toxicity is becoming apparent. Problems identified from SSRI use at the end of pregnancy include signs and symptoms of withdrawal, feeding problems, and poor respiratory adaptation (Webster, 1973; Pastuszak *et al.*, 1993; Oberlander *et al.*, 2003). SSRI use during pregnancy was reported to be associated with increased REM sleep, motor activity, tremulousness, and startles in newborns on Day 1 or 2 of life (Zeskind and Stephens, 2003). Experts suggest discontinuing antidepressant medication near the end of the third trimester to minimize this factor (Wisner *et al.*, 2000).

These studies have not systematically examined single exposure to the drug without depression (effectively treated depression) compared to the combined effect of fetal exposure to both the drug and depression. They have also not examined the effects on the fetus, prior to potential confounding factors inherent in the delivery process: preterm delivery, anesthesia, medications, birthweight, and continued exposure through breastmilk. There is a growing need to study the exposure of the fetus to mental health conditions, both treated and untreated, in conjunction with postnatal development, environment, and long-term developmental psychopathology.

Current and future directions

We are currently examining the effects of Major Depressive Disorder, Anxiety Disorders, and SSRI medication on the fetus and the newborn in a prospective study. The Structured Clinical Interview for the DSM-IV (SCID-I/NP, Nov. 1999) is being used to diagnose or confirm a previous diagnosis (Spitzer *et al.*, 1992; Williams *et al.*, 1992). The 60-minute ultrasound and FHR monitoring protocol is given at 26 and 36 weeks of gestational age. The infant is then observed at birth using the NICU Network Neurobehavioural Scale (NNNS), as well as a 2-hour sleep state observation. These data will provide critical information regarding the potential effects of SSRI exposure and MDD on fetal and newborn neurobehavioural development. The data will provide information about how the fetal CNS responds to the two maternal biological environments, as well as contribute to the urgently needed information for treatment guidelines of mood disorders during pregnancy. We are also examining the stability of individual differences of neurobehavioural measures from the fetal to newborn period.

Future longitudinal studies may provide information about the moderators of these effects and what contributes to resiliency among children born to women with antenatal and postpartum mental health diagnoses. Research in the prenatal period will need to focus on fetal behaviour and physiology, as well as the confounding and moderating effects of maternal nutritional intake, substance use, sleep (both ultradian and circadian rhythms), and SES on fetal development and the protective factors that may enhance coping skills.

Conclusions

Neurotransmitter receptors change as a result of exposure to a particular medication or other altered physiological milieu (Cooper *et al.*, 1991). These changes are dependent upon the timing and duration of the exposure. For example, minor physical anomalies (no functional defects), have been found with SSRI use in weeks 2–8 of pregnancy, but not for any other time in gestation (Chambers *et al.*, 1996). Central nervous system development also has critical periods, or a point in time most vulnerable to insult or change. Prenatal mental illness exposes the fetus to altered biochemistry, which has an effect on HPA activity and CNS receptor density in certain areas of the fetus' brain. How and when exposure occurs is likely to be of great significance. It is reasonable to speculate that prenatal exposure to active major depressive disorder and/or anxiety disorders, and all that this implies could be a primary contributor to development of emotional disorders in the child. Therefore, the use of medications and psychosocial interventions to modulate or ameliorate the biochemical effects of mental illnesses may be of value not only to the mother, but also to the fetus.

References

Allister, L., Lester, B. M., Carr, S., *et al.* (2001). The effects of maternal depression on foetal heart rate response to vibroacoustic stimulation. *Developmental Neuropsychology*, **20(3)**, 639–51.

Altshuler, L. L., Cohen, L., Szuba, M. P., *et al.* (1996). Pharmacologic management of psychiatric illness during pregnancy: dilemmas and guidelines [see comments]. *American Journal of Psychiatry*, **153(5)**, 592–606.

Altshuler, L. L., Cohen, L. S., Moline, M. L., *et al.* (2001). Treatment of depression in women. *Postgraduate Medicine, Special Report* (The Expert Consensus Guideline Series), 1–28.

Armstrong, K. L., O'Donnell, H., McCallum, R., *et al.* (1998). Childhood sleep problems: association with prenatal factors and maternal distress/depression. *Journal of Paediatric Child Health*, **34(3)**, 263–6.

Atkinson, A. K. and Rickel, A. U. (1984). Postpartum depression in primiparous parents. *Journal Abnormal Psychology*, **93(1)**, 115–19.

Beardslee, W. R., Bemporad, J., Keller, M. B., *et al.* (1983). Children of parents with major affective disorder: a review. *American Journal of Psychiatry*, **140(7)**, 825–32.

Beck, A. T., Ward, C. H., Mendelson, M., *et al.* (1961). An inventory for measuring depression. *Archives of General Psychiatry*, **4**, 561–71.

Beck, C. T. (1995). The effects of postpartum depression on maternal-infant interaction: a meta-analysis. *Nursing Research*, **44(5)**, 298–304.

Biederman, J., Faraone, S. V., Hirshfeld-Becker, D. R., *et al.* (2001). Patterns of psychopathology and dysfunction in high-risk children of parents with panic disorder and major depression. *American Journal of Psychiatry*, **158(1)**, 49–57.

Blackburn, S. T. (2003). Placental physiology. In *Maternal, Fetal and neonatal physiology: a clinical perspective* (ed. S. T. Blackburn), pp. 95–111. St Louis, MO: W. D. Saunders.

Brazelton, T. B. (1973). Neonatal Behavioural Assessment Scale. Clinics on developmental medicine. *Journal of Development and Behavioural Pediatrics*, **50(2)**, 1–66.

Brazelton, T. B. (1978). The Brazelton Neonatal Behaviour Assessment Scale: introduction. *Monographs in Social Research in Child Development*, **43(5–6)**, 1–13.

Bremner, J. D. (2003). Long-term effects of childhood abuse on brain and neurobiology. *Child and Adolescent Psychiatric Clinics in North America*, **12(2)**, 271–92.

Bremner, J. D., Krystal, J. H., Southwick, S. M., *et al.* (1995). Functional neuroanatomical correlates of the effects of stress on memory. *Journal of Trauma Stress*, **8**(4), 527–53.

Bremner, J. D., Innis, R. B., Southwick, S. M., *et al.* (2000a). Decreased benzodiazepine receptor binding in prefrontal cortex in combat-related posttraumatic stress disorder. *American Journal of Psychiatry*, **157**(7), 1120–6.

Bremner, J. D., Innis, R. B., White, T., *et al.* (2000b). SPECT [I-123]iomazenil measurement of the benzodiazepine receptor in panic disorder. *Biological Psychiatry*, **47**(2), 96–106.

Brunson, K. L., Eghbal-Ahmadi, M., Bender, R., *et al.* (2001). Long-term, progressive hippocampal cell loss and dysfunction induced by early-life administration of corticotropin-releasing hormone reproduce the effects of early-life stress. *Proceedings of the National Academy of Sciences USA*, **98**(15), 8856–61.

Cameron, O. G., Smith, C. B., Lee, M. A., *et al.* (1990). Adrenergic status in anxiety disorders: platelet alpha 2-adrenergic receptor binding, blood pressure, pulse, and plasma catecholamines in panic and generalized anxiety disorder patients and in normal subjects. *Biological Psychiatry*, **28**(1), 3–20.

Caspi, A., Sugden, K., Moffitt, T. E., *et al.* (2003). Influence of life stress on depression: moderation by a polymorphism in the 5-HTT gene. *Science*, **301**(5631), 386–9.

Chambers, C. D., Johnson, K. A., Dick, L. M., *et al.* (1996). Birth outcomes in pregnant women taking fluoxetine. *New England Journal of Medicine*, **335**(14), 1010–15.

Chapillon, P., Patin, V., Roy, V., *et al.* (2002). Effects of pre- and postnatal stimulation on developmental, emotional, and cognitive aspects in rodents: a review. *Developmental Psychobiology*, **41**(4), 373–87.

Charney, D. S., Woods, S. W., and Heninger, G. R. (1989). Noradrenergic function in generalized anxiety disorder: effects of yohimbine in healthy subjects and patients with generalized anxiety disorder. *Psychiatry Research*, **27**(2), 173–82.

Chrousos, G. P., Torpy, D. J., and Gold, P. W. (1998). Interactions between the hypothalamic-pituitary-adrenal axis and the female reproductive system: clinical implications. *Annals of Internal Medicine*, **129**(3), 229–40.

Clarke, A. S., Wittwer, D. J., Abbott, D. H., *et al.* (1994). Long-term effects of prenatal stress on HPA axis activity in juvenile rhesus monkeys. *Developmental Psychobiology*, **27**(5), 257–69.

Cooper, J. R., Bloom, F. E., and Roth, R. H. (1991). *The biochemical basis of neuropsychopharmacology*, 6th edn. New York, NY: Oxford University Press.

Coplan, J. D., Trost, R. C., Owens, M. J., *et al.* (1998). Cerebrospinal fluid concentrations of somatostatin and biogenic amines in grown primates reared by mothers exposed to manipulated foraging conditions. *Archives of General Psychiatry*, **55**(5), 473–7.

Coste, S. C., Kesterson, R. A., Heldwein, K. A., *et al.* (2000). Abnormal adaptations to stress and impaired cardiovascular function in mice lacking corticotropin-releasing hormone receptor-2. *Natural Genetics*, **24**(4), 403–9.

Coste, S. C., Murray, S. E., and Stenzel-Poore, M. P. (2001). Animal models of CRH excess and CRH receptor deficiency display altered adaptations to stress. *Peptides*, **22**(5), 733–41.

Da Costa, D., Larouche, J., Dritsa, M., *et al.* (2000). Psychosocial correlates of prepartum and postpartum depressed mood. *Journal of Affective Disorders*, **59**(1), 31–40.

Davis, M. (1992). The role of the amygdala in fear-potentiated startle: implications for animal models of anxiety. *Trends in Pharmacological Science*, **13**(1), 35–41.

Devoe, L. D., Murray, C., Youssif, A., *et al.* (1993). Maternal caffeine consumption and foetal behaviour in normal third-trimester pregnancy. *American Journal of Obstetrics and Gynecology*, **168**(4), 1105–12.

DiPietro, J. (2001). Foetal neurobehavioural assessment. In *Biobehavioural assessment* (ed. P. S. Zeskind and J. E. Singer), pp. 43–80. New York: Guilford Press.

DiPietro, J. A., Bornstein, M. H., Costigan, K. A., *et al.* (2002). What does foetal movement predict about behaviour during the first two years of life? *Developmental Psychobiology*, **40**(4), 358–71.

El-Haddad, M. A., Ismail, Y., Guerra, C., *et al.* (2002). Effect of oral sucrose on ingestive behaviour in the near-term ovine foetus. *American Journal of Obstetrics and Gynecology*, **187**(4), 898–901.

Feldman, S., Newman, M. E., Gur, E., *et al.* (1998). Role of serotonin in the amygdala in hypothalamo-pituitary-adrenocortical responses. *Neuroreport*, **9**(9), 2007–9.

Field, T. (1984). Early interactions between infants and their postpartum depressed mothers. *Infant Behaviour and Development*, **7**, 517–22.

Field, T. (1998). Maternal depression effects on infants and early interventions. *Preventive Medicine*, **27**(2), 200–3.

Field, T., Diego, M., Hernandez-Reif, M., *et al.* (2002). Relative right versus left frontal EEG in neonates. *Developmental Psychobiology*, **41**(2), 147–55.

Field, T., Diego, M., Hernandez-Reif, M., *et al.* (2003). Pregnancy anxiety and comorbid depression and anger: effects on the foetus and neonate. *Depress Anxiety*, **17**(3), 140–51.

Finnegan, L. P., Connaughton, J. F., Jr., Kron, R. E., *et al.* (1975). Neonatal abstinence syndrome: assessment and management. *Addictive Disorders*, **2**(1–2), 141–58.

Fossey, M. D., Lydiard, R. B., Ballenger, J. C., *et al.* (1996). Cerebrospinal fluid corticotropin-releasing factor concentrations in patients with anxiety disorders and normal comparison subjects. *Biological Psychiatry*, **39**(8), 703–7.

Fowles, E. (1988). The development of maternal–foetal attachment during pregnancy. *Chart*, **85**(7), 15.

Frodl, T., Meisenzahl, E. M., Zetzsche, T., *et al.* (2002). Hippocampal changes in patients with a first episode of major depression. *American Journal of Psychiatry*, **159**(7), 1112–18.

Fuller, K. H., Waters, W. F., Binks, P. G., *et al.* (1997). Generalized anxiety and sleep architecture: a polysomnographic investigation. *Sleep*, **20**(5), 370–6.

Gaffney, K. F. (1986). Maternal–foetal attachment in relation to self-concept and anxiety. *Maternal and Child Nursing Journal*, **15**(2), 91–101.

Gagnon, R. (1995). Developmental aspects of alterations in foetal behavioural states. In *Foetal development: a psychobiological perspective* (ed. J. P. Lecanuet, W. P. Fifer, N. A. Krasnegor and W. P. Smotherman), p. 129. Hillsdale, NJ: Lawrence Erlbaum Ass.

Gingras, J. L. and O'Donnell, K. J. (1998). State control in the substance-exposed foetus. I. The foetal neurobehavioural profile: an assessment of foetal state, arousal, and regulation competency. *Annals of the New York Academy of Sciences*, **846**, 262–76.

Gold, P. W., Licinio, J., Wong, M. L., *et al.* (1995). Corticotropin releasing hormone in the pathophysiology of melancholic and atypical depression and in the mechanism of action of antidepressant drugs. *Annals of the New York Academy of Sciences*, **771**, 716–29.

Gotlib, I. H., Whiffen, V. E., Mount, J. H., *et al.* (1989). Prevalence rates and demographic characteristics associated with depression in pregnancy and the postpartum. *Journal of Consulting and Clinical Psychology*, **57**(2), 269–74.

Gould, E., Tanapat, P., McEwen, B. S., *et al.* (1998). Proliferation of granule cell precursors in the dentate gyrus of adult monkeys is diminished by stress. *Proceedings of the National Academy of Sciences USA*, **95**(6), 3168–71.

Grace, J. (1989). Correlates of maternal–foetal attachment. *Birth*, **16**(2), 87–8.

Gray, T. S. and Bingaman, E. W. (1996). The amygdala: corticotropin-releasing factor, steroids, and stress. *Critical Reviews in Neurobiology*, **10**(2), 155–68.

Groome, L. J., Swiber, M. J., Bentz, L. S., *et al.* (1995). Maternal anxiety during pregnancy: effect on foetal behaviour at 38 to 40 weeks of gestation. *Journal of Developmental and Behavioural Pediatrics*, **16**(6), 391–6.

Grossman, R., Yehuda, R., New, A., *et al.* (2003). Dexamethasone suppression test findings in subjects with personality disorders: associations with posttraumatic stress disorder and major depression. *American Journal of Psychiatry*, **160**(7), 1291–8.

Gurguis, G. N., Vitton, B. J., and Uhde, T. W. (1997). Behavioural, sympathetic and adrenocortical responses to yohimbine in panic disorder patients and normal controls. *Psychiatry Research*, **71**(1), 27–39.

Gurvits, T., V., Shenton, M. E., and Hokoama, H. (1996). Magnetic resonance imaging study of hippocampal volume in chronic combat-related post-traumatic stress disorder. *Biological Psychiatry*, **40**(11), 1091–9.

Harnish, J. D., Dodge, K. A., and Valente, E. (1995). Mother–child interaction quality as a partial mediator of the roles of maternal depressive symptomatology and socioeconomic status in the development of child behaviour problems.Conduct Problems Prevention Research Group. *Child Development*, **66**(3), 739–53.

Hayashi, A., Nagaoka, M., Yamada, K., *et al.* (1998). Maternal stress induces synaptic loss and developmental disabilities of offspring. *International Journal of Developmental Neuroscience*, **16**(3–4), 209–16.

Heim, C., Newport, D. J., Bonsall, R., *et al.* (2001). Altered pituitary-adrenal axis responses to provocative challenge tests in adult survivors of childhood abuse. *American Journal of Psychiatry*, **158**(4), 575–81.

Heim, C., Newport, D. J., Miller, A. H., *et al.* (2000). Long-term neuroendocrine effects of childhood maltreatment. *Journal of the American Medical Association*, **284**(18), 2321.

Heimer, L. (1983). *The human brain and spinal cord*. New York, NY: Springer-Verlag.

Henry, C., Kabbaj, M., Simon, H., *et al.* (1994). Prenatal stress increases the hypothalamo-pituitary-adrenal axis response in young and adult rats. *Journal of Neuroendocrinology*, **6**(3), 341–5.

Herman, J. P. and Cullinan, W. E. (1997). Neurocircuitry of stress: central control of the hypothalamo-pituitary-adrenocortical axis. *Trends in Neuroscience*, **20**(2), 78–84.

Heslegrave, R. J., Ogilvie, J. C., and Furedy, J. J. (1979). Measuring baseline-treatment differences in heart rate variability: variance versus successive difference mean square and beats per minute versus interbeat intervals. *Psychophysiology*, **16**(2), 151–7.

Jacobson, L. and Sapolsky, R. (1991). The role of the hippocampus in feedback regulation of the hypothalamic-pituitary-adrenocortical axis. *Endocrinology Review*, **12**(2), 118–34.

Jolkkonen, L., Lepola, U., Bisette, G., *et al.* (1993). CSF corticotropin-releasing factor is not affected in panic disorder. *Biological Psychiatry*, **33**, 136–8.

Jones, N. A., Field, T., Fox, N., *et al.* (1998). Newborns of mothers with depressive symptoms are physiologically less developed. *Infant Behaviour and Development*, **21**(3), 537–41.

Josefsson, A., Berg, G., Nordin, C., *et al.* (2001). Prevalence of depressive symptoms in late pregnancy and postpartum. *Acta Obstetrics Gynecologica Scandinavica*, **80**(3), 251–5.

Josten, L. (1982). Contrast in prenatal preparation for mothering. *Maternal and Child Nursing Journal*, **11**(2), 65–73.

Kendler, K. S., Neale, M. C., Kessler, R. C., *et al.* (1992a). Childhood parental loss and adult psychopathology in women. A twin study perspective. *Archives in General Psychiatry*, **49**(2), 109–16.

Kendler, K. S., Neale, M. C., Kessler, R. C., *et al.* (1992b). Generalized anxiety disorder in women. A population-based twin study. *Archives in General Psychiatry*, **49**(4), 267–72.

Kennaway, D. J. (2000). Melatonin and development: physiology and pharmacology. *Seminars in Perinatology*, **24**(4), 258–66.

Kennaway, D. J. (2002). Programming of the foetal suprachiasmatic nucleus and subsequent adult rhythmicity. *Trends in Endocrinology and Metabolism*, **13**(9), 398–402.

Kennaway, D. J., Goble, F. C., and Stamp, G. E. (1996). Factors influencing the development of melatonin rhythmicity in humans. *Journal of Clinical Endocrinology and Metabolism*, **81**(4), 1525–32.

Kisilevsky, B. (1990). Vibroacoustic stimulation can pose risks. *Journal of Obstetrics, Gynecology and Neonatal Nursing*, **19**(6), 469–70.

Kisilevsky, B. S. (1995). The influence of stimulus and subject variables on human foetal responses to sound and vibration. In *Foetal Development: A Psychobiological Perspective* (ed. J. P. Lecanuet, W. P. Fifer, N. A. Krasnegor, *et al.*), pp. 243–78. Hillsdale, NJ: Lawrence Erlbaum.

Kisilevsky, B. S. and Muir, D. W. (1991). Human foetal and subsequent newborn responses to sound and vibration. *Infant Behaviour and Development*, **14**, 1–26.

Kisilevsky, B. S., Muir, D. W., and Low, J. A. (1990). Maturation of responses elicited by a vibroacoustic stimulus in a group of high-risk foetuses. *Maternal and Child Nursing Journal*, **19**(3), 239–50.

Kisilevsky, B. S., Muir, D. W., and Low, J. A. (1992). Maturation of human foetal responses to vibroacoustic stimulation. *Child Development*, **63**(6), 1497–508.

Kiuchi, M., Nagata, N., Ikeno, S., *et al.* (2000). The relationship between the response to external light stimulation and behavioural states in the human foetus: how it differs from vibroacoustic stimulation. *Early Human Development*, **58**(2), 153–65.

Ladd, C. O., Owens, M. J., and Nemeroff, C. B. (1996). Persistent changes in corticotropin-releasing factor neuronal systems induced by maternal deprivation. *Endocrinology*, **137**(4), 1212–18.

LaGasse, L. L., Seifer, R., and Lester, B. M. (1999). Interpreting research on prenatal substance exposure in the context of multiple confounding factors. *Clinical Perinatology*, **26**(1), 39–54, vi.

Lahey, B. B., Flagg, E. W., Bird, H. R., *et al.* (1996). The NIMH Methods for the Epidemiology of Child and Adolescent Mental Disorders (MECA) Study: background and methodology. *Journal of the American Academy of Child and Adolescent Psychiatry*, **35**(7), 855–64.

Lecanuet, J. P., Fifer, W., Krasenegor, N. A., *et al.* (ed.) (1995). *Foetal development: a psychobiological perspective*. Hillsdale, NJ: Lawrence Erlbaum Associates.

Lecanuet, J. P., Graniere-Deferre, C., Jacquet, A. Y., *et al.* (2000). Foetal discrimination of low-pitched musical notes. *Developmental Psychobiology*, **36**(1), 29–39.

Leifer, M. (1977). Psychological changes accompanying pregnancy and motherhood. *Genetics and Psychology Monographs*, **95**(1), 55–96.

Lester, B. M. (1998). The Maternal Lifestyles Study. *Annals of the New York Academy of Sciences*, **846**, 296–305.

Lester, B. M. and Tronick, E. Z. (2004). The Neonatal Intensive care unit Network Neurobehavioral Scale. *Pediatrics*, **113** (3 Pt2), 1–631.

Lindgren, K. (2001). Relationships among maternal–foetal attachment, prenatal depression, and health practices in pregnancy. *Research in Nursing and Health*, **24**(3), 203–17.

Lobel, M., Dunkel-Schetter, C., and Scrimshaw, S. C. (1992). Prenatal maternal stress and prematurity: a prospective study of socioeconomically disadvantaged women. *Health and Psychology*, **11**(1), 32–40.

Lovejoy, M. C., Graczyk, P. A., O'Hare, E., *et al.* (2000). Maternal depression and parenting behaviour: a meta-analytic review. *Clinical Psychology Review*, **20**(5), 561–92.

Marshall, R. D., Blanco, C., Printz, D., *et al.* (2002). A pilot study of noradrenergic and HPA axis functioning in PTSD vs. panic disorder. *Psychiatry Research*, **110**(3), 219–30.

Mastorakos, G., Magiakou, M. A., and Chrousos, G. P. (1995). Effects of the immune/inflammatory reaction on the hypothalamic- pituitary-adrenal axis. *Annals of the New York Academy of Sciences*, **771**, 438–48.

Matthews, S. G. (2002). Early programming of the hypothalamo-pituitary-adrenal axis. *Trends in Endocrinology and Metabolism*, **13(9)**, 373–80.

McAnarney, E. R. and Stevens-Simon, C. (1990). Maternal psychological stress/depression and low birth weight. Is there a relationship? *American Journal of Diseases of Childhood*, **144(7)**, 789–92.

McCauley, J., Kern, D. E., Kolodner, K., *et al.* (1997). Clinical characteristics of women with a history of childhood abuse: unhealed wounds. *Journal of the American Medical Association*, **277(17)**, 1362–8.

Merialdi, M., Caulfield, L. E., Zavaleta, N., *et al.* (1999). Adding zinc to prenatal iron and folate tablets improves foetal neurobehavioural development. *American Journal of Obstetrics and Gynecology*, **180(2 Pt 1)**, 483–90.

Monk, C., Fifer, W. P., Myers, M. M., *et al.* (2000). Maternal stress responses and anxiety during pregnancy: effects on foetal heart rate. *Developmental Psychobiology*, **36(1)**, 67–77.

Monk, C., Myers, M. M., Sloan, R. P., *et al.* (2003). Effects of women's stress-elicited physiological activity and chronic anxiety on foetal heart rate. *Journal of Developmental and Behavioural Pediatrics*, **24(1)**, 32–8.

Mulder, E. J., Morssink, L. P., van der Schee, T., *et al.* (1998). Acute maternal alcohol consumption disrupts behavioural state organization in the near-term foetus. *Pediatric Research*, **44(5)**, 774–9.

Nijhuis, I. J., ten Hof, J., Nijhuis, J. G., *et al.* (1999). Temporal organization of foetal behaviour from 24-weeks gestation onwards in normal and complicated pregnancies. *Developmental Psychobiology*, **34(4)**, 257–68.

Nijhuis, J. G. (1986). Behavioural states: concomitants, clinical implications and the assessment of the condition of the nervous system. *European Journal of Obstetrics, Gynecology and Reproductive Biology*, **21(5–6)**, 301–8.

Nijhuis, J. G., Prechtl, H. F., Martin, C. B., Jr., *et al.* (1982). Are there behavioural states in the human foetus? *Early Human Development*, **6(2)**, 177–95.

Oberlander, T. F., Misri, S., Fitzgerald, C. E., *et al.* (2004). Pharmacologic factors associated with transient neonatal symptoms following prenatal psychotropic medication exposure. *Journal of Clinical Psychiatry*, **45(2)**, 230–7.

O'Connor, T., O'Halloran, D. J., and Shanahan, F. (2000). The stress response and the hypothalamic-pituitary-adrenal axis: from molecule to melancholia. *Quarterly Journal of Medicine*, **93(6)**, 323–33.

O'Connor, T. G., Heron, J., and Glover, V. (2002). Antenatal anxiety predicts child behavioural/emotional problems independently of postnatal depression. *Journal of the American Academy of Child and Adolescent Psychiatry*, **41(12)**, 1470–7.

O'Hara, M. W., Neunaber, D. J., and Zekoski, E. M. (1984). Prospective study of postpartum depression: prevalence, course, and predictive factors. *Journal of Abnormal Psychology*, **93(2)**, 158–171.

O'Hara, M. W., Zekoski, E. M., Philipps, L. H., *et al.* (1990). Controlled prospective study of postpartum mood disorders: comparison of childbearing and nonchildbearing women. *Journal of Abnormal Psychology*, **99(1)**, 3–15.

O'Hara, M. W., Schlete, J. A., Lewis, D. A., *et al.* (1991). Controlled prospective study of postpartum mood disorders: psychological, environmental, and hormonal variables. *Journal of Abnormal Psychology*, **100(1)**, 63–73.

Orr, S. T., James, S. A., and Blackmore Prince, C. (2002). Maternal prenatal depressive symptoms and spontaneous preterm births among African-American women in Baltimore, Maryland. *American Journal of Epidemiology*, **156(9)**, 797–802.

Papadimitriou, G. N., Kerkhofs, M., Kempenaers, C., *et al.* (1988). EEG sleep studies in patients with generalized anxiety disorder. *Psychiatry Research*, **26(2)**, 183–90.

Pastuszak, A., Schick-Boschetto, B., Zuber, C., *et al.* (1993). Pregnancy outcome following first-trimester exposure to fluoxetine (Prozac). *Journal of the American Medical Association*, **269(17)**, 2246–8.

Pillai, M. and James, D. (1990). Development of human foetal behaviour: a review. *Foetal Diagnosis and Therapy*, **5(1)**, 15–32.

Pillai, M., James, D. K., and Parker, M. (1992). The development of ultradian rhythms in the human foetus. *American Journal of Obstetrics and Gynecology*, **167(1)**, 172–7.

Plotsky, P. M. and Meaney, M. J. (1993). Early, postnatal experience alters hypothalamic corticotropin-releasing factor (CRF) mRNA, median eminence CRF content and stress-induced release in adult rats. *Brain Research and Molecular Brain Research*, **18(3)**, 195–200.

Post, R. M., Weiss, S. R., Smith, M., *et al.* (1995). Stress, conditioning, and the temporal aspects of affective disorders. *Annals of the New York Academy of Sciences*, **771**, 677–96.

Prechtl, H. F. R. (1969). Brain and behavioural mechanisms in the human newborn infant. In *Brain and early behaviour: development in the foetus and infant* (ed. R. J. Robinson), pp. 115–31. London: Academic Press.

Prechtl, H. F. and Einspieler, C. (1997). Is neurological assessment of the foetus possible? *European Journal of Obstetrics, Gynecology and Reproductive Biology*, **75(1)**, 81–4.

Reppert, S. M., Duncan, M. J., and Weaver, D. R. (1987). Maternal influences on the developing circadian system. In *Perinatal development: a psychobiological perspective* (ed. N. A. Krasnegor, E. M. Blass, M. A. Hofer, and W. P. Smotherman), pp. 343–56. New York, NY: Academic Press, Inc.

Riemann, D., Berger, M., and Voderholzer, U. (2001). Sleep and depression–results from psychobiological studies: an overview. *Biological Psychology*, **57(1–3)**, 67–103.

Rini, C. K., Dunkel-Schetter, C., Wadhwa, P. D., *et al.* (1999). Psychological adaptation and birth outcomes: the role of personal resources, stress, and sociocultural context in pregnancy. *Health Psychology*, **18(4)**, 333–45.

Rivkees, S. A. and Hao, H. (2000). Developing circadian rhythmicity. *Seminars in Perinatology*, **24(4)**, 232–42.

Rubin, R. (1972). Fantasy and object constancy in maternal relationships. *Maternal and Child Nursing Journal*, **1(2)**, 101–11.

Rubin, R. (1975). Maternal tasks in pregnancy. *Maternal and Child Nursing Journal*, **4(3)**, 143–53.

Salisbury, A., Lester, B., Tronick, E., *et al.* (2002). The Maternal Lifestyle Study: maternal depression and cocaine effects on infant neurobehaviour. *Pediatric Academic Societies Annual Meeting Program Issue*, **51(suppl)**.

Salisbury, A., Law, K., LaGasse, L., *et al.* (2003). Maternal–foetal attachment. *Journal of the American Medical Association*, **289(13)**, 1701.

Sandman, C. A., Wadhwa, P., Hetrick, W., *et al.* (1997). Human foetal heart rate dishabituation between thirty and thirty-two weeks gestation. *Child Development*, **68(6)**, 1031–40.

Sandman, C. A., Wadhwa, P. D., Dunkel-Schetter, C., *et al.* (1994). Psychobiological influences of stress and HPA regulation on the human foetus and infant birth outcomes. *Annals of the New York Academy of Sciences*, **739**, 198–210.

Sandman, C. A., Wadhwa, P. D., Chicz-DeMet, A., *et al.* (1997). Maternal stress, HPA activity, and foetal/infant outcome. *Annals of the New York Academy of Sciences*, **814**, 266–75.

Sandman, C. A., Wadhwa, P. D., Chicz-DeMet, A., *et al.* (1999). Maternal corticotropin-releasing hormone and habituation in the human foetus. *Developmental Psychobiology*, **34(3)**, 163–73.

Sapolsky, R. M. (1996). Why stress is bad for your brain. *Science*, **273(5276)**, 749–50.

Saraceno, B. (2002). The WHO World Health Report 2001 on mental health. *Epidemiological Psychiatry Society*, **11(2)**, 83–7.

Schneider, M. L. (1992a). The effect of mild stress during pregnancy on birth weight and neuromotor maturation in rhesus monkey infants (*Macaca mulatta*). *Infant Behaviour and Development*, **15**, 389–403.

Schneider, M. L. (1992b). Prenatal stress exposure alters postnatal behavioural expression under conditions of novelty challenge in rhesus monkey infants. *Developmental Psychobiology*, **25**(7), 529–40.

Schneider, M. L. and Coe, C. L. (1993). Repeated social stress during pregnancy impairs neuromotor development of the primate infant. *Journal of Developmental and Behavioural Pediatrics*, **14**(2), 81–7.

Schneider, M. L., Clarke, A. S., Kraemer, G. W., *et al.* (1998). Prenatal stress alters brain biogenic amine levels in primates. *Developmental Psychopathology*, **10**(3), 427–40.

Schneider, M. L., Roughton, E. C., Koehler, A. J., *et al.* (1999). Growth and development following prenatal stress exposure in primates: an examination of ontogenetic vulnerability. *Child Development*, **70**(2), 263–74.

Seckl, J. R. (1998). Physiologic programming of the foetus. *Clinical Perinatology*, **25**(4), 939–62, vii.

Seckl, J. R. (2001). Glucocorticoid programming of the foetus; adult phenotypes and molecular mechanisms. *Molecular and Cell Endocrinology*, **185**(1–2), 61–71.

Shaffer, D., Gould, M. S., Fisher, P., *et al.* (1996). Psychiatric diagnosis in child and adolescent suicide. *Archives of General Psychiatry*, **53**(4), 339–48.

Shieh, C. and Kravitz, M. (2002). Maternal–foetal attachment in pregnant women who use illicit drugs. *Journal of Obstetrics, Gynecology and Neonatal Nursing*, **31**(2), 156–64.

Smagin, G. N., Heinrichs, S. C., and Dunn, A. J. (2001). The role of CRH in behavioural responses to stress. *Peptides*, **22**(5), 713–24.

Smith, C. V. (1995). Vibroacoustic stimulation. *Clinical Obstetrics and Gynecology*, **38**(1), 68–77.

Smith, C. V., Phelan, J. P., Platt, L. D., *et al.* (1986). Foetal acoustic stimulation testing. II. A randomized clinical comparison with the nonstress test. *American Journal of Obstetrics and Gynecology*, **155**(1), 131–4.

Smith, C. V., Phelan, J. P., Broussard, P., *et al.* (1988). Foetal acoustic stimulation testing. III. Predictive value of a reactive test. *Journal of Reproductive Medicine*, **33**(2), 217–18.

Smith, E., Batuman, O., Trost, R., *et al.* (2002). Transforming growth factor-beta 1 and cortisol in differentially reared primates. *Brain, Behaviour and Immunity*, **16**, 140–9.

Smith, G. W., Aubry, J. M., Dellu, F., *et al.* (1998). Corticotropin releasing factor receptor 1-deficient mice display decreased anxiety, impaired stress response, and aberrant neuroendocrine development. *Neuron*, **20**(6), 1093–102.

Smotherman, W. P. and Robinson, S. R. (1988). Behaviour of rat foetuses following chemical or tactile stimulation. *Behavioural Neuroscience*, **102**(1), 24–34.

Spielberger, C. (1983). *Manual for the state-trait anxiety inventory*. Palo Alto, CA: Consulting Psychologists Press.

Spitzer, R. L., Williams, J. B., Gibbon, M., *et al.* (1992). The structured clinical interview for DSM-III-R (SCID). I: History, rationale, and description. *Archives of General Psychiatry*, **49**(8), 624–9.

Steer, R. A., Scholl, T. O., Hediger, M. L., *et al.* (1992). Self-reported depression and negative pregnancy outcomes. *Journal of Clinical Epidemiology*, **45**(10), 1093–9.

Stein, M. B., Hanna, C., Koverola, C., *et al.* (1997). Structural brain changes in PTSD. Does trauma alter neuroanatomy? *Annals of the New York Academy of Sciences*, **821**, 76–82.

Stratakis, C. A. and Chrousos, G. P. (1995). Neuroendocrinology and pathophysiology of the stress system. *Annals of the New York Academy of Sciences*, **771**, 1–18.

Stratakis, C. A., Gold, P. W., and Chrousos, G. P. (1995). Neuroendocrinology of stress: implications for growth and development. *Hormone Research*, **43**(4), 162–7.

Stratakis, C. A., Mastorakos, G., Magiakou, M. A., *et al.* (1996). 24-hour secretion of growth hormone (GH), insulin-like growth factors-I and -II (IGF-I, -II), prolactin (PRL) and thyrotropin (TSH) in young adults of normal and tall stature. *Endocrine Research*, **22**(3), 261–76.

Stuart, S., Couser, G., Schilder, K., *et al.* (1998). Postpartum anxiety and depression: onset and comorbidity in a community sample. *Journal of Nervous and Mental Disorders*, **186**(7), 420–4.

Sundstrom, I. M., Bixo, M., Bjorn, I. I., *et al.* (2001). Prevalence of psychiatric disorders in gynecologic outpatients. *American Journal of Obstetrics and Gynecology*, **184**(2), 8–13.

Swinkels, J. A. and de Jonghe, F. (1995). Safety of antidepressants. *International Clinical Psychopharmacology*, **9**(Suppl 4), 19–25.

Takahashi, L. K., Haglin, C., and Kalin, N. H. (1992). Prenatal stress potentiates stress-induced behaviour and reduces the propensity to play in juvenile rats. *Physiological Behaviour*, **51**(2), 319–23.

Takahashi, L. K., Turner, J. G., and Kalin, N. H. (1992). Prenatal stress alters brain catecholaminergic activity and potentiates stress-induced behaviour in adult rats. *Brain Research*, **574**(1–2), 131–7.

Thoman, E. B., Korner, A. F., and Kraemer, H. C. (1976). Individual consistency in behavioural states in neonates. *Developmental Psychobiology*, **9**(3), 271–83.

Timor-Tritsch, I. E. (1986). The effect of external stimuli on foetal behaviour. *European Journal of Obstetrics, Gynecology and Reproductive Biology*, **21**(5–6), 321–9.

Torpy, D. J. (1998). Hypothalamic-pituitary-adrenal axis and the female reproductive system. *Annals of Internal Medicine*, **129**, 229–40.

Vallee, M., Mayo, W., Dellu, F., *et al.* (1997). Prenatal stress induces high anxiety and postnatal handling induces low anxiety in adult offspring: correlation with stress-induced corticosterone secretion. *Journal of Neuroscience*, **17**(7), 2626–36.

Varni, J. G., Clark, E., and Giddon, D. B. (1971). Analysis of cyclic heart rate variability. *Psychophysiology*, **8**(3), 406–13.

Visser, G. H. and Mulder, E. J. (1993). The effect of vibro-acoustic stimulation on foetal behavioural state organization. *American Journal of Indian Medicine*, **23**(4), 531–9.

de Vries, J. I. P., Visser, G. H. A., and Prechtl, H. F. R. (1982). The emergence of foetal behaviour. I. Qualitative aspects. *Early Human Development*, **7**, 301–22.

Wadhwa, P. D. (1993). *Prenatal psychosocial factors, neuroendocrine parameters, and birth outcomes: a prospective investigation*. Ann Arbor, MI: University Microfilms.

Wadhwa, P. D., Sandman, C. A., Porto, M., *et al.* (1993). The association between prenatal stress and infant birth weight and gestational age at birth: a prospective investigation. *American Journal of Obstetrics and Gynecology*, **169**(4), 858–65.

Wadhwa, P. D., Dunkel-Schetter, C., Chicz-DeMet, A., *et al.* (1996). Prenatal psychosocial factors and the neuroendocrine axis in human pregnancy. *Psychosomatic Medicine*, **58**(5), 432–46.

Wadhwa, P. D., Porto, M., Garite, T. J., *et al.* (1998). Maternal corticotropin-releasing hormone levels in the early third trimester predict length of gestation in human pregnancy. *American Journal of Obstetrics and Gynecology*, **179**(4), 1079–85.

Webster, P. A. (1973). Withdrawal symptoms in neonates associated with maternal antidepressant therapy. *Lancet*, **2**(7824), 318–19.

Weinstein, A. G., Chenkin, C., and Faust, D. (1997). Caring for the severely asthmatic child and family. I. The rationale for family systems integrated medical/psychological treatment. *Journal of Asthma*, **34**(4), 345–52.

Weinstock, M., Matlina, E., Maor, G. I., *et al.* (1992). Prenatal stress selectively alters the reactivity of the hypothalamic-pituitary adrenal system in the female rat. *Brain Res*, **595**(2), 195–200.

Welberg, L. A. and Seckl, J. R. (2001). Prenatal stress, glucocorticoids and the programming of the brain. *Journal of Neuroendocrinology*, **13**(2), 113–28.

Welberg, L. A., Seckl, J. R., and Holmes, M. C. (2001). Prenatal glucocorticoid programming of brain corticosteroid receptors and corticotrophin-releasing hormone: possible implications for behaviour. *Neuroscience*, **104(1)**, 71–9.

Williams, J. B., Gibbon, M., First, M. B., *et al.* (1992). The structured clinical interview for DSM-III-R (SCID). II. Multisite test-retest reliability. *Archives of General Psychiatry*, **49(8)**, 630–6.

Williams, M. T., Hennessy, M. B., and Davis, H. N. (1998). Stress during pregnancy alters rat offspring morphology and ultrasonic vocalizations. *Physiological Behaviour*, **63(3)**, 337–43.

Wisner, K. L., Peindl, K. S., and Hanusa, B. H. (1995). Psychiatric episodes in women with young children. *Journal of Affective Disorders*, **34(1)**, 1–11.

Wisner, K. L., Zarin, D. A., Holmboe, E. S., *et al.* (2000). Risk-benefit decision making for treatment of depression during pregnancy. *American Journal of Psychiatry*, **157(12)**, 1933–40.

Wolff, P. H. (1959). Observation on newborn infants. *Psychosomatic Medicine*, **21**, 110–18.

Wolff, P. H. (1965). The development of attention in young infants. *Annals of the New York Academy of Sciences*, **118**, 815–30.

Wolff, P. H. (1967). The role of biological rhythms in early psychological development. *Bulletin Menninger Clinic*, **31**, 197–218.

Yehuda, R., Southwick, S. D., Krystal, J. H., *et al.* (1993). Enhanced suppression of cortisol following dexamethasone administration in posttraumatic stress disorder. *American Journal of Psychiatry*, **150**, 83–6.

Zeskind, P. S. and Stephens, L. E. (2004). Maternal selective serotonin reuptake inhibitor use during pregnancy and newborn neurobehavior. *Pediatrics*, **113**, 368–75.

Zuckerman, B., Amaro, H., Bauchner, H., *et al.* (1989). Depressive symptoms during pregnancy: relationship to poor health behaviours. *American Journal of Obstetrics and Gynecology*, **160(5 Pt 1)**, 1107–11.

Zuckerman, B., Bauchner, H., Parker, S., *et al.* (1990). Maternal depressive symptoms during pregnancy, and newborn irritability. *Journal of Developmental and Behavioural Pediatrics*, **11(4)**, 190–4.

Chapter 5

Emotional processes in human newborns: a functionalist perspective

Robert Soussignan and Benoist Schaal

Interest in the ontogeny of emotional expressions has a long history first pioneered by Darwin (1872/1965, 1877) and a handful of precursors (e.g. Watson and Morgan, 1917; Sherman, 1927; Bridges, 1932). It is somewhat surprising that, until recently, only a few empirical investigations have explored the processes underlying expressive behaviours during the first postnatal weeks, despite numerous theoretical frameworks providing varied ways to conceptualize the emergence and early changes of affective expression and integration (e.g. Lewis and Michalson, 1983; Izard and Malatesta, 1987; Fogel and Thelen, 1987; Barrett and Campos, 1987; Fisher *et al.*, 1990; Camras *et al.*, 1991; Trevarthen, 1993; Sroufe, 1996; Mascolo and Griffin, 1998; Lafrenière, 2000). These conceptualizations have been the focus of ongoing controversies between differential (Izard and Malatesta, 1987; Ackerman *et al.*, 1998), cognitive (Lewis, 1993; Sroufe, 1996), dynamic system (Fogel and Thelen, 1987; Camras, 1992; Lewis and Douglas, 1998), and functionalist perspectives to emotional development (Campos *et al.*, 1989; Barrett, 1998). Although all these perspectives acknowledge that early expressive behaviours serve internal and external regulatory functions that support survival and well-being (e.g. regulation of sensory input, comfort, suckling, communication, attachment), no consensus is reached on whether:

◆ behavioural expressions of young infants are initially undifferentiated or emerge full-blown in an adult-like form;

◆ expressive behaviours at birth are stereotyped, reflex-like actions that depend only on the sensory parameters of stimulations;

◆ young infants' facial behaviours reflect internal states of feeling;

◆ the cognitive appraisal of events is required for the emergence of infants' emotional expressions;

◆ motivational and experiential factors influence the onset of newborns' expressive reactions;

◆ complex subjective processes (such as self or interpersonal awareness) may underlie expressive behaviours during the first weeks of life.

The aim of this chapter is to address these points in regard of recent research on emotional responses during very early development. After surveying some key issues raised by traditional views of emotional development (i.e. differential versus cognitive perspectives), we will examine how the reconceptualization of emotion within a functionalist perspective can provide guidance for a discussion on emotional processes in neonates. In contrast to theories in which emotion during the neonatal period is seen either as the product of hard-wired mechanisms (e.g. differential emotions theory; Izard and Malatesta, 1987), or as unlikely because newborns lack the cognitive prerequisites for experiencing feelings (Sroufe 1979, 1996; Lewis and Michalson, 1983; Lewis, 1993), the functionalist approach conceives emotion as relational processes deriving from significant transactions between the individual and the environment (e.g. Campos *et al.*, 1989; Saarni *et al.*, 1998). Within this perspective, we will gather available evidence suggesting that events acquire relevance for the newborn as a function of available sensorimotor abilities in interaction with maturational, motivational, and environmental constraints. To develop that view, we will capitalize on empirical data from behavioural research with more emphasis on the role of olfaction and taste. Although research in the early development of audition and vision has been plentiful, the chemosensory modalities have received attention only recently and the discussion of related results is of great interest in regard with emotional responsiveness on several grounds. First, the chemosensory modalities differentiate structurally very early during embryonic and fetal development (Schaal, 1988). Secondly, newborn infants display odour and taste elicited facial expressions that vary along the pleasant–unpleasant dimension (Steiner, 1979; Soussignan *et al.*, 1997). Finally, the chemosensory functions are motivation- and experience-dependent in various animal neonates (Schaal and Orgeur, 1992; Smotherman and Robinson, 1996); thus, they can be used as model systems to explore some processes underlying expressive behaviours in human newborns.

Traditional views on the ontogenetic origins of emotion

For the last decades, two prevailing theoretical views have guided infancy research on emotion. The first, named *Differential emotions theory* is enrooted in Darwinian thinking. It conceptualizes emotions as resulting from the interplay of independent, discrete, and integrated systems with modular properties serving adaptive functions and organizing cognition, action, and communication (Izard and Malatesta, 1987; Izard, 1991; Ackerman *et al.*, 1998). Following this perspective, basic emotions (i.e. disgust, joy, sadness, interest, anger, fear, surprise) emerge in an already differentiated form according to a predictable timetable as the product of the maturation of dedicated neural circuits and adaptation demands, but independent from cognitive development[1]

---

[1] According to the theory of differential emotions, although cognitive processes (e.g. appraisal, anticipation, understanding, and learning) appear crucial to activate emotional behaviour or foster emotion regulation during development, they are not viewed as a necessary component for experiencing or inducing an emotion, particularly during early life.

(Izard and Malatesta, 1987; Malatesta *et al.*, 1989). Some of these basic emotions are presumed to be fully functional at birth (e.g. disgust, interest) and their corresponding neuromuscular efferents are viewed as reflex-like patterns elicited by certain biologically relevant stimuli. This theory also conjectures that components of emotions (e.g. expressive behaviours, feeling states) are originally concordant, thus justifying the use of facial behaviour as an expressive signature of discrete subjective feelings (i.e. automatic read-outs of emotion). For instance, differential facial responses to nociceptive or bitter stimuli at birth have been interpreted as the surface manifestation of disgust or pain feelings in neonates (Steiner, 1977; Grunau and Craig, 1987; Izard, 1991; Delevati and Bergamasco, 1999). Other nativist-orientated theorists also hold that differentiated emotions are present at birth and do not require higher representational cognition (Trevarthen, 1993; Trevarthen and Aitken, 2001). They also conceived of newborns as possessing rudimentary skills in the perception of self as an agent capable of experiencing and sharing emotions with others (i.e. 'interpersonal awareness' or 'primary intersubjectivity'), especially during face-to-face communication with a conspecific. Trevarthen (1993) suggests that this primary intersubjectivity takes root in the innate capacity for empathetic relatedness with conspecifics.

The second perspective is cognitively orientated. It assumes that basic emotions do not exist in the first months of life because feeling, which represents the core of emotion for these theorists[2], comes about only after the infant has acquired the capacity to attribute a cognitive meaning to an event or to distinguish self from other (Lewis and Michalson, 1983; Lewis, 1993; Sroufe, 1996). Within this framework, neonatal actions and states are described as undifferentiated (e.g. global distress), diffuse, and bipolar (i.e. negative and positive states). Neonatal reactivity is considered to be based on physiological processes (e.g. hunger, pain), reflexively activated by quantitative parameters of stimulation (i.e. intensity), or by endogenous CNS fluctuations, rather than having qualitative content or event meaning. For instance, Sroufe (1996) proposed a tripartite model of emotional development in infancy. Following this model, affective life begins in the newborn period with undifferentiated 'physiological prototypes' (e.g. endogenous smile, distress) that have a purely reflexive base. For example, the neonatal smile during rapid-eye-movement sleep is considered as reflecting spontaneous fluctuations in CNS arousal, whereas stereotyped facial responses to bitter or sour tastes are considered as defensive reactions to noxious stimuli, rather than expressions of disgust as an emotion (Lazarus, 1991; Sroufe, 1996). These behaviours are thus conceived in terms of reflexive brainstem activities produced in the absence of forebrain-mediated affective or cognitive processing (Joseph, 2000). These neonatal prototypes differentiate over the first months of infancy into precursors of emotions (e.g. pleasure, frustration, and wariness), which are seen as diffuse, but psychologically-relevant responses (i.e. meaning or event-related). Finally, the basic emotions (e.g. joy,

---

[2] Feeling is usually defined as 'the irreducible quality of consciousness accompanying evaluations' (Saarni *et al.*, 1998).

anger, fear)—involving more precise, anticipated, or immediate reactions and specific meaning—are supposed to emerge in the second half of the first year of life as the result of a progressive differentiation between self and the environment due to developments in memory and explicit recognition[3].

In summary, whereas the differential emotions theory assumes that discrete facial expressions emerge without facial-movement precursors, cognitively-orientated theorists argue that expressions are undifferentiated during early infancy. Furthermore, according to the cognitive theorists, mental prerequisites (i.e. emerging conscience, cognitive appraisal) are needed for the generation of the subjective experience of emotion to a salient event, and that the mere presence of adult-like facial templates of expressive movements at birth is not a sufficient criterion for inferring feeling states or discrete emotional experience.

Although these theoretical frameworks raise ontological issues about the origins of human mind and subjective experience, a number of their statements (e.g. expression-feeling congruence, intersubjectivity, self-awareness) appear difficult to test during early infancy. Nevertheless, the assumption of the differential emotions theory for an innate concordance between specific expressions and discrete feelings has been indirectly explored by testing falsifiable hypotheses based on several criteria of differentiation (Izard and Malatesta, 1987; Camras *et al.*, 1991; Izard, 1994; Izard *et al.*, 1995). This issue has been approached by examining whether infant facial patterns:

- remain stable with age (developmental stability);
- communicate recognizable signals of basic emotions to adult receivers (signalling value);
- resemble the morphology of adult facial expressions of basic emotions (morphological similarity);
- are differentially produced by appropriate emotion elicitors (situational specificity).

So far no research has systematically examined the ontogeny of facial expressions from birth to the first half-year of life, but existing studies may provide insights to the issue of the differentiation of emotions. Arguments in favour of the differential emotions hypothesis mainly stem from data indicating not only differential facial responses in 10-week-old infants to specific emotional expressions of their mothers, but also a morphological continuity of discrete emotion expressions between this age

---

[3] Lewis (1993) distinguishes between emotional states and emotional experiences. An emotional state is defined as a particular constellation of changes in somatic and/or neurophysiological activity; emotional experience is seen as the subject's interpretation and evaluation of the perceived emotional state and expression. From his view, although basic emotional states emerge between 2 and 6 months, they cannot be experienced because infants are not capable of self-referential behaviour or consciousness during the first half-year of life (but see Rochat, 1999). However, Lewis also suggested that individuals might experience internal states and expressions without being necessarily aware of them. Accordingly, different levels of consciousness might be present during infancy.

and 9 months (Haviland and Lelwica, 1987; Izard *et al.*, 1995). For example, Izard *et al.* (1995) microanalysed infants' facial expressions (via the Maximally Discriminative Facial Movement Coding System: MAX) throughout the first 9 months of life during mother-infant, face-to-face interactions (still-face, contingent play, expressions of sadness and anger posed by the mother). They reported that, as early as 2.5 months, infants responded differentially to their mother's facially- and vocally-expressed emotions for joy, interest, sadness and anger, and that the basic morphology of their facial patterns remained stable through the first 9 months of life.

The innate status of the discrete patterning of emotional expressions during early infancy has been questioned on the basis of the empirical evidence showing that all the criteria for inferring differentiated processes (developmental stability, signalling value, morphological similarity, situational specificity) are rarely satisfied. In a research aimed to study the development of anger expression during early infancy, Stenberg and Campos (1990) recorded facial and bodily expressions of 1-, 4- and 7-month-olds to an experimental anger-eliciting situation (arms restraint) in the presence of social targets (mother or unfamiliar person). Using the MAX coding system, they revealed that 1-month-olds showed only facial components indicative of negative expressions, whereas the 4- and 7-month-olds displayed specific facial patterning of anger. Interestingly, the directionality of anger faces was age-dependent, since the expressions became socially directed only between 4 and 7 months. The developmental course of MAX-specified facial expressions has also been examined longitudinally at 2, 4, and 6 months during face-to face play, and the still-face procedure (Matias and Cohn, 1993). Although discrete facial expressions were frequent in positive social conditions, no age difference was detected between the discrete and blended negative expressions during the still-face procedure. These expressive blends were interpreted as indicative of undifferentiated affect, evidence not entirely compatible with the assumption of developmentally stable facial expressions for discrete emotion. Matias and Cohn suggested there is a progressive ontogenetic differentiation of both the morphology and signalling function of infants' facial expressions.

The signalling value of infant facial expressions has been investigated by testing the social validity of the MAX coding system using adult judgments. When adult receivers were required to recognize the signalling value of infant facial templates, the expressions of anger, disgust, fear and sadness were judged as emotion blends or could not be reliably distinguished from global distress (Oster *et al.*, 1992). In addition, when MAX-specified infant facial expressions were decoded with the Facial Action Coding System (FACS; Ekman and Friesen, 1978) and the baby-FACS (Oster and Rosenstein, in press), the infants' expressions of discrete negative emotions failed to match adult prototypes, except for disgust (Oster *et al.*, 1992). Thus, for negative emotional expressions, the infant–adult similarity and social validity can be used as evidence against the differential emotions theory postulate that negative facial expressions are fully differentiated in young infants.

Finally, concerning the last criterion—situational specificity—although some degree of specificity was previously reported for some emotional expressions (joy, surprise, anger; Hiatt *et al.*, 1979; Stenberg and Campos, 1990), studies on very young infants did not confirm that distinct negative facial expressions are produced in response to a variety of emotion-eliciting situations (inoculation, arm restraint, cookie removal, separation from mother, contingency interruption, see Camras *et al.*, 1991). For instance, in Camras's (1992) detailed single case study of an infant, conducted over the first postnatal weeks and in a wide range of contexts, there was considerable overlap in facial expressions, scored with the Izard's Affex coding system, among a variety of emotion-inducing situations (Camras, 1992). Interestingly, the same expressions of distress-pain or disgust were associated with a wide range of emotion elicitors (such as bathing, pacifier removal, waking up, termination of physical contact), whereas a number of facial templates of emotion (anger, sadness, distress-pain) were observed in response to the same eliciting circumstance. Components of the disgust-like expression (wrinkled nose and lifted upper lip) were also reported in newborns and very young infants in response to manipulations considered as intrusive, but not necessarily disgusting (e.g. oral insertion of an object, bath, nasal aspiration; Rosenstein and Oster, 1988; Camras *et al.*, 1991; Camras, 1992).

In summary, the available evidence suggests that the facial patterns displayed by young infants clearly are not like those of adults, which are fully differentiated expressions with specific emotions. A process of differentiation of facial expression of basic emotions should therefore operate during early infancy. However, one must regard the current findings as suggestive. Various reasons for the disagreement between infant and adult facial configurations for various emotions must be considered further. First, a great part of the disagreements may be linked with unresolved issues concerning:

- the validity of adult coding systems for measuring infant emotion expressions;
- the exact number of facial prototypes hypothesized to be associated with particular emotions;
- the way to interpret partial or composite expressions.

For example, it is unclear whether blended expressions encode signals of distinct emotions, undifferentiated states, or specific appraisal dimensions (e.g. pleasantness, novelty, arousal, attention, goal obstacle, personal agency; Scherer, 1992; Matias and Cohn, 1993; Izard *et al.*, 1995; Smith and Scott, 1997; Kaiser and Wehrle, 2001).

Secondly, using facial movements as the sole index of emotion may obscure the differentiation issue because emotions recruit flexible, multiple-response systems. Their components (e.g. physiological responsiveness, action tendency, facial, vocal and gestural expressions) may be differentially related to specific contexts as a function of the relevance of an event to infant goals and adaptive demands of the environment (Campos *et al.*, 1975; Hiatt *et al.*, 1979; Campos *et al.*, 1989; Barrett, 1993;

Weinberg and Tronick, 1994). For example, contexts presumed to be appropriate to elicit fear (e.g. visual cliff, stranger approach) rarely induced facial fear expressions from 10- to 12-month-olds, but they often elicit withdrawal behaviours allowing the infant to avoid a potential danger (Hiatt *et al.*, 1979).

Finally, existing findings do not necessarily mean that facial expressions are fully undifferentiated and functionally unorganized during early infancy or that young infants do not experience some form of feeling. Because ontogenetic heterochrony is a general principle of development, it may be expected that distinct components could initially be independent and follow separate developmental pathways to later become organized into functionally coherent systems (Fogel and Thelen, 1987). It is also assumed that some expressive components during early ontogeny, although morphologically differentiated, might be more or less functionally organized according to the maturational status of processing systems, the infant experience, and the adaptive value of the current action. For example, while smiling may be seen as an 'anticipatory' or 'prefunctional' movement pattern in the early repertoire before serving a true communicative function, neonatal disgust like-actions (gaping, tongue protrusion, nose wrinkling, head turning) may be described as ontogenetic precursors pertaining to a defensive system regulating inhalation and intake (Peiper, 1963). In that line, the nose wrinkling in the newborn, which is also characteristic of adult disgust expressions, could reduce the inflow of unpleasant or irritant airborne molecules and protect the olfactory receptors (Darwin 1872/1965). As will be illustrated below, the emergence of these actions during the newborn period is mediated by both motivational and experiential factors.

A functionalist perspective of the origin of emotion

Proponents of the functionalist perspective define emotion as processes designated to establish, maintain, or change the relations between the person and the environment, when such relations are significant to the individual[4] (Barrett and Campos, 1987; Campos *et al.*, 1989). There are at least four major processes through which stimuli or events become significant and powerful elicitors of emotion:[5]

- their intrinsic hedonic value;
- their relevance to motivational goals;

---

[4] See also Scherer (2000) who defined emotions as episodes of coordinated changes in several components (e.g. neurophysiological activation, motor expression, subjective feeling) in response to external or internal events of major significance to the organism.

[5] Although these processes are distinct they do not necessarily function independently from each other during early infancy. For example, as it will be shown from our overview, memory processes may be jointly involved with motivational, hedonic or social processes in the onset of newborns' expressive responses. However, for clarity reasons, they will be reviewed in separate sections.

- their relevance with regard to past experience;
- their communicative value or social relevance (Campos *et al.*, 1989, Saarni *et al.*, 1998).

Thus, neither facial expressions nor feelings are required for inferring emotions. Because facial expressions are not necessarily elicited in emotionally-loaded situations, the functionalist view considers that several components of the emotional system (e.g. facial behaviour, vocalization, action tendency, physiological patterning) must be explored during early infancy to illuminate the significance of the transactions between the individual and the environment (Campos *et al.*, 1989; Barrett, 1993). Moreover, a feeling (i.e. a subjectively conscious experience) is not viewed as the core of emotion and implicit experiences of affective states (pain, pleasure, disgust) are supposed to be present at birth, although they are likely distinct from the subjective experience of adults. Rather than postulating that emotions are organized into a limited set of innate discrete categories, it is assumed that they emerge across development in different forms and distinct contexts as members of a particular emotion family (Barrett, 1993). For example, disgust-like responses observed during distinct phases of ontogeny (newborn period, infancy, childhood, adolescence) are viewed as 'members of a disgust family' because they share crucial features (e.g. facial movements, physiological patterning, regulatory functions), but may also differ in other features (e.g. morphological complexity, co-occurring cognitive appraisal, dissociation between facial expressions and subjective experience) as a function of the developmental abilities of the organism, contextual demands, and socio-cultural history (Soussignan and Schaal, 1996a,b). For example, 5-years-olds can exhibit disgust expressions using smiles, while smelling unpleasant odours in the presence of an unfamiliar adult, and not when they are alone, in an attempt to cover or dissimulate an unpleasant feeling (Soussignan and Schaal, 1996a). This ability to dissociate facial expressions from their corresponding emotional experience is lacking in children with autism spectrum disorder, reflecting the role of socialization factors and socio-cognitive development in the control of expressive behaviours (Soussignan *et al.*, 1995).

Emotional processes are also viewed as organized at birth in a fluid, task-specific manner in accordance with the maturational state of sensory and motor systems, current motivational and ecological constraints, and the infants' previous experience. The view of a flexible organization of behavioural systems during the neonatal period has been substantially supported by the extensive research on neonatal perceptual and cognitive competence. For example, in the haptic-proprioceptive realm, newborn infants were shown to be able to:

- modulate oral and hand activities according to the texture, rigidity and shape of objects (Rochat, 1987; Molina and Jouen, 1998; Streri *et al.*, 2000);
- discriminate external from self-administered tactile stimulations (Rochat and Hespos, 1997);
- rely on proprioception for matching the actions produced by a model (e.g. Meltzoff and Moore, 1977; Kugiumutzakis, 1993);

- display elementary forms of hand-mouth coordination (Butterworth and Hopkins, 1988).

This set of findings led the above investigators to argue that neonatal actions are neither completely reflex-like nor wholly undifferentiated, but are, in great part, goal-orientated.

This view is also raised by scholars who share an evolutionary stance of behavioural development. They stressed that, although not fully differentiated, neonatal responsiveness to environmental stimuli is shaped by natural history constraints and adaptive needs (e.g. Alberts, 1987; Hall and Oppenheim, 1987; Lecanuet et al., 1995; Smotherman and Robinson, 1996). The perceptual and cognitive abilities of young infants are considered as adaptive in their own right or as precursors of future abilities, but not just as immature versions of adult abilities. Developmental psychobiologists propose the notion of ontogenetic adaptation defined as morphological, behavioural or cognitive devices specialized to solve ecological demands and immediate adaptive needs during transitions from early life (Alberts, 1987; Hall and Oppenheim, 1987; Smotherman and Robinson, 1996). For example, as a case of ontogenetic adaptation, the behavioural complex around sucking does not only serve nutritional needs, but it also has short-term regulatory functions (e.g. soothing) that allow coordinated transactions with the social environment, as well as long-term regulation of preferences by its involvement in reinforcement and learning (Blass, 1990). Although sucking appears at first sight to be stereotyped in form and eliciting stimuli, it is morphologically flexible at birth and can be used to control incoming stimuli (e.g. in an operant reinforcement procedure, Rochat, 1987, Lipsitt and Behl, 1990). Other neonatal actions such as facial patterns function more as ontogenetic precursors or as members of an emerging expression family related to hedonic, motivational, memorial and communicative processes. They may thus be considered as elements of primitive emotional systems providing valuable information on meaningful transactions between the neonatal organism and its environment.

Hedonic processes

Hedonic processes are usually invoked when sensory stimulation intrinsically produces irreducible sensations of pleasure or displeasure and induces preferential responding in terms of approach/acceptance or withdrawal/rejection (Schneirla, 1967; Steiner, 1977; Kahneman et al., 1999). Most theorists consider hedonic valence as a salient feature of emotion experience, that plays a central role in the regulatory processes of behaviour (e.g. Frijda, 1986; Campos et al., 1989). Hedonic processes have been investigated during the neonatal period:

- to assess the initial state of preferences and aversions, and to specify whether they are modality-dependent;
- to clarify their role in the early growth of emotion regulation;
- to provide insights into the origins of emotional expressions.

Considerable evidence now indicates that inborn hedonic responses to taste stimuli are responses that develop independently during postnatal experience. Several reports using various behavioural and physiological measures (e.g. facial expressions, sucking, heart rate, EEG asymmetry) have shown differential responsiveness to hedonically-positive (sucrose) and -negative (quinine, citric acid) solutions in both animal and human newborns (Crook and Lipsitt, 1976; Steiner, 1977; Fox and Davidson, 1986; Lipsitt and Behl, 1990). For example, shortly after birth, facial responses to sweet solutions were more often characterized by relaxation, sucking, tongue protrusion, and licking, whereas non sweet stimuli (bitter and sour) induce more often negatively-valenced actions (e.g. gaping, lip pursing, lip corners depressing, brow raising, nose wrinkling, head retraction; Steiner, 1979; Ganchrow et al., 1983; Fox and Davidson, 1986; Rosenstein and Oster, 1988; Bergamasco and Beraldo, 1990). Facial patterns of interest and left-frontal EEG activation were also described in 2-to-3-day olds in response to sucrose, as opposed to citric acid solutions (Fox and Davidson, 1986).

It is interesting to stress that a phylogenetic continuity of taste-elicited affective reactivity between humans, other primates and rats has been suggested (Berridge, 2000, Steiner et al., 2001). For example, the comparative analysis of the microstructure of taste-elicited facial responses indicates that some components are universal among all primates, such as gapes to bitter or rhythmic tongue protrusions to sweet, whereas other components seem to belong only to humans and great apes (e.g. complex lip smacking to sweet tastes; movements involving musculature of the brows, nose and middle face to bitter tastes). From an evolutionary perspective, these innate and universal preferences for, or aversions to, particular taste stimuli, are considered as adaptive. The taste of sweetness usually signals a substance of high caloric value, whereas the taste of bitter often signals potential toxicity.

The issue of whether hedonic responses to olfactory stimuli are present at birth or whether they are acquired postnatally, as a function of experience or cultural modelling, remains controversial (Steiner, 1979; Rozin and Fallon, 1987; Engen, 1988). Odours are salient sensory cues that can evoke species typical-behaviours in human neonates (sucking, disgust-like expressions), as well as facial behaviours that are mediated by both cortical inhibitory mechanisms and socialization processes during development (Soussignan et al., 1995; Soussignan and Schaal, 1996a). Although, some authors reported that hedonically contrasted odours trigger stereotyped facial patterns (enjoyment vs. disgust-like expressions) in neonates younger than 12 hours old (Steiner, 1979), others found no clear behavioural and autonomic differentiation between odorants adults considered to be pleasant or unpleasant (Engen et al., 1963; Engen and Lipsitt, 1965; Self et al., 1972). This inconsistency most probably reflects procedural differences and methodological shortcomings (cf. Soussignan et al., 1997). For example, because the smell experience involves the co-activation of olfactory and trigeminal systems, particularly with high-concentration odorants, intranasal irritation may account for the infants' responses reported in the above studies.

To sort out these inconsistencies the issue of odour hedonics in infants was recently reconsidered. Infant facial and autonomic (respiratory rate and body temperature) responsiveness was recorded during various behavioural states to the presentation of hedonically-contrasted odour qualities (vanillin vs. butyric acid). The odorants were matched for intensity and irritating power to ecologically-relevant substrates (i.e. breast milk, formula milks, amniotic fluid), and were thus delivered at low-to-very low intensities (Soussignan *et al.*, 1997). The odour-elicited facial configurations were micro-analysed with the Baby-FACS (Oster and Rosenstein, in press) and revealed the following results:

- the markers of 'disgust' (nose wrinkling, upper lip raising) discriminated between odours that adults judged either as pleasant (vanillin) or unpleasant (butyric acid), with significantly more of such negative actions to the unpleasant odour, but note that there was considerable inter-individual variability in infant facial patterns (see Fig. 5.1);

- the autonomic responses also differentiated the odorants since pleasant ones increased the respiration rate more than unpleasant ones.

However, although some early disposition to reliably process odour-related hedonics were suggested, these data did not provide strong evidence that neonates organize odours within the same perceptual space as adults. That is, odours that were pleasant (vanillin) or unpleasant (butyric acid, formula milk) to adults did not univocally elicit positive (i.e. smiling, sucking) or negative expressions in neonates. For example, in sleeping and awake 3-day-old newborns, Fig. 5.1 provides evidence that smelling butyric acid may elicit disgust-like responses (a,b) or smiling (c), whereas odours of formula milks (judged as negative by adults, see Soussignan *et al.*, 1997) may induce smiling and sucking (d,f).

The lack of clear hedonic differentiation of odours in newborns seems to stand at odds with the above-reported findings on taste. Accordingly, both sensory systems may be differently articulated with response systems. Although taste reception is considered to be reliably connected with differentiated, opposite expressive response systems, olfaction seems to be only partly canalized in that way. This is suggested by two points. First, our data imply that (at least some) odorants that are unpleasant to adults elicit negatively-valenced facial expressions in newborns. As these stimulations were administered at very weak intensity, one may assume that sensory components of the smell experience reputed to elicit rejection (viz. high intensity, irritation) are not prerequisites for inducing disgust-like facial patterns. The tendency to respond negatively to some odorants could be seen as part of an emesis system designed to reject unpalatable food (Darwin 1872/1965; Rozin and Fallon, 1987). Thus, one cannot rule out the possibility that some odorants would be inherently aversive. This hypothesis is also supported by cross-cultural studies on odour hedonics which provide substantial evidence for an invariant tendency to value negatively a large set of unpleasant odours associated

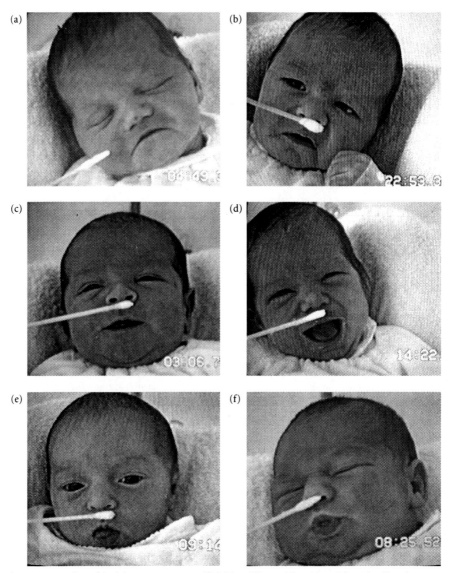

Fig. 5.1 Examples of facial responses to artificial (vanillin and butyric acid) and milk odours in sleeping and waking 3-day-old newborns. (a) AU 10 + 15 (butyric acid at 0.0039%). (b) AU 10 + 20 + 26 (butyric acid at 0.125%). (c) AU 12 + 26 (butyric acid at 0.0078%). (d) AU 6 + 12 + 27 (formula milk). (e) Licking (vanillin at 1.25%). (f) Sucking (formula milk). AU, action unit; AU 6, cheek raising; AU 10, upper lip raising; AU 12, lip corner pulling; AU 15, lip corner depressing; AU 20, lip stretching; AU 26, jaw dropping; AU 27, mouth stretching. Vanillin was rated as pleasant, while butyric acid and formula milk were rated as unpleasant by an adult panel.

with decay or body exudates (Schaal *et al.*, 1998b). Second, there is no strong evidence that newborns do respond appetitively to odorants considered to be very pleasant for adults. Variability in early olfactory preferences is not surprising since a salient characteristic of the infants' chemosensory environments (viz., amniotic and lacteal fluids) is their variability (Mennella and Beauchamp, 1991, Schaal and Orgeur, 1992, Mennella *et al.*, 1995, Schaal *et al.*, 2002). Such unpredictable developmental niches are completely incompatible with hard-wired stimulation-response pairings. So, it may be expected that neonatal preferences for odours may be shaped in part by innate predispositions (which await better specifications) and in part by experience gathered from prenatal and postnatal learning.

Whether positive hedonic stimuli regulate affective states in a reliable way during early development comes mainly from work on taste. For instance, sucrose and other carbohydrates applied on the anterior tongue elevate threshold for pain with sustained effects in reducing crying, and transiently increasing mouthing and hand-mouth contacts (Blass and Hoffmeyer, 1991; Barr *et al.*, 1994; Blass and Shah, 1995). The reduction of distress vocalizations that follows sweet taste stimulation is likely mediated by endogenous opioid systems, because the effects of sucrose are blocked by the administration of opioid antagonists in neonatal rats (Blass *et al.*, 1987; Shide and Blass, 1989) and are absent in human neonates born to women who were methadone-treated during pregnancy (Blass and Ciaramitaro, 1994). However, this calming effect of sucrose appears to be transient during development as it is effective only on the first presentations during the first 2 weeks of life. At 4 weeks of age a sweet taste loses its consoling power unless infants have engaged visually with the experimenter (Zeifman *et al.*, 1996). This ontogenetic shift may reflect the emergence of an integrative system combining visual and orogustatory afferents in the regulation of distress and crying.

It should be stressed that the soothing effect of nasally-administered chemosensory stimuli has been demonstrated recently in human newborns for both maternal odours (milk, body odour, and amniotic fluid) and familiar artificial odours (Schaal *et al.*, 1980; Sullivan and Toubas, 1998; Varendi *et al.*, 1998; Goubet *et al.*, 2003). For example, preterm newborns previously familiarized with vanillin showed no increase in crying and grimacing during a blood test in presence of the familiar odour as compared with control groups (Goubet *et al.*, 2003).

Finally, the study of hedonic processes in human neonates raises fundamental questions about the origins and development of facial expressions of emotion (e.g. Rosenstein and Oster, 1988). More specifically, because some neonatal facial patterns (e.g. lowered brows, raised cheeks, wrinkled nose, lifted upper lip) are morphologically similar to adult disgust expressions, it may be debated whether they are to be viewed as components of a defensive reflex to intrusive/intense stimulations (as suggested by Bridges, 1932; Lazarus, 1991; Sroufe, 1996) or as expressions innately connected with the subjective experience of disgust in response to given stimuli (as suggested by Steiner, 1977; Fox and Davidson, 1986; Izard, 1991). Existing data do not allow us to address the issue of the specificity between sensory elicitors and facial expressions during the newborn period. Some evidence suggest that disgust-related facial patterns can occur in intrusive situations which are not necessarily to be considered as disgusting (Rosenstein and Oster, 1988; Camras, 1992). Thus, the mere presence of facial expressions is not sufficient to draw inferences about underlying internal states. A conservative approach to the presence of differentiated emotional states in newborns would be to take into account cognitive criteria in the onset of emotional responses. For example, appraisal theorists have suggested that the minimal cognitive prerequisite for the elicitation of an emotion is the evaluation of an event or the relevance of a stimulus for the organism's goals and needs (Scherer, 1994; Frijda, 1994). From this perspective, low level cognitive processing should be active (e.g. implicit learning) and a certain form of emotion may be experienced at birth. As we shall see in the next sections, there is some evidence that newborn infants can extract the meanings of events which appears relevant in the context of the organism's needs (see motivational processes) and ontogenetic history (see memory processes).

Motivational processes

The concept of motivation usually refers to psychobiological processes that play a major role in goal-directed behaviours as a function of variations of internal physiological states (e.g. metabolic, hormonal) and/or cognitive representations (e.g. expectancies, memory; Toates, 1986). From a functionalist view, the neonatal repertoire includes actions that are goal-orientated because they are part of affordance systems enabling the organism to respond adaptively toward specific features of the environment. These goal-directed actions are possible without postulating deliberate planning or explicit awareness of self and others (Rochat and Striano, 1999). For example, calming, feeding, exploring and communicating may be proposed as functional goals underlying the infant behaviours at birth. The construct of motivation may explain why the same environmental event can elicit different emotional reactions across time or contexts, or why the same behavioural pattern can be recruited to express different bodily and mental processes. Despite the paucity of data on early motivational processes, there is some evidence that neonatal behaviour can be mediated by both internal physiological signals and experiential processes (Lipsitt and Behl, 1990). For example, taste responsiveness and hand-mouth coordination in newborn infants appear to be influenced by motivational mechanisms underlying feeding behaviour (Jensen, 1932; Lew and Butterworth, 1995). Feeding in infancy also represents a salient context for the evaluation of biologically meaningful stimuli (e.g. milk) and thus for experiencing hedonically-valenced stimulations.

An excellent illustration of the role of motivational factors in hedonic processing comes from experiments on the phenomenon named 'alliesthesia'. Olfactory alliesthesia refers to the change in pleasure of food-related odours after a meal, a process that has been well studied in both human and animal models (Cabanac, 1971, 1979).

For example, in human adults, either eating a meal or an intragastric infusion of glucose produced a shift from pleasant to unpleasant valence of food-related odours. This negative alliesthesia reaches its maximum within 45–60 minutes following ingestion (Cabanac and Fantino, 1977). Does such a phenomenon operate from birth onwards, and if so what can it tell us about the nature and significance of the emotional processes at work? In a recent study, we recorded facial and autonomic responsiveness to an artificial odorant (vanillin) and to food-related odours (familiar formula milk, unfamiliar formula milks) during active sleep in 3-day-old, bottle-fed neonates (Soussignan *et al.*, 1999). These infants were tested for preferential responses to the various stimuli 50 minutes before and after a feed, with the aim of examining whether the shift in motivational states (from hunger to satiety) was related to a change in hedonic responsiveness to food-related odours differing in familiarity. Several findings emerged from this study. Increases in heart rate were detected only when the infants smelled their familiar milk during the post-prandial condition (i.e. satiety state). The Baby-FACS analysis also indicated that they exhibited more negative and disgust-like facial responses to the odour of their familiar formula during the post-prandial condition only (Fig. 5.2).

The odour of the stimuli that were not related to satiation did not bring about any change in facial responses between the pre- and post-prandial conditions. These findings are consistent with the view that 3-day-old neonates selectively process the odour of the milk, which satiated them and produces emotional responses adapted to their motivational state and stimulus familiarity. They suggest that neonates can display:

◆ motor components of negative emotion to a familiar stimulus (a milk odour) that is not intrinsically unpleasant;

◆ differentiated affective reactions (i.e. heart-rate change, disgust-like facial reactions) to olfactory cues that have acquired a meaning in the context of feeding.

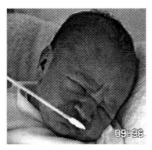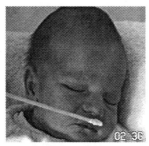

Fig. 5.2 Samples of facial responses of sleeping 3-day-old newborns exposed to the odour of their familiar formula during a post-prandial condition. Each facial response involves the action unit 10 (AU 10) produced by the contraction of *levator labii superioris* muscle (FACS name, upper lip raising). AU 10 and AU 9 (nose wrinkling) are usually considered as facial markers of the disgust expression.

Thus, some of the criteria (e.g. appreciation of the meaning of an event, event-response decoupling), proposed by appraisal theorists (e.g. Leventhal and Scherer, 1987; Lazarus, 1991; Scherer et al., 2001), for inferring emotional processes are present at birth.[6]

Memory-dependent processes

Infancy research has clearly demonstrated that human newborns are endowed with learning abilities involving implicit memory. Newborns can be habituated, classically or instrumentally conditioned to various stimuli (odours, sounds, touch), and acquire sensory information through mere exposure (e.g. Slater et al., 1984; De Casper and Spence, 1986; Balogh and Porter, 1986; Sullivan et al., 1991; Faas et al., 2000). The issue of whether memory-dependent processes can be affectively-loaded during early development is critical for the emotion-cognition debate, as it could illuminate how implicit cognitive appraisals might be involved in the onset of expressive responses at birth. An interesting study by Blass et al. (1984) addressed directly that issue. These investigators reported that 2-hour-old babies respond affectively to the violation of a learned expectation. The newborns were subjected to a classical conditioning paradigm in which they received several trials of forehead stroking immediately followed by the delivery of a minute dose of sucrose. Their expressive behaviour (pucker-suck, mouthing, chewing, lips turning down, frowning, crying) and head orientation were carefully coded and compared with that of two control groups. Only infants in the experimental group exhibited increased sucking and positive head-turning during the first conditioning trials of the tactile stimulus. More interestingly, when extinction trials (sucrose undelivered) were run, only two such violations sufficed to strongly diminish the hedonically-positive oral responses and to increase signs of negative facial expressions and crying. This rapid onset of negative expressions after discontinuation of a potent reinforcer raises the possibility that newly born infants easily form memories and expectancies about the consequences of a gustatory event (i.e. positive hedonic experience). Because the failure to satisfy such an expectation induced crying, it is possible that cognitive appraisals are already involved in emotional processing during the first postnatal days. Thus, the congruence of an actual event to a memorized template may be a powerful pathway to generate contrasted affect (Lazarus, 1991).

The above result suggests that newborn infants are able to retain the meaning of a past event with regard to hedonic valence. This is compatible with a theoretical framework viewing emotional processing as already hierarchically organized at two levels during the neonatal period: a sensory-motor level including inborn expressive-motor programs to significant events (e.g. hedonic stimulation) or to unconditional stimuli, and a schematic level based on implicit memories of previous emotional experience

---

[6] For a number of theorists, appraisal does not necessarily involve explicit or complex cognitive processing (Leventhal and Scherer, 1987; Scherer et al., 2001).

(Leventhal and Scherer, 1987). Whether the expressive changes noted during the extinction trials in Blass *et al*.'s (1984) study correspond to global states (e.g. distress) or to discrete emotional experiences remains unresolved. Although these authors indicated that the infant's expressions were also composed of surprise actions, frowning and angry faces, their study unfortunately did not report data on the morphology of facial patterns of basic emotions. Given that surprise faces may be linked with violation of expectancies, and anger faces are produced after frustration or restraint to goal attainment (Stenberg and Campos, 1990), the demonstration of such facial expressions in future studies would be a strong argument in favour of the operation of appraisal processes specifically related to appropriate elicitors of emotion at birth. Further investigations using reliable facial measurement techniques (e.g. FACS) within the same experimental paradigm are thus required to clarify whether they correspond to specific facial expressions of emotion.

There is also evidence suggesting that memory processes based on prior contingent experience can generate affective responses from birth onwards. De Casper and Carstens (1981) used an operant conditioning paradigm in infants aged less than 3 days. In the first session, the infants in the experimental group could produce vocal music only if non-nutritive sucking met an appropriate criterion (contingent on singing). In a second session, the same singing was presented non-contingently. Infants in a control group were exposed to the same condition in a reverse order, and thus were unable to induce singing (non-contingent singing) in the first session. Infants exposed to contingent stimulation were able to change their sucking behaviour to produce singing compared with the control group. More interestingly, there was an order effect: when the singing was presented non-contingently, only newborns with a history of contingent stimulation displayed increases of negative expressions (vocalizations, grimaces). These findings are consistent with the view that losing control over a reinforcing stimulus could be involved in the onset of negative affect.

In summary, the above studies using classical or operant conditioning procedures suggest that human newborns can negatively evaluate stimulation that is not intrinsically aversive (stroking, vocal singing) when a discrepancy is detected between familiar information (e.g. previous episodes of reinforcement) and ongoing stimulation. Thus, affective life of newborns is not reducible to purely physiological processes (e.g. Sroufe, 1996), but appears to be event-related, psychologically-based, and relatively organized with respect to context.

The existence of emotional responses and learning abilities in the newborn raises questions about their ontogenetic origin. It has become clear that sensory and cognitive competences and behavioural organization are not present at the moment of birth, but have their roots in prenatal development (Lecanuet *et al.*, 1995; Schaal *et al.*, 1995b; Smotherman and Robinson, 1996). In humans, the strongest evidence for fetal learning and memory has been demonstrated with the auditory modality through paradigms of classical and operant conditioning, habituation, and mere exposure

(Lecanuet *et al.*, 1995; Hepper, 1996). For example, the way vocal and speech sounds are processed by the newborn depends on prenatal exposure to maternal voice or specific language (e.g. DeCasper and Spence, 1986). Abilities to learn olfactory cues have been extensively documented in mammalian fetuses, such as rats (Smotherman, 1982; Hepper, 1988), rabbits (Bilko *et al.*, 1994; Coureaud *et al.*, 2002) and sheep (Schaal *et al.*, 1995a, 1999). In these species, the fetus is exposed during late gestation to a wide range of odorants brought into the amniotic pool through the mother's diet. Antenatal experience with such odorants affects neonatal responses to the same stimuli. For example, fetal rats, rabbits and lambs exposed only *in utero* to given odorants (such as citral, garlic, cumin, juniper) display preferences for the same odorants as neonates, weanlings, or even adults. Thus, mammalian fetuses are able to extract information from their prenatal chemical ecology and newborns retain that information for long postnatal periods, in certain cases until adulthood (Schaal and Orgeur, 1992).

Similar facilitative or inductive processes operate in human fetuses and influence hedonic reactions to olfactory stimuli in neonates. The chemosensory systems are mature enough for functional activity prior to birth (Schaal, 1988) and odorous compounds are present in the fetal compartment (Schaal and Orgeur, 1992; Mennella *et al.*, 1995). There is evidence suggesting that human fetuses can learn odours *in utero* and that neonates can retain such odours. For example, 4-day-olds can retain the odour profile of their familiar amniotic fluid (Schaal *et al.*, 1998a) or of odorant substances (alcohol, garlic) consumed by their mothers during pregnancy (Hepper, 1995; Faas *et al.*, 2000).

Prenatal learning in the human fetus was recently tested in looking for the formation of hedonic responses to odours introduced *in utero* through the mother's diet during the last 2 weeks of pregnancy (Schaal *et al.*, 2000). Taking advantage of the widespread use of anise in the local cuisine and the fact that it is readily perceived by newborns, we studied odour-elicited facial responses in two groups of neonates born to mothers who had or had not consumed anise flavour. Facial responsiveness to anise and a control odour, and preferential head orientation in a paired-odour test, were recorded 3 hours and 4 days after birth in both groups of infants. Those born to anise-consuming mothers evinced appetitive responses for the anise odour over this period (sucking, licking, chewing, head orientation), whereas those born to anise non-consuming mothers displayed more frequent negative facial responses (e.g. nose wrinkling, gaping, upper lip raising, frowning) on the day of birth (see Fig. 5.3). These data indicate that the dietary odorants of the pregnant mothers influence the hedonic polarity of their neonates' initial olfactory responses. Thus, fetal learning and long-term memorization of intrauterine chemosensory information modulate later facial expressiveness. Although the acquisition processes and the hedonic integration on which this learning is based remain unclear (e.g. non-associative versus associative encoding), one may hypothesize that the matching between a prenatally established olfactory template and postnatal odour cues may be essential to elicit positive responses.

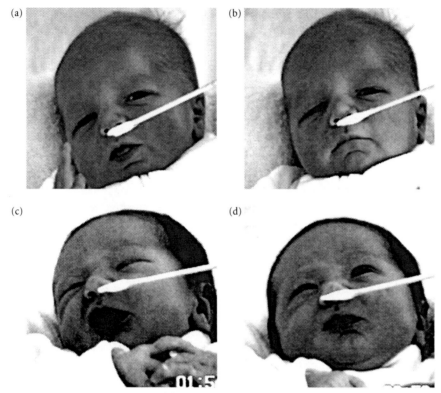

Fig. 5.3 Representative examples of facial responses to odours of a 4-hour-old born to an anise-consuming mother (a,b) and of an 8-hour-old newborn born to an anise non-consuming mother (c,d). (a) Facial response to anise odour: tongue protruding and licking. (b) Facial response to the control stimulus: no action unit. (c) Facial response to anise odour: brow lowering, cheek raising, upper lid lowering, nose wrinkling, jaw dropping. (d) Facial response to control stimulus: no action unit.

Conversely, a discrepancy in perinatal chemosensory information may tend to generate negative responses.

It is interesting to note that brain regions essential to the processing of the emotional significance of environmental events (e.g. the amygdala) are functional during the newborn period, at least for olfactory inputs (in the rat, Wilson & Sullivan, 1994). The olfactory bulb projections to the amygdala are present at birth, and some amygdaloid nuclei (e.g. cortical, basomedial, basolateral) are viewed as an integral component of the main olfactory system (Swanson and Petrovich, 1998). The amygdala appears to be involved in hedonically-valenced olfactory learning in neonate rats (Wilson and Sullivan, 1994). For example, bilateral lesions of the amygdala in 1-day-old rat pups impair associative conditioning of an odour preference, but not conditioned behavioural activation (Sullivan and Wilson, 1993). Interestingly, in human newborns the recording of cerebral haemodynamic response to unpleasant and pleasant odorants revealed a differential pattern of activation in the cortical region (i.e. orbitofrontal cortex; Bartocci et al., 2000, 2001) usually involved in olfactory processing in adults (e.g. Royet et al., 2000). While the unpleasant odour induced a haemodynamic decrease over the right side of the orbitofrontal region, the pleasant odour produced an increase over the left orbitofrontal area in all babies. Although further studies are required to confirm these previous findings in human newborns, one cannot rule out that the anatomical organization of the mammalian brain at birth might be sufficient for processing olfactory information involved in the formation of implicit affective memory.

In summary, despite the paucity of data on perinatal learning in humans, the existing findings suggest the critical role of memory and implicit appraisal processes in the early development of affective responses. These differentiated postnatal responses provide valuable information on the dynamics of behavioural organization and support the view that neonatal emotional systems are contextually flexible.

Sensitivity to human expressive signals

A pre-adaptation for emotional communication probably originates from the propensity of the human newborn to respond selectively to human stimuli or to nurturing signals through visual, auditory, olfactory, and tactile modalities. Despite limited visual acuity, immediately after birth, infants prefer to look at face-like patterns over non-face-like patterns, at their mother's face than at a stranger's face, and at a face with eyes open than at a face with eyes closed (Field et al., 1984; Johnson et al., 1991; Walton et al., 1992; Pascalis et al., 1995; Batki et al., 2000; Cassia et al., 2001). Whether these findings reflect an inborn tendency to orientate towards salient features of the human face (e.g. configural properties of internal features, detection of eyes or gaze direction) or rather a sensitivity of the neonatal visual system to energy properties of the stimulus (e.g. contrast sensitivity, movement sensitivity) remains to be settled (Johnson and Morton, 1991; Valenza et al., 1996; Simion et al., 2001).

Current debates focus on whether domain-specific cognitive mechanisms are involved since birth using specialized neural systems dedicated to the processing of specific features (e.g. gaze module, detector of face orientation) or whether human faces are perceived by domain-general mechanisms (e.g. a processing system non specific to faces; Johnson and Morton, 1991; Batki et al., 2000; Kanwisher, 2000). When dynamic components of complex social stimuli are taken into account, neonates seem able to respond selectively to human models by imitating facial movements such as tongue protrusion (Meltzoff and Moore, 1977; Legerstee, 1991; Kugiumutzakis, 1993). The processes at the origin of this early ability continue to be debated (Meltzoff and Moore, 1997; Nadel and Butterworth, 1999; Bremner, 2002). Do they simply reflect low-level mechanisms based on specialized perceptual-motor couplings or more sophisticated systems, involving supra-modal representations and active intermodal mappings between the sight of a facial action, and the feelings that accompany the self-production of the same action?

Newborns are also particularly sensitive to the human voice in responding to stimuli such as speech sounds (e.g. vowels; Aldridge et al., 2001). In an operant-choice procedure, they prefer their mother's voices to those of other females (De Casper and Fifer, 1980). This mother-infant discrimination appears to be influenced by prenatal experience with maternal speech (De Casper and Spence, 1986). They also selectively respond to their own mother's body odour (originating from the neck, breast, axillae) and to the odour of amniotic fluid, and may rely on olfactory cues to locate the breast within the first postnatal hours or days (MacFarlane, 1975; Schaal et al., 1980, 1998a; Makin and Porter, 1989; Varendi et al. 1994; Marlier et al., 1998).

Whereas the above brief overview suggests rudimentary forms of early competence in the domain of 'social perception', the question of whether newborn infants can perceive or respond to human expressive signals has been less systematically investigated. There are at least three types of research suggesting that newborn infants are sensitive to expressive cues carried in conspecific social displays, although the significance and processes underlying this early sensitivity remain unclear so far. The first element concerns the phenomenon of emotional contagion. During the neonatal period, infants are able to produce different types of cries (e.g. 'hunger' cry, 'pain' cry) that can be related with specific environmental stimuli (Wolff, 1987). They also seem reactive to the communicative value of cries produced by other newborns. For example, infants were more likely to cry when listening to tape-recorded cries of other newborns than when listening their own cry or an equally loud and intense nonhuman sound in the same conditions (Simner, 1971; Sagi and Hoffman, 1976; Martin and Clark, 1982). Furthermore, playbacks of distress vocalizations of other infants were shown to be highly effective in inducing facial signs of distress (i.e. brows lowered, eye fissure tightly closed, cheek raised), and in reducing non-nutritive sucking in both awake and sleeping newborns (Dondi et al., 1999). These findings not only suggest that newborns are able to discriminate fairly similar acoustic parameters, but also that they might be sensitive to emotional cues carried in conspecific vocalizations (e.g. negative tone of human cry). Although the functional value of such distress reactivity to expressive displays of other newborns is unclear, it may be considered a precursor of emotional contagion (Moore, 1990; Zahn-Waxler and Radke-Yarrow, 1990). The underlying mechanisms of this precocious phenomenon are not clearly understood, but one explanation may be based on the neonatal tendency to discriminate familiar from unfamiliar vocal stimuli and to automatically mimic particular features of the human cry (perception–action coupling).

Research on imitation and discrimination of facial expressions also suggests neonatal sensitivity to the communicative value of expressive behaviour. Using a trial-to-criterion habituation procedure, Field et al. (1982, 1983) reported that neonates (term and preterm) were able to discriminate shortly after birth facial expressions of happiness, sadness, and surprise posed by a live female model. More interestingly, these infants displayed differential facial movements in response to the three facial expressions. While the happy expression elicited more frequently widening of the lips, the sad expression induced more often protruded lips and furrowed brows, and the expression of surprise produced more wide-open mouths. It was also shown that infants born to mothers having had depressive symptoms during gestation were less facially expressive in response to the modelled expressions of happiness and surprise (Lindy and Field, 1996).

Such findings are to be interpreted with caution and require replication with methodological improvements (e.g. inclusion of control groups including neutral faces or faces without emotional actions, fine-grained coding of neonatal facial patterns) before concluding that infant newborns are able to decode and encode expressive signals. Furthermore, due to functional limitations of the neonatal visual system, such differential responsiveness does not necessarily imply that newborns actually discriminate facial configurations of basic emotions (see Nelson, 1987), but that they respond to local features of the face (e.g. sensitivity to appearance changes of the mouth and lips) without extracting any emotional meaning.

Finally, the question of whether the neonate is pre-adapted to decode emotional cues transmitted by human voice has also been recently investigated. Using a cross-linguistic approach, Mastropieri and Turkewitz (1999) videotaped newborns of Spanish and English-speaking American mothers, while listening to speech stimuli in each language that varied in prosody. Intonation patterns were selected to convey happy, sad, angry, and neutral feelings, and were low-pass filtered to align them with speech sounds experienced prenatally. Newborns evinced increased eye opening in response only to the presentation of the happy condition. Interestingly, this differentiation was noted when the infants were exposed to voicing in their maternal language, but not when exposed to the same vocal expressions in an unfamiliar language. These findings do not demonstrate that newborns actually perceive the tone (e.g. valence) or intentional meaning (e.g. affiliation) of human expressions of happiness, but they do suggest that they might be sensitive to the prosodic cues of a familiar language as a possible consequence of prenatal auditory experience.

Conclusions

Our review suggests that the four processes (i.e. sensory hedonism, motivation, memory, and communication) proposed by the functionalist perspective for inducing emotional responses operate from birth onwards. Each process is part of critical transactions with the environment in organizing action, and allowing events to acquire meaning and saliency for newborns. Central to this approach is the view that these processes emerge in response to adaptive needs/functional goals specified within the evolved niche of the newborn. Guided by this perspective, we also provided evidence from our own research, which revealed that neonatal olfaction can be used as a model system to explore hedonic, motivational, and memory-based processes involved in the onset of emotional responses. For instance, the fact that the familiar milk odour can elicit disgust-like responses when internal organic variables shift or that a prenatally-experienced odorant can induce postnatal preferences, are clearly compatible with the view that, right at birth, affective responses are embedded within motivational (prandial state) and memory processes (prenatal and postnatal learning). The view that emotional systems are flexible, rather than hard-wired at birth raises interesting issues for future research. For example, the demonstration of a prenatal mother-to-infant transmission of chemosensory information pertaining to food or self raises the possibility that an infant's affective reactions and preferences are primed in part before birth.

Hedonic processes constitute essential determinants of early emotional life that play a critical role in the regulation of psychobiological states. Research in neonatology has highlighted the powerful regulatory effect of positive hedonic stimulations (taste, odour and touch, exercising sucking) on well-being, and the reduction of undesirable affective states in both premature and full-term neonates. However, much remains to be known about the mediating mechanisms and the differential comforting impact of a range of hedonic and ecologically-relevant stimuli. The research conducted on emotional communication during the newborn period (e.g. emotional contagion, imitation, social discrimination) at this point is only suggestive, but it opens up the possibility that newborn infants could decode and encode emotional cues from facial and vocal expressions displayed by conspecifics. However, what remains unclear is whether infants are really sensitive to the hedonic tone or meaning carried by the emotional signal displayed by other persons. Replications of Field's experiments are needed before we can reach any conclusion about imitation of emotional expressions at birth.

Another issue that remains unsettled concerns the level of differentiation of emotional facial patterns during the newborn period. Although clear correspondence is lacking between specific elicitors and facial templates of emotion, the low coherence detected in the few existing studies (Camras, 1992) could reflect difficulties in specifying the appropriate situation/event related to a given facial expression as a function of the infants' current abilities. One important direction for future research would be to test within appropriate ecological contexts (e.g. Soussignan *et al.*, 1999; Schaal *et al.*, 2000) and emotionally-relevant paradigms (e.g. De Casper and Carstens, 1981; Blass *et al.*, 1984) whether the patterning of facial movements corresponds to specific templates of emotion when compared with stimuli irrelevant to the situation.

The ontogenetic perspective of emotional development may also help to clarify definitional issues that are hotly debated in emotion psychology, such as minimal cognitive requirements, or the status of the subjective experience of emotion (Ekman and Davidson, 1994). First, cognitively-orientated theorists emphasize the process of 'meaning analysis' in the inception of emotion (e.g. Lazarus, 1991; Sroufe, 1996).

Although it has been suggested that representational cognition is needed for inducing emotion, our overview highlights the point that appraisal processes are operating at a certain level in the neonatal period and are involved in the onset of emotional responses, or at least of emotional expressivity. For instance, some ecologically-relevant stimuli that are not intrinsically unpleasant (e.g. stroking, singing voice, milk odour) may generate negative facial responses when they are related to the violation of an expectancy (Blass et al., 1984), the loss of a contingency (De Casper and Carstens, 1981), or when they have acquired a meaning in the context of feeding (Soussignan et al., 1999). Thus, affective responses do not appear, at birth, to be strongly stereotyped or reflex-like, but rather as part of an organized cognitive system devised to register the relevance of environmental events in function of the individual's history and current needs. One can assume that emotion and cognition, at least under their implicit form, appear already at birth as interdependent processes with causal reciprocity. On the one hand, cognitive processing, based on memory of past events, may trigger emotional responses. On the other hand, emotion in signalling events that are hedonically loaded (pleasant versus unpleasant) and relevant to adaptive purposes and individual well-being (bodily needs, goals) influences cognitive processing in rending a situation more strongly salient to an organism.

Secondly, cognitively-orientated investigators have stressed the importance of emergent conscience in the subjective experience of emotion. Consciousness is traditionally viewed as a hallmark of human cognition and the core element of feeling (e.g. Clore, 1994). The question of whether newborns have rudiments of self-representation or awareness of others, and thus evince feeling, may be difficult to resolve empirically. Although a number of authors speculate that infants' facial and vocal imitation during the first days of life reflect a certain level of consciousness, voluntary behaviour, or signs of shared experience with others (Kugiumutzakis, 1999; Trevarthen and Aitken, 2001), more parsimonious interpretations have been provided to explain these neonatal abilities (Rochat and Striano, 1999; Nadel and Potier, 2002). However, the existing findings do not rule out the hypothesis that some forms of implicit experience of self, objects, or persons could be present at birth.

An intriguing study conducted by Rochat and Hespos (1997) showed that newborn infants tend to display more rooting responses to external tactile stimulation on the perioral region than to self-produced stimulation. These findings were taken as evidence that newborns express rudiments of discrimination between their own body and their environment (i.e. ecological self). However, it is not entirely clear in this study whether newborns were really sensitive to their proprioceptive stimulations because they could also have responded differentially to their own- versus experimenter-induced touch as a possible consequence of differences in tactile parameter (e.g. intensity and temporal dynamics of pressure). Given that such findings have great momentum for a theory on the origin of subjective experience of emotion, replication is required with a more controlled experimental design. Another indirect line of evidence exists when one assume that proprioceptive feedbacks generated by facial expressions could contribute to the subjective experience of emotion. Although not testable in newborns, an intra-individual function of facial expressions cannot be rejected in children and adults. Substantial evidence is indeed at hand that sensory feedback from muscular actions is involved in subjective feelings (Adelmann and Zajonc, 1989; McIntosh, 1996; Ceschi and Scherer, 2001). For example, some results suggest that the proprioceptive/cutaneous cues produced by smiling contribute to the experience of positive emotion (Strack *et al.*, 1988, Soussignan, 2002). There is no a priori reason that similar processes do not operate from early infancy onwards.

It is clear from this brief survey that neonatal emotion must not be seen as resulting from the operation of either entirely unorganized or as entirely structured/hard-wired entities, but rather from integrative processes embedded in the infant's ontogenetic capacities, and the demands of its internal and external environment. Given the scarceness of experimental data on emotion during the newborn period, future research should investigate key processes underlying infant–environment transactions. A functionalist approach to emotional development yields not only a dynamic toolkit for exploring the processes mediating the emergence of behaviour, but also sheds light on the origins of cognitive and social development.

Acknowledgements

The research on neonatal olfaction reported in this chapter was partially funded by the Direction Générale de l'Alimentation (programme 'Aliment Demain'), Ministères de la Recherche et de la Technologie, et de l'Agriculture. Drs Luc Marlier and Tao Jiang are acknowledged for their help.

References

Ackerman, B. P., Abe, J. A., and Izard, C. E. (1998). Differential emotion theory and emotional development: mindful and modularity. In *What develops in emotional development?* (ed. M. F. Mascolo and S. Griffin), pp. 85–106. New York, NY: Plenum Press.

Adelman, P. K. and Zajonc, R. (1989). Facial efference and the experience of emotion. *Annual Review of Psychology*, **40**, 249–80.

Alberts, J. R. (1987). Early learning and ontogenetic adaptation. In *Perinatal development. A psychobiological perspective* (ed. N. A. Krasnegor, E. M. Blass, M. A. Hofer, and W. P. Smotherman), pp. 11–37. Orlando, FL: Academic Press.

Aldridge, M. A., Stillman, R. D., and Bower, T. G. R. (2001). Newborn categorization of vowels-like sounds. *Developmental Science*, **4(2)**, 20–32.

Balogh, R. D. and Porter, R. H. (1986). Olfactory preferences resulting from mere exposure in human neonates. *Infant Behavior and Development*, **9**, 395–401.

Barr, R. G., Quek, V., Cousineau, D., *et al.* (1994). Effects of intraoral sucrose on crying, mouthing, and mouth-hand contact in newborn and six-weeks old infants. *Developmental Medicine and Child Neurology*, **36**, 606–18.

Barrett, K. (1993). The development of nonverbal communication of emotion: a functionalist perspective. *Journal of Nonverbal Behavior*, **17**, 145–69.

Barrett, K. (1998). A functionalist perspective to the development of emotions. In *What develops in emotional development?* (ed. M. F. Mascolo and S. Griffin), pp. 109–33. New York, NY: Plenum Press.

Barrett, K. C. and Campos, J. (1987). Perspectives on emotional development: II. A functionalist approach to emotions. In *Handbook of infant development* (ed. J. D. Osofsky), pp. 555–78. New York, NY: Wiley.

Bartocci, M., Winberg, J., Ruggiero, C., *et al.* (2000). Activation of olfactory cortex in newborn infants after odor stimulation: a functional near-infrared spectroscopy study. *Pediatric Research*, **48**, 18–23.

Bartocci, M., Winberg, J., Papendieck, G., *et al.* (2001). Cerebral hemodynamic response to unpleasant odors in the preterm newborn measured by near-infrared spectroscopy. *Pediatric Research*, **50**, 324–30.

Batki, A., Baron-Cohen, S., Wheelwright, S., *et al.* (2000). Is there an innate gaze module? Evidence from human neonates. *Infant Behavior and Development*, **23**, 223–9.

Bergamasco, N. H. P. and Beraldo, K. E. A. (1990). Facial expressions of neonates infants in response to gustatory stimuli. *Brazilian Journal of Medical Biological Research*, **23**, 245–9.

Berridge, K. C. (2000). Taste reactivity: Measuring hedonic impact in human infants and animals. *Neuroscience Biobehavioral Reviews*, **24**, 173–98.

Bilko, A., Altbäcker, V., and Hudson, R. (1994). Transmission of food preference in the rabbit: the means of information transfer. *Physiology and Behavior*, **56**, 907–12.

Blass, E. M. (1990). Suckling: determinants, changes, mechanisms, and lasting impressions. *Developmental Psychology*, **26(5)**, 20–33.

Blass, E. M. and Ciaramitaro, V. (1994). Oral determinants of state, affect, and action in newborn humans. *Monographs of the Society for Research in Child Development*, **59**, 1–96.

Blass, E. M. and Hoffmeyer, L. B. (1991). Sucrose as an analgesic in newborn infants. *Pediatrics*, **87**, 215–18.

Blass, E. M. and Shah, A. (1995). Pain-reducing properties off sucrose in human newborns. *Chemical Senses*, **20**, 29–35.

Blass, E. M., Ganchrow, J. R., and Steiner, J. E. (1984). Classical conditioning in newborn humans 2–48 hours of age. *Infant behavior and Development*, **7**, 223–35.

Blass, E. M., Fitzgerald, E., and Kehoe, P. (1987). Interactions between sucrose, pain and isolation distress. *Pharmacology Biochemestry and behavior*, **26**, 483–9.

Bremner, J. G. (2002). The nature of imitation by infants. *Infant Behavior and Development*, **141**, 1–3.

Bridges, K. M. B. (1932). Emotional development in early infancy. *Child Development*, **3**, 324–41.

Butterworth, G. and Hopkins, B. (1988). Hand-mouth coordination in the newborn baby. *British Journal of Developmental Psychology*, **6**, 303–14.

Cabanac, M. (1971). Physiological role of pleasure. *Science*, **173**, 1103–7.

Cabanac, M. (1979). Sensory pleasure. *Quarterly Review of Biology*, **54**, 1–29.

Cabanac, M. and Fantino, M. (1977). Origin of olfacto-gustatory alliesthesia: intestinal sensitivity to carbohydrate concentration? *Physiology and Behavior*, **18**, 1039–45.

Campos, J. J., Emde, R. R., Gaensbauer, T., *et al.* (1975). Cardiac and behavioral interrelationships in the reactions of infants to strangers. *Developmental Psychology*, **11**, 589–601.

Campos, J., Campos, R., and Barrett, K. (1989). Emergent themes in the study of emotional development and emotion regulation. *Developmental Psychology*, **25**, 394–402.

Camras, L. A. (1992). Expressive development and basic emotions. *Cognition and Emotion*, **6**, 269–83.

Camras, L. A., Malatesta, C., and Izard, C. E. (1991). The development of facial expressions in infancy. In *Fundamentals of nonverbal behavior* (ed. S. Feldman and B. Rimé), pp. 73–105. Cambridge: Cambridge University Press.

Cassia, V. M., Simion, F., and Umiltà, C. (2001). Face preference at birth: the role of an orienting mechanism. *Developmental Science*, **4**, 101–8.

Ceschi, G. and Scherer, K. (2001). Contrôler l'expression faciale et changer l'émotion: une approche développementale. N° thématique: Émotion et Développement, *Enfance*, **3**, 257–69.

Clore, G. L. (1994). Why emotions are never unconscious. In *The nature of emotion* (ed. P. Ekman and R. J. Davidson), pp. 285–90. New York, NY: Oxford University Press.

Coureaud, G., Schaal, B., Hudson, R., *et al.* (2002). Transnatal olfactory continuity in the rabbit: behavioral evidence and short-term consequence of its disruption, *Developmental Psychobiology*, **40**, 372–90.

Crook, C. K. and Lipsitt, L. P. (1976). Neonatal nutritive sucking: effect of taste stimulation upon sucking and heart rate. *Child Development*, **47**, 518–22.

Darwin, C. (1965). *The expression of the emotion in man and animals.* Chicago: University of Chicago Press (originally published 1872).

Darwin, C. (1877). A biographical sketch of an infant. *Mind*, **2**, 285–94.

De Casper, A. J. and Carstens, A. A. (1981). Contingencies of stimulation: effects on learning and emotion in neonates. *Infant Behavior and Development*, **4**, 19–35.

De Casper, A. J. and Fifer, W. P. (1980). Of human bonding: newborns prefer their mother's voices. *Science*, **208**, 1174–6.

De Casper, A. J. and Spence, M. J. (1986). Prenatal maternal speech influences newborns' perception of speech sounds. *Infant Behavior and Development*, **9**, 133–50.

Delevati, N. M. and Bergamasco, H. P. (1999). Pain in the neonate: an analysis of facial movements and crying in response to nociceptive stimuli. *Infant Behavior and Development*, **22**, 137–43.

Dondi, M., Simion, F., and Caltran, G. (1999). Can newborns discriminate between their own cry and the cry of another newborn infant? *Developmental Psychology*, **2**, 418–26.

Ekman, P. and Davidson, R. J. (1994). *The nature of emotion.* New York, NY: Oxford University Press.

Ekman, P. and Friesen, W. (1978) *Facial Action Coding System: a technique for measurement of facial movement.* Palo Alto, CA: Consulting Psychologist Press.

Engen, T. (1988). The acquisition of odour hedonics. In *Perfurmery: the psychology and biology of fragrance* (ed. S. Van Toller and G. H. Dodd), pp. 79–90. London: Chapman and Hall.

Engen, T. and Lipsitt, L. P. (1965). Decrement and recovery of responses to olfactory stimuli in the human neonate. *Journal of Comparative and Physiological Psychology*, **59**, 312–16.

Engen, T., Lipsitt, L. P., and Kaye, H. (1963). Olfactory responses and adaptation in the human neonate. *Journal of Comparative and Physiological Psychology*, **56**, 73–7.

Faas, A. E., Sponton, E. D., Moya, P. R., *et al.* (2000). Differential responsiveness to alcohol odor in human neonates. Effects of maternal consumption during gestation. *Alcohol*, **22**, 7–17.

Field, T. M., Woodson, R., Greenberg, R., *et al.* (1982). Discrimination and imitation of facial expressions by neonates. *Science*, **218**, 179–81.

Field, T. M., Woodson, R., Cohen, D., *et al.* (1983). Discrimination and imitation of facial expressions by term and preterm neonates. *Infant Behavior and Development*, **6**, 485–9.

Field, T. M., Cohen, D., Garcia, R., *et al.* (1984). Mother-stranger discrimination the newborn. *Infant Behavior and Development*, **7**, 19–25.

Fisher, K. W., Shaver, P. R., and Carnochan, P. (1990). How emotions develop and how they organise development. *Cognition and Emotion*, **4**, 81–127.

Fogel, A. and Thelen, E. (1987). Development of early expressive and communicative action: Reinterpreting the evidence from the dynamic systems perspective. *Developmental Psychology*, **23**, 747–61.

Fox, N. and Davidson, R. J. (1986). Taste elicited changes in facial signs of emotion and the asymmetry of brain electrical activity in human newborns. *Neuropsychologia*, **24**, 417–22.

Frijda, N. H. (1986). *The emotions.* Cambridge: Cambridge University Press.

Frijda, N. H. (1994). Emotions require cognitions, even if simple ones. In *The nature of emotion* (ed. P. Ekman and R. J. Davidson), pp. 197–202. New York, NY: Oxford University Press.

Ganchrow, J. R., Steiner, J. E., and Daher, M. (1983). Neonatal facial expressions in response to different qualities and intensities of gustatory stimuli. *Infant Behavior and Development*, **6**, 189–200.

Goubet, N., Rattaz, C., Pierrat, V., *et al.* (2003). Olfactory experience mediates response to pain in preterm newborns. *Developmental Psychobiology*, **42**, 171–80.

Grunau, R. V. E. and Craig, K. D. (1987). Pain expression in neonates: facial action and cry. *Pain*, **28**, 395–410.

Hall, W. G. and Oppenheim, R. W. (1987). Developmental psychobiology: prenatal, perinatal and early postnatal aspects. *Annual Review of Psychology*, **38**, 91–128.

Haviland, J. M. and Lelwica, M. (1987). The induced affect response: 10-week-old infants' responses to three emotional expressions. *Developmental Psychology*, **23**, 97–104.

Hepper, P. G. (1988). Adaptive fetal learning: prenatal exposure to garlic affects postnatal preferences. *Animal Behavior*, **36**, 935–6.

Hepper, P. G. (1995). Human fetal olfactory learning. *International Journal of Prenatal and Perinatal Psychology and Medicine*, **7**, 147–51.

Hepper, P. G. (1996). Fetal memory: does it exist? What does it do? *Acta Paediatrica*, **416**, 16–20.

Hiatt, S., Campos, J., and Emde, R. (1979). Facial patterning and infant emotional expression: Happiness, surprise, and fear. *Child Development*, **50**(10), 20–35.

Izard, C. E. (1991). *The psychology of emotions.* New York, NY: Plenum Press.

Izard, C. E. (1994). Innate and universal facial expressions: evidence from developmental and cross-cultural research. *Psychological Bulletin*, **115**, 288–99.

Izard, C. E. and Malatesta, C. Z. (1987). Perspectives on emotional development I: differential emotions theory of early emotional development. In *Handbook of infant development*, 2nd edn (ed. J. D. Osofsky), pp. 494–554. New York, NY: Wiley Interscience.

Izard, C. E., Fantauzzo, C. A., Castle, J. M., *et al.* (1995). The ontogeny and significance of infants' facial expressions in the first 9 months of life. *Developmental Psychology*, **31**, 997–1013.

Jensen, K. (1932). Differential reactions to taste and temperature stimuli in newborn infants. *Genetic Psychology Monographs*, **12**, 363–479.

Johnson, M. H. and Morton, J. (1991). *Biology and cognitive development.* Oxford: Blackwell.

Johnson, M. H., Dziurawiec, S., Ellis, H., *et al.* (1991). Newborns' preferential tracking of face-like stimuli and its subsequent decline. *Cognition*, **40**, 1–19.

Joseph, R. (2000). Fetal brain and cognitive development. *Developmental Review*, **20**, 81–98.

Kaiser, S. and Wehrle, T. (2001). Facial expressions as indicators of appraisal processes. In *Appraisal processes in emotion* (ed. K. R. Scherer, A. Schorr, and T, Johnstone), pp. 285–300. Oxford: Oxford University Press.

Kahneman, D., Diener, E., and Schwarz, N. (1999). *Well-being: the foundations of hedonic psychology.* New York, NY: Russel Stage Foundation.

Kanwisher, N. (2000). Domain specificity in face perception. *Trends in Cognitive Science*, **3**, 759–62.

Kugiumutzakis, G. (1993). Intersubjective vocal imitation in early mother-infant interaction. In *New perspective in early communicative development* (ed. J. Nadel and L. Camaioni), pp. 23–47. London: Routledge.

Kugiumutzakis, G. (1999). Genesis and development of early infant mimesis to facial and vocal models. In *Imitation in infancy* (ed. J. Nadel and G. Butterworth), pp. 36–59. Cambridge: Cambridge University Press.

Lafreniere, P. J. (2000). *Emotional development: a biosocial perspective*. Belmont: Wadsworth.

Lazarus, R. S. (1991). *Emotion and adaptation*. New York, NY: Oxford University Press.

Lecanuet, J. P., Fifer, W. P., Krasnegor, N. A., *et al.* (1995). *Fetal development: a psychobiological perspective*. Hillsdale: LEA.

Legerstee, M. (1991). The role of person and object in eliciting early imitation. *Journal of Experimental Child Psychology*, **51**, 423–33.

Leventhal, H. and Scherer, K. S. (1987). The relationship of emotion to cognition: a functional approach to a semantic controversy. *Cognition and Emotion*, **1**, 3–28.

Lew, A. R. and Butterworth, G. (1995). The effects of hunger on hand-mouth coordination in newborn infants. *Developmental Psychology*, **31**, 456–63.

Lewis, M. (1993). The emergence of human emotions. In *Emotions* (ed. M. Lewis and M. Haviland), pp. 223–35. New York, NY: Guilford Press.

Lewis, M. D. and Douglas, L. (1998). A dynamic systems approach to cognition-emotion interactions in development. In *What develops in emotional development?* (ed. M. F. Mascolo and S. Griffin), pp. 159–188. New York: Plenum Press.

Lewis, M. and Michalson, L. (1983). *Children's emotions and moods: development theory and measurement*. New York, NY: Plenum.

Lindy, B. and Field, T. (1996). Newborns of mothers with depressive symptoms are less expressive. *Infant Behavior and Development*, **19**, 419–24.

Lipsitt, L. P. and Behl, G. (1990). Taste-mediated differences in the sucking behavior of human newborns. In *Taste, experience and feeding* (ed. E. D. Capaldi and T. L. Powley), pp. 77–93. Washington, DC: American Psychological Association.

Macfarlane, A. J. (1975). Olfaction in the development of social preferences in the human neonate. *Ciba Foundation Symposia*, **33**, 103–17.

Makin, J. W. and Porter, R. H. (1989). Attractiveness of lactating females' breast odors to neonates. *Child Development*, **60**, 803–10.

Malatesta, C. Z., Culver, C., Tesman, J. R., *et al.* (1989). The development of emotion expression during the first two years of life. *Monographs of the Society for the Research in Child Development*, Serial No. **219**, Vol. 54.

Marlier, L., Schaal, B., and Soussignan, R. (1998). Neonatal responsiveness to the odor of amniotic fluid and lacteal fluids: A test of perinatal chemosensory continuity. *Child Development*, **69**, 611–23.

Martin, G. B. and Clark, R. D. (1982). Distress crying in neonates: species and peer specificity. *Developmental Psychology*, **18**, 3–9.

Mascolo, M. F. and Griffin, S. (1998). *What develops in emotional development?* New York, NY: Plenum Press.

Mastropieri, D. and Turkewitz, G. (1999). Prenatal experience and neonatal responsiveness to vocal expressions of emotion. *Developmental Psychobiology*, **35**, 204–11.

Matias, R. and Cohn, J. F. (1993). Are Max-specified infant facial expressions during face-to-face interaction consistent with differential emotions theory? *Developmental Psychology*, **29**, 524–31.

McIntosh, D. N. (1996) Facial feedback hypotheses: evidence, implications, and directions. *Motivation and Emotion*, **20**, 121–47.

Meltzoff, A. N. and Moore, M. K. (1977). Imitation of facial and manual gestures by human neonates. *Science*, **198**, 75–8.

Meltzoff, A. N. and Moore, M. K. (1997). Explaining facial imitation: a theoretical model. *Early Development and Parenting*, **6**, 179–92.

Mennella, J. A. and Beauchamp, G. (1991). Maternal diet alters the sensory qualities of human milk and the nursling's behavior. *Pediatrics*, **88**, 737–44.

Mennella, J. A., Johnson, A., and Beauchamp, G. K. (1995). Garlic ingestion by pregnant women alters the odor of amniotic fluid. *Chemical Senses*, **20**, 207–09.

Molina, M. and Jouen, F. (1998). Modulation of the palmar grasp behavior in neonates according to texture property. *Infant Behavior and Development*, **21**, 659–67.

Moore, B. S. (1990). The origins and development of empathy. *Motivation and Emotion*, **14**, 75–80.

Nadel, J. and Butterworth, G. (1999). *Imitation in infancy*. Cambridge, MA: Cambridge University Press.

Nadel, J. and Potier, C. (2002). Imiter et être imité dans le développement de l'intentionnalité. In *Imiter pour découvrir l'humain* (ed. J. Nadel and J. Decety), pp. 83–104. Paris: PUF.

Nelson, C. A. (1987). The recognition of facial expressions in the first two years of life: mechanisms and development. *Child Development*, **58**, 889–909.

Oster, H. and Rosenstein, D. (in press). Baby-FACS: *analyzing facial movement in infants*. Palto Alto, CA: Consulting Psychologists Press.

Oster, H., Hegley, D., and Nagel, L. (1992). Adult judgments and fine-grained analysis of infant-facial expressions: testing the validity of a priori coding formulas. *Developmental Psychology*, **28**, 1115–31.

Pascalis, O., de Schonen, S., Morton, J., *et al.* (1995). Mother's face recognition by neonates: a replication and extension. *Infant Behavior and Development*, **18**, 79–85.

Peiper, A. (1963). *Cerebral function in infancy and childhood*. New York, NY: Consultants Bureau.

Rochat, P. (1987). Mouthing and grasping in neonates: evidence for the early detection of what hard or soft substances afford for action. *Infant Behavior and Development*, **10**, 435–49.

Rochat, P. and Hespos, S. J. (1997). Differential rooting response to neonates: evidence for an early sense. *Early Development and Parenting*, **6**, 105–12.

Rochat, P. and Striano, T. (1999). Socio-cognitive development in the first year. In *Early social cognition: understanding others in the first month of life* (ed. P. Rochat), pp. 3–34. Mahwah, NJ: Erlbaum.

Rosenstein, D. and Oster, H. (1988). Differential facial responses to four basic tastes in newborns. *Child Development*, **59**, 1555–68.

Royet, J. P., Zald, D., Versace, R., *et al.* (2000). Emotional responses to pleasant and unpleasant olfactory, visual, and auditory stimuli: a positron emission tomography study. *Journal of Neuroscience*, **15**, 7752–9.

Rozin, P. and Fallon, A. E. (1987). A perspective on disgust. *Psychological Review*, **94**, 23–41.

Saarni, C., Mumme, D. L., and Campos, J. J. (1998). Emotional development: action, communication, and understanding. In *Handbook of child psychology: social, emotional, and personality development* (ed. W. Damon and N. Eisenberg), Vol. 3, pp. 237–309. New York, NY: John Wiley.

Sagi, A. and Hoffman, M. L. (1976). Empathic distress in the newborn. *Developmental Psychology*, **12**, 175–6.

Schaal, B. (1988). Olfaction in infants and children: developmental and functional perspectives. *Chemical Senses*, **13**, 145–90.

Schaal, B. and Orgeur, P. (1992). Olfaction *in utero*: can the rodent model be generalized? *Quarterly Journal of Experimental Psychology*, **44B**, 245–78.

Schaal, B., Montagner, H., Hertling, E., *et al.* (1980). Les stimulations olfactives dans les relations entre l'enfant et sa mère. *Reproduction, Nutrition, Développement*, **20**, 843–58.

Schaal, B., Orgeur, P., and Arnould, C. (1995a). Chemosensory preferences in newborn lambs: Prenatal and perinatal determinants. *Behaviour*, **132**, 352–65.

Schaal, B., Orgeur, P., and Rognon, C. (1995b). Odor sensing in the human fetus: anatomical, functional and chemo-ecological bases. In *Prenatal development: A psychobiological perspective* (ed. J-P. Lecanuet, N. A. Krasnegor, W. A. Fifer, and W, Smotherman), pp., 205–37. Erlbaum, Hillsdale, NJ.

Schaal, B., Marlier, L., and Soussignan, R. (1998a). Olfactory function in the human fetus: evidence from selective neonatal responsiveness to the odor of amniotic fluid. *Behavioral Neuroscience*, **112**, 1438–49.

Schaal, B., Rouby, C., Marlier, L., *et al.* (1998b). Variabilité et universaux au sein de l'espace perçu des odeurs: approches inter-culturelles de l'hédonisme olfactif. In *Géographie des odeurs* (ed. R. Dulau and J. R. Pitte), pp. 25–47. Paris: L'Harmattan.

Schaal, B., Lecanuet, J. P., and Granier-Deferre, C. (1999). Sensory and integrative development in the human fetus and perinate: the usefulness of animal models. In *Animal models of human cognition and emotion* (ed. M. Haug and R. E. Whalen), pp. 119–42. Washington, DC: American Psychological Association.

Schaal, B., Marlier, L., and Soussignan, R. (2000). Human fetuses learn odours from their pregnant mother's diet. *Chemical Senses*, **25**, 729–37.

Schaal, B., Soussignan, R., and Marlier, L. (2002). Olfactory cognition at the start of life: the perinatal shaping of selective odor responsiveness. In *Olfaction, gustation and cognition* (ed. C. Rouby, B. Schaal, D. Dubois, R. Gervais and A. Holley), pp. 421–40. New York, NY: Cambridge University Press.

Scherer, K. R. (1992). What does a facial expression express? In *International review of studies of emotion* (ed. K. T. Strongman), Vol. 2, pp. 139–65. New York: Wiley.

Scherer, K. R. (1994). An emotion's occurrence depends on the relevance of an event to the organism's goal/need hierarchy. In *The nature of emotion* (ed. P. Ekman and R. J. Davidson), pp. 227–31. New York: Oxford University Press.

Scherer, K. R. (2000). Psychological models of emotion. In *The neuropsychology of emotion* (J. C. Borod), pp. 137–62. Oxford: Oxford University Press.

Scherer, K. R., Schorr, A., and Johnstone, T. (2001). *Appraisal processes in emotion*. Oxford: Oxford University Press.

Schneirla, T. C. (1967). Aspects of stimulation and organization in approach-withdrawal processes underlying vertebrate behavioral development. In *Advances in the study of behaviour* (ed. D. S. Lehrman, R. A. Hinde, and E. Schaw), pp. 1–74, vol.1. Academic Press, New York.

Self, P. A., Horowitz, F. D., and Paden, L. Y. (1972). Olfaction in newborn infants. *Developmental Psychology*, **7**, 349–63.

Sherman, M. C. (1927). The differentiation of emotional responses in infants. I. Judgments of emotional responses from motion picture views and from actual observations. *Journal of Comparative Psychology*, **7**, 265–84.

Shide, D. J. and Blass, E. M. (1989). Opioid-like effects of intraoral infusions of corn oil and polycose on stress reactions in 10-day-old rats. *Behavioral Neuroscience*, **103**, 1168–75.

Simion, F., Cassia, V. M., Turati, C., *et al.* (2001). The origins of face perception: specific versus non-specific mechanisms. *Infant and Child Development*, 10, 59–65.

Simner, M. L. (1971). Newborns' response to the cry of another infant. *Developmental Psychology*, 5, 136–50.

Slater, A., Morison, V., and Rose, D. (1984). Habituation in the newborn. *Infant Behavior and Development*, 7, 183–200.

Smith, C. A. and Scott, H. S. (1997). A componential approach to the meaning of facial expressions. In *The psychology of facial expression* (ed. J. A. Russell and J. M. Fernandez-Dols), pp. 229–54. Cambridge: Cambridge University Press.

Smotherman, W. P. (1982). Odor aversion learning by the rat fetus. *Physiology and Behavior*, 29, 769–71.

Smotherman, W. P. and Robinson, S. R. (1996). The development of behavior before birth. *Developmental Psychology*, 32, 425–34.

Soussignan. R. (2002). Duchenne smile, emotional experience and autonomic reactivity: a test of the facial feedback hypothesis. *Emotion*, 2, 52–74.

Soussignan. R. and Schaal, B. (1996a). Children's facial responsiveness to odors: Influences of hedonic valence of odor, gender, age and social presence. *Developmental Psychology*, 32, 367–79.

Soussignan. R. and Schaal, B. (1996b). Forms and social signal value of smiles associated with pleasant and unpleasant sensory experience. *Ethology*, 102, 10, 20–41.

Soussignan. R., Schaal, B., Schmit, G., *et al.* (1995). Facial responsiveness to odours in normal and pervasively developmentally disordered children. *Chemical Senses*, 25, 47–59.

Soussignan. R., Schaal, B., Marlier, L., *et al.* (1997). Facial and autonomic responses to biological and artificial olfactory stimuli in human neonates: re-examining early hedonic discrimination of odors. *Physiology and Behavior*, 62, 745–58.

Soussignan. R., Schaal, B., and Marlier, L. (1999). Olfactory alliesthesia in human neonates: Prandial state and stimulus familiarity modulate facial and autonomic responses to milk odors. *Developmental Psychobiology*, 35, 3–14.

Sroufe, L. A. (1979). *Socioemotional development*. In *Handbook of infant development* (ed. J. Osofsky), pp. 462–516. New York, NY: Wiley.

Sroufe, L. A. (1996). *Emotional development: the organization of emotional life in the early years.* Cambridge: Cambridge University Press.

Steiner, J. E. (1977). Facial expressions of the neonate infant indicating the hedonics of food-related chemical stimuli. In *Taste and development: the genesis of sweet preference* (ed. J. M. Weiffenbach), pp. 173–88. Bethesda: DHEW.

Steiner, J. E. (1979). Human facial expressions in response to taste and smell stimulation. In *Advances in Child Development and Behavior* (ed. H. W. Reese and L. P. Lipsitt), Vol. 13, pp. 257–93. New York, NY: Academic Press.

Steiner, J. E., Glaser, D., Hawilo, M. E., *et al.* (2001). Comparative evidence of hedonic impact: affective reactions to taste by human infants and other primates. *Neuroscience and Biobehavioral Reviews*, 25, 53–74.

Stenberg, C. and Campos, J. (1990). The development of anger expressions in infancy. In *Psychobiological and biological approaches to emotion* (ed. N. Stein, B. Leventhal, and T. Trabasso), pp. 247–82. Hillsdalle, NJ: Erlbaum.

Strack, F., Martin, L. L., and Stepper, S. (1988). Inhibiting and facilitating conditions of the human smile: a nonobstrusive test of the facial feedback hypothesis. *Journal of Personality and Social Psychology*, 54, 768–77.

Streri, A., Lhote, M., and Dutilleul, S. (2000). Haptic perception in newborns. *Developmental Science*, 3, 319–27.

Sullivan, R. and Toubas, P. (1998). Clinical usefulness of maternal odor in newborns: soothing and feeding preparatory responses. *Biology of the Neonate*, **74**, 402–8.

Sullivan, R. M. and Wilson, D. A. (1993). The role of the amygdala complex in early olfactory associative learning. *Behavioral Neuroscience*, **107**, 254–63.

Sullivan, R. M., Taborsky-Barba, S., Mendoza, R., *et al.* (1991). Olfactory classical conditioning in neonates. *Pediatrics*, **87**, 511–18.

Swanson, L. W. and Petrovich, G. D. (1998). What's the amygdala? *Trends in Neuroscience*, **21**, 323–31.

Toates, T. (1986). *Motivational systems*. Cambridge: Cambridge University Press.

Trevarthen, C. (1993). The function of emotions in early infant communication and development. In *New perspective in early communicative development* (ed. J. Nadel and L. Camaioni), pp 48–81. London: Routledge.

Trevarthen, C. and Aitken, K. (2001). Infant intersubjectivity: research, theory, and clinical applications. *Journal of Child Psychology and Child Psychiatry*, **42**, 3–48.

Valenza, E., Simion, F., Cassia, U., *et al.* (1996). Face preference at birth. *Journal of Experimental Psychology*, **22**, 892–903.

Varendi, H., Porter, R. H., and Winberg, J. (1994). Does the newborn baby find the nipple by smell? *Lancet*, **344**, 989–90.

Varendi, H., Christensson, K., Porter, R. H., *et al.* (1998). Soothing effect of amniotic fluid smell in newborn infants. *Early Human Development*, **51**, 47–55.

Walton, G. E., Bower, N. J. A., and Bower, T. G. R. (1992). Recognition of familiar faces by newborns. *Infant Behavior and Development*, **15**, 265–89.

Watson, J. B. and Morgan, J. J. (1917). Emotional reactions and psychological experimentation. *American Journal of Psychology*, **28**, 161–74.

Weinberg, K. M. and Tronick, E. Z. (1994). Beyond the face: an empirical study of infant affective configurations of facial, vocal, gestural, and regulatory behavior. *Child Development*, **65**, 1503–15.

Wilson, D. A. and Sullivan, R. M. (1994). Neurobiology of associate learning in the neonate: early olfactory learning. *Behavioral and Neural Biology*, **61**, 1–18.

Wolff, P. H. (1987). *The behavioral states and the expressions of emotion in early infancy*. Chicago: University of Chicago Press.

Zahn-Waxler, C. and Radke-Yarrow, M. (1990). The origins of emphatic concern. *Motivation and Emotion*, **14**, 107–30.

Zeifman, D., Delaney, S., and Blass, E. M. (1996). Sweet taste, looking, and calm in two and four-week-old infants: the eyes have it. *Developmental Psychology*, **32**, 1090–9.

Chapter 6

Emotions in early mimesis

Giannis Kugiumutzakis, Theano Kokkinaki,
Maria Makrodimitraki, and Elena Vitalaki

Introduction

The aim of the present chapter is to stress the role of emotion as one of the main components of imitation. Within this framework, we will describe evidence of emotions observed before, during and after imitative encounters in naturalistic or experimental settings, from birth up to 10 months of age (Kugiumutzakis, 1985, 1993, 1998, 1999; Kokkinaki, 1998; Trevarthen et al., 1999; Kokkinaki and Kuginmutzakis, 2000; Vitalaki, 2002; Markodimitraki, 2003).

According to ancient Greek thinkers, mimesis could not occur between emotionless persons (Kugiumutzakis, 1998; Bruner, 2002). Over the last 100 years, the emotional aspect of early mimesis has been noted by many developmentalists. Baldwin (1896) described the emotional origin of circular reaction/self-imitation—a non-random response 'selected' because of its increased vitality, represented by *pleasure*. Freud (1921) noted that there exists a path leading from identification by way of imitation to empathy and that identification is the original form of emotional tie with an 'object'. Guillaume (1926) considered mimesis in the context of smiles, fear, sympathy, etc., concluding that, while early imitation leads to sympathy, sympathy does not constitute the emotional aspect of early mimesis. Wallon described the sharing of emotions (through bodily and facial expressions) between adults and infants after their third month of life, and noted the emotional nature of early imitation, which he regarded as source of sympathy (see Nadel, 1994; Tremblay et al., this volume). Later, the hypothesis of a strong link between emotion and imitation was forgotten under the influence of Piaget.

The emotionless mimesis of the object

As Bruner (1983) notes, Piaget's contribution to our understanding of how the child's mind grows is tremendous. Piaget (1950, 1968; Piaget and Inhelder, 1969) gives equal status to cognitive and emotional aspects of every action. He assumes that the cognitive aspect provides the structure, and the emotional aspect provides the motives and the energetic force of behaviour. At the same time Piaget stresses that the source of motive for infant imitation, namely, the source of the emotion of 'interest' has a purely cognitive origin. In Stage IV of sensorimotor imitation he notes:

> The interest thus appears to come from a kind of conflict between the partial resemblance which makes the child want to assimilate, and the partial difference which attracts his attention the more because it is an obstacle to immediate reproduction. It is therefore this two-fold character of resemblance and opposition which seems to be the incentive for imitation' (Piaget, 1962, p. 51).

Not merely the interest of the infant in imitation, but mimesis itself results from intrapsychic, individual processes, which according to Piaget (1962, p. 2) dominate and lead to inter-personal relationships. At the root of Piaget's cognitivism is Baldwin's notion of initial a-dualism, Freud' s notion of narcissism (but without Narcissus) and the core idea of circular reaction/self-imitation. For Piaget, circular reaction is not to be equated with Baldwin's 'loose sense' of the term, but with Wallon's 'limited sense', namely, '… the functional use leading to the preservation or the rediscovery of a new result' (1936, p. 70). Unlike Piaget, however, both Baldwin and Wallon considered the emotional aspect of circular reaction/self-imitation. Piaget ignored emotion or, when he recognized it, it had to lead in automatic contagious crying (1962, p. 10) or (as in the case of interest) to have a cognitive origin.

Indeed, Piaget's views on the 'emotional' aspect of infant mimesis are in full agreement with his radical, emotionless, and utilitarian cognitivism. For Piaget (1968, p. 128), the common element between his cognitivism and Marx's 'primary proposition' is the interaction between the properties of human productivity and the properties of the object. It was the mimesis of an object (not of a person) that interested Piaget. For more than 40 years he emphasized the role played by imitation of an object and its usable properties in the genesis of representation and language (Piaget, 1936, pp. 375–6; 1962, pp. 65–6; 1980, p. 166). He portrayed the human infant as a lone, egocentric, chaotic, asocial, emotionless being, '… in a world of objects that he must array in space, time and causal relations …', as Bruner (1983) correctly observed. His baby was unable to discriminate the self from the other/model, because the object notion had not yet been formed, and for that reason mimesis of objects, up to the fourth stage, was both a part of circular reactions and accompanied by a 'causality through imitation, which is itself a device for making what looks interesting continue' (Piaget, 1962, pp. 71, 85). It was not a real, human baby. It was a constructed baby, at the mercy of a constructed a-dualism, 'amid the chaos of impressions by which he is beset' (Piaget, 1962, p. 83). It was the object notion and the imitation of objects that interested the constructed Piagetian baby—not the social reciprocity that Wallon discussed, the same Wallon who was accused by Piaget of leaping suddenly from neurology to sociology (Piaget, 1962, p. 68; Hobson, 2002, pp. 103–4)!

Wallon's voice was ignored in Anglophone Psychology (Nadel, 1994; Nadel and Butterworth, 1999) and the predominance of the Piagetian theory in Developmental Psychology brought about a long period of apathetic cognitivism. For many followers of Piaget, this characterization may appear to be unduly harsh, but in our opinion, it is obviously true for the following reason. Piaget (1962) made 58 general observations and more than 533 specific observations on infant imitation. Only seven of these observations were imitations of objects while the rest involved either imitation of persons (n = 479) or imitation of persons and objects (n = 47). However, Piaget focused on the object imitations. The rest were important to him only to stress, on the one hand, the role of assimilation in early cognitive development and, on the other hand, the way mimesis gives rise to representations. For Piaget (1962) the most interesting model was not an acting or interacting person, but the properties of an object. The most 'striking example of intelligent investigation' was when L tried to depict the solution she sought by mimicking with her mouth the opening of a match-box (Piaget, 1962, p. 65). We cannot imagine that his own three infants, as well as their mother and father (and some other persons in the family), did not smile or laugh during these 533 imitative episodes. However, Piaget (1962) only observed smiling in his own three infants on 13 occasions (obs. 2, 6, 8, 10, 23, 27, 34, 37), laughter on 20 occasions (obs. 4, 9, 14, 18, 20, 22, 23, 24, 25, 28, 40, 49), pleasure on three occasions (obs. 11, 44, 58), and crying on six occasions (obs. 1, 2). Emotions had to be there, but were ignored by Piaget, despite his thesis that all behaviour presupposes intelligence and motives in the form of emotions (1968, p. 15).

To paraphrase Bruner (1990, p. 1), in the last 30 years a silent (infant), but very expressive revolution has brought the inter-subjective infant mind back into the human sciences after a long period of apathetic cognitivism (e.g. Trevarthen 1977; Murray and Trevarthen, 1985; Stern, 1985; Nadel, 1994; Reddy et al., 1997; Braten, 1998; Butterworth, 1999; Reddy, 1999; Bruner, 2002; Hobson, 2002). Even students and supporters of Piaget admit that he disregarded the social and emotional factors of human development (Maratos, 1996, 1998).

Over the last 30 years there have been a number of comprehensive reviews of infant imitation (e.g. Zazzo, 1957; Maratos, 1973, 1982; Meltzoff and Moore, 1983; Nadel and Butterworth, 1999; Uzgiris, 1999). The majority of the studies cited were experimental attempts to establish the existence of neonatal mimesis, and its development during infancy and early childhood in both typical and atypical human populations, and in non-human species. Here, we present observations concerning the emotions that accompany mimesis during the first 10 months of human infancy.

Studying early mimesis

In an effort to understand the genesis and development of human mimesis we have conducted 11 empirical studies. Given the general aim of this chapter, we can only summarize the main results, especially those that are related to the emotional aspects of mimesis. In Table 6.1 there is a description of basic characteristics of each study.

In the first four experimental studies the neonates were examined in the maternity hospital immediately after birth and in the rest seven, longitudinal studies (Studies 5–11)

Table 6.1 The 11 studies on early imitation

Studies	Kind of study	Partners	n	Range of infant age	Kind of imitation	Study of emotions	Place
1. Kugiumutzakis 1985	Experimental cross-sectional	Neonate–experimenter	98	10–45 min	Facial	Descriptive	Crete
2. Kugiumutzakis 1985	Experimental cross-sectional	Neonate–experimenter	11	15–40 min	Facial	Descriptive	Crete
3. Kugiumutzakis 1985	Experimental cross-sectional	Neonate–experimenter	12	13–35 min	Facial	Descriptive	Crete
4. Kugiumutzakis 1985	Experimental cross-sectional	Neonate–experimenter	49	14–42 min	Facial, vocal	Descriptive	Crete
5. Kugiumutzakis 1985	Field study longitudinal	Infant–experimenter	14	1st h–6 months	Facial, vocal	Descriptive	Crete
6. Kugiumutzakis 1993	Naturalistic longitudinal	Mother–infant	42	15 days–6 months	Vocal	Descriptive	Crete
7. Kokkinaki 1998	Naturalistic longitudinal	Mother–infant, father–infant	45	2–6 months	All kinds	Systematic	Scotland
8. Kokkinaki 1998	Naturalistic longitudinal	Mother–infant father–infant	45	2–6 months	All kinds	Systematic	Crete
9. Vitalaki 2002	Naturalistic longitudinal	Grandmother–infant, mother–infant	48	2–10 months	All kinds	Descriptive	Crete
10. Vitalaki 2002	Naturalistic longitudinal	Mother–infant	26	2–10 months	All kinds	Descriptive	Crete
11. Markodimitraki 2003	Naturalistic longitudinal	Twin–twin, each twin with each parent and grandparent	8	1–10 months	All kinds	Systematic	Crete

we investigated the development of imitation, in the home setting, every 15 days, in dyadic interactions of the infants with the experimenter (Study 5) and with their mothers, fathers, grandmothers (Studies 6–10). In Study 11 we investigated the development of mimesis in the inter-actions of one pair of non-identical twins (a girl and a boy), as well as in the interactions of each twin with her/his mother, father, maternal grandmother and grandfather, and paternal grandmother and grandfather.

In the first three experimental studies neonates, regardless of whether they were born vaginally or by caesarian section and regardless of whether they were full- or preterms (32 weeks) imitated the facial models of tongue protrusion (TP) and mouth opening (MO). In the fourth experimental study, in addition to the above two models, full-term neonates imitated the model of eye movements (EM) and they clearly tried to imitate the vowel 'a', but not the consonant 'm' and the complex sound 'ang'.

The infant imitators used two strategies of attention to the models and three forms of reproductive behaviour. The fifth, longitudinal study added the finding that infant imitative ability remains constant during the first 6 months, but what will or will not be imitated changes. Imitation of TP and MO develops according to a U-shaped curve, imitation of the vocal models in an inversely U-shaped manner and imitation of EM in a negative linear fashion (Kugiumutzakis, 1985, 1998, 1999).

In the above six studies (Studies 6–11) parents and grandparents tended to imitate infants significantly more than *vice versa*. Vocal imitations were significantly more frequent than the other kinds of mimesis (facial imitation, etc.). The majority of the vocal sounds imitated were vowels (about 70%), and the remainder was consonant and vowel-consonant sounds. Mimesis took place more often in turn-takings than in co-actions or in combinations of turn-takings with co-actions. The ability of infants and adults to imitate remained constant during the first 10 months (Kugiumutzakis, 1985, 1993, 1998, 1999; Kokkinaki, 1998; Trevarthen *et al.*, 1999; Vitalaki, 2002; Markodimitraki, 2003).

Emotions in early mimesis: 'uncontrolled observations'

Elsewhere (Kugiumutzakis, 1983, 1985, 1998) we have described the relevance of the ancient 'anecdotal' observations on early imitation made by Darwin (1872), Preyer (1892), and other observers during the last three centuries. These observations have been confirmed in the last 30 years (Butterworth, 1999). What are missing are reports of the complex regulatory behaviour that accompany target behaviours in experimental studies of imitation which go mostly unnoted and unreported. To his credit, Trevarthen (1977) has stressed the value of descriptive observations of these collateral behaviours some of which we will discuss below.

'Interest' as part of neonatal imitation

The following three observations indicate that the emotion of interest is present before imitation, and directs the infant's attention either to the moving part of the experimenter's face in the case of the facial models or to the source of the sound in the case of the vocal models. It is also present during imitation, when the infant explores, corrects, or stops the imitative activity. During the model's action, the infant's interest functions in an inter-mental level, while during the reproduction of the models it functions intra-mentally. In both cases, interest seems to be a precondition for neonatal mimesis (Kugiumutzakis, 1985, 1988, 1998).

Observation 1

The great majority of the neonates directed their attention, in an effortful way, to the moving part of the adult model's face during presentations of tongue protrusion (TP), mouth-opening (MO), and eye movements (EM). The infants' attention intensified from a relatively fixed gaze to selective visual exploration of the moving part of the experimenter's face with clear interest while frowning. Visual exploration and frowning of preterm neonates lasted longer than those of full-term newborns. According to Darwin 'the frown shows that the mind is intent on one object'. (Darwin, 1938, in N Notebook, obs. 58, cited in Gruber, 1974, p. 341; see also Darwin, 1872, pp. 220–6)

Observation 2

During the presentation of the vocal model for 'a', we observed that the majority of imitators turned their heads to localize the sound source that was accompanied by eye widening and elevated brows. According to Rinn (1984) the latter expressions occur in attentive listening.

Observation 3

We noticed three forms of reproductive behaviour of the adult's facial expressions. In the first form, they simply approximated a replication of the facial model. In the second form, called 'improvement of imitation after several trials', the neonates reproduced the model a number of times, and on each successive trial they converged towards a more precise match. To achieve this aim their attention had to be directed upon every step in their imitative activity and their face looked very 'serious' during these moments. In the third form, we called 'deterioration of imitation after several trials', the first imitative effort was a satisfactory reproduction of the model, but as the newborns continued their actions, they did not produce a more accurate replication of the model's expressions. Instead, in every additional 'effort' they depart more and more from their first successful effort, as if they had lost interest in imitating the model. The fleeting nature of interest during this form of imitation seemed apparent.

Bodily postures in neonatal imitation

Observation 4

The postural comfort of the neonates was crucial during the presentation of the facial models. During the presentation of the vocal models the neonates were lying down on their bed. It seems that this posture helped them more than the upright position to observe and reproduce the sound 'a'.

Observation 5

The imitative responses to sound 'a' were strained. The neonates appeared to be trying hard to emit the sound; the result was usually an intense explosion of a prolonged and unstructured 'a' sound. The response of the neonates frequently was accompanied by stretching hand movements and closed eyes. Not only their face, but their whole body appeared to be involved in this selective imitation of sound.

The above two observations indicate that an appropriate posture during testing seems to be a precondition for the appearance of Behavioural State 3 (open eyes, regular respiration, and lack of gross movements and vocalization) and for the emergence of interest. Posture may help or hinder the neonate ability to perceive and react to the model's target behaviour. Furthermore, along with parts of the face the whole body participates in neonatal facial imitation; this occurs to an even greater extent during vocal mimesis of 'a' (Kugiumutzakis, 1985, 1988, 1998). Our observations support Wallon's thesis concerning the role of bodily postures in emotional expression and in the regulation of the intensity of social involvement (see Nadel, 1994, p. 180).

Pleasure in early mimesis

In Study 5 we observed the first appearance of infant pleasure before, during and after imitation, mimesis of the rhythm of the vocal models, as well as clear avoidance reactions. Additional examples are given in the next three observations.

Observation 6

The first appearance of infant smiling in response to the models was observed 15 days after birth. After this age, the smile appeared continuously through 6 months of age; many infants smiled before, during, and after mimesis—which we interpreted to reflect their pleasure associated with the interaction. Almost 10 years after the completion of Study 5, we observed a smile after the presentation of the model to a 2-day-old (Kugiumutzakis, 1994). It was not an endogenous, but an exogenous, social smile, addressed to the experimenter (not the mother) in the maternity hospital. This newborn infant violated the doctrine stating that the exogenous smile is not present at birth, but begins to appear around the first or the second month of life (Plutchik, 1994, p. 208). We wonder whether it was only this neonate (and not many generations of newborns) that had violated this theoretical rule.

Observation 7

When imitation decreased as a response to the modeling of different facial models, the infants, instead of imitating, smiled to the experimenter or reacted by cooing and clear vocalizations, as if they wanted to 'express something' when they could not imitate him. During periods of both increased and decreased vocal imitation several infants reacted with *mimesis of the rhythm* of the vocal models. Thus, the smile (with or without vocal responses) either accompanied imitation or substituted for it, and the imitation of the rhythm likewise either accompanied vocal mimesis or substituted for it.

Observation 8

Sometimes, infants, even neonates, showed avoidance responses when an adult modeled an action. They moved their heads or their eyes or turned their whole body away from the experimenter's face. The message was clear to the experimenter, who either had to wait a few minutes until the baby re-engaged in the interaction or had to give up testing until the next day. The infants' involvement in the inter-subjective imitative games clearly depended on their transient emotions at the moment of the test.

The last three observations make several points. First, for the infant, by 15 days of age (if not earlier), the imitative interaction is usually a pleasurable experience, evidenced by clear, exogenous, social smiles, which either accompany mimesis (with or without vocal sounds) or substitute for it. Secondly, the substitution itself, during periods of decreased infant mimesis, may indicate intrinsic regulation of infant awareness (Trevarthen, 1998) as they display emotions of enjoyment and interest. The message received by the adult models is: 'At present I cannot share with you the same action, but still there exists something communicable between us—the pleasure to be, feel and act together, and its expression are my ways to sustain our communication'. Of course, adultomorphic terms cannot express precisely either the meaning of the infants' smiles or the feelings of the experimenter during the moments of substitution which may be something like: 'She/he is participating by offering "something" in our contact, she/he is "in"; *we are* an interacting unit'. And this "something" probably is equally, or even more, important to sharing the same action as the model. Thirdly, the mimesis of rhythm of the vocal models by a minority of infants both neonates (<45 minutes old) and older babies may indicate that an infant's musical and imitative abilities are somehow connected from the start (see Trevarthen, 2000, 2001, this volume). Fourthly, the intentional avoidance responses clearly indicate the core role of the infants' emotions in initiating and maintaining imitative communication—an infant's willingness to participate in imitative contacts seems to be regulated by her/his transient emotions or mood at the time of the test (Kugiumutzakis, 1985, 1988, 1998).

Confirming an 'uncontrolled' observation

Charles Darwin, when his son was a few days over six months of age, made the following observation:

> '... when a child cries or laughs, he knows in a general manner what he is doing and what he feels ... When a few days over six months old, his nurse pretended to cry, and I saw that his face instantly assumed a melancholy expression, with the corners of the mouth strongly depressed; now this child could rarely have seen any other child crying, never a grown-up person crying, and I should doubt whether at so early an age he could have reasoned on the subject. Therefore it seems to me that an innate feeling must have told him that the pretended crying of his nurse expressed grief; and this through the instinct of sympathy excited grief in him. (Darwin, 1872, pp. 357–358)

In our naturalistic Study 9, Vitalaki (2002) made the following observation.

Observation 9

> The infant (six-and-half months old) and her grandmother enjoyed a very playful communication. The grandmother, suddenly, with a smiling face, asked the baby 'Shall we pretend to cry?' and she started pretending to cry. For tenths of a second the baby's face assumed an expression of a 'mocking smile', and then, while the grandmother continued pretending to cry, the infant's face assumed an expression of sadness and she started crying. The grandmother stopped her 'crying' and instantly the infant did the same. The grandmother [as so often Piaget (1962) did] repeated the 'experiment' and the infant's reactions were the same—a mocking smile followed by an

expression of sadness and then crying. After the 'confirmation of her hypothesis', the grandmother initiated other playful activities and the interaction ended with laughs. (Vitalaki, 2002, p. 256)

The above observation is similar to the one Darwin made 130 years ago. The only difference is that the infant in Crete initially seemed to understand that the grandmother was only pretending, as evidenced by her mocking smile, but when the grandmother continued to 'cry', the infant expressed sympathy. Elsewhere, Kugiumutzakis (1993, 1998) suggested that emotions involved in early mimesis can be either 'negative or 'positive' and that detection of another's sorrow, specified from the acoustical and visual invariants, cannot be excluded. When neonates imitate other newborns' cries they appear to attempt empathic communication (Sagi and Hoffman, 1976; Martin and Clark, 1982). Mimesis in early infancy appears to be mainly a pleasurable experience, but both infants and adult partners also exhibit moments of sympathetic imitation of sad feelings. The effects of a mother's depression on the behaviour of an infant is well known (e.g. Field, 1992; Murray, 1998; Chatzinikolaou, 2002).

Emotions in mimesis of twins

In the majority of cases imitation between the non-identical twins (Study 11; Markodimitraki, 2003) was accompanied by more or less the same emotions shared by both infants (mostly interest, pleasure and a mixture of the two emotions, see below). However, there were a few cases when the twins' emotions with mimesis were not similar, as in the following example.

Observation 10

One summer afternoon, the twin 3-month-olds were sitting half-naked on a sofa looking at each other. The girl started pushing the soles of her feet (first the right and then the left) rhythmically against the boy's legs and soles of his feet. The boy instantly imitated his sister. The girl appeared to enjoy this imitative game, but her brother's face remained very serious. After several mutual mimeses, the boy stopped imitating his sister, but the girl continued her rhythmical movements. The boy looked directly at her eyes. His unmoving body, his frozen face, but mainly his censorious eyes expressed a kind of 'restrained anger', which extinguished the communicative interest of his sister, who stopped moving her legs and looked away from her twin brother.

The above observation indicates that the twins' emotions before and during imitation were clearly different. Although they shared the same action of mutual mimesis, they did not share the same emotions. Probably the lack of emotional sharing put an end to their communication. Not only in adult–infant mimesis, but also in infant–infant imitation, as Fiamenghi (1997) and Trevarthen et al. (1999) have shown, emotions are *there* all the time to make the imitative interaction possible or to negate it. The same held true in the imitative interaction of the twins in our sample (Markodimitraki, 2003), although in the case of the twins one must take into account certain critical aspects peculiar to twinship (Piontelli, 2002).

Adult pleasure expressed during imitative communications with infants

Observation 11

In Study 7 (Kokkinaki, 1998), a father and his three-and-half-month-old son had a pleasurable interaction. The infant uttered a prolonged, well-structured vowel sound 'aa-aa-aa-aa-aa', coming from the back of the mouth. Father, laughed and imitated the model, adding a movement to it (he raised the head up). The infant instantly laughed and imitated the complex model. In this very long imitative episode (it lasted 3 minutes), the more the father repeated the funny model the more the infant imitated him and the more both partners laughed. At the end, in their 'confluent', hilarious laughter we cannot discriminate who enjoyed this imitative interaction the most. According to the researcher and other observers the paternal model produced the sounds and characteristic movements of a very alert billy goat—later we were informed that father was from a Cretan mountain village, where he spent his childhood years. In Crete villages, the young often imitate the funny expressions of many animals, including billy-goats. Our observation was of a very 'male' mimesis: from male infant vocal model to a paternal, funny, animal-like imitation/new model, which was, in turn, imitated by his son, and so on. In such a case parent–infant mimesis is a social event that mixes emotions from the past with the present, both of which are shared with the infant. We assume that the infant vocal model gave rise to a paternal, playful, comical memory of the characteristic vocal and facial expressions of an animal. Not the content of the paternal memory, but its emotional quality was shared by the infant. The original, natural model for the father was probably an animal expression—a case of inter-species mimesis nicely described by Democritus (humans imitate animals, see Kugiumutzakis, 1998) and Darwin (1872—dogs imitate humans), and recently by Bard (1998; Bard and Russell, 1999), who has documented inter-species inter-subjectivity between newborn chimpanzees and their human caretakers. Imitation seems to be a very ancient inter-subjective mode of 'transference' of actions, knowledge, and emotions at intra-species, inter-generational, and sometimes even inter-species levels.

Observation 12

In our naturalistic studies we have observed cases where, after a successful infant mimesis, parents and grandparents both asked and answered their own questions, in a virtual dialogue with their real, but non-verbal baby. In one case (Study 6, Kugiumutzakis, 1993) after the successful vocal imitation of her daughter, one mother said: 'Is that you talking little one? Are you talking to mummy? Yes-yes-yes-yes, mummy, it's me. What did you think? Did you think I'm dumb?'. Such 'virtual dialogues' are very simple, but common, forms of parental and grandparental empathy, originating from successful infant mimesis and expressing expectations about the mental and language development of the non-speaking infant.

The last two observations serve to remind us, that the adults' pleasure (approving remarks, smiles, laughs, virtual empathic dialogues, expression of expectations, comments expressing strong emotions like parental love, teasing, etc.) is so obvious and so common that it escapes our notice—one just accepts that parents and grandparents enjoy the imitative communication 'more' than their infants. Also, the personal emotional memories and the expectations of the parents and grandparents for the infant's future are often present in the 'immediate' mimesis, emotions that are usually shared by the infants. When parental memories are pleasurable and funny, imitative interactions are pleasurable and comical for the baby as well—even though the baby does not know the content of the adult memory, which may involve activities or experiences the adult has had with human adults and other animals.

Emotions in early mimesis: systematic observations

In six naturalistic studies (Studies 6–11, see Table 6.1) we tested Darwin's (1872) hypothesis about the emotional nature of mimesis; in three naturalistic studies (Studies 7, 8, 11, see Table 6.1) we investigated the emotions before, during, and after imitation.

Vowels expressing emotions

Vocal imitation was regarded by Aristotle (1964, *Rhetoric, 1140A*) as the most precise form of mimesis, because the vocal organs are the most accurately reproductive of all parts of the body. Darwin (1872, pp. 83–93) assumed that the vocal organs are efficient in the highest degree as a means of expression and that vowel sounds carry the affective values important for inter-personal exchanges.

In the fourth experimental study (see Table 6.1; Kugiumutzakis, 1985), we found that neonates tried to imitate only the sound 'a'. Moreover, micro-analyses and statistical analyses of the data from the six naturalistic studies (Studies 6–11; see Table 6.1) indicated that vocal imitation prevailed over other kinds of mimesis and that more that 50% of the vocal imitations were of vowel sounds (range: 52–76%). In Table 6.2 we summarize (in relative frequencies) the findings from the six studies.

Table 6.2 Categories of vocal sounds imitated in the six naturalistic studies

Naturalistic longitudinal studies	n	Vowels		Consonants		Vowel-consonant combinations	
		n	%	n	%	n	%
6 Kugiumutzakis (1993)	42	572	76	25	3	150	21
7/8 Kokkinaki (1998)	90	1036	61.7	314	18,7	329	19.6
9 and 10 Vitalaki (2002)	74	686	52	85	6	554	42
11 Markodimitraki (2003)	8	220	71.4	9	2,9	79	25.7

If we take into account that vowels also appeared in combination with consonants, then vowel sounds (alone or in combination) appeared in more than 80% of vocal mimeses across the six studies (range: 81.3–97%, in Table 6.2). Although the there is no satisfactory standard coding for the emotional content for vocal expressions, the above results seems to support Darwin' s (1872) suggestion that vowels, more than consonants, carry emotional meaning for intra-species interaction, including, in our case, imitative communication during early human infancy.

In one of our studies, we investigated systematically the different vocal sounds imitated during mother–infant interactions. A classification was employed to distinguish 36 Greek speech sounds and their standard phonetic equivalents. Among the vowel sounds with more than 10 occurrences in the 747 vocal imitative episodes the sounds 'a', 'e', 'o', and 'ae' occurred with statistically the same frequency for infant and maternal imitations (Kugiumutzakis, 1993, pp. 30–1). This finding supports Darwin' s suggestion that the vowel sounds 'a', 'o', 'e', and 'i' appear in pleasurable communication, especially in laughter (1872, p. 88). The role of vowels in early mimesis seems to be extremely important.

Emotional matching in early mimesis

Ten years ago Kugiumutzakis (1994) proposed that the nature of early mimesis is emotional and that in dyadic interactions both partners feel at least two interacting emotions—enjoyment and interest—which motivate the inter-subjective game of imitation. The idea is, of course, very old; it is found in Brandl's question: 'Why does the infant imitate the acts of a person, but not the movements of a curtain?' (quoted by Guillaume, 1926).

In her naturalistic, longitudinal and inter-cultural studies (Studies 7 and 8) Kokkinaki (1998, 2001) coded the emotional expressions of infants and parents 10 seconds before imitation, during imitation, and 10 seconds after imitation. Microanalyses were conducted using a time-unit of a 25th of a second with Video-Logger Event Recorder software. Cohen's Kappas for intrascorer reliability ranged from $k = 0.82$ to 0.89, and for the inter-scorer reliabilities from $k = 0.70$ to 0.85 (Kokkinaki, 1998, 2001).

Both infants' and adults' emotional expressive behaviour were coded before, during, and after imitation. The coding of the emotional expressions was based on observation of facial and vocal expressions. Pleasure or happy facial expression was coded when the face of one partner had open eyes, an elongated mouth that was closed or slightly open in the horizontal plane, while the corners of the mouth were drawn upwards, the lips were stretched causing wrinkles on each side of the mouth and the cheeks were slightly drawn upwards. Interest was defined according to eye contact, gaze, or orientation to the other partner' s face or body, accompanied by an unsmiling face, open eyes, and lips usually open or at other times loosely closed. When the lips were open, the corners of the mouth were slightly downward, with the upper lip in a reversed U-shape, and the lower lip was relaxed or slightly stretched. In addition to gaze behaviour, one or a combination of the following facial expressions also occurred: raised or knitted eye-brows, wide open eyes, blinking, cooing, or pre-speech mouth movements (for the infant), and other vocalizations or baby talk (for the parent). A neutral expression was coded when the infant or adult was not looking or orientating herself/himself to the partner's face or body. The expression was that of an unsmiling, relaxed face, with no signs of vocalizations or intent to vocalize (such as pre-speech mouth movements; for more details see Kokkinaki, 1998, 2001). Many emotions in single or combinatory form were observed. The great majority were 'positive', transient emotions. The emotions of pleasure, interest, and the non-emotional, 'neutral' expression prevailed before, during, and after imitation. Due to the low frequency or absence of other emotional expressions in many cells, we only considered the three categories defined above.

Kokkinaki found 'emotional matching', namely imitation of the emotions before, during and after mimesis. It was confirmed that:

- the emotions of interest and pleasure predominated and emotional matching preceded, accompanied and followed the reproduction of the models actions;
- when both partners (infant–father/mother) displayed interest or pleasure before mimesis, they were both likely to remain in the same emotional state during and after imitation;
- when the parent was showing pleasure and the infant was showing interest before imitation, it was more likely that both would show pleasure during mimesis;
- when both partners displayed interest during mimesis, it was more likely that the infant would remain in the same state and that parent would express pleasure after imitation;
- no significant differences were found in the emotional matching 'during', 'before-and-during', 'during-and-after', or 'before-and-after' mimesis between parents and infants of both sexes in Scotland and Crete.

The above results show that emotions may constitute the recognizable form of expression of partner's motives and that, for mimesis to begin, these motives must be reciprocated. We suggest that this is a case of direct perception and imitation/sharing of the other's motives (Kokkinaki, 1998, 2001; Kugiumutzakis, 1998; Trevarthen *et al.*, 1999, p. 129). Both parents and infants are able to share the emotions experienced, before making their first, accurate, imitative action, and this sharing of transient emotions is an ever-present element preceding imitation and cognition (Kugiumutzakis, 1994, 1998). The uniformity of the emotions in parent–infant mimesis in Scotland and Crete provides cross-cultural evidence for the universality of the inter-subjective nature of imitation during early human infancy.

Early mimesis 'swims' in emotions

In the naturalistic, longitudinal Study 11, Markodimitraki (2003) used the same method as Kokkinaki (1998). Cohen's Kappas for intrascorer reliability ranged from

$k = 0.80$ to 0.88 and for the inter-scorer reliabilities from $k = 0.79$ to 0.90. Pleasure and interest predominated among the emotions observed before, during and after imitation. Additionally, Markodimitraki observed a 'mixed emotion', called 'pleasure-and-interest', namely, a transient emotional state involving elements of both pleasure (smile, with the mouth very slightly open) and interest (intense gazing at the partner's face or body) before, during, and after mimesis. During mimesis, this mixed emotion was found to increase, like pleasure, while interest and neutral expressions decreased (see Fig. 6.1.)

This pattern of increases and decreases remained stable:

- in imitation of the five kinds of models (vocal sounds, facial movements, non-speech sounds, body movements and combinations);
- in imitation occurring in the context of turn taking, co-action and combinations;
- in mimesis during the time of the study (from 1st to 10th months).

The emotional increases and decreases mentioned fluctuated from 58% (non-speech sounds) to 100% (vocal models) in the five kinds of models and in the three communicative structures they fluctuated from 58% (turn takings with co-actions) to 92% (co-actions) to 100% (turn takings). There was a steady increase of smiling and smile-interest emotions across age. For example, from the first to the 10th month, the pleasure during mimesis was found to increase in 12 out of 19 time points (63% stability of the pattern) and the mixed emotion during mimesis was found to increase in 16 out of 19 time points (84% stability of the pattern; for more details see Markodimitraki, 2003).

The above results indicate that mimesis in early infancy does not occur in an emotionless vacuum. When twins are tested, together and separately, with each parent and each grandparent share more or less the same actions and the same transient (usually 'positive') emotions. The stability of the pattern of increases and decreases of the four emotions as a function of the kinds of mimesis, and the timing of their occurrences during the study may indicate that the emotional sharing is a constituent part (a part of the content) of both mimesis itself and 'scaffolding' surrounding the imitative act for young infants. This scaffolding is both flexible, as indicated by the transient nature

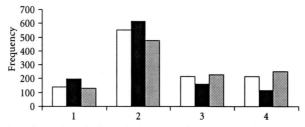

Fig. 6.1 Distribution of emotions before, during, and after imitation. 1, Pleasure; 2, mixed emotions; 3, interest; and 4, neutral expression. White bars, before; black bars, during; and grey bars, after imitation in Study 11.

(a)  (b)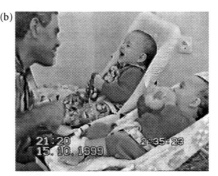

Fig. 6.2 (a) Twin boy (3.5 months old) is imitating the movements of his paternal grandfather. Both partners share the mixing emotion of 'pleasure-and-interest' (Markodimitraki, 2003). (b) Maternal grandfather is imitating the vowel sound of the twin girl (4 months old). Both partners display expressions of pleasure, while the twin boy watches with interest their dyadic communication in this triadic interaction (Markodimitraki, 2003).

of the emotions, and steady, as evidenced by the stability of the pattern of increases and decreases of the positive emotions during imitation. The sharing of the same pattern of increases and decreases of emotions suggests that this emotional scaffolding is built by both communicative partners—infant and parent/grandparent, or infant and her/his co-twin (Fig. 6.2; see also Fiamenghi, 1997). As seen in Fig. 6.1 (black bars) the act of mimesis itself 'swims' in emotions during the first ten months of life (Markodimitraki, 2003).

Discussion

Our quantitative data confirmed many of our qualitative observations. Both converge to the same conclusion: mimesis in infant–adult and infant–infant interaction is not an apathetic, sensorimotor event, but is a clear case of inter-subjective communication. The emotional nature of early mimesis is complex and has many interconnected aspects. Five aspects will be discussed next.

Redefining mimesis

Mimesis is defined as the reproduction of a model's action (Piaget, 1962, p. 2). From our own research and that of others' we know that the infant's reproduction of the model's action is rarely an exact copy of the model. We may characterize the reproduction as precise or 'good enough', but we must admit (indeed, we see or hear) that it is not an exact copy. Above, we described three types of reproductive behaviour. Only the first type characterizes the newborn's mimesis as being precise, and even that is not an exact copy. This is the reason why we often stress that in early mimesis the two partners share more or less the same action. As Trevarthen *et al.* (1999) emphasize, imitations are of greater interest when they are not exact copies of the model, because differences between the imitator's and the model's actions 'may constitute not errors, but significant information in their co-operation' (p. 141). Piaget (1962, p. 84) also recognized that infant reproductions are 'more or less exact copies', although he used the metaphor of photographic art to describe the 'positives' of imitation, the 'negatives' of accommodation, and the 'printing' that is the result of reproductive assimilation.

Our observations suggest that surrounding more or less similar actions, communicative partners generally share similar emotions. Also, they share the intention and motivation for communication through mimesis, namely, both partners appear to perceive directly the intention and motivation attached in the model movements and sounds, and to return them with more or less the same actions and emotions by which they were perceived (Kugiumutzakis, 1985, 1998). Imitation in early infancy seems to be something more than simple reproductions of another's action. Thus, we propose a 'new' definition of imitation that replaces the notion of 'reproduction' with that of sharing, because this latter term better reflects the inter-subjective nature of neonatal and early mimesis, and because sharing in human evolution and development is as fundamental as the air we breathe (Kugiumutzakis, 2002). We suggest defining mimesis in early infancy as 'the sharing of more or less the same actions, intention, motivation and emotions between two communicating partners.' Partners in this sharing can be newborns or young infants and their significant others, including a twin.

Role of emotions

The core role of the emotional engagement between infants and mothers/others in the development of thought, self-awareness and language is described by Hobson (2002) in his thought-provoking, fascinating book entitled *The cradle of thought*. In this challenging work, after he describes our studies on neonatal mimesis, Hobson comments on our thesis about the phenomenon. We have assumed (Kugiumutzakis, 1998, p. 80) that the newborn baby's mimesis is the result of a drive for inter-mental and behavioural matching, originated in a neonatal exploratory motive system that seeks another *emotional being* to engage in a cooperative, complementary, inter-subjective game. Commenting on this thesis Hobson notes:

> For many scientists this is going too far. Justified skepticism is a worthy hallmark of the scientific endeavor, and here is a case where skepticism is understandable. There is a wide gap between observations of an infant's imitation of someone else and claims about the infant's motives to seek engagement with another being. Besides, there is only so much we can say with confidence on the basis of studies of imitation alone. So we need to look elsewhere to corroborate or contradict the idea that infants engages in cooperative and complementary relations with others. (Hobson, 2002, p. 33)

Looking elsewhere, namely, at other infant research studies of the last 30 years as well as at studies on children with autism, Hobson (2002) concludes that even a very young infant has an organized mental life, which is 'expressed in behaviour that is innately fashioned to coordinate with the social behaviour of other people', that infants have an active social life right from the start, which is highly emotional, and it is through emotional connectedness that an infant discovers the kind of thing a person is. He continues:

> A person is the kind of thing with which one can feel and share things, and the kind of thing with which one can communicate (p. 59) ... We have a basic human response to expressions of feeling in others—a response that is more basic than thought. (Hobson, 2002, p. 60)

Hobson's theory is a good alternative to Piaget's object-orientated infant mind. In the present work, we have tried the cover part of the 'wide gap' of knowledge about the infant's motives to seek engagement with another emotional being. Given that we agree with Hobson (2002, p. 252) that human infants have to be endowed with the capacity to respond with feelings to the feelings of others (the first step towards understanding minds), we would like to add that this is exactly what seems to happen in early mimesis 'right from the start': sharing more or less the same feelings, plus sharing more or less the same action. In the experimental studies on neonatal imitation the sharing occurs not with the mother, but with the experimenter. It is an interpretive challenge, especially when it occurs in babies 10–45 minutes after their birth. Sharing appears before the understanding of sharing, as Hobson (2002) notes when he describes the developmental steps from the inter-personal cradle to symbolic and imaginative thought. Neonatal mimesis with persons less than 45 minutes old is, as far as we know, a good example of this inter-subjective sharing (Trevarthen, 1998; Trevarthen *et al.* 1999). In order to reduce 'the scientific skepticism' and close part of the 'wide gap', we summarize below our observations and assumptions.

Pleasure and interest during mimesis

Our observations in a naturalistic context suggest that interest is present and functional in an inter-mental level before and in an intra-mental level during neonatal mimesis. The emotion of interest is a precondition for neonatal mimesis. The appearance of interest depends on the presence of another person/model and on the posture of the baby during the test. Posture seems to be a precondition for both interest and neonatal and early mimesis. Both facial parts and the whole body participate in neonatal mimesis, with the bodily postures expressing emotions and their intensity, as Wallon once suggested. Infant exogenous, social smiles, signifying pleasure, were observed during the first 15 days after delivery, either accompanying or substituting for mimesis, with substitution to denote the intrinsic regulation of the infant's awareness, by the interacting emotions of pleasure and interest. The infant mimesis of rhythm of the vocal models may indicate the common emotional core, and intuitive rhythms of both infant musicality and mimesis. The imitative communication often appears to have rhythmical movements and sounds from the model and the imitator, despite the fact that they are less melodic than the rhythms occurring in musical interactions. Infant intentional avoidance movements indicate the role of the transient emotions or even moods before or during imitation. Human infants are not apathetic copy machines. Most of the time early mimesis is a pleasurable experience, but often infants experience moments of sympathetic imitation, as two 'uncontrolled' observations (Darwin, 1872; Vitalaki, 2002) and five systematic studies (Sagi and Hoffman, 1976; Martin and Clark, 1982; Field, 1992; Murray, 1998; Chatzinicolaou, 2003) show. The core role of the emotions in early mimesis is evidenced in the case of the twins, whose imitative interaction stopped because they could not share the same emotions (Markodimitraki, 2003). Imitative interaction is also pleasurable for parents and grandparents, as shown by their approving remarks, smiles, laughs, virtual empathic dialogues, and comments denoting expectations, love, teasing, etc. An infant's activities/models may give rise to the adult partner's pleasurable memories, the emotional quality of which is shared by the infant (Kugiumutzakis, 1985, 1992, 1998, 1999, 2002; Kokkinaki, 1998).

Our data confirm the central role for vowels in early mimesis (Darwin, 1872) and the predominance of the transient emotions of pleasure, interest, pleasure-and-interest, as well as neutral expressions before, during, and after mimetic act in naturalistic settings. Beyond their central role in imitative interactions, the uniformity of emotions in two cultures (Crete and Scotland) suggest that there is a common, unlearned origin and natural foundation for emotions during mimesis. As Aristotle once noted (Kugiumutzakis, 1995, 1998), emotions are embedded in the matter of the body. For seconds, or even tenths of a second, emotional matching starts before action matching, accompanies it, and continues after it. Emotional sharing seems to be an ever-present prior element of early inter-subjective mimesis. The stable pattern of increases in the expression of pleasure (and pleasure-interest), and decreases in interest and neutral expressions may show the flexibility and the stability of a common, built-in, emotional scaffolding, itself both a constitutive part and a 'sea' within which imitation 'swims', at least during the first 10 months of life (Kokkinaki, 1998; Kugiumutzakis, 2002; Markodimitraki, 2003). More naturalistic and more controlled studies are clearly desirable, using more specific coding systems, like Oster's FACS (see Oster, this volume) and investigating in parallel the 'vitality affects' (Stern, 1985) in naturalistic, dynamic contexts. We hope that this chapter will encourage the study of the emotional aspects of human mimesis, in order to regain the time lost during the long, apathetic cognitive period in developmental psychology.

Emotions in playfulness and musicality

Like Hobson (2002), we have 'looked elsewhere to corroborate or contradict the idea that infants engages in cooperative and complementary relations with others'. Two other members of our research group have investigated emotions before, during, and after playfulness and rhythmic activity in infants, and have found similar increases and decreases in the above emotions during such activities. Semitekolou (2003) studied from the seventh to the twelfth month the playful episodes in dyadic and triadic interactions (mother–infant, father–infant and mother–father–infant). It was found that during the occurrence of the playful communicative activities, in both dyadic and triadic interactions, pleasure and joy increased, while interest decreased and neutral and negative emotions disappeared. Mazokopaki (unpublished) investigated, among other things, infant rhythmical activities in the absence and presence of musical stimulation during their second to the 10th month of life. In both conditions, it was found that during infant rhythmical body, dance movements, and rhythmical vocalizations, their pleasure and joy increased, while interest and neutral expressions decreased. Although more investigations are needed to clarify the crucial role of emotions in early development (Trevarthen, 1993, 1998), it seems that this emotional pattern is to be found during inter-subjective imitation, playfulness, and infant rhythmic activity, throughout the first ten months of life.

A pluralist perspective

To understand by reason (up to a point) the fundamental role of emotions in human evolution, development and future, it is necessary to adopt a pluralist theoretical and methodological perspective, which has to go beyond biological reductionism and anthropological relativism. Such a perspective gives plenty of space for the role of emotion in areas as diverse as Poetry and Robotics. Darwin (1872) used many kinds of data, including the forgotten Voice of the Poets (Homer, Shakespeare) to persuade us, that emotions reveal intentions and thoughts of others 'more truly than do words' (p. 364). In the future we will understand more about the neuroanatomy and neuro-chemistry of our emotions, and this will be an extremely useful knowledge for our species. We already know that 'emotional' genes and 'emotional' neural systems do not have emotions. We, in our subjectivity and inter-subjectivity, exhibit our emotions and share them with others. Perhaps we share 'emotional' genes that help us to express spontaneously our feelings, but simultaneously we share 'imitative' genes and many 'mimetic'/theatrical cultural means to hide and deliberately control them (Bruner, 2002). Just as there is no reason for the primacy of cognition over emotion, perception and action (Kugiumutzakis, 1998), there is no reason for the primacy of biology over culture. In their endless inter-weaving, all voices are crucial, including the voice of the Poet (Elytis, 1979) who says (p. 150) to reductionists : 'with the traps you can capture birds, but you never capture their singing'.

References

Aristotle (1964). *Rhitoriki* (Rhetoric). Athens: Zacharopoulos.

Baldwin, J. M. (1896). Consciousness and evolution. *Psychological Review*, **3**, 300–9.

Bard, K. (1998). Social-experiental contributions to imitation and emotion in chimpanzees. In *Inter-subjective communication and emotion in ontogeny* (ed. S. Braten), pp. 208–27. Cambridge: Cambridge University Press.

Bard, A. K. and Russell, L. C. (1999). Evolutionary foundations of imitation: social cognitive and developmental aspects of imitative process in non-human primates. In *Imitation in infancy* (ed. J. Nadel and G. Butterworth), pp. 89–123. Cambridge: Cambridge University Press.

Braten, S. (1998). Inter-subjective communion and understanding:development and perturbation In *Inter-subjective communication and emotion in ontogeny* (ed. S. Braten), pp. 372–82. Cambridge: Cambridge University Press.

Bruner, J. (1983). *In search of mind. Essays in autobiography.* New York, NY: Harper and Row.

Bruner, J. (1990). *Acts of meaning.* Cambridge, MA: Harvard University Press.

Bruner, J. (2002). *Making stories, law, literature, life.* New York, NY: Farrar, Straus and Giroux.

Butterworth, G. (1999). Neonatal imitation: existence, mechanisms and motives. In *Imitation in infancy* (ed. J. Nadel and G. Butterworth), pp. (63–88). Cambridge: Cambridge University Press.

Chatzinikolaou, K. (2002). *The development of empathy and sympathy in the first Year.* PhD thesis, School of Psychology, University of Reading.

Darwin, C. (1872/1965). *The expression of the emotions in man and animals.* Chicago: University of Chicago Press.

Elytis, O. (1979). *Anikta chartia (An open game).* Athens: Akmon.

Field, T. (1992). Infants of depressed mothers. *Development and Psychopathology,* **4,** 49–66.

Fiamenghi, G. A. (1997). Inter-subjectivity and infant–infant interaction: imitation as a way of making contact. *Annual Report, Research and Clinical Center for Child Development,* **19,** 15–21. Sapporo: Hokkaido University.

Freud, S. (1921/1986). *Group psychology and the analysis of ego,* Vol. **12.** London: Penguin Books.

Gruber, H. E. (1974). *Darwin on man: a psychological study of scientific creativity.* London: Wildwood.

Guillaume, P. (1926/1971). *Imitation in children.* Chicago: University of Chicago Press.

Hobson, P. (2002). *The cradle of thought. Exploring the origins of thinking.* London: MacMillan.

Kokkinaki, T. (1998). *Emotion and imitation in early infant–parent interaction. A longitudinal and cross-cultural study.* PhD thesis, Department of Psychology, University of Edinburgh, Scotland, UK.

Kokkinaki, T. (2001). A longitudinal, naturalistic and cross-cultural study on emotions in early infant–parent imitative interactions. *British Journal of Developmental Psychology* **21,** 243–58.

Kokkinaki, T. and Kugiumutzakis, G. (2000). Basic aspects of vocal imitation in infant–parent interaction during the first six months. *Journal of Reproductive and Infant Psychology,* **18(3),** 173–87.

Kugiumutzakis, G. (1983). *Imitative phenomena: a new challenge.* MA thesis, Department of Psychology, Uppsala University, Sweden.

Kugiumutzakis, G. (1985). *The origin, development and function of the early infant imitation.* PhD thesis, Department of Psychology, Uppsala University, Sweden.

Kugiumutzakis, G. (1988). Genesis tis anthropinis mimesis (Genesis of human mimesis). *Psychologika Themata,* **1(1),** 5–21.

Kugiumutzakis, G. (1992). Phonitikes mimeses stin epikoinonia miteras-vrefous (Vocal mimeses in mother-infant communication). In *Proodos stin Anaptixiaki Psychologia ton Proton Chronon (Progress in Developmental Psychology of the Early Years)* (ed. G. Kugiumutzakis), pp. 93–137. Iraklion: Crete University Press.

Kugiumutzakis, G. (1993). Inter-subjective vocal imitation in early mother–infant interaction. In *New perspective in early communication development* (ed. J. Nadel and L. Camaioni), pp. 22–47. London: Routlege.

Kugiumutzakis, G. (1994). Is early human imitation an emotional phenomenon? Paper presented at the *Symposium on inter-subjective communication and emotion in ontogeny,* Norwegian Academy of Science and Letters, Oslo, 25–30 August.

Kugiumutzakis, G. (1995). Anthropini anaptyxi: to klouvi ke ta poulia (Human development: The cage and the birds). In *Anaptyxiaki Psychologia. Parelthon, Paron ke Mellon (Developmental psychology. past, present and future)* (ed. G. Kugiumutzakis), pp. (663–704). Iraklion: Crete University Cress.

Kugiumutzakis, G. (1998). Neonatal Imitation in the Inter-Subjective Companion Space. In *Inter-subjective Communication and Emotion in Ontogeny* (ed. S. Braten), pp. (63–88). Cambridge: Cambridge University Press.

Kugiumutzakis, G. (1999). Genesis and development of early infant mimesis to facial and vocal models. In *Imitation in infancy* (ed. J. Nadel and G. Butterworth), pp. 22–47. London: Routledge.

Kugiumutzakis, G. (2002). Sharing in mimesis during infancy. Paper presented at the symposium in honour of Jerome Brumer on *We share, therefore we are: on human development, education and culture*, University of Crete, Greece, Heraklion, 21–2 October.

Maratos, O. (1973). *The origin and development of imitation in the first six months of life*. Ph.D thesis, University of Geneva, Switzerland.

Maratos, O. (1982). Trends in the development of imitation in early infancy. In *Regressions in mental development: Basic phenomena and theories* (ed. T. G. Bever), pp. 81–102. Hillsdale, NJ: Erlbaum.

Maratos, O. (1996). Newborn and infant imitation: a case of inter-subjective communication. Invited talk at the Second European Research Conference on *The development of sensory, motor and cognitive abilities in early infancy: Antecedents of language and the symbolic function*, Barcelona, Spain, April, 1996.

Maratos, O. (1998). *Paidi, Epistimi ke Psychanalysi. I diadromes tou Jean Piaget (Child, science and psychoanalysis: the routes of Jean Piaget)*. Athens:Kastaniotis.

Markodimitraki, M. (2003). *H Psychologia ton Didymon: Mimisi ke synaisthimata se ena zeygos heterozygotikon didymon (Psychology of twins: mimesis and emotions in one pair of non identical twins)*. PhD thesis, Department of Philosophy and Social Studies, University of Crete, Greece.

Martin, G. B. and Clark, R. D. (1982). Distress crying in neonates: species and peer specificity. *Developmental Psychology*, **18**, 1–9.

Meltzoff, A. and Moore, M. (1983). Newborn infants imitate adult facial gestures. *Child Development*, **54**, 702–9.

Murray, L. (1998). Contributions of experimental and clinical perturbations of mother-infant communication to the understanding of infant inter-subjectivity. In *Inter-subjective communication and emotion in ontogeny* (Ed. S. Braten), pp. 127–43. Cambridge: Cambridge University Press.

Murray, L. and Trevarthen, C. (1985). Emotional regulation of interaction between two-month-olds infants and their mother. In *Social perception in infants* (ed. T. M. Field and N. A. Fox), pp. 177–97. Norwood, NJ: Ablex.

Nadel, J. (1994). Wallon' s framework and influence. In *Early child development in the french tradition: contributions from current research* (ed. A. Vyt, H. Bloch, and M. H. Bornstein), pp. 177–90. Norwood, NJ: Erlbaum.

Nadel, J. and Butterworth, G. (1999). Introduction. Immediate imitation rehabilitated at last. In *Imitation in infancy* (ed. J. Nadel and G. Butterworth), pp. 1–5. Cambridge: Cambridge University Press.

Piaget, J. (1936/1977). *The origin of intelligence in the child*. London: Penguin Books.

Piaget, J. (1950). *The psychology of intelligence*. London: Routledge and Kegan.

Piaget, J. (1962). *Play, dreams and imitation in childhood*. London: Routledge and Kegan.

Piaget, J. (1968). *Six psychological studies*. New York, NY: Vintage Books.

Piaget, J. (1980). Schemes of action and language learning. In *Language and learning. The debate between Jean Piaget and Noam Chomsky* (ed. M. Piattelli-Palmarini), pp 164–7. London: Routledge.

Piaget, J. and Inhelder, B. (1969). *The psychology of the child*. London: Routledge and Kegan.

Piontelli, A. (2002). *Twins. From fetus to child*. London: Routledge.

Plutchik, R. (1994). *The psychology and biology of emotion*. New York, NY: Harber Collins.

Preyer, W. (1892). *The mind of the child*. New York, NY: Appleton.

Reddy, V. (1999). Prelinguistic communication. In *The development of language: studies in developmental psychology* (ed. M. Barrett), pp. 25–50. Hovey: Psychology Press.

Reddy, V., Hay, D., Murray, L., *et al.* (1997). Communication in infancy: mutual regulation of affect and attention. In *Infant development: recent advances* (ed. G. Bremmer, A. Slater, and G. Butterworth), pp. 247–74. Hovey: Psychology Press.

Rinn, W. E. (1984). The neuropsychology of facial expression: a review of the neurological and psychological mechanisms for producing facial expressions. *Psychological Bulletin*, 1, 52–77.

Sagi, A. and Hoffman, M. L. (1976). Empathic distress in the newborn. *Developmental Psychology*, 12(2), 175–6.

Semitekolou, M. (2003). I anaptyxi ton dyadikon ke ton triadikon pechniodon allilepidraseon metaxi goneon-vrefon apo ton 7o eos ton 12o mina (*Development of playful dyadic and triadic parent–infant interactions from 7th to 12th months*). PhD thesis, Department of Philosophy and Social Studies, University of Crete, Greece.

Stern, D. (1985). *The interpersonal world of the infant: a view from psychoanalysis and developmental psychology*. New York, NY: Basic Books.

Trevarthen, C. (1977). Descriptive analysis of infant communicative behaviour. In *Mother–infant interaction* (ed. H. R. Schaffer), pp. 227–69. London: Academic Press.

Trevarthen, C. (1993). The function of emotions in early infant communication and development. In *New perspective in early communication development* (ed. J. Nadel and L. Camaioni), pp. 48–81. London: Routlege.

Trevarthen, C. (1998). The Concept and Foundations of Infant Inter-subjectivity. In *Inter-subjectivity Communication and Emotion in Early Ontogeny* (ed. S. Braten), pp. (15–46). Cambridge: Cambridge University Press.

Trevarthen, C. (2001). The neurobiology of early communication: Inter-subjective regulations in human brain development. In *Handbook of brain and behaviour in human development* (ed. A. F. Kalverboer and A. Gramsbergen), pp. 841–81. Dordrecht: Kluver Scsdemic Publishers.

Trevarthen, C., Kokkinaki, T., and Fiamenghi, G. (1999). What infants' imitations communicate: with mothers, with fathers and with peers. In *Imitation in infancy* (ed. J. Nadel and G. Butterworth), pp. 127–85. Cambridge: Cambridge University Press.

Uzgiris, I. (1999). Imitation as activity: its developmental aspects. In *Imitation in infancy* (J. Nadel and G. Butterworth), pp. 186–206. Cambridge: Cambridge University Press.

Vitalaki, E. (2002). *I anaptyxi tis mimisis stin allilepidrasi giagias-vrefous* (*Development of mimesis in grandmother–infant interaction*). PhD thesis, Department of Philosophy and Social Studies, University of Crete, Greece.

Zazzo, R. (1957). Le problème de l' imitation chez le nouveau-ne. *Enfance*, 10, 135–42.

Chapter 7

Feeling shy and showing-off: Self-conscious emotions must regulate self-awareness

Vasudevi Reddy

This paper seeks a re-examination of the nature and development of self-conscious emotions. It argues that we should consider two phenomena from infancy—shyness and showing-off—as forms of self-conscious emotionality. These behaviours occur in the first year of infancy, before infants have developed the 'idea of me' and before they are believed to be capable of self-conscious affects (Lewis, 1994). An alternative developmental scheme is proposed in which, far from being ruled inadmissible on *a priori* grounds, such phenomena are argued to reveal the infant's awareness of the attention and evaluation of other persons towards the self, indicative simultaneously of self- and other-consciousness. Two theoretical points are argued. One, that self-consciousness is, in the first instance, not an idea, but an emotion. Secondly, related to this, that being self-conscious emerges from and is evident in other-consciousness.

When we encounter shyness or showing-off in our everyday lives we are rarely unmoved. We could be moved, of course, to revulsion or distaste, as well as to attraction or sympathy, but moved we usually are. These behaviours affect us so directly because they are dynamic attempts to regulate the intimacy or attraction in our relationship with the other person. Both are traditionally recognized 'symptoms' of self-awareness and of self-conscious affect—of embarrassment or pride, of a desire to impress or to hide, or both. Both could even be considered at the extreme ends of the same dimension—in which the attention of the other person, and the intimacy of or evaluation in that attention, are being responded to and played with—one in pulling back from and the other in coming forward towards the other.

Mainstream cognitive developmental theory argues that in order for self-conscious emotions to exist, there must first exist a concept of self from which the emotions can develop and around which they can cohere. It is argued, human infants do not possess or become capable of possessing a concept of self until the middle of the second year of their lives. The emotions that go with hiding from or revealing the self to others, it is therefore argued, cannot emerge until around this age.

Although in a way totally logical, and possessed of impeccable philosophical credentials (e.g. Mead, 1936) this theory and the causal direction it posits has been challenged from many different directions. Some of these challenges seek a re-conceptualization of what it means to be 'conscious' of something (e.g. James, 1905), some a re-conceptualization of the meaning of 'self' and, simultaneously, of the 'other' in relation to self (e.g. Neisser, 1993; Trevarthen, 1993). Others suggest the possibility of the reverse causal influence in which emotionality, even of the self-conscious type, is seen not as derivative of cognition (involving a concept of self), but rather as a simultaneously emerging or mutually interdependent phenomenon (e.g. Izard and Hyson, 1986; Hobson, 1990). Given these challenges, the nature and developmental path of self-conscious emotionality is, therefore, far from clear.

In this chapter, I will explore continuities in the development of expressions of shyness and showing-off, which I will argue show more than merely superficial similarities over time and constitute significant evidence that whatever we refer to as self-conscious affects do not emerge from representations of the self in the middle of the second year of human infancy, but significantly precede and very likely inform them.

Feeling shy

Writings on shyness normally divide it into two types: to put it very simply, into positive shyness and fearful shyness. Although different authors might place its age of onset at different points in time, fearful shyness is normally seen as an early and rather primitive phenomenon both in phylogeny and in human development, with no serious implications for self-consciousness. Positive shyness, on the other hand, despite its age of onset placed at many different age points (and described variously as coyness, bashfulness, embarrassment) is often seen as involving an awareness of self as object to the other (Buss, 1986; Lewis, 1994; Miller, 1996; see Reddy, 2001, for a review). This distinction has emerged as much from theoretical intuitions about the cognitive bases of self-conscious affects as it has from rather patchy evidence available suggesting that fearful shyness occurs earlier and positive shyness later, in development.

Positive shyness: coyness, bashfulness, and embarrassment

Despite its apparent developmental significance the findings on the age of emergence of positive shyness (smiling with averting of gaze and increased touching of body and face) are, in fact, far from clear. Although some evidence (Lewis et al., 1989) suggests a close association between passing the mirror self-recognition test at around 18 months and showing signs of positive shyness, there are reasons to be cautious in accepting this link. There are reports of coyness to strangers at 12 months (Bretherton and Ainsworth, 1974) and to the self in a mirror at 14 months (Amsterdam, 1972; Amsterdam and Greenberg, 1977). There are also two studies from early in infancy that show that smiling and, simultaneously, smilingly averting gaze are behaviours that can be seen in 5-month-olds (Stifter and Moyer, 1991) and in 2-month-olds (Reddy, 2000), and that they occur more in first contact after a break in interaction (Reddy, 2000), a situation that is also productive of signs of self-consciousness in adults (e.g. see Leary et al., 1992 on blushing and unexpected positive attention).

However, what are these behavioural reactions? First, can we call them emotional reactions at all? Secondly, can they be called self-conscious emotional reactions when there is no self to be conscious of?

Positive shyness in 2-month-olds

Coyness, bashfulness and embarrassment are usually identified by a central core of features: they must include an ambivalence of the positive with the negative, both more or less simultaneously directed towards the other person. While an ambivalence of the interpersonally positive and negative is involved in many other emotional engagements—e.g. in teasing, in jealousy or in conflicting emotions—the expression of positive shyness is unmistakable. It consists of a positive approach towards the other person with a simultaneous brief withdrawal. In its simplest form it can be seen in smiling with simultaneous gaze or head aversion. In adults such smiles are perceived by other adults as embarrassed smiles, but primarily if the withdrawal begins *before* the peak of the smile begins to decline (Asendorpf, 1990). In addition to this facial expression, positive shyness is often characterized by arm or hand movements, which serve to further occlude the smile from the attention of the other person, often stereotyped in flirtatious movements of the hand, the fan or the large kimono sleeve held in front of the smiling mouth. Embarrassed smiles may also involve more direct attempts to obscure the smile, for example by directly compressing or biting the lips (Keltner, 1995). In all, this is the central ambivalence that Izard and Hyson (1986) identify as the characterizing feature of shyness—the (often futile) attempt to *prevent* communication.

Smiling gaze or head aversions showing narrowed eyelids and open mouths, more similar to coy smiles than to shy smiles as described in 9-month-olds by Young and Decarie (1977), were observed in 2-month-olds (Reddy, 2000). The following is a description of an interaction between an infant at 10 weeks, 6 days and his mother:

> Rohan lying on carpet, mother leaning over him. Mother says 'Hello. Hello love' and chats in a very quiet and subdued manner for about a minute. Infant looking at her, vocalizes, but not smiling. Then he begins 'singing' vocalizations. As these increase, with a lot of looking around and more vigorous movements of the limbs, the mother's voice becomes happier and more animated. She begins to say 'Hiya, Hiya' in a teasing voice with a rising intonation overlapping with the beginning of a smile from the infant. As the smile begins, the hands which had been clasped together at midline, come down to the sides, the smile widens, the torso and head turn to the side with the smile still broad and the arms come rising up in a curve, before head and gaze return, with a reduced smile, to the mother.

Several structural and functional features of these smiles are worth examining in detail, most showing similarities, as well as differences from those in older children and adults (see Table 7.1).

Table 7.1 Similarities and differences between coy smiles in 2-month-olds and in toddlers/adults

	2-Month-olds	Toddlers/adults	Similarities	Differences
Temporal dynamics	Smiling with gaze or head aversion before end of peak of smile	Smiling with gaze aversion before end of peak of smile	Similar combination of smile with aversion and similar temporal dynamics	
Arms, hands	Arms raising and curving above the midline near the face	Hand movements towards face and body, sometimes hand covering mouth	Movements serving to come between own face and other	Infants: more gross movements
Smile controls	No smile controls	Smile controls evident in adults, possibly in toddlers		Infants: no smile controls evident
Gaze aversion and gaze return	Quick gaze return in majority of cases, especially in younger infants	Quick gaze return indicative of ambivalence rather than avoidance	Quick gaze return in infants and in older children and adults	

Head aversion	Head frequently averted in addition to gaze. Direction most frequently side and down	Head sometimes averted in addition to gaze. Direction most frequently side and down	Involved in infants and older children and adults. Most frequently to side and down in infants as well as in adults	Infants: more frequent; possible differences in angle of head aversion (no evidence)
Identity of Interactant	With familiar people, with Self in mirror, with strangers (especially from 4 months)	With familiar people, with Self in mirror, with strangers	Not just within one relationship	
Context	At perceived onset of others' attention	At perceived onset of others' attention. At perceived (potential) evaluation of specific acts	Onset of attention	Infants: only at onset of attention, not at attention to specific acts

Structural features

First, the majority of smiling gaze aversions (58%) were followed by return of gaze to the interactant either immediately after or just before the end of the smile; this pattern was identified by Lewis (1995) as a significant indicator in toddlers of ambivalence, rather than avoidance, the latter being more likely to be displayed with gaze remaining averted. With increasing age there was a higher incidence of delayed gaze return, suggesting an increasing control of attention to targets (see also Lamb *et al.*, 1987, cited by Ruff and Rothbart, 1996) and possibly also an increasing control of the actions involved in the expression. Secondly, head aversion was frequent (in about 85% of these smiles) in addition to gaze aversion, more frequent than in embarrassed reactions in adults (about 57%, Keltner, 1995; see Table 7.1).

Thirdly, some of these smiles (about 25%) involved a distinctive raising and curving of the arms, often noticed and remarked on by the parents. Adults and older children also move their hands to cover their faces or their mouths in accompaniment of embarrassed smiles. However, while the infant arm movements were gross and impulsive, those in toddlers (Lewis *et al.*, 1989) and adults (Keltner, 1995) appear to be more isolated and controlled, involving nervous self-exploration or face-touching, although this may not always be the case (Eibl-Eibesfeldt, 1990). The difference between infant arm movements and hand movements in older children and adults suggests a more massive emotional reaction to the other in the infants, perhaps indicative of an attentional focus more on the other than on the self (Lewis, 1995). Fourthly, these smiles did not involve any attempt to suppress the smile, a characteristic of several of the embarrassed smiles observed in adults by Keltner (1995) and anecdotally in 18-month-olds (Reddy, 2001). The absence of smile controls once again suggests a lower degree of control and differentiation in the pattern, as well as a lower degree of reflective consciousness in the infants of their bodies.

Functional features

Several functional aspects of these smiles are also important for understanding their relationship to such expressions in older children and adults. First, coy smiles were not only responses to strangers, but were elicited by familiar people (in fact, primarily by familiar people in the early months), as well as by themselves in a mirror. This is the case in adulthood as well; while we may mainly show positive shyness with strangers, we also show it with people we are intimate with, for example, in response to a deep compliment, to unexpected attention from the other, to a knowing tease, etc[1].

---

[1] Shyness, coyness and embarrassment in adults can occur in relation to a stranger or to the remarks of friends and intimates, but rarely in relation to watching the self in a mirror while alone (Miller, 1996). In toddlers, these expressions have been reported in relation to the self in a mirror, to strangers and to the mother and other familiar persons. In the very young infants, only relatively familiar interpersonal partners appear to elicit these expressions; the stranger only elicited them if she first elicited positive interaction rather than just blank looks or avoidance, and the self in a

Secondly, the eliciting events were 'greetings', always involving mutual gaze and often a vocalization from the other. It is justifiable to call these acts of mutual gaze 'greetings' partly because adult speech to infants might be more characterized by 'hello's even during a conversation, than is adult speech to other adults, and partly because the incidence of coy smiles was highest immediately following the renewal of interaction after a brief break. Furthermore, the first smile following renewal of interaction was more likely than the second or later smiles to be a coy smile. In older children and adults too, the onset of attention can be a significant elicitor of embarrassment and blushing, even when this attention is positive and appreciative (Lewis *et al.*, 1989; Leary *et al.*, 1992). However, the infant coy smiles were all elicited in this one context alone—i.e. onset of attention—and not by attention to specific acts or performances by the infant, as can be the case with older children and adults. The infant's presence, rather than the infant's acts, appears to be the focus of the attention to which these smiles are reactions.

Positive shyness towards the end of the first year

Although there is no study directly focusing on positive shyness towards the end of the first year, anecdotal evidence suggests that coy smiles towards strangers, indeed coy games with strangers, abound from the middle of the first year where the infant looks at the stranger, inviting a response and then looks away seemingly shyly. Furthermore, parents report that their infants sometimes refuse to perform on demand; on some occasions refusals are perceived to be deliberate negativeness, whereas on others they are perceived to be the result of a shy or coy embarrassment at performing and being viewed, especially by strangers. Examples of infants letting down proud first-time parents by steadfastly refusing to wave for the visitors until the front door shuts behind them, are familiar to all of us.

Positive shyness and affective self-consciousness

Coy smiles are evident much earlier than cognitive developmental theory predicts and before the development of mirror self-recognition; they have been observed at 14, 12, 9, 5, and even 2 months. What do they signify in terms of affective self-consciousness? These reactions clearly involve expressions of affect (smiles, rather than indifference or disinterest) and occur within social interaction even in 2-month-olds. Their structural

---

mirror only worked to elicit interaction after previous exposure to the self in the mirror (there is no assumption here that the self in a mirror is seen as anything more than another familiar person). By the end of the fourth month, parental reports suggest that the expression is increasingly elicited by complete strangers. So, early in infancy, these expressions appear to occur in intimate interactions rather than as a response to novelty or ambivalence towards strangers. It makes psychological sense that familiar contexts reveal such ambivalent expressions earlier in infancy than do strange or novel contexts—confident responsiveness to familiar persons and styles of interaction may be more likely to yield a greater variety of emotional expressions.

and functional similarity to the embarrassed reactions reported in older infants suggests that they must belong to the same family of emotional expressions. The differences between these reactions and those later in development suggests that as is the with many other emotional reactions from early infancy (Oster, 1997), its affective-contextual meaning, as well as its morphological features inevitably expands and changes with age. That even at 2 months these are not simply automatic or reflexive reactions is evident in the fact that their occurrence, their frequency, and their intensity varies between individual infants, between different moods and social circumstances within individuals, and between the effectiveness of different 'stimuli' in leading to them. The presence of arousal and arousal regulation in these reactions is not a contra-indication for the existence of affect: arousal is involved in many emotional reactions always needing to be qualified with more details about its emotional tone. Of course, arousal is involved in adult self-conscious emotions, too.

That self-conscious affects may be evident earlier than hitherto suggested is supported by several recent empirical developments, e.g. that the actions of the self are recognized very early in life (Bahrick *et al.*, 1996) and by recent theoretical arguments, e.g. about the interconnected understanding of self and other (Stern, 1985; Trevarthen, 1993; Butterworth, 1995; Neisser, 1997). The evidence of continuities in the expression of positive shyness suggests a gradual development of self-conscious affects from early infancy rather than their emergence from a late developing 'idea of me' (Lewis, 1994).

Showing-off

Showing-off is not often discussed as an indicator of self-consciousness. The term pride is normally invoked as the self-conscious emotion which occupies the other end of the interpersonal dimension from positive shyness. Nobody would argue, however, with the view that pride may, and often does, lead to showing-off. It makes little sense, in fact, to describe a behaviour as showing-off unless it is seen as stemming from a desire to elicit or retain the (positive) attentional evaluations of others. Pride is typically described as an emotion that is about the self, in fact about one's representation of the self, and seen as resulting from the internalization of the standards and goals that surround one (Lewis *et al.*, 1989). Pride, then, unlike embarrassment, depends for its emergence not only on the capacity to be aware of others' attention directed to oneself, but additionally on the awareness of goals and standards to evaluate one's actions. Lewis and colleagues suggest that pride as an emotion does not develop until about 3 years of age. Mastery motivation, however, and the behaviour associated with seeking and showing mastery is reported to be present in human infants from at least around the end of the first year (e.g. Messer, 1995). One reading of this discrepancy in developmental age between the two concepts could be that mastery behaviour may result from an intrinsic pleasure in achievement without a grasp of independent standards by which this achievement can be evaluated (or because of which one might be judged positively).

Showing-off—highlighting aspects of the self for the purpose of obtaining positive evaluation or positive attention from others—is, in fact, reported to occur even earlier than mastery behaviour in human infancy; in fact, from the third quarter of the first year (Bates *et al.*, 1976; Trevarthen and Hubley, 1978; Reddy, 1991). Before considering the implications of showing-off for self-conscious emotionality, let us first take a look at what these behaviours look like and the contexts in which they occur.

Showing-off in the first year

The actions involved in infant showing-off may be silly (e.g. throwing the self around roughly on the floor, knocking down a tower of bricks as soon as it is built by the other, etc.), clever (e.g. newly developed clapping with two hands, newly learned standing up, picking up and waving bricks in both hands after some effort, etc.) or even naughty (deliberately violating routines or rules, although this is better discussed as teasing). Showing-off can occur in order to gain attention when it is absent, to retain it when one is already the centre of attention, or to gain approval for 'cleverness'. The following excerpts from interviews with parents (Reddy, 1998; Reddy and Williams, in preparation) give a flavour of the kinds of things infants did to gain and manipulate attention, and the simple everyday contexts in which these occurred

Trying odd and extreme actions to gain attention

This category describes infant actions when they are not already being attended to:

> Stephanie developed a very high-pitched shrill shriek at 7 months, which she used primarily in situations when she was getting no attention. 'Yes, like you're pushing her around in a supermarket trolley, and you hear this . . . (and you're) thinking something awful's happened, and . . . nothing. She's sitting there just grinning at you, waiting for a response. (Mother of Stephanie, 7 months, 3 days, during interview)
>
> Alec's just had lunch and he displayed some strange behaviour. I had been feeding him and he'll stop and take a spoonful of his dinner and then after the spoon has come out he'll start banging his head against the back of his highchair and sticking his tongue out, but still smiling at the same time and watching me. Again, when I bring a spoon up to his mouth he'll stop, take what's off the spoon and start head banging again. (Mother of 8-month-old Alec, speaking into a dictaphone)

Although the mother does not report her reaction to this behaviour in the example above, the infant's focus on the mother's attention to him in general and his use of his unusual actions in order to manipulate that attention seems clear. Consider also the following example from an 11-month-old girl:

> She'll put things on her head or something . . . And she'll just sit there in the middle of the room . . . and sort of you'll look up from your book or something, and she's just sat there quietly and you burst into laughter, its like you start laughing and she goes like that, smiles at you from under her dress as if to say 'ha, ha, got you' but she (makes a noise like saying 'look at me'). (Mother of 11-month-old Anna)

Displaying a repertoire of tricks when the centre of positive attention

Infants also seem to recognize being the centre of attention—from one person or several—and are commonly reported to engage in actions seemingly to exploit this attention. The actions tend to involve either just anything which maintains or increases the attention in the moment, or those that have succeeded in the past. Sometimes infants produce a string of actions from their 'bag of tricks'. For example:

> Mother reports that Rebecca definitely shows-off. 'Well, in fact, when I went to the Poly last week . . . She's really quite shy, and I thought she'd be getting worried about these four strangers coming into the room, but she just sat there beaming at them all, she just sat there holding the stage. I think she kind of knew it was her they were interested in, and far from making a beeline for me, she just sat there. She was a movie star . . . (Mother of Rebecca, aged 7 months, 7 days)
>
> I think she's showing-off now . . . she's putting her arms up . . . and she's walking along like this . . . she does show off quite a lot . . . like we've got a little foot stool and now . . . and now the latest thing is now . . . Is she'll climb up on this stool to show off to everybody . . . she now stands up . . . I've got a cardboard box with her toys in and she turns it on its side and she climbs up and sits on it and she's got one leg hanging over the side (looking at you). (Parents of 11-month-old Vicky)
>
> If any adult, or any new adult especially, comes into the room he tries to get their attention (on dictaphone) . . . If its other people, then he suddenly goes into this whole kind of clapping, waving hands (repertoire of things) . . . Well I went up to my Mum's the weekend before last and he had a massive audience there, cos they haven't seen him for 6 weeks, my family, and he was on cloud nine all weekend. So he was . . . he was just showing off the whole weekend. (Mother of 11-month-old Alec)

Repeating clever or difficult actions for approval

In addition to the use of actions to get or retain general positive attention, infants also display from around 8 months, actions which are deemed 'clever' by those around them or are intrinsically difficult, and seek praise for them, looking around for attention when done. Some of them are idiosyncratic acts, while others are conventional forms of action:

> She is also now starting to stand up a lot and seeking for you to tell her what a clever girl she is. She'll pull herself up and then look round to see who is looking at her. (Mother of Vicky, 8 months)
>
> Freya was very pleased with herself because she put, she was holding two little shapes, little plastic shapes in one hand, and she was showing it to us, grinning. (4 days later, mother records that now Freya is continually trying to hold two objects in one hand, or trying to pick up and hold two things in one hand instead of in two; Mother of 8-month-old Freya on dictaphone)
>
> She does sort of sigh as if . . . as if she's achieved something . . . you know . . . I mean the other day she managed to get her dress over her head so her head popped through the other side and she made a sound for me to look at her and I said 'oh aren't you a clever girl . . . or she managed to get her sock the other day on her arm like a glove puppet and she's walking around

the room sort of waving her arm, you know, to say 'look I've done this, I've got it on my arm'. (Mother of 11-month-old Anna)

In one longitudinal study based on interviews with parents when their infants were aged 8, 11, and 14 months, we found that even at 8 months, over three-quarters of the infants were reported to be definitely engaging in some form of showing-off. About half of the 8-month-olds were also engaging in clever showing-off, which involved actions such as putting shapes in, doing appropriate actions on objects, dancing, clapping , waving, pulling self up. These acts were judged to be done for praise—therefore, counting as clever showing-off—because the infants looked to the parent after the act 'expecting praise'. By 14 months, clever showing-off, which was reported by all but one parent, involved a richer variety of actions within each infant. The clever actions included dancing, throwing a ball, using the telephone, kissing for praise, climbing the stairs, doing puzzles, cleaning teeth, feeding self with a spoon, as well as clapping, waving, etc. All of these acts were judged by the parents to be done for praise involving looking back to the parent during the act or after it was completed.

Showing-off and affective self-consciousness

What does infant showing-off tell us about self-conscious emotionality? First of all, do these actions reveal an emotion at all? There is unlikely to be any theoretical resistance in accepting the emotionality of these behaviours. The infants are evidently acting intentionally in a conscious sense, selecting their actions for repetition with immense sensitivity to situations and to persons. They reveal many different signs of emotion in their faces, voices, and bodies, the expression itself is intensely positive and anticipatory of the response of the other. That these reactions are emotional, therefore, seems to be little in doubt.

However, is the emotion involved a self-conscious emotion akin to pride in response to achievement or praise? Is there an incipient awareness of a self that can be appreciated or approved developing before the end of the first year? Although these simple achievements that the infants are showing-off with are not the same as the evaluations in terms of detached standards, which Michael Lewis argues develop around 3 years of age, they are nonetheless achievements, and known by the child as achievements in the eyes of others as well as (in the case of the 'difficult' actions) of the self. Standards in terms of objectively existing criteria for good and bad may, indeed, not become available to the child until 3 years of age. However, markers for achievement within engagement seem available from at least the latter part of the first year in the form of appreciation from others for specific acts and in terms of success following difficulty. The use of these acts to re-elicit such appreciation cannot be ignored in the context of the development of a self that seeks to present itself in a certain way. From this perspective, it could be argued that showing-off or pride-like affect is present within interpersonal engagements from the second half of the first year.

However, what about first half of the first year? Is it the case that, as Michael Lewis suggests in talking about two sorts of embarrassment, the awareness of the evaluativeness of others' attention emerges much later than the awareness of its directedness?

Effortful seeking and retaining of attention from 2 months

Tentative evidence from the first half of the first year, about infants calling others to attend to them and 'performing' conversationally is worth looking at a little further (see Trevarthen, 1977). Here is one excerpt from a 13 week-old infant during a face to face 'chat' with his mother. Since such behaviour is rarely directly explored, such excerpts serve at the moment as suggestions for further research:

> Mother calls to infant for a chat. Infant busy looking around at sister and father and actions around. Turns to Mother on her initiation and responds with smiles and coos. She tickles him and talks playfully, he responds with near laughs and smiles. Her energy seems to wear out and she quietens down, but still looking at him. She stops tickling him. After a brief pause the infant, eyes still on mother with a pleasant expression, initiates a long effortful vocalization to her with protruding lips and pauses. She responds with a slightly querying tone 'Noooo!? Don't you pretend!' then resumes her tickling, saying 'What're you trying to say? What're you trying to say?' with a rising intensity. The infant responds once again with cooing, and a smile, but with lower intensity, and then looks around. (Rohan, 13 weeks interacting with mother)

The infant was in a very positive mood—not boisterous, but pleasant and interested in everything around, and willing to engage. The infant's behaviour could be described as a kind of performing. That it occurred during a pause in the intensity of the mother's efforts and was an initiation by the infant, rather than a response to the mother's immediate act is evident. The effortful, trilling vocalization seems to have been done in order to regain the mother's attention and engagement. The infant was not, however, keen to intensify the engagement, as was evident when the mother responded to his effort, and the infant smiled and then looked around elsewhere. This act of the infant's is not 'showing-off' as normally understood, i.e. it was simply an effortful performance, trying to regain attention to the self. Nonetheless, it could be placed on one end of a developmental continuum of showing-off, where the positive attention of another is elicited with an effortful performance for no reason other than to engage in pleasant interaction. It was certainly an effortful heightening of the visibility of the self to the other.

Reducing and heightening visibility of the self in autism

If it is the case that others' appreciation and attention is available to the infant very early in life, leading to self–other conscious affects, what happens in cases where children are known to have difficulty in perceiving such emotional qualities in others? Autism provides a case in point. One would expect that children with autism would show deficits both in terms of displays of coyness and in terms of displays of showing-off. Regardless of whether they can recognize themselves in mirrors (which previous research shows that they can, at the appropriate developmental age, Dawson and McKissick, 1984), they should nonetheless be unable to respond with feelings of positive shyness to attention from others or to act in order to re-elicit or maintain appreciation from others. Pride as manifest in achieving or in overcoming difficulties may well be present, but pride as expressed in showing-off for others' attention should be seriously impaired.

Do children with autism express positive shyness and showing-off? There is not very much research in this area, but what little there is suggests that they do not, or at least, not in the way that typically developing infants and children do. Chidambi (2003) in a unique study attempting to elicit coy reactions in children with autism and other learning disabilities found that while the majority (9 out of 13) of the control group of learning disabled children reacted clearly coyly to a gradual build up of positive appraisal from a stranger via a teddy bear, only one (one out of 12) of the children with autism did so. In one study comparing pre-school children with autism with those with Down Syndrome, we found that independent of whether the children had passed the mirror self-recognition task or not, the children with autism never showed coy reactions either to themselves or to others in the mirror, while some of the children with DS did (Reddy *et al.*, in preparation). The following description is an example:

> Conor looks in the mirror, leans close and smiling broadly puts his face next to his face in the mirror; still smiling he turns his face and looks at his mother in the mirror; he then leans back and points to himself in the mirror. His mother says 'Are you in there?' He looks at himself, smiling, and claps his hand over his mouth. Then his attention is caught by something else in the mirror. (Conor, 3 years, with DS, passed the mirror test)

The lack of self-conscious affects in children with autism has also been reported by Dawson (Dawson *et al.*, 1990; Hobson, 1990). On the other hand, fearful shyness as described in the literature, i.e. an avoidant kind of self-consciousness, is known to be shown by some children with autism, and is familiar to most carers, expressed, e.g. in the refusal to engage with strangers, to run away when being looked at, etc. If this differential pattern is really valid (and further exploration is needed in order to be sure that children with autism do, indeed, show fearful shyness, but not positive shyness) then the distinction made by theorists about only positive shyness being indicative of self-consciousness is given some support.

What about showing-off? Do children with autism show-off? The answer in general (and there are, in fact, very few formal answers to this question) is that they do, but much less than and differently from other children. In one study (Reddy, 1998), based on interviews with parents of pre-school children with autism and children with Down syndrome matched on developmental age, we found that less than 50% of the children with autism were reported to show any interest at all in showing-off of any kind, as opposed to 78% of the children with Down syndrome. Under a quarter of the children with autism were reported to engage in some kind of clever showing-off, as opposed to two-thirds of the children with DS. In the children with autism, the clever showing-off was generally limited to saying words 'with a smirk'. Only in one of these children (out of a sample of 19 children with autism) was there anything like a variety of acts, involving saying action rhymes, using the potty and whipping the hat off appropriately in a song. In contrast, in the children with DS, clever showing-off when it occurred was rich and varied in each child, ranging from singing, playing the piano, doing jigsaws, using the potty, clapping, and waving, etc.

Developing awareness of attention and evaluation

Both shyness and showing-off are argued here to require an awareness of the attention of others. What does this awareness of attention consist of? If Michael Lewis' argument (1995) about two different kinds of embarrassment is correct, it could be argued that there are two aspects of others' attention that infants become aware of: first, of its directedness (towards the infant) and later of its evaluativeness (Reddy, 2001). At first glance, this sequence seems supported by the present data. It could be argued that at 2 months, the infant is aware of the directedness of others' attention to him/herself and can respond with positive shyness; not being aware of its evaluativeness, however, the infant is not yet capable of showing-off. This could be seen as developing later, towards the end of the first year.

However, is it ever possible, least of all in infancy, to experience something without experiencing its emotional valence, even if that valence is one of neutrality or indifference? Particularly for infants, it could be argued that emotional valence is the most salient and most easily available perceptual information. Stern (1985), for instance, argues that such information may be perceivable independent of modality of expression. If this is the case and if the emotional valence of attention is available to infants from early in life, then why is it the case that infants in the early months appear to respond to others' attention, but not to its evaluativeness? One explanation could be that infants are, in fact, responding to the evaluativeness of attention right from the start. It is the objects to which others' evaluative attention is directed, which they may not be able to perceive. Another person's appreciation, for example, may initially only be perceivable by an infant if it is directed to the infant herself. Only later might the infant perceive others' appreciation directed to her specific performances.

If this alternative account of the developing awareness of evaluative attention is valid, then it ought to be the case, first of all, that infant actions upon others' attention show a development in the objects to which the attention is directed. Table 7.2 suggests that this is indeed the case. Secondly, it ought also to be the case that the evaluativeness of others' attention is affectively engaged with from the start. Table 7.3 summarizes two kinds of engagement with positive evaluativeness in others' attention—one involving a reduction in the visibility and the other a heightening of the visibility of the targets to which positive evaluation is directed. Both kinds of engagement can be seen to be present from the early months; the developmental change involves the targets whose visibility is heightened or reduced.

Table 7.2 Expanding awareness of the objects of others' attention

From age	The object of the other's attention	Infant response to and action upon other's attention
2–4 months	Self	*Responding:* to others' gaze to self with interest, pleasure, distress, ambivalence, indifference, and co-ordinated expressions.
		Directing: making 'utterances', 'calling' attention to self, seeking face-to-face engagement.
6–8 months	Frontal events and targets	*Responding:* Following others' gaze to frontal targets; gaze alternation between target and attentive other person, with interest, pleasure, anxiety, indifference.
		Directing: No known evidence.
7–10 months	Acts by self	*Responding:* to others' attention to acts by self with pleasure interest, anxiety.
		Directing: repetition of acts that elicit laughter/attention/praise, with gaze to others' faces.
9–11 months	Objects in hand	*Responding:* to others' gaze at objects in hand? Evidence unclear.
		Directing: Beginning of showing/giving objects in hand.
10–14 months	Distal targets	*Responding:* Following others' gaze to distal targets.
		Directing: Going across room to fetch objects to give; pointing to distant objects
15–20 months	Past events, absent targets	*Responding:* attending to others' reports of past events? Evidence unclear. Following gaze to targets behind self.
		Directing: Discriminating absence of attention, reference to past events

Table 7.3 Developments in affective self-consciousness

	Embarrassment-like displays: hiding the Self	Pride-like displays: exposing the Self
2–4 months	Coy smiles (with smiling gaze aversion and curving arm movements) at onset of attention from self or familiar others.	Calling others to engagement with loud squeals. Games inviting mutual attention followed by turning away.
7–12 months	Coy or watchful refusals to 'perform' on request. Coy looks, alternation of smiling and gaze aversion and wariness to greetings from strangers.	Showing-off through silly, exaggerated, or vigorous actions to retain or attract attention. Repetition of 'clever' acts for re-eliciting others' appreciation. Games involving hiding and revealing the self.
18 months	Coyness and embarrassment to being observed and being over-complimented (with smiling gaze aversion and face touching)	Preening, admiring self in mirror, 'cute' looks. Games involving hide and seek and surprising actions.
36 months	Displays of embarrassment or shame in response to others' evaluation, actual or anticipated. Extended coy smiles involving lengthier expressions.	Displays of pride in response to others' evaluation, actual or anticipated

Implications for theories of self-conscious emotions: an alternative story

These data from the first year of infancy pose a challenge to the idea that what have been called self-conscious emotions are the result of the development of a concept of self. Embarrassment-like displays are evident from far too early in development in appropriate contexts and develop in systematic differentiation of the display, as well as of the context, to be dismissed as mere 'biological' phenomena. Displays akin to pride and preening are, similarly, evident from well before the end of the first year. That these affective reactions can be called self-conscious affects psychologically (as well through resemblance) is justified by their clear regulation of the visibility of the self as an object of the other's attention. It seems that the emotions typically called 'self-conscious' are rooted in perceptions of the others' attention and emotion, rather than in thought about the self. Since there is no evidence that conceptualization of the self develops any earlier than 18 months (or 12 months at the earliest) the direction of effect proposed by cognitive-developmental theory must be challenged. The 'secondary' emotions seem to be secondary neither in terms of developmental age nor in terms of derivativeness.

The case for a reversal of the direction of effect, i.e. that self-conscious affects lead to, rather than result from a concept of self, which has been made by developmental psychologists such as Carroll Izard and Peter Hobson (see Draghi-Lorenz *et al.*, 2000 for a critical review of theories in this area) seems worth examining. This reversed direction

EMBARRASSMENT-LIKE DISPLAYS: HIDING THE SELF

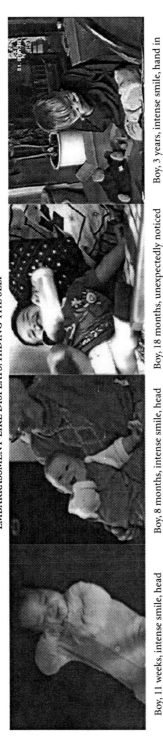

Boy, 11 weeks, intense smile, head and gaze aversion, , arms curving up, response to greeting by mother at onset of interaction.

Boy, 8 months, intense smile, head and subsequent gaze, aversion, arm curving up, in response to greeting by visitor.

Boy, 18 months, unexpectedly noticed by grandfather while speaking; intense smile, head and gaze aversion, body curving away and arm rising up

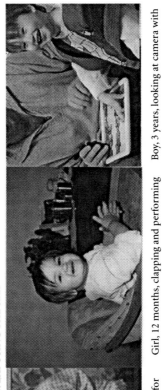

Boy, 3 years, intense smile, hand in front of mouth, looking in mirror at self with dot on face.

PRIDE-LIKE DISPLAYS: EXPOSING THE SELF

Boy, 13 weeks, effortful trilling, vocalisation during face-to-face chat with mother, pleased expression

Girl, 6 months, demonstrating for mother new skill at clapping, expression of pride.

Girl, 12 months, clapping and performing to camera and to praise from grand-mother

Boy, 3 years, looking at camera with pride on succeeding in placing a piece of the puzzle.

of effect means that the occurrence and meaningfulness of these emotions must be crucial in shaping self-awareness. How might this work?

Commonplace in early (and later) interpersonal interactions is a continual ebb and flow of increasing and decreasing visibility of one or other of the partners. Most of these changes in visibility involve some minimal level of affect. Some of them, however, involve clear forms of affect such as embarrassment at being praised, coyness at being greeted, pleasure in receiving appreciation, pride in overcoming a difficulty, etc., which we identify as self-conscious emotions. Consider the following sequences:

> She approaches and says hello, I look up with a smile, she compliments my appearance, I drop my gaze smilingly, she changes the subject.
>
> He comes up close and greets me, smiling. I am startled, look up and smile and turn away briefly, then step back and talk about the weather.
>
> He smiles and turns away coyly when she speaks to him, she is charmed by the reaction and laughs lightly.
>
> She sees the appreciation in his face and confidently cracks a joke, he laughs, she cracks another one.
>
> He adjusts his hair in the window before walking into the room to greet her.

If these affective interplays are, indeed, common in interpersonal interaction what consequences do they have? First, they are clearly helpful in achieving a comfortable balance of affective tension both within and between individuals. Secondly, they perform a constitutive role, defining and redefining the people who are thus engaged. They change within the engagement, from moment to moment, the nature of the individuals and the nature of their engagement.

So what implications do the regulatory and constitutive roles of such affective interchanges have for the development of awareness of the self and of other? Two answers follow: in order to become aware of the self (or the other) the infant must also become aware of their affective aspects. In other words, the self (and the other) must be known as affective creatures. Secondly, more importantly, it is through the medium of these affective states that the infant becomes aware of her self (or of the other). This is true of any affective state that the infant is in while interacting with another person, or that the infant perceives the other person to be in during interaction. But it is also, and importantly true of self-conscious affective states: to be joyfully aware of someone's appreciation or shyly aware of someone's attention cannot but shape the awareness we develop of the self or of the other in that interaction. In other words, the self (and the other) are to be known through the experience of the affects. The infant, then, is faced with the task of becoming aware of a self and of an other who often manifest affective reactions and who are affected by each other while experiencing these affective interchanges.

The idea that self-conscious affects arise after and because of the development of a concept of self seems to be to put the cart before the horse. Neither in terms of chronology nor in terms of a plausible explanatory story, do we need to adopt that position. A simpler and more fitting explanation would be to see self-conscious affects as leading to (both because of chronological sequence and because of the their influence upon) the development of a concept of self.

However, what of the case of autism? Clearly, these children show evidence of a concept of self; they pass the mirror self-recognition test, they refer to themselves (albeit with some pronominal confusion in their language), but they do not show the kind of self-conscious affects described above. This could on the face of it be interpreted as evidence against the reversed direction of effects suggested above. Alternatively, the sense of self that children with autism are reported to develop could be seen as exemplifying the inadequacies of the developmental route suggested by cognitive developmental theory. They do, indeed, develop a concept of self, but one that has certain deficits. If a sense of self is developed without experiencing or perceiving the kinds of self-conscious affects discussed here (involving a positive heightening or reducing of the visibility of the self), as it must often be in autism, that sense of self cannot include those aspects of self or other, and must have developed without the medium of experiencing those affects. The concept of self these children must be developing must in respect of affects be a bystander concept; they are conceiving of the self and of the other without the advantage of feeling what the self and the other in typical development can feel towards each other. Literal heightening and reducing of the visibility of the self is unproblematic in autism—the attraction of peekaboo with accompanying affect is well documented in children with autism. Similarly, the presence of what might be called negative self-consciousness or distressed avoidance of the gaze or attention of others, has been documented in autism. This suggests that it is not a problem of literal perspectives on themselves that is impaired or that there is no awareness of the self as an object of others' attention. It seems that the capacity to feel self-conscious affects in positive engagement is what is impaired. A concept of self can thus be developed with or without prior experience of self-conscious affects; however, quite different consequences ensue for each.

If an organism approached the task of developing an awareness of itself without already feeling emotions that we call self-conscious, that organism would be unable to develop a sense of self or of other as we understand it; the self which the organism was to become aware of would itself be an emotionally isolated self not an emotionally related self. Such a view of self–other conscious emotions as the medium for self-awareness makes it difficult to explain self-awareness as a representational achievement. The medium ebbs and flows and constantly changes as the emotional relation changes; the self itself is simply a point of relational flux, constantly being re-shaped as an entity in relation. Self-consciousness, therefore, is inseparable from other-consciousness.

William James puts another slant on the inseparability of self-consciousness and other-consciousness. He wrote that his search for consciousness left him only with the objects which entered into consciousness. The more he tried to catch consciousness the less he could (despite a Cartesian confidence that the existence of the inner world cannot be doubted). 'Whenever I try to become sensible of my thinking activity as such, what I catch is some bodily fact, an impression coming from my brow, or head, or throat, or nose' (James, 1905, p. 467). Being self-conscious, similarly, might leave us not with images of the self, but instead with images of the things and people that stirred the 'self-conscious' feelings or thoughts. These early reactions (and their similarities and differences) may initially originate, not in an understanding of the self as an object of attention, nor solely of the other as a giver of attention, but of the other-in-relation-to-self.

Managing intimacy and attraction in interpersonal relations

'We are "seen" when our feelings are understood, or when something that is meaning-ful to us is empathically felt by the other person' (Amodeo and Wentworth, 1986, p. 95). 'Touching another's felt experience' suggest the relationship manuals, can disarm us. There are two aspects to this experience of being touched, both of which are relevant to engagements involving shyness and showing-off in infancy. In shyness, the infant is revealing having been touched by being seen. The recipient of the shyness is both the toucher, and the person who has seen and then been touched by the infant's affect. Within a sensitive relationship positive shyness can work dramatically to deepen intimacy. Showing-off, with its lower degree of vulnerability, is much less moving and deepening of intimacy. Although it, too, can touch the adult with its evidence of caring for one's approval. In another sense, however, showing-off genuinely is the other side of the coin of shyness: it reveals a confidence in taking the risk of rejection

Why is it significant that infants are capable of managing intimacy and attraction in relations with others from so early in life? Clearly, it matters for survival. The appeal of infants to adults is evidently not just in static displays of baby-facedness; they have to do something to hold us. This something could be the way in which they not only engage with us, but show that they themselves are engaged with us through demonstrations of positive shyness and show that they want to impress us—through demonstrations of showing off. Embarrassment and pride could, as has been the case so far, be conceived of as individual emotions. Things that develop inside the individual infant or child as a result of a growing awareness of the self and of invisible psychological aspects of others, and that lead to emotional experiences that were not hitherto possible.

Alternatively, once could conceive of embarrassment and pride and other self-conscious emotions as relational emotions. They emerge because we have relations which we manage in particular ways. They are not internal states, they are ways of being with another person, and they lead to rather than result from, conceptual awareness of the self and of the psychological states of the other. This explanation handles the data described here without doing violence to the chronology and without treating the infant's early attempts to affect or be affected by us with cavalier dismissiveness.

Summary

Using evidence of two familiar phenomena in infancy—positive shyness and showing-off, the paper argues that self-conscious affects are better considered in terms of emotional continuities than in terms of distinct differences. This suggests (a) a gradually increasing awareness of self and other rather than a sharp onset of this awareness late in infancy, and (b) that feeling self-conscious is not developmentally dependent upon a specific conceptual awareness of self (and is either independent of it or mutually interdependent) but is dependent upon an ability to perceive attention towards self and to feel appropriately in response, (c) that self-conscious affects may be better re-named self-other conscious affects and (d) that the interpersonal presence of these emotional reactions and the responses they elicit from others may, in fact, be essential to the further development of self-consciousness.

References

Amodeo, J. and Wentworth, K. (1986). *Being intimate: a guide to successful relationships*. London: Arkana.

Amsterdam, B. (1972). Mirror self-image reactions before age two. *Developmental Psychobiology*, 5(4), 297–305.

Amsterdam, B. and Greenberg, L. M. (1977). Self-conscious behaviour of infants. *Developmental Psychobiology*, 10(1), 1–6.

Asendorpf, J. B. (1990). The expression of shyness and embarrassment. In *Shyness and embarrassment* (ed. W. R. Crozier), pp. 87–118. Cambridge: Cambridge University Press.

Bahrick, L. E., Moss, L., and Fadil, C. (1996). Development of visual self-recognition in infancy. *Ecological Psychology*, 8(3), 189–208.

Bates, E., Camaioni, L., and Volterra, V. (1976). Sensorimotor performatives. In *Language and context: the acquisition of pragmatics* (ed. E. Bates), pp. 49–71. New York, NY: Academic Press.

Bretherton, I. and Ainsworth, M. (1974). Responses of one-year-olds to a stranger in a strange situation. In *The origins of fear* (ed. M. Lewis and L. A. Rosenblum), pp. 131–164. New York: Wiley.

Buss, A. H. (1986). A theory of shyness. In *Shyness: perspectives on research and treatment* (ed. W. H. Jones, J. M. Cheek, and S. R. Briggs), pp. 39–46. New York: Plenum Press.

Butterworth, G. (1995). An ecological perspective on the origins of self. In *The body and the self* (ed. J. L. Bermudez and A. J. Marcel), pp. 87–105. Cambridge, MA: MIT Press.

Chidambi, G. (2003). Autism and self-conscious emotions. Unpublished PhD Thesis. University of London: University College.

Dawson, G. H., Hill, D., Spencer, A., *et al.* (1990). Affective exchanges between young autistic children and their mothers. *Journal of Abnormal Child Psychology*, 18(3), 335–45.

Dawson, G. and McKissick, F. C. (1984). Self-recognition in autistic children. *Journal of Autism and Developmental Disorders*, 14(4), 383–94.

Draghi-Lorenz, R., Reddy, V., and Costall, A. (2001). Rethinking the development of 'non-basic emotions': a critical review of existing theories. *Developmental Review*, 21, 263–304.

Eibl-Eibesfeldt, I. (1989) *Human ethology*. Hawthorne, NY: Aldine de Gruyter.

Hobson, R. P. (1990). On the origins of self and the case of autism. *Development and Psychopathology*, 2(2), 163–81.

Hobson, R. P. (1998). The intersubjective foundations of thought. In *Intersubjective communication and emotion in early ontogeny. Studies in emotion and social interaction* (ed. S. Braten), pp. 283–96. New York, NY: Cambridge University Press.

Izard, C. E. and Hyson, M. C. (1986). Shyness as a discrete emotion. In *Shyness: perspectives on research and treatment* (ed. W. H. Jones, J. M. Cheek, and S. R. Briggs), pp. 147–60. New York: Plenum Press.

James, W. (1905). *Textbook of psychology*. London: Macmillan and Co.

Keltner, D. (1995). Signs of appeasement: evidence for the distinct displays of embarrassment, amusement and shame. *Journal of Personality and Social Psychology*, **68(3)**, 441–54.

Leary, M. R., Britt, T. W., and Cutlip, W. D. (1992). Social blushing. *Psychological Bulletin*, **112(3)**, 446–60.

Lewis, M. (1994). Myself and me. In *Self-awareness in animals and humans: developmental perspectives* (ed. S. T. Parker, R. W. Mitchell, and M. L. Boccia), pp. 20–34. New York, NY, US: Cambridge University Press.

Lewis, M. (1995). Embarrassment: the emotion of self-exposure and evaluation. In *Self-conscious emotions: the psychology of shame, guilt, pride and embarrassment* (ed. J. P. Tangney and K. W. Fischer), pp. 199–218. New York, NY: Guildford Press.

Lewis, M., Sullivan, M. W., Stanger, C., *et al.* (1989). Self development and self-conscious emotions *Child Development*, **60(1)**, 146–56.

Mead, G. H. (1934). *Mind, self and society* (ed. C.W. Morris). Chicago, IL: University of Chicago Press.

Messer, D. J. (1995). Mastery motivation: past, present and future. In *Mastery motivation: origins, conceptualizations, and applications. Advances in applied developmental psychology*, Vol. **12** (ed. R. H. MacTurk and G. A. Morgan), pp. 293–316. Westport, CT: Ablex.

Miller, R. S. (1996). *Embarrassment: poise and peril in everyday life*. New York, NY: Guildford Press.

Neisser, U. (1993). *The perceived self: ecological and interpersonal sources of self-knowledge*. New York, NY: Cambridge University Press.

Oster, H. (1997). Facial expression as a window on sensory experience and affect in newborn infants. In *What the face reveals: basic and applied studies of spontaneous expression using the Facial Action Coding System* (ed. P. Ekman and E. L. Rosenberg), pp. 320–7. New York, NY: Oxford University Press.

Reddy, V. (1991). Playing with others' expectations: teasing and mucking about in the first year. In *Natural Theories of Mind* (ed. A. Whiten), pp. 143–58. Oxford: Blackwell.

Reddy, V. (1998). *Person-directed play: humour and teasing in infants and young children*. Research report to the Economic and Social Research Council. London: ESRC.

Reddy, V. (2000). Coyness in early infancy. *Developmental Science*, **3(2)**, 186–92.

Reddy, V. (2001). Positively shy! Developmental continuities in the expression of shyness, coyness, and embarrassment. In *International handbook of social anxiety: concepts, research and interventions relating to the self and shyness* (ed. R. W. Crozier and L. E. Alden), pp. 77–99. New York, NY: John Wiley and Sons Ltd.

Reddy, V., Williams, E., and Lang, B. (in preparation). Engaging with the self in a mirror.

Ruff, H. A. and Rothbart, M. K. (1996). *Attention in early development*. New York, NY: Oxford University Press.

Shotter, J. (1998). Agency and identity: A relational approach. In *The social child*. (ed. A. Campbell, and E. Muncer), (pp. 271–291). Hove, England: Psychology Press.

Stern, D. (1985). *The interpersonal world of the infant*. New York, NY: Basic Books.

Stifter, C. A. and Moyer, D. (1991). The regulation of positive affect: gaze aversion during mother-infant interaction. *Infant Behaviour and Development*, **14(1)**, 111–23.

Trevarthen, C. (1977). Descriptive analyses of infant communication behavior. In *Studies in Mother-Infant Interaction: The Loch Lomond Symposium* (ed. H. R. Schaffer), pp. 227–70. London: Academic Press.

Trevarthen, C. (1993). The self born in intersubjectivity. In *The perceived self: ecological and interpersonal sources of self-knowledge* (ed. U. Neisser), pp. 121–73. New York, NY: Cambridge University Press.

Trevarthen, C. and Hubley, P. (1978). Secondary intersubjectivity: confidence, confiding and acts of meaning in the first year. In *Action, Gesture and Symbol* (ed. A. Lock), pp. 183–229. London: Academic Press.

Young, G. and Decarie, T. G. (1977). An ethology-based catalogue of facial/vocal behaviour in infancy. *Animal Behaviour*, **25(1)**, 95–107.

New technology

Chapter 8

Infant perception and production of emotions during face-to-face interactions with live and 'virtual' adults

Darwin Muir, Kang Lee, Christine Hains, and Sylvia Hains

Overview

In this chapter, we will discuss research on the emergence and development of infants' competence in social perception—their ability to perceive, understand, and react to people as opposed to objects. In particular, we examine the infants' ability to react differentially to adult emotional expressions with responses that reflect their own emotional state. We begin by briefly reviewing evidence from studies in which both static and dynamic stimuli were presented to infants and infant visual attention was measured. Next, we describe studies in which adult facial and vocal displays were manipulated during face-to-face interactions with live and televised adults. We end by describing a new method for studying infant social perception using a computer driven 'virtual' adult. Two major points concerning the development of infant social perception of adult emotional expressions emerge from our research. To obtain a complete picture of infant social perception, researchers need to test infants in an interactive, dynamic context and must include measures of infant emotional responses, as well as measures of visual attention. Finally, we suggest several future directions for research on emotional development using both live and virtual adult technology.

Introduction

The traditional methods for studying infant social perception are based on static displays. An excellent review of infants' discrimination and categorization of facial expressions of emotion during infancy is provided by de Haan and Nelson (1998) and Bornstein and Arterberry (2003). The studies they reviewed measured infant competence using visual fixation time measures (e.g. visual habituation and preferential looking procedures) and physiological (event-related potential) responses to static stimuli (pictures). Such procedures are very effective tools to estimate when infants can discriminate between certain adult emotional expressions, and when they can generalize among various exemplars of particular emotional expressions in categorical perception studies. Although results are somewhat mixed, overall, the evidence suggests that the infants are able to discriminate between specific exemplars of adult emotional expressions (e.g. happy versus fear or anger) by 3 to 4 months of age. However, their ability to generalize among exemplars of a given emotional category (happy, sad, or angry) emerges gradually during the second 6 months of life. The first emotion to be categorized is happy (e.g. smiling) which according to Bornstein and Arterberry (2003), emerges in infants at 5 months of age.

The ability to discriminate and categorize static pictures is not necessarily a prerequisite of social perception. Our studies of infant emotion perception and production were inspired by social interaction theorists, such as Lewis and Goldberg (1969), Trevarthen (1974), Brazelton et al. (1974), and Tronick (1989). These theorists have suggested that very young infants not only discriminate between adult facial and vocal emotional expressions, but they actually understand the 'social message' being conveyed by the adult during face-to-face interactions. Infants express their understanding by engaging in reciprocal responses to the adult's social signals. For example, Tronick asserts that during face-to-face interactions 'infant smiles and vocalizations (and looks) are contingent on specific maternal affective turn-taking signals . . . adults make similar modifications' (p. 115, our italics emphasize procedural aspects below). Evidence for Tronick's theory is readily available in the natural world. When we casually interact with young infants in places such as grocery stores, they clearly display a rich repertoire of responses to our tactile, facial and vocal stimulation (see also chapters by Kugiumutzakis et al., Trevarthen, and Tronick, this volume). Based on these observations, we began designing studies to examine infants' appreciation of adult emotional expressions within the context of a social interaction.

Still-face paradigm: a model design to study infant emotion perception and production.

Tronick et al. (1978) were the first to describe a phenomenon that illustrates infants' sensitivity to a change in an adult's social responses during face-to-face interactions. They reported that infants stopped smiling and averted their gaze when their mothers posed a neutral, still-face after a few minutes of normal interaction. An example is shown in Fig. 8.1. Similar still-face effects have been found for mothers, fathers, and strangers across several cultures including US, Canadian, French, and Chinese cultures (e.g. Kisilevsky et al., 1998). Possible mechanisms underlying the still-face effect were reviewed recently by Adamson and Frick (2003) and Tronick (2003), and discussed briefly by Tronick and Tremblay et al. (this volume). We suggest that the still-face effect is more than a social phenomenon. The still-face procedure itself, along with its variations, can serve as a powerful research tool for studying early social, perceptual, and cognitive development. This methodology complements more traditional infant research techniques, such as visual preference and habituation methods (e.g. Bornstein and Arterberry, 2003). In this chapter, we will focus on the methodological advantages for using variations in the still-face procedure to study infant emotion perception and production.

Muir and Lee (2003) referred to the general procedure used to produce a still-face effect as an interaction-perturbation paradigm, and listed three advantages for using this paradigm to study infant social perception (see also Muir and Nadel, 1998; Muir and Hains, 1999). First, the paradigm consists of a very simple experimental design involving two groups of infants. In the no-change control group, the adult engages

A
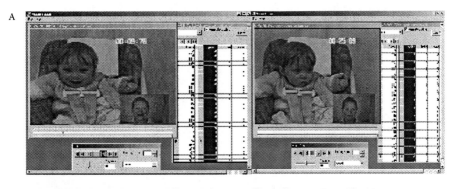

B
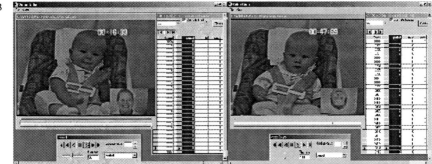

Fig. 8.1 Demonstrations of two effects in A and B recorded using our VideoCoding program discussed in the text. (It is free on the web at the Queen's University home page or at http://psyc.queensu,ca/~vidcoder). (A) Example of an infant displaying the still-face effect. Normal interaction: infant looks and smiles. Still face: infant stops looking and smiling. (B) Example of an infant displaying the inverted face effect. Normal interaction: infant looks and smiles. Inverted face: infant looks, but stops smiling. (C) Picture of the control room showing computer keyboard, special effects mixer and picture of infant and VIA displayed on the TV monitor. (D) Pictures of an infant in the experimental chamber interacting with a VIA presented on a 19-inch TV monitor, 1 m away at eye level. The infant is being recorded by the camera on top of the monitor. The picture on the left shows the infant smiling and looking at the VIA. The picture on the right shows the infant's view of the VIA (note: line on screen from camera).

C

D

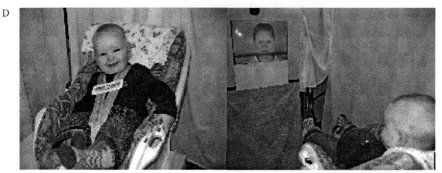

Fig. 8.1 (continued)

infants in three periods of normal face-to-face interaction (NNN) to provide a baseline comparison for the experimental group. In the experimental group (NPN) the adult engages in a normal, face-to-face interaction with infants in Period 1 (N), introduces some perturbation in her behaviour in Period 2 (the P period), and resumes a normal interaction with the infant in Period 3 (N).

The most important attribute of this design is that it overcomes, to some extent, the problem of how to explain the requirements of the study to a pre-verbal infant. The first interaction period can be seen as a non-verbal instructional period, the second period introduces the infant to the experimental manipulation, and the final period is akin to a debriefing period.

A second advantage of this NPN/NNN design is that it allows for comparisons between infant behaviours in two different ways, both intra-subject and between groups. The intra-subject comparison allows one to examine the change in infant behaviour from the normal interaction to the experimental condition and back again (seen as a quadratic trend across periods in a data analysis). The inter subject comparison allows one to compare infant performance in the control versus experimental groups (seen as a group by period interaction in a data analysis). Fig. 8.4A illustrates the typical behavioural functions we find for experimental (still-face) and control groups for measures of infant attention and smiling duration during each period (see Kisilevsky *et al.*, 1998, for many examples).

The third advantage to the interaction/perturbation paradigm is the emphasis experimenters place on using multiple measures of infant social engagement. While researchers generally acknowledge that infant reactions to environmental stimulation are complex, and consist of more than a single type of response, in many cases only one response is recorded (e.g. visual attention). By contrast, the interaction/perturbation procedure produces a rich array of infant responses to various perturbations in adult stimulation, leading researchers to record several infant responses. As noted below, when an interacting adult changes some aspects of her communicative signals (e.g. varying her tactile, facial, and/or vocal expressions), measures of infant visual attention to the adult's face may be entirely insensitive to such changes, while affect measures can reveal large perturbation effects.

Modifying the still-face procedure to test infant emotion perception and production

We have conducted a number of experiments on infant social perception using the interaction/perturbation paradigm. Theoretical rationales, procedural details, and results of the live interaction studies have been summarized by Muir and Hains (1999), and Muir and Nadel (1998), and will not be repeated here. We will give more procedural details in the section where we discuss the experiments using our 'virtual adult'. First, we will describe the effects of several perturbations in adult behaviour that illustrate the importance of measuring infant emotional responses in studies of social perception.

Adult touch can regulate infant emotional responses

In the standard still-face procedure, adults use touch, as well as vocal and facial expressions to engage infants in the N periods. Adult touch on its own is a powerful elicitor of both infant attention and positive affect (Muir, 2002). Stack and Muir (1990, 1992) found that when adults were allowed to continue touching infants during the still-face period, with their hands covered, the still-face effect was reduced or eliminated (i.e. infants continued to look and smile at the adult's still-face in response to the adult's touch). However, a large still-face effect can be produced when adult touch is eliminated from the procedure (Gusella et al., 1988; Ellsworth et al., 1993). Thus, to better isolate perturbation effects due to changes in adult facial and vocal stimulation, we eliminated adult touch in the all of the studies discussed below.

Adult eye direction regulates infant emotional responses

Adults use eye contact as a cue to potential social interaction. The importance of this cue has been examined in a number of ways. Blass and Camp (2001) reported that 2–3-month-olds showed a visual preference for a stranger who had previously made eye contact while feeding them over a stranger who fed them without eye contact. Caron et al. (1997) presented infants with a movie of an actress who smiled and talked using infant directed speech while she looked toward and away from the camera. Their 5-month-olds, but not 3-month-olds, smiled more when the adult's eyes were forward. We used the NPN design to study the infants' responses to eye contact with the P representing a period of no eye contact (Hains and Muir, 1996a; Symons *et al.*, 1998). Three- to 5-month-olds' smiling dropped reliably (~50%) during the P period, when the adult's eyes were averted. By contrast, visual attention remained constant across periods, similar to no-change controls. If we only measured visual attention, we would have concluded that infants are not affected by adult eye contact. However, clearly that is not the case; eye contact is an important cue used by infants to regulate their emotional behaviour during interactions with adults. The importance of manipulating adult behaviour during interactions is emphasized by Delgado *et al*.'s (2002) failure to find any differences in the still-face effect produced by mothers who either maintained or broke eye contact during the still-face period.

Indirect evidence that infants perceive adult facial emotions: the inverted face effect

According to many early theoretical accounts (e.g. Tronick, 1989), the still-face effect is generated because infants read and react in a reciprocal manner to the adult's positive emotional expressions during normal face-to-face interactions. When the adult poses a neutral, non-responsive facial expression it violates the infant's expectations for the adult to exhibit positive emotional expressions. Infants respond by becoming upset or at the very least they stop trying to engage the adult in reciprocal social exchanges. To test infants' sensitivity to adult facial emotional expressions *per se*, we designed a study in which the adult maintained contingent interactions with the infant but her facial emotions were hard to read. It is well known that adults have difficulty reading emotional expressions in inverted faces (Thompson, 1980; Rhodes, Brake, and Atkinson, 1993). By inverting an adult's face, while maintaining all other aspects of the interaction, the infant's ability to process the emotional content of the adult's face might be destroyed, which we hypothesized would produce a reduction in infant visual attention and smiling during the perturbation.

Muir and Nadel (1998) reviewed a series of infant face inversion studies. A typical set of results are shown in Fig. 8.5A. Across studies, infant visual attention always remained high during P, and did not differ across periods or from the control groups (NNN). In contrast, almost every infant showed a large drop in smiling during the perturbation. This result emphasizes the importance of measuring infant emotional responses such as smiling in conjunction with visual attention in social perception studies. If we had only measured visual attention, we would have concluded that infants did not perceive the inversion of a face during face-to-face interactions. By contrast, changes in infants' smiling indexed their strong reaction to the change in facial orientation. These results were found in infants between 3- and 6-months of age who interacted with mothers or with strangers.

To continue to investigate the regulation of infant smiling as a sensitive index of infant social perception, Rach-Longman (1991) conducted a head orientation study. Infants were placed in an infant seat on the floor, surrounded by a circular screen approximately 1 m high and 1 m in diameter, that was open at the top. The experimenter's head and shoulders were visible when she leaned over the top of the screen to interact with infants. By randomly changing her position around the perimeter of the screen, she varied her facial orientation from upright, to 45°, 90°, and 180° to the infant's perspective. Rach-Longman found no differences in infants' visual attention as a function of adult head orientation, but their smiling dropped significantly when she changed her head orientation from upright to 45°, and even further at 90° and 180°. Thus, the size of perturbation effects on smiling can be used to derive tuning functions for at least one perceptual manipulation (head orientation).

Finally, the inverted face effect also is generated by a silent adult face, i.e. when the adult mimes her speech throughout the procedure. Again, positive affect drops to inverted faces relative to upright faces, while visual attention remains unaffected by facial orientation (Cao et al., 1992). Thus, we concluded that the reduction in smiling caused by inverting the adult's face provided indirect evidence that infants are able to read positive affect in the adult's face by 3-months of age (Muir and Rach-Longman, 1989; Muir et al., 1994).

Direct evidence that infants differentiate happy and sad facial expressions

The inverted face effect only provides indirect evidence that infants are sensitive to adult facial emotional expressions. For example, the novelty of inverting the adult's head may interfere with the infant's social response of smiling—i.e. it may be hard for them to process the face cognitively and socially at the same time. A more direct test of their ability would be to manipulate the adult's facial expressions of emotion directly. Using the NPN design, D'Entremont and Muir (1997) varied the adult's emotional expression during the still-face period posing neutral, happy, or sad expressions. They produced a large still-face effect irrespective of the still-face's emotional expression. The drop in visual attention did not differ for any of the still-face expressions; however, there was slightly, but significantly, more infant smiling to the happy still-face than to the sad or neutral ones. Thus, infants do react differentially to static facial expressions of smiling by 5-months of age in the still-face procedure, the same age as Bornstein and Arterberry (2003) found when they tested static faces using visual habituation.

Of course, the failure of the adult to react at all during the still-face period may have overshadowed the infant's perception of the different emotional expressions in the still-face. Thus, D'Entremont and Muir (1999) conducted a series of experiments to manipulate the adult's emotional expressions during an ongoing interaction (NPN design). A stranger engaged 5-month-olds in face-to-face interactions, while exhibiting a sad expression in the P period. During P, the adult imagined an occasion when she

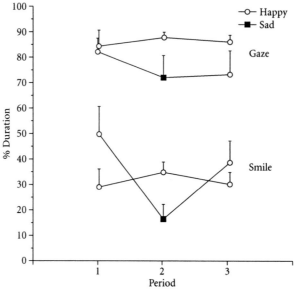

Fig. 8.2 The happy–sad face effect. These data are derived from D'Entremont and Muir (1999, Table 8.1). Percentage duration of gaze and smiling for each of the three 60-minute periods are shown for a no-change control group (NNN; the adult interacted with happy emotional expressions for all three periods) versus the experimental group (NPN; the adult interacted with happy expressions in Periods 1 and 3, and with sad expressions in Period 2). Standard errors for each point are indicated by the vertical bars.

was feeling sad and expressed her emotions accordingly. As shown in Fig. 8.2, there was a significant drop in infant smiling during the experimental period (significant quadratic function) relative to the controls revealing the infants' sensitivity to a change from happy to sad adult emotional expressions. Visual attention remained high across periods for the experimental group. As was the case for the inverted face effect, if we had only measured visual attention we would have concluded that 5-month-olds were relatively insensitive to the affective message in the adult's facial and vocal expressions.

To ensure that the sad-face effect could be produced by changes in facial expression alone, D'Entremont and Muir ran a second study in which the adult remained silent, miming her words in both conditions. Shorter periods (30 seconds) were used because pilot tests indicated that infants become fussy after about 90 seconds of interaction with a silent adult. In this case, infant visual attention dropped significantly over time, but no effect of the perturbation was found. By contrast smiling dropped from 25% during N to 2% when the adult expressed sad emotions.

Finally, D'Entremont (1995) conducted a longitudinal study on eight infants who were tested in their homes (no subject loss) each month from 1 to 5 months of age with the happy–sad face procedure described above. For this study there was no control condition; instead, infants received two sets of three 1-minute periods (NPN).

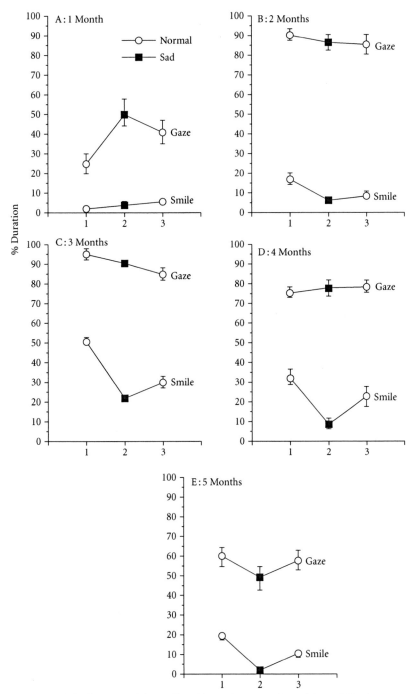

Fig. 8.3 Onset of the happy–sad face effect. These data are adapted from D'Entremont (1995). Percentage duration of gaze and smiling for each of the three 60 minute periods are shown for eight infants tested in an NPN design (happy-sad-happy expressions) monthly from 1 to 5 months of age. Standard errors for each point are indicated by the vertical bars. Significant quadratic trends for smiling as a function of period, defining the happy-sad face perturbation effect, occurred at 3, 4, and 5 months of age; no quadratic trends were shown for gaze durations.

During one of the sad face perturbation periods, D'Entremont silently mimed her words and during the other one she spoke out loud to infants (order counterbalanced). The average infant looking and smiling durations across periods are shown in Fig. 8.3 for the voice condition (voice and no-voice conditions did not differ) for each age. Total looking time increased from 1 to 2 months, peaked at 3 and 4 months, and decreased again at 5 months (a significant quadratic trend). However, there were no significant quadratic trends for visual attention across periods at any age—i.e. no happy–sad face perturbation effect for visual attention—replicating D'Entremont and Muir (1999). These results compliment those of researchers who use visual attention measures and static facial displays (e.g. Bornstein and Arterberry, 2003), and find that infants fail to categorize happy facial expressions until at least 5 months of age. Thus, by using the interaction/perturbation procedure, D'Entremont was able to show that infants can discriminate between multiple exemplars of an adult's happy versus sad facial emotional expressions when a smiling index is used, several months earlier than visual attention measures indicate.

The TV interactive/perturbation procedure

To this point, we have shown that the interactive/perturbation procedure is an effective way to demonstrate young infants' sensitivity to a variety of adult cues. However, there are limitations on the types of manipulations possible in a live interaction. To partially overcome this, we attempted to replicate our effects by having adults interact with infants while they were seated in separate rooms, looking at each other on TV monitors (for procedural details see Muir and Hains, 1999, and Gusella et al., 1988). Using our TV interaction procedure, we produced the large still-face effect shown in Fig. 8.4A.

We also replicated the averted eye effect described above using the TV interaction procedure and our NPN design. We had adult strangers interact over TV with 5-month-olds for all three periods, except that during the P period, the adult averted her eyes horizontally by about 40° to look at the infant on a TV monitor. During the averted eye period, infant smiling, but not attention, dropped significantly relative to N periods, almost matching the results obtained when the adult averted her eyes while seated in front of the infant (Hains and Muir, 1996a; Symons et al., 1998).

The TV technique originally was designed by Murray and Trevarthen (1985) to study the impact of non-contingent maternal social stimulation on infant emotional responses. They compared a live, contingent TV interaction period with one where a recording of the adult's previous behaviour was replayed to the infant (making it non-contingent). In general, researchers have reported a significant drop in infant smiling and visual attention during replay compared to N periods for mothers (Murray and Trevarthen, 1985; Nadel et al., 1999) and strangers (Hains and Muir, 1996b; Bigelow and Birch, 1999). However, there are some contradictory results. Hains and Muir (1996b) did not find a negative response by 5-month-olds to non-contingent mothers and Rochat et al. (1998) failed to replicate Murray and Trevarthen's (1985) results with 6-week-olds. Possible reasons for these failures to replicate are discussed by Muir and Nadel (1998).

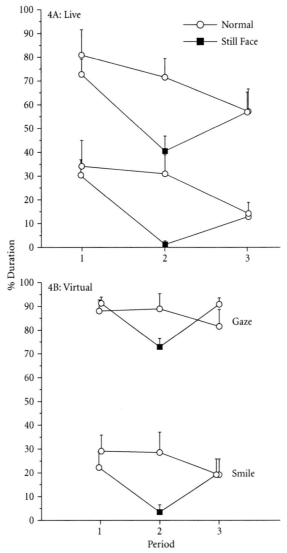

Fig. 8.4 The still-face effect for a live over TV (A) and virtual interactive (B) adults. The data plotted in A are adapted from Gusella *et al.* (1988). Control (*n* = 8) mothers interacted 'normally' for three 90-second periods with their infants over TV. Mothers in the experimental group (*n* = 8) engaged in normal interactions during Periods 1 and 3, and posed a still-face during Period 2. In B, the same comparisons are made using a virtual interacting adult (VIA) for 60 seconds periods (from Muir *et al.*, 2002). Durations of smiling and visual attention are indicted by open circles during 'normal' periods, and during the still-face condition by the filled squares with standard errors indicated by the vertical lines on each point. A large still-face effect [a significant condition: experimental (*n* = 8) versus control (*n* = 8); X period interaction, with a significant quadratic trend only for the experimental (NPN) groups] was found in both live over TV and virtual adult experiments. While the smiling results are almost identical in the two experiments, the VIA appeared overall to generate more infant attention than the live adult here and in Figs. 8.5 and 8.6.

Adult facial emotions: the inverted face effect

In several studies we reproduced the inverted face effect discussed using TV interactions (e.g. Rach-Longman, 1991). In fact, in our first inverted face study, Roman (1986) had mothers and their 5-month-olds interact over TV for three periods (NPN), with the mother's face inverted electronically on the infant's TV screen as the perturbation. We used this procedure to insure that the mother remained naïve to the perturbation. The results from this study are those plotted in Fig. 8.5A (discussed earlier).

Direct evidence that infants differentiate happy from sad facial expressions

D'Entremont (personal communication, 2000) replicated the happy-sad effect on positive affect described above for interactions with a stranger seated in front of the infants using the TV interaction procedure. Using the NPN design she had both mothers and strangers interact with infants over TV. Overall, infants smiled less during sad-P periods (6% duration averaged across the two adults) than during the happy-N periods ($M = 22\%$). However, in this case, the infants also showed significantly less visual attention during P ($M = 50\%$) than during N periods ($M = 72\%$).

Creating a 'virtual' adult (VIA) to interact with young infants

The five examples discussed above demonstrate that infants will engage in interactions with televised adults and will show perturbation effects similar to those produced with an adult seated in front of them. However, the use of the TV interaction procedure only solved some of our stimulus control problems. One of our research goals was to examine infants' sensitivity to affective messages carried by an adult's face and voice during a natural face-to-face interaction. We noted that differences in adult interaction styles could influence infants' reactions, confounding our results. Furthermore, some perturbations in adult social signals that are of theoretical interest cannot be performed by live adults (e.g. presenting infants with conflicting vocal and facial emotional expressions). Given that infants so readily interact with our televised, live strangers, and given the increasing power and decreasing cost of personal computers, we developed a computer-driven Virtual Interactive Adult (VIA) to obtain better stimulus control (Muir *et al.*, 2002; Semcesen *et al.*, 2000).

Our VIA was designed to present a dynamic, life-like female head and shoulders that could be driven by an experimenter in response to infants' social signals to simulate an adult's contingent social responses to infants during a normal face-to-face interaction. The VIA evolved in several stages. In our first attempt, Semcesen *et al.* (2000) created a VIA by video-recording the head and shoulders of two experienced female experimenters while they each interacted with an infant over TV for 3 minutes. From this video-record, Semcesen selected 14 segments for each interactor, which included the following comment categories: one greeting, one consoling, one surprise and 11 'positive' clips (e.g. 'You're

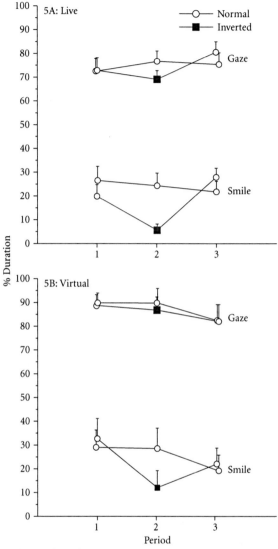

Fig. 8.5 The inverted face effects for live over TV (A) and virtual interactive (B) adults. The data are plotted for durations of infant visual attention and smiling in A and B, with standard errors shown by the vertical bars. In A for the experimental group (*n* = 8) mothers interacted for three 90-second periods with their infants over TV; in Periods 1 and 3, their faces were upright on the TV (open circles) while in Period 2, unbeknown to the mothers, their faces were inverted (filled squares) on the infants' TV monitors electronically. The no-change control data for 3 periods of normal interaction using both live over TV and VIA adults (*n* = 8 for each group) were collected recently by C. Hains, and are shown for comparison with experimental live (A) and VIA (B) groups. In this Figure, the reliable quadratic trends for smiling defined the inverted face effect for experimental live and VIA adults, while there were no perturbation effects for infant visual attention.

Table 8.1 In A, a list of video clips used by to construct the initial Virtual Adult Interacter (VIA). In B, the clips in the final version of the VIA

(A) Clips used for the VIA for experimenter 1 in Semcesen *et al.* (2000)

Type of Clip	Clip	Keyboard letter	Duration (seconds)
Greeting	Hello. Hi baby.	z	5
Positive	How are you? How are you?	a	4
Positive	Babababa. Abagoobee.	s	3
Positive	Abadoobadabadee.	d	4
Positive	Am I making no sense?	f	3
Positive	You're such a pretty baby.	g	3
Positive	You're such a pretty baby aren't you? Yes you are.	h	4
Positive	That's a good baby.	j	3
Positive	Oh, you're telling me a little story.	l	5
Positive	Oh. Ooooh. That's a funny story.	;	5
Positive	Do you think I'm funny? Agadabadoo. Adoobadoobadoo.	r	7
Positive	What are you doing? Are you going to tell me a little story?	m	5
Surprise	Oh, whatcha doing. Whatcha doing.	k	5
Consoling	Oh. Oooh. Don't cry. Don't cry.	c	6
Still-face	Still-face	p	60
Silent smiling face	Silent smiling face	Space bar	10

(B) The set of clips for the VIA (Muir *et al.*, 2003) that optimized infant visual attention and smiling during 'normal' interaction periods (N), and produced almost identical still-face, inverted face, and voice perturbations effects in validity studies. Note that the clips are clustered together on the keyboard according to their general function, to facilitate ease of presentation by the experimenter during contingent interactions with infants.

Key	Script (first few words)
Z	Hello Baby
X	Reunite
P	I never knew that
I	Are you talking to me
U	Are you telling me something
O	That's a funny story
A	Ah bababa
Y	Can you tell me a story
Q	Can you look at me
G	Ohhhh

Table 8.1 (continued)

Key	Script (first few words)
F	Wonderful baby
S	Silly baby
D	Such a good baby
L	Show me another smile
K	Play a smiling game
J	Beautiful smile
H	Wonderful smile
B	Don't cry
N	What's wrong
W	What do you have
E	What do you see
R	What have you got
T	Where are you going
C	We are all done

such a pretty baby') listed for Experimenter 1 in Table 8.1A. Semcesen digitized the video-record using a Matrox video capture device and edited the clips using Adobe Premier software. A computer programme called 'KeyClips' was developed by Baron *et al.* (2002) to control the presentation of the VIA's clips. The Key Clips software allows the experimenter to choose an appropriate contingent response for each of the infants' behaviours by striking the appropriate key on the computer keyboard (see Table 8.1).

Semcesen had each experimenter use the VIA, constructed from their own clips, to interact for 1 minute with eight infants, while standing in the control room, shown in Fig. 8.1C. After considerable practice operating the VIA, the experimenter watched the infant on a TV monitor and pressed the appropriate keys on the computer keyboard below the TV in response to the infant's social signals. An example of an infant smiling at the VIA during such an interaction is shown in Fig. 8.1D. Cameras recorded both the infants' behaviour and the VIA displays; the two records were combined using a special effects generator and digitized into our videocoding programme described below and illustrated in Fig. 8.1A,B.

Semcesen found experimenter differences: experimenter 1 presented slightly more positive affect ($Ms = 96\%$ versus 88%), was more vocal ($Ms = 81\%$ versus 75%), and made more head movements ($Ms = 50\%$ versus 22%) than experimenter 2. Infants were more responsive to experimenter 1 than to experimenter 2; they looked longer ($M = 95\%$ versus 78%, respectively) and smiled more ($M = 48\%$ versus 12%, respectively) at experimenter 1. When compared with the experimenter's behaviour in previous live TV studies, the adults' response latency to the infants' social signals was significantly longer when driving the VIA (1.6 seconds) than when they interacted live over TV (0.9 seconds). Infants smiled and looked longer at experimenter 1 than experimenter 2 in the live TV procedure as well. Thus, despite differences in the experimenters' behaviour and the delayed response of the VIA compared to live interacters, Semcesen's VIAs did generate infant social responses that appeared to be comparable to those generated by the same adults during live interactions.

Validation studies using the VIA

C. Hains (personal communication) noted several problems with Semcesen's version of the VIA. The size of the set of adult responses (clips) culled from 3 minutes of interaction with a single infant was too small. Semcesen's VIAs were missing a number of critical clips that experimenters needed to cover the range of responses they normally would use to interact with infants. Semcesen had each of her adults interact with four other infants, but she could not use any of these clips because of noticeable differences between recordings in the adult's dress, hair, and posture. Also, the failure of the adults to centre their heads at the end of each response to the infant resulted in jerky head movement between each clip and the default or the next action sequence. Thus, for our validation studies, Muir *et al.* (2002) reconstructed a single, standard VIA to increase the number of clips and to control head position. They used experimenter 1 (CH) as the VIA, given that she generated the highest degree of positive affect, which was one of our major dependant variables. Finally, CH did not actually interact with an infant; she was recorded in the TV interaction setting while viewing herself on the TV monitor as she perfected the script for each clip, and ensured that each segment began and ended with her head centred on the screen. CH produced 26 different video segments (3–8 seconds in length) listed in Table 8.1B. The clips included one greeting, one ending, and one reunion clip, plus groups of clips that we classified as general banter, response to a talking baby, and reacting to smiling, upset, or distracted babies. The clips in each category were clustered on the keyboard, as shown in Table 8.1, to facilitate presenting different exemplars for the same infant behaviour (to minimize habituation) during the interaction. Finally, CH morphed the digitized segments at the beginning and the end of each action to create an almost seamless transition between clips.

The VIA still-face effect

In our first validation study, sixteen 4–6-month-olds were tested using the still-face (NPN) procedure with the new VIA. Experimental infants ($n = 8$) viewed the adult posing a neutral still-face during the P period and controls ($n = 8$) received contingent VIA stimulation for three periods (NNN). Infants were recorded, and the video records were digitized and coded using another software package we designed. The Queen's University Video Coding System is a coding shareware programme that allows the user to unite an *avi* video file with a Microsoft Access database to score any behaviour at the rate from single frames to 200% of real time (Baron *et al.*, 2001; http://psyc.queensu.ca/~vidcoder

provides a free copy of the programme and instruction manual). Fig. 8.1 shows example frames from this programme to illustrate the still-face and inverted face effects. In this and all other studies scoring was blind as to condition by covering the adult's face and turning off the sound.

The infants' smiling and visual attention during the live TV and VIA still-face procedures are shown in Fig. 8.4A,B. The VIA generated a significant amount of smiling (~25%) and high levels of visual attention (over 90%) in Period 1, replicating Simcesen's results. The VIA still-face effect matched the live still-face effect (compare Figs. 8.4A,B). The only obvious difference between the two procedures was a smaller decline (about 20% drop) in visual attention for the VIA compared to the live, TV still-face (about 40% drop). However, the shape of the still-face effect was similar for both live and VIA procedures.

The VIA inverted face effect

Our second validation study tested the inverted face effect using the VIA procedure with 4–6-month-olds. Evans (2001) created a VIA file that inverted the faces of all of the VIA video clips and tested 8 infants using the NPN design. They interacted with the upright VIA's face in Periods 1 and 3, and the VIA's inverted face in Period 2. Evans used the same recording and scoring procedures as in previous studies; the durations of visual attention and smiling at the VIA are shown in Fig. 8.5B, along with no-change controls. Comparing Fig. 8.5 A and B, the significant inverted face effects for both procedures are strikingly similar.

The role of the adult voice in infant social perception

Here, we will briefly discuss infant sensitivity to adult speech, and intermodal perception of emotions, followed by illustrations of how the VIA can be used to advance research in this area.

It is well established that infants respond differentially to speech over non-speech sounds at birth, even when non-speech sounds are matched for many of the spectral and temporal properties of the speech signal (e.g. Vouloumanos and Werker, 2004). Fetuses discriminate between their mother's voice and a stranger's voice (Kisilevsky *et al.*, 2003) and newborns prefer to listen to the mother's voice over a stranger's (DeCasper and Fifer, 1980), as well as maternal over nonmaternal language (Moon *et al.*, 1993).

In non-interaction studies, it has been shown that very young infants are sensitive to various relationships between characteristics of the adult's face and voice (see Bahrick, 2000, for a review). For example, infants react to disruptions in the temporal synchrony of the face and voice (Dodd, 1979), and a discrepancy between the shape of the lip movements and corresponding vowel sounds (Kuhl and Meltzoff, 1982). Burnham (1993) found that 1-month-olds discriminated between dynamic displays of mothers' and strangers' faces, but only if the faces were accompanied by the voices (i.e. they did not discriminate between silent faces).

Effects of removing the voice during face-to-face interactions

We hoped that our interaction/perturbation procedure would provide a more sensitive index of infants' ability to respond to changes in adults' voices, as well as their faces. However, in our initial studies, infants appeared to be relatively insensitive to voice perturbations during face-to-face interactions. For example, Gusella et al. (1988) compared the data for the still-face and control groups shown in Fig. 8.4A with two other manipulations. When a mother's interactive face was presented without vocal accompaniment (TV sound turned off), her 5-month-old continued to smile and look at her. By contrast, when her pre-recorded still-face was accompanied by her interactive voice, infants showed a large still-face effect. Also, recall that when D'Entremont and Muir (1999) had adult strangers shift from happy to sad emotional expressions, the drop in smiling was similar with or without an accompanying voice, although the face plus voice conditions did generate more visual attention than face alone conditions. The voice also makes a difference in generating the inverted face effect; infants did smile at a relatively low level to a live, talking inverted face and this smiling disappeared when the adult stopped talking (see Muir and Nadel, 1998). In their review of these studies, Muir and Nadel (1998) concluded that the adult's face appears to be the major force driving positive affect in young infants, while the adult's voice operates primarily to maintain infant visual attention, although on its own the voice can elicit some positive affect when facial expressions become hard to decipher.

Effects of vocal perturbations during live and VIA face-to-face interactions

While eliminating the adult's voice during face-to-face engagements has minimal impact on infant emotional responses directed towards the adult's face, altering the adult's voice during the interaction can result in a dramatic drop in infant positive affect. This work was initiated by Barbara D'Entremont (1997; details in Muir and Nadel, 1998) who tried to engage 5-month-olds in a live, face-to-face interaction by miming her words while playing a 5-tone tune on a synthesizer in synchrony with her lip movements, effectively replacing her voice. She stopped the experiment after testing only five babies because they all became upset.

Patterson and Hains (unpublished, cited in Muir et al., 2002) tried to replicate D'Entremont's observations using our standard NPN design. Seventeen 4–6-month-olds were introduced to one of two interacters who replaced their voices in the perturbation period with the same five synthesizer tones used in the previous study. The results are presented in Fig. 8.6A. While infants did not become upset when the synthesizer tones replaced the voice, their smiling dropped significantly during the perturbation and infant visual attention significantly increased.

Moulson et al. (2004) attempted to replicate this effect using our VIA with one major procedural difference. She carefully played the synthesizer tones in synchrony with the

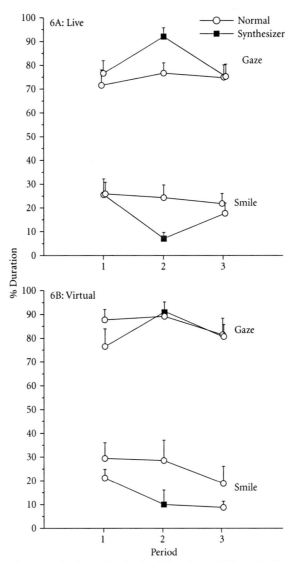

Fig. 8.6 The synthesizer perturbation effect for live (A) and virtual (B) adults. The data are plotted for durations of infant visual attention and smiling in A and B, with standard errors shown by the vertical bars. The filled squares indicate the voice was replaced by synthesizer tones. In both A (n = 17 for the experimental group tested by Patterson and Hains, unpublished; n = 8 for the control group from Fig. 8.5A) and B (n = 8 for both groups; experimental group from Moulson, et al., 2004; controls from Fig. 8.5B), infants showed a significant increase in visual attention and decrease in smiling when the adults' facial expressions were accompanied by tones; indeed, the means almost overlay each other for the two experimental groups in the first two periods. However, the live synthesizer group recovered smiling in Period 3, while the VIA synthesizer group did not. The synthesizer groups' performance contrasts with that of controls that showed little change gaze and smiling across periods.

onset and offset of the VIA's mouth movements, and maintained the gross pitch contour for each vocal passage. These tones were better matched to vocalizations for the VIA than was possible in the live procedure. The major effects of replacing the VIA's voice were a significant increase in visual attention and a decline in smiling during the synthesizer period. In fact, the means from Fig. 8.6A,B for the first two periods for both measures are almost identical. However, in Period 3 smiling remained depressed for the VIA (Fig. 8.6B), while smiling recovered for the live interacters (Fig. 8.6A). This particular vocal perturbation by our VIA appears to have made a more lasting impact on infant positive affect than a similar vocal perturbation during live interactions. Moulson *et al.* obtained further evidence to support this conclusion when she presented the same perturbation in a PNP design. In this case, visual attention remained high across periods, while smiling was significantly lower in Period 1 (about 8% duration) than for the VIA with normal vocalizations, and remained depressed throughout Periods 2 and 3. Clearly, some perturbations in the adult's voice during face-to-face interactions can depress infant positive affect.

The role of vocal emotional expression

Recently, Mastrophieri and Turkewitz (1999) reported that newborns also respond differentially to the affect in female voices. Their infants displayed more eye-opening responses to low-pass filtered female voices when they expressed happy emotions than when they expressed sad, angry, or neutral emotions. Furthermore, this affect discrimination was present for emotional speech in the mother's native language (e.g. English), but not for the same emotional expressions in a novel language (e.g. Spanish), suggesting that the discrimination was learned during the fetal period.

Caron *et al.* (1988), using visual habituation procedures, showed that infants as young as 4 months of age discriminated between several dynamic emotional expressions in the face of a videotaped model, but only when her facial expressions were accompanied by her voice. In older infants, speech sounds also facilitate the recognition of adult facial expressions of emotions. Fernald (1993) presented recordings of adult approval vocalizations alternated with prohibition vocalizations while 5-month-olds viewed a picture of a female face posing a neutral expression. Her infants' positive affect was higher during the approval than during the prohibitive vocalizations. Taken together, this research suggests that infants may be tuned to perceive and respond to emotional expressions in adults' voices early in life, perhaps at birth.

Walker-Andrews (1997) provides an excellent literature review on infant intermodal perception of facial and vocal expressions of emotions. In her own work, she presented pre-recorded faces expressing different emotions (e.g. happy versus sad) on two adjacent TV monitors, accompanied by a single vocal track that matched the emotions in one of the faces. She found that infants looked longer at the face that matched the happy expressions in the voice by 4–5 months of age- and voice-matched other expressions (e.g. sad) at slightly older ages. This inter-modal matching of affect in the face and voice disappeared when she inverted the faces, consistent with the inverted face effect we described above. However, Kahana-Kalman and Walker-Andrews (2001) and Montague and Walker-Andrews (2002) reported that 3.5-month-olds will look longer at the face matching the happy or sad vocal tracks, but only with mothers' faces; they did not sound-match strangers' or fathers' faces. Furthermore, there was a difference in intermodal matching for different maternal expressions; 3.5-month-olds looked longer at the miss-matched face when they were tested with happy versus angry emotional expressions (e.g. they looked longer at the mother's happy face while listening to her angry voice).

Although Walker-Andrews' voice-matching preferential looking procedure can be used to assess infant reactions to conflicting emotions in the face and voice indirectly, it is not possible to conduct direct tests because a live adult cannot express happiness in her face and sadness in her voice at the same time. We hoped to provide a more direct test using the VIA given that our validation studies showed it could act as a substitute for a live adult.

The VIA with a happy face and sad voice

To test infant sensitivity to conflicts in the emotions expressed by an adult's face versus voice, we created a new VIA that used the same list of expressions as those listed in Table 8.1B. This time a sad face and voice was recorded. Hains created a set of clips for the VIA that had a happy face and sad voice by inserting the sad vocal track onto the happy face for each clip, using Adobe Premiere. In this experiment, using the NPN design, in P we used the VIA with the happy face paired with the sad voice. Because sad speech is slower than happy speech, perfect synchrony between all aspects of the lip movements and speech sounds was not possible. To counter this problem, she also created a slightly modified happy face-happy voice VIA by randomly shifting the vocal tracks for each clip slightly (mean temporal mismatch of ~150 ms, i.e. 4 frame offset at 30 frames per second) from the original set of matched face-voice video clips. This was used during Period 2 in our no-change control group to rule out the possibility that any perturbation effect might be due to the mismatched timing of the lips and speech sounds, rather than the mismatched emotional content. Although infants do perceive desynchronized faces and voices (Dodd, 1979), disruption in social interactions was slight and only found during live TV interactions when the voice was delayed by more than 1 second (Cao, 1994).

The infants' behaviour and the VIA display were recorded, digitized and scored as described above; the average durations of visual attention and smiling are shown in Fig. 8.7. In this case infants' positive affect and attention did not change across periods and were similar to controls. This result may have occurred because the infants could not discriminate the VIA's happy and sad vocal emotions. This has not been tested yet, but adults rated the positive affect in the VIA's happy face as being less positive when the face was paired with the sad voice than with the happy voice (Smith, 2003, unpublished). Another alternative, one that we favour, is that in the VIA interactive context, infants simply were captured by the happy facial expressions in the VIA's face

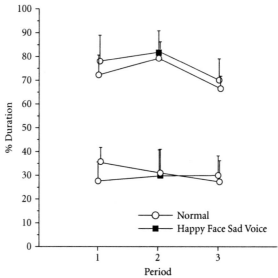

Fig. 8.7 The happy face-sad voice perturbation effect for virtual interactive adults. The data collected by Rianne Hastie (unpublished) are plotted for durations of infant visual attention and smiling for experimental (NPN) and control (NNN) groups, with standard errors shown by the vertical bars. The filled squares indicate that the happy voice was paired with a sad voice in Period 2 for the experimental group (n = 8). The VIA for this control group (n = 8) had synchronized happy facial and vocal expressions in Periods 1 and 3, as did the experimental group; however, in Period 2 the VIA's matching happy face-happy voice expressions had a randomized delay introduced between the face and voice (M = 150 ms) to approximate the temporal asynchrony that occurred when the happy face was paired with the sad voice in Period 2 for the experimental group. Clearly, there was no difference between experimental and control groups for this perturbation.

and ignored the discrepant vocal affect. A third possibility is that the VIA will not generate the happy versus sad facial expression effect described by D'Entremont and Muir (1989) for live interaction/perturbation procedures and by D'Entremont (personal communication) for TV interactions. Experiments currently are in progress to examine these possibilities and preliminary results rule out the third possibility. A group of 5-month-olds (n = 8) have shown a significant drop in smiling, but no change in visual attention, when the VIA's face shifted from happy expressions in Period 1 to sad expressions in Period 2 while the voice remained happy. These results almost match those of D'Entremont and Muir (1999) when their adult's emotional facial and vocal expressions changed from happy in Period 1 to sad in Period 2 (see Fig. 8.2).

Summary and future research directions

In this chapter, we described an interactive/perturbation experimental method that can be used to study infant social perception, including emotion perception. It was derived from the still-face paradigm where adults first engage the infant in face-to-face interactions followed by a perturbation in their behaviour and then the resumption of a normal interaction. We focused on two primary infant behaviours, positive emotional expressions and visual attention, to assess the impact of various perturbations in adult behaviour on the infant.

Use of the interactive/perturbation design (NPN/NNN)

We used this design to demonstrate infant sensitivity to perturbations in adult behaviour. We showed that 3–7-month-olds reduced both smiling and looking at adults who either stopped responding and posed a neutral facial expression, or continued to stimulate them with positive facial and vocal emotional expressions that were not contingent on the infants' behaviour (i.e. non-contingency effect). Infants were also found to be sensitive to changes in other aspects of adult social stimulation such as shifts in head orientation, eye direction, affect (happy to sad emotions), and vocalizations (voice to tones). However, their sensitivity to these manipulations was only indexed by a decline in positive affect during the perturbation period—visual attention measures revealed either no reaction or a very weak one to such perturbations.

There are additional advantages to the use of this procedure for studying infant social perception. First, because most infants show the perturbation effects, relatively few subjects are required ($n \sim 8$ infants per group in most of our studies). Also, we can examine the infant's sensitivity to perturbations by comparing the size of the change in positive emotions during different perturbations. Preliminary attempts to compare perturbations suggest that effects are greatest for the still-face and non-contingency, and are much less dramatic to shifts in eye direction and emotional and vocal expressions (see Muir and Hains, 1999 for details) . Furthermore, at least for the inverted face effect, the degree of decline in smiling is directly related to the size of the perturbation, allowing us to calculate an orientation tuning function. Similar sensitivity functions should be present for different degrees of eye rotation (Symons et al., 1998), emotional expressions of sadness, and other perturbations.

Use of the virtual interactive adult (VIA) to test infant social perception

Perhaps our most exciting research advance is that infants can be engaged in relatively natural dyadic exchanges with a 'virtual' interactive adult we called the VIA. We described how we constructed a VIA that produced perturbation effects similar to those produced by live interacters (e.g. the still face, inverted face, and altered voice effects). This technology allows us to digitally alter aspects of the adult's facial and vocal signals (e.g. inverting the eyes/mouth, rotating the head gradually, moving the pupils, altering the VIA's emotional expressions) to test the threshold of infant sensitivity to these and other perturbations in adult behaviour. Some examples of studies with the VIA are perturbations in:

Adult emotional expressions

For the first time we can test infant reactions to perturbations that are of theoretical interest but are impossible to produce using live adults. For example, Papoušek *et al.* (1990) found that 4-month-olds could not discriminate adult approving (happy sounds) from disapproving (negative emotional vocalizations) infant directed speech when the vocal contours were reversed. We expect infant social engagement also will be dampened if the virtual adult's contingent facial or vocal displays are presented backwards—a test that can only be accomplished using our interactive virtual adult procedure.

Contingency

The sensitivity of infants to variations in the timing of the VIA's responses to infants can be evaluated in a variety of ways. For example, a previous record of the VIA's responses to a different infant can be played to the infant to replicate the contingency effects found using the TV interactions discussed above. Also, the importance of the timing of adult responses to infant signals can be assessed by imposing variable or constant delays in the VIA's response following the experimenter's key strike.

Individual differences

The VIA can serve as a standardized stimulus to investigate cross-cultural similarities and differences in infant competence in social perception. For example, the universal nature of emotion perception and production during social interactions can be examined cross-culturally by testing infants from other cultures for still-face, inverted face, and happy-sad effects using our current, Canadian VIA. If we obtain different functions, other VIAs can be constructed to see if, for example, the difference is due to physical differences in the face, or the nature of the facial and verbal emotional expressions, or language differences, etc. The VIA also can provide a standardized stimulus to assess individual differences in infants' reactions to social stimulation for early diagnosis of infants at risk for later social-cognitive deficits, such as autism spectrum disorder (discussed by Loveland, this volume).

In conclusion, we hope that the use of an interaction/perturbation procedure and the VIA technology described in this chapter will help researchers to provide converging evidence for a comprehensive description of the development of infants' perception and production of emotional expressions by social stimuli.

Acknowledgments

The research at Queen's University, discussed in this chapter, was supported by Natural Sciences and Engineering Research Council grants awarded to Darwin Muir and to Kang Lee. We wish to thank the parents and infants who participated in the studies, for

Rianne Hastie for her help collecting the data in Fig. 8.7, and Ann Muir for proof reading the manuscript.

For a free copy of the Virtual Interactive Adult and KeyClips Software contact C. Hains by e-mail at tabie@psyc.queensu.ca.

References

Adamson, L. B. and Frick, J. E. (2003). The still-face: a history of a shared experimental paradigm. *Infancy*, **4**, 451–73.

Bahrick, L. E. (2000). Increasing specificity in the development of intermodal perception. In *Infant development: the essential readings* (ed. D. Muir and A. Slater), pp. 119–36. Oxford: Blackwell.

Baron, M. J., Wheatley, J., Symons, L., *et al.* (2001). *The Queen's video coder*. Department of Psychology, Queen's University, Kingston, Canada. Available at: http://psyc.queensu.ca/~vidcoder.

Baron, M. J., Hains, C. R., and Muir, D. (2002). *The virtual interactive adult and keyclips software*. Available from C. Hains, tabie@psyc.queensu.ca.

Bigelow, A. E. and Birch, S. A. J. (1999). The effects of contingency in previous interactions on infants' preference for social partners. *Infant Behaviour and Development*, **22**, 367–82.

Blass, E. and Camp, C. (2001). The ontogeny of face recognition: eye contact and sweet taste induced preference in 9- and 12-week-old human infants. *Developmental Psychology*, **37**, 762–74.

Bornstein, M. H. and Arterberry, M. E. (2003). Recognition, discrimination and categorization of smiling by 5-month-old infants. *Developmental Science*, **6**, 585–99.

Brazelton, T. B., Koslowski, B., and Main, W. (1974). The origins of reciprocity: The early mother-infant interaction. In *The effect of the infant on its caregiver* (ed. M. Lewis and L. A. Rosenblum), pp. 49–76. New York: Wiley.

Burnham, D. (1993). Visual recognition of mother by young infants: facilitation by speech. *Perception*, **22**, 1133–53.

Caron, A., Caron, R., and MacLean, D. (1988). Infant discrimination of naturalistic emotional expressions: the role of face and voice. *Child Development*, **59**, 604–16.

Caron, A., Caron, R., Roberts, J., *et al.* (1997). Infant sensitivity to deviations in dynamic facial-vocal displays: the role of eye regard. *Developmental Psychology*, **33**, 802–13.

Cao, Y. (1994). Five month-olds' perception of asynchrony between face and voice during social interactions. *Infant Behaviour and Development*, **17**, 555.

Cao, Y., Hains, S., and Muir, D. (1992). Isolating the effects of adult vocal and facial stimulation during interactions with 4- to 6-month-olds. *Infant Behaviour and Development*, **15**, 334.

DeCasper, A. J. and Fifer, W. P. (1980). Of human bonding: newborns prefer their mothers' voices. *Science*, **208**, 1174–6.

de Haan, M. and Nelson, C. (1988). Discrimination and categorization of facial expressions of emotion during infancy. In *Perceptual development: visual auditory, and speech perception in infancy* (ed. A. Slater), pp. 247–86. East Sussex: Psychology Press.

D'Entremont, B. (1995). *One- to six-month-olds' attention and affective responding to adults' happy and sad expressions: the role of face and voice*. Unpublished Doctoral Dissertation, Queen's University, Kingston, Ontario.

Delgado, C. E. F., Messinger, D. S., and Yale, M. E. (2002). Infant responses to direction of parental gaze: a comparison of two still-face conditions. *Infant Behaviour and Development*, **25**, 311–18.

D'Entremont, B. and Muir, D. (1997). Five-month-olds' attention and affective responses to still-faced emotional expressions. *Infant Behaviour and Development*, **20**, 563–8.

D'Entremont, B. and Muir, D. (1999). Infants' responding to adult's happy and sad expressions during contingent interactions. *Infant Behaviour and Development*, **22**, 527–39.

Dodd, B. (1979). Lip reading in infants: attention to speech. *Canadian Psychologist*, **11**, 478–84.

Ellsworth, C. P., Muir, D. W., and Hains, S. M. J. (1993). Social competence and person-object differentiation: an analysis of the still-face effect. *Developmental Psychology*, **29**, 63–73.

Evens, E. M. (2001). *Infant face perception: the effect of inversion involving a virtual interacter.* Unpublished Honours Thesis, Queen's University, Kingston, Ontario.

Fernald, A. (1993). Approval and disapproval: infant responsiveness to vocal affect in familiar and unfamiliar languages. *Child Development*, **64**, 657–74.

Gusella, J. L., Muir, D. W., and Tronick, E. A. (1988). The effect of manipulating maternal behaviour during an interaction on three- and six-month-olds' affect and attention. *Child Development*, **59**, 1111–24.

Hains, S. M. J. and Muir, D. W. (1996a). Infant sensitivity to adult eye direction. *Child Development*, **67**, 1940–51.

Hains, S. M. J. and Muir, D. W. (1996b). Effects of stimulus contingency in infant-adult interactions. *Infant Behaviour and Development*, **19**, 49–61.

Kahana-Kalman, R. and Walker-Andrews, A. (2001). The role of person familiarity in young infants' perception of emotional expressions. *Child Development*, **72**, 352–69.

Kisilevsky, B. S., Hains, S. M., Lee, K., *et al.* (1998). The still-face effect in Chinese and Canadian 3- to 6-month-old infants. *Child Development*, **34**, 629–39.

Kisilevsky, B. S., Hains, S. M., Lee, K., *et al.* (2003). Effects of experience on foetal voice recognition. *Psychological Science*, **14**, 220–4.

Kuhl, P. K. and Meltzoff, A. N. (1982). The bimodal perception of speech in infancy. *Science*, **218**, 1138–41.

Lewis, M. and Goldberg, S. (1969). Perceptual-cognitive development in infancy: a generalized expectancy model as a function of mother-infant interaction. *Merrill-Palmer Quarterly*, **15**, 745–51.

Mastrophieri, D. and Turkewitz, G. (1999). Prenatal experience and neonatal responsiveness to vocal expressions of emotion. *Developmental Psychobiology*, **35**, 204–14.

Moon, C., Cooper, R. P., and Fifer, W. (1993). Two-day-olds prefer their native language. *Infant Behaviour and Development*, **16**, 495–500.

Montague, D. and Walker-Andrews, A. (2002). Mothers, fathers, and infants: the role of person familiarity and parental involvement in infants' perception of emotional expressions. *Child Development*, **73**, 1339–52.

Moulson, M., Lee, K., and Muir, D. (2004). *5-month-olds' reactions to vocal perturbations during face-to-face interactions with a virtual adult.* Presented at the May, 2004 International Conference for Infant Studies, Chicago, Ill.

Muir, D. W. (2002). Adult communications with infants through touch: The forgotten sense. *Human Development*, **45**, 95–99.

Muir, D. W. and Hains, S. (1999). Young infants' perception of adult intentionality: adult contingency and eye direction. In *Early social cognition: understanding others in the first months of life* (ed. P. Rochat), pp. 155–84. Mahwah, NJ: Erlbaum.

Muir, D. W. and Nadel, J. (1998). Infant social perception. In *Perceptual development: visual auditory, and speech perception in infancy* (ed. A. Slater), pp. 247–86. East Sussex: Psychology Press.

Muir, D. and Lee, K. (2003). The still-face effect: methodological issues and new applications. *Infancy*, **4**, 483–91.

Muir, D. W. and Rach-Longman, K. (1989). Once more with expression: on de Schonen and Mathivet's (1989) model for the development of face perception in human infants. *Cahiers de Psychologie Cognitive (European Bulletin of Cognitive Psychology)*, **9**, 103–9.

Muir, D. W., Humphrey, D. E., and Humphrey, G. K. (1994). Pattern and space perception in young infants. Special issue: invariance, recognition, and perception: in honor of Peter C. Dodwell. *Spatial Vision*, **8**, 141–65.

Muir, D. W., Hains, C., Hains, S. M., *et al.* (2002). *Infant interactions with a virtual adult: the still-face effect and other perturbation effects*. Poster presented at the International Society for Infant Studies, Toronto.

Murray, L. and Trevarthen, C. (1985). Emotional regulation of interaction between two-montholds and their mothers. In *Social perception in infants* (ed. T. M. Field and N. A. Fox), pp. 101–25. Norwood, NJ: Ablex.

Nadel, J., Carchon, I, Kervella, C., *et al.* (1999). Expectancies for social contingency in 2-month-olds. *Developmental Science*, **2**, 164–73.

Papoušek, M., Bornstein, M. H., Nuzzo, C., *et al.* (1990). Infant responses to prototypical melodic contours in parental speech. *Infant Behaviour and Development*, **13**, 539–45.

Rach-Longman, K. (1991). *The effect of adult face orientation on human infant affect and attention within the first half year of life*. Unpublished Doctoral Dissertation, Queen's University, Kingston, Ontario.

Rhodes, G., Brake, S., and Atkinson, A. P. (1993). What's lost in inverted faces? *Cognition*, **47**, 25–57.

Rochat, P., Neisser, U., and Marian, V. (1998). Are young infants sensitive to interpersonal contingency? *Infant Behaviour and Development*, **21**, 355–66.

Roman, J. (1986). *Six-month-olds' responses to an inverted image of their mothers' face during social interactions*. Unpublished honours thesis, Queen's University, Kingston, Ontario, Canada.

Semcesen, T., Muir, D., Symons, L., *et al.* (2000). *Contingent fact-to-face interactions with 5-month-olds over TV: live versus computer presentations*. Poster at the International Conference for Infant Studies, Brighton, UK.

Stack, D. M. and Muir, D. W. (1990). Tactile stimulation as a component of social interchange: New interpretation for the still-face effect. *British Journal of Developmental Psychology*, **8**, 131–45.

Stack, D. M. and Muir, D. W. (1992). The effect of manipulating adult tactile stimulation during an interaction of 5-month-olds' affect and attention. *Child Development*, **63**, 1509–25.

Symons, L., Hains, S., and Muir, D. (1998). Look at me: 5-month-old infant's sensitivity to very small deviations in eye-gaze during social interactions. *Infant Behaviour and Development*, **21**, 531–6.

Thompson, P. (1980). Margaret Thatcher: a new illusion. *Perception*, **9**, 483–4.

Trevarthen, C. (1974). Conversations with a 2-month-old. *New Scientist*, May, 230–5.

Tronick, E. Z. (1989). Emotions and emotional communication in infants. *American Psychologist*, **44**, 112–19.

Tronick, E. Z. (2003). Thoughts on the still-face: disconnection and dyadic expansion of consciousness. *Infancy*, **4**, 475–82.

Tronick, E., Als, H., Adamson, L., *et al.* (1978). The infants' response to entrapment between contradictory messages in face-to-face interactions. *Journal of the American Academy of Child Psychiatry*, **17**, 1–13.

Walker-Andrews, A. (1997). Infants' perception of expressive behaviours: differentiation of multimodal information. *Psychological Bulletin*, **121**, 437–56.

Vouloumanos, A. and Werker, J. F. (2004). Tuned to the signal: the privileged status of speech for young infants. *Developmental Science*, **7**, 270–6.

Chapter 9

Emotion understanding: robots as tools and models

Lola Cañamero and Philippe Gaussier

Is there a place for emotions in robotics?

To many, the title of this chapter might sound like a complete nonsense—after all, what do emotions have to do with robots? How could robots possibly tell us anything about them and, more generally, about us? Science fiction has typically portrayed robots as prototypes of the unemotional and this vision largely prevails in science, as well as for the layperson, in spite of the proliferation of 'affective' toys and robots. Admittedly, many of these 'affective devices' are little more than 'bags of tricks' aimed at entertaining the young (and not so young) and technically-orientated sectors of the population, rather than pieces of scientific research trying to take a step towards a broader understanding of what emotional phenomena can be, yet these devices can be extremely efficient at achieving their goal, offering us good opportunities to reflect on the human tendency to anthropomorphize even with dealing with the dullest technology (Reeves and Nass, 1996) and to perceive the world as emotionally coloured. However, shedding light on human perception of affect is neither the only, nor the main, contribution that robots can make to the study of emotions. Artifacts—computers or robots—can also be valuable tools to support scientists in their investigation of human emotions and, more fundamentally, they permit scientists to model and test hypotheses about affective phenomena. The investigation of all of these issues is the domain of a new research area, generally known as 'affective computing', which departs from and complements other disciplines traditionally concerned with the study of emotions in important ways. Rosalind Picard points out:

> This is different from presenting a theory of emotions; the latter usually focuses on what human emotions are, how and when they are produced, and what they accomplish. Affective computing includes implementing emotions, and therefore can aid the development and testing of new and old emotion theories. However, affective computing also includes many other things, such as giving a computer the ability to recognize and express emotions, developing its ability to respond intelligently to human emotion, and enabling it to regulate and utilize its emotions. (Picard, 1997, p. 3)

In this chapter, we focus on autonomous robots, as opposed to other artifacts such as computers, to sketch our views on how they can be meaningful tools and models for the study of emotion. Autonomous robots are especially interesting since they are physical devices moving around, making decisions, solving problems, and interacting in the real world—the same world humans and animals inhabit. Therefore, autonomous robots are particularly suited to study two fundamental aspects of emotions:

- Their role as mechanisms for adaptation to the environment and behaviour control.
- Their role in social interaction and communication.

Robotic systems offer the possibility to approach these issues in different ways. On the one hand, models of some emotion 'components' can be explicitly included in the architecture of the robot to give rise to behaviour that appears to arise from an emotional system. On the other hand, autonomous robots allow us to investigate how emotions can be an emergent property of a dynamical system, without having to model an 'emotional system' explicitly. In this latter case, the lack of an explicit emotional system does not imply that emotions are considered as phenomena that only exist in the eye of the beholder. On the contrary, we believe that understanding what kinds of problems can be solved without the involvement of an emotional system will help us delineate the functions of emotions in cognitive processing. We will therefore present some of the problems that autonomous robots currently tackle without any kind of emotion model, before discussing some cases in which it might make sense to bring emotions into play.

State-of-the-art problems in behaviour-based robotics

As we mentioned previously, most of the state-of-the-art work in autonomous robotics does not use any emotional mechanism at all. Let us first briefly consider the design philosophy underlying autonomous robots and then provide some illustrative examples of typical problems they have to solve.

Behaviour-based paradigm in robotics

Robot architectures are based on the idea that real time reaction capabilities are crucial for good robot/environment interaction, in particular when the environment is dynamic or *a priori* unknown. To take into account the effect of the interactions with the environment, most robotic architectures use some kind of behaviour-based approach (Brooks, 1991; Arkin, 1998). In this paradigm, which draws on ideas from biology, ethology, and neuroscience, the control architecture is divided into different loops of processes running in parallel and corresponding to the different kinds of behaviours[1] and time scales the robot has to manage. For instance, it is important to introduce a fast reaction mechanism allowing robots to avoid obstacles while they are moving. At the same time (i.e. in parallel with this activity) other processes are being

---

[1] The term 'behaviour(s)' is used in a technical sense in behaviour-based robotics to denote different competencies or activities that the robot is able to perform in its environment.

executed 'independently'. For example, information from images can be analysed to control much more complex activities like homing, object grasping, or planning. All these processes can issue different motor commands, some of which might be incompatible and 'compete' for the same actuator for their execution. Merging this asynchronous flow of parallel information can be performed via a prioritization mechanism.

As an example, in the subsumption architecture (Brooks, 1986), one of the earliest types of behaviour-based architectures, behaviours are organized in layers running in parallel, each of them with its own perception and action capabilities that are 'loosely coupled' with minimal interaction limited to the inhibition of the perceptual input or the suppression of the motor output of one layer by another. Using these inhibition and suppression mechanisms, layers are arranged in a hierarchy with fixed priorities that reflect the importance that each layer (behaviour) carries for the survival of the robot in that particular environment and, therefore, determine which behaviour(s) to execute given the presence of relevant stimuli in the environment. This allows, for instance, for the robot to decide that going to a planned position is less important for the survival of the robot than avoiding an important danger. In this case, the 'warning' of a danger will suppress the output of the planning system. Therefore, the decision making process is completely decentralized and much more robust than the sequential 'perception-reasoning-action' process used in classical artificial intelligence and robotics, since any low-level process can take over the control of the robot's behaviour if necessary. The behaviour of the robot can also be highly opportunistic.

Many other behaviour-based architectures and 'decision making' (or action selection) strategies can be used (see Arkin, 1998; Pfeifer and Schreier, 1999, for overviews). Some architectures include various 'internal goals' or 'motivations' to drive the behaviour of the robot, as we will see later. All of them share the basic philosophy of using parallel, loosely coupled perception-action loops, decentralized decision-making, action-orientated perception, and lack of (or use of very minimal, coarse, and distributed) representations. This way of designing control architectures attempts to avoid the symbol grounding problem (Harnad, 1990) and other difficulties of the traditional approach (see Pfeifer and Schreier, 1999).

Sensory-motor and reinforcement learning

Let us suppose that an autonomous robot has to learn how to return to a particular location. If the robot is equipped with a visual mechanism to recognize particular objects in the visual scene, it can use this mechanism to localize where different objects are in a room. Hence, we can design a group of neurons to learn that a given location is characterized by a particular conjunction of landmarks and azimuths. When the robot is near the learned location, the mismatch between the learned configuration and the current situation will be very low. By contrast, when the robot is far away from the learned location the mismatch will be high (Gaussier and Zrehen, 1995; Gaussier et al., 1999). This place recognition mechanism can be used to build a homing behaviour.

The robot has to learn at least three locations/actions in the neighbourhood of its home in order to reach it (see Fig. 9.1).

Such an architecture consists in a fairly direct coupling of perception and action, as shown in Fig. 9.2. When the robot is facing its home base, it can learn to recognize the landmark-azimuth configuration and associate it to the direction of motion in order to reach its home (using a simple conditioning rule).

If the robot is far from its home base—and supposing it cannot see it—it tries to recognize its current location. Due to the generalization capabilities of the place recognition system, the 'winner-takes-all' mechanism used for the place recognition group will activate the neuron associated with the learned place that is nearest to the place where the robot is current located. This neuron will then trigger the learned motor action and the robot will move in a direction that decreases its distance to its home base. After several movements, the robot will enter an area where another place cell wins, triggering another movement that will allow it to move in a more appropriate direction to reach its home. Hence, perception–action learning can be seen as a way to create an attraction basin: our robot is no more than a ball falling in the learned attraction basin.

Now, if we want our robot to move between places, for example, going from one place where it can drink to another place where it can eat, using a simple Hebbian learning algorithm we can associate the place cells around each goal to a particular 'motivation' or internal variable. The motivation and the place cell are supposed to be simultaneously active during the learning phase to allow for an easy association. This motivation signal acts as a bias in the competition for place recognition. It changes the shape of the attraction basin and, instead of going to the nearest learned goal, our robot becomes capable of going to another goal (location) due to the modification in the shape of the attraction basin (see Fig. 9.3).

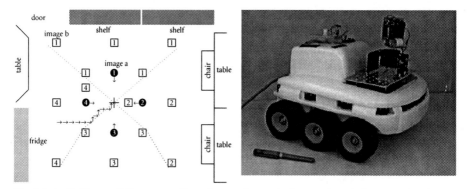

Fig. 9.1 Left: Place cell-like segregation of space in a robotic experiment. Four panoramic images are learned (circles), others are associated with one of these learned panorama (boxes). As we can see, if the robot learns to reach the cross from each learned panorama it can reach the cross from any other panorama associated with the learned one (generalization). The set of arrows represents an example of robot trajectory (see Gaussier et al., 1999 for details). **Right:** Photo of the Koala robot used in the visual navigation experiments.

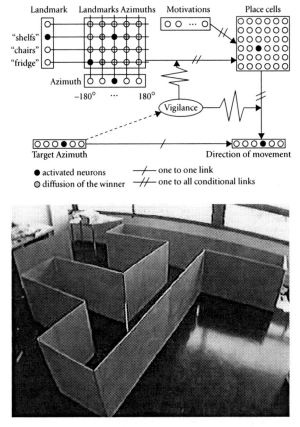

Fig. 9.2. Top: Schematic representation of the PerAc block. From the perceived situation, the reflex system extracts information to control directly the actions. Concurrently, the recognition system learns sensory input patterns and how to link them to actions by associative or reinforcement learning. The system adapts itself dynamically to the environment. **Bottom**: An example of maze learning where a delayed reward signal was used to learn to associate particular signs in the maze with an action allowing to reach a 'goal' location where the reward was received.

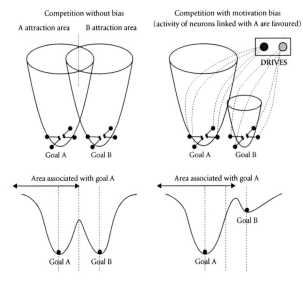

Fig. 9.3 Bias introduced by motivations in goal selection.

In the case of an open environment, simple Hebbian learning is sufficient to build interesting behaviours. Obviously, if we want our robot to avoid a particular area because it is associated with a 'punishment', it has to be able to avoid the ongoing action. This learning needs to use the punishment signal as a modulator factor of the Hebbian learning, in this case, to learn an inhibitory link between a place cell and the ongoing action. Other kinds of reinforcement learning rules (Barto *et al.*, 1983; Watkins and Dayan, 1992; Weaver *et al.*, 1993; Gaussier *et al.*, 1997) can be used to associate the recognition of any perceived information to an arbitrary action according to a reward signal that can be delayed in the most complex cases: for instance the robot is only rewarded if it succeeds in performing a particular sequence of actions (see Fig. 9.2).

Action selection, planning and internal values

In more complex cases, for instance when the robot has learned several actions in a given place and has to choose one of them according to a particular goal, more complex mechanisms must be used. One solution consists of learning a cognitive map of the environment (Tolman, 1948; Revel *et al.*, 1998). This learning can be performed without any reinforcement signal (latent learning), since it relies on the learning of some kind of environment causality: 'from here, I can go there'. The almost co-activation of a departure node and an arrival node leads to the strengthening of the connections between these two nodes. After a while, the robot builds a graph or a map coding for the topological relationship between the different places it knows in its environment (see Fig. 9.4).

When an interesting place is found, the robot can learn to associate the satisfaction of this goal to the node corresponding to that place on its cognitive map. Later, when the robot is at another place, if the previous goal is activated, it triggers a diffusion mechanism from node to node all along the cognitive map. Then, with the appropriate

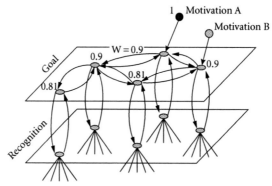

Fig. 9.4 Global architecture of the planning system. When a motivation 'A' activates a goal, a back-propagation of the information is performed in direction to all the nodes of the graph (all the weights are equal to 0.9). The recognition level allows the system to identify the situations when the robot arrives in the vicinity of a learned place. Those situations are directly linked to the goal level, which allows the system to plan a route from one attractor to the next.

mechanism, it is easy to choose from the current robot location the action that will allow it to go to the place corresponding to the most activated node in the direct neighborhood of the current node on the cognitive map. Gradually, the robot will rise in the gradient direction and reach the goal. If several goals are activated at the same time, the robot will choose the nearest goal location in terms of the minimum number of intermediate nodes on the map (cognitive distance).

This means that, in a first approximation, the robot should not be able to solve difficult choices such as going to a more distant place to satisfy two goals at the same time, thereby minimizing the global cost of the complete journey, instead of going to a nearer

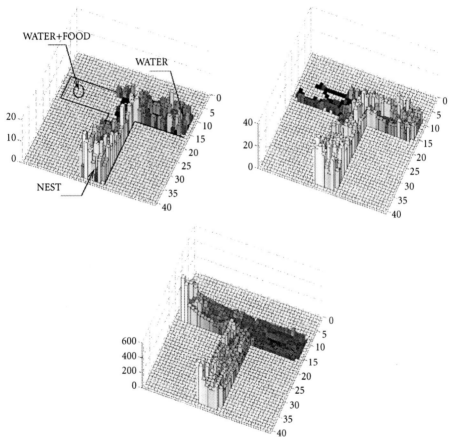

Fig. 9.5 Histograms representing the evolution of the robot's behavior in a T-maze. At the beginning (left) the robot tries the right arm, finds the water and moves between the water and the nest (it does not succeed to explore the left arm). By chance, it begins to explore the right arm and finds water and food (center). Then very quickly it only uses that arm. At last (right), it almost never returns in the right arm except during the exploration phases.
The histogram shows the cumulate number of crossing in a given area since the beginning of the exploration. The levels are normalized.

place where it can only satisfy one. However, the coupling of the dynamics between the robot's motivations (such as going regularly to eat and to drink) allows one to reinforce particular links in the cognitive map. As a result, when the robot discovers randomly an 'interesting' route (e.g. a route leading to a place where it can satisfy both goals simultaneously), the synchronization of motivations leads to a higher probability of using this new path: to satisfy the second goal the robot has to use this path. By the way, it satisfies the first motivation, so the new route is more and more reinforced until a definitive bifurcation of the robot behaviour in favour of the solution that maximize both motivations at the same time (best compromise; Quoy et al., 1999; Gaussier et al., 2000). Figure 9.5 shows how the path that the robot follows to satisfy both goals changes when it tries by chance the new pathway, which changes the timing of the activation of motivations for both pathways.

More complex action selection mechanisms have been used to manage and sequence complex behaviours (see e.g. Maes, 1991; Tyrrell, 1993; Donnart and Meyer, 1996; Cañamero, 1997) or to combine the effects of various motivations (e.g. Spier and McFarland, 1997; Avila-García et al., 2003), but the principles underlying these mechanisms remain the same. In all these cases, the use of a behaviour-based approach that grants dynamical and continuous control to the robot also leads to simplification of the work of the robot designer (Kelso, 1995; Schöner et al., 1995). However, these architectures are not devoid of problems. For example, due to the use of local information, it may happen that the robot remains stuck in local minima and deadlock situations, such as switching rapidly and unproductively between alternative actions (dithering). As we will see, this is a typical problem that an emotion-based mechanism could help to solve in a more satisfactory way.

Emotions in autonomy, adaptation, and survival in the solitary robot

In the previous section we illustrated some of the typical problems addressed in behaviour-based robotics without resorting to any explicit 'affective' mechanism in the architecture of the robot. However, for certain types of situations, it might make sense to use 'emotion-based' mechanisms and strategies akin to those found in animals and humans when dealing with similar kinds of situations, in particular when problems of autonomy, adaptation, and survival are at stake. Emotions are interesting to roboticists in various fundamental ways, by virtue of the main functions that they play as regulatory systems at different levels.

Mechanisms for (bodily) adaptation

By producing (rapid) bodily and cognitive changes, emotions constitute mechanisms that allow an agent to deal better (faster or more appropriately) with events, both internal and external, which are important for its (and the species) survival in particular contexts.

These contexts include situations that are dangerous, or that include unexpected events or opportunities.

Motivating and guiding actions

As Frijda puts it 'What emotions are about is action (or motivation for action) and action control' (1995, p. 506). At the simplest level, the categorization of events as pleasant/unpleasant, beneficial/noxious, turns neutral stimuli into something to be pursued or avoided. Due to their generality of object, time, intensity, and density, emotions amplify the effects of motivations, which are stimulus-specific and need an urgent satisfaction (Tomkins, 1984). As a consequence, they can change goal or motivation priorities (overriding 'decisions' arising from the motivational state) to deal with situations that need an urgent response.

Expressive and communicative function

Emotions and their expression are also of paramount importance in communication and in the regulation of social interactions.

All of these different functions could contribute to enhance the adaptation capabilities and autonomy of robots in one way or another (see Cañamero, 2001c, 2003, for a discussion of these issues). The next section provides some concrete examples regarding the roles of emotions in adaptation and in motivation and guidance of actions and we will touch upon applications of the expressive and communicative role of emotions in the context of human-robot interaction.

Where could emotions help?

We will now consider some of the major problems faced by autonomous robots for which emotions could help provide better solutions.

Management of goals

Robots endowed with some sort of 'motivational system' that sets and prioritizes 'internal' goals to drive their decision-making processes enjoy greater autonomy than purely reactive robots that only respond to the presence of external stimuli. However, in some cases, in particular in rapidly changing dynamic environments that presents threats to the survival of the robot, it can be disadvantageous to follow strictly the dictates of the motivational system, since goal priorities might need to be changed to address a new and urgent problem (e.g. to escape from a danger) before having satisfied the current need. As we noted at the beginning of this section, emotions can produce changes in goal priorities, and several models of emotions considered as 'interrupts' (Simon, 1967) have been implemented in robots.

Repetitive and inefficient behaviour

Due to various features such as the use of local information, and poor or noisy sensors and actuators, autonomous robots can engage in repetitive activities ('loops' or 'deadlocks') that fail to achieve the pursued goal and at the same time involve a cost (e.g. in terms of energy consumption), e.g. a robot that repeatedly tries to obtain an object out of reach. A 'second order' control mechanism that could monitor performance and goal achievement to detect inefficient behaviour due to deadlocks would provide a solution to this problem. Rather than a burdensome 'meta-reasoning' system, a more appropriate solution for these robots would be the use of internal states, such as 'boredom', 'frustration', or 'anger' arising from inefficient behaviour and failure to achieve the current goal. This system could lead rapidly to a change in the goal and a behavioural change that ends the deadlock.

Autonomous learning

As has already been noted, learning in autonomous robots typically follows association or reinforcement models, and makes use of some kind of external signals (arising from the environment or supplied by a 'critic') that provide reward or punishment. Other models include learning by imitation (see below) of the actions of another agent (human or robot), usually called the 'demonstrator'. One of the main problems underlying all these models is how to make those signals truly meaningful to the robot so that the learning process is more autonomous and grounded in the architecture of the robot. In other words, how can a robot make sense of the perceived signals by itself, as opposed to using reward information provided by some sort of 'external teacher'? How can it decide what to learn and what *not* to learn? A mechanism rooted in an internal 'value system' would be needed to provide internal signals regarding the 'positive' or 'negative' qualities of actions and stimuli, giving them a meaning with respect to the values, needs, and goals of the robot beyond a metaphoric use of the terms 'pain' and 'pleasure' to refer to rewards and punishments that allow the robot to learn the appropriate valence of the events. Initial attempts to solve these problems are given by Andry *et al.* (2001) and Cos-Aguilera *et al.* (2003), and later in this chapter.

Cognitive overload

Management of memory is another major problem in autonomous robots. If the robot lacks appropriate criteria to filter out information, its memory is then too global, causing problems of cognitive overload and very long recall times. Mechanisms for selective memory inspired from emotional memory in humans (e.g. phenomena like mood-congruent recall of past memories) and the related notion of autobiographic memory, would help to solve some of these problems and also provide generally coherent responses to a wide range of situations.

It can be argued that it should be possible to conceive of different mechanisms to 'fix' the above problems independently in a more or less *ad hoc* way without having to resort to any emotion-like system and without using the term 'emotion' for those mechanisms. However, our interest in using an emotional system (or, for that matter, implementing that metaphor) lies in the fact that the same system is intertwined with and can affect various other subsystems simultaneously. Although we will not attempt to define the term 'emotion,' we consider that, in this context, emotions can be appropriately characterized as processes of a dynamic nature that integrate causally related processes of several subsystems (Mandler, 1985) including: the physiological, the cognitive-evaluative, and the communicative-expressive.[2] Emotions then can be seen as 'constructs that allow causally related, complex, dynamic states of the subsystems to be characterized and identified simultaneously' (Pfeifer, 1991).

We will illustrate some of these ideas using the particular case of action selection in the next section.

Emotions for action selection in autonomous robots

What do robot emotions look like? Robotic emotional systems are no magic tricks: like everything in robots, they consist of some form of 'algorithm' or program. What is important in this 'program' is how it affects the behaviour and cognitive processing of the robot. Different types of models and approaches can be used to model emotions, as discussed by Cañamero (2001c; see also Cañamero, 1998, 2001b), but here we adopt the perspective of behaviour-based robotics. Within this approach, if emotions are to be meaningful to the robot, they must be an integral part of its architecture and must be grounded in an internal value system that is adaptive for the robot's physical and social niche. It is this internal value system that is at the heart of the creature's autonomy and produces the valenced reactions that characterize emotions. As Wehrle suggests: 'grounding somehow implies that we allow the robot to establish its own emotional categorization which refers to its own physical properties, the task, properties of the environment, and the ongoing interaction with its environment' (Wehrle, 2001, p. 576).

As an example, the architecture proposed by Cañamero (1997) and analyzed recently (Cañamero, 2003) relies on both motivations and emotions to perform behaviour selection. Initially implemented in simulated robots, this architecture is now being adapted to real robots as part of Orlando Avila-García's Ph.D. thesis at the University of Hertfordshire. The robots inhabit a typical action selection environment containing various types of resources, obstacles that hamper their activities, and predators. They must choose among and perform different activities in order to maintain their well-being (the stability of their internal milieu) and survive-remain viable in their environment, following Ashby (1952), as long as possible-their ultimate goal. The architecture of the robots is behaviour-based and consists of five systems. First, there is a synthetic physiology of survival-related variables controlled homeostatically (e.g. blood sugar, vascular volume, energy, etc.). Secondly, there are 'hormones' that can alter the levels of the controlled variables. Thirdly, there is a set of motivations

---

[2] When considering emotions in humans, the subjective experience subsystem is also included. However, we prefer not to talk about subjective experience in the case of robots.

(aggression, cold, curiosity, fatigue, hunger, self-protection, thirst, and warm) that are activated by 'errors' (deficit or excess) in the levels of the controlled variables when these depart from their ideal values, thereby setting the internal needs of the robot. Fourthly, there is a repertoire of behaviours that can satisfy those internal needs or motivations (and also create new ones), as their execution carries a modification (increase or decrease) in the levels of specific variables. Finally, there is a set of 'basic' emotions (anger, boredom, fear, happiness, interest, and sadness) that can be activated as a result of interactions between the robot and the world—the presence of external objects or the occurrence of internal events caused by these interactions—which release 'hormones' when activated.

Under 'normal' circumstances, behaviour selection is driven by the motivational state of the robot—at each point in time, normally the motivation with the highest need to be satisfied will be in charge of selecting the behaviour that can best correct its related physiological error. Emotions constitute a 'second order' control mechanism running in parallel with the motivational control system to continuously 'monitor' the external and internal environment for significant events. They can alter motivational priorities and behaviour execution through the effect of released hormones on the physiology, arousal, attention, and (internal and external) perception of the robot. This emotional system was specifically designed to overcome some of the major problems of reactive and motivated behaviour selection architectures, such as lack of flexibility in overall behaviour due to a rigid link between a stimulus and a response, repetitive and inefficient behaviour, inefficient treatment of emergency situations, etc. Therefore, the different emotions were designed to act as mechanisms for fast adaptation to particularly significant circumstances from the point of view of the survival of the robot in a highly dynamic environment, namely:

- *Anger*: A mechanism to block the influences from the environment by abruptly stopping the current situation. Its triggering event is the fact that the accomplishment of a goal (a motivation) is menaced or undone.

- *Boredom*: A mechanism to stop inefficient behaviour that does not contribute to satisfy any of the robot's needs. Its triggering event is prolonged repetitive activity.

- *Fear*: A defence mechanism against external threats. Its triggering event is the presence of predators.

- *Happiness*: A form of re-equilibration triggered by the achievement of a goal.

- *Interest*: A mechanism for the robot to engage in interaction with the world. Its triggering event is the presence of a novel object.

- *Sadness*: A mechanism to stop an active relation with the environment when the robot is not in a condition to get a need satisfied; it acts by slowing down the metabolism and motor system of the robot.

This architecture was designed to show how the use of emotions can improve action selection in autonomous robots by solving some of the problems present in more traditional architectures. It could also be useful to study how emotions can be maladaptive by simulating (via modification of relevant parameters) various emotional disorders. However, since it was designed (hand-coded) to meet particular requirements, it cannot tell us why emotions are adaptive or how they evolved to be so. Using evolutionary techniques to generate different emotional systems, therefore, seems a very interesting direction to explore, as it would also allow us to evaluate the performance and adaptive value of emotions for different action selection tasks and environments. Different aspects of emotion-based learning also need to be investigated in this context. Using a simplified version of this architecture, ongoing work as part of Ignasi Cos-Aguilera's PhD thesis includes learning object affordances in the context of behaviour selection based on internal homeostatic and hormonal (valenced) feedback resulting from interaction episodes with objects in the environment (Cos-Aguilera *et al.*, 2003).

Issues in human-robot interaction

The models and architectures seen in previous sections lack any mechanisms to allow social interactions with other entities—humans or robots. To interact socially, many other aspects and cognitive capabilities have to be incorporated in the robot. In some cases, interaction can result as a side-effect of clever sensory-motor couplings, as we will see in the next section. In other cases, we might want to endow our robots with explicit, expressive capabilities that will make humans attribute emotional states to robots and react to them according to these attributions.

Side-effects of sensory-motor systems

Robot learning has been studied for a long time in the case of an isolated robot. Algorithms have become more and more efficient, but after a while it became obvious that an isolated system, even with the best algorithms, cannot discover very complex strategies or behaviours on its own. The combinatorial explosion is simply to huge and time-consuming. Imitation appears to be a powerful tool for learning. The problem is that in most of the work on imitation (e.g. Meltzoff and Moore, 1977) it is assumed that the imitator tries to copy the actions of the demonstrator to achieve a common goal, which implies the presence of a complex internal (and innate) mechanism to manage the imitation process.

Our Neurocybernetics Team's idea was to develop a simple, sensory-motor regulation system, somewhat like a homeostat (Ashby, 1952), to learn the correspondence between the visual position of the robot arm and its proprioception. In this architecture, the robot simply detects the area in the image where more motion is occurring and tries to learn to associate this location with the different possible proprioceptions. If the robot perceives a difference between its proprioception and its image, it tries to reduce it. An interesting side-effect is that if a human is moving his arm in the robot field of view, the robot perceives the motion, and tries to reduce the error between its

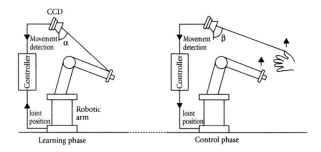

Fig. 9.6 Low-level imitation principle applied to a robotic arm.

proprioception and the visual information. As a result, the robot arm begins moving, following the movement of the human demonstrator. Therefore, external observers have the impression that our robot is imitating them, while all it tries to do is remain in a fixed position while moving to reduce the error between its proprioception and its visual image (see Fig. 9.6).

Here, perceptual ambiguity is used to bootstrap the imitative behaviour, which only relies on a very simple sensory-motor strategy. The neural network used for this is not so obvious, although, since it works with a single camera, an arm with 5 degrees of freedom, and it builds a multi-modal map (Gaussier *et al.*, 1998; Andry *et al.*, 2000, 2002). Learning the complete movement is easy since the robot does not try to learn the trajectory of the demonstrator's arm trajectory, but it simply needs to store its own sequence of actions. Unfortunately, an external reward is needed to decide if the trajectory has to be stored or not—i.e. was it a good imitation? Was it a real demonstrator or just a shadow our robot arm was following? We will see latter how to avoid the use of an explicit learning signal.

Another interesting example is the work of Takanishi *et al.* (1997). They designed a robotic head with a neck and an active visual system that controlled the gaze of two CCD cameras. Their system was tested in different situations to show that active movements of the robot cameras plus active movements of the head/neck in the direction of the target produced better target localizations. An interesting side-effect was how much this simple sensory-motor coupling appealed to the observers. They expressed their feelings that the robot 'wanted' to look at something. Moreover, when the object was too near to the head, the head was moving back and the observer had the impression that the robot was trying to avoid an unpleasant situation. It was a clear case of a robotic system being able to trigger some empathic behaviours from humans due to their tendency to assign intentions to others.

This system was able to trigger an emotional response in the human observers with a simple hardwired sensory-motor mechanism. This result opens the door to the development of non-conventional human/machine interfaces by showing how powerful the evocation of emotional feeling can be when a robot interacts with a human—even if the robot does not have any emotional system at all.

Imitation as a communication tool

As seen in the previous section, passive imitation can trigger some basic social interactions. However, in baby/parents relations there is no need for an explicit reward to learn a particular behaviour. Consequently, in the case of a robot, the question is: how could internal reward be produced that does not depend on a symbolic signal? The solution is found in the study of baby/parent interaction, in particular, the evidence that response synchrony was crucial to maintain the attention of the baby (Nadel, 2000). We proposed a simple mechanism that merges all of the input data in order to try to predict the rhythm of the global incoming flow of sensory data. If the system succeeds in predicting the rhythm, we consider that the robot has successfully tuned into the rhythm of the interaction: this allows the robot to generate, by itself, a positive reward that reinforces its current behaviour. By contrast, if the robot fails to predict the rhythm of the exchange we consider that the robot has failed to engage in the rhythm of the exchange, producing a negative valence (punishment), which inhibits the current behaviour.

We were able to show that this kind of mechanism can be used to teach an arbitrary set of sensory-motor rules to a computer without giving it any reward (Andry et al., 2001). The frequency of the trials with the human demonstrator was used by the computer to decide whether or not to reinforce its current behaviour. In order to close this 'interaction loop' between the robot (or computer) and the human, we would need to endow the artifact with the ability to display the 'internal state' induced by this reward in a way that is not only efficient, but also intuitive and acceptable to humans. Next, we will consider how roboticists approach the design of expressive artifacts.

Emotions in human-robot interaction

Whereas researchers modelling emotion for individual robots have focused on the design of architectures, i.e. the 'inner' aspect of emotions, researchers modelling emotions for robots interacting socially have focused primarily on the 'external' features of emotional expression. Emotional expression is certainly a key factor in social communication and interaction, since the external manifestations of emotions can play a major role as 'signaling' mechanisms, at several levels. For example, the emotional expression of an individual can be used by another as social reference, to 'assess' the type of situation it is confronted with and the appropriate response to it. In some cases, an emotional expression carries some 'information content', and it can then be said to play a communicative role; it can be controlled to some extent and can be intentionally used to let others know one's emotional state so that they can predict the person's future actions and adjust their own reactions accordingly. Emotions also contribute to the construction of intersubjectivity.

Ideally, we would like to see these 'internal' and 'external' aspects fully integrated in the same robotic architectures in the not too distant future. For the time being, however, the enormous challenges that each of these problems poses in robotics has produced a variety of relatively simple and rather 'ad hoc' attempts to arrive at solutions. Therefore, in the next section we will deal with only the 'external manifestations' of emotions in the context of human-robot interaction.

Why have expressive robots?

Work on expressive robots for interaction with humans is receiving increasing attention. Intuitively, we can think of different roles that emotional expressions can play in social interactions between humans and robots.

Conveying intentionality

People need to understand the behaviour observed in their social (human or artificial) partners results from causes or intentions that allow them to form coherent explanations for their past behaviour and to predict their future behaviour. Emotions and personalities are often postulated as such causes of behaviour and sources of intentions. Autonomous robots might, in addition, use their own emotional expressions to convey their intentions or needs to humans.

Eliciting emotions

In the same way as other people's emotions elicit emotional responses from humans, emotions in robots can be used with the same purpose, to elicit responses that either match the robot's emotional state (e.g. a pilot assistant that tries to bring the pilot to an alert state) or are instrumental to it (e.g. a robot expressing sadness due to its inability to accomplish a task can receive the help of a 'moved' human).

Human comfort

Robots that are able to express emotions and adapt their interactions to the emotional state of their social partners can be expected to make humans feel more comfortable during interaction. One obvious reason is that this interaction is tailored to meet the emotional needs of the human. Another important reason is that when a robot displays emotional behaviour and expressions, it appears to be more human-like or at least it becomes an animate object.

Enhanced communication

Endowing a robot with emotional expressions, a key element in non-verbal communication, can make communication cognitively less costly for the human partner. If emotional robots are to achieve a sufficient level of sophistication to interpret our subtle expressions and obtain relevant information from contextual clues, at some point in the future we might also want them to 'understand' what we *mean*, not (only) what we say.

The main features that expressive robots should show to be accepted as 'social partners' are: giving the impression of being alive, being believable, and displaying interactive behaviour adapted to humans. How can this be implemented in robots?

Designing emotional expressions for robots

Building a 'believable' expressive robot that can interact with humans poses many challenges that, in our opinion, need to be approached from a multi-disciplinary perspective. In addition to the more technical aspects, robot designers are confronted with a number of conceptual problems for which psychological theories and models, conceived to analyse existing (biological) systems, rather than to build artificial ones, do not provide much guidance. Let us examine some of them.

Features

Human emotional expression is multi-modal, highly complex, and very difficult to reproduce in robots in its entirety. Researchers have to select a subset of features to convey emotion in a way that makes such expressions believable—although not necessarily realistic—to the human observer. Inspiration and data are usually sought from psychology, classical animation (e.g. Thomas and Johnston, 1981), and very often empirical testing. Faces are the most commonly used means of expression, usually in a simplified (and caricaturized) version with schematic eyes and a mouth, and in the most complex versions with eyebrows and eyelids. Very few attempts exist to produce highly realistic faces that include elements such as artificial skin (see Menzel and d'Aluisio, 2000 for examples). Posture and movement (of the elements of the face and sometimes of other body parts, e.g. the neck) are regarded as highly important for expression; in particular, movement must be coherent, well synchronized, and have the right timing. Some researchers (e.g. Breazeal, 2002) put forward the use of features activating the 'baby scheme'—features that make adults react to the face as they would to a baby. While it has been suggested that such features are not necessary for emotional expression (Cañamero, 2002) they might make the robot itself more appealing or 'cute' to the human eye. Expressive faces are sometimes combined with vocal inflexions (see e.g. Picard, 1997; Breazeal, 2002), although current speech synthesis systems still cannot produce a voice of human quality and tend to sound too artificial.

Underlying model

Is facial emotional expression better modeled as a discrete set of prototypical expressions or as points in a space with continuous dimensions? The choice of one or the other model has an impact on the type and quality of the expressions produced. However, again, the literature does not provide much guidance and roboticists must generally resort to the use of their own intuition and much empirical testing. Most

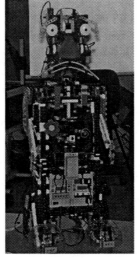

Fig. 9.7 Expressive robots. **Left**: Sparky. **Center**: Feelix. **Right**: Kismet.

robotic faces follow the discrete categories approach and use few degrees of freedom (typically four to six) and few expressive features (typically two to four) to produce highly stereotyped, but easily readable expressions. The example of Sparky (Scheeff *et al.*, 2002) is shown in Fig. 9.7(left). Other robots also allow researchers to blend prototypical expressions to form more complex and 'chimeric' ones, such Feelix (Cañamero and Fredslund, 2001), depicted in Fig. 9.7(centre). The fact that stereotyped expressions are easily readable makes these robots suitable for simple interactions when it is important to avoid putting strong cognitive demands on the human user, such as when the robot interacts with children or people with cognitive disabilities, or when the user must simultaneously engage in another task, while the face serving as an expressive 'interface.' Other robots have been designed to engage in more complex interactions and to produce more subtle expressions follow a dimensional approach. For example, Kismet (Breazeal, 2002) was a robotic head designed with many degrees of freedom, many expressive features, and carefully timed movements (Fig. 9.7, right) to serve as a test-bed to investigate infant–caretaker interactions. The expressions of this robot are not always easily interpretable; however, it can produce more subtle expressions that engage adult humans to interact with it as they would with an infant.

Level of complexity

The fact that the emotional expressions of the robot have to be believable to humans does not imply that they must be realistic. As a matter of fact, most expressive robots have caricaturized faces rather than detailed reproductions of human faces. Although some researchers struggle to achieve realistic human-like faces, there seems to be a good reason to prefer simplicity unless a nearly perfect level of realism can be attained.

This idea is reflected in the 'uncanny valley' hypothesis put forward by the Japanese roboticist Masahiro Mori (summarized in Reichard, 1978). The emotional reaction of humans to human appearance and movement in robots is not linear. It increases positively with similarity. However, a chasm is found when similarity is high enough for the face to appear human, but imperfections in shape or movement are perceived as being very disturbing and produce a negative emotional reaction in the observer. A strong positive emotional reaction reappears when similarity is perfect. According to Mori, movement seems to have more weight in this reaction than appearance. Thus, a cartoon-like, very caricaturized face with rudimentary movement can be more effective than a very sophisticated robotic face given that the state of the art in robotics is still far from producing the required level of accuracy in the complexity of real, dynamic, human facial expressions.

'Shallow' versus 'deep' modelling

Is it enough to model the external features of emotional expressions to achieve believable interactions between robots and humans or should these external manifestations be produced by an underlying emotional system? As we have seen in the case of the active vision head, simple, but cleverly engineered, sensory-motor coupling can result in very believable emotional reactions by robots even if they were not designed with that purpose in mind. Therefore, in the case of sporadic or short-term interactions, a 'shallow modeling' approach can be very effective. However, to produce believable, long-term interactions between robots and people, the external behaviour of the robot must not only be coherent, but also be flexible and adapted to that of its partner. Such features can only be achieved if external robot behaviour is generated by a 'deep' internal model.

Robots as useful tools for studying human interactions

Earlier, we sketched some of the reasons for our interest in designing expressive robots that can interact with humans from both practical and engineering perspectives. However, expressive robots can also be useful tools to facilitate and support the investigation of research questions regarding human emotions. In this respect, we have developed a very simple expressive head (Fig. 9.8) in the context of an ongoing collaboration with psychologist Philippe Brun of University of Rouen. This head is being used as a tool to study imitation and evocation of emotional expressions by typical and autistic children. Therefore, the features and expressions of the head need to be very simple—only 5 degrees of freedom, three in the mouth and two in the eyebrows, are used to display a small subset of emotional expressions. However, even a simple robot like this presents a number of features that makes it an interesting tool for research, such as:

- A few parameters can be modified to control movement, speed, timing, etc., in order to vary the dynamics of the expressions.

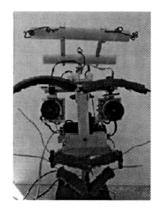 

Fig. 9.8 Our expressive head. **Left:** bare version. **Right:** covered with a mask.

- A wide range of expressions, both typical and atypical, can be formed.
- The robot can display still or dynamic emotional expressions.
- It can be used as a tool to display expressions alone or while interacting with humans.
- The degree of similarity with a human face can be varied easily in the caricature mode by adding other features, in order to assess the degree of complexity needed for a 'humanoid' to be perceived as 'human.'
- A physical device usually is perceived as more appealing and life-like than a video image. However, it is not clear whether this is always the case or whether this always a positive feature—for example, this might be questionable with autistic people.

Such a simple robot allows investigators to address a number of questions that would be difficult to study otherwise. A more interesting tool, which would also be a model of theories on emotion understanding, should be capable of reacting to human expressions and behaviour, therefore closing the interaction loop. This issue is an important item on our agenda for future research.

Concluding remarks

In this chapter, we reviewed state-of-the art research on behaviour-based robotics with a focus on the contributions of our understanding of how emotions lead to adaptive behaviour and are fundamental to human social interaction. We suggested that robots can be useful as tools and models for emotion research. The emphasis that the behaviour-based paradigm puts on the construction of 'complete' creatures that can participate in closed-loop bodily interaction with their environment has important implications for the design of artificial emotional systems (Cañamero, 2001a). The following conclusions were reached:

- To be meaningful to the robot emotions must be an integral part of its architecture rather than an *ad hoc* appendage. This means that emotions must be grounded in an internal value system that is meaningful (adaptive) for the robot's physical and social niche. It is this internal value system that is at the heart of the creature's autonomy and produces the valenced reactions that characterize emotions.

- ◆ Emotion grounding requires that our model clearly establishes a link between emotions, motivation, behaviour (including expressive behaviour), perception, and various aspects of 'cognition', so that these elements can affect and feed back into one another.

- ◆ This link must be rooted in the body of the agent, since it is through the body that agents interact with the physical and social world.

This approach does not imply that only by including explicit 'emotion machinery' in the architecture of robots can researchers produce emotion-orientated behaviour or provide useful hints for the investigation of emotional phenomena. On the contrary, we have seen through several examples of active vision, reinforcement learning and imitation, that the use of simple sensory-motor couplings induces emergent behaviours or side-effects that create emotional reactions in the human observer. These systems can also provide valuable feedback for modelling purposes, since the emergent properties introduced by the effects of dynamical interaction can simplify the design process and the emotion model itself. Nevertheless, to achieve long-term and flexible adaptation to the environment, and to the dynamics of social interactions, emotional systems appear to be a fundamental constituent of the control architectures of robots confronted with the same types of situations for which emotions provide a useful adaptation mechanism in humans and other animals. Building such artificial emotional systems is an example of synthetic psychology in which robots constitute efficient tools to simulate and investigate the dynamic effects of cognitive models of the brain, and, in particular, of emotional phenomena.

Acknowledgements

Lola Cañamero wishes to acknowledge the contributions of Jakob Fredslund and Henrik Lund, for the work on Feelix; Orlando Avila-García and Ignasi Cos-Aguilera for the work on motivation- and emotion-based action selection, and learning architectures.

Philippe Gaussier wishes to acknowledge the contributions of Pierre Andry and Jacqueline Nadel for the work on imitation, Arnaud Revel for the work on reinforcement learning, and Mathias Quoy, Sacha Leprêtre, and Philippe Laroque for the work on planning. The work of the Neurocybernetics group has received support from various French research programmes, including Cognitique action, several ACI groups on computational neuroscience and the team-project Gaussier-Nadel EPML38 on 'imitation in robotics and psychology'.

Both authors wish to acknowledge Daniel Viezzi and Philippe Brun for their work on the expressive head, and are grateful to Jacqueline Nadel for her support and constructive feedback.

References

Andry, P., Moga, S., Gaussier, P., *et al.* (2000). Imitation: learning and communication. In *Proceedings of the Sixth International Conference on Simulation for Adaptive Behaviour* (SAB 2000), pp. 353–62. Cambridge, MA: MIT Press.

Andry, P., Gaussier, P., Moga, S., *et al.* (2001). Learning and communication in imitation: an autonomous robot perspective. *IEEE Transactions on Systems, Man and Cybernetics, Part A,* **31(5),** 431–44.

Andry, P., Gaussier, P., and Nadel, J. (2002). From sensory-motor coordination to low-level imitation. In *Proceedings of the Second International Workshop on Epigenetic Robotics* (ed. G. Prince, Y. Demiris, Y. Marom, *et al.*). *Lund University Cognitive Studies,* **94,** 7–15.

Arkin, R. (1998). *Behavior-based robotics.* Cambridge, MA: MIT Press.

Ashby, W. (1952). *Design for a brain: the origin of adaptive behaviour.* London: Chapman and Hall.

Avila-García, O., Cañamero, L., and te Boekhorst, R. (2003). Analyzing the performance of 'winner-take-all' and 'voting-based' action selection policies within the two-resource problem. In *Advances in artificial life. Proceedings of the 7th European Conference (ECAL 2003),* LNAI 2801 (ed. W. Banzhaf, T. Christaller, P. Dittrich, *et al.*), pp. 733–42. Berlin: Springer-Verlag.

Barto, A., Sutton, R., and Anderson, C. (1983). Neuronlike adaptive elements that can solve difficult control problems. *IEEE Transactions on Systems, Man and Cybernetics,* **13(5),** 834–46.

Breazeal, C. (2002). *Designing sociable robots.* Cambridge, MA: MIT Press.

Brooks, R. A. (1986). A robust layered control system for a mobile robot. *IEEE Journal of Robotics and Automation,* 2(1), 14–23.

Brooks, R. A. (1991). Intelligence without representation. *Artificial Intelligence,* **47(2),** 139–59.

Cañamero, L. D. (1997). Modeling motivations and emotions as a basis for intelligent behavior. In *Proceedings of the First International Conference on Autonomous Agents* (ed. W. L. Johnson), pp. 148–55. New York, NY: ACM Press.

Cañamero, L. D. (ed.) (1998). *Emotional and intelligent: the tangled knot of cognition.* Papers from the 1998 AAAI Fall Symposium. Menlo Park, CA: AAAI Press.

Cañamero, L. D. (2001a). Building emotional artifacts in social worlds: challenges and perspectives. In *Emotional and intelligent II: the tangled knot of social cognition.* Papers from the 2001 AAAI Fall Symposium, 22–30. Menlo Park, CA: AAAI Press.

Cañamero, L. D. (ed.) (2001b). *Emotional and intelligent II: the tangled knot of social cognition.* Papers from the 2001 AAAI Fall Symposium. Menlo Park, CA: AAAI Press.

Cañamero, L. D. (2001c). Emotions and adaptation in autonomous agents: a design perspective. *Cybernetics and Systems,* **32(5),** 507–29.

Cañamero, L. D. (2002). Playing the emotion game with Feelix: what can a LEGO robot tell us about emotion? In *Socially Intelligent Agents: Creating Relationships with Computers and Robots* (ed. K. Dautenhahn, A. Bond, L. D. Cañamero, *et al.*), pp. 69–76. Norwell, MA: Kluwer Academic Publishers.

Cañamero, L. D. (2003). Designing emotions for activity selection in autonomous agents. In *Emotions in Humans and Artifacts* (ed. R. Trappl, P. Petta, and S. Payr), pp. 115–48. Cambridge, MA: MIT Press.

Cañamero, L. D. and Fredslund, J. (2001). I show you how i like you—can you read it in my face? *IEEE Transactions on Systems, Man and Cybernetics, Part A,* **31(5),** 454–9.

Cos-Aguilera, I., Cañamero, L., and Hayes, G. (2003). Learning object functionalities in the context of behaviour selection. In *Proceedings of Towards Intelligent Mobile Robots (TIMR'03): 4th British Conference on Mobile Robotics* (ed. U. Nehmzow and C. Melhuish), University of the West of England, Bristol, UK, 28–29 August, 2003.

Donnart, J-Y. and Meyer, J-A. (1996). Hierarchical map building and self-positioning with MonaLysa. *Adaptive Behavior*, **5(1)**, 29–74.

Frijda, N. H. (1995). Emotions in robots. In *Comparative Approaches to Cognitive Science* (ed. H. L. Roitblat and J-A. Meyer), pp. 501–16. Cambridge, MA: MIT Press.

Gaussier, P. and Zrehen, S. (1995). Perac: a neural architecture to control artificial animals. *Robotics and Autonomous System*, **16(2–4)**, 91–320.

Gaussier, P., Revel, A., Joulain, C., *et al.* (1997). Living in a partially structured environment: How to bypass the limitation of classical reinforcement techniques. *Robotics and Autonomous Systems*, **20**, 225–50.

Gaussier, P., Moga, S., Quoy, M., *et al.* (1998). From perception-action loops to imitation processes: a bottom-up approach of learning by imitation. *Applied Artificial Intelligence*, **12(7/8)**, 701–27.

Gaussier, P., Joulain, C., Banquet, J., *et al.* (1999). The visual homing problem: an example of robotics/biology cross-fertilization. *Robotics and Autonomous Systems*, **30**, 155–80.

Gaussier, P., Leprêtre, S., Quoy, M., *et al.* (2000). Experiments and models about cognitive map learning for motivated navigation. In *Interdisciplinary approaches to robot learning*, volume 24 (ed. J. Demiris and A. Birk), pp. 53–94. Robotics and Intelligent Systems Series, World Scientific.

Harnad, S. (1990). The symbol grounding problem. *Physica D*, **42**, 335–46.

Kelso, J. S. (1995). *Dynamic patterns: the self-organization of brain and behaviour*. Cambridge, MA: MIT Press.

Maes, P. (1991). A bottom-up mechanism for behavior selection in an artificial creature. In *Proceedings of the First International Conference on Simulation of Adaptive Behaviour* (ed. J. A. Meyer and S. W. Wilson), pp. 238–46. Cambridge, MA: MIT Press.

Mandler, G. (1985). *Mind and body*. New York, NY: W. W. Norton.

Meltzoff, N. and Moore, M-K. (1977). Imitation of facial and manual gestures by human neonates. *Science*, **198**, 75–82.

Menzel, P. and d'Aluisio, F. (2000). *Robo sapiens: evolution of a new species*. Cambridge, MA: MIT Press.

Nadel, J. (2000). The functional use of imitation in preverbal infants and nonverbal children with autism. In *The imitative mind: development, evolution and brain bases* (ed. A. Meltzoff and W. Prinz), pp. 42–62. Cambridge: Cambridge University Press.

Pfeifer, R. (1991). *A dynamic view of emotion with an application to the classification of emotional disorders*. Vrije: Universiteit Brussel, AI Memo.

Pfeifer, R. and Schreier, C. (1999). *Understanding intelligence*. Cambridge, MA: MIT Press.

Picard, R. W. (1997). *Affective computing*. Cambridge, MA: MIT Press.

Quoy, M., Gaussier, P., Leprêtre, S., *et al.* (1999). A neural model for the visual navigation and planning of a mobile robot. In *Advances in artificial life, ECAL99*, LNAI volume **1674**, pp. 319–23. Berlin: Springer-Verlag.

Reeves, B. and Nass, C. (1996). *The media equation. How people treat computers, television and new media like real people and places*. New York, NY: Cambridge University Press/CSLI Publications.

Reichard, J. (1978). *Robots: fact, fiction + prediction*. London: Thames and Hudson Ltd.

Revel, A., Gaussier, P., Leprêtre, S., *et al.* (1998). Planning versus sensory-motor conditioning: what are the issues? In *Proceedings of SAB'98: from animals to animats*, **5**, pp. 129–38. Cambridge, MA: MIT Press.

Scheeff, M., Pinto, M., Rahardja, K., *et al.* (2002). Experiences with Sparky, a social robot. In *Socially intelligent agents: creating relationships with computers and robots* (ed. K. Dautenhahn, A. Bond, L. D. Cañamero, *et al.*), pp. 173–80. Norwell, MA: Kluwer Academic Publishers.

Schöner, G., Dose, M., and Engels, C. (1995). Dynamics of behaviour: theory and applications for autonomous robot architectures. *Robotics and Autonomous System*, **16(2–4)**, 213–45.

Simon, H. A. (1967). Motivational and emotional controls of cognition. *Psychological Review*, 74(1), 29–39.

Spier, E. and McFarland, D. (1997). Possibly optimal decision making under self-sufficiency and autonomy. *Journal of Theoretical Biology*, 189, 317–31.

Takanishi, A., Matsuno, T., and Kato, A. (1997). *Development of an anthropomorphic head-eye robot with two eyes—coordinated head-eyes motion and pursuing motion in the depth direction* (Wasada University Japan). IEEE RSJ, IROS 97 Grenoble France, video proceedings.

Thomas, F. and Johnston, O. (1981). *Disney animation: the illusion of life*. New York, NY: Abbeville Press.

Tolman, E. (1948). Cognitive maps in rats and men. *Psychological Review*, 55(4), 189–208.

Tomkins, S. S. (1984). Affect theory. In *Approaches to emotion* (ed. K. R. Scherer and P. Ekman), pp. 163–95. Hillsdale, NJ: Lawrence Erlbaum Associates.

Tyrrell, T. (1993). The use of hierarchies for action selection. *Adaptive Behavior*, 1(4), 387–419.

Watkins, C. and Dayan, P. (1992). Q-learning. *Machine Learning*, 8(3), 279–92.

Weaver, S., Klopf, A., and Morgan, J. (1993). A hierarchical network of control systems that learn: modeling nervous system function during classical and instrumental conditioning. *Adaptive Behavior*, 1(3), 263–319.

Wehrle, T. (2001). The grounding problem of modeling emotions in adaptive systems. *Cybernetics and Systems*, 32(5), 561–80.

Comparative approaches: typical and impaired emotional development

Chapter 10

The repertoire of infant facial expressions: an ontogenetic perspective

Harriet Oster

My ongoing research on infant facial expressions has been guided by the view that the facial expressions shown by young infants are neither global and diffuse precursors of adult facial expressions, nor precocious, fully formed versions of those expressions. Instead, I have argued (Oster *et al.*, 1992; Oster, 1997) that infant facial expressions and other communicative behaviours should be examined in their own right as biologically-based adaptations crucial for the infant's survival and normal development. In this sense, some of the most characteristic facial expressions shown by young infants may be thought of as ontogenetic adaptations—a term used by Oppenheim (1980, 1981) to designate neurobehavioural attributes and capacities of immature animals, which may have evolved because of the adaptive functions they serve in ontogeny. From this perspective, certain universally recognized facial expressions in adults might represent 'metamorphoses' of facial expressions that evolved originally to serve as communicative signals in infants. Darwin (1872/1998) also recognized this possibility, as discussed below.

An ontogenetic perspective on the development of emotional expressions implies that there are likely to be changes as well as continuities in the morphology, affective meaning, and communicative function of some facial expressions. For that reason, we need precise and objective measures to describe the patterns of expression actually shown by infants—regardless of whether they resemble prototypical adult expressions—and to trace developmental changes in facial expression. Similarly, we need an empirical approach to understand infant facial expressions in terms of their adaptive significance in infant–caregiver communication—not just in terms of adult emotion categories. Fine-grained measures of infant expression are also needed to capture subtle variations in the patterning and coordination of facial expressions, and to investigate individual differences in facial expressiveness and emotion regulation, particularly in at-risk or atypical populations.

Baby FACS (Oster, 2004), a fine-grained, anatomically based coding system, is uniquely suited to all of these tasks, as discussed in the third part of this chapter. However, because there has been continuing disagreement about the nature of infant facial expressions and the measurement systems used to study them, I begin this chapter by re-examining long-standing theoretical and methodological issues in this ongoing debate, and I attempt to clarify misconceptions that have arisen in the recent literature. An alternative, ontogenetic perspective and an ethological approach to studying infant facial expressions are outlined in the second section. I next describe the Baby FACS coding system, and discuss its advantages for basic research on emotional development and for research on individual differences in emotional expressiveness and affective communication in normative and at-risk populations. The use of Baby FACS in basic and applied research is illustrated in the following section, which summarizes two ongoing studies: a collaborative, cross-cultural study of 11-month-old infants in different emotion-eliciting situations (Camras *et al.*, 1998, 2004) and a short-term longitudinal study of infants with craniofacial anomalies and their mothers (Oster *et al.*, 2000, 2003; Oster, 2003). A description of the basic repertoire of infant facial expressions follows, with illustrations of several distinctive infant facial configurations, including variants and intensities of positive and negative affect expressions. The chapter concludes with an outline of critical questions for future research.

The nature and measurement of infant facial expressions

Most developmental psychologists today agree that affective communication plays a crucial role in early social, emotional, and cognitive development (Bowlby, 1969; Oster and Ekman, 1978; Cicchetti and Schneider-Rosen, 1984; Izard and Malatesta, 1987; Campos *et al.*, 1989; Oster *et al.*, 1992; Sroufe, 1995). Despite differing theoretical perspectives, most investigators also agree that infants are preadapted for social interaction, and that their facial expressions and other expressive behaviours have a biological basis. Researchers studying mother–infant interaction have been struck by the rich and varied repertoire of facial expressions shown by young infants, and by their caretakers' seemingly intuitive responses to those signals (cf. Hinde, 1974; Papousek and Papousek, 1987; Trevarthen, 1998). At the same time, it is clear that cognitive development and experience also play a role in the elaboration and refinement of emotions and emotional expressions.

Measures of infant facial expression have been used in a wide variety of research paradigms as indicators of infants' perceptual and cognitive processes, emotional responses, and capacities for emotion regulation and reciprocal social interaction. Implicit in these studies is the belief that infant facial expressions are capable of conveying reliable information about the infant's 'state of mind' and behavioural predispositions. Many developmental psychologists would also agree that facial expression serves intra-psychic signalling and motivational functions (Campos and Barrett, 1984; Cicchetti and Schneider-Rosen, 1984; Izard and Malatesta, 1987; Oster, 1992). Disagreements have focused primarily on the nature of the information we can infer from infant facial expressions, and the nature of developmental changes in facial expressions and emotions.

Three related, but independent questions have dominated debates about the development of facial expressions:

- Do specific, discrete emotions and expressions develop through a process of differentiation from more global affective responses?
- Are the universally recognized facial expressions of basic emotions (cf. Ekman, 1989) present in their adult-like form from early infancy?
- Do facial expressions reliably reflect the infant's affective state and/or emotional experience from the beginning of life?[1]

In the following discussion, I focus primarily on issues related to facial expression and facial measurement, omitting detailed discussion of broader issues of emotional development. (See Campos and Barrett, 1984; Cicchetti and Schneider-Rosen, 1984; Barrett and Campos, 1987; Izard and Malatesta, 1987; Camras, 1991; Lewis, 1993; Sroufe, 1995 for more comprehensive examination of these issues.) This is not because I view facial expressions as the only window on emotional development or necessarily the most reliable window, but because I believe that a clarification of the issues relating to facial expression can contribute to progress in addressing the broader developmental issues.

Emotional development as a process of gradual differentiation

According to traditional views, the basic human emotions develop through a gradual process of differentiation from more diffuse and undifferentiated emotional reactions in the newborn. According to Bridges' (1932) classic model, newborns display only global excitement, followed within the first 2–3 weeks of life by distress in response to 'disagreeably painful and unsatisfying experiences' (p. 327). Delight differentiates from 'agitated excitement on the one hand and non-emotional quiescence and passivity on the other' around 3 months (p. 334). These primitive emotional reactions progressively differentiate into specific, discrete emotions over the first 2 years of life. Bridges has been rightfully criticized for her unrepresentative research sample (infants in a foundling hospital, including only three less than 1 month old) and unsystematic observations. However, the general notion that emotional reactions become increasingly differentiated with development was widely accepted until it was challenged by differential emotions theory (DET), as discussed below.

----

[1] In this paper I use the term emotional experience loosely, to mean experience at some level of awareness. A discussion of whether young infants have the presumed cognitive prerequisites for experiencing particular emotions (or any emotion at all) is beyond the scope of this paper. However, in my own view, emotion does not require self-conscious awareness (Lewis, 1993) or deliberate, conscious appraisal of the eliciting event. At the same time, I agree that the meaning of an event for the infant—at some level of information processing—determines the nature of the emotion experienced, and that the quality of emotional experience changes with increasing cognitive development (cf. Barrett and Campos, 1987; Sroufe, 1995).

Sroufe (1979, 1995), while agreeing with the basic notion that emotions become more finely differentiated with age, modified Bridges' model in several respects. In his model, distress is present from birth as a reaction to excessive physiological arousal, whatever the cause. Although discrete negative emotions, such as anger and fear, do not emerge until the second half-year, precursors of those emotions are present in the first months of life. These precursors differ from each other in the source of distress, for example, frustration or rage in response to physical restraint and wariness in response to discrepant or arresting stimulation, but they are expressed, behaviourally, by non-specific reactions such as crying. Sroufe viewed the endogenous sleep smiles of newborns as precursors of later smiles of delight and joy, which emerge at 2–3 and 7 months, respectively. Further differentiation and elaboration of emotions occur over the course of the first 3 years, with the emergence of emotions such as pride, shame, and guilt from origins in earlier joy, fear, and anger, respectively.

With regard to the second question raised above, Sroufe (1979, 1995) reported that discrete, adult-like facial expressions of emotions such as surprise, anger, and fear were rarely observed in young infants in contexts believed to elicit those emotions. With regard to the third question, Sroufe (1979, 1995) has maintained that facial expressions are neither necessary nor sufficient to infer an infant's emotional response. Thus, although the endogenous sleep smiles of newborns involve the same facial muscle actions as adult smiles, Sroufe did not regard them as expressions of delight or joy, but as precocious precursors of these emotions. On the other hand, we might be justified in inferring the emotion of fear in a 10-month-old who responds to an approaching stranger by turning away and crying, although the infant does not show a differentiated, adult-like facial expression of fear. In this case, the emotion would be inferred from other behavioural and physiological indicators, taking into account the infant's age and level of cognitive development.

My own observations are consistent with Sroufe's (1995) conclusion that adult-like facial expressions of discrete negative emotions are absent in early infancy, as discussed below, and I am in general agreement with his broader organizational perspective on emotional development. One limitation of Sroufe's model is that all emotions and expressions may not stem from two or three non-specific precursors of positive and negative affect. For example, expressions associated with alert, focused attention (interpreted as interest or puzzlement) and disgust-like expressions to negative tastes are present from the beginning of life, as discussed further below. Surprise may have a separate origin, and the development of grief and sadness in response to the experience of loss needs closer examination, as Sroufe (1995, p. 68) acknowledged. Finally, potentially meaningful variations in distress expressions or negative emotion precursors are ignored in this model.

Differential emotions theory

In sharp contrast to traditional views, Izard and his collaborators have rejected the idea that emotions and their facial expressions develop through a process of differentiation from more global and undifferentiated precursors. Citing Darwin (1872/1998), Izard *et al.* (1995, p. 997) maintain that the universally recognized facial expressions of certain basic emotions are largely innate, and that these facial expressions emerge 'without facial-movement precursors' within the first 2–7 months of life. According to Izard and Malatesta (1987, p. 531), 'the facial expressions of young infants are identical in all essential aspects to adult expressions that have been shown to be universal'. These investigators acknowledge a few exceptions to this general rule, noted below, but otherwise maintain that young infants show adult-like expressions of the basic emotions, including discrete negative emotions. Indeed, Izard and Malatesta have maintained that because infants have been only minimally influenced by socialization and cultural learning, and have limited ability to mask or feign their emotions, they show more extreme and stereotyped expressions of the basic emotions than do adults. According to DET, the underlying feeling states accompanying universal facial expressions are also invariant throughout life, and there is an innate concordance between expressions and feeling states.

Together, these assumptions of DET form the basis for two coding systems, Max (The Maximally Discriminative Facial Movement Coding System; Izard, 1995) and Affex (A System for Identifying Affect Expressions by Holistic Judgements; Izard *et al.*, 1983). Max and Affex use facial movement formulas derived from prototypical, universally recognized adult facial expressions to specify the appearance changes presumed to signal eight discrete emotions in infants: interest, surprise, joy, sadness, anger, fear, disgust, and contempt. Izard based the formula for interest on observation of infants, because this expression has not been studied in adults. An additional formula, specifying the expression of 'discomfort-pain' (DP) in infants, was based on observations of infants' responses to the pain of inoculation. According to DET, this expression is a specific response to physical pain or discomfort; there is no generalized expression of distress in the Max coding system. Partial expressions, involving only one of the component actions specified in the formula for an emotion, are also recognized in DET as discrete emotion expressions, while expressions with components of two or more different emotions are classified as blends.

According to the Max manual (revised edition, Izard, 1995, p. 1), 'with some modifications in the descriptions of appearance changes, the system can be used to measure emotion signals at any age'. Infant–adult differences are attributed primarily to the amount of subcutaneous fat in infants' faces (e.g. bulges in infants' faces where lines and wrinkles would appear in adult faces). In addition, Izard (1983) acknowledges that the Max-specified expression of physical pain differs from adult pain expressions, and that infants do not show a variant of adult anger expressions with pressed lips and raised upper eyelids. According to DET, the increasing capacity for regulating emotion results in a reduction in the frequency of full-face expressions with age, but not a differentiation of discrete expressions from less differentiated precursors (e.g. Izard *et al.*, 1995, p. 1011). Thus, according to DET the facial expressions of the basic emotions are 'morphologically stable', and Max formulas for discrete negative emotions such as anger, fear, sadness, and disgust are presumed to apply to infants and adults alike.

Criticisms of DET

Critics of DET do not question the general view that emotions and emotional expressions have a biological basis and serve important adaptive functions during early development. However, this does not necessarily imply, as Izard and his colleagues have maintained (Izard and Malatesta, 1987; Izard *et al.*, 1995), that facial expressions should emerge full-blown in their adult-like form in early infancy or that there should be no developmental changes in the morphology, signal value, or affective meaning of facial expressions (cf. Oster and Ekman, 1978; Fridlund *et al.*, 1987; Oster *et al.*, 1992). Recent findings, from my own and other investigators' laboratories, have challenged the empirical evidence for these assumptions of DET, and for the Max and Affex formulas based on them. Most critics have focused on the failure to find independent evidence that infant facial expressions identified by Max and Affex formulas reflect the corresponding discrete emotions in infants. Much less attention has been paid to evidence that the expressions themselves are not, in fact, morphologically the same as their adult prototypes.

Smiling and expressions of interest have been found to be reliably associated with positive 'incentive events', such as mother–infant interaction. However, the results of experimental studies and studies involving naturalistic observations have shown that infants do not differentially produce Max-specified expressions of surprise or discrete negative emotions in situations believed to elicit the corresponding emotions, even when other behavioural or physiological measures indicate the presence of the target emotion (e.g. Matias and Cohn, 1993; Camras *et al.*, 1998; see reviews by Camras, 1991; Oster *et al.*, 1992; Sroufe, 1995). The use of Max and Affex formulas as the sole measure of infants' emotional responses can result in errors of both omission and commission. For example, many researchers have reported that the Max-specified anger expression is the predominant response in a wide variety of eliciting situations, including situations designed to elicit fear or sadness rather than anger (e.g. Camras, 1991; Matias and Cohn, 1993; Sroufe, 1995; Sullivan and Lewis, 2003). Attributing anger to infants in those contexts without independent evidence that anger (and not another emotion) is present could lead to questionable conclusions about normative responses or individual differences (cf. Oster *et al.*, 1992; Sroufe, 1995). Izard's own studies (e.g. Izard *et al.*, 1995) have failed to provide rigorous tests of the external validity of Max formulas for discrete negative emotions. The interpretation of facial expressions identified by Max formulas as partial expressions or blends of discrete negative emotions is especially problematic, because it presupposes the validity of the Max formulas for full-face expressions.

Several investigators have suggested that facial configurations identified by Max as expressions of specific, discrete negative emotions represent more generalized distress in young infants (Camras, 1991; Oster *et al.*, 1992; Matias and Cohn, 1993; Sroufe, 1995). Consistent with this view, many researchers report only composite measures of Max-specified negative affect expressions rather than data on specific negative expressions. If Max-specified facial expressions of discrete negative emotions such as anger, fear, and sadness do not represent those specific emotions, does that mean that facial expressions and emotions are not reliably linked in early infancy, as suggested by supporters of dynamical systems, functionalist, and cognitive developmental perspectives (cf. Campos and, Barrett 1984; Barrett and Campos, 1987; Fogel and Thelen, 1987; Camras, 1991; Lewis, 1993; Sullivan and Lewis, 2003)? Although this conclusion may be justified in some cases, I do not believe that it is a necessary conclusion, because it is based in part on acceptance of the 'face validity' of Max formulas for infant expressions of emotion.

The problem is not just that Max-specified facial expressions of discrete negative emotions do not reliably occur in contexts where those emotions would be expected—but also that the Max-specified expressions are not, in fact, morphologically the same as their presumed adult prototypes. This conclusion was indirectly suggested by Oster *et al.*'s (1992) finding that untrained observers perceived distress or blends of two or more negative emotions in slides (most from the Max training set) showing infant facial expressions that fit Max formulas for discrete negative emotions. A more recent study by Izard *et al.* (1995) largely replicated these results. The facial measurement study reported by Oster *et al.* (1992) provided more direct evidence that Max-specified infant expressions of discrete negative emotions do not involve the same patterns of facial muscle action as their presumed adult prototypes.

In the measurement study, the Max-specified infant facial expressions and prototypical adult expressions used in the observer judgment study were coded with Baby FACS (for infant slides) and FACS (for the adult slides), and the raw coding of facial muscle configurations was independently analysed in Ekman's lab, without information about their source, by the FACS interpretation dictionary—a database of cross-culturally validated, prototypical adult expressions. Consistent with the observer judgment data, the infant expressions of 'discomfort-pain' were interpreted as pain or non-specific negative affect, but only three of 19 Max-specified expressions of discrete negative emotions (two of sadness and one of disgust) fit adult templates for those discrete emotions. None of the Max-specified anger or fear expressions were identified as such.[2] The Baby FACS coding showed that infant facial expressions classified by Max formulas as expressions of discrete negative emotions involved components of

---

[2] Izard *et al.* (1995) discounted these findings on the grounds that different coding systems have different prototypes for universally recognized facial expressions. However, this should not be the case if both systems are based on cross-culturally validated examples of adult facial expressions. In fact, the adult slides of discrete negative emotions (including a slide from Izard's laboratory of an open-mouth anger expression) were accurately judged by the naïve observers and were accurately identified by the FACS Interpretation Dictionary.

cry faces that are not present in adult expressions of those emotions (e.g. raised cheeks and upper lip, squinted lower eyelids), and that certain salient components of prototypical adult expressions of discrete negative emotions were not present in the infants' faces (e.g. raised upper eyelids in fear and anger). In brief, what this study demonstrated was that adults showing the same configurations of facial muscle actions as infants whose expressions fit Max formulas for discrete negative emotions would not look angry, afraid, or sad—but rather as though they were crying or about to cry.

Max-specified facial expressions of anger (AR), discomfort/pain (DP), and fear (FT) are in fact variants of the classic cry face described by Darwin (1872/1998). In both AR and DP the brows are lowered and drawn together (AC 25), the cheeks and lower eyelids are raised, the upper lip is raised, the nasolabial furrow is bowed outward, and the mouth is opened and horizontally stretched, producing a squarish appearance (AC 54). The only difference between Max AR and DP is that in AR the eyes are narrowly open and squinted (AC 33), while in DP they are tightly closed (AC 37).[3] AC 53, the mouth component of the Max fear formula, is a cry mouth with a horizontally stretched mouth and a slightly opened jaw. The still photographs and video clips illustrating AC 53 on the Max training tape show cry face components (raised cheeks, nasolabial furrow deepening), although they are not specified in the Max formula for fear. Full-faced, discrete fear expressions (involving raised and drawn together brows and raised upper eyelids along with the horizontally stretched mouth) are rarely observed in infants, so in most cases infant expressions with AC 53 would be coded as blends with AR, DP, or SD, depending on the upper face components. Illustrations of infant cry faces that fit Max formulas for full-faced DP, AR, and an AR/FT blend are shown in Fig. 10.1.

Variations in the degree of mouth and eye opening during periods of fussiness or crying in infants are more parsimoniously explained as reflecting fluctuations in the intensity of distress, not alternations between different discrete negative emotions. Such variations are probably also related to vocalizations, respiration, ongoing motor activity, and varying degrees of emotion regulation. Older infants and adults have a greater capacity to keep their eyes open when they are crying, but this does not necessarily indicate the discrete emotion of anger (as suggested by Izard et al., 1987). Similarly, a cry face with closed eyes (in a child or in a grieving adult) does not necessarily indicate physical pain, and a cry face with a slightly opened mouth does not necessarily indicate fear.

....

[3] Both AC 33 and AC 37 raise the cheeks and produce 'narrowed or squinted eyes' (Max manual, 1995, pp. 69 and 71). However, cheek raising is coded as AC 33 when the eyes are open (as in the Max AR formula) and as AC 37 when they are tightly closed (as in the Max DP formula). This distinction is likely to be ignored in studies where physical pain is not expected. For example, the photo used to illustrate a discrete, Max-coded anger expression in Sullivan and Lewis (2003, p. 699) shows a cry face with tightly closed eyes, which would fit the formula for DP not AR.

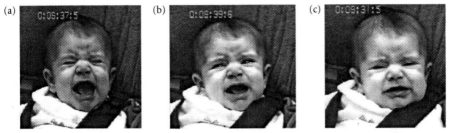

(a) 0:09:37:5   (b) 0:09:39:6   (c) 0:09:31:5

Fig. 10.1 Cry face configurations in a 6-month-old in the Still Face paradigm. In all three photos, the brows are lowered and drawn together at their inner corners, the cheeks are raised, the nasolabial furrow is deepened, and the mouth corners are stretched horizontally. (a) Cry face with tightly closed eyes and a squarish mouth—a discomfort-pain (DP) expression according to Max formulas. (b) Cry face with narrowly open eyes and a squarish open mouth—an anger (AR) expression according to Max. (c) Cry face with narrowly open eyes with a slightly open, horizontally stretched mouth—an anger/fear (AR/FT) blend according to Max.

The evidence cited by Izard *et al.* (1995) for the 'morphological stability' of discrete emotion expressions comes from descriptive data on the rate of occurrence of infant facial configurations that fit Max and Affex criteria for full-face, partial, and blended expressions of discrete emotions from 2.5 to 9 months of age. The formulas themselves were presumed to be stable. However, because Max is not a comprehensive coding system, coders it ignores infant–adult differences and age-related changes in facial expression. According to Izard (1995, p. 2), Max 'focuses only on facial behaviours or appearance changes, which . . . have been hypothesized to identify emotion or affect signals'. Certain facial muscle actions or combinations seen in adult and infant emotional expressions are omitted from Max formulas, or cannot be independently and unambiguously coded because they are part of compound ACs that include several independent muscle actions.[4] The more general point—and my reason for going into

----

4 As seen in Table 1 of the revised Max manual (Izard, 1995), AC 54 in Max represents a complex combination of facial actions that combine to produce the angular, squarish mouth that is a component of Max-specified anger and discomfort/pain expressions. Although the drawings, still photographs, and video excerpts illustrating AC 54 in the Max training materials clearly show a horizontally stretched mouth, an action produced by risorius, this muscle is not listed as a component of AC 54 in Table 1, but only as a component of AC 53 (a fear component) and AC 55 (an alternative mouth component in AR formulas). As noted above, in AC 54 and 55, the jaw is widely opened, while in AC 53 it is only slightly opened. Thus, degrees of horizontal mouth stretching and mouth opening cannot be independently coded. Another muscle action comprising AC 54 is levator labii superioris, alaeque nasi, which raises the upper lip and wrinkles the nose. This muscle action is also a component of AC 59B (part of the Max disgust formula), but cannot be independently coded in Max. Two other muscle actions that raise the upper lip and deepen the nasolabial furrow in infant cry faces, levator labii superioris (also seen in variants of adult anger and disgust according to Ekman) and zygomaticus minor (a salient component of sadness and grief expressions according to Darwin and Ekman), are likely to be involved in infant facial expressions coded as AR, DP, FT, and SD, but

these details—is that we cannot describe infant–adult differences or developmental changes and continuities in facial expression unless we can comprehensively and unambiguously describe the patterns of facial expression produced by infants and adults. In other words, if we only code the presence or absence of infant facial expressions that fit *a priori* formulas, we will not be able to test the assumption that infant and adult expressions are morphologically the same.

In summary, the evidence to date does not support the claim that the universally recognized facial expressions of discrete negative emotions are present in their adult-like form from early infancy—the second question raised at the beginning of this chapter. Although it is also clear that negative affect expressions are less finely differentiated in early infancy than in adults, it is not yet clear whether the facial expressions of specific negative emotions such as anger and fear develop through a process of differentiation from the pre-cry and cry face configurations of young infants or whether these expressions emerge full-blown without precursors, as claimed by DET, but at some point later in development. One hypothesis suggested by Sroufe's model is that infants may first begin to show more discrete expressions of negative emotion (i.e. expressions with fewer components of cry faces and more components of prototypical adult expressions) in contexts that elicit less intense negative emotion. The possibility that infants show different variants of cry face or pre-cry face configurations in situations thought to elicit different negative emotions was examined in detailed analyses of videotapes from a collaborative cross-cultural study involving Chinese, Japanese, and American 11-month-olds in anger- and fear-eliciting situations. The results to date, summarized below, do not provide clear evidence for this idea (Camras *et al.*, 1998, 2004).

With regard to the question of whether facial expressions reliably reflect an infant's emotional feeling state in early infancy, the answer depends in part on the answers to the first two questions. It is possible that facial expressions and emotions are reliably linked in infants, but that negative emotions and facial expressions are both less finely differentiated in young infants than in older infants and children. However, evidence that 10–12-month-old infants show clear behavioural signs of fear and anger in contexts believed to elicit those specific emotions would suggest that facial expressions may be less finely differentiated than negative affect states. At this point we can only speculate about why this might be. Some suggestions are offered in the final section of this chapter.

An ontogenetic perspective

Investigators on both sides of the differentiation versus discrete emotions debate have tended to view infants' facial expressions from the vantage point of the adult repertoire of facial expressions. While acknowledging the importance of affective communication

---

these actions are not specified in the formulas for these expressions, and they cannot be independently coded in Max because they are part of other compound ACs used in different emotion formulas.

in early social interaction, emotion researchers have mostly asked when in development the universally recognized expressions of basic emotions can be seen in infants and young children, and when in development infants are capable of experiencing the corresponding emotions. In contrast, an ontogenetic perspective (Oster, 1997; Oster *et al.*, 1992) takes as its starting point the organized patterns of facial expression produced by young infants and attempts to determine their origins, causes, signal value, and affective meaning for the infant and their caregivers. This perspective allows us to trace changes and continuities in the repertoire of infant facial expressions without making prior assumptions about the developmental processes involved.

This approach differs in obvious ways from DET, which assumes, in effect, that there are no distinctive infant expressions—that the facial expressions shown by young infants are essentially the same as their adult prototypes in their morphology, social signal value, and affective meaning. It differs in more subtle ways from Sroufe's organizational view, which views the emotional reactions of young infants as relatively non-specific precursors of more differentiated and specific emotions and emotional expressions that unfold later in development. Although young infants do not show finely differentiated facial expressions of specific negative emotions they show a variety of distinctive facial expressions that are not just precursors of later discrete emotional expressions. Such expressions are also interesting for what they are in infancy—distinctive signals crucial in infant–caregiver communication, which may have evolved because of their adaptive functions in infancy (cf. Oppenheim, 1980). Detailed measurement of infant expressions reveals greater organization and specificity than is apparent from a classification of these expressions as global positive or negative affect, or as emotion precursors. An empirical, ethological approach to studying infant facial expressions suggests that in addition to communicating information about emotion, narrowly defined, facial displays may convey information about other aspects of the infant's 'state of mind', such as state of alertness, perceptual and cognitive processes, behavioural predispositions, and efforts to control emotion.

To discover the message a facial expression or other signal communicates to caregivers, and its meaning for the caregiver and infant, the traditional ethological approach is to study the context in which the signal occurs, the antecedent events, the infant's other behaviour before, during, and following the signal, and the caregivers' responses. In addition, the component facial muscle actions themselves can sometimes provide clues to the origins and meaning of certain facial expressions in infants and adults. That is because, as Charles Darwin (1872/1998) appreciated, emotional expressions are not arbitrary, God-given creations (or products of a rational, abstract developmental scheme), but rather the products of natural evolutionary and developmental processes. For Darwin, the challenging task was to explain how particular muscle actions came to be associated with particular emotions. According to Darwin and later evolutionary biologists, most emotional expressions had their origins in adaptive behaviours that originally served some direct biological function and that later became specialized (or ritualized) for communication because their communicative function (e.g. signalling the sender's behavioural disposition) had survival value (see Altman, 1967; Smith, 1977; Hinde, 1982, for detailed discussion).

Certain human expressions like smiling and crying are completely specialized for communication from the beginning of life. However, components of other facial expressions in infants and adults might retain some of their direct biological or physiological regulatory function, as well as serving a signal function, for example, actions related to information seeking (raised brows, widened eyes, visual fixation) versus rejection (gaze aversion, narrowed or closed eyes, mouth gaping to eject a bad-tasting substance). Darwin (1872/1998) also observed that 'some of the most characteristic expressions exhibited by man are derived from the act of screaming' (p. 356), and from efforts to prevent or check crying (p. 350). These observations suggest that differing negative affect expressions in infants may reflect differences in the intensity or source of distress, the infant's behavioural predispositions, or efforts to regulate emotion. Labelling these configurations in terms of discrete negative emotions ignores potentially meaningful differences in their functions and meaning, as well as observable differences in morphology between the infant expressions and prototypical adult expressions. Detailed coding of the actual facial configurations shown by infants in different contexts is needed to understand the expressions in their own right as well as in terms of their relation to later expressions of discrete negative emotions.

Baby FACS

Baby FACS (Facial Action Coding System for Infants and Young Children; Oster, 2004) is a fine-grained, anatomically-based coding system adapted from Ekman and Friesen's (1978) Facial Action Coding System for adults (revised edition, Ekman *et al.*, 2002). The basic Action Units (AUs) correspond to discrete, minimally distinguishable actions of the facial muscles. Because the basic coding units of Baby FACS are exhaustive and mutually exclusive, any complex facial movement can be precisely and unambiguously identified in terms of combinations and sequences of its constituent actions. For example, four independent muscle actions in the brow region raise the inner and outer corners of the brows (AU 1 and 2, respectively), draw together or 'knit' the inner corners of the brows (AU 3), lower the brows, and 'knot' the skin above the nasal root (AU 4). (The adult FACS does not separately code brow knitting but includes it in AU 4.) These separate actions and their combinations can produce 15 different unique brow configurations. The three muscles that raise the upper lip and deepen the nasolabial furrow produce distinct appearance changes and are therefore designated by different AUs:

- AU 9 (levator labii superioris, alaeque nasi), which wrinkles the nose and raises the nostril wings and central portion of the upper lip and produces a bulging of the skin above the root of the nose;
- AU 10 (levator labii superioris), which raises the middle portion of the upper lip in a sneer-like action and causes an angular bend in the upper lip and nasolabial furrow;

◆ AU 11 (zygomaticus minor), which raises the outermost portion of the upper lip, flattening the plane of the lip and producing an outward bowing of the nasolabial furrow.

As discussed below, these upper lip actions may occur separately or together in infants' facial expressions. Degrees of mouth opening are coded independently of other actions, such as raising the lip corners (AU 12, the principal component of smiling) or horizontal stretching of the mouth (AU 20, the principal component of cry faces).

Embryological studies (reviewed by Oster and Ekman, 1978; Oster, 2004) have shown that all of the muscles of facial expression are formed and innervated by the facial nerve (7th cranial) prior to term. The prenatal functioning of the facial muscles was demonstrated in the remarkable studies of Hooker and Humphrey (cf. Humphrey, 1970). Squint- and scowl-like actions of the muscles around the eyes, and movements involving puckering and protrusion of the upper and lower lips, sucking, gag reflexes, and cry faces were observed in response to stimulation in fetuses 10 to 29 weeks of menstrual age. These studies show that the facial muscle actions produced by pre- and full-term infants can be described in terms of the same basic action units (AUs) as adult facial actions (Oster and Ekman, 1978; Oster, 2004). However, infants' faces differ considerably from adults' faces in the proportions and dimensions of the bony structures of the face, in the (full-term) infant's extensive subcutaneous fat deposits and thick, highly elastic skin, and in the presence of specialized features such as the sucking lip and buccal sucking pad. Because of these differences, the appearance changes produced by facial muscle actions differ in infants and adults. The Baby FACS manual describes in detail the surface cues produced by individual AUs and combinations of AUs.

FACS and Baby FACS coding are based on functional anatomy, that is, the mechanics of facial muscle action. In scoring facial movements, the coder takes into account multiple changes in facial appearance produced by a given Action Unit or combination. These may include changes in the shape and position of facial landmarks (the brows, lip corners, etc.) as well as characteristic patterns of wrinkling, creasing, dimpling, bulging, and stretching of the skin. Because Baby FACS coding is based on multiple and redundant cues to each facial action, facial muscle actions can be reliably identified despite age differences, racial and individual differences, and abnormalities in facial morphology or neuromuscular abnormalities. For these reasons, Baby FACS can be used with pre-, as well as full-term infants, and with toddlers and young children.

FACS and Baby FACS (unlike Max) include codes for all visible actions of the facial muscles, whether or not they are presumed to be related to emotion. For that reason, we can use Baby FACS to study a wide range of facial behaviour in addition to emotion-related behaviour, such as the facial actions accompanying neonatal reflexes (e.g. rooting, startles), the facial movements occurring during REM sleep, facial responses to sensory stimulation, and responses related to cognitive information processing. Baby FACS does not provide formulas for coding discrete negative emotions, such as fear and anger in infants, for the reasons discussed above. However, Baby FACS does include descriptions of salient infant facial expressions and explicit guidelines for coding intensities and variants of smiles and cry faces.

In addition to its usefulness for basic research on emotional development, Baby FACS is ideally suited to research on individual and cultural differences in infant facial expression, including dynamic aspects of facial expression, as discussed below. Baby FACS is the only available coding system that can be used to describe and analyse subtle individual, group, or age differences in facial expressions. If we want to know how the smiles of blind, pre-term, or facially disfigured infants differ from those of normal, full-term infants, we need to be able to identify the specific facial actions involved in the behaviour grossly labelled 'smiling'. Measures of qualitative differences in the intensity and modulation of positive and negative affect expressions are particularly useful for research with atypical and clinical samples.

Two research strategies

In describing the repertoire of infant facial expressions, I draw examples from my earlier research and from two ongoing studies. These two studies represent complementary research strategies for addressing the long-standing questions discussed above: a cross-cultural experimental study, and a longitudinal study of infants with craniofacial anomalies and their mothers, an 'experiment in nature'.

Responses to fear and anger elicitors in three cultures

The cross-cultural project, conducted in collaboration with Linda Camras, Joseph and Rosemary Campos, Meng Zhao Lan, Lei Wang, Tatsuo Ujiee, and Kazuo Miyake, was designed to provide a rigorous test of the first two questions raised at the beginning of this chapter: whether infants less than 1 year of age show adult-like facial expressions of specific negative emotions in experimental situations designed to elicit those emotions, and whether they show differentiated facial expressions of negative emotion, regardless of whether their expressions resemble adult-like prototypes. In addition, we asked whether the facial expressions produced by infants in the United States, Japan, and China in the three paradigms differ in any way.

The infants (12 males and 12 females in Berkeley, California, Fukushima, Japan, and Beijing, China) were each videotaped in three different emotion-eliciting situations:

- a female experimenter who gently encircled the infant's wrists and held their hands to the tray top (a hypothesized anger or frustration elicitor);
- a toy gorilla head that emitted raspy, growling noises (a hypothesized fear elicitor);
- a yipping toy dog that appeared to vanish (a hypothesized surprise elicitor).

A 10-second baseline period involving the friendly experimenter, silent gorilla, and visible toy dog preceded the stimulus episode. The infants' facial expressions were comprehensively coded with Baby FACS during a 10-second baseline and the first 20 seconds of the stimulus episode (see Camras *et al.*, 1998, 2004 for procedural details).

The results of our ongoing analyses of the fear and anger situations have shown that the 11-month-old infants did not produce discrete, adult-like facial expressions of these emotions in either situation. Instead, when upset, they showed varying intensities of distress, with facial actions (e.g. cheeks raised, eyes narrowly squinted, nasolabial furrow bowed, and horizontal mouth stretching) that are components of infant and adult cry faces, but not prototypical adult expressions of anger and fear. The brow and mouth configurations identified by Max as specific fear and anger components were not differentially produced in the fear and anger paradigms, either as full-face or partial configurations (Camras *et al.*, 1998, 2004; Oster *et al.*, 1996).

With respect to the second question, we have not yet found evidence for any facial expressions specific to the fear vs. anger paradigms. However, there were significant paradigm differences in visual fixation, facial stilling, and body movements (Camras *et al.*, 2004; Oster *et al.*, 1996). In all three cultures, infants looked significantly longer at the eliciting stimulus in the fear than in the anger paradigm, and they showed significantly more facial and bodily stilling in response to the growling gorilla. The infants' fixed attention and cessation of facial and bodily movement in the gorilla paradigm are consistent with the interpretation of their responses to a highly novel and potentially threatening stimulus as wariness (cf. Sroufe, 1995). In contrast, the infants in all three cultures showed more extreme gaze aversion, referencing of the mother, and struggling in the arm restraint than in the gorilla paradigm. These responses may reflect specific aspects of the arm restraint paradigm (e.g. attempts to escape physical restraint), as well as more general frustration. American and Japanese infants also smiled more in the arm restraint than in the gorilla paradigm, reflecting the more social (and perhaps more ambiguous) nature of arm restraint, which may enlist more social coping strategies. Thus, although we have not yet found evidence for differentiated fear and anger expressions, significant paradigm differences in attention and body movements indicate that the gorilla and arm restraint paradigms elicited different subjective feeling states, and different emotion regulation and coping strategies. Observers' judgments of the infants' behaviour (from tapes not showing the infants' faces) were consistent with the interpretation of their responses to the growling gorilla as wary or fearful and to arm restraint as frustrated (Camras *et al.*, 1997).

With respect to our third question, the repertoire of infant facial expressions did not differ across cultures. Infants in all three cultures produced subtle variants of smiles and cry faces and distinctive infant expressions, such as brow knitting, pouts, and jaw thrusts; there were no culture-specific facial configurations. The differences we observed were quantitative in nature: differences in the amount of positive and negative expressions and differences in measures of overall 'expressiveness'. Unexpectedly, the Chinese infants smiled less and showed less intense negative affect than the American and Japanese infants, who did not differ significantly. The Chinese infants also produced fewer facial movements overall, and were less variable and less labile in their expressions than the American and Japanese infants (Camras *et al.*, 1998).

Because of the highly structured experimental paradigms used in this study, and because we did not obtain any data on caregiving practices or experiences in early infancy, we cannot explain the cultural differences we observed. Longitudinal studies and studies of emotional expression in naturalistic environments are needed to discover the origins of these cultural differences.

Infants with a facial difference

Infants with craniofacial anomalies are of interest for research on emotional development because morphological abnormalities can lead to distortions, ambiguities, or deficits in the infants' facial expressions, which could make it difficult for caregivers to read and respond sensitively to their facial signals. My ongoing longitudinal study of infants with facial anomalies (Oster et al., 2000; Oster et al., 2003; Oster, 2003) was designed to investigate the direct effects of craniofacial abnormalities on the morphology of the infants' facial expressions and the clarity of the infants' facial signals, as well as the 'transactional' effects of maternal depression, anxiety, and other psychosocial factors on the quality of mother–infant interactions and the infants' emotional expressiveness.

Research on children, adolescents, and adults with cleft lip and palate, and other congenital craniofacial conditions has consistently shown that facial disfigurement can have a negative impact on psychosocial adjustment and emotional well-being. However, there is considerable individual variability in outcomes, and the evidence indicates that facial appearance is not, by itself, a reliable predictor of an individual's adjustment or psychological well-being (cf. Pope, 1999). Several investigators have hypothesized that individual differences in psychosocial adjustment have their roots in the quality of early relationships with caregivers (cf. Speltz et al., 1994b). The results of earlier studies (Field and Vega-Lahr, 1984; Barden et al., 1989; Speltz et al., 1994a) indicated that infants with facial anomalies smile less and show less clear-cut signalling than comparison infants, and that their mothers show less affectionate and sensitive interactive behaviour. These earlier studies had two serious limitations: first, they either focused exclusively on cleft lip and palate or lumped different kinds of facial conditions together; and secondly, they did not use fine-grained, anatomically-based measures of the infants' facial behaviour. Thus, it is not clear whether the infants actually smiled less, or whether their smiles were ambiguous, or simply different in appearance from comparison infants' smiles.

In my ongoing longitudinal study, I have distinguished between uncomplicated cleft lip and palate—the most common facial anomaly and one of the most common birth defects—and a variety of other, often more severe and complicated congenital facial conditions, including deformities of the skull and bony structures of the face, asymmetries, multiple facial clefts, partial facial paralysis, and hemangiomas (vascular malformations). The 51 infants in the study include 15 with cleft lip and palate (CLP), 18 with other craniofacial anomalies or facial hemangiomas (CFH), and 18 unaffected comparison infants (COMP) infants.[5] Infants with evidence of neurological abnormalities or generalized developmental delays were excluded. However, infants in the CFH group were more likely to have associated birth defects. The infants were videotaped at target ages of 1½, 3, 6, 9, and 12 months during unstructured social interaction with the mother and (except at 12 months) in the Still Face paradigm, and their facial expressions were coded with Baby FACS. During each visit, the mothers completed self-report questionnaires assessing depression, anxiety, social support, and other variables believed to affect the quality of the mother's interactive behaviour. I summarize here preliminary findings from the 3- and 6-month sessions.

Our first important finding was that the facial expressions of infants with craniofacial anomalies can be reliably coded with Baby FACS (Oster *et al.*, 2000). Because Baby FACS coding is based on multiple and redundant cues to each facial action and takes variations in facial morphology into account, the infants' facial muscle actions can be accurately identified in terms of FACS AUs, and deficits or abnormalities in facial movement can be objectively specified. Baby FACS coding revealed that the basic repertoire of infant facial expressions is largely preserved even in infants with severe facial anomalies.[6] However, morphological abnormalities affect the functioning of the facial muscles in one or more regions of the face, as well as the outward appearance of facial muscle actions. For example, actions such as lip pursing, funneling, and tightening are restricted to the lower lip or absent in infants with a bilateral cleft lip, while cheek raising is less apparent in infants with craniosynostosis, whose cheekbones tend to be flattened. Both kinds of conditions can affect the appearance of smiles and cry faces. Hemangiomas can mask facial features, and partial facial paralysis can distort facial movements on the contralateral side of the face, as well as limiting actions on the affected side.

The signal value of the infants' facial expressions

The next question we addressed was whether these objectively specified differences in the appearance of infants' facial expressions made a difference in their social signal value. Handler and Oster (2001) found that mothers of infants with craniofacial anomalies were as accurate as mothers of comparison infants in attributing positive or negative affect to their infants' emotional expressions. In this study, verbatim transcripts of the mothers' spontaneous emotion attributions during unstructured face-to-face interactions were made from videotapes that did not show the infants' faces, and the infants' facial expressions were coded from time-linked tapes with the sound turned off. However, the mothers' emotion attributions in this study could have

---

[5] Because the conditions grouped together into the heterogeneous CFH group are rare, it would have been impossible in a single-site study to find enough infants with any one condition to divide the participants more finely according to specific diagnostic categories.

[6] The exception was an infant with Mobius syndrome, which involves a total paralysis of the muscles of facial expression. This infant was not included in analyses involving measures of facial expression.

been based on the infants' other behavior, such as vocalizations and body movements, as well as facial expressions.

An observer judgment study (Oster, 2003) provided a more stringent test of the social signal value of the facial expressions produced by infants with facially disfiguring conditions. In this study, 38 undergraduates unfamiliar with facial anomalies or infant facial expressions viewed 37 slides showing the faces of infants in four groups (cleft lip, craniofacial anomaly, hemangioma, and comparison). Explicit Baby FACS criteria were used to classify the infants' facial expressions into four categories (Cry Face, Negative Face, Interest, and Smile) and to rate them on a 7-point scale ranging from intense cry face to intense smile, with interest expressions at the midpoint. The judges rated the emotion shown in each slide on a corresponding 7-point scale ranging from intense distress to intense happiness. Their emotion ratings significantly differentiated the four expression categories and were significantly correlated with ratings based on objective Baby FACS criteria ($r > 0.95, p = 0.000$) in all four infant groups. There were no significant infant group differences in emotion ratings. The judges were thus highly accurate in rating the hedonic valence, and the magnitude of positive and negative affect expressions shown in the facial expressions of infants with facial anomalies, despite differences in the superficial appearance of their expressions (see Oster, 2003, for details of the procedures and findings of this study).

Group differences in facial expression

Our coding of the infants' facial expressions and the observer judgment study demonstrated that infants with even severe facial anomalies are capable of communicating both positive and negative affect. At the same time, we have found significant group differences in the amount of smiling displayed by infants in the Still Face paradigm at 6 months (Oster et al., 2000). For these analyses, interobserver agreement on the identification and precise location (to within 0.10 second) of smiles averaged 0.86 (Kappa).

A repeated-measures ANOVA revealed significant group ($p = 0.002$) and episode ($p = 0.000$) effects for the rate of smiling (mean smiles per minute). Univariate ANOVAs revealed significant or near significant group differences in the rate of smiling in all three episodes: $F(2, 39) = 3.27, p = 0.049$ in the Baseline, $F(2, 39) = 2.97$, $p = 0.063$ in the Still Face, and $F(2, 39) = 6.17, p = 0.005$ in the Recovery episode. *Post hoc* analyses revealed that comparison group infants (COMP, $n = 15$) smiled significantly more often in the Baseline, Still Face, and Recovery episodes (2.82, 1.61, and 3.07 smiles per minute, respectively) than infants in the combined craniofacial-hemangioma group (CFH, $n = 14$, 1.56, 0.49, and 0.96 smiles per minute), all $p < 0.05$. Infants in the cleft lip group (CLP, $n = 13$) were intermediate (2.4, 1.04, and 1.96 smiles per minute). Paired-samples t-tests showed that infants in all three groups showed a significant decrease in the rate of smiling from the Baseline to the Still Face Episode ($p < 0.05$), but only comparison group infants showed a significant increase in smiling from Still-Face to Recovery, ($t(14) = 2.37, p = 0.033$). The increase from Still Face to Recovery in the CLP group approached significance, $t(12) = 2.064$,

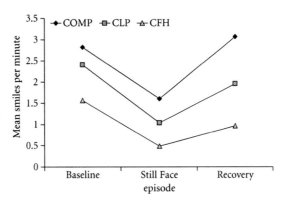

Fig. 10.2 Rate of smiling in the three episodes of the Still Face paradigm in three groups of 6-month-old infants. COMP = comparison infants; CLP = infants with uncomplicated cleft lip or cleft lip and palate; CFH = infants with other craniofacial anomalies or hemangiomas.

$p = 0.061$. In all of these comparisons, infants in the CFH group smiled less than infants in the CLP and COMP groups. Episode effects and group differences in infant smiling are shown in Fig. 10.2.

Maternal depression

With regard to the third issue examined in this study, mothers of infants in the CFH group reported significantly higher levels of depression on the CES-D (Radloff and Wales, 1977) than mothers in the two other groups at both 3 months, $F(2, 35) = 4.17$, $p = 0.024$; and 6 months, $F(2, 41) = 8.45$, $p = 0.001$. CESD scores at 3 and 6 months were significantly positively correlated, $r(n = 34) = 0.500$, $p = 0.003$, indicating continuity in maternal distress symptoms. The increased level of depressive symptoms in mothers in the CFH group is plausibly related to the fact that infants in this group had rarer and often more severe or complicated conditions than infants in the CLP group and in many cases would require more extensive, prolonged, and riskier interventions throughout childhood and sometimes adolescence. Whatever the explanation, maternal depressive symptoms at both 3 and 6 months had a negative impact on maternal sensitivity and responsiveness (Oster *et al.*, 2003) and on the infants' social responsiveness. Maternal depression at both 3 and 6 months was significantly negatively correlated with infant smiling at 6 months. CESD scores at 3 months were correlated with the rate of infant smiling in both the baseline and still face episodes of the Still Face paradigm at 6 months, $r(n = 32) = -0.483$, $p = 0.005$ and $r(n = 32) = -0.350$, $p = 0.050$, respectively. The 6-month CESD scores were significantly correlated with infant smiling only in the baseline episode, $r(n = 42) = -0.392$, $p = 0.010$.

What our findings to date indicate is that the decreased smiling observed in the CFH group is an indirect effect of maternal distress, rather than a direct effect of the infants' facial condition. These findings suggest the need for early assessment to detect clinically significant levels of maternal psychological distress in mothers of infants with birth defects, to address their emotional problems, and to provide guidance and support for their interactions with the infant. The finding that the basic repertoire of infant facial expressions is largely intact in infants with craniofacial anomalies further suggests that, except in rare cases, an absence or muting of facial expressiveness is a cause for concern, and not the inevitable result of a craniofacial anomaly. More detailed coding and analysis of facial expressiveness in this population (e.g. measures of the intensity of positive and negative facial expressions, and measures of the coordination of their facial expressions with other expressive modalities) might provide sensitive tools for assessing their developing capacity for emotional communication and emotion regulation.

The repertoire of infant facial expressions

As discussed above, although young infants do not show fully differentiated, adult-like facial expressions of discrete negative emotions such as fear, anger, and sadness, their facial expressions are not global and diffuse, as Bridges (1932) and other early observers believed. Young infants have a rich and varied repertoire of facial expressions, including expressions accompanying alert attention or 'interest' and subtle variants and modulations of positive and negative affect expressions. These facial configurations do not result from random firing of the facial muscles; only a fraction of the combinations of facial muscle actions that can physically co-occur actually do occur with any frequency (cf. Camras et al., 1998). Young infants sometimes do produce fleeting, isolated facial muscle actions or seemingly uncoordinated facial movements, especially during transitional states like drowsiness and mild fussiness. However, they also produce organized patterns and sequences of facial muscle activity, which are coordinated with breathing, vocalizing, and body movements, and which are meaningfully related to eliciting situations—although not necessarily specific, discrete emotion elicitors. As Thompson (1990) has noted, infants' facial expressions communicate both graded and categorical information. Examples of both types of signal are described below. However, this is not meant to be an exhaustive catalogue of infant facial expressions.

Hedonic valence

Infant facial expressions can be reliably coded in terms of their hedonic valence. Naïve observers readily distinguish between affectively positive, neutral, and negative expressions (e.g. Oster et al., 1992), and observers show agreement in judging intensities of positive and negative affect (e.g. Messinger, 2002; Oster, 2003). Because the emotion signalled by a particular facial muscle action usually depends on the co-occurring facial actions, isolated actions are usually ambiguous, even with respect to positive and negative hedonic tone. For example, as part of a Duchenne smile cheek raising (AU 6, orbicularis oculi, pars orbitalis) intensifies the positive valence of the smile; as part of a cry face, it intensifies the negative valence of that expression (Messinger, 2002). Nose wrinkling (AU 9), alone or in combination with negative affect components in the

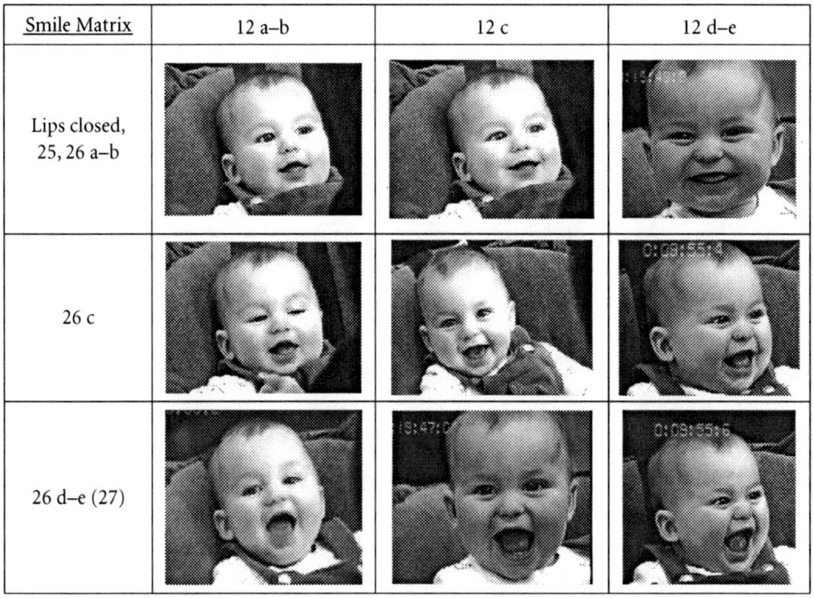

Fig. 10.3 Baby FACS matrix for coding intensities and variants of smiles. The smiles in this 3 × 3 array, produced by a 6-month-old engaged in social interaction with his mother, vary in the intensities of the two principal components of smiles. Zygomaticus major (AU 12), which raises the lip corners obliquelyupward, increases in intensity from left to right. Jaw opening (AUs 25/26/27) increases from top to bottom. The smiles along the diagonal from upper left to lower right are good examples of small, medium, and big smiles. Other actions accompanying these two smile components may contribute to their perceived intensity and are separately coded, such as cheek raising (AU 6), seen in the three cells on the right; brow raising (Aus 1 + 2), seen in the lower left cell; and nose wrinkling (AU 9), seen in the smile in the lower right cell. The Baby FACS manual suggests strategies for using the smile and cry mouth matrices.

brows, and lower face is a component of adult disgust expressions and infant responses to negative tastes (Rosenstein and Oster, 1988). However, smiles with nose wrinkling (as in the lower right photo in Fig. 10.3) are not perceived as expressions of negative affect or as blends of positive and negative affect.

Nevertheless, certain muscle actions are associated almost exclusively with positive or negative affect when contradictory actions are not present. The principal component of smiling (AU 12, zygomaticus major) is an unambiguously positive signal in the sense that it communicates positive affect when no other actions are present, and it is not a component of any negative affect expressions. Brow lowering (AU 4, depressor supercilli and/or procerus), alone or in combination with brow raising (AU 1 and/or 2) and/or brow knitting (AU 3) is a component of several different negative affect expressions and virtually never co-occurs with smiles. However, brow knitting alone without other brow actions or other negative AUs is not necessarily a sign of negative affect

(Oster, 1978), as discussed below. AU 10 (levator labii superioris), unlike AU 9, also seems to be an unambiguously negative signal.

Distaste expressions

Interestingly, the strongest evidence for differentiated negative affect expressions has come from newborn infants' taste-elicited facial expressions. In Rosenstein and Oster's (1988) study, 2-hour-old infants produced differential facial responses to bitter, sour, and salty tastes (dilute quinine, citric acid, and saline solutions, respectively), as well as differential facial responses to sweet (sucrose) versus non-sweet tastes. The infants' responses to all three non-sweet solutions involved hedonically negative actions in the mid and upper face, including nose wrinkling (AU 9) and/or upper lip raising (AU 10), which are components of adult disgust expressions—consistent with Darwin's (1872/1998) hypothesis that disgust expressions have their origins in the rejection of bad tastes. In addition, the sour solution elicited lip pursing, while the bitter solution elicited mouth gaping. These taste-specific components demonstrated a built-in capacity for taste discrimination. They can also be viewed in terms of their possible adaptive functions in either preventing ingestion of a potentially harmful bitter substance (mouth gaping) or diluting a potentially palatable liquid (lip pursing and sucking, which press the cheeks against the gums, stimulating salivation). Although the infants showed negative affect components in all three regions of the face, they did not cry or show the classic cry face involving a squared open mouth. Therefore, we did not believe these expressions represented undifferentiated distress. However, the precise nature of the infants' subjective feeling states could not be inferred with certainty (see Oster, 1997, for discussion).

Cry faces

Cry faces, with or without cry vocalizations, are present from birth if not prenatally (cf. Humphrey, 1970) and remain in the repertoire throughout life, with little or no change in their morphological appearance. The classic squarish, open mouth cry face described by Darwin (1872/1998) results from the combined activation of muscles that raise the upper lip (AUs 9, 10, 11, or a combination of these), stretch the mouth corners horizontally (AU 20), and lower the mandible (AU 26–27). The cry mouth is accompanied by one or more muscle actions in the brows, cheeks, and lower face.

The brows may be lowered and drawn together (AUs 3 and/or 4), obliquely raised (AUs 1 + 3), or raised and straightened (AUs 1 + 2 + 3/4). The cheeks and/or lower eyelids may be raised (AU 6), with eyes narrowly squinted (AU 7) or closed (AU 43).

The lower lip may be pulled down (AU 16), the lip corners may be pulled down (AU 15), and the red part of the lips may be tightened (AU 23). Thus, 10 or more independent muscle actions may co-occur in a single cry face configuration. These are not static configurations, however, as there are moment-to-moment fluctuations in the degree of eye and mouth opening, and in the onset and offset of different muscle actions within a single bout of fussing or crying. As noted above, there is no evidence that these modulations represent fluctuations between different discrete negative emotions.

The Baby FACS manual includes explicit criteria for coding intensities and variants of cry faces. The mouth component is represented by a 3 × 3 matrix, analogous to the smile matrix shown in Fig. 10.3. In the cry mouth matrix, the intensity of horizontal lip stretching (AU 20) increases in the horizontal dimension from left to right, and the degree of mouth opening increases in the vertical dimension from top to bottom, from a slightly open mouth (AU 26 a or b) to a widely stretched open jaw (26 d, e or 27). The three cry face expressions in Fig. 10.1 involve moderate to intense levels of AU 20. However, the mouth is widely open in Fig. 10.1a, moderately open in 10.1b, and only slightly open in 10.1c. Other actions present along with the cry mouth component (brow and eyelid actions, midface actions, lip muscle actions) are separately coded. Pre-cry faces or grimaces, involving affectively negative components in the upper, mid, and lower face but not an actual cry mouth, are quite variable in their morphology.

The cry face is not specific to a particular eliciting situation, as discussed above. However, the lack of situational specificity does not mean that it is not a meaningful social signal or that it does not reflect the infant's emotional feeling state. Cry faces of increasing intensity signal increasing levels of distress to naïve observers (cf. Oster et al., 1992; Oster, 2003) and undoubtedly to caregivers. It is also possible that different variants of cry face reflect qualitatively different 'states of mind' in infants, but the evidence to date is inconclusive.

Modulated negative expressions

Darwin (1872/1998) noted that some of our most characteristic facial expressions are related to crying and to efforts to control crying. Pouting is particularly intriguing, because it involves facial muscle actions that oppose the strong, involuntary muscle actions that pull the mouth into a cry face. In a pouting expression, shown in Fig. 10.4a, the action of mentalis (AU 17) raises the lower lip, often pushing it forward, and the upper lip is pulled down and tightened (AU 8, the proverbial 'stiff upper lip'); the lip corners may be slightly lowered (triangularis, AU15), and the jaw closes partially or completely. The upper and midface components are variable but usually involve negative affect components. The brows may be knit and lowered (as in adult anger expressions) or obliquely raised (as in adult sad expressions), and the cheeks and lower eyelids may be raised, narrowing the eye opening. In a majority of cases, pouts occur either immediately preceding or following a cry face, or both, particularly when the infant is just beginning to become upset. However, pouts are not intrinsic components of cry faces. Pouts are typically 'directed' at a social partner. When the eyes are closed during a cry face, they tend to open and focus on the caregiver (or experimental elicitor) during a pout. Pouts would be considered components of sad expressions or sadness

(a) 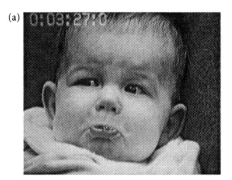 (b)

Fig. 10.4 Modulated negative expressions in a 6-month-old in the Still Face paradigm.
(a) Pouting expression with raised chin boss, protruding lower lip, and tense, pulled-down
upper lip. (b) Intense cry face with raised chin boss and depressed mouth corners, forming
a kidney-mouth configuration.

blends in Max (Izard, 1995), but they are frequently observed in frustration situations
(e.g. Sullivan and Lewis, 2003) and situations believed to elicit fear, as well as during
the Still-Face and unstructured social interactions. Thus, the label of sadness fails to
capture their distinctive meaning.

Based on the facial muscles involved in pouting and its temporal relation to crying,
I have hypothesized (Oster, 1982, 2004) that this expression reflects an effort (not necessarily conscious) to regulate distress. More parsimoniously, it may reflect an internal
struggle between competing tendencies to cry and to keep from crying, or to stop crying
once crying has begun. In Darwin's words, the infant seems to be trying 'to prevent a
crying fit from coming on, or to stop crying' (Darwin, 1872/1998, p. 188), although
there is no conscious awareness of the muscle actions brought into play in this struggle.
A capacity to regulate crying is adaptive because it allows the infant to maintain behavioural organization, and (during social interaction) to maintain contact with the mother and the physical environment. Pouting is also a salient signal to caregivers that the
infant is upset (for whatever reason) and is likely to cry if the situation is not improved.
Toddlers and young adults may use a pout as a 'warning' that they will cry unless they
get their way. However, the fact that the facial configuration of pouting can be observed
in newborn infants and in premature infants prior to expected due date suggests that
this facial expression is not initially acquired through experience during social interactions. Instead, the coordinated facial actions seen in pouting expressions seem to be
associated with modulations of crying and gaze from the beginning of life.

A burst-pause pattern of cry vocalizations may have evolved as part of an internal
self-regulatory process (perhaps serving to interrupt intense crying, which can deplete
oxygen or lead to physical exhaustion). Alternatively, it may have evolved as a specialized signal in infant–caregiver interaction that enables the caregiver to intervene before
the infant begins to cry uncontrollably. This would be particularly useful both to the
infant and to caregivers sensitive to subtle infant signals, since sensory thresholds are

elevated during intense crying, making it more difficult to intervene once full-blown crying has begun. I am not suggesting here that the facial actions involved in pouting directly regulate emotion or interrupt crying, but that they reflect an internal self-regulatory process or competing tendencies. Pouting can also be seen in adults struggling to keep from crying, along with unambiguous signs of efforts to regulate or mask distress such as covering the mouth with the hands.

I have observed pouting in all of the samples of infants I have studied, including the 11-month-old Chinese, Japanese, and American infants in my collaborative cross-cultural study with Joseph Campos, Linda Camras, and our collaborators in Japan and China (Meng Zhao Lin, Tatsuo Ujiee, and Kazuo Miyake). In that sample, pouting was produced by infants in all three cultures in response to both the anger and fear elicitors. More than 64% of the pouts produced in the two paradigms by infants in the 3 cultures were preceded or followed within 1 second by a cry face. We are currently examining the coordination of pouting with cry faces, vocalizations, visual fixation, and other self-regulatory behaviours to test the hypothesis that pouting reflects emotion regulation.

Another variant of cry faces seen in young infants has been called a kidney mouth face (Young and Decarie, 1977), because the raised chin and pulled down upper lip occur during a cry face with the mouth open and the mouth corners stretched horizontally, resulting in a kidney shaped mouth opening. This configuration virtually always occurs during a cry face and may be accompanied by closed eyes, as in Fig. 10.4b. It may reflect a weaker tendency to modulate crying, but the evidence for emotion regulation is less clear for this expression than for pouting expressions. The brow and midface components are variable, but generally involve intense negative affect components (e.g. brows strongly lowered and drawn together, cheeks and lower eyelids raised, deepened nasolabial furrow).

Attention-related expressions

Infants show a variety of facial expressions accompanying alert, focused attention. According to the Max coding system (Izard, 1995), components of the interest expression include any one or more of a variety of actions in the brows, midface, and mouth region: e.g. brows raised or drawn together, mouth slightly opened and relaxed, pursed, or funneled. I have suggested (Oster, 1978), following Darwin (1872/1998), that brow knitting (corrugator, AU 3) in the absence of affectively negative components may represent a distinct variant of focused attention corresponding to 'puzzlement', or an effort to assimilate a novel or discrepant event. This interpretation was suggested by the finding that brow knitting frequently precedes or follows smiles during social interactions between young infants and their mothers, and that the brows relax as soon as the smile begins. Whereas the brows may be raised throughout a smile, brow knitting almost never accompanies smiles. Brow knitting and brow raising overlap in terms of the general contexts in which they occur, and in terms of the lower-face actions that may accompany them. However, we can only find out whether they differ in their signal value or affective meaning if we code them separately, rather than lumping them together as 'interest' expressions. The different variants of attention-related expressions are considered hedonically neutral. Consistent with this interpretation, in Oster's (2003) judgment study involving infants with craniofacial anomalies and unaffected infants, naïve observers' ratings of the emotion shown in infant expressions classified by Baby FACS criteria as interest/puzzlement averaged 4.13 (range 3.82–4.59) on a 7-point scale ranging from intense distress to intense happiness.

Smiles

The principal component of smiling is the action of zygomaticus major (AU 12 in FACS), which raises the lip corners obliquely upward. Simple smiles may involve only a slight action of AU 12, but more complex or intense smiles may involve a wide variety of other facial actions, including varying degrees of mouth opening. Duchenne smiles (cf. Ekman, 1989), involving contraction of orbicularis oculi pars orbitalis (AU 6), which raises the cheeks and crinkles the skin below the eyes, can occasionally be seen in newborn infants as part of sleep smiles (Oster, 1978). They are more often seen beginning around 2 months during social interactions. The presence of AU 6 serves to intensify the positive signal value of a smile (Messinger, 2002). What is particularly striking about smiling in infants is that combinations of zygomaticus major with other facial actions are not random (Oster and Ekman, 1978). As noted above, infants may raise their brows (AUs 1 + 2) while smiling, but knit or lowered brows (corrugator, depressor supercilii, or procerus, AUs 3 and/or 4 in Baby FACS), alone or in combination with brow raising, almost never accompany smiles, except during fleeting transitions between brow knitting (AU 3) and smiling (Oster, 1978). Smiles can physically co-occur with triangularis (AU 15), which pulls down the mouth corners, and although this combination is not uncommon in adults, I have never seen it in infants. Smiling in infants may be accompanied by nose wrinkling (levator labii superioris, alaeque nasi) (AU 9), as shown in Fig. 10.3, and by varying degrees of tongue protrusion. As noted above, such smiles are not perceived as negative expressions or as blends of joy and disgust. However, smiles are rarely if ever accompanied by the adjacent muscle action, levator labii superioris (AU 10), which raises the upper lip in a sneer-like action. Lower face actions that are components of 'interest' or 'puzzlement' do co-occur with smiling, for example pursing or rolling in the lips. The specific meanings communicated by the variants of smiling have not been investigated.

The 'combination rules' involving smiling, especially those involving adjacent muscles, cannot be explained on purely neuromuscular grounds, as the actions not seen with smiles can physically co-occur with them. Instead, they seem to be related to the fact that the 'disallowed' actions involve components of negative affect expressions. These regularities suggest that positive and negative affect are centrally organized at a finer level than global, all-or-none displays.

Infants' smiles vary in their intensity as well as in the presence or absence of other facial actions. The Baby FACS manual specifies explicit guidelines for coding the intensity of smiles. The mouth component is represented by a 3 × 3 matrix representing the intensities of the two major components of smiles. As illustrated in Fig. 10.3, zygomaticus major (AU 12, which raises the lip corners obliquely upward) increases from left to right; and the degree of mouth opening increases from a slightly opened jaw in the top row to a jaw that is stretched widely open in the bottom row. As in the case of the cry mouth matrix, cheek raising (AU 6) and other actions that accompany AU 12, are separately coded. The usefulness of the Baby FACS smile matrix was demonstrated in a study comparing the smiles produced by 7-month-old pre- and full-term black infants in the Still Face paradigm (Segal *et al.*, 1995). In that study, the two groups of infants did not differ in the overall amount of time they spent smiling, but pre-term infants spent significantly less time displaying the most intense smiles, suggesting a muting of positive affect in these infants.

Questions for future research

In this final section, I outline some questions for future research, including still unanswered questions about the nature and origins of universally recognized facial expressions of emotion, and I suggest some new directions for applying research on facial expressions to clinical and at-risk populations.

The first question, still unresolved after decades of research, concerns the development of differentiated facial expressions of specific, discrete negative emotions. It is clear that these expressions are not present in their adult-like form in infants in the first year of life. It is also clear that infants' facial expressions are not global and diffuse. We still do not know when or how more discrete expressions of fear, anger, and sadness begin to replace more generalized distress expressions. To answer that question, we need detailed longitudinal studies to trace the development of children's emotional responses (including facial and non-facial responses) in contexts that reliably evoke particular emotions in natural, as well as experimental settings. One hypothesis is that discrete expressions of specific negative emotions gradually emerge from more generalized cry faces as children develop more effective instrumental behaviors and a greater capacity to regulate distress. As suggested above, we can begin to look for facial expressions with more specific anger or fear components, and less intense or fewer distress components in contexts in which negative affect is less strongly aroused or in the brief interval before distress overwhelms the infant's coping capacity.

We might ask why infants apparently do not display clearly differentiated facial expressions of basic emotions like anger and fear, if the communication of emotion serves an important adaptive function. We can speculate that discrete, adult-like facial expressions of negative emotions such as anger and fear are not necessary for an infant's survival. Infants are incapable of fighting or fleeing, and the only plausible threat an infant can make is to cry. In situations that are frustrating or frightening, infants need an attentive adult to remove a source of frustration or rescue them from potential harm. In most cases, the context and non-facial behaviors allow caregivers to identify the source of distress. Adult-like displays of anger might even provoke attack.

(There is some evidence that adults prone to child abuse misinterpret the signals of infants and young children, attributing intentional malice or defiance to infants' cries.) Similarly, fear faces that were too adult-like could trigger automatic fearful responses in recipients in response to events that would only be threatening to an infant. These are just speculations, but they are as plausible as the *a priori* assumption that universally recognized facial expressions should all be present in their adult-like form within the first 7 months of life.

I have already discussed the apparent lack of isomorphism between facial expressions and inferred emotional states. To some extent, this is more apparent than real, since Max-specified facial expressions of emotions, such as anger and fear, are not, in fact, morphologically the same as their presumed adult counterparts. In some cases, therefore, infants' cry faces may accurately reflect an internal state of distress, produced by overwhelming negative affect–whatever the original source. However, in cases where there are clear behavioral indicators that an older infant in a particular context is experiencing a specific negative emotion such as fear, the lack of isomorphism between facial expression and feeling state may be real. However, even here the infant's facial expression would communicate the vital information that the infant needs help.

Although we cannot code young infants' facial expressions in terms of discrete adult emotion categories, we can reliably code distinctive infant expressions, including variants and modulations of positive and negative affect expressions. One task for future research is to define aspects of infant emotional expression that will be potentially useful for describing clinically significant individual or group differences. I suggest that, in addition to measures of the frequency and duration of specific facial configurations, measures that tap dynamic features of infants' facial expressions could be potentially very useful (cf. Thompson, 1990). For example, measures of facial expressiveness, such as the measures of lability and variability used by Camras *et al.* (1998) to compare Chinese, Japanese, and American infants, could be used in research on infants with regulatory disorders (cf. Papousek and Papousek, 1983) or movement disorders, or in research on normative individual differences in temperament. Measures of the timing and coordination of the component actions of facial expressions (e.g. their relative coherence or disorganization) could be useful in studying children with attention-deficit hyperactivity disorders, or to specify the specific characteristics that make a child's facial expressions appear odd, or unnatural, or ambivalent (for example, abused children classified as disorganized disorientated). Detailed and precise measures of the component actions of facial expressions are needed for all of these purposes.

Finally, detailed measures of facial expression are needed for research on emotion regulation. Too often, emotion regulation is identified by the absence of negative affect expressions in situations in which negative emotion would be expected. However, independent evidence is needed in these cases to establish that the infant experienced negative affect or avoided experiencing negative affect in specific ways (e.g. gaze aversion). Coding subtle or fleeting cues to negative affect can help to provide evidence of regulation in progress. In addition, as noted above, efforts to regulate emotion may be reflected in components of certain negative affect expressions themselves, such as pouting or (as Darwin suggested) oblique eyebrows. In addition to providing possible insight into the meaning of such facial configurations, they might provide clues to the origins of adult facial expressions of which they are components.

References

Altman, S. A. (1967). *Social communication among primates*. Chicago: University of Chicago Press.

Barden, R. C., Ford, M. E., Jensen, A. G., *et al.* (1989). Effects of craniofacial deformity in infancy on the quality of mother–infant interactions. *Child Development*, **60**, 819–24.

Barrett, K. and Campos, J. (1987). Perspectives on emotional development II: A functionalist approach to emotions. In *Handbook of infant development*, 2nd edn (ed. J. Osofsky), pp. 555–78. New York, NY: John Wiley and Sons.

Bridges, K. (1932). Emotional development in early infancy. *Child Development*, **3**, 324–41.

Campos, J. J. and Barrett, K. C. (1984). Toward a new understanding of emotions and their development. In *Emotions, cognition, and behaviour* (ed. C. E. Izard, J. Kagan, and R. B. Zajonc), pp. 229–63. New York, NY: Cambridge University Press.

Camras, L. A. (1991). A dynamic systems perspective on expressive development. In *International review of studies on emotion* (ed. K. Strongman), pp. 1–36. New York, NY: Wiley.

Camras, L. A. (1991). Conceptualizing early infant affect: view II and reply. In *International review of studies on emotion* (ed. K. Strongman), pp. 16–28, 33–6. New York, NY: John Wiley and Sons.

Camras, L. A., Malatesta, C., and Izard, C. (1991). The development of facial expressions in infancy. In *Fundamentals of nonverbal behaviour* (ed. R. Feldman and B. Rime), pp. 73–105. Cambridge: Cambridge University Press.

Camras, L. A., Oster, H., Campos, J., *et al.* (1997). Observer judgments of emotion in American, Japanese, and Chinese infants. In *New directions in child development: No. 4. The communication of emotion* (ed. W. Damen and K. Barrett), pp. 89–105. San Francisco, CA: Jossey-Bass.

Camras, L. A., Oster, H., Campos, J., *et al.* (1998). Production of emotional facial expressions in American, Japanese, and Chinese infants. *Developmental Psychology*, **34**, 616–28.

Camras, L. A., Meng, Z., Ujiie, T., *et al.* (2002). Observing emotion in infants: facial expression, body behaviour, and rater judgments of responses to an expectancy-violating event. *Emotion*, **2(2)**, 179–193.

Camras, L. A., Oster, H., Bakeman, R., *et al.* (2004). Do infants show distinct negative facial expressions for fear and anger? Emotional expression in 11-month-old European-American, Chinese, and Japanese Infants. Manuscript submitted for publication.

Cicchetti, D. and Schneider-Rosen, K. (1984). Theoretical and empirical considerations in the investigation of the relationship between affect and cognition in atypical populations of infants. In *Emotions, cognition, and behaviour* (ed. C. E. Izard, J. Kagan, and R. B. Zajonc), pp. 366–406. New York, NY: Cambridge University Press.

Darwin, C. (1872/1998). *The expression of the emotions in man and animals*, 3rd edn. New York, NY: Oxford University Press. (Original work published 1872.)

Ekman, P. (1989). The argument and evidence about universals in facial expressions of emotion. In *Handbook of psychophysiology: The biological psychology of the emotions and social processes* (ed. H. Wagner and A. Mansted), pp. 143–164. New York: Wiley.

Ekman, P. and Friesen, W. V. (1978). *Facial Action Coding System*. Palo Alto, CA: Consulting Psychologists Press.

Ekman, P., Friesen, W. V., and Hager, J. (2002). *Facial Action Coding System*. [CD ROM] Salt Lake City: Research Nexus, Subsidiary of Network Information Research Corporation.

Field, T. M. and Vega-Lahr, N. (1984). Early interactions between infants with cranio-facial anomalies and their mothers. *Infant Behaviour and Development*, **7**, 527–30.

Fogel, A. and Thelen, E. (1987). The development of early expressive and communicative action. *Developmental Psychology*, **23**, 747–61.

Fridlund, A., Ekman, P., and Oster, H. (1987). Facial expressions of emotion: Review of literature. In *Nonverbal behavior and* communication, 2nd edn (ed. A. Siegman and S. Feldstein), pp. 143–224. Hillsdale, NJ: Lawrence Erlbaum Associates.

Handler, M. K. and Oster, H. (April, 2001). Mothers' spontaneous attributions of emotion to infants' expressions: effects of craniofacial anomalies and maternal depression. In *Cues to 'intuitive' responses to infant signals: converging evidence from adults' attributions and detailed coding* (co-chair D. Messinger and H. Oster), Symposium conducted at the Meeting of the Society for Research in Child Development, Minneapolis.

Hinde, R. (1974). *Biological bases of human social behaviour*. New York, NY: McGraw Hill.

Hinde, R. A. (1982). *Ethology: its nature and relations with other sciences*. New York, NY: Oxford University Press.

Humphrey, T. (1970). Function of the nervous system during prenatal life. In *Physiology of the prenatal period: functional and biochemical development in mammals*, Vol. **2** (ed. U. Stave), pp. 751–96. New York, NY: Appleton-Century-Crofts.

Izard, C. E. (1983). *The maximally discriminative facial movement coding system*, rev. edn. Newark, DE: Instructional Resources Center.

Izard, C. E. and Malatesta, C. Z. (1987). Perspectives on emotional development I: Differential emotions theory of early emotional development. In *Handbook of infant development*, 2nd edn (ed. J. D. Osofsky), pp. 494–554. New York, NY: Wiley.

Izard, C. E., Dougherty, L. M., and Hembree, E. A. (1983). *A system for identifying affect expressions by holistic judgements (Affex)* (Rev. ed. D. E. Newerk). Instructional Resources Center, University of Delaware.

Izard, C. E., Hembree, E. A., and Huebner, R. R. (1987). Infants' emotion expressions to acute pain: Developmental change and stability in individual differences. *Developmental Psychology*, **23**, 105–13.

Izard, C. E., Fantauzzo, C. A., Castle, J. M., *et al.* (1995). The ontogeny and significance of infants' facial expressions in the first 9 months of life. *Developmental Psychology*, **31**, 997–1013.

Lewis, M. (1993). The emergence of human emotions. In *Handbook of emotions* (ed. M. Lewis and J. M. Haviland), pp. 223–35. New York, NY: Guilford Press.

Matias, R. and Cohn, J. F. (1993). Are Max-specified infant facial expressions during face-to-face interactions consistent with Differential Emotions Theory? *Developmental Psychology*, **29**, 524–31.

Messinger, D. S. (2002). Positive and negative: Infant facial expressions and emotions. *Current Directions in Psychological Science*, **11**, 1–6.

Oppenheim, R. W. (1980). Metamorphosis and adaptation in the behaviour of developing organisms. *Developmental Psychobiology*, **13**, 353–6.

Oster, H. (1978). Facial expression and affect development. In M. Lewis and L. A. Rosenblum (ed.), *The development of affect* (pp. 43–75). New York: Plenum Press.

Oster, H. (1982, March). *Pouts and horseshoe mouth faces: their determinants, affective meaning, and signal value in infants*. Paper presented at the biennial meeting of the International Conference on Infant Studies, Austin, TX.

Oster, H. (1997). Facial expression as a window on sensory experience and affect in newborn infants. In *What the face reveals: Basic and applied studies of spontaneous expression using the Facial Action*

Coding System (FACS) (ed. P. Ekman and E. Rosenberg), pp. 320–7. New York, NY: Oxford University Press.

Oster, H. (2003). Emotion in the infant's face: Insights from the Study of Infants with Facial Anomalies. In *Emotions inside out: 130 years after Darwin's 'Expression of the Emotions in Man and Animals'* (ed. P. Ekman, J. Campos, R. Davidson, and F. de Waal). *Annals of the New York Academy of Sciences*.

Oster, H. (2004). *Baby FACS: Facial Action Coding System for infants and young children*. Unpublished monograph and coding manual. New York, NY: New York University.

Oster, H. and Ekman, P. (1978). Facial behaviour in child development. In *Minnesota Symposia on Child Psychology*, Vol. **11** (ed. A. Collins), pp. 231–76. Hillsdale, NJ: Lawrence Erlbaum.

Oster, H., Hegley, D., and Nagel, L. (1992). Adult judgments and fine-grained analysis of infant facial expressions: testing the validity of *a priori* coding formulas. *Developmental Psychology*, **28**, 1115–31.

Oster, H., Camras, L., Campos, J., *et al.* (1996, April). *The patterning of facial expressions in Chinese, Japanese, and American Infants in fear- and anger-eliciting situations*. Poster presented at the International Conference on Infant Studies, Providence, RI. [Abstract, *Infant Behaviour and Development*, April, 1996, **19**, p. 665.]

Oster, H., Taufique, S., Grinberg, A., *et al.* (2000). *Mothers and infants at play: the effects of infant facial anomalies and maternal depression on affective communication*. Paper presented at the XVIth Biennial Meeting of the International Society for the Study of Behavioural Development, Beijing, China.

Oster, H., Klein, J., and Sagee, N. (2003). *The effects of maternal distress and type of infant facial anomaly on maternal sensitivity and mother–infant interaction*. Poster presented at the Biennial Meeting of the Society for Research in Child Development, Tampa FL.

Papousek, H. and Papousek, M. (1983). Interactional failures: Their origins and significance in infant psychiatry. In *Frontiers of infant psychiatry* (ed. J. D. Call, E. Galenson, and R. L. Tyson), pp. 31–7. New York, NY: Basic Books,.

Papousek, H. and Papousek, M. (1987). Intuitive parenting: a dialectic counterpart to the infant's integrative competence. In *Handbook of infant development*, 2nd edn (ed. J. D. Osofsky), pp. 669–720. New York, NY: Wiley.

Pope, A.W. (1999). Points of risk and opportunity for parents of children with craniofacial conditions. *Cleft Palate-Craniofacial Journal*, **35**, 36–9.

Radloff, P. J. and Wales, J. B. (1977). The CES-D scale: a self-report depression scale for research in the general population. *Applied Psychological Measurement*, **1**, 385–401.

Rosenstein, D. and Oster, H. (1988). Differential facial responses to four basic tastes in newborns. *Child Development*, **59**, 1555–68.

Segal, L., Oster, H., Cohen, M., *et al.* (1995). Smiling and fussing in seven-month-old preterm and full-term Black infants in the Still-Face situation. *Child Development*, **66**, 1829–43.

Smith, J. S. (1977). *The behaviour of communicating*. Cambridge, MA: Harvard University Press.

Speltz, M. L., Goodell, E. W., Endriga, M. C., *et al.* (1994a). Feeding interactions of infants with unrepaired cleft lip and/or palate. *Infant Behaviour and Development*, **17**, 131–9.

Speltz, M. L., Greenberg, M. T., Endriga, M. C., *et al.* (1994b). Developmental approach to the psychology of craniofacial anomalies. *Cleft Palate-Craniofacial Journal*, **31**, 61–7.

Sroufe, L. A. (1979). The ontogenesis of emotion. In *Handbook of Infant Development*, (ed. J. D. Osofsky), pp. 462–516. New York, NY: Wiley.

Sroufe, L. A. (1995). *Emotional development: the organization of emotional life in the early years*. New York, NY: Cambridge University Press.

Sullivan, M. and Lewis, M. (2003). Contextual determinants of anger and other negative expressions in young infants. *Developmental Psychology*, **39**, 693–705.

Thompson, R. A. (1990). Emotion and self-regulation. In *Socioemotional development* (ed. R. A. Thompson), *Nebraska Symposium on Motivation*, **36**, pp. 366–467. Lincoln: University of Nebraska Press.

Trevarthen, C. (1998). The concept and foundation of infant intersubjectivity. In *Intersubjective communication and emotion in early ontogeny* (ed. S. Braten), pp. 15–46. New York, NY: Cambridge University Press.

Young, G. and Decarie, T. G. (1977). An ethology-based catalogue of facial/vocal behaviour in infancy. *Animal Behaviour*, **25**, 95–107.

Chapter 11

Why is connection with others so critical? The formation of dyadic states of consciousness and the expansion of individuals' states of consciousness: coherence governed selection and the co-creation of meaning out of messy meaning making

Edward Tronick

Why do infants, indeed all people, so strongly seek states of interpersonal connectedness, and why does the failure to achieve connectedness wreak such damage on their mental and physical health? When the break in connection is chronic, as occurs in some orphanages, infants and children become distressed, depressed, listless, and fail to develop. In less extreme situations, where caregivers are withdrawn and emotionally unavailable, infants go into sad withdrawn mood states. Even in experimental manipulations that briefly break the interactive connection between infants or children and others, such as the Face-to-Face Still-Face Paradigm or the Strange Situation Procedure, infants and children become angry, distressed, frustrated, and/or withdrawn and apathetic. No less dramatic are the exuberant smiles and giggles of infants and children when they are connected to others, a phenomenon which also needs explanation. Furthermore, the contrast between the subjective experience of connection and disconnection is vivid. When connection is made with another person there is an experience of growth and exuberance, a sense of continuity, and a feeling of being in synch along with a sense of knowing the other's sense of the world. With disconnection there is an experience of shrinking, a loss of continuity, a senselessness of the other. Feeling disconnected is painful and in the extreme there may be terrifying feelings of annihilation. However, what makes this contrast between connection and disconnection so objectively and phenomenologically powerful? Why does connection have such a profound effect on the body, brain, behaviour, and experience in the moment and over time? Indeed, what do we mean by connection? What *is* being connected, and *how* is connection made?

Dyadic States of Consciousness Model (DSCM)

The hypothesis I want to explore is the Dyadic States of Consciousness Model (DSCM). The DSCM assumes that humans are complex and open psychobiological systems. As open systems, humans must garner energy from the environment to maintain and increase their organization and complexity—that is, to reduce their entropy. At the top of the human hierarchy of the complexly assembled multitude of psychobiological subsystems are emergent psychobiological states of consciousness (SOCs). The content of an SOC is the individual's age-possible implicit and explicit sense of the world, and their relation to it. An SOC is also an anticipation of how to move into the future. SOCs are linked and dependent on all the psychobiological levels below it (e.g. physiological, neuronal, neuronal group, whole brain processes), and in a circular (downward) causal manner SOCs affect the lower levels. SOCs are generated with the purpose of making as coherent and complex a sense of the world as possible at every moment by garnering meaning from the world. However, as we shall see, the sense made of the world is at best messily coherent and continuously changing.

Though SOCs are 'in the individual' and individuals have self-organizing meaning making capacities for creating them, these capacities are limited compared with dyadic meaning making regulatory processes. Thus, as with many other psychobiological states (e.g. states of hunger, sleep, moods, temperature, metabolism), SOCs are created by a dyadic regulatory system that operates to make meaning within and between individuals. The successful regulation of meaning leads to the emergence of a mutually induced dyadic state of meaning, what I call dyadic state of consciousness (DSC). When a DSC is formed, new meanings are created, and these meanings are incorporated into the SOCs of both (or more) individuals. As a consequence, the coherence and complexity of each individual's sense of the world increases, a process I refer to as the dyadic expansion of consciousness model (DECM). Thus, the successful creation of SOCs fulfills the open system principle to garner energy and increase complexity. Connection then is the dyadic regulation meaning to form a DSC, and the creation and incorporation of meaning with its consequent increase in the coherence and complexity of the individual's SOC. An unfortunate implication of the DECM derived from open systems theory is that, when individuals chronically fail to create DSCs, there is a dissipation (loss) of their coherence and complexity; they move closer to entropy (i.e. death). Disconnection is the failure of the dyadic meaning-making system. Meaning is not created, exchanged, and incorporated, and consequently the coherence of individual's SOC incrementally dissipates.

At the outset, I want to acknowledge that this paper draws heavily on the work of Bruner (1970, 1972, 1990) on meaning making and my discussions with him on co-creative processes; Freeman (1994, 2000) for his ideas on the purposive functioning of the brain; Prigogine (Stengers and Prigogine, 1997) and Per Bak (Bak, 1996) for their descriptions of open and complex systems; Edelman (1987) for his ideas on neuronal selection; and my collaborator Brazelton (Brazelton *et al.*, 1974; Brazelton, 1992) for his perspective on development and dyadic processes. Of further importance to the conceptualizations in this paper are the works and thinking of Hofer (1994a,b), Trevarthen (1980, 1990, 1993), Kagan (1998), Fogel (1993), LeVine (LeVine, 1977; Levine and Coe, 1985; LeVine and Leiderman, 1994), and my work with Sander (1976, 1977, 1988, 1995) and the Process of Change Group (Stern *et al.*, 1998; Tronick, 1998).

What is a state of consciousness (SOC)?

What is an SOC? The literature is filled with varying definitions and meanings about consciousness, and it is foolhardy to try and make coherent sense of them. As used here, an SOC is seen as a psychobiological state, which is derived from the medical and developmental literature, and not from the typical dictionary definition that often equates consciousness with the sole characteristic of awareness. The dictionary definition is somewhat all-or-none, and once consciousness is attained it is seen as much the same even with development. In fact, although there may be different levels or kinds of consciousness, this unchanging a-developmental quality permeates much of neuroscience models of consciousness. By contrast, a psychobiological definition encourages the examination of components and elements of states, their coherence and complexity, their linkage and organization, and most importantly their development. Thus, an SOC is a psychobiological state with a distinct complex organization of body, brain, behaviour, and experience. It is a distinct assemblage of implicit and explicit meanings, intentions and procedures. SOCs are individuals' private, continuously-changing knowledge of the world and their relationship to it.

SOCs are purposive, and organize internal and external actions toward some end. Freeman (2000) sees individuals as operating with intentionality, but what the individual intends and does is only sensible in the context of the individual's SOC—sense of the world at that moment. There is no necessity for awareness in an SOC as demonstrated by the fact that most daily activities are purposive and carried out without awareness. With or without awareness, SOCs have an impelling certitude about the way the world is (Harrison, personal communication, 2003). What is meant by an impelling certitude? Freeman refers to our 'brains and bodies [as being] committed to the action of projecting ourselves corporeally into the world' (Freeman, 2000, p.18). Impelling certitude is that sort of commitment, an empowering of intentions and actions. Like the air we breathe, it is likely to be out of awareness, but it is always present with greater or lesser intensity. However, when an impelling certitude is violated, it comes into awareness. Think of the impelling certitude about the reality of wholeness that is violated when a magician makes a body separate from a head, or a New Englander's discomfort when confronted by a Californian's desire for sharing personal stories, or an adolescent's insistence that it is realistic to achieve peace by everyone just agreeing to it. Thus,

SOCs might be thought of as unique gestalts of meaning that have an impelling certitude about the way things are for the individual. They are the meaning the individual has for being in and acting on the world in the present as he/she moves into the future.

Age-possible SOCs

A critical feature of SOCs is that they can only be 'age-possible', though as we shall see, age-possible is hardly the only constraint on SOCs. The concept of 'age-possible' SOCs is needed to take into account the developmentally possible sense individuals are capable of making, given their meaning-making processes. For example, the sense of the world that is in a baseball player's muscles (sometimes referred to as muscle memory) when he catches a ball is qualitatively different from the knowing that is in a toddler's body when she catches a ball. Yet, both of their SOCs make coherent sense of what they are doing. Furthermore, the concept of age-possibility makes explicit that the interpersonal connection, the DSC made between an infant and adult versus a child and adult, will be qualitatively different. Thus, SOCs and connectedness are not fixed, but dynamically changing with development.

Young infants' SOCs are psychobiological assemblages of affect, actions, and experience. The meaning is in what their body and brain do, and their subjective experience. It is *of* and *in* the moment, although the moment soon integrates personal experience and lengthens with development. For example, the alert newborn has an SOC that might be something like 'there are things to look at'. This SOC of the world is an integration of the circadian rhythms of their bodily (i.e. the biorhythmic flow of sleep and awake states) and brain processes (i.e. occipital processing of visual input), and their perceptual activity (e.g. visual exploration of the world) for gaining meaning. Of course, a 'look-for-things' SOC is difficult for the young infant to maintain given their self-organizing capacities (e.g. head movements go in a different direction than eye movements, their intention switches, their bowels act up), and it deteriorates into distress and crying, a rather different SOC.

For older infants, Piaget (1954) described how the meaning of an object is what infants can do with it—an object is 'graspable' or 'bangable'—and their action and intention of repetitive banging make sense once we appreciate their SOC. The Piagetian infant's SOC is qualitatively different if she can reach and grasp an object with one hand, and explore it with the other while sitting from the SOC of infant who has to hold objects with two hands while lying on his back because the meaning is *in* the action. Take another example: infants' SOC about a (virtual) looming object is that it is 'dangerous' and ducking out of its way makes sense given their meaning making. If this ascription of meaning to the infant's actions seems over the top, realize that the infant could apprehend the looming event in other ways—it might be interesting, novel, or make no sense at all. Moving into the domain of social interactions, but still holding to Piaget's ideas, infants smiling back at a smiling adult apprehend that there is a general affordance for connection, but infants have more specific and different SOCs for different people. Forgive the grammar, but for the infant the SOC of one 'liked-familiar-person' is simultaneously 'huggable', 'communicable-with', 'synchroniz-able-with', 'happy- and cryable-with', and 'sing-songable-with', whereas a different liked-familiar person is 'exciting', 'not-to-be irritable with', 'too-arousing-with', 'bouncable-with', and 'peek-a-boo-able-with'.

Infant SOCs also have an impelling certitude. Observe the young infant who fails to search for a hidden object to see that she is 'absolutely certain' that it is gone. Another example is the total distress of the infant separated from the mother—the certitude that not only is she gone forever, but the certitude that he will be annihilated, or the absolute thrill an infant experiences being tossed into the air by an older sibling (and the parents' impelling certitude that the infant will be dropped). Of course, I recognize that we are inferring infants' SOCs about the world, and we cannot truly know them. However, in different contexts we can see what infants do, as well as what they do not do, which gives our inference power, but our inference does not tell us if they are conscious or not, self-aware or self-reflective, which is a different problem to our infer-ring their SOCs. If this still seems difficult, we must realize that, if infants did not have age-possible SOCs about themselves in the world, they could not function in it. Their actions would be incoherent and unpredictable, a veritable Jamesian 'bloomin buzzin confusion', a view that is no longer tenable given the past 50 years of research on infant competencies.

The toddler and young child have qualitatively different SOCs from those of the infant. Their meaning-making tools include language and symbols, and complex body skills (e.g. finger movements to running) and body micro-practices (e.g. false coyness). In pretend play, toddlers assemble fantasy, reality, and their age-possible memories into new SOCs. They are not only in the moment, but their meanings are disjunctive and assemblages of illogical narratives. The SOCs of toddlers are complex, and have an '*and ___, and ____, and ___, . . .*' organization of apprehension that places no demand for the possible or the logical. Think only of a toddler's impelling certitude when he loudly demands to have the identical berries that fell from a branch back on the tree the way they were, and his utter distress when he says a different branch is bad and he does not want it . . . ever! (A. Bergman, personal communication).

There is little need to further elaborate the idea that SOCs are different for older chil-dren, adolescents, and adults. Nonetheless, it is worth noting, because developmental and neuro-scientists tend not to attend to it; at some point in development, SOCs assemble meanings from psychodynamic processes including a psycho-dynamic uncon-scious. These dynamic processes are not equivalent to the passionless non-conscious or implicit processes invoked by developmental psychologists, cognitive neuroscientists or even some psychoanalytic writers. I believe that unconscious dynamic processes are inherent to the SOCs of children and adults. Dynamic unconscious processes make someone's knowing what is in another person's SOC cryptic, and as problematic as knowing the SOC of an infant, yet somehow we do come to apprehend the SOC of another. How we come to have that apprehension is based on understanding how SOCs are formed and what principles govern their formation.

Dyadic regulation: open systems and complexity

The coherence of an individual's sense of the world is both regulated and increased by internal self-organizing and dyadic regulatory processes. Prigogine states that a primary principle governing the activities of open biological systems is that they must acquire energy from the environment to maintain and increase their coherence, complexity, and distance from entropy. The energy for a biological system must have a particular form to be useful [i.e. have meaning or what Sander (1988) calls fittedness for the organism]. For example, although the food that prey eats has plenty of energy, if predators eat what their prey eats, they cannot utilize that energy—it has no 'meaning' for them. Complexity refers to a hierarchical system exhibiting emergent systems properties. It is neither fixed nor chaotic. It is information rich with local contextual interactions. Self-organizing processes that increase complexity have limits that put a ceiling on a systems' maximum complexity. These limitations of self-organization are an inherent characteristic of all open systems. Humans have developed an exceptional (though hardly unique) way to overcome these limits by forming synergistic relationships with others, what I refer to as a dyadic regulatory system. Though dyadic regulation also has limits, this dyadic system is able to garner more resources than each individual's self-organizing processes could on their own. As a consequence, the complexity of each individual as a complex psychobiological system is increased.

Dyadic regulation: psychobiological states

To understand mutual regulation, I want to start with an example far from the regulation of SOCs—infant temperature regulation. I choose this example because it illustrates the dyadic regulatory process for a psychobiological state that is most typically seen as a self-organized process. Temperature regulation is a complex system with a singular purpose: maintaining homeothermic status. This regulatory system is hierarchically organized with a multitude of subsystems, from metabolic processes to behavioural systems. It is a system that operates to maintain equilibrium, and although it changes with development (e.g. the loss of brown fat) and is influenced by environmental factors (e.g. the increase in capillary networks in the hand in cold environments), its change and development is limited compared with other psychobiological systems (e.g. respiratory systems, or motor systems, or SOCs). Infants have self-organizing capacities to regulate below normal temperature, such as increasing their activity level, preferentially metabolizing high energy brown fat or moving into less energetic behavioural states. However, these self-organized capacities are limited and immature, and will eventually fail, an especially quick event for infants with their high surface to volume ratio. However, although Claude Bernard saw temperature regulation as a within individual process, it is not. It is a dyadic process.

Infants' self-organized regulatory capacities for operating on temperature control are supplemented by external regulatory input by caregivers that is specifically fitted to overcome the infant's limitations (Hofer, 1984). For example, caregivers place infants against their chests, share their body heat with their infants, which in turn reduces their infants' surface heat loss. This dyadic regulatory process itself is guided by communicative signals from the infant. These communicative signals induce the implicit purpose and intentions of the infant into the caregiver's sense of what is going on with the infant. 'I'm cold, help me'. Adult, 'Got it!' When done successfully, the input provided is fitted (meaningful) to the infant's temperature regulatory system and the system becomes more coherently organized than the infant would be on its own.

Additionally, the capacities for self-regulation actually grow with the acquisition of meaningful input from the caregiver, such that later in development, the infant will be able to self-regulate temperature without as much external regulatory scaffolding, an idea not unlike Vygotsky's (1978) concept of the zone of proximal development. Alternatively, were the formation of a dyadic state to fail, the infant would lose control of his temperature and his homeostatic state would dissipate. When the failure is chronic, the infant's self-regulatory capacities would not grow. Furthermore, even this equilibrium system is not fully predictable. The infant actions that induced the infant's intent into the caregiver may have one form one day and another form another day. The caregiver's apprehension of it and the caregiver's input to the infant might also vary. Moreover, the infant signal that worked one time may not work the next time, and the same is true for the caregiver's response, as most parents have experienced. Nonetheless, it is likely that the activities that work more often will become more and more a part of the workings of the dyadic regulatory process.

Dyadic regulation: SOCs and actions in the world

Dyadic processes more effectively regulate the infants' SOCs than the infant can do on his or her own, even when the infant is doing something that seems to be an individual task. Take, for example, a not-yet-independently-reaching infant who tries to reach an object. The infant has an intent that is beyond his own self-regulatory capacities. At first, his SOC is organized, and his looking and intent are coherently organized. However, once he attempts to get his hands to the object he is unable to coherently organize his actions, looking, and intent. The organization of his SOC is decreased. He becomes distressed, loses what motor control he had, but he does not necessarily give up the intent. In a way, the infant can no longer make sense of the world and his relation to it. His SOC loses some coherence and complexity. By contrast, as part of a dyadic system with a caregiver who, by apprehending the infant's intent, provides postural support and the infant is able to free up his arms, control his posture, and bat at the object. The infant engages in a more complex action than he would be capable of on his own.

Dyadic regulation: individual SOCs and the emergence of DSCs

Bullowa (1979) described this phenomenon when she documented the greater complexity of the infant's behaviour in the presence of others compared with the infant alone. In the example given, had the mother's apprehension of the infant's SOC been that the infant intended to reach for the object when, in fact, he intended to stroke her face, the infant and mother would remain separate and uncoordinated. Then again, when there is a successful mutual mapping of (some of) the constituent meanings in their individual SOCs into the other's SOC, there is the emergence of a dyadic state of shared meaning, a DSC. This DSC is more complex and information-rich than individual SOCs. It is more complex because it is made up of more systems, the infant and the mother, and their hierarchically arranged subsystems, and it is information-rich because it contains meanings from both the infant's and the mother's SOCs. Critically, the effect of being subcomponents of a DSC is that the infant and the mother can appropriate information from it into their own SOCs. A critical consequence of this appropriation is the expansion of their individual SOCs. Namely, by being connected, their sense of themselves in the world expands and becomes more coherent and complex.

Dyadic regulation: SOCs, DSCs and social interactions

Infant–adult interaction, or for that matter any dyadic human interaction, is perhaps the quintessential example of dyadic regulation of meaning-making (Fogel, 1993). In interaction each individual attempts to increase the coherence of their sense of themself, the other and what they are doing together. When an interaction is dyadically well regulated, there is an emergence of a more coherent and complex sense of the world. For example, in an infant–mother interaction, each individual communicates their affective evaluation of the state of what is going on in the interaction: relational affects (e.g. feeling apart from, feeling in synch with [Foscha, 2000]) and their relational intention (e.g. continue, stop, change [Weinberg and Tronick, 1994]). These communications simultaneously express what they are experiencing in the moment and what they intend to do. In response to the induction of meaning in the other, infants and mothers attempt to adjust their behaviour to maintain a coordinated dyadic state. When the mutual induction is successful, a DSC is formed, meanings from the other's SOC are incorporated and their SOCs gain coherence and complexity.

Figure 11.1 illustrates the process of mutual regulation, formation, and breaking of dyadic DSCs. A 6-month-old infant and his mother are playing a game, and the mother leans in to nuzzle the baby. The infant takes hold of the mother's hair and they are both joyful. The infant's age-possible SOC is in his actions and his affect. He has yet to make sense of the game as a game, echoing Piaget's argument that objects are not yet objects for infants, but only what they do to them. His impelling certitude is something like, 'This is the greatest thing I have ever done!' The mother's more complex SOC includes a similar age-possible feeling (i.e. 'the joy of him!'), as well as her greater knowledge of the game, how to make it work, their other games, and many other implicit and unconscious things. Collaborating together they create a DSC by inducing some of these meanings into the SOC of the other person.

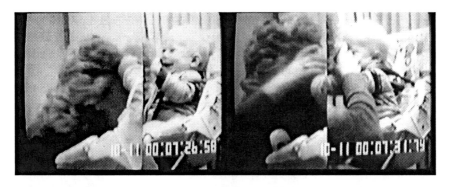

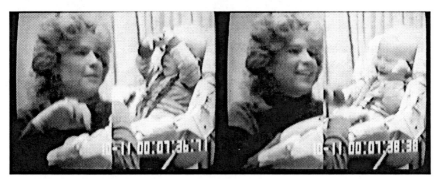

Fig. 11.1 Sequence of infant responding to mother's anger facial expression. In the first images the infant is pulling on the mother's hair. She then takes his hands and disengages, and then makes an angry face and vocalization. The infant brings his hands and arms up to his face in a defensive manoeuvre, and then looks at her from under his arms. The mother backs away and then attempts to elicit his attention by touching his legs. In the last frame they have resumed their playful interaction.

When she pulls away he does not let go. In pain, the mother responds with a bare-toothed angry facial expression and angry vocalizations—'Ouch, ouch!!'. The infant immediately sobers and brings his hand up to his face in a defensive move. His SOC changes to something like 'this is threatening' and he defensively ducks behind his hands. The meaning is in the ducking and the feeling of threat. The mother almost immediately pulls back. The mother's own mentalization (Fonagy and Target, 1998) of her action (an age-possible knowing that the infant is not yet able to do) and the infant's induction of meaning into her SOC, changes her SOC. They disconnect, the hair-pulling DSC is broken and each is left to self-organize their SOCs. The infant's SOC is now *in* his sober wary face and his looking away from behind his hands. His impelling certitude perhaps is something like 'I'm confused, this doesn't happen!' Likely the mother is feeling something like 'concern' or 'apology', and age-possible meanings such as 'I scared him. I messed up our good time' and maybe meanings out of her own past ('I always felt apologetic to my mother'.) The mother pauses and then slowly approaches the infant again. The infant drops his hands with a number of coy moves that convey his intent to cautiously re-engage. The mother, too, makes a slow approach and they reconnect with joyful smiles. A DSC is restored: 'Whew!' They again induce meaningful elements of each of their SOCs in the other. Specifically, the infant's emotional reaction is determined by his own meaning-making capacities, his capacities for effectively apprehending his mother's affective displays and reactions.

Human connection: DSCs and the expansion of SOCs

We can now return to the opening question: 'Why do infants, indeed all people, so strongly seek states of connectedness, and why does the failure to achieve connectedness wreak such damage on their mental and physical health?' Connection is the formation of a DSC, and it is critical because it expands the coherence and complexity of individuals' SOCs. Normal interactions are examples of the creation of DSCs. The mutual smiling and cooing of mother and infant in face-to-face interactions is an example of a DSC. So too, is the pretend play of the toddler with another person and the all night conversations of adolescents. Social referencing by infants, children, and adults is a way to gain meaning about ambiguous events that leads to a new impelling certitude about its meaning (Campos and Lucariello, 1999). The 12-month-old who backs away from the visual cliff in apprehension of the mother's expression of fear has used her expressed meaning to form his sense of the event. Similarly, the 2-year-old's laughing at the mother who makes a fear face in the visual cliff reflects his certitude about the situation and her actions—this is pretend! By being in a DSC, individuals experience a growth in the coherence and complexity of their SOC. Thus, forming DSCs is not an exotic state or an exceptional moment in time, but very much the chronic experience of normal development (but see below as regards their 'intensity').

Human connection: the Still-Face as a breaking of connection

The still-face (SF) is an example of a failure to create a DSC and dissipation of the individuals' SOC (Tronick *et al.*, 1978a,b; Vygotsky, 1978; Adamson and Frick, 2003). The still-faced mother precludes the formation of a DSC because there is no exchange or creation of meaning. The recipient of the SF has to make meaning with their own

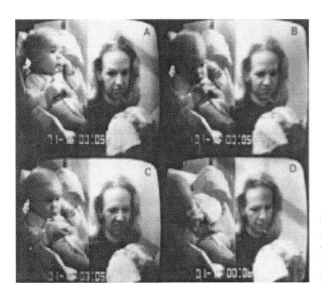

Fig. 11.2 An infant losing postural control and turning to self-comforting behaviours in response to the mother being still-faced.

self-organizing abilities. In response to the SF, infants act to acquire and re-instate their exchange of meaning, but with the mother's continued lack of response they engage in self-organized regulatory behaviours to maintain their coherence and complexity, to avoid the dissipation of their SOC. Figure 11.2 shows how an infant during the SF literally losses postural control, turns away, has a sad facial expression, and is self-comforting with his hands in his mouth. The age-possible impelling certitude of the infant's SOC is something like, '[this is] threatening'. This certitude is both in and expressed by his posture and actions. As the SF continues, the infant's SOC is likely to change to something like 'I must try to hold myself together'. This certitude is similar to the earlier examples—the infants' apprehension of the looming object or the mother's anger expression as dangerous. If one doubts these or similar interpretations, simply consider that the infant could apprehend the still-faced mother in other ways—as boring, playful, or novel—all of which would result in different behaviours by infants, none of which happen in the SF.

More recent work on the SF with young children and adults makes it even clearer how the SF is failing to form DSCs. In my laboratory, we have developed a procedure for using the SF with children 18–54 months of age (Weinberg *et al.*, 2002). In the first episode of this procedure, the child and the adult engage in floor-play with toys. This episode is followed by an SF episode in which the mother 'freezes' and does not respond to the infant. In a third episode, the mother resumes her normal play. The findings are as striking as our original SF findings with infants. Young children respond to the maternal SF with heightened negative affect, and expressions of confusion and demands for change. The toddlers ask 'Why don't you talk to me?' or command, 'Talk to me!', while soliciting the mother's interactive behaviour (e.g. pointing at her eyes, tapping or almost hitting the mother, making repeated louder and louder requests), and then distancing themselves from her. Importantly, and in keeping with their greater age-possible meaning-making capacities, preschoolers may attribute states of mind to the mother (e.g. 'Are you sleeping? Wake up!' or 'Don't be afraid of the alligator [toy]!'). Thus, there is meaning in their affect and actions (similar to the age-possible meanings of the infant), but also in their age-possible capacities for pretend play, cognitions, language, mentalization, and complex affects. Their impelling certitude is one of confusion and fearfulness at the break in connection. When play is resumed, the child asks questions that attempt to make coherent sense of what happened (e.g. 'Why didn't you talk to me?') even though it brings back the painfulness of the experience.

In further extension of the SF to adults, a research assistant Lisa Bohne interviewed college sophomores after they participated in an experimental role-play of an adult version of the SF. One student role played an unresponsive mother and the other simulated being 'in the mind of an infant'. The infant-persons who experienced the SF reported feeling anxious and vulnerable, angry, frustrated, sad, afraid, confused, even 'panicky'. The students who acted out the SF mother reported feeling guilty, distressed, anxious, depressed, shamed, vulnerable, and confused. One reported, 'It felt terrible to be so closed off from the infant. It made me feel depressed and I'm sure the infant did too after our interaction'. Preventing an exchange meanings and the formation of a DSC disorganized each adult's own SOC, and generated a fearful, confused, and less coherent sense of the world. Importantly, these adults did not try to step away from their negative experience, but in more sophisticated ways than the toddlers, continued to try to make coherent sense of what they had experienced after the procedure was terminated. Some of them actually apologized for what they had done. It is unfortunate that we cannot know what sense the infant makes of the SF some time after it is terminated.

Human connection: the chronic breaking of connection and downward causation

An extreme example of the failure to form DSCs is the chronic deprivation of infants in orphanages described by Spitz (Spitz and Cobliner, 1965). For these infants I believe that the complexity of their SOCs actually dissipated. Perhaps, still more compromising, their self-organizing and dyadic capacities were stunted such that they could hardly make coherent sense of their place in the world. Of note is the general finding of their apathy, an extremely pathological state for infants in which there is a reduction of attempts to acquire meaningful input from others or the environment to expand their SOC. Nonetheless, the apathy may be a protective state in which the infants self-organized themselves to maintain whatever remnant of a coherent sense of the world they have. However, I believe the compromise is so great that there was an ongoing dissipation of their SOCs and further diminishment of their self-organizing abilities.

It is easy to think that compromising the food intake of the Spitz's infants would lead to their kind of 'malnourished' body, brain, and SOC. However, in many cases we know that the nutrition and other 'necessities' were adequate, and that the necessity that was unavailable was connection with others, namely the establishment and maintenance of DSCs. These infants were not able to exchange meanings with others. This deprivation of meaning led not only to the failure to maintain and expand their SOCs, but also to the disorganization of many of the lower level psychobiological states, such as metabolic systems and immune system. This 'downward causation', what Freeman (2000) calls 'circular causality' is a characteristic of complex systems.

Downward causation occurs when the operation of the emergent properties at higher levels (e.g. SOCs) in the hierarchical assembling of subsystems constrain and impact the actions of the lower level systems (e.g. motor systems). For Spitz's infants the downward causal effect of being unable to form DSCs was to downwardly cause systems such as their immune system to dissipate, resulting for many in death by opportunistic infections. In the infants who were physiological survivors of the deprivation of meaning, their capacity for acquiring resources was so damaged that they failed to grow and develop. We also see damaged self-organizing capacities for acquiring resources in the reports on the Romanian orphans who as older children are not able to engage in forms of normal exchange. Thus, Spitz's infants are an example of a failing open system—human systems that were deprived of connection and could not increase the complexity of their SOCs and could not maintain their complexity. In a sense, these infants as systems lost much of their capacity to generate the most human of characteristics.

Human connection: the distortion of connection

Distortion of DSCs can help us understand the effects of parental affective disorders on infants and children in two ways. First, a mother with an affective disorder (e.g. a depressed mother) is often an inadequate external regulator of the infant. Her responsiveness and her apprehension of communications are limited, her communications are harder for the infant to apprehend, and her responses are less likely to fit to the infant's regulatory needs. Forming a DSC with her is difficult and it is self-amplifying— the initial difficulties increases the effects of later exchanges. Secondly, despite these dyadic regulatory problems, the mothers and the infants' capacities are not so compromised that they cannot form a DSC, but the formation of a DSC insidiously compromises the infant.

The DSC between a depressed mother and her infants contains sad and angry affect, melancholic feelings, and gloomy meanings. Were this depressed DSC restricted to the connection between the children and their mothers, its toxicity might be restricted as well, but lamentably it is not. Field (Field *et al.*, 1988) found that the interactions of infants of depressed mothers with others was sadder.

My hypothesis is that the impelling certitude of children of depressed mothers is that connection can only be made in sadness and their self-organizing capacities for creating DSCs aim to create or re-instate this kind of DSC with others. For example, in our laboratory, infants of depressed mothers have more dysregulated interactions with our experienced research assistants who are blind to the depressive status. The RAs feel that the infant induces an experience of 'stay away, don't connect', and the RAs touch the infant less and maintain a greater distance from the infant. In the interactions with their mothers there is a growth of complexity and coherence of these infants' SOC, but their impelling certitude limits the child's acquiring of resources from non-depressed others.

Human connection: the blind selective operation of coherence on messy meaning systems

The SOCs of infants of depressed mothers clearly are not growth promoting in the long run, but the alternative would be to not form a DSC at all. From the perspective of open systems, what the infant does is to choose the lesser of two evils: either grow complexity now or dissipate now. As a consequence, the child's experience of expansion becomes focused on the sharing 'depressed' states. Thus, the more general question is 'How is an individual's sense of the world put together?' My proposal is that SOCs emerge from selective processes operating to increase the coherence and complexity of the individual's age-possible sense of the world. However, we must first understand that selection has to repetitively activate SOCs and DSCs—meanings, as well as meaning-making processes—that are messy.

This argument is analogous to the argument made by neuroscientists that initially disordered arrays of neurons are selected to form Hebbian circuits or cell groups because of repetitive co-occurring activation. Edelman (1987) sees selection operating on neurons to form neuronal groups. Cells that fire together in relation to sensory input, motor output, and all the other forms of input and output in the brain, and its subsystems (e.g. reafferent signals) come to form coherent cell groups. More specifically, selection operates to maximize the coherence of the relations among brain and bodily processes, and structures from the level of neurons to neuronal groups to activation patterns in different areas of the brain to the autonomic nervous system to homeostatic physiological systems to endocrine systems, to metabolic processes, to bodily movements and behaviour, in order to make these systems into a functioning whole in an environmental context. Coherence means that there is a growth of relations (correlations) among previously unrelated internal and external variables. These new relations can be thought of as a pattern in space and/or time (e.g. unrelated neurons become a cell group by having a coordinated pattern of firing) which may have greater complexity and emergent properties.

Learning peek-a-boo: selective coherence and messy systems

Let me begin with an example of selection from messiness: the infant learning to play peek-a-boo. The learning of peek-a-boo emerges through the repetitive operation of coherence on the messiness of the infant's actions, intentions, and apprehensions in an incremental bit-by-bit and moment-by-moment manner. Initially, the infant makes a large number and variety of behaviours, and has lots of varying intentions and apprehension of what is going on. Most of these actions are unrelated to each other or to the adult's game playing actions. The infant looks away when he should be looking toward, or he raises his shoe, or he wants the light and reaches for it. What he is doing is messy—variable, unstable, disorganized. There is no coherence in what he is doing in relation to the game, though, of course, he is making some sort of sense of what is going. Nonetheless, over time and with repetition, some of the infant's behaviours, intentions, and apprehensions of the adult's actions and intentions come to be related to one another. The infant looks at the same time the adult places their hands over their eyes or looks back at them after the adult says 'boo'. Furthermore, the adult makes adjustments (e.g. holding positions longer) in what she does in relation to the infants' actions and her apprehension of his intent to increase the likelihood and maintenance of the coordination.

The selective assembling of these co-occurrences of the infant's self-organized actions and intentions and his apprehension of the adult's intentions and actions becomes incrementally more coherent than what was assembled in prior moments. There is still lots of messiness to the actions and intentions of his sense-making, but without belabouring the process, with an enormous number of repetitions, the messiness is pared away over weeks and months, and finally the 'game' is put together. The infant's SOC and his DSC of the game become more coherent (see Thelen, 1995 for a similar example as regards reaching).

The example can help us to understand that selection of new meanings about the world cannot increase the coherence of SOCs with too little messiness or too much messiness. A low coherence state of meanings is unpredictable, and constantly randomly changing and self-organizing, and external processes are unable to generate order. The peek-a-boo infant's actions are messy, but not random. By contrast, a highly coherent organization of meanings is predictable and static, but the infant's initial actions are hardly fixed. Perhaps when the game is learned they do become fixed and unchanging (do we all play peek-a-boo the way we did when we were 15 months old?), but by then the infant will have new intentions.

The ubiquitousness of messiness

Fortunately, messiness is ubiquitous in development. The expression of meaning and intent does not have fixed forms. Infants have sets of affective configurations for expressing meanings but they are expressed by a variable assembling of expressive modalities. 'Stop' is expressed by turning away one time or pushing away another time or with cries and flailing arms another time. For toddlers, the same word can express different intents. 'Ball' means 'there is the ball', or 'give me the ball', or 'you have the ball', or 'ball?' Older children and adults seem to express meaning more clearly, but there is much that is cryptic. Also, whatever the age of the individuals, meanings are missed or misread, responses are inappropriate, do not fit to the expressed meaning, or are mistimed. Importantly, meanings and intentions are not fully formed, they change from one moment to the next and, of course, there are differences in the intent of the two individuals and intention often exceeds capacities. Even without these difficulties that create messiness the expression of meaning operates at tenths of seconds or faster, a rate that cannot be maintained for sustained periods. Furthermore, because SOCs are age-appropriate, and are assemblages of implicit, non-conscious, and dynamically unconscious meanings, the individuals have a problem of fathoming intent across age- and 'explicitness' gaps. Indeed, one can wonder how can infants induce meaning in adults when their meaning-making systems are qualitatively different? This accounting leaves out the meanings that are purely personal and individually historical. Messiness, indeed!

For SOCs, when an individual is engaged with things, there is a selective assembling of intentions, information garnered by exploratory behaviours and from the effects of instrumental behaviours on the environment that enhances their coherence. When the individual is with another person, there is more stuff to work on and more relations to bring together for incrementing coherence. In a dyad, coherence comes with the apprehension of mutual intentions, and the coordination of their behaviours and their mutual effects on each other. When one of the individuals is an infant or child, and the other individual an adult, coordination can be easier because the adult adjusts their activities to better fit to the child's SOCs. With mutual apprehension, the SOCs of each individual become increasingly well-fitted together. When the coherence of their intentionalizing, talking, looking, touching, moving is increased sufficiently, a DSC is formed. In this DSC, age-possible meanings that are expressed with their bodies, movements, and intentions, can be appropriated by the two individuals to increase the coherence of their own SOC.

Blind selection and compromises of development

In the moment-to-moment of the SF to the chronic failure to form DSC in Spitz's orphans to the derailment of 'normal' SOCs in children of depressed mothers, selection operates to make more coherent meaning of infants' or children's place in the world. When the SF is done, children and adults struggle to find a coherent sense of what happened to them to overcome their confused and disjointed (i.e. in-coherent) SOC. In the depressed dyads, increasing the coherence of the meaning being made in the moment, selects an assemblage of meanings from those available that are the most coherent: 'We can be sad together (or not make sense of things at all)'. These SOCs are more coherent *now*, but in the long run they will become increasingly problematic as they limit the resources available to the infant or child. However, that is the rub of maximizing the coherence of meaning moment-by-moment. Selecting meanings to increase coherence is blind to the meaning assembled in an SOC and blind to its long-term impact. It simply operates to maximize what better fits together from what is available *now*. It operates even if the long run costs are extremely high, not only because the long run is unknowable, but also because in the moment the alternative is to dissipate, to lose coherence, and complexity about the world, a loss that must be avoided by open systems.

Blind selection and the co-creation of the varieties of normal development

Blind as it is, selection to increase coherence of the individual's sense-making is not the only generator of pathology. It is ubiquitously 'normal'. I have observed a surprising example of how coherence governed selection-operating in the face-to-face interactions of Gusii mothers and their infants. This example also illustrates how what emerges from selective processes is a co-creation of the two individuals. It also shows how different age-possible SOCs, in this example the acultural infant and the acculturated adult, as well as other constraints interplay with one another to affect development. The Gusii are agriculturalists in the Western highlands in Kenya (LeVine and Leiderman, 1994). Although face-to-face play is a rare activity, when asked to engage in it the Gusii infants and mothers do it much like we observe in our Boston studies. However, what was surprising in their interaction was that at the moment when the Gusii infants were getting most excited, and about to express a big greeting with a smile and a hand wave, the mothers looked away. In response, the infant greeting dissolved mid-stream. The infant looked away and actually looked deflated. It is as if the mother made a SF. The infants' SOC dissipated because his intent and actions were assembled to 'greet' the mother, but the mother's intention was to *not* engage in mutual excited affective greeting. There was a lack of coherence between the infant's and the mother's SOCs, but over time a coherent way of greeting emerged. How does the infant come to know her intention and get his intention coordinated with hers?

My sense is that in the next exchange as they move into play and the infant greets her again, the mother turns away and they remain disconnected, but bit-by-bit the infant no longer goes into a big gaping smile, as well as doing a lot of other messy things (e.g. squirming, looking at his feet). At one point he may look at her briefly and soberly. The mother responds in a reciprocal manner—soberly. Their intentions and actions have relations that were not there previously. From this small increment in coherence they select mutual actions and intentions so that they develop a different way of how to greet—a kind of somber looking at each other that has greater coherence and complexity.

Making sense of this co-creation requires knowing that the mother's SOC was constrained by a cultural rule about who can look at whom and with what affect. Women, for example, do not share heightened affect with others and, although this rule is relaxed with infants, it still operates. The mother's impelling certitude of what makes sense guides her actions. On the infant side, after repetitions of the interaction he too comes to know in an age-possible way—perhaps with a body micro-practice—what gaze and affect to assemble to maximize the coherence he experiences with the mother.

This way of greeting takes on an age-possible and, can we say, age-possible cultural impelling certitude.

This example is very surprising when we think of the mutually exuberant smiles that mothers and infants in communities in the West assemble with one another into DSCs. To make sense of Western mothers and infants, mutual gaping, we need to know that the Western mother's sense of her infant is that he is a social partner who needs to express emotions. Consequently, bit-by-bit with repetition of interactions, they assemble a heightened way of being together. On the Boston infants' side, they come to know this meaning in an age-possible (cultural) form of affect, behaviour and expectation. Despite these stunning differences, both the Western shared exuberant dyadic greetings and the Gusii sober greetings, both are assembled through a reiterated selective process of increasing the coherence of the sense of what their shared greeting is. Thus, despite claims to the contrary, neither greeting is 'natural' in the sense of innate and neither pattern, or for that matter the thousands of other greeting patterns seen in other cultures, are universal. They are co-created by individuals. The Gusii and Western greetings are distinct SOCs co-created by Gusii mothers and infants, and Western mothers and infants. Neither infant came into the world armed with a Gusii or Western greeting. The greetings had to be co-created.

Co-creation and prior constraints

It is critical to note that the greetings created are not simply *de novo* creations. One of the powerful constraints is the adult's cultural meaning. It affects what the mothers do and what will 'feel natural' and be coherently assembled with their infants. As cultural forms they are an example of Tomesello's (2001) view that culture is created over historical time spans in a bit-by-bit bootstrapping process. Another constraint is mood. The depressed mothers' mood operates as a constraint on how the infant and the mother can form DSCs in the same manner as non-depressed mothers' joyful mood acts as a constraint.

It is beyond the scope of this paper to elaborate on the issue of constraints, but there are numerous constraints including age-possible meanings, personal history and experience, temperament, and personality. However, even with constraints, coherence governed selection out of messiness and the co-creation of meaning emphasizes the dynamic and unpredictable changes of meaning-making. Meaning-making is always in process, taking form, and changing. It is *not* simply an exchange of pre-formed meanings from one brain into another brain, a common, but false view in fields from linguistics to brain sciences. Instead, there is a mutual induction of not yet fully formed constituents of meaning from each individual's SOC into the other's SOC. These not-so-well-formed meanings are then selectively assembled to increase the coherence of the meaning being created. Elements that do not increase the coherence meaning are not selected (neurons that don't fire together don't get linked together). Furthermore, co-creation also is not a process of co-construction of meaning. Co-construction implies a pre-existing plan or, more specifically, preformed meanings that are put together to build a larger and shared meaning. Co-creation, in contrast, emphasizes that the meaning made is a process in which each individual's meaning is changed and created into a new meaning. The still-in-process eventual shared meaning, that is created by both of them, is also new. However, the concept of co-creation does not question that meaning-making is also private (Modell, 1993). Private meaning-making is undeniable and when brought into dyadic processes it affects the meanings that are co-created.

Conclusion

I would like to cautiously assert the possibility that many psychobiological states are SOCs because it may give us a more unified way to think about development. It is easy to see SOCs as ways of making implicit sense of the world and for organizing action to gain meaning from the world when there *is* awareness or even when there is no awareness. Although perhaps more difficult to conceptualize, other psychobiological states, such as sleep and hunger, may also be thought of as SOCs or at least as somewhat similar. These states are not regulating meaning, but they too organize brain, body, behaviour, and experience. Actions in these states are purposive and operate to maintain the organization of the state, change it, or change the world. Furthermore, in these states individuals garner specific ('meaningful') input from the world leading to an increase in the coherence of the organization of the state. For example, when core body temperature drops, infants adjust their posture to minimize surface heat loss, they switch to metabolizing brown fat, and they may fall asleep to minimize energy consumption. Thus, even at the 'mechanical' psychobiological level states are purposive, have an implicit intended end state, organize behaviour and experience, and require 'meaningful' input to operate. This way of thinking about psychobiological states as SOCs is not unlike the ethnologists term *Umwelt*, the way the world is to an animal in its niche.

I make this suggestion because an advantage of even weakly accepting this argument is that development from infancy through adulthood can be viewed as the development of specific characteristics of SOCs, and the specifics of their self and dyadic regulatory processes. Moreover, regulatory processes, especially dyadic regulatory processes for these more 'mechanical' psychobiological states, can aid us in thinking about the dyadic regulation of SOCs. Nonetheless, a key difference between psychobiological SOCs and other psychobiological states is that SOCs are non-equilibrium states that are often in a state of criticality. They go through qualitative developmental changes, whereas many other psychobiological states are equilibrium states that tend not to qualitatively change.

Over the past 50 years of infancy research we have demonstrated the competencies of the infant. The implication is that the subjective experience of the infant was orderly as well. However, understanding that meaning is made out of messiness and while coherence is increased it is never perfect, I would hypothesize that the infant's experience of the world is messy as well. It is not a Jamesian confusion, but I think that it can be disjointed, contradictory, and confusing. For example, remembering that infant meanings are in their bodies, actions, intents and affects, what is the not-yet-reaching infant's sense of the world when they fall over as they reach toward an object with both hands and throw their head back? 'Where did it all go? What is happening?'

Simply put, I think we have overestimated the continuity and orderliness of experience, and the experience of states such as dissociation may be more common and 'normal' than we have previously thought (as suggested by Fisher, see Noam, 1996), but there can be abnormal effects as well. Incoherent SOCs will lack impelling certitude and because of their incoherence will be experienced as threatening to the integrity of the individual. Both of these experiential aspects will have profound effects, including the sudden total distress of the infant or the toddler in a situation that, to adults, appears to be a 'normal' event (e.g. the berries falling off the branch) to what we used to call nervous breakdowns, de-compensation, and perhaps some psychoses.

Another point and one that contrasts with some of the work I have done in the past that emphasized high experiential moments—Now Moments and Moments of Meeting—is that in this paper I have emphasized that the formation of DSCs is a common phenomenon (Tronick, 1998). I think the ordinariness of dyadic meaning-making is obvious, but equally obvious is that not all DSCs are experienced the same way; they do not have the same incremental effect on the coherence and complexity of SOCs. Rather, it seems that DSCs and SOCs have an intensity and force. The emotion brought into an SOC may be one variable affecting intensity. Another may be differences in the meanings being worked on. Based on the idea of coherence-governed selection, I would suggest that the DSCs with greater force and intensity are ones that assemble more private meanings from each individual into shared meanings. Such assemblages are most likely to lead to an increase in complexity of each individual's SOC, an emergence of something new and unexpected. For example, when an infant and a mother both engage in simultaneous huge gaping smiles, 'everything' about them and between them—actions, intentions, apprehensions—are coherently organized. They both experience expansion and connectedness. Another example of an intense and forceful DSC is a psychodynamic interpretation. Its effect is to bring together into a single coherent insight a vast variety of explicit and implicit and dynamically unconscious meanings in the patient's SOC that will generate a powerful feeling of connection to the therapist (transference) and an experience of expansion.

Connection is the regulation and co-creation of the age-possible meanings individuals make of the world and their place in it. The making of meanings is dyadic and continuous. The meaning emerges out of the messiness of individuals' SOC and the DSC that is created. Neither SOC nor the DSC are perfectly coherent. At best in the moment, and with development they become increasingly coherent and complex. Perhaps more important, the experience itself has to be seen as messily coherent. Even more important is to recognize that no connection between individuals is ever perfect, but out of all this imperfection unique meanings and connections emerge. Such is the wonder of the human condition—the emergence of the new out of messiness.

Acknowledgements

I would like to acknowledge the invaluable work on this paper by Jacob Ham and my discussion with my colleagues Marilyn Davillier, George Downing, and Alexandre Harrison.

References

Adamson, L. and Frick, J. (2003). Research with the Face-to-Face Still-Face paradigm: a review. *Infancy*, **4(4)**, 451–73.

Bak, P. (1996). *How Nature Works*. New York: Springer-Verlag.

Brazelton, T. B. (1990). *The earliest relationship: parents, infants, and the drama of early attachment*. Reading, MA: Addison-Wesley Publishing Co, Inc.

Brazelton, T. B. (1992). *Touchpoints: your child's emotional and behavioural development*. Reading, MA: Addison-Wesley.

Brazelton, T. B., Koslowski, B., and Main, M. (1974). The origins of reciprocity: the early mother-infant interaction. In *The effect of the infant on its caregiver* (ed. M. Lewis and L. A. Rosenblum), pp. 49–76. New York, NY: John Wiley Interscience.

Bruner, J. (1990). *Acts of meaning*. Cambridge, MA: Harvard University Press.

Bruner, J. S. (1970). The growth and structure of skill. In *Mechanisms of motor skill development* (ed. K. J. Connoly), pp. 63–94. London: Academic Press.

Bruner, J. S. (1972). Nature and uses of immaturity. *American Psychologist*, **27**, 687–702.

Bullowa, M. (1979). Prelinguistic communication: a field for scientific research. In *Before Speech: the Beginning of Interpersonal Communication* (ed. M. Bullowa), pp. 1–62. Cambridge: Cambridge University Press.

Campos, J. J. and Lucariello, J. (1999). Origins and consequences of social signaling. Paper presented at the National Conference on Child and Human Development, Rockville, MD, USA.

Edelman, G. M. (1987). *Neural Darwinism: the theory of neuronal group selection*. New York, NY: Basic Books.

Field, T., Healy, B., Goldstein, S., *et al.* (1988). Infants of depressed mothers show 'depressed' behaviour even with nondepressed adults. *Child Development*, **59**, 1569–79.

Fogel, A. (1993). Two principles of communication: co-regulation and framing. In *New perspectives in early communicative development* (ed. J. Nadel and L. Camaioni), pp. 9–21. London: Routledge and Kegan Paul.

Fonagy, P. and Target, M. (1998). Mentalization and the changing aims of child psychoanalysis. *Psychoanalytical dialogues*, **8**, 87–114.

Foscha, D. (2000). *The transforming power of affect*. New York: Basic Books.

Freeman, W. (1994). *Societies of brains*. Hillside, NJ: Erlbaum.

Freeman, W. J. (2000). *How brains make up their mind*. New York, NY: Columbia University Press.

Hofer, M. A. (1984). Relationships as regulators: a psychobiologic perspective on bereavement. *Psychosomatic Medicine*, **46**, 183–97.

Hofer, M. A. (1994a). The development of emotion regulation: biological and behavioural considerations. *Monographs of the Society for Research in Child Development*, 192–207.

Hofer, M. A. (1994b). Hidden regulation in attachment, separation, and loss. In *The development of emotion regulation. Biological and behavioural considerations*, **59(2–3)**, (ed. N. A. Fox), pp. 192–207. Chicago: University of Chicago Press.

Kagan, J. (1998). *Three seductive ideas*. Cambridge, MA: Harvard University Press.

LeVine, R. A. (1977). Child rearing as a cultural adaptation. In *Culture and Infancy: variations in the human experience* (ed. B. A. Rosenfield), pp. 15–28. New York: New York Academic Press.

LeVine, R. A. and Leiderman, P. H. (1994). *Child care and culture: lessons from Africa*. New York, NY: Cambridge University Press.

Levine, S. and Coe, C. L. (1985). The use and abuse of cortisol as a measure of stress. In *Stress and Coping* (ed. T. Field, P. McCabe, and N. Schneiderman), pp. 19–23. Mahwah, NJ: Lawrence Erlbaum Associates.

Modell, A. (1993). *The private self*. Cambridge, MA: Harvard University Press.

Noam, G. F. K. (1996). *Development and vulnerability in close relationships*. Mahwah: Lawrence Erlbaum Associates.

Piaget, J. (1954). *The construction of reality in the child*, 8th edn. New York, NY: Basic Books.

Sander, L. (1988). Reflections on self-psychology and infancy. In *Frontiers in self psychology*, vol 3 (ed. A. Goldberg), pp. 64–77. Mahwah, NJ: Atlantic Press.

Sander, L. (1995). *Thinking about developmental process: wholeness, specificity, and the organization of conscious experiencing*. New York, NY: American Psychological Association.

Sander, L. W. (1976). Issues in early mother–child interaction. In *Infant psychiatry. a new synthesis* (ed. E. N. Rexford, L. W. Sander, and S. T), pp. 127–47. Yale: Yale University Press.

Sander, L. W. (1977). The regulation of exchange in the infant-caretaker system and some aspects of the context-content relationship. In *Interaction, conversation, and the development of language* (ed. M. Lewis and L. A. Rosenblum), pp. 133–55. Harlow: John Wiley and Sons, Inc.

Spitz, R. A. and Cobliner, W. G. (1965). Emotional deficiency diseases of the infant. In *The first year of life. a psychoanalytic study of normal and deviant developmnent of object relations* (ed. R. A. Spitz), pp. 267–84. Guilford, CT: International Universities Press, Inc.

Stengers, I. and Prigogine, I. (1997). *The end of certainty*. New York, NY: Simon and Schuster.

Stern, D., Sander, L., Nahum, J. P., *et al.* (1998). Non-interpretive mechanisms in psychoanalytic therapy. *International Journal of Psychoanalysis*, **79**, 903–21.

Thelen, E. (1995). Motor development a new synthesis. In *American psychologist* (ed. F. D. Horowitz), pp. 79–95. New York, NY: American Psycholgoical Association, Inc.

Tomasello, M. (2001). *The cultural origins of human cognition*. Cambridge, MA: Harvard University Press.

Trevarthen, C. (1980). The foundations of intersubjectivity: Development of interpersonal and cooperative understanding in infants. In *The social foundations of language and thought: Essays in honor of J. S. Bruner* (ed. D. Olsen), pp. 316–42. New York, NY: W. W. Norton.

Trevarthen, C. (1990). Growth and education of the hemispheres. In *Brain circuits and functions of the mind* (ed. C. Trevarthen), pp. 334–63. Cambridge: Cambridge University Press.

Trevarthen, C. (1993). The function of emotions in early infant communication and development. In *New perspectives in early communicative development* (ed. J. Nadel and L. Camaioni), pp. 48–81. London: Routledge.

Tronick, E. Z. (1998). Interactions that effect change in psychotherapy: a model based on infant research. *Infant Mental Health Journal*, **19**, 1–290.

Tronick, E. Z., Als, H., and Adamson, L. (1978a). Structure of early face-to-face communicative interactions. In *Before speech: the beginning of interpersonal communication* (ed. M. Bullowa). Cambridge: Cambridge University Press.

Tronick, E. Z., Als, H., Adamson, L., *et al.* (1978b). The infant's response to entrapment between contradictory messages in face-to-face interaction. *Journal of the American Academy of Child and Adolescent Psychiatry*, **17**, 1–13.

Tronick, E. Z., Brushweiller-Stern, N., Harrison, A. M., *et al.* (1998). Dyadically expanded states of consciousness and the process of therapeutic change. *Infant Mental Health Journal*, **19**, 290–9.

Vygotsky, L. (1978). *Mind in society*. Cambridge, MA: Harvard University Press.

Weinberg, M. K. and Tronick, E. Z. (1994). Beyond the face: an empirical study of infant affective configurations of facial, vocal, gestural, and regulatory behaviors. *Child Development*, **65**, 1503–15.

Weinberg, M. K., Beeghly, M., and Olson, K. I., *et al.* (2002). Preschoolers reactions to their still-faced mother. *International conference in infant studies*, Toronto, Canada, April.

Chapter 12

Prenatal depression effects on the fetus and neonate

Tiffany Field

Introduction

Prenatal depression effects include excessive activity in the fetus and unresponsive behaviour, low activity levels, indeterminate sleep, low vagal tone, and atypical patterns of frontal EEG activation in the newborn. The fetuses and neonates of depressed mothers differ as a function of their mothers' type of depressive behaviour, including withdrawn or intrusive behaviour. The different neurotransmitter imbalance in withdrawn and intrusive depressed mothers during pregnancy (elevated norepinephrine, depressed serotonin, and depressed dopamine in withdrawn mothers and elevated norepinephrine, depressed serotonin, but elevated dopamine in the intrusive mothers) may contribute to the differences noted in their fetuses and neonates. Fetal activity is greater in the fetuses of withdrawn mothers than the fetuses of intrusive mothers. By the neonatal stage, the physiological and biochemical profiles of these infants match their mothers' profiles. The differential dysregulation pattern noted at the neonatal period is then compounded by inadequate stimulation and arousal modulation from the depressed mothers, with the intrusive mothers being overstimulating and the withdrawn mothers being understimulating. By preschool, the children of withdrawn mothers are exhibiting internalizing problems and the children of intrusive mothers are showing externalizing problems. This review is uniquely focused on prenatal depression effects, and highlights the need for early identification and intervention for prenatal depression.

Long-term effects of maternal depression in general

The negative effects of maternal depression in general are increasingly documented including growth and immune problems in the form of failure-to-thrive (Raynor and Rudolf, 1996), malnutrition (Guedeney, 1997) and significantly greater illness in the infants of depressed mothers during the first year of life (Francois et al., 1996), non-optimal cognitive outcomes at toddlerhood (Murray and Cooper, 1997), to behaviour problems (Mohan et al., 1998), hyperactivity and aggression (Stormont and Zentall, 1995), repeat injuries (Russell, 1998), and an increased incidence of child maltreatment

(Runyan *et al.*, 1997) by the preschool stage. Most of the longer-term outcome studies have involved single time point studies of preschool and grade school aged children of depressed mothers. The general conclusion of this literature is that the children of depressed mothers have internalizing and externalizing problems, and these often affect school performance, as well as lead to more serious problems such as conduct disorder. Later at school age, significant adjustment problems occur (Sinclair and Murray, 1998), including increased depression and anxiety (Aslan *et al.*, 1998), reduced popularity (Goodman *et al.*, 1993) and conduct problems at 8–12 years, and conduct disorder after age 12 (Downey and Coyne, 1990; Boyle and Pickles, 1997).

Non-optimal early interactions

For almost two decades, the non-optimal outcomes for children of depressed mothers have generally been attributed to the depressed mothers being emotionally unavailable and unresponsive during their early interactions with their infants (see Field, 1998, for a review). Innumerable early interaction studies documented those effects, and the examples have continued including recent data on depressed mothers having longer switching pauses that are more variable and less consistent, again suggesting that these mothers are not contingently responsive (Zlochower and Cohn, 1996) and are less coordinated in their interactions with their infants and toddlers (Jameson *et al.*, 1997). Only rarely have depressed mothers been described as 'looking normal' (Frankel and Harmon, 1996).

Effects noted earlier at the neonatal stage

Recent data suggest that maternal depression effects emerge as early as the neonatal period including inferior scores on the Brazelton orientation, motor and irritability scales (Murray and Cooper, 1997). In addition, their prematurity and very low birth weight rates are higher (Singer *et al.*, 1999), and they are noted to experience a greater incidence of postnatal complications including bronchopulmonary dysplasia and intraventricular haemorrhage (Locke *et al.*, 1997).

Stress and anxiety effects on the fetus

These very early neonatal differences suggest prenatal depression effects on the fetus. Although very little research has been conducted on prenatal depression effects, prenatal anxiety effects have been studied for decades. In the most recent studies, Glover and her colleagues have documented an association between maternal anxiety and increased uterine artery resistance, an effect that would be expected to reduce blood flow to the fetus (Glover *et al.*, 1999; Teixeira *et al.*, 1999). In this research, the mean uterine artery resistance index was higher in women who had high state anxiety and heart rate (27% versus 4%). In regression analyses, state anxiety and maternal heart rate were the most significant predictors of mean uterine artery resistance, and trait anxiety was the most significant predictor of maximum uterine artery resistance.

The authors suggested that the hypothalamic-pituitary-adrenocortical (HPA) system, as manifested by elevated cortisol levels, or sympathetic activation, as manifested by elevated norepinephrine levels, contributed to these effects in the 32-week-old fetuses.

They subsequently went on to explore maternal cortisol effects on the fetus (Gitau et al., 1998). Fetal concentrations of cortisol were significantly related to maternal cortisol concentrations ($r = 0.62$) in their 30–35-week-old fetuses. Forty per cent of the variance in fetal cortisol levels could be explained by the maternal concentrations. In a similar study (Wadhwa et al., 1998), corticotropin releasing hormone (CRH, an hypothalamic neuropeptide that has a major role in regulating pituitary-adrenal function and the release of cortisol) increased in pregnant women in response to stress at 28–30 weeks gestation. The CRH levels significantly predicted pre-term delivery at 0.98 reliability. In turn, those infants who were delivered prematurely had significantly greater corticotropin releasing hormone levels than those who delivered at term. These studies combined could explain the relationships reported between prenatal stress, pre-term delivery, low birth weight, and low head circumference (Lou et al., 1992).

Differential effects of anxiety and depression

Prenatal depression effects have not been much studied except for our pilot research showing greater activity in the fetuses of our prenatally depressed mothers (Dieter et al., 2001). Although prenatal depression might be expected to have similar effects as prenatal anxiety, the most recent data from the Glover et al. (1999) laboratory suggest that anxiety and depression may have different effects, and operate by different mechanisms. As already noted, maternal anxiety has been associated with increased uterine artery resistance (Teixeira et al., 1999). In turn, the presumed reduction of fetal blood flow associated with increased uterine artery resistance may contribute to the low birth weight noted following high anxiety pregnancies. Thus, increased uterine artery resistance appears to be mediated by maternal anxiety. On the other hand, increased cortisol in the fetus may be mediated by maternal depression. Glover and her colleagues (Gitau et al., 1998) presented strong relationships between maternal cortisol levels and fetal cortisol levels. However, in another study they (Glover et al., 1999) showed no correlation between norepinephrine levels in the mother and fetus, suggesting that only the cortisol stress hormone is being directly transported across the placenta in amounts sufficient to affect the fetus. However, because there was no relationship between maternal anxiety and cortisol levels in that study, even though there was a relationship between maternal anxiety and impaired blood flow (i.e. increased uterine artery resistance), the maternal cortisol–infant cortisol relationship may be less related to anxiety effects than to maternal depression effects, depression being typically accompanied by elevated cortisol levels.

In still other mothers, anxiety and depression may combine to affect the fetus by a third possible mechanism. In the Glover et al. studies just reviewed, maternal anxiety was associated with the activation of the sympathetic-adrenal axis manifested by

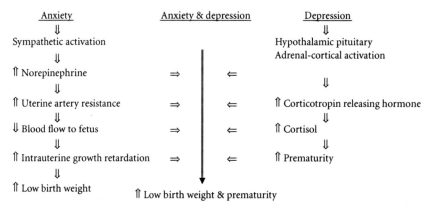

Fig. 12.1 Potential pathways for effects of prenatal anxiety on low birthweight and prenatal depression on prematurity.

elevated norepinephrine levels, which in turn were associated with increased uterine artery resistance, presumed to impair blood flow. Impaired fetal blood flow can lead to pre-eclampsia and intrauterine growth retardation. In contrast, maternal depression effects on the fetus may be mediated by the hypothalamic-pituitary-adrenal (HPA) axis associated elevations in cortisol levels in both the mother and the fetus. In the offspring of mothers with high anxiety, unconfounded by depression, a reduction in birth weight might be expected due to intrauterine growth retardation associated with increased uterine artery resistance. In mothers with high depression, the offspring might be expected to have reduced gestational age, as was reported following elevated cortisol (Wadhwa *et al.*, 1998; see Fig. 12.1). The more typical chronically depressed mothers, however, experience both depression and anxiety, and their newborns may show both shorter gestational age and reduced birth weight.

The problem in this research to date has been that maternal stress, anxiety, and depression have all been confounded, as they may be in nature. Profiles of maternal anxiety alone, maternal depression alone, and maternal anxiety combined with maternal depression may take different forms in maternal behaviour, and they may conform to different physiological and biochemical profiles that, in turn, have differential effects on the fetus.

Confounding effects of fetal malnutrition and drug use exposure

Another problem with the existing research is that prenatal depression and anxiety effects have often been further confounded by other risk variables, such as low socio-economic status and its associated problems including drug use, alcohol use, and smoking, resulting in fetal malnutrition. Some have reported that smoking alone may explain more of the variance in pre-term gestation and low birth weight than anxiety and depression combined (Lou *et al.*, 1992). In those studies where investigators have recruited relatively homogeneous groups unconfounded by these other 'nuisance' variables, prenatal stress (which we are suggesting may have similar effects as prenatal depression) was related to reduced gestational age and pregnancy-related anxiety was correlated with reduced birth weight (Wadhwa *et al.*, 1998). Outcomes such as pre-term birth and low birth weight are presently the most common causes of mortality and morbidity in newborns, and are also associated with significantly higher rates of long-term neurodevelopmental impairments and disabilities (Creasy, 1994). Biomedical or obstetric risk factors, however, predict only a small proportion of the variance in these outcomes (Shiono and Klebanoff, 1993), leaving prenatal depression and anxiety as important risk factors worthy of further exploration.

Depression and anxiety in intrusive and withdrawn types

Intrusive and withdrawn types of prenatal depression may reflect different combinations of depression and anxiety. The two types of prenatally depressed women may be experiencing different stressors, the withdrawn both depression and anxiety, and the intrusive may be experiencing depression without anxiety, but with anger. The intrusive women's depression would have less severe effects on the fetus because those women have normal dopamine levels, which in turn have behaviour activation effects. The withdrawn mothers, in contrast, may be experiencing combined depression and anxiety, leading to their withdrawn pattern, and more severe 'depression' effects due to depleted dopamine, behavioural inactivation, and anhedonia.

The withdrawn and intrusive behaviour styles of depressed mothers were described several years ago by Tronick, Cohn and our own investigative team (Tronick and Field, 1986), with the different style mothers showing different interaction behaviour with their infants. More recently, we have documented generalization of these behaviour styles to their significant others (Hart *et al.*, 1999a). These different style depressed mothers not only have different interaction styles with their infants and significant others, but they also have different physiological and biochemical profiles that are mirrored in their infants. If depression and anxiety, and their combination, can differentially contribute to fetal development, then it is important to identify the effects of those different combinations (e.g. withdrawn depressed mothers who may have high anxiety and intrusive depressed mothers who may have low anxiety) to determine:

- their differential effects on their fetuses and infants, and the degree to which their infants' biochemistry and physiology conform to their mothers' profiles;
- the degree to which this behavioural/physiological/ biochemical profile is stable across infancy and into early pre-school/grade school;
- the degree to which prenatal, perinatal, post partum, and early infancy interventions could help prevent the pre-school internalizing/externalizing problems, and the grade school depression/conduct disorder problems that seem to be emerging in the offspring of depressed mothers.

Fetal development highlights the need for early identification

The data just reviewed suggesting that anxiety and depression may be sole or co-morbid diagnoses certainly complicate screening and early identification as well as the selection of appropriate intervention strategies. Litmus tests are needed like the levels of corticotropin hormone reliably predicting premature deliveries (Wadhwa *et al.*, 1998). Our research suggests that left frontal/right frontal EEG activation, neurotransmitter patterns and scores on the BIS/BAS (Carver and White, 1994) showing approach/withdrawal tendencies could be added to depression and anxiety measures to more accurately identify different types of depressed mothers during pregnancy (Diego *et al.*, 2001). The mothers could then be given prenatal intervention.

The need for prenatal intervention is highlighted by the fact that most chronically depressed women are unwilling to take medications during pregnancy. Psychology is therefore challenged to find alternative preventative treatments. The need for prenatal identification and intervention is also highlighted by a large group of research summarized in a volume called *Fetal Development: A Psychobiological Perspective* (edited by Lecanuet *et al.*, 1995) suggesting that significant learning occurs prenatally. Research by DeCasper and Spence (1986), for example, documented newborns' preference for their mother's voice versus the voices of other women, and particularly when it was electronically altered to sound as if the newborn was again in the womb as opposed to hearing the mother's extrauterine voice. These data were not surprising given the data of DeCasper and Fifer (1980) showing that newborns discriminated a Dr Seuss story that they had heard prenatally from another that they had not heard prenatally. They would suck harder or less hard depending upon the conditions of the experiment to hear the preferred familiar Dr Seuss story 'To think I saw it on Mulberry Street' (DeCasper and Fifer, 1980).

More direct evidence for fetal learning comes from studies on habituation, the most primitive form of learning. A stimulus is applied, typically a vibrotactile stimulus using a vibrator, to the pregnant woman's abdomen. The fetus first moves in response to that stimulus and, after repeated presentations of the stimulus, the fetus pays less attention or stops responding, having 'habituated' the stimulus or having learned that it is not relevant. Several studies of this kind appear in the volume by Lecanuet *et al.* (1995).

Fetal behaviour is also predictive of later temperament. For example, in one study, 20–60% of the variation in infant temperament could be predicted in fetuses of mothers experiencing depressed mood, movement and heartrate (DiPietro *et al.*, 1996). Fetal recordings were made at six points during prenatal development, and then the infants' mothers completed temperament questionnaires at 3 and 6 months after birth. Babies who were more active *in utero* were more irritable and active on the temperament assessments. Babies who had irregular sleep-wake patterns in utero also showed sleep problems at 3–6 months. Even small changes in the mother's mood in that study seemed to directly affect fetal activity.

The mechanisms by which these effects are transmitted are unclear. The mother's activity level, heart rate, and intrauterine hormones may all be involved in these effects. Some offspring of depressed women may be more vulnerable to the impact of environmental factors such as these because of some underlying genetic predisposition (Kendler *et al.*, 1992). The possibility that maternal depression effects are genetically mediated has been raised by many (McGuffin *et al.*, 1994; Plomin *et al.*, 1997; Rutter *et al.*, 1997). This will require genetic research strategies such as twin and adoptee designs. In the interim, the data from the fetal research and the ultrasound study on fetuses of different style depressed mothers highlighted the need for studying these different styles, and the profiles of early dysregulation in the infants that might relate to their prenatal experience and might help explain their less optimal early interaction behaviour.

Prenatal depression in intrusive and withdrawn mothers

Most of the studies on prenatal depression in intrusive and withdrawn mothers were conducted by our group, and are detailed here. Studies from other laboratories are also briefly reviewed whenever relevant or if they served as models for our studies. In most of these studies the mothers were not only chronically depressed (dysthymic), but also had other risk factors including being low socioeconomic status. In some studies the mothers were adolescent, another notable risk factor for infant development. These risk factors are, of course, potential confounds and their effects cannot be underestimated, although they are difficult to measure or control. However, both the depressed and non-depressed mothers came from the same SES and same age group so that depression was an additional factor for the group labelled depressed, and seemingly the only way in which the depressed and non-depressed groups differed. In most of the studies reviewed here, depression was defined as protracted depressive mood state or dysthymia, typically determined by the BDI or CES-D combined with a diagnostic interview (the Diagnostic Interview Schedule or the Diagnostic Interview Schedule for Children in the case of adolescent mothers). Although these measures have been noted to be significantly correlated (Wilcox *et al.*, 1996), more mothers have been classified as depressed on the basis of the BDI or CES-D alone versus the DIS or DISC, leading to the frequently reported problem that the self-report instruments may be yielding false positives. Differential diagnosis is one of the primary methodological difficulties conducting research with this population. Another is non-compliance with the treatment and the research assessment process, a problem that probably relates to those other risk factors including the poverty, minority status, lack of education, and learned helplessness of the women, and in some cases the adolescent parenthood of the sample, factors that are common in the studies reviewed here.

Incidence of different types of depressed mothers based on interaction behaviour

First, data are presented from a longitudinal study that we began during pregnancy, but one in which the mothers were not identified as intrusive or withdrawn until their infants were 3–6-months-old (Field, 2001). Throughout, only statistically significant findings are presented. In this study, the mothers had been classified as depressed during the prenatal period based on a diagnosis of dysthymia on the Diagnostic Interview Schedule (DIS, or the DISC if they were adolescent mothers; Robins *et al.*, 1981; Shaffer *et al.*, 1991). We elected to recruit chronically depressed pregnant women because several investigators have documented the more severe effects of chronic maternal depression (Frankel and Harmon, 1996; Campbell and Cohen, 1997; NICHD Early Child Care Research Network, 1999), and we had found similar results in a study comparing prenatally depressed women, postpartum depressed women, and chronically depressed women (Diego *et al.*, 2004). The data from that study suggested that on behavioural, physiological, and biochemical variables, both the chronically depressed mothers and their infants showed the most dysregulation. However, at this time we were not able to classify the mothers as intrusive or withdrawn until we could observe their face-to-face interaction behaviour with their infants at 3-months-old, which is the context in which we had first observed the different styles of depressed mothers (Field *et al.*, 1990). At the 3-month-period, 41% of the depressed mothers were identified as intrusive (having demonstrated rough physical contact, including tickling, poking, tugging, using rapid staccato actions, and tense or fake facial expressions), 38% were identified as withdrawn (flat affect, rare touching, rare vocalizing, disengaged behaviour, looking away from the infant), and 21% were classified as good (non-intrusive/non-withdrawn).

Withdrawn mothers are inferior interaction partners and intrusive mothers are less empathetic

At the 3–6-month period the assessment that was conducted to classify these mothers as intrusive or withdrawn included videotaping the mothers and infants during face-to-face interactions (Jones *et al.*, 2001). In addition, we attempted to determine whether the mothers recognized their interaction styles as being overstimulating or understimulating. This information was felt to be useful for tailoring intervention strategies for depressed mothers and their infants. In an earlier study, we had noted that interaction coaching strategies were more effective when tailored to the behaviour style of the mother (Malphurs *et al.*, 1996).

The videotapes were first made of the mothers and their infants interacting, and then independent observers coded the videotapes. The mother was then asked to code her own behaviour with her infant, and then to code two model mothers (withdrawn and intrusive) and their infants on a videotape. The mothers were then shown a video of a crying infant interacting with an intrusive or withdrawn mother, and then they were asked whether the crying infant distressed or annoyed them to determine whether the different style mothers differed in empathy. In this empathy study, the withdrawn mothers were noted to be less expressive and they showed a more negative pattern of interaction with their infants than the intrusive mothers (Jones *et al.*, 2001). Furthermore, unlike the intrusive mothers who recognized their behaviour as being overstimulating, the withdrawn mothers did not perceive their own behaviours as withdrawn and understimulating. The withdrawn mothers, nonetheless, recognized withdrawn behaviour in the model mothers. The pattern shown by the withdrawn mothers is consistent with reports that depressed mothers recognize negative behaviours of others, but fail to recognize negative behaviours in themselves (Field *et al.*, 1993). Thus, the withdrawn mothers might be less likely to implement new interaction patterns following interaction coaching unless they are also taught to recognize their own understimulating behaviour. Intrusive mothers may recognize their intrusive behaviour and report greater levels of these behaviours, but not view these behaviours as unusual or harmful.

Despite their negative interaction behaviour, both groups of mothers in this study (Jones *et al.*, 1997a) perceived their infants in a positive manner, as in fact being more outgoing and less shy than they were coded by the independent observer. Finally, the withdrawn mothers reported that they were more disturbed and expressed more anxiety about the crying infant, whereas the intrusive mothers reported more irritation/annoyance and expressed more anger about the crying infant, suggesting that the withdrawn mothers were more empathetic than the intrusive mothers.

In this sample of intrusive mothers, the incidence of reported infant abuse was greater (5%), in contrast to the greater incidence of neglect reported in the withdrawn mother sample (3%). Examples of these kinds of maltreatment could be seen as early as the 3–6-month-old infant–mother interactions. The extremely withdrawn mothers behaved like statues with virtually no interaction with their infants. In contrast, the extremely intrusive mothers behaved like 'wood–pecking, boxing machines' poking and 'boxing' their infants' faces and jerking their infants' heads, such that the sessions needed to be interrupted and referrals made to protective services.

Others have noted that intrusive mothers were involved with their infants to the point of interfering (Egeland *et al.*, 1993), and exhibiting anger, hostility, and high levels of irritability (Weissman and Paykel, 1974; Lyons-Ruth *et al.*, 1986). Some associated this pattern with greater covert hostility, affectivity and more interference with the infants' goal-directed activity (Lyons-Ruth *et al.*, 1986). Others described this behaviour as overstimulation and physical intrusiveness (Panaccione and Wahler, 1986; Malphurs *et al.*, 1996).

Reports on the infants' behaviour have been somewhat conflicting. Cohn and his colleagues (Cohn *et al.*, 1986) noted that withdrawn mothers spent approximately 80% of their time disengaged from their infants, and responded to their infants only when the infants were distressed. Intrusive mothers showed anger and irritation, or roughly handled their infants 40% of the time. The infants of intrusive mothers protested less than 5% of the time, but spent 55% of the time avoiding their mothers. On the other hand, infants of withdrawn mothers protested 30% of the time and watched their mothers less than 5% of the time. In contrast, data from our laboratory indicated that infants of withdrawn mothers were inactive and spent a majority of their time looking around, whereas infants of intrusive mothers fussed for a greater proportion of the time (Field *et al.*, 1990).

These different maternal interaction styles also appear to differentially affect boy and girl infants. In at least one study, boys appeared to be more vulnerable than girls to the withdrawn state (Weinberg and Tronick, 1998). The authors suggested that when the mother's regulatory support was missing, this was particularly problematic for boys because of their typically being less developmentally mature and needing more regulation than girl infants. The girl infants, in contrast, seemed to be more vulnerable to the intrusive type interaction, perhaps, as the authors suggested, because it interferes with their more developed exploratory activities. Independent of the infants' gender, the long-term outcomes appear to be less favourable for infants of withdrawn mothers (Field, 2001). In early infancy they had less optimal interaction behaviour and in later infancy their Bayley Mental Scale scores were lower.

Different EEG patterns in withdrawn and intrusive depressed mothers and their infants

EEG patterns also differentiate these different style depressed mothers and their infants. EEG researchers have documented associations between approach emotions such as happy and angry, and greater relative left frontal EEG activation; between withdrawal emotions such as sadness and greater relative right frontal EEG activation; and between adult depression and greater relative right frontal EEG activation (Davidson and Fox, 1982, 1989; Henriques and Davidson, 1990). Our group has shown that depressed mothers have greater relative right frontal EEG activation and their infants have the same pattern when their infants are 3 months old (Field *et al.*, 1995), 1-month-old (Jones *et al.*, 1996b), and even as young as 1-week (Jones *et al.*, 1996a). An earlier study by Dawson and her colleagues (Dawson *et al.*, 1992) and a more recent study (Dawson *et al.*, 1999) revealed this phenomenon at 18 months. Greater relative right frontal EEG activation at 1 month in our study was also related to indeterminate sleep patterns and negative affect at the neonatal period (Jones *et al.*, 1996b). That the depressed mothers showed greater relative right frontal EEG activation is not surprising, but the appearance of this pattern as early as 1 week in their infants was very unexpected given the supposed plasticity of brain development during the first several months of life. The literature had suggested that the frontal cortex was very slow to develop and would not be expected to reveal patterns of this kind until at least 6 months of life. In addition, this pattern appeared to be stable in infants of depressed mothers, at least from 3 months to 3 years of age (Jones *et al.*, 1997b). In this longitudinal study depressed mothers and their infants consistently showed greater relative right frontal EEG activation from 3 months to 3 years. Recent data suggest, however, that the two different style depressed mothers and their infants have different EEG patterns (Jones *et al.*, 1997b). Withdrawn depressed mothers and their infants show greater relative right frontal EEG activation patterns, while the intrusive depressed mothers and their infants show greater relative left frontal EEG activation.

Infants of intrusive mothers are more exploratory and have better developmental scores at 1 year old

At 1 year old, the infants' exploratory behaviour and their performance on developmental assessments were investigated (Hart *et al.*, 1999b). At this time, the infants of the intrusive mothers were noted to be more exploratory (manipulate a jack-in-the-box) during a teaching interaction. Also, at this time, the intrusive mothers were showing significantly lower depression scores than the withdrawn mothers (18 versus 27 on the Beck Depression Inventory), although they still met the >16 BDI score criterion for depression. The infants of the intrusive mothers also showed superior performance on the Bayley mental scales. The infants of intrusive mothers' superior performance on the Bayley was highly correlated with their exploratory behaviour during the teaching interaction.

Across infancy and into early preschool the stability of these classifications, and their corresponding biochemical and EEG profiles were noted (Jones *et al.*, 1997b). Unfortunately, the attrition rate was high for the 'good' mothers, who would hopefully be maintained in a future sample because of the useful information they may provide on how depressed mothers, despite their depression, can engage in optimal behaviour for their children's development.

Non-empathy, internalizing, and externalizing problems at preschool age

At the 3-year stage, in addition to recording EEG activity, the empathetic reactions to emotion-inducing situations and the ability to complete a learning task were examined in the preschool children (Jones *et al.*, 2000). The children of the depressed mothers showed greater relative right frontal EEG activation, were slower in completing the teaching task and they spent more time asking for help. The depressed mothers stated their approval less often and spent less time helping their child complete the task. The children of the depressed mothers also showed fewer empathetic responses to a crying infant, as well as to their own mothers' simulated distress. The children showed two styles of non-empathy, one marked by aggressive non-empathy behaviour (e.g. shouting at their mothers or kicking them), and the other marked by apathetic non-empathy behaviour (e.g. ignoring her), behaviours that might be expected, based on their mothers' classification as intrusive or withdrawn. In addition, the children of intrusive mothers were showing externalizing behaviours and the children of the withdrawn mothers were showing internalizing behaviours. The differences between the children's non-empathetic responding mirrored the differences noted in the earlier 3-month period when the intrusive mothers appeared to have angry reactions, while the withdrawn mothers appeared to have more apathetic, but more empathetic reactions. It should be noted, however, that this sample was limited to younger mothers from a lower socioeconomic status group. Nonetheless, these different profiles of depression highlight the need for developing treatments that are tailored to the different profiles the mothers and infants are displaying. Of importance for the longitudinal follow-up of this sample to school age is whether the internalizing behaviour at preschool becomes depression at school age and whether the externalizing behaviour at preschool turns into conduct disorder by school age.

The same longitudinal sample retrospectively analysed for neonatal and prenatal predictors

Once the mothers' depression style had been classified, based on their interactions with their 3-month-old infants (Jones et al., 2001), we were able to retrospectively analyse the neonatal and prenatal data on this longitudinal sample. The neonates of the depressed mothers showed inferior performance on the orientation, motor, reflex, excitability, withdrawal, and depression clusters of the Brazelton, with the newborns of the withdrawn mothers showing the least optimal performance.

Table 12.1 Stepwise regression for the depressed group using maternal predictor variables and newborn outcome variables

Step #	Maternal Predictor variables	Neonatal Outcome variables	Multiple		F-to-enter
			R	R2	
1	CES-D	Orientation	0.64	0.41	4.20
2	Norepinephrine		0.79	0.63	6.50
1	Cortisol	Abnormal reflexes	0.43	0.18	5.11
1	CES-D	Depression	0.54	0.29	16.95
1	CES-D	Excitability	0.43	0.19	8.45
2	Dopamine		0.82	0.67	9.64
1	CES-D	Withdrawal	0.69	0.47	9.22
2	Dopamine		0.80	0.64	9.71
1	CES-D	Cortisol	0.59	0.35	14.60
1	Trait anxiety	Norepinephrine	0.57	0.33	12.82
2	Norepinephrine		0.66	0.44	9.77
1	CES-D	Epinephrine	0.62	0.38	7.99
1	Dopamine	Dopamine	0.49	0.24	8.50

Looking at relationships between the mothers' prenatal data and their offsprings' neonatal data (Jones *et al.*, 1997a; Lundy *et al.*, 1998), the depressed mothers as a group had higher cortisol and norepinephrine levels during pregnancy. Although the mothers from both the withdrawn and intrusive groups had been diagnosed as dysthymic on the DIS (or DISC if they were adolescents), and had equivalently high BDI scores, the withdrawn mothers had lower dopamine levels than the intrusive mothers. The neonates had biochemical profiles similar to their different classification mothers. The newborns of the withdrawn mothers had lower dopamine levels, like their mothers, and the newborns of intrusive mothers had higher dopamine levels, like their mothers. Otherwise, the profiles were similar, with both groups of mothers and infants having similarly high norepinephrine and cortisol levels, and similarly low serotonin levels. Stepwise regression analyses revealed that the depressed mothers' prenatal norepinephrine and dopamine levels significantly predicted the newborns' norepinephrine and dopamine levels, as well as their Brazelton scores (Lundy *et al.*, 1998; see Table 12.1).

Confounding risk factors

In this programme of studies, as already noted, most of our samples were not only depressed, but high-risk for other reasons including being low socioeconomic status and having associated problems such as prenatal exposure to malnutrition and drug exposure. Thus, much of the data just reviewed needs to be considered in that context and is significantly limited in its generalizability. Also, several of the samples were cross-sectional as opposed to longitudinal because of compliance problems with the low SES, relatively uneducated samples of mothers. Having recognized that these factors significantly confound the effects of maternal depression on fetal and infant development, we recruited a new sample of mothers who were experiencing depression, but were not experiencing the confounding and compounding effects of low socioeconomic status, and the related malnutrition and drug use effects.

Identification of mothers in new sample by BIS/BAS during the prenatal period

During the course of the previous studies we were able to explore various assessment procedures that might distinguish the intrusive and withdrawn depressed mothers prior to their interactions with their 3-month-old infants, so that they could be classified during pregnancy. Earlier we had only been able to distinguish them at their infants' 3–6-month assessment based on their interaction behaviours. However, in a comprehensive assessment study (Diego *et al.*, 2001), we were able to document high correlations between the mothers' different interaction styles at 3–6 months, and their EEG patterns and scores they had received on the Behavioural Inhibition Scale/Behavioural Activation Scale (BIS/BAS; Carver and White, 1994) at the prenatal period. As might have been expected, the mothers with high BIS (behavioural inhibition) scores were those showing withdrawn interaction behaviour and greater relative right frontal EEG activation in contrast to those with high BAS (behavioural approach) scores showing greater relative left frontal EEG activation and intrusive interaction patterns.

Sample recruited prenatally shows differential biochemical profiles in mothers and differential fetal activity

With these new identification procedures (the EEG patterns and BIS/BAS scores), we were able to reliably identify chronically depressed women with these different styles during the early pregnancy period. Their biochemical profiles were tracked at monthly intervals from month four to month eight of pregnancy and fetal activity was recorded during ultrasound sessions at the same intervals (Dieter *et al.*, 2001). Significantly higher activity levels were noted in the fetuses of depressed mothers at 5, 6 and 7 months gestation (see Fig. 12.2), with the activity levels of the withdrawn mothers' fetuses being more elevated than those of the intrusive mothers. The mothers' depression scores on the CES-D and anxiety scores on the STAI predicted 58% of the variance in fetal activity.

The already documented biochemical profiles emerged again in this new low-risk sample, with the withdrawn mothers having lower dopamine levels and both style mothers having elevated norepinephrine, epinephrine and cortisol levels (Field *et al.*, 2001). Both the intrusive and withdrawn mothers had lower serotonin levels than the non-depressed mothers. Activity levels were higher in the fetuses of mothers with higher cortisol levels and lower serotonin levels. Low serotonin was, in turn, related to low dopamine and low dopamine to elevated cortisol. Based on Wadhwa *et al.*'s 1998 data showing the 0.98 relationship between maternal cortisol (ACTH) and rate of prematurity, these high activity (high maternal cortisol level) fetuses would be considered at risk for premature delivery.

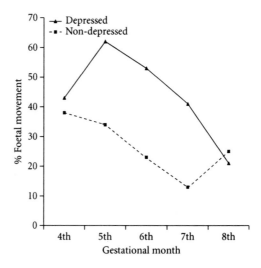

Fig. 12.2 Fetal movement during 4–8 months gestation in fetuses of depressed and non-depressed pregnant women.

Mothers' prenatal biochemistry predicts neonatal biochemistry, EEG and behaviour

In this same sample, significant correlations were noted again between the mothers' neurotransmitter and hormone levels prenatally and the infants' levels at birth (Field *et al.*, 2001). These included significant correlations between the prenatal mothers' and the newborns' norepinephrine, epinephrine, cortisol, dopamine and serotonin levels. The intrusive mothers' and infants' serotonin levels were lower relative to the non-depressed sample, and their dopamine levels higher than the withdrawn dyads. The withdrawn mothers and their infants had significantly lower levels of dopamine, as well as serotonin. Low levels of dopamine and serotonin in the mothers prenatally were correlated with greater relative right frontal EEG activation in the neonates. The newborns of withdrawn mothers also had lower scores on state regulation and higher withdrawal scores on the Brazelton Neonatal Behaviour Assessment.

Depleted dopamine in withdrawn mothers and infants

The lower dopamine in the withdrawn mothers and their infants is perhaps not surprising given that they are less active (dopamine being an activating transmitter). Dopamine has been considered a pivotal neurotransmitter in the model being investigated on children's psychiatric disorders by Rogeness *et al.* (1992). In that model, derived from an extensive database on multiple disorders in children, high norepinephrine, high dopamine, and high serotonin levels are typically associated with normal, extraverted, high energy traits (see Table 12.2). Children, however, with elevated norepinephrine and dopamine, but low serotonin levels often have externalizing problems. In our longitudinal study already described, the children of the intrusive mothers were showing externalizing problems (Jones *et al.*, 2000), as might have been predicted by their neurotransmitter pattern. In contrast, high norepinephrine accompanied by

Table 12.2 Hypothetical characteristics associated with functional balance among NT Systems

	High DA	Low DA
Low NE, Low 5HT	Aggressive CD, ADD with hyperactivity, irritable, no anxiety or depression	Generally 'normal,' low motivation, schizoid, possible attentional problems
High NE, low 5HT	Aggressive, anxious/depressed CD, mild hyperactivity, adequate concentration	Overly inhibited and anxious, tendency to withdraw
Low NE, high 5HT	Non-aggressive CD, mild ADD with mild hyperactivity	ADD without hyperactivity, inhibited
High NE, high 5HT	Normal, extroverted and anxious, high energy, obsessive compulsive traits	Anxious, inhibited, depressed

ADD = attention deficit disorder, CD = conduct disorder.

low dopamine is associated in the Rogeness *et al.* (1992) model with anxious, inhibited, depressed behaviour. Again, the neurotransmitter profile matched the internalizing problems of our sample of children of withdrawn mothers. Even as early as birth, the newborns of the withdrawn mothers in our study not only showed lower activity levels and less responsivity to social stimulation, but also greater relative right frontal EEG activation and lower dopamine levels, typically associated with inhibition and withdrawn behaviour. In contrast, the newborns of intrusive mothers showed more active approach behaviour, greater relative left frontal EEG activation and higher dopamine levels, typically associated with active, aggressive behaviour.

An animal model on norepinephrine and dopamine in depression

An animal model (the rat) developed by Jay Weiss and his colleagues (Weiss *et al.*, 1998) has linked the noradrenergic and dopaminergic systems in depression. In this model, dopamine is implicated as much if not more so than norepinephrine in depression-related responses including low activity levels and anhedonic responses. Depressive symptomatology in that model has been traced to abnormal activity (hyper-responsivity) of the locus coeruleus neurons which then release galanin from the locus coeruleus access terminals, in turn inhibiting (hyperpolarizing) dopamine neurons in the ventral tegmentum to mediate depression-related changes. The elevated norepinephrine levels and the depressed dopamine levels in the withdrawn mothers relative to the intrusive mothers suggest a greater degree of depression, at least depression that dampens activity and hedonic levels. The pattern of elevated norepinephrine and depressed dopamine in their neonates might explain their lower activity levels and lesser responsiveness to social stimulation on the Brazelton Neonatal Behaviour Assessment, as well as, their greater relative right frontal EEG activation.

Potential origins of differences in withdrawn and intrusive mothers

The different forms of maternal depression including withdrawn and intrusive styles may derive from different neurotransmitter profiles, as already mentioned, and from different temperaments/personality styles with an approach/withdrawal orientation to life, much as in the extraverted/introverted or the externalizer/internalizer dimensions discussed by Eysenck (1967). Others have described similar subtypes of depressive behaviour including one type that is characterized by dependency and self-criticism (Luthar and Blatt, 1995), and another by sociotropy and autonomy (Beck, 1967). On top of the depression common to both groups, the mothers may be experiencing additional emotions that are unique to their different style, for example, anger in the intrusive mothers and anxiety in the withdrawn mothers, and they may have developed different coping-with-depression styles including 'anger out' versus 'anger in' or 'active coping' versus 'passive coping'. These could also be representative of different types of pathology including the old nomenclature of the 'active/endogenous' depression or they could simply represent different stages of severity such as the intrusive behaviour happening at an earlier stage, and the withdrawn stage occurring later as learned helplessness and vegetative symptoms, such as psychomotor retardation and anhedonia develop. Because we have also seen more intrusive behaviour in younger depressed mothers, this contrast in style may reflect maternal age differences.

Our intent has not been to determine the origins of these different styles, but rather the effects of these different styles on the mothers' infants. To date we have focused on the differential effects of the different styles of maternal depression on the infants including the relationship between the mothers' prenatal biochemical and physiological profiles, and that of their infants at the neonatal stage and the compounding effects of their different interaction styles on the infants' behaviour during early infancy. However, because our data suggest that these styles are stable at least across the first few years of life (Jones *et al.*, 1999), because these styles have different effects on their infants (Field, 1998), and because the styles generalize to interactions with other people including the mothers' significant others (boyfriends and spouses; Hart *et al.*, 1999a), we are becoming mindful of the importance of exploring the potential underlying mechanisms of these different depressed mother interaction styles.

Psychobiological attunement model reconsidered

In the interim, these data suggest a reconsideration of our 'psychobiological attunement' model. In that model we had argued that the infants of depressed mothers experience dysregulation, and that that dysregulation is later compounded by inadequate stimulation and arousal modulation from their mothers (Field, 1985, 1992, 1995, 1998). Whether the mothers had a withdrawn (understimulating) or intrusive (overstimulating) interaction style, their stimulation was considered non-optimal in that model. The more recent data showing better developmental outcomes for the infants of intrusive mothers (at least their better development scores at one year) raise questions about some of the assumptions of the original model.

The new data suggest that:

- The excessive stimulation of the intrusive mothers, in particular their verbal stimulation, may be facilitating better cognitive development of their infants as compared to the infants of withdrawn mothers. The better cognitive development might also result from these infants being more active (higher dopamine levels) and having to actively respond to their mothers, as opposed to the infants of withdrawn mothers who can be inactive in response to their mothers' inactivity. The more actively responding infants might be processing more stimulation and in turn becoming more exploratory (as suggested by their greater exploratory behaviour at one year), suggesting a more indirect pathway for the mothers' effect on the infants' development.

• The neonatal data showing more optimal Brazelton performance and greater relative left frontal EEG activation in infants of intrusive mothers suggest that the infants of intrusive mothers may themselves be less dysregulated than the infants of withdrawn mothers as early as the neonatal period. This may not be surprising because their mothers had a more balanced (less depressed) neurotransmitter pattern (elevated dopamine), which in turn would affect fetal development and contribute to that pattern in their infants. Replication data are needed, however, to determine whether the Bayley scale differences are robust at 1 year and whether, despite their cognitive advantage as infants, the children of intrusive mothers continue to show externalizing problems at the preschool stage.

Future directions

The data just reviewed suggest the need for the following future directions:

• As already indicated, samples of depressed mothers need to be studied without the confounding effects of low socioeconomic status and related malnutrition and substance use problems. A larger sample of less impoverished mothers would also enable recruitment and maintaining a sample of 'good' interaction depressed mothers. Nonetheless, the high and low-risk samples could be compared across assessment periods to address the question of the added contribution of these high risk factors to maternal depression effects.

• Samples already assessed at the preschool age need to be followed into the grade school years to determine whether the internalizing and externalizing behaviours evidenced at the pre-school stage continue into the early grade school years, manifesting as the more serious depression and conduct disorder problems.

• The prenatal development protocol needs to be expanded to track the fetus from earlier in pregnancy in a longitudinal versus cross-sectional sample across pregnancy with a more extensive biochemical battery, as well as additional confirmatory fetal measures. Corticotropin releasing hormone (CRH) and oxytocin should be added, CRH because of its relationship to prematurity (Wadhwa *et al.*, 1998), and oxytocin because of its critical importance for growth and for the mother-infant relationship (Uvnas-Moberg, 1997). Monitoring several fetal measures, including the uterine artery resistance index, fetal heart rate, fetal activity, and fetal responses to stimulation measures would strengthen the data.

• Additional data are needed on the perceptual skills of those infants who have been compromised by unfavourable biochemical influences during pregnancy. The data already published on the inferior performance on the Brazelton Neonatal Behaviour Assessment (Abrams *et al.*, 1995; Lundy *et al.*, 1996), and lesser responsivity to social stimulation both from an attentive and expressive side (Lundy *et al.*, 1996), suggest that the perceptual skills of these infants may be limited from the newborn stage. Some very recent data show, for example, that newborns of depressed mothers are slower to habituate different sensory stimuli including textures (Hernandez-Reif *et al.*, 2001b) and temperatures (Hernandez-Reif *et al.*, 2001a). If the biochemical influences are present from the beginning of pregnancy and much of the senses are developed early in pregnancy, it is conceivable that these newborns may be limited in their perception of tactile, olfactory, gustatory, auditory, and visual stimulation from birth.

◆ It would appear from our pilot data that the mother's perception of her own behaviour is distorted and could benefit from feedback not only about her own behaviour, but about her infant's behaviour from birth.

◆ Interventions appear to be needed as early as the prenatal period to reduce the biochemical imbalance affecting fetal and later newborn behaviour, and to continue the intervention across infancy and pre-school to avoid the problems of regression associated with early termination of intervention programmes. These future directions highlight the need for clinicians and researchers alike to collaborate on this far-reaching problem.

Acknowledgments

We would like to thank the mothers and infants who participated in these studies. This research was supported by an NIMH Merit Award (MH#46586) and by an NIMH Senior Research Scientist Award (MH#00331) to Tiffany Field, and funding from Johnson and Johnson to the Touch Research Institutes.

References

Abrams, S. M., Field, T., Scafidi, F., *et al.* (1995). Maternal 'depression' effects on infants' Brazelton Scale performance. *Infant Mental Health Journal*, **16**, 231–5.

Aslan, S. H., Aslan, O., and Alparslan, Z. (1998). Effects of chronic maternal depression on children's depression and anxiety: a comparative study. *Tuerk Psikiyatri Dergisi*, **9**, 32–7.

Beck, A. T. (1967). The past and future of cognitive therapy. *Journal of Psychotherapy Practice and Research*, **6**, 276–84.

Boyle, M. and Pickles, A. R. (1997). Influence of maternal depressive symptoms on ratings of childhood behaviour. *Journal of Abnormal Child Psychology*, **25**, 399–412.

Brazelton, T. B. (1973). *The Neonatal Behaviour Assessment Scale*. New York, NY: Heineman.

Campbell, S. B. and Cohn, J. F. (1997). The timing and chronicity of postpartum depression: implication for infant development. In *Postpartum depression and child development* (ed. L. Murray, P. Cooper), pp. 165–97. New York, NY: Guilford Press.

Carver, C. and White, T. (1994). Behavioural inhibition, behavioural activation, and affective responses to impending reward and punishment: the BIS/BAS Scale. *Journal of Personality and Social Psychology*, **67**, 319–33.

Cohn, J. F., Matias, R., Tronick, E. Z., *et al.* (1986). Face-to-face interactions of depressed mothers and their infants. In *Maternal Depression and Infant Disturbance* (ed. E. Z. Tronick and T. Field), pp. 31–45. San Francisco: Jossey-Bass.

Creasy, R. K. (1994). Pre-term labor and delivery. In *Maternal foetal medicine: principles and practice* (ed. R. K. Creasy and R. Resnik), pp. 494–520. Philadelphia: WB Saunders Company.

Davidson, R. J. and Fox, N. A. (1982). Asymmetrical brain activity discriminates between positive versus negative affect in human infants. *Science*, **218**, 1235–7.

Davidson, R. J. and Fox, N. A. (1989). Frontal brain asymmetry predicts infants' response to maternal separation. *Journal of Abnormal Psychology*, **98**, 127–31.

Dawson, G., Klinger, L. G., Panagitotides, H., *et al.* (1992). Frontal lobe activity and affective behaviour of infants of mothers with depressive symptoms. *Child Development*, **63**, 725–37.

Dawson, G., Frey, K., Panagitotides, H., *et al.* (1999). Infants of depressed mothers exhibit atypical frontal electrical brain activity during interactions with mother and with a familiar, nondepressed adult. *Child Development*, **70**, 1058–66.

DeCasper, A. J. and Fifer, W. P. (1980). Of human bonding: newborns prefer their mothers' voice. *Science*, **208**, 1174–6.

DeCasper, A. J. and Spence, M. J. (1986). Prenatal maternal speech influences newborns' perception of speech sounds. *Infant Behaviour and Development*, **9**, 133–50.

Diego, M. A., Field, T., and Hernandez-Reif, M. (2001). BIS/BAS scores are correlated with frontal EEG-asymmetry in intrusive and withdrawn mothers. *Infant Mental Health Journal*, **22**, 665–75.

Diego, M. A., Field, T., Cullen, C., *et al.* (2004). Prepartum, postpartum and chronic depression effects on infants. *Psychiatry*, **67**, 63–80.

Dieter, J., Field, T., Hernandez-Reif, M., *et al.* (2001). Maternal depression and increased fetal activity. *Journal of Obstetrics and Gynaecology*, **21**, 468–73.

Di Pietro, J. A., Hodgson, D. M., Costigan, K. A., *et al.* (1996). Foetal neurobehavioural development. *Child Development*, **67**, 2553–67.

Downey, G. and Coyne, J. C. (1990). Children of depressed parents: An integrative review. *Psychological Bulletin*, **108**, 50–76.

Egeland, B., Pianta, R., and O'Brian, M. (1993). Maternal intrusiveness in infancy and child maladaptation in early school years. *Development and Psychopathology*, **5**, 359–70.

Eysenck, J. J. (1967). *The biological basis of personality*. Springfield, IL: Thomas.

Field, T. (1985). Attachment as psychobiological attunement: being on the same wavelength. In *Psychobiology of attachment* (ed. M. Reite and T. Field), pp. 415–54. New York, NY: Academic Press.

Field, T. (1992). Infants of depressed mothers. *Development and Psychopathology*, **4**, 49–66.

Field, T. (1995). Infants of depressed mothers. *Infant Behaviour and Development*, **18**, 1–13.

Field, T. (1998). Maternal depression effects on infants and early intervention. *Preventive Medicine*, **27**, 200–3.

Field, T., Diego, M., Hernandez-Reif, M., *et al.* (2001). Depressed, withdrawn and intrusive mothers' effect on their fetuses and neonates. *Infant Behavior and Development*, **24**, 27–39.

Field, T., Healy, B., Goldstein, S., *et al.* (1990). Behaviour state matching and synchrony in mother-infant interactions of nondepressed versus depressed dyads. *Developmental Psychology*, **26**, 7–14.

Field, T., Morrow, C., and Adlestein, D. (1993). 'Depressed' mothers' perceptions of infant behaviour. *Infant Behaviour and Development*, **16**, 99–108.

Field, T., Fox, N., Pickens, J., *et al.* (1995). Right frontal EEG activation in 3- to 6-month-old infants of 'depressed' mothers. *Developmental Psychology*, **31**, 358–63.

Francois, J., Haab, C., Montes de Oca, M., *et al.* (1996). Maternal depression and somatic troubles of the infant. *Psychiatrie de l'Enfant*, **39**, 103–36.

Frankel, K. A. and Harmon, R. J. (1996). Depressed mothers: they don't always look as bad as they feel. *Journal of the American Academy of Child and Adolescent Psychiatry*, **35**, 289–98.

Gitau, R., Cameron, A., Fisk, N., *et al.* (1998). Foetal exposure to maternal cortisol. *Lancet*, **352**, 707.

Glover, V., Teixeira, J., Gitau, R., *et al.* (1999). Mechanisms by which maternal mood in pregnancy may affect the foetus. *Contemporary Reviews in Obstetrics and Gynecology*, **Sept**, 155–60.

Goodman, S. H., Brogan, D., Lynch, M., *et al.* (1993). Social and emotional competence in children of depressed mothers. *Child Development*, **64**, 516–31.

Guedeney, A. (1997). From early withdrawal reaction to infant depression: a baby alone does exist. *Infant Mental Health Journal*, **18**, 339–49.

Hart, S., Field, T., Jones, N. A., *et al.* (1999a). Intrusive and withdrawn behaviours of mothers interacting with their infants and boyfriends. *Journal of child Psychology and Psychiatry*, **40**, 239–45.

Hart, S., Jones, N. A., Field, T., *et al.* (1999b). One-year-old infants of intrusive and withdrawn depressed mothers. *Child Psychiatry and Human Development*, **30**, 111–20.

Henriques, J. B. and Davidson, R. J. (1990). Regional brain electrical asymmetries discriminate between previously depressed and healthy control subjects. *Journal of Abnormal Psychology*, **99**, 22–31.

Hernandez-Reif, M., Field, T., Diego, M., *et al.* (2003). Haptic habituation to temperature is slower in newborns of depressed mothers. *Infancy*, **4**, 47–63.

Hossain, Z. and Roopnarine, J. (1993). Division of household labor and child care in dual-earner African-American families with infants. *Sex Roles*, **29**, 571–83.

Humphrey, T. (1967). Some correlations between the appearance of human foetal reflexes and the development of the nervous system. *Progressive Brain Research*, **4**, 93–135.

Insel, T. R., Kuisley, G., Mam, P., *et al.* (1990). Prenatal stress has long term effects on brain opiate receptors. *Brain Research*, **511**, 93–7.

Jameson, P., Gelfand, D., Kulcsar, E., *et al.* (1997). Mother-toddler interaction patterns associated with maternal depression. *Development and Psychopathology*, **9**, 537–50.

Jones, N. and Field, T. (1999). Right frontal EEG asymmetry is attenuated by massage and music therapy. *Adolescence*, **34**, 529–34.

Jones, N. A., Field, T., and Fox, N. A. (1996a). Greater right frontal EEG activation in one-week-old infants of depressed mothers. *Infant Behaviour and Development*, **21**, 527–30.

Jones, N., Field, T., Fox, N. A., *et al.* (1996b). EEG activation in one-month-old infants of depressed mothers. *Development and Psychopathology*, **9**, 491–505.

Jones, N., Field, T., Fox, N. A., *et al.* (1997a). Infants of intrusive and withdrawn mothers. *Infant Behaviour and Development*, **20**, 17–8.

Jones, N., Field, T., Fox, N. A., *et al.* (1997b). Brain electrical activity stability in infants/children of depressed mothers. *Child Psychiatry and Human Development*, **28**.

Jones, N. A., Field, T., Fox, N. A., *et al.* (1998). Newborns of mothers with depressive symptoms are physiologically less developed. *Infant Behaviour and Development*, **21**, 537–41.

Jones, N., Field, T., and Davalos, M. (2000). Right frontal EEG asymmetry and lack of empathy in preschool children of depressed mothers. *Child Psychiatry and Human Development*, **30**, 189–204.

Jones, N. A., Field, T., Hart, S., *et al.* (2001). Maternal self-perceptions and reactions to infant crying among intrusive and withdrawn depressed mothers. *Infant mental Health Journal*, **22**, 576–86.

Kendler, K. S., Neale, M. C., Kessler, R. C., *et al.* (1992). Familial influences on the clinical characteristics of major depression: a twin study. *Acta Psychiarica Scandinavica*, **86**, 371–8.

Lecanuet, J., Fifer, W. P., Krasnegor, N. A., *et al.* (1995). *Foetal development: a psychobiological perspective*. Hillsdale, NJ: Lawrence Erlbaum Associates, Inc.

Locke, R., Baumgart, S., Locke, K., *et al.* (1997). Effect of maternal depression on premature infant health during initial hospitalization. *Journal of American Osteopathic Association*, **97**, 136–9.

Lou, H. C., Nordentoft, M., Jensen, F., *et al.* (1992). Psychosocial stress and severe prematurity. *Lancet*, **340**, 54.

Lundy, B., Field, T., and Pickens, J. (1996). Newborns of mothers with depressive symptoms are less expressive. *Infant Behaviour and Development*, **19**, 419–24.

Lundy, B., Jones, N. A., Field, T., *et al.* (1998). Prenatal depressive symptoms and neonatal outcome. *Infant Behaviour and Development*, **22**, 121–37.

Luthar, S. and Blatt, S. (1995). Differential vulnerability of dependency and self-criticism among disadvantaged teenagers. *Journal of Research on Adolescence*, **5**, 431–49.

Lyons-Ruth, K., Zoll, D. L., Connell, D., *et al.* (1986). The depressed mother and her one-year-old infant: Environment, interaction, attachment and infant development. In *Maternal depression and infant disturbance* (ed. E. Tronick and T. Field), pp. 61–3. New York, NY: Jossey Bass.

Malphurs, J., Larrain, C. M., Field, T., *et al.* (1996). Altering withdrawn and intrusive interaction behaviours of depressed mothers. *Infant Mental Health Journal*, **17**, 152–60.

McGuffen, P., Owen, M. J., O'Donovan, M. C., *et al.* (1994). *Seminars in psychiatric genetics*. London: Royal College of Psychiatrists.

Mohan, D., Fitzgerald, M., and Collins, C. (1998). The relationship between maternal depression: Antenatal and pre-school stage and childhood behavioural problems. *Irish Journal of Psychological Medicine*, **15**, 10–13.

Murray, L. and Cooper, P. J. (1997). *Postpartum depression and child development*. New York, NY: Guilford Press.

Panaccione, V. F. and Wahler, R. G. (1986). Child behaviour, maternal depression, and social coercion as factors in the quality of care. *Journal of Abnormal Child Psychology*, **14**, 263–78.

Plomin, E., DeFries, J. C., McClearn, G., *et al.* (1997). *Behavioural genetics*. New York, NY: W. H. Freeman.

Raynor, P. and Rudolf, M. (1996). What do we know about children who fail to thrive? *Child: Care, Health and Development*, **22**, 241–50.

Robins, L., Helzer, J., Croughan, J., *et al.* (1981). National Institute of Mental Health Diagnostic Interview Schedule. *Archives of General Psychiatry*, **38**, 381–390.

Rogeness, G. A., Javors, M. A., and Pliszka, S. R. (1992). Neurochemistry and child adolescent psychiatry. *Journal of the American Academy of Child and Adolescent Psychiatry*, **31**, 765–81.

Russell, K. M. (1998). Preschool children at risk for repeat injuries. *Journal of Community Health Nursing*, **15**, 179–90.

Rutter, M., Maughan, B., Meyer, J., *et al.* (1997). Heterogeneity of antisocial behaviour: causes, continuities, and consequences. In *Nebraska Symposium on Motivation*, Vol. **44**, *Motivation and delinquency* (ed. D. W. Osgood), pp. 45–118. Lincoln: University of Nebraska Press.

Runyan, D. K., Hunter, W. M., Everson, M. D., *et al.* (1997). *Longitudinal studies of child abuse and neglect, longscan: the first five years at the coordinating center, North Carolina Site and Seattle Site*. Washington, DC: Clearinghouse on Child Abuse and Neglect Information.

Shaffer. T., Fisher, P., Piacentini, J., *et al.* (1991). *DISC-2.25*. Unpublished manuscript, New York State Psychiatric Institute, New York.

Shiono, P. H. and Klebanoff, M. A. (1993). A review of risk scoring for pre-term birth. *Clinics in Perinatology*, **20**, 107–25.

Sinclair, D. and Murray, L. (1998). Effects of postnatal depression on children's adjustment to school. Teacher's reports. *British Journal of Psychiatry*, **172**, 58–63.

Singer, L. T., Salvator, A., Guo, S., *et al.* (1999). Maternal psychological distress and parenting stress after the birth of a very low-birth-weight infant. *Journal of the American Medical Association*, **281**, 799–805.

Stormont, S. M. and Zentall, S. (1995). Contributing factors in the manifestation of aggression in preschoolers with hyperactivity. *Journal of Child Psychology and Psychiatry and Allied Disciplines*, **36**, 491–509.

Teixeira, J., Fisk, N. and Glover, V. (1999). Association between maternal anxiety in pregnancy and increased uterine artery resistance index: cohort based study. *British Medical Journal*, **318**, 153–7.

Tronick, E. and Field, T. (1986). *Maternal depression and infant disturbance*. San Francisco, CA: Jossey-Bass

Uvnas-Moberg, K. (1997). Oxytocin linked antistress effects—the relaxation and growth response. *Acta Psysiologica Scandinavica*. Supplementum, **640**, 38–42.

Wadhwa, P., Garite, P. D., Porto, M., *et al.* (1998). Maternal corticotropin-releasing hormone levels in the early third trimester predict length of gestation in human pregnancy. *American Journal of Obstetrics and Gynecology*, **179**, 1079–85.

Weinberg, M. and Tronick, E. Z. (1998). The impact of maternal psychiatric illness on infant development. *Journal of Clinical Psychiatry*, **59**, 53–61.

Weiss, J. M., Bonsall, R., Demetrikopoulos, M. K., *et al.* (1998). Galanin: a significant role in depression? *Annals of the New York Academy of Science*, **21**, 364–82.

Weissman, M. and Paykel, E. (1974). *The depressed woman: a study of social relationships*. Chicago: University of Chicago Press.

Wilcox, H., Field, T., Prodromidis, M., *et al.* (1996). Correlations between the BDI and CES-D in a sample of adolescent mothers. *Adolescents*, **33**, 565–74.

Zlochower, A. J. and Cohn, J. F. (1996). Vocal timing in face-to-face interaction of clinically depressed and non-depressed mothers and their 4-month-old infants. *Infant Behaviour and Development*, **19**, 371–4.

Chapter 13

Emotion sharing and emotion knowledge: typical and impaired development

Helene Tremblay, Philippe Brun, and Jacqueline Nadel

In this chapter, we argue that emotional development is a main component of an evolving self–other system. On the same lines as Wallon's theory (Wallon, 1938; see Nadel, 1994, for a review), we propose that infants at start belong to their social world before they belong to themselves. Within this framework, the process in play is one of learning to distinguish what is mine and what is yours, to attribute to others feelings and mental states that are different from ours, through complementary roles, simultaneously gaining both self-awareness and awareness of others. We suggest that the later cognitive ability to decouple what we actually feel and what our face reveals to others is an emerging property of this process. The first 5 years of life may offer a dialectic spiral involving emotional sharing and understanding of emotions as mental states that may differ in self and in others. We present current research showing how these different facets of emotion evolve during infancy and early childhood.

First expectancies: emotional sharing through other's social contingency

During the very first months of life, body movements, tone intensity, and facial expressions have an emotional value for others, and affective encounters with others create the best context for emotional sharing (Bruner, 1975), but is it enough to start building the self–other distinction (Neisser, 1999; Stern, 1993, Trevarthen *et al.*, 1999)?

We suggest that the infants' ability to extract contingency from emotional interaction leads them to anticipate interactivity and agency as the main distinction between what the self does and what another does. Expecting contingency may be considered as a first milestone in the development of a capacity to attribute intentionality to others. The underlying proposition is that typical young infants, far from being solely reactive to emotional contingency, also are contingency expectant.

How does one test such an option before language develops? A solution is to offer non-contingent interaction to infants (Gusella *et al.*, 1988; see Muir and Nadel, 1998, for a review). To do so, two types of designs are available: designs that disrupt the interactive flow by posing a Still face, and designs that manipulate technically the interactive flow. The later are televised devices pioneered by Murray and Trevarthen (1985). More recently, we improved on their procedure with our equipment inspired by teleprompter technique. This new device allows us to maintain a continuous interactive flow between the mother's behaviour, and to present to the infant either a contingent episode of her mother's interaction, or a non-contingent voice with a contingent face, or a non-contingent face with a contingent voice, or a non-contingent episode for both face and voice. In our non-contingent replay studies, instead of stopping a videotaped interaction, rewinding the video recording and then presenting the replay to the young infant, we presented our infants with a seamless shift from contingent to non-contingent maternal behaviour followed by a seamless shift from non-contingent to contingent maternal interaction.

When mothers interacted with their 2-month-old infants through this device, the results were clear-cut. We found frequent gaze to mother, smile and imitation during the maternal contingent episode, as Fig. 13.1 shows, while the infants gazed away and displayed intense negative emotional reactions during non-contingent maternal interactions, as illustrated by Fig. 13.2. An increase in attention to the mother was noted during the second contingent episode, compared to the first one (Nadel *et al.*, 1999a). The increase in infant visual attention during the second contingent episode suggested to us that infants were engaged in a careful exploration of their newly contingent mother; perhaps it was a necessary precursor to re-engaging in communication after a significant disruption in maternal behaviour.

Gaze away during replay indicated that the infants detected non-contingency. Negative emotional reactions during replay were seen as an index of infant's disappointment when facing a non-contingent mother. Is this a general picture of how early

Fig. 13.1 Positive emotional sharing at 2 months during a TV contingent interaction with mother.

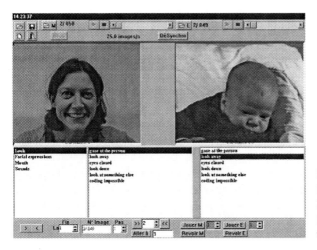

Fig. 13.2 Negative emotional responses of a 2-month-old boy to a TV non-contingent interaction with mother.

emotional sharing works as a detector of social contingency and of social agency, or are there conditions that favour or even support the rise of expectancies in infants as young as 2 months of age?

Infants at risk

Maternal depression offers a research case for further knowledge concerning such questions. Indeed, in the case of depression, maternal partnership is disturbed by personal problems, which may lessen the attention given to the infant's emotional tone and willingness to share emotions. What is the effect of repeatedly experiencing occasional non-contingent behaviour on the development of the infants' ability to form expectancies? When infants of depressed mothers were presented with the non-contingent episode, they lessened their visual attention to the mother (which indicates that they detected non-contingency), but did not show negative emotional reactions. This finding with 2-month-olds totally converges with Field (1984)'s results with 3-month-olds. Field showed that infants with depressed mothers differed significantly from infants of non-depressed mothers, in that they did not show any change in ECG rate when their mother displayed a non-contingent (still) face.

If infants do not protest, it does not follow that they are not upset. On the contrary, it may well be that their capacity to expect is in danger. Field argues that the effects of long exposure to stress, likely to generate passive and depressed coping strategies. This hypothesis implicitly relies on the distinction between interactions and relations (Nadel, 2002a). In cases of durable relationships between partners, the interactions developed take account of past history. Infants of depressed mothers have a past history of relative unresponsiveness on the part of their mother. Infants of non-depressed mothers have no past history of this kind. Within this framework, infants of depressed mothers may be thought to have learnt early to disengage from stressful situations on which they have no control.

Table 13.1 Communicative patterns of healthy and depressed mothers interacting with their 2-month-old infants via audiovideo monitors

Behaviours	ND mothers	p	D mothers
% Gaze	96.4	—	93.2
	(3.6)		(3.3)
% Smile	90.7	—	68.3
	(27.7)		(24.4)
% Speak	92.5	—	75.7
	(6.0)		(20.2)
%Motherese	82.5	**	27.2
	(2.4)		(43.6)
% Imitate	11.6	**	0.7
	(6.7)		( )

** p < 0.001

Televised communication of depressed mothers was compared with those of non-depressed mothers. Depressed and non-depressed mothers similarly gazed, smiled, and spoke to their infant. However, depressed mothers rarely comment synchronously upon their infant's behaviour by motherese or imitation, like non-depressed mothers do.

Besides the influence of past history, some features of depressed maternal behaviour may contribute to cause the infants to be emotionally insensitive to non-contingency. Comparing the communicative behaviour of depressed and non-depressed mothers for 40/100 seconds, we found no difference between the two groups concerning the amount of gaze, smile, and speech. However, as shown in Table 13.1, microcontingent behaviours, namely 'motherese' and imitation were significantly less used by depressed mothers. We considered 'motherese' and 'imitation' as microcontingent behaviours because they require a moment-by-moment attention to any emotional, gestural, and vocal expression of the child. Motherese has been described as a marker of synchrony, as far as it is a verbal comment of the on-going state of the infant (Stern, 1977). Imitation may be considered as an almost perfect search of behavioural synchrony (Gergely and Watson, 1999).

We concluded that depressed mothers do not offer many synchronous signals to their infants, which may lessen the infant's sensitivity to synchrony. Murray's findings (1992) fit with this suggestion: her longitudinal studies showed long-lasting problems of social attunement and self- assertiveness in children with depressed mothers.

Appreciation of others' emotions

As noted above, dyadic contexts are classical ways to explore the early signals of awareness of other's emotional contingency. A new procedure involves studying infant response to social interactions within triads (Nadel and Tremblay-Leveau, 1999). This procedure is based on the general claim in socio-cognitive development that there is a shift around 8–9 months when social interaction between an infant and another may be extended to include a third event in the environment. At this age, infants begin to appreciate the environmental target of the other person's emotional reaction, and can understand if the referent of the adult's gaze behaviour is either an object (Scaife and Bruner, 1975) or a person. It was first suggested that the opening of the communicative structure to a third element stood as a precursor of language development (Bruner, 1981). Today, developmental models propose, in addition, that joint attention and joint activities are early markers of the infant's understanding of attentional mental states that can be predictive of the other's actions and intentions (Baron-Cohen, 1995; Barresi and Moore, 1996; Tomasello, 1999).

If the cognitive and meta-cognitive facets of the triadic communicative structure have been well triggered, others aspects have been neglected. Two striking omissions surround the study of the triadic communicative development. First, very few researchers focused on the very young infants' abilities not only to experience, but also to master triadic communication. Secondly, the interest allowed to the emotional load embedded in triadic exchanges concerned mainly joint activities of an adult and an infant toward an object (Bates *et al.*, 1975; Bruner, 1981; Adamson and Bakeman, 1985; Mundy *et al.*, 1992; Mundy, 1995); rarely have joint activities of the participants toward a third person been studied, although it is a common experience in the infants' social world, i.e. when friends and strangers are visiting.

One attempt to fill the gap in our knowledge was made by Fivaz-Depeursinge and Corboz-Warnery (1999), who studied communicative and affective aspects of the mother–father–infant triangle. The paradigm involved observing the three actors in four successive 1–2-minute settings and is proto-typical of a family life: two successive dyadic parent–child interaction in the presence of the other parent as a kindly observer, a triadic father–mother–child interaction followed by a father–mother conversation with the child as an observer. The results of studies of both clinical and non-clinical families suggest that, by 3 months of age, infants perceive tensions and conflicts between parents, alternate their attention between both parents, produce emotional and communicative signals towards each or both parents, and express relevant emotional signals as a function of the parents' attitudes (Fivaz-Depeursinge and Corboz-Warnery, 1999).

What if the social triad is not the family unit? To test this question, one of us created a design that allows the appreciation of the infant's emotional behaviour according to the nature of the triadic context. Eleven 3-month-old infants were observed in two triadic conditions: one with an infant, an adult, and an object (person-person-object, PPO condition), another with an infant and two adults that were familiar to the infant, but not caregivers (person-person-person, PPP condition). In both conditions, the adult interacted with the infant until she turned her attention towards the object (PPO condition) or towards the second adult (PPP condition). The infants produced significantly more socially-directed behaviours in the PPP condition ($M = 1.5$) than in the PPO condition ($M = 0.8$). When examining the nature of the socially-directed behaviours that redirected the adult's attention towards the infant, it was observed that 3-month-old infants doubled socially-directed facial and bodily movements in the condition where the adult talked to another adult ($M = 2.0$) compared to the condition where the adult talked to an object ($M = 1.1$). Such behavioural differences according to the context suggest that 3-month-olds already capture the interactive nature of human encounters and are much more motivated to participate when the triadic context is a social one. Their sensitivity to species-specific emotional patterns of interaction may play a formative role in the development of referential communication (Bruner, 1975; Baron-Cohen, 1989; Tager-Flusberg, 1989; Karmiloff-Smith, 1992) and in the development of emotional knowledge.

Sharing emotion and self-awareness

Typical development

By the end of the first year of life, in social encounters infants tackle the same question of identity within emotional context, but the social means to assert it are more sophisticated. For instance, they are now able to take account of their position in a social triad to pilot successfully others' attention into communication with self. Our 'exclusion' design allows us to uncover evidence of the infant's growing sensitivity to the question of 'who shares with whom'(Tremblay-Leveau and Nadel, 1995, 1996). With this design, two familiar infants of the same age meet an acquainted experimenter who interacts with only one of them. Thus, one of the infants is included in an interaction with the adult, while the other is excluded from the ongoing interaction. As soon as the excluded infant has efficiently commanded the adult's attention, the adult turns toward her, excluding from her attention the infant that was her previous unique partner. This way, both infants are successively included and excluded, and we are able to compare their social behaviours in the two conditions.

Studies were conducted with children aged 11, 16, and 23 months. Comparisons of bodily movements of the same infant when excluded and when included provide developmental evidence of a repertoire adapted to the interactive position of the child in a multi-participant context. When included, the infant devoted her attention to the interactive adult, while she gazed alternatively at the adult and at the other infant when excluded. When excluded, the infant proposed new targets to the occupied infant and adult, while when included the infant was totally involved in turn-taking with the adult. Even if the attempts to involve the two others in a new topic were more numerous in the older infants, 11 month-olds were already able to act this way.

What we would like to emphasize here is that these triadic social encounters were not only playful, but also loaded of positive emotion mainly when children tried to attract the two others' attention in order to be included in the communicative flow. Two aspects of children's behaviours were particularly significant at this regard. The first one concerned 'showing-off' behaviours, considered as social behaviours that typically induce emotional interactions (Bates et al., 1975; Reddy, 1991; Reddy, this volume). The second one concerned emotional facial expressiveness addressed to the two other partners.

Table 13.2 Gestural and emotional initiatives in (relative frequency for infant)

	Age		
	11 months	16 months	23 months
Handles the target of the	33	**28	19
interacting dyad	(3.1)	(1.1)	(4.9)
Referrential gestures	20	28	35
	(7.0)	(5.8)	(9.12)
Showing-off gestures	31	24	32
	(4.2)	(2.5)	(3.5)
Smiles	20	37	29
	(2.8)	(4.0)	(4.1)
	****	****	**
Laughs	1	4	18
	(0.9)	(1.58)	(3.0)
	*	*/*	****
Protest	8	8	** 3
	(1.5)	(1.0)	(1)

* <.05   ** <.02   */* <.02   *** <.001   **** <.0005

During the momentary exclusion period, as shown in Table 13.2, a third of the social gestures directed toward the two others were showing-off gestures such as banging objects repetitively, jumping, making funny noises, laughing noisily. These data suggest a remarkably precocious understanding of the fact that, when excluded from an ongoing interaction, the best is to focus on the actual script of the dyad, in order to complement it with functional or referential and declarative gestures. Infants also understand early that they can disrupt the others' attention by the means of funny show-off gestures, which will be accepted as positive initiatives. Even more, positive triadic affect increased significantly during the second year, while negative emotional expressions were rarely produced.

Atypical development

It has been suggested that children with autism may show quite normal understanding of facial, vocal and gestural expression of emotions but may not normally recognize intentions of con-specifics in their affective interactions, which would further interfere with the development of a theory of mind (Baron-Cohen, 1991; Karmiloff-Smith, 1992).

In an attempt to explore this hypothesis, Tremblay used the 'Person-Person-Person' (P-P-P) versus 'person-person-object' (PPO) design for young infants previously described. Eight low-functioning and non-verbal children with autism diagnosed according to DSM-IV and the Child Autistic Rating Scale (CARS; Schopler *et al.*, 1988), participated to the study. They were aged 4.7–11.2 and their mental age ranged from 12 to 24 months according to Psychoeducational Profile-R (Schopler and Reichler, 1979). Gaze to the experimenter was significantly higher in the PPP condition than in the PPO condition. All children modified their visual attention and their social behaviours when the interactive adult turned her attention towards either the object or the other person. However, they produced more frequent behaviour such as taking the adult's hand or making eye contact to the occupied adult in the PPP context ($M = 11$) than in the PPO context ($M = 3.8$). Another notable difference according to the triadic context concerned positive affective expressions ($M = 8.0$) in the PPP condition versus the PPO condition ($M = 2.0$).

These results pointed out a paradox: in the PPP context, more than in the PPO context, children with autism acted markedly as if they dissociated attentional sharing and referential sharing. It was not the rupture of the interactive synchrony that entailed the production of ostensible behaviours accompanied by facial emotional expressions, since the eight children, in or out of an ongoing affective interaction, reacted more precisely to the change of the ongoing adults' attentional flow. This is in agreement with findings by Mundy *et al.* (1986) who showed that autistic children tended to address similar or even higher amount of social behaviours with eye contact to a quiet or inactive adult than to an interactive one. The same phenomenon was observed in the separation paradigm (Shapiro *et al.*, 1987; Capps *et al.*, 1994). In contrast, efforts to actually participate in an active communicative structure, with the production of socially-directed behaviours referred to an object or a person, were seldom in the two conditions.

These works suggest that, for children with autism, emotional activation arises when humans in dyadic or triadic social contexts do not directly look, talk, or express emotions at them. The main social experiences may be limited to passive, quiet or indirect emotional interaction, just as the main experiences specific to non-social environment may be limited to requesting versus indicating behaviours (Mundy, 1995). This kind of interaction with others is not referential, but enhances an affective process that may lay foundations for an understanding of contingency via emotional sharing. Such appreciation is suggested by the results of one of our experiment conducted with a revised version of the Still face paradigm (Nadel *et al.*, 2000) described next.

Sharing emotion and awareness of other as an interactive agent

Typical development

Posing a Still Face generates a violation of basic principles of social contingency (Cohn and Tronick, 1982; Murray and Trevarthen, 1985; Tronick, this volume). Classically, it is part of a three-condition design posed by the mother in the following order: contingent–non-contingent–contingent episode. The episodes are of equal duration. During the non-contingent episode, the mother poses a Still Face, whatever the infant's behaviour. As early as 2 months of age, the infant of a healthy mother will gaze away, withdraw, and look upset: her negative response to the Still Face informs us about her capacity to detect non-contingency. It is one thing, however, to detect contingency and another to expect contingency as a general property of human behaviour. When infants start expecting contingency from strangers, they demonstrate that they are aware of a specific feature of human beings: intentional interactivity. By 5–6 months of age, infants react negatively to strangers who stare at them with a Still Face (e.g. Rochat and Striano, 1999) and to strangers who display non-contingent social signals (Hains and Muir, 1996).

Atypical development

If children with autism generally ignore strangers and seem to appreciate passive persons, it may be because they have not formed an understanding of what to expect from human beings. One test of this question we developed is an examination of their reaction to a revised version of the Still Face paradigm. Our modified design is also composed of three 3-minute episodes, but this time the first period is a Still Face episode (SF1) followed by an Imitative Interaction (II), followed by a second Still Face episode (SF2), all acted by a stranger. Such a modification allows us to evaluate whether the children will react negatively to the first non-contingent behaviour (SF1) of a person that they have never experienced as a contingent partner. If so, this demonstrates that they have formed general expectancies about human intentional interactivity during face-to-face engagements. Additionally, the design answers the question addressed by the classical version of the still paradigm: does the child detect a change from a contingent (II) to a non-contingent (SF2) episode?

In a pilot study including eight low-functioning non-verbal children with autism and eight MA matched typical children, we found that the children with autism (mean Developmental Age, $M = 30$ months) all ignored the stranger and did not show any concern about her still behaviour during the first Still episode (Fig. 13.4a). After a 3-minute imitative interaction of the stranger, during the second Still episode, the children showed contingency awareness when they displayed strong negative reactions to the violation of contingency reactions from the stranger. Indeed, the strong differences in autistic social behaviours that were found between the two Still Face conditions suggest that the adult had to prove to be a contingent partner before some social expectancy can take place. This contrasts strongly with the reactions of 30-month-olds, who tried to get in touch with the Still Face stranger, and then left the room or even refused from the start to stay alone in the room with her. In a recent study led by Maurer and Nadel, children with Down Syndrome, matched on Developmental Age with the autistic group, also showed strong aversive reactions to the Still Face stranger: they alternately gazed at the stranger and then hid their faces, stood far away from the stranger, and expressed negative emotions of fear or angst, after short attempts to interact (Figs. 13.3 and 13.4b).

An important aspect to underline concerns the interactive episode: indeed, all children with autism paid much more attention to the stranger during this episode, and displayed some positive reaction to their being imitated. As imitation is a case of almost perfect contingency, this may explain why they were able to form some social expectancy for

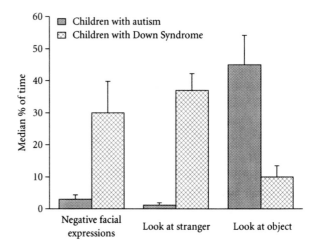

Fig. 13.3 Comparison of behaviours of MA-matched children with autism and children with Down Syndrome during the first Still Face of a stranger.

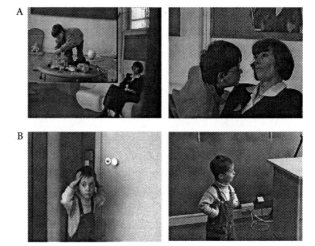

Fig. 13.4 Facing a still stranger in a room furnished with attractive toys. (A) A child with autism. (B) A child with Down Syndrome.

contingency after only three minutes of exposure to an interaction with the stranger. To explore this question, another study was conducted using the same revised paradigm to evaluate the effect of an imitative interaction compared to a non-imitative interaction. In that study, the group of children who were imitated spent more time being close to the adult and touching the adult during the second Still Face period, and also showed significantly more negative facial expressions (Escalona *et al.*, 2000). We conclude that this reflects the children expressing more of disappointed expectancy when the experimenter has been an imitator. The role of imitation in the development of tight relationships is evaluated in a second study with repeated imitation sessions, where we found that social behaviours, like looking at the adult, smiling and vocalizing toward the adult, as well as recognizing being imitated increased significantly throughout the sessions (Field *et al.*, 2001).

In summary, our results suggest that low-functioning children with autism do not form a generalized expectancy for contingency when they face strangers, but they do enjoy synchronous behaviours from strangers, and come to expect sharing synchrony after they experience a contingent engagement with strangers, especially ones who imitate them. Consequently, if children are able to develop expectancies for imitation, they therefore are able to recognize been imitated. They can establish a relationship between self and other's actions, link self-agency to other's agency, and feel emotions conveyed by bodily postures seen in others. From there, a sense of feeling the same, of experiencing the same, of sharing, arises. As there exists a strong link between the ability to imitate and to recognize being imitated, we expect autistic children to be able to use the imitative system as a way to communicate (Nadel, 2002b).

Self and other cohering through an objective motive for shared emotion

Before mastering language, children communicate with their age-peers via postural imitation (Nadel, 1986; Nadel-Brulfert and Baudonnière, 1982). Postures have two functions: they scaffold movements in the physical world and they generate expressive signals toward the human world. Not surprisingly, postural imitation also has two functions: it helps children learn new procedures (Gergely *et al.*, 2002) and it facilitates sharing mental representations of emotions. Using our paradigm of identical sets of objects, we provided evidence that the children's target during synchronic imitations is to match the other's bodily postures. Children imitated clumsiness, failures to achieve a goal, as well as successful novel or familiar actions. The highly significant increase in smiling and laughter in dyads of 2-year-olds when two sets of ten similar objects were available, instead of one set of twenty different objects, shows the efficiency of synchronic imitation to share others' emotions and scripts before the use of language (Nadel, 2002b). Gestural imitation is not simply a social behaviour that attracts and focuses social attention. It also presents the key-features of a language in so far as it involves shared monitoring of synchrony, shared monitoring of turn-taking between imitator and model, explicit understanding of the partner's intentionality to be imitated or to imitate, and joint attention to the same topic via the use of identical objects (Nadel *et al.*, 1999b). For these reasons, imitative language may be seen as a late achievement of the like-me mechanism (Meltzoff and Gopnik, 1993). Both gestural and vocal imitation require some cognitive and meta-cognitive ingredients, such as the capacities to attribute intentions to the model, to plan and produce imitative behaviours, to understand cues to imitate the model's actions, and to negotiate turn-taking and role-switching. Imitation allows children to represent events, roles, and pretend goals and feelings. It adds a representational dimension to emotional sharing.

Emotion knowledge in self and other

Typical development

By 3 years of age, children start renewing their representational abilities to talk about or to label emotional states apart from a here-and-now emotional context. They undertake a cognitive re-description of their first emotional inter-subjective experiences. They start developing a complex knowledge of emotions that favour cognitive appraisal of events, and emotional adjustment to social contexts. Harris (1989) suggests that emotion knowledge and, in particular, emotion mind-reading capacity is one aspect of the general knowledge of mind in children. In a similar vein, Lemerise and Arsenio (2000), inspired by Crick and Dodge's model (1994), propose that social and emotional understanding of behaviours and events require emotion processes to be combined with cognitive processes. Halberstadt *et al.* (2001) see emotion knowledge as an important part of a capacity to appropriately identify and interpret emotional information expressed by others, and by themselves, according to the context. Saarni's model (1999) of emotional competence also stresses the role of cognitive and metacognitive aspects, such as the awareness of one's emotional state, the ability to discern and understand others' emotions, to use emotion words, to show empathic involvement, to differentiate emotional mental states from emotional expressions, and to cope with aversive or distressing emotional events.

The cognitive and metacognitive factors of emotional development should not lead however to forget that emotion knowledge is embedded in biological substrates (Panksepp, 1998, this volume) and in inter-subjective sharing (Trevarthen, 1993, this volume). The re-description of emotional experiences is not a solitary cognitive adventure. It is a novel way to share emotions with others through the elaboration of scripts inspired by past emotional history and pretend future events.

Emotions are verbally expressed

A number of studies have investigated the development of children's abilities to talk about emotions (Bretherton *et al.*, 1986; Bullock and Russell, 1986), to verbally identify basic emotions from facial and contextual cues (Field and Walden, 1982; Reichenbach and Masters, 1983), or to label mixed emotions pictures (Kestenbaum, and Gelman, 1995). Recently, Russell and Widen (2002) investigated the nature of the mental category evoked by a facial expression of emotion in children aged 2–7 years. Using a non-narrative sorting task (emotion categories were presented to children as boxes into which people who feel only a certain way could go), they showed that emotion labels resulted in more accurate categorization than did the corresponding facial expression. According to Russell and Widen (2002), this superiority of labelling feelings over faces suggests that the role of emotion labels in children's construct of emotion knowledge needs to be considered further.

Intersubjective emotional contexts are explicitly commented

Dunn *et al.* (1991) focused on capacities of children from 3 to 6 years of age and their mothers to talk about causes and consequences of emotional mental states. They observed that mothers' speech about emotion can improve emotion perspective-taking in children.

Several studies stressing the inextricable link between emotional competence and social competence have shown that preschool children can identify emotion-eliciting situations, and can make inferences about the relationships between these emotion-eliciting situations and appropriate basic expressions of emotions (Denham, 1986; Gross and Ballif, 1991; Dunn and Hughes, 1998; Smith and Walden, 1998; LaFreniere, 2000; Denham *et al.*, 2003).

Cutting and Dunn (2002) investigated the still unclear relation between false-belief understanding and emotion understanding in 4-year-olds. Children's meta-cognitive knowledge appeared to be highly correlated with their understanding of the emotional consequences of social events. They argued that false belief competence and emotion understanding may be considered as related, but distinct dimensions of social cognition.

Emotional states are distinct from other mental states

Young preschool children start understanding that emotional mental states of others can differ from their own. Around 30 months, they can infer connections between desires, perceptive behaviours, and emotions in others (Wellman *et al.*, 2000). At three, they are able to predict a protagonist's emotion based on the protagonist's desire (Harris *et al.*, 1989; Wellman, 1990). However, their capacity to infer others' emotions can be influenced by their own desire (Rieffe *et al.*, 2001). Bratmetz and Schneider (1999) discussed the status of emotion attributed to a desire that is counterfactually satisfied. Rather than a conception of emotional response as an expression of irrational thinking, their data support a conception linking desire, belief, and emotion.

Emotional mental states are differentiated (decoupled) from emotional expressions

There is a growing body of evidence showing the development of preschoolers' decoupling (or dissemblance) competence (Denham, 1998; Saarni, 1999). They are able to exhibit facial expressions of emotions that do not correspond to their emotional mental states (Saarni, 1984; Underwood *et al.*, 1992; Zeman and Garber, 1996; Garner, 1999; McDowell *et al.*, 2000; Parker *et al.*, 2001). Children of 7 years old also learn to hide negative emotions and pose positive expressions when this pattern of emotional displays is socially appropriate (Saarni, 1984). Preschoolers' dissemblance knowledge appears not to be dependent on their facial expression knowledge (Garner, 1999) and is preferentially used in the presence of an adult (Cole, 1986; Josephs, 1994; Soussignan *et al.*, 1995).

The development of children's dissemblance capacity may be evaluated also through their understanding of the distinction between real and apparent emotions. For instance, Harris (1989) asked preschoolers to say how the protagonist in stories appeared to feel and how he really felt. Four-year-olds, as well as six-year-olds, demonstrated their understanding of the distinction between real and apparent emotions.

Emotional mental states can be bodily expressed

Another way to test children's decoupling capacity is to ask children to display labeled facial expressions of emotions in the absence of any emotional event. Using a task created by Loveland *et al.* (1995), Brun (1999) asked 80 children from 3 to 6 years of age to express facial expressions of happiness, anger, sadness, surprise labelled by an adult. At age 3, children successfully expressed happiness only. Anger and sadness were not successfully displayed before 6 years of age. Hence, the capacity to evoke negative emotions appears late in development just as the dissemblance competence of negative expressions, mentioned earlier.

A similar pattern of performances was observed in another group of 80 children, aged 3–6, who were asked to express the facial expression corresponding to a vocal expression of happiness, surprise, anger, or sadness. For all age groups, only the percentage of correct responses concerning happiness were significantly different from chance responses. Anger, sadness, fear and surprise were far from being successfully expressed even at 6 years (Brun, 2001).

Atypical development

A focus on emotion knowledge is also noticeable in the field of developmental psychopathology. For instance, Izard *et al.* (2001) have shown that emotion knowledge can be considered as a good predictor of social and academic competence in children at risk. Turk and Cornish (1998) have explored facial and vocal recognition of emotions and emotion understanding in boys with fragile-X syndrome. Hosie *et al.* (1998) examined emotion understanding capacities in preschool deaf and hearing children. Smith and Walden (1999) compared emotion knowledge performances of maltreated and non-maltreated preschool children. In all these studies, no difference between groups was noted. By contrast, a number of studies have found impairments of emotion knowledge in children with mental retardation (Stewart and Singh, 1995; Moore, 2001), in socially anxious children (Melfsen and Florin, 2002), in children with externalizing behaviour disorders (Egan *et al.*, 1998), and in children with Down syndrome (Kasari *et al.*, 2001, 2003).

Children with autism also show impaired emotion knowledge and social understanding (Snow *et al.*, 1987; Sigman *et al.*, 1992; Loveland *et al.*, 1995, 2001; Celani *et al.*, 1999; Travis *et al.*, 2001). Hobson (1993) has developed an emotional theory to account for the autistic children's impaired emotional knowledge. Hobson suggests that children with autism are specifically deficient early in their expressiveness and later in their emotion knowledge, and therefore in their Theory of Mind understanding. In order to test this hypothesis, Hobson (1986a,b) had children with autism and typical children match facial expressions of emotions to auditory expressions of emotion, and also label facial expressions of emotions (Hobson *et al.*, 1989), and react to emotion-related concepts (Hobson and Lee, 1989). This series of studies showed that children with autism, with a mental age of between 5 and 7 years have severe difficulties to perform emotional tasks, hence, supporting the hypothesis of a specific emotional impairment in autism. However, several studies have failed to replicate Hobson's findings when the autistic group's performance was compared with that of children matched on mental age (Braverman *et al.*, 1989; Prior *et al.*, 1990) and that of typical preschool children (Brun *et al.*, 1998).

Emotion knowledge has also been tested in high-functioning children with pervasive disorders of the autistic spectrum. An impairment was found in the ability to draw a coherent relation between a situation and an emotional state (Rieffe *et al.*, 2000). Similarly, understanding that emotion may originate from beliefs was shown to be specifically difficult for children with autism, while understanding that emotion is caused by desires and events was not different in the MA-matched group of mentally retarded adolescents (Baron-Cohen, 1991).

In order to investigate what about emotion is specifically impaired in children with autism, Brun (2003) asked children with autism (MA = 3 years) to pose facial expressions of emotions (happiness, anger, sadness, fear, or surprise) corresponding to vocal emotional stimuli. Children's expressions were videotaped and analysed with the coding scale proposed by Loveland and colleagues (Loveland *et al.*,1994). Data were coded by two independent coders (Cohen's kappa: 0.84). Brun reported that emotional performances of children with autism were similar to those of typical 3-year-olds, i.e. children who have not mastered the ability to represent emotions out of context (Fig. 13.5). This suggests that there is a need for further investigation of how children with autism react to emotions in context. We have seen earlier that even low-functioning

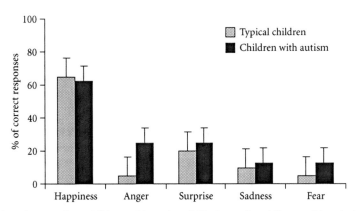

Fig. 13.5 Posed expressions children with autism (MA: 3 years) and 3-year-old typical children.

children with autism react to an occupied adult and initiate interaction toward a Still Face adult that has previously been interactive. They are sensitive to emotional contingency. It remains to assess whether their emotional impairment is a primary impairment, as hypothesized by Hobson, or a secondary impairment, due to a paucity of social experience and an impoverished representation of social experiences.

Final comments

Some movements of the face and of the body differ from the others for the sole reason that they express. Darwin (1872) did not fail to notice this point and made it one of the key-criteria of evolution. However, his perspective did not immediately cause a disappearance of the powerful Cartesian tradition, which attributes devastating results to emotion. Wallon (1934), following Darwin, opened up a functionalist perspective where the developmental role of emotions is to scaffold the building of a meta-representational inner world composed of motives, emotional representations, logical predictions, and causal inferences that deeply influence the interactions with the social world (see Nadel, 1994, for a review). Finally, we have recently learnt from cognitive and neurocognitive sciences that emotion is a complex phenomenon involving brain activity, physiological and behavioural reactions, providing informations about current situations, representations of what is felt by self, and what others can observe of our emotional outputs. How do these different facets of emotion evolve throughout infancy and early childhood?

In this chapter, we argued that emotional development is a main component of the self–other system, and evolves through early social and affective encounters. Early in development, young infants can detect and discriminate others' emotional engagement. Infants expect emotional resonance from others. On the one hand, infants' emotional expressions are easily understood since they look similar to adults' expressions (see Oster, this volume). On the other hand, infants' implicit understanding of emotions in others is an early component of sensitivity to social contingency. Emotional sharing is a primitive aspect of communication (Wallon, 1934; Bruner, 1981); however, there may be facets of emotional sharing during the first and the second year of life, which have been neglected by researchers. Sharing the other's emotional presence, sharing their emotional engagement for an object of interest or sharing their concern for another person are examples of experiences that emerge simultaneously with emotional behaviour: that is, with the construction of self–other concepts. At this point, the function of emotion is to guarantee the process of intuitive evaluation of self and other, which assures behavioural regulation and communication with others.

We suggest that a decisive turning point occurs around the end of the second year. Now the function of emotion evolves into a process that not only permits the evaluation of the consequences of another's behaviour, but also aids in the prediction of another's emotional behaviour. Indeed imitative communication between peers illustrates how 2-year-old children skillfully, but cautiously, integrate the peer's non-verbal means, mimics, postures, gestural, and vocal features in order to distribute and maintain (and eventually resume if the prediction was false) communicative roles between themselves and their peers. The advance observed here is the redescription of prior emotional experiences organized by children themselves through imitative communication.

Then another change concerning emotion arises. Around 4 years of age, a revolution occurs that is related to an emerging capacity to represent emotions, to decouple emotional expressions displayed and expressions felt, and to react to disembedded emotions. The function of emotion now serves to edify an enlarged map of human encounters, including evaluating emotional indices, elaborating factual and mental predictions about emotional behaviours, and conceiving plans for virtual emotional encounters.

When expression and understanding of emotions are impaired, social exchanges are deeply altered. Impairment in emotional knowledge also has important consequences for social interactions. However, it is important to note that children with autism are not completely ignorant about self–other construction, communication and emotion. When opportunities are correctly given, children with autism can detect and discriminate other's emotional engagement, can expect emotional resonance from others, can take into account the other's concern for another person, can distribute and maintain imitative communicative roles, and can even evaluate disembedded emotional indices. The main difficulty of children with autism is that they seem dependent of here-and-now emotional cues without creating relations between prior and future events (see Loveland, this volume).

In future studies, researchers need to compare emotional behaviour when embedded in self–other (interactive) systems and when disembedded. This is an important task to fulfill, especially if we want to know more about the link between emotional experience and emotional knowledge. Only a handful of designs are available to study emotions in communicative context. We have adapted or designed four of them so that they can be used with infants before language operates, and with non-verbal children. By contrast, numerous designs are available that use disembedded perceptual or verbal stimuli to explore the capacities to discriminate or represent emotions without an interactive context. A neglect follows in the investigation of the children's evolving repertory of emotional responses in communicative context. In addition, the paucity of designs allowing the study of emotions within social contexts limits the exploration of emotional experience in children that have representational impairments, like children with autism and other developmental psychopathologies.

At this point, we expect important advances to be generated by the use of hypermedia techniques, which will allow, in the near future, to picture virtual environments simulating real emotional events. Virtual environments are interesting experimental tools because they allow us to control and manipulate parameters of the self–other system that may inform about necessary conditions of emotional involvement. Already some studies are in progress with young infants facing a virtual adult (see Muir *et al.*, this volume) and with persons with an Asperger Syndrome facing social events in a virtual environment (Parsons and Mitchell, 2002). No doubt, the study of emotion in typical and impaired development will benefit from these technical advances. Robots also provide consistent new methodological tools (Dautenhahn, 1999), especially when we plan to compare interactions with mechanical animates to interactions with biological animates: for instance, in front of a mechanical animate designed by Viezzi and Gaussier so as to protrude its tongue, 6-month-olds complain or cry while they smile in front of a human face producing the same tonguing (Nadel and Revel, 2003). So far, artifacts are excellent tools and models, as convincingly stressed by Canamero and Gaussier (this volume), and affective computing will certainly add valuable information to our understanding of emotional mechanisms. However, it may do little to improve our understanding of the infants' and children's ability to share and expect another's emotional behaviour. For we need partners to feel: mapping our own behaviours onto that of another person's behaviour is a unique way to experience the other's and our own emotions.

References

Adamson, L. and Bakeman, R. (1985). Affect and attention: infants observed with mothers and peers. *Child Development*, **56**, 582–93.

Baron-Cohen, S. (1989). Joint-attention deficits in autism: toward a cognitive analysis. *Development and Psychopathology*, **3**, 185–90.

Baron-Cohen, S. (1991). Do people with autism understand what causes emotion? *Child Development*, **62**, 385–95.

Baron-Cohen, S. (1995). *Mindblindness: an essay on autism and theory of mind*. Cambridge, MA: MIT Press/Bradford Books.

Barresi, J. and Moore, C. (1996). Intentional relations and social understanding. *Behavioural and Brain Sciences*, **19**, 107–54.

Bates, E., Camaioni, L., and Volterra, V. (1975). The acquisition of performatives prior to language. *Merrill-Palmer Quarterly*, **21**, 205–24.

Bradmetz, J. and Schneider, R. (1999). Is Little Red Hiding Hood afraid by her grand mother? Cognitive versus emotional response to a false belief. *British Journal of Developmental Psychology*, **17**, 501–14.

Braverman, M., Fein, D., Lucci, D., *et al.* (1989). Affect comprehension in children with pervasive developmental disorders. *Journal of Autism and Developmental Disorders*, **19(2)**, 301–16.

Bretherton, I., Fritz, J., Zahn-Waxler, C., *et al.* (1986). Learning to talk about emotions: A functionalist perspective. *Child Development*, **57**, 529–48.

Brun, Ph. (1999). L'évocation des expressions faciales émotionnelles chez le jeune enfant et chez l'enfant autiste. *Bulletin de l'ARAPI*, **4**, 37–40.

Brun, Ph. (2001). Psychopathologie des émotions chez l'enfant: l'importance des données développementales typiques. *Enfance*, **3**, 281–91.

Brun, Ph. (2003). *Posed expressions of emotions in typical preschool children and in children with autism*. Poster presented at the XIth European Conference on Developmental Psychology, 27–31 August, Milan.

Brun, Ph., Nadel, J., and Mattlinger, M-J. (1998). L'hypothèse émotionnelle dans l'autisme. *Psychologie Française*, **43(2)**, 147–56.

Bruner, J. (1975). From communication to language: a psychological perspective. *Cognition*, **3**, 255–87.

Bruner, J. (1981). Learning how to do things with words. In *Human growth and development* (ed. J. Bruner and A. Garton), pp. 62–84. London: Oxford University Press.

Bullock, M. and Russell, J. A. (1986). Concepts of emotion in developmental psychology. In *Measuring emotions in infants and children*, Vol. **2** (ed. C. E. Izard and P. B. Read), pp. 203–37. Cambridge: Cambridge University Press.

Capps, L., Sigman, M., and Mundy, P. (1994). Attachment security in children with autism. *Development and Psychopathology*, **6**, 249–61.

Celani, G., Battacchi, M. W., and Arcidiacono, L. (1999). The understanding of the emotional meaning of facial expressions in people with autism. *Journal of Autism and Developmental Disorders*, **29**, 57–66.

Cole, P. M. (1986). Children's spontaneous control of facial expression. *Child Development*, **57**, 1309–21.

Cohn, J. F. and Tronick, E. Z. (1982). Communicative rules and sequential structure of infant behaviour during normal and depressed interaction. In *Social interchange in infancy: affect, cognition, and communication* (ed. E. Tronick), pp. 59–77. Baltimore, MD: University Park Press.

Crick, N. R. and Dodge, K. A. (1994). A review and reformation of social information-processing mechanisms in children's social adjustment. *Psychological Bulletin*, **115**, 74–101.

Cutting, A. L. and Dunn, J. (2002). The cost of understanding other people: social cognition predicts young children's sensitivity to criticism. *Journal of Child Psychology and Psychiatry*, **43(7)**, 849–60.

Dautenhahn, K. (1999). Robots as social actors: Aurora and the case of Autism. *Proceedings CT99, The Third International cognitive Technology Conference*. 359–74.

Darwin, C. (1872/1965). *The expression of emotion in man and animals*. Chicago: University of Chicago Press.

Denham, S. A. (1986). Social cognition, social behaviour, and emotion in preschoolers: contextual validation. *Child Development*, **57**, 194–201.

Denham, S. A. (1998). *Emotional development in young children*. New York, NY: Guilford Press.

Denham, S. A., Blair, K. A., DeMulder, E., *et al.* (2003). Preschool emotional competence: Pathway to social competence? *Child Development*, **74(1)**, 238–56.

Dunn, J. and Hughes, C. (1998). Young children's understanding of emotions within close relationships. *Cognition and Emotion*, **12**, 171–90.

Dunn, J., Brown, J. R., and Beardsall, L. (1991). Family talk about feeling states and children's later understanding of other's emotions. *Developmental Psychology*, **27**, 448–55.

Egan, G. J., Brown, R. T., Goonan, L., *et al.* (1998). The development of decoding emotions in children with externalizing behavioural disturbances and their normally developing peers. *Archives of Clinical Neuropsychology*, **13(4)**, 383–96.

Escalona, A., Field, T., Nadel, J., *et al.* (2000). Brief report: imitation effects on children with autism. *Journal of Autism and Developmental Disorders*, **32(2)**, 141–4.

Field, T. (1984). Early interactions between infants and their postpartum depressed mothers. *Infant Behaviour and Development*, **7**, 527–32.

Field, T. M. and Walden, T. A. (1982). Production and discrimination of facial expressions by preschool children. *Child Development*, **53**, 1299–300.

Field, T., Sanders, C., and Nadel, J. (2001). Children with autism display more social behaviours after repeated imitation sessions. *Autism*, **5(3)**, 317–24.

Fivaz-Depeursinge, E. and Corboz-Warnery, A. (1999). *The primary triangle: a developmental system view of mothers, fathers and infants*. New York, NY: Plenum Press.

Garner, P. W. (1999). Continuity in emotion knowledge from preschool to middle-childhood and relation to emotion socialization. *Motivation and Emotion*, **23(4)**, 247–65.

Gergely, G. and Watson, J. S. (1999). Infant's sensitivity to imperfect contingency in social interaction. In *Early social cognition* (ed. P. Rochat), pp. 101–36. Hillsdale, NJ: Erlbaum.

Gergely, G., Bekkering, H., and Kiraly, I. (2002). Rational imitation in preverbal infants. *Nature*, **415**, 755.

Gross, A. L. and Ballif, B. (1991). Children's understanding of emotion from facial expressions and situations: a review. *Developmental Review*, **11**, 368–98.

Gusella, J., Muir, D. W., and Tronick, E. (1988). The effect of manipulating maternal behaviour during an interaction on three- and six-month-olds' affect and attention. *Child Development*, **59(4)**, 1111–24.

Hains, S. and Muir, D. (1996). Effects of stimulus contingency in infant-adult interactions. *Infant Behaviour and Development*, **19**, 49–61.

Halberstadt, A. G., Denham, S. A., and Dunsmore, J. C. (2001). Affective social competence. *Social Development*, **10**, 79–119.

Harris, P. L. (1989). *Children and emotion*. Oxford: Blackwell Publishers.

Harris, P. L., Johnson, C., Hutton, D., *et al.* (1989). Young children's theory of mind and emotion. *Cognition and Emotion*, **3**, 379–401.

Hobson, R. P. (1993). *Autism and the development of mind*. Hove: Lawrence Erlbaum Associates.

Hobson, R. P. (1986a). The autistic child's appraisal of expressions of emotion. *Journal of Child Psychology and Psychiatry*, **27(3)**, 321–42.

Hobson, R. P. (1986b). The autistic child's appraisal of expressions of emotion: A further study. *Journal of Child Psychology and Psychiatry*, **27(5)**, 671–80.

Hobson, R. P. and Lee, A. (1989). Emotion related and abstract concepts in autistic people: evidence from the British Picture Vocabulary Scale. *Journal of Autism and Developmental Disorders*, **19**, 601–23.

Hobson, R. P., Ouston, J., and Lee, A. (1989). Naming emotion in faces and voices: Abilities and disabilities in autism and mental retardation. *British Journal of Developmental Psychology*, **7**, 237–50.

Hosie, J. A., Gray, C. D., Russell, P. A., *et al.* (1998). The matching of facial expressions by deaf and hearing children and their production and comprehension of emotion labels. *Motivation and Emotion*, **22(4)**, 293–312.

Izard, C., Fine, S., Schultz, D., *et al.* (2001). Emotion knowledge as a predictor of social behaviour and academic competence in children at risk. *Psychological Science*, **12**, 18–23.

Josephs, I. (1994). Display rule behaviour and understanding in preschool children. *Journal of Nonverbal Behaviour*, **18**, 301–26.

Karmiloff-Smith, A. (1992). *Beyond modularity*. Cambridge, MA: MIT Press.

Kasari, C., Freeman, S. F., and Hughes, M. A. (2001). Emotion recognition by children with Down syndrome. *American Journal of Mental Retardation*, **106**, 59–72.

Kasari, C., Freeman, S. F., and Bass, W. (2003). Empathy and response to distress in children with Down syndrome. *Journal of Child Psychology and Psychiatry*, **44(3)**, 424–31.

Kestenbaum, R. and Gelman, S. (1995). Preschool children's identification and understanding of mixed emotions. *Cognitive Development*, **10**, 443–58.

LaFrenière, P. J. (2000). *Emotional development: a biosocial perspective*. Belmont, CA: Wadsworth.

Lemerise, E. A. and Arsenio, W. F. (2000). An integrated model of emotion processes and cognition in social information processing. *Child Development*, **71**, 107–18.

Loveland, K. A., Tunali-Kotoski, B., Pearson, D. A., *et al.* (1994). Imitation and expression of facial affect in autism. *Development and Psychopathology*, **6**, 433–44.

Loveland, K. A., Tunali-Kotoski, B., Chen, R., *et al.* (1995). Intermodal perception of affect in persons with autism or Down syndrome. *Development and Psychopathology*, **7**, 409–18.

Loveland, K. A., Pearson, D. A., Tunali-Kotoski, B., *et al.* (2001). Judgments of social appropriateness by children and adolescents with autism. *Journal of Autism and Developmental Disorders*, **31**(4), 367–76.

McDowell, D. J., O'Neil, R., and Parke, R. D. (2000). Display rule application in a disappointing situation and children's emotional reactivity: Relations with social competence. *Merill-Palmer Quarterly*, **46**(2), 306–24.

Melfsen, S. and Florin, I. (2002). Do socially anxious children show deficits in classifying facial expressions of emotions. *Journal of Nonverbal Behaviour*, **26**(2), 109–26.

Meltzoff, A. N. and Gopnik, A. (1993). The role of imitation in understanding persons and developing a theory of mind. In *Understanding other minds* (ed. S. Baron-Cohen, H. Flusberg and D. Cohen), pp. 335–66. Oxford: Oxford University Press.

Moore, D. G. (2001). Reassessing emotion recognition performance in people with mental retardation: a review. *American Journal on Mental Retardation*, **106**(6), 481–502.

Muir, D.W. and Nadel, J. (1998). Infant social perception. In *Perceptual development: visual, auditory, and speech perception in infancy* (ed. A. Slater), pp. 247–85. London: Psychology Press.

Mundy, P. (1995). Joint attention and social-emotional approach behaviour in children with autism. *Development and Psychopathology*, **7**, 63–82.

Mundy, P., Sigman, M., Ungerer, J. A., *et al.* (1986). Defining the social deficits in autism: the contribution of nonverbal communication measures. *Journal of Child Psychology and Psychiatry*, **27**, 657–69.

Mundy, P., Kasari, C., and Sigman, M. (1992). Nonverbal communication, affective sharing, and intersubjectivity. *Infant Behaviour and Development*, **15**, 377–81.

Murray, L. (1992). The impact of postnatal depression on infant development. *Journal of Child Psychology and Psychiatry*, **33**, 543–61.

Murray, L. and Trevarthen, C. (1985). Emotional regulation of interactions between two-month-olds and their mothers. In *Social perception in infants* (ed. T. M. Field and N. Fox), pp. 101–25. Norwood, NJ: Ablex.

Nadel, J. (1986). *Imitation et communication entre jeunes enfants*. Paris: PUF.

Nadel, J. (1994). The development of communication: Wallon's framework and influence. In *Early child development in the French tradition* (ed. A. Vyt, H. Bloch, and M. Bornstein), pp. 177–89, Hillsdale, NJ: Lawrence Erlbaum Ass.

Nadel, J. (2002a). When do infants expect ? *Infant Behaviour and Development*, **25**, 30–3.

Nadel, J. (2002b). Imitation and imitation recognition: Functional use in preverbal infants and nonverbal children with autism. In *The imitative mind* (ed. A. Meltzoff and W. Prinz), pp. 42–62. Cambridge: Cambridge University Press.

Nadel, J. (2002c). Some reasons to link imitation and imitation recognition into theory of mind. In *Simulation and knowledge of action* (ed. J. Dokic and J. Proust), pp. 119–35. Amsterdam: John Benjamins.

Nadel, J. and Revel, A. (2003). How to build an imitator ? *Proceedings of the AISB'03*, 2nd International Symposium on Imitation in Animals and Artefacts, Aberystwyth, 120–4.

Nadel, J. and Tremblay-Leveau, H. (1999). Early perception of social contingencies and interpersonal intentionality: dyadic and triadic paradigms. In *Early social cognition* (ed. P. Rochat), pp. 189–212. Mahwah, NJ: Lawrence Erlbaum Associates.

Nadel, J., Carchon, I., Kervella, C., *et al.* (1999a). Expectancies for social contingency in 2-months-olds. *Developmental Science*, **2(2)**, 164–73.

Nadel, J., Guérini, C., Pézé, A., *et al.* (1999b). The evolving nature of imitation as a transitory means of communication. In *Imitation in infancy* (ed. J. Nadel and G. Butterworth), pp. 209–34. Cambridge: Cambridge University Press.

Nadel, J., Croué, S., Kervella, C., *et al.* (2000). Do autistic children have ontological expectancies concerning human behaviour? *Autism*, **4(2)**, 133–45.

Nadel-Brulfert, J. and Baudonnière, P. M. (1982). The social function of reciprocal imitation in 2-year-old peers. *International Journal of Behavioural Development*, **5**, 95–109.

Neisser, U. (1999). The perceived self: Ecological and interpersonnel sources of self-knowledge. Cambridge University Press.

Panksepp, J. (1998). *Affective neuroscience. The foundations of human and animal emotions*. New York, NY: Oxford University Press.

Parker, E. H., Hubbard, J. A., Ramsden, S. R., *et al.* (2001). Children's use and knowledge of display rules for anger following hypothetical vignettes versus following live peer interaction. *Social Development*, **10(4)**, 528–57.

Parsons, S. and Mitchell, P. (2002). The AS interactive project. *Journal of Intellectual Disability Research*, **46**, 430–43.

Prior, M., Dahlstrom, B., and Squires, T-L. (1990). Autistic children's knowledge of thinking and feeling states in other people. *Journal of Child Psychology and Psychiatry*, **31(4)**, 587–601.

Reddy, V. (1991). Playing with others' expectancies: teasing and mucking about in the first year. In, *Natural theories of mind* (ed. A. Whiten), pp. 143–58. Oxford: Basil Blackwell.

Reichenbach, L. and Masters, J. C. (1983). Children's use of expressive and contextual cues in judgments of emotion. *Child Development*, **54**, 993–1004.

Rieffe, C., Meerum Terwogt, M., and Stockmann, L. (2000). Understanding atypical emotions among children with autism. *Journal of Autism and Developmental Disorders*, **30(3)**, 195–203.

Rieffe, C., Meerum Terwogt, M., Koops, W., *et al.* (2001). Preschoolers' appreciation of uncommon desires and subsequent emotions. *British Journal of Developmental Psychology*, **19**, 259–74.

Russell, J. A. and Widen, S. C. (2002). A label superiority effect in children's categorization of facial expressions. *Social Development*, **11**, 30–52.

Saarni, C. (1999). *The development of emotional competence*. New York, NY: Guilford Press.

Saarni, C. (1984). An observational study of children's attempts to monitor their expressive behaviour. *Child Development*, **55**, 1504–13.

Scaife, M. and Bruner, J. (1975). The capacity of joint visual attention in the infant. *Nature*, **253**, 265–6.

Schopler, E. and Reichler, R. J. (1979). Individualised assessment and treatment for autistic and developmentally disabled children, vol 1. *Psycho-educational profile*. Austin, TX. PRO-ED.

Schopler, E., Reichler, R. J., and Rochen-Renner, B. (1988). *The childhood Autism Rating Scale (CARS)*. Los Angeles: Western Psychological Services.

Shapiro, R., Sherman, M., Clamari, G., *et al.* (1987). Attachment in autism and other developmental disorders. *Journal of the American Academy of Child and Adolescent Psychiatry*, **26**, 485–90.

Sigman, M., Kasari, C., Kwon, J-H., *et al.* (1992). Responses to the negative emotions of others by autistic, mentally retarded, and normal children. *Child Development*, **63**, 796–807.

Smith, M. and Walden, T. (1998). Developmental trends in emotion understanding among a diverse sample of African-American preschool children. *Journal of Applied Developmental Psychology*, **19(2)**, 177–97.

Smith, M. and Walden, T. (1999). Understanding feelings and coping with emotional situations: A comparison of maltreated and nonmaltreated preschoolers. *Social Development*, **8**, 93–116.

Snow, M., Hertzig, M. E., and Shapiro, T. (1987). Expression of emotion in young autistic children. *Journal of American Academy of Child and Adolescent Psychiatry*, **26**, 836–8.

Soussignan, R., Schaal, B., Schmit, G., *et al.* (1995). Facial responsiveness to odours in normal and pervasively developmentally disordered children. *Chemical Senses*, **25**, 47–59.

Stern, D. (1977). *The first relationship: Infant and mother*. Cambridge, Mass.: Harvard University Press.

Stern, D. N. (1999). The role of feelings in an interpersonnel self. In *The perceived self: ecological and interpersonnel sources of self-knowledge* (ed. U. Neisser), pp. 205–15. Cambridge: Cambridge University Press.

Stewart, C. A. and Singh, N. N. (1995). Enhancing the recognition and production of facial expressions of emotion by children with mental retardation. *Research in Developmental Disabilities*, **16**(5), 365–82.

Tager-Flusberg, H. (1989). A psycholinguistic perspective on language development in the autistic child. In *Autism: Nature, diagnosis and treatment* (ed. G. Dawson), pp. 92–115. New York, NY: Guilford.

Tomasello, M. (1999). Social cognition before the revolution. In *Early social cognition* (ed. P. Rochat). Mahwah, NJ: Lawrence Erlbaum Associates.

Travis, L., Sigman, M., and Ruskin, E. (2001). Links between social understanding and social behaviour in verbally able children with autism. *Journal of Autism and Developmental Disorders*, **31**(2), 119–30.

Tremblay-Leveau, H. and Nadel, J. (1995). Young children's communication skills in triads. *International Journal of Behavioural Development*, **18**(2), 227–42.

Tremblay-Leveau, H. and Nadel, J. (1996). Exclusion in triads: Can it serve <<metacommunicative >> knowledge in 11- and 23-month-old children ? *British Journal of Developmental Psychology*, **14**, 145–58.

Trevarthen, C. (1993). The function of emotion in early infant communication and development. In *New perspectives in early communicative development* (ed. J. Nadel and L. Camaioni), pp. 48–81. New York, NY: Routledge Press.

Trevarthen, C., Kokkinaki, T., and Fiamenghi, G. A. (1999). What infants' imitation communicates. In *Imitation in infancy* (ed. J. Nadel and G. Butterworth), pp. 127–85. Cambridge: Cambridge University Press.

Turk, J. and Cornish, K. (1998). Face recognition and emotion perception in boys with fragile-X syndrome. *Journal of Intellectual Disability Research*, **42**(6), 490–9.

Underwood, M. K., Cole, J. D., and Herbsman, C. R. (1992). Display rules for anger and aggression in school-age children. *Child Development*, **63**, 366–80.

Wallon, H. (1934). *Les origines du caractère chez l'enfant*. Paris: Alcan.

Wallon, H. (ed.) (1938). L'activité proprioplastique. In *La vie mentale, tome VIII* (ed. H. Wallon), pp. 201–23. Paris: Société de Gestion de l'Encyclopédie Française.

Wellman, H. M. (1990). *The child's theory of mind*. Cambridge, MA: MIT Press.

Wellman, H. M., Phillips, A. T., and Rodriguez, T. (2000). Young children's understanding of perception, desire, and emotion. *Child Development*, **71**(4), 895–912.

Zeman, J. and Garber, J. (1996). Display rules for anger, sadness, and pain: It depends on who is watching. *Child Development*, **67**, 957–73.

Chapter 14

Social-emotional impairment and self-regulation in autism spectrum disorders

Katherine A. Loveland

The autistic spectrum of disorder has been of special interest to investigators studying emotional development because of the severe emotional and social deficits associated with it. In this chapter I review evidence concerning impairment of social-emotional functioning and self-regulation in children with autism spectrum disorders. I will argue that existing evidence about autism points not only to a failure of mechanisms to perceive and understand social and emotional events, but also to a failure of self-regulation of behaviour and emotion that leads both to inappropriate, 'autistic' behaviour and to elevated risk for co-morbid psychopathology.

Emotional functioning in autism and related disorders

Evidence about the emotional functioning of individuals with autism spectrum disorders (here referred to as *autism*) has come from both clinical observation and research studies. From early in life, persons with autism typically have difficulty understanding the emotional behaviour of others, as self-reports of their life experience have shown (Grandin, 1995; Jones *et al.*, 2001). In natural settings, individuals with autism are observed to express emotion differently than do other people (Yirmiya *et al.*, 1989; Capps *et al.*, 1993; Joseph and Tager-Flusberg, 1997). For example, some display flattened affect except when highly emotionally aroused, expressing only the 'highs' and the 'lows' of emotional experience. Other individuals with autism are highly expressive of emotion, but not always in appropriate ways (e.g. laughing when laughter is clearly inappropriate; Reddy *et al.*, 2002). Several studies have found less positive expression of emotion and more negative expression of emotion in children with autism in natural interactions with caregivers (Yirmiya *et al.*, 1989; Joseph and Tager-Flusberg, 1997; Bieberich and Morgan, 1998). Some families report that children with autism do not express affection readily, or only do so in response to reminders, or as part of a learned or stereotyped sequence of behaviour. Failure to cry when hurt or otherwise express suffering is also frequently reported in children with autism. Similarly, a lack of fear that would ordinarily be appropriate in a situation is characteristic of some children with autism. Such children may fearlessly enter dangerous situations, such as climbing in high places or walking out into traffic on busy streets.

In general, a particularly striking feature of autism is the tendency for affected individuals to have different emotional reactions to those expected to things and events they experience. For example, a child who shows no fear of climbing on a high fence might, nonetheless, be terrified of running water in the bathroom sink. The obvious emotional differences between persons with and without autism have led to a great deal of interest in the study of emotion in this population, both from the standpoint of the amelioration of autistic behavioural deficits, and from the standpoint of scientific interest in the basis for such a profound disorder of emotional functioning.

The great majority of research studies on emotion in persons with autism have dealt with the understanding or recognition of emotions, rather than expression of emotion. Many studies have found poorer performance by persons with autism relative to comparable persons without autism on tasks such as recognizing, labelling, or categorizing emotion in still pictures (Weeks and Hobson, 1987; Hobson, 1986a,b; Bormann-Kischkel et al., 1995; Assumpcao et al., 1999; Garcia-Villamisar and Polaino-Lorente, 1999a,b), matching emotions to contexts (Fein et al., 1992), and matching emotions within and across modalities (Kitlowski, 1995; Loveland et al., 1995.) Individuals with autism have been found to have particular difficulty identifying and attributing emotion when it is placed in a context that is more cognitively complex, such as a false belief task (Garcia-Villamisar and Polaino-Lorente, 1999a), or when it involves a cognitive component, such as in the emotion of surprise (Baron-Cohen et al., 1993).

Some evidence suggests persons with autism may use different strategies to perform social-emotional tasks (Bormann-Kischkel et al., 1995; Grossman et al., 2000; Pelphrey et al., 2002). For example, Pelphrey et al. (2002) studied the visual scanpaths of five adults with autism and five controls who were looking at pictures of human faces. Adults with autism looked less at core features of the faces and more at the nonfeatural areas. Klin et al. (2002) also found that, while viewing a movie of a social scene, individuals with autism looked less at eye regions, and more at mouths and other areas; scores on their task were also related to social competence. Both Pierce et al. (2001) and Schultz et al. (2000a) found that brain activation on fMRI differed between subjects with and without autism, viewing facial and emotional stimuli, suggesting that different processes are occurring as these stimuli are perceived. Although there is evidence that persons with autism can make use of both verbal and non-verbal sources of information about emotion (Loveland et al., 1997), Grossman et al. (2000) found that in more challenging emotional tasks, subjects with autism may tend to rely on verbal information for emotion. Similarly, some investigators have suggested that persons with autism use verbal strategies to help compensate for deficiencies in emotion perception (MacDonald et al., 1989). Findings such as these may point to fundamental differences in the ways persons with autism perceive and use emotional information.

Nevertheless, emotional impairments in autism have sometimes been hard to document in laboratory studies. Differences in performance between people with and without autism are not always found to be present, particularly in tasks of simple emotion recognition or labeling. The methods used to test emotion performance have varied widely, and such design issues as the choice of comparison group can make a great difference in findings (Hobson, 1991a). When groups are comparable in language level (Ozonoff *et al.*, 1990; Prior *et al.*, 1990; Loveland *et al.*, 1997; Buitelaar *et al.*, 1999a,b; Grossman *et al.*, 2000), or when very young normal children or children with other psychopathologies are the comparison group (Brun *et al.*, 1998; Buitelaar *et al.*, 1999a,b), emotion task differences may be reduced or absent. In fact, typically developing children as old as 6 years may still be struggling with correctly matching facial and auditory expressions of some emotions, particularly anger, sadness and surprise (Brun, 2001). Also, groups other than those on the autism spectrum have been found to have deficiencies on emotion tasks (e.g. Hobson *et al.*, 1989; Minter *et al.*, 1991.) These findings suggest that, although emotional deficits are characteristic of persons with autism, they are neither specific to the autism spectrum nor independent of developmental factors.

Differences between individuals with and without autism are more likely to be found in studies where tasks deal with perception of complex, dynamic or subtle emotional states (Capps *et al.*, 1992; Loveland *et al.*, 1995, 2001a; Haviland *et al.*, 1996), emotional verbal memory (Beversdorf *et al.*, 1998), social judgments (Pierce *et al.*, 1997; Klin, 2000; Loveland *et al.*, 2001c), non-facial expressions of emotion or attitude (Moore *et al.*, 1997), or imitation and expression of emotion (Loveland *et al.*, 1994; Adolphs *et al.*, 2001; Celani *et al.*, 2001). Thus, both the nature of the task and the cognitive complexity of the situation tested play a role in determining the ability of persons with autism to perform emotion-related tasks.

For many years a key issue in the study of emotion in autism was the question of whether emotion or cognition is more 'central' to explaining the characteristic social deficits of autism (e.g. Hobson, 1991b). At this point, the field seems to have moved beyond this question, just as the larger field of developmental psychology no longer asks whether development occurs because of nature or nurture, construed narrowly. Rather, the mounting evidence that deficits in both areas are present and that these deficits are related, has shifted the focus of inquiry in new directions. Among these are efforts to identify the brain substrates of emotional differences in autism, the developmental course of such differences and their relationship to the larger question of a 'mind-reading' deficit in autism (reflecting the fact that at present, impairments of social and emotional functioning in autism are usually attributed to the presence of deficits in understanding others' mental states; Baron-Cohen, 1995). However, as yet little attention has been given to specifying the link between failure to understand the social and emotional world, and the behavioural expression of inappropriate social and emotional behaviour, including not only characteristically 'autistic' behaviours, but also co-morbid psychopathologies. In the section that follows, I explore this important, but little-studied aspect of emotional development in persons with autism.

Self-regulation of behaviour and emotion in autism

A number of studies have provided evidence that individuals with autism, even when they do have the ability to identify others' emotional states, may nonetheless be relatively poor at determining their functional significance, that is, their implications for behaviour. In particular, individuals with autism often do not use information about other people's emotional states to select or adjust their own actions in ongoing social situations (Loveland and Tunali, 1991; Kamio, 1998). Thus, they might recognize, if explicitly asked about it in an experiment, that a particular facial expression denotes a certain emotional or motivational state, yet not know, in real situations, how this fact affects how they themselves should behave toward someone showing that expression. For example, a study by Adolphs *et al.* (2001) found that higher IQ persons with autism were impaired in judging the trustworthiness of faces based on pictures, a judgment that has important implications for social action. This finding suggests people with autism are poor at using information in facial expressions to determine who does and does not offer a potential threat to them, and thus they may display poor social judgment in some situations.

Similarly, studies on empathy have found that children with autism may not respond to other people's distress, even when there is reason to think they are aware of it (Loveland and Tunali, 1991; Sigman *et al.*, 1992; Yirmiya *et al.*, 1992; Bacon *et al.*, 1998; Corona *et al.*, 1998), suggesting that they may not know how to respond. Children with autism have been reported to differ in empathy responses from a variety of comparison populations, including persons with MR, ADHD, anxiety disorder or no disorder (Dyck *et al.*, 2001.) They have been found to make fewer empathic responses and to pay greater attention to toys than to persons when others display distress; and to make significantly fewer sympathetic verbal responses to a distressed examiner than subjects with Down syndrome (Loveland and Tunali, 1991; Sigman *et al.*, 1992). They have also been found to be less able to respond empathically to videotaped depictions of other people in emotionally-charged situations or showing emotions (Yirmiya *et al.*, 1992; Walker-Andrews *et al.*, 1994). Interestingly, recent research on intellectually able individuals with autism shows that at least some of them have the ability to identify others' mental states (what others think, know, believe, intend or feel), even though they do not always do so in their daily lives (Serra *et al.*, 1999; Rieffe *et al.*, 2000). These findings on reduced empathy in autism might be explained in part by a lack of awareness of other persons' mental states (Baron-Cohen, 1989), but they may also be explained by an inability to determine how to respond to others' mental states (Loveland, 1991, 2001). Thus, there is a need for better understanding of the processes by which people with autism use what information they do have about the social-emotional world to regulate their own responses, both behavioural and emotional.

Although there is now abundant evidence that individuals with autism do have impairments in understanding others' mental states, there is clearly also reason to think that they are impaired in the self-regulation of social-emotional behaviour (Loveland, 2001; Bachevalier and Loveland, 2003). The term self-regulation has been used in a variety of ways by investigators in different fields (cf. Cicchetti and Tucker, 1994). It has been used to mean strategies for self-monitoring to improve performance in educational (Wehmeyer *et al.*, 2003) or athletic (Behncke, 2002) contexts; homeostatic mechanisms to regulate biological states such as elevated cortisol (Quas *et al.*, 2002); cognitive and attentional mechanisms for regulating behaviour and choice (Bush *et al.*, 2000; Posner and Rothbart, 2000; Stevens *et al.*, 2002); explicit metacognitive strategies that can affect behaviour, cognition and affect (Miller and Byrnes, 2001; Armor and Taylor, 2003); affective abilities consequent to differences in personality and temperament (Lengua *et al.*, 1999; Baumann and Kul, 2002); and the ability to regulate emotional responses to environmental events, particularly those that are stressful (Schore, 2000; Mendolia, 2002; Rosenblum *et al.*, 2002). A few authors have also used the term self-regulation to refer more broadly to the adaptive regulation of behaviour across a number of domains, including both social and emotional behaviour (e.g. Loveland, 2001; Barkley *et al.*, 2002; Glenn and Cunningham, 2002). It is in this broader sense that I adopt the term self-regulation here, applying it to the regulation of social responding and of emotional reactivity. I would argue that both of these areas of self-regulation are impaired in persons with autism, and that both contribute to the impairment of social-emotional behaviour observed in persons with autism, as well as to their increased vulnerability to co-morbid psychopathology.

Self-regulation in response to the continuously changing conditions of the social world is an essential process for survival, that depends not only on the ability to perceive or infer relevant information about other people, but also on the ability to evaluate and modify our own behaviour and responses in light of what we know (Loveland, 2001). For example, in a social situation, each person must continuously assess not only what is said, but the emotional context of speech (how are conversational partners reacting to each other and to what is said and done?), the situational context (e.g. where and when is the interaction taking place, and what are the social constraints that apply? what social relationship exists between those interacting?), and any changes in conditions that might take place. Assessment of this type requires a sensitive awareness of social-emotional information, as well as cultural and other factors that help to govern its interpretation. Thus, successful self-regulation requires a rapid assessment of one's own behaviour and reactions, as well as their effects on others and the situation.

Some research suggests that persons with autism typically deal with complex social-emotional situations by applying explicit rules or cognitive strategies that they have learned from past experience (Yirmiya *et al.*, 1992; Hadwin *et al.*, 1996), rather than by identifying and responding to the unique nature of each situation in a flexible way.

Unfortunately, such rules or strategies do not allow the person with autism to adapt well to a wide range of situations, and they may be especially ineffective when new conditions are encountered. Thus, people with autism appear to lack the fine-grained, flexible, fully developed ability to self-regulate social, and emotional behaviour, that is present in typically developing persons.

Seen from this perspective, we may say that persons with autism have special difficulty not only with perceiving social and emotional aspects of the world, but also with using this information to regulate their own behaviour and emotions in appropriate ways. Unlike most laboratory tasks of emotion, however, real social interactions are complex, rapidly changing and embedded within social-cultural context. Such conditions thus severely challenge the ability of the person with autism to self-regulate social and emotional responses.

Consequences of social and emotional dysregulation in autism

Research suggests that the development of self-regulatory social competence is dependent in part on the development of emotional self-regulation (Calkins, 1994; Bradley, 2000; Denham *et al.*, 2003). Emotional self-regulation involves the ability to modify one's own emotional reactions in response to perceived challenge (Denham *et al.*, 2003). The process of self-regulation of emotion begins very early in life, with the infant's arousal in response to various environmental events. An important developmental task is to attain the capacity to re-establish equilibrium after an arousing or upsetting event (Als *et al.*, 1977). There are wide individual differences in the degree of irritability infants display, their reactivity to events, and their capacity to self-regulate and return to a baseline state. Although these skills develop gradually in all, infants also differ in the rate at which self-regulation abilities are attained. Self-regulation of emotion and behaviour is also intimately involved in those characteristic patterns of behaviour and responsivity subsumed under the concept of 'temperament' (Kagan *et al.*, 1998). There is evidence that children described as 'high-reactivity' or 'high inhibition' are predisposed to anxiety and depression (Kagan *et al.*, 1999). High reactivity has been found to be a relatively stable trait over development. Highly reactive or behaviourally 'inhibited' children find environmental events more arousing, and perhaps threatening, than other children do. They tend to react more strongly to such events, and they frequently show social withdrawal and difficulty self-regulating emotion. The reactivity of children to stress may be better gauged not by the level of cortisol per se but by the ability to bring elevated cortisol back to a baseline level rapidly (Gunnar and Barr, 1998). Thus, highly reactive children function best when they learn to use self-regulatory strategies that buffer the affective effects of stressful experiences, rather than simply withdrawing (Manassis and Bradley, 1994; Stewart and Rubin, 1995). Attachment ordinarily plays a role in the development of the child's ability to cope successfully with stress, such that children who less successfully form attachments to caregivers may be at increased risk for later psychopathology (Bradley, 2000). The caregiver's degree of responsiveness, in turn, interacts with the child's behaviours to help or hinder the development of the ability to regulate affect appropriately; a number of authors have argued that the ability to modulate arousal is a complex product of maternal behaviour in caregiving combined with biological predispositions in the child and situational factors, such as deprivation, conflict between adults in the home, or other environmental stressors (Belsky *et al.*, 1995; Calkins and Fox, 1992; Field, 1994).

What are the implications for the person with autism who has, in addition to deficits in perceiving and understanding the human social-emotional world, only limited insight into his own emotional behaviour and its effects on others, and a limited ability to modify it? Children with autism, as described above, tend to respond emotionally to different experiences and in different ways than do other people. This makes their behaviour seem idiosyncratic, inappropriate, and often, out-of-control. Unfortunately, many individuals with autism, once emotionally upset by something, find it very difficult to re-establish a state of equilibrium; especially in young children this tendency can be manifested as lengthy tantrums during which it is difficult to calm the child. If adults and peers perceive that the child's behaviour is unpredictable or not readily controlled, this can lead to frustration, as well as hostile or inconsistent caregiving, which in turn can exacerbate the child's tendency to act out or withdraw, increasing frustration, etc., in a spiral of increasingly maladaptive behaviour. If not assisted by effective caregiving and interventions, such a child will gradually become less and less able to manage in a social environment that increases in complexity as the child grows older and social expectations for age-appropriate behaviour change. Over time, one would also expect a child with such a condition to be highly vulnerable to developing additional psychopathology because of the significant neurobehavioural insult associated with years of high emotional stress. In fact, persons with autism are at high risk for co-morbid psychopathologies such as anxiety and depression (Lainhart and Folstein, 1994; Lainhart, 1999), which may be expressed in a variety of ways, depending on the individual's developmental level. In the section that follows I briefly review some of what is known about anxiety in autism, and show that inability to effectively self-regulate behaviour and emotion is an important factor in the frequent occurrence of co-morbid psychopathology in persons with autism.

Anxiety in autism spectrum disorders

Brian is nine years old and has autism. Although he is of average IQ and speaks fluently, he has some difficulty with organized oral expression and becomes anxious when required to answer questions aloud on any topic. This is one of several situations that his family recognizes can easily push Brian to a level of anxiety that he cannot seem to control. Brian has a history of lengthy and uncontrollable tantrums when his anxiety becomes too great. As a result, his family has become accustomed to avoiding circumstances that might tend to make Brian feel stressed, in order to prevent him from having an outburst. On the first day of testing with Brian, he receives an IQ test that requires him to answer questions he finds challenging. After gradually escalating signs of anxiety (foot tapping, agitated movement in his chair, refusal, shrill vocal tone), Brian erupts into screaming and tantruming, and the test session is terminated for the day. After about a half hour he curls up in the corner in the fetal position and after a time is able to leave the room quietly. On the second day, Brian works with a different examiner who administers the Autism Diagnostic Observation Schedule (ADOS) (Module 3). Although Brian works cooperatively at first, he responds negatively to the ADOS questions about social relationships, and his anxiety begins to escalate visibly. This time the examiner re-directs him to different activities (blocks, a toy car) before his anxiety can reach too high a level for him to control. She then returns to the questions a little at a time only after Brian has re-established emotional control, re-directing him again as needed, multiple times. In this manner the ADOS is completed without interruption.

Anxiety can be described as a state of apprehensiveness or uncertainty associated with the anticipation of negative outcome; it can be expressed through both voluntary and involuntary mechanisms and behaviours. For example, involuntary expressions of anxiety may include sweating, trembling, flushing or pallor, changes in breathing and heart rate. Since anxiety is generally experienced by humans as an unpleasant emotional state, it can serve as a motive for complex voluntary activity aimed at avoiding or reducing negative outcomes (e.g. studying harder for a test). However, anxiety is often manifested when the individual cannot find a ready means of reducing or avoiding the anticipated negative outcome. In this case, activity may be expressed in the form of habitual or stereotyped behaviours ranging from mild (e.g. pacing, nail-biting) to severe (e.g. the hair-pulling of trichotillomania). These behaviours do not usually remove the source of the anxiety and, in fact, can result in other problems, but they may, nonetheless, serve a kind of self-regulatory function, in that they may help to reduce anxiety by allowing the individual to self-comfort or to re-direct a state of agitation into motor activity.

Although some authors (cf Damasio, 2000) view anxiety not as an emotion, but as a neurobiologically induced tendency or state, I take the view that anxiety is a type of negative affect that reflects distress related to uncertainty or anticipation of negative outcome, or confusion/conflict about a course of action. Anxiety in people with autism seems to differ from anxiety in typically developing people in several ways:

- The source of anxiety in people with autism can be idiosyncratic. People with autism may experience anxiety in response to experiences that would not ordinarily be anxiety provoking to other people, e.g. being with a large group of people at church or a sporting event, hearing a vacuum cleaner. At the same time, people with autism may fail to experience or express anxiety in situations that would provoke it in most others, e.g. apparent fearlessness in situations of danger, or lack of concern about the social consequences of acting inappropriately.

- Even when the source of anxiety is one typically shared by others (e.g. a sudden change in plans, fear of thunderstorms or dogs), the degree of anxiety people with autism experience in a given situation may be much greater than ordinarily expected.

For example, families frequently report that children with autism become very upset when minor, unexpected changes in routine occur.

◆ People with autism have greater difficulty than typically developing people in self-regulating emotion and behaviour, especially in response to negatively valenced experiences. Individuals with autism appear to lack effective coping mechanisms for dealing with stress. Thus, for them, anxiety tends to 'spiral out of control', instead of being successfully regulated through internal control (homeostatic) mechanisms, resulting in an escalating state of emotional distress that is frequently accompanied by inappropriate behaviours (tantruming, aggression, other acting out). In many people with autism, even external help in self-regulating emotion is not completely successful, as when children tantrum for extended periods and do not respond well to attempts to calm them. Thus, the manifestation of anxiety in persons with autism resembles in some ways that seen in children without autism who are 'highly reactive', not only because of the tendency to react more strongly to any given stressor, but also because of their difficulty in self-regulating emotion through age-appropriate internal or external homeostatic mechanisms.

The few studies of anxiety in individuals with autism suggest that anxiety is very common in this population, particularly among more intellectually able individuals (Lainhart, 1999; Gillott et al., 2000; Kim et al., 2000). Martin et al. (1999) found that among those children with autism in their sample who were being treated with psychotropic medication, about 65% were being treated for anxiety. Anxiety in autism may manifest as a general tendency to high reactivity in response to any stressful experience or as a pattern of anxiety connected with specific experiences (such as crowds, noise, or social situations), or as a behaviour pattern suggestive of a specific anxiety disorder (e.g. Obsessive Compulsive Disorder, trichtillomania; Loveland et al., 2003). There is some disagreement about the relationship of the repetitive and stereotyped behaviour patterns of autism to those of Obsessive Compulsive Disorder (Baron-Cohen, 1989; Swedo and Rapoport, 1989; Tsai, 1992), since, for example, not all of these behaviour patterns are accompanied by apparent emotional distress. However, anxiety and stress in daily life very likely contribute to inappropriate and challenging behaviour by persons with autism (Groden et al., 1994). Among the other factors that may contribute to anxiety in persons with autism are their cognitive limitations. Impairment in executive functioning (Pennington and Ozonoff, 1996) can lead to difficulty planning and organizing of behaviour in adaptive ways, particularly when old strategies do not work and new solutions to problems must be found. Cognitive conflict about a course of action, or frustration when familiar strategies are not successful, can lead to anxiety, and in the absence of flexible means for modulating emotion, can lead to outbursts or other behavioural problems.

As I have argued at greater length elsewhere (Loveland, 2001), the difficulties of persons with autism in emotional and behavioural self-regulation outlined above may be seen as reflecting the disruption of a cycle of perception and action (Gibson, 1979) that ordinarily serves to regulate the relationship of person and environment. In a perception-action cycle, perception guides action and action provides new opportunities for perception, in a reciprocal fashion. Thus, persons with autism may fail to detect relevant information about social and emotional aspects of their environment, leading to a distorted understanding of other people and social situations. In addition to this problem, persons with autism are not skilled at using what they do know to adjust their own behaviour appropriately and they often do not benefit from social feedback (e.g. the disapproval of others) that would ordinarily help them learn how to behave more appropriately. At the same time, integrally linked with the problem of self-regulation of social behaviour, persons with autism have a very significant deficit in the ability to regulate their own affective states. This deficit contributes to the inability of persons with autism to deal effectively with social situations, especially those they find challenging. Although the specific experiences that lead to stress and anxiety for individuals with autism vary a great deal, affective dysregulation seems to be characteristic of them and is most likely a major contributor to the development of secondary psychopathologies.

Social-emotional self-regulation and the brain in autism

The view of social-emotional impairment in autism that I have offered has implications for the ways one might construct a neurodevelopmental account of autism. In this view, a model of the brain in autism must deal not only with those brain systems that subserve social-emotional understanding, but also those that subserve the self-regulation of emotion and behaviour.

Recent years have seen an explosion of research studies on the brain in autism. Because autism is a developmental disorder that begins early in life and affects subsequent brain development, one would expect its brain substrate to be diffuse, complex, varying among individuals and changing with development (Bachevalier and Loveland, 2003). The variety of results found in studies on possible brain differences in autism has suggested this is so. As a consequence, a complete model of the developing brain in autism will be difficult to attain. At the same time, converging evidence from human and animal studies supports a model of the brain in which the major social-emotional deficits of autism are linked to developmental dysfunction of a brain circuit including the amygdala (an early-developing medial temporal lobe structure involved in detecting the emotional valence and the functional significance of things experienced) and the orbitofrontal cortex (a later-developing structure involved in executive control of social behaviour and social judgment; Bachevalier, 1991, 1994, 2000; Schore, 1994, 1996; Saunders et al., 1998; Bachevalier et al., 2001) This brain circuit can be seen as regulating the perception-action cycle of social-emotional behaviour: The amygdala detects information about the mental states, emotions, attitudes, and intentions of others, and their significance for the self, whereas the orbitofrontal cortex is involved in using this information to select and adjust behaviour in response to ongoing changes in the behaviour of other people (Rolls, 1990; Damasio and Tranel, 1992; Rolls *et al.*, 1994; Schultz *et al.*, 2000a,b; see Bachevalier and Loveland, 2003, for a fuller discussion of this point.) Evidence from studies of persons with autism supports the hypothesized role of this circuit; for example, individuals with autism studied with structural and functional MRI have been found to have differences in the amygdala and other temporal lobe regions, associated with impaired performance on emotional tasks (Critchley *et al.*, 2000; Howard *et al.*, 2000; Schultz *et al.*, 2000a,b). Several authors have suggested that impairment of the amygdala in autism results in an inability to appreciate the meaning of social and emotional stimuli (Fein *et al.*, 1987; Fotheringham, 1991; Loveland, 1991, 2001; Hobson, 1992). Similarly, structural and functional differences in the frontal lobe have been found in studies of autism (Kawasaki *et al.*, 1997; Harrison *et al.*, 1998; Minshew *et al.*, 1999; Carper and Courchesne, 2000).

Results from our laboratory have supported the hypothesis of prefrontal-limbic dysfunction in autism (Loveland *et al.*, 2001a,b). In a pilot study, we found that higher IQ subjects with autism performed more poorly than typically developing controls on tests specific to the orbitofrontal cortex and amygdala. By contrast, tests specific to a parallel brain circuit including the dorsolateral prefrontal cortex and hippocampus were sensitive to IQ level, but not to diagnosis. Thus, impairment of a prefrontal-limbic circuit or circuits may be specific to the social-emotional deficits of autism and may also help to account for the prominent deficits in self-regulation that accompany deficits in social-emotional understanding.

Further directions

This discussion of the emotional functioning of persons with autistic spectrum disorders raises a number of directions for further study. The review of literature in this area suggests that interventions aimed at improving social-emotional functioning should avoid relying on teaching emotion recognition as a primary method. Rather, research is needed to develop more techniques to encourage self-monitoring, and the ability to modify behaviour and regulate affect.

It is also time to move beyond a dominant focus on mental contents in the study of emotional functioning, and toward research that more clearly emphasizes the embeddedness of the person with autism within a social and cultural environment. Current research on infants (see Muir, Nadel, Oster, Trevarthen, Tronick, and others, this volume) has already demonstrated the importance of studying the dyad as a context for social-emotional and communicative behaviour, whereas studies of autism have rarely done so. Thus, there is a need for more study of the ways emotion occurs in the natural interactions of people with autism, and the role it plays in communication and social behaviour.

Research is also needed on the factors that predispose children with autism to developing co-morbid psychopathologies, particularly anxiety and depression. It seems likely that the impairment of brain structures that underlie autism itself may leave the child with extreme vulnerability to these and other disorders, because of a limited ability to regulate affective responses. Nevertheless, with the development of interventions to encourage early coping and self-management, as well as other forms of treatment, the risk for additional psychopathology might be lessened.

Finally, research on the autistic spectrum must aim at vertical integration, bringing together basic research on neural and biochemical substrates with laboratory experimental studies of cognitive and social-emotional behaviour, naturalistic research and clinical studies, to examine common hypotheses. In particular, future research should link together our rapidly expanding knowledge of the brain in autism with studies on the development of social-emotional behaviour and its self-regulation, within the context of the perception-action cycle.

Acknowledgements

Preparation of this work was supported in part by grant to the author P01 HD35471 from the National Institute on Child Health and Human Development.

References

Adolphs, R., Sears, L., and Piven, J. (2001). Abnormal processing of social information from faces in autism. *Journal of Cognitive Neuroscience*, **13(2)**, 232–40.

Als, H., Tronick, E., Lester, B. M., *et al.* (1977). The Brazelton Neonatal Behavioural Assessment Scale (BNBAS). *Journal of Abnormal Child Psychology*, **5(3)**, 215–31.

Armor, D. A. and Taylor, S. E. (2003). The effects of mindset on behavior: self-regulation in deliberative and implemental frames of mind. *Personality and Social Psychology Bulletin*, **29(1)**, 86–95.

Assumpcao, F. B. Jr., Sprovieri, M. H., Kuczynski, E., *et al.* (1999). Reconhecimento facial e autismo [Facial recognizing and autism]. *Arquivos de Neuro-Psiquiatria*, **57(4)**, 944–9.

Bachevalier, J. (1991). An animal model for childhood autism: memory loss and socioemotional disturbances following neonatal damage to the limbic system in monkeys. In *Advances in neuropsychiatry and psychopharmacology, Volume 1: schizophrenia research* (ed. C. A. Tamminga and S. C. Schulz), pp. 129–40. New York, NY: Raven Press.

Bachevalier, J. (1994). Medial temporal lobe structures and autism: a review of clinical and experimental findings. *Neuropsychologia*, **32**, 627–48.

Bachevalier, J. (2000). The amygdala, social behaviour, and autism. In *The amygdala: a functional analysis*, 2nd edn (ed. J. P. Aggleton), pp. 509–44. New York, NY: Oxford University Press.

Bachevalier, J. and Loveland, K. (2003). Early orbitofrontal-limbic dysfunction and autism. In *Neurodevelopmental mechanisms in genesis and epigenesis of psychopathology: future research directions* (ed. D. Cicchetti), pp. 215–36. New York: Cambridge University Press.

Bacon, A., Fein, D., Morris, R., *et al.* (1998). The responses of autistic children to the distress of others. *Journal of Autism and Developmental Disorders*, **28**, 129–42.

Barkley, R. A., Shelton, T. L., Crosswait, C., *et al.* (2002). Preschool children with disruptive behavior: three-year outcome as a function of adaptive disability. *Development and Psychopathology*, **14(1)**, 45–67.

Baron-Cohen, S. (1989). Do autistic children have obsessions and compulsions? *British Journal of Child Psychology*, **28**, 193–200.

Baron-Cohen, S. (1995). *Mindblindness: an essay on autism and theory of mind*. Cambridge, MA: MIT Press/Bradford Books.

Baron-Cohen, S., Spitz, A., and Cross, P. (1993). Do children with autism recognize surprise? A research note. *Cognition and Emotion*, **7**(6), 507–16.

Baumann, N. and Kuhl, J. (2002). Intuition, affect, and personality: unconscious coherence judgments and self-regulation of negative affect. *Journal of Personality and Social Psychology*, **83**(5), 1213–23.

Behncke, L. (2002). Self-regulation: a brief review. *Athletic Insight: Online Journal of Sport Psychology*, **4**(1), Available: *http://www.athleticinsight.com/Vol4Iss1/SelfRegulation.htm*.

Belsky, J., Rosenberger, K., and Crnic, K. (1995). The origins of attachment security: 'classical' and contextual determinants. In *Attachment theory: Social, developmental, and clinical perspectives* (ed. S. Goldberg, R. Muir, and J. Kerr), pp. 153–83. Hillsdale, NJ: Analytic Press.

Beversdorf, D. Q., Anderson, J. M., Manning, S. E., *et al.* (1998). The effect of semantic and emotional context on written recall for verbal language in high functioning adults with autism spectrum disorder. *Journal of Neurology, Neurosurgery and Psychiatry*, **65**(5), 685–92.

Bieberich, A. A. and Morgan, S. B. (1998). Affective expression in children with autism or down syndrome. *Journal of Autism and Developmental Disorders*, **28**(4), 333–8.

Bormann-Kischkel, C., Vilsmeier, M., *et al.* (1995). The development of emotional concepts in autism. *Journal of Child Psychology and Psychiatry and Allied Disciplines*, **36**(7), 1243–59.

Bradley, S. J. (2000). *Affect regulation and the development of psychopathology*. New York, NY: Guilford Press.

Brun, P. (2001). Psychopathologie de l'emotion chez l'enfant: L'importance des donnees developpementales typiques [The psychopathology of emotions in children: the importance of typical developmental data]. *Enfance*, **53**(3), 281–91.

Brun, P., Nadel, J., and Mattlinger, M. (1998). L'hypothese emotionnelle dans l'autisme [The emotional hypothesis in autism]. *Psychologie Francaise*, **43**, 147–56.

Buitelaar, J. K., Van der Wees, M., Swabb-Barneveld, H., *et al.* (1999a). Theory of mind and emotion-recognition functioning in autistic spectrum disorders and in psychiatric control and normal children. *Development and Psychopathology*, **11**(1), 39–58.

Buitelaar, J. K., van der Wees, M., Swaab-Barneveld, H., *et al.* (1999b). Verbal memory and performance IQ predict theory of mind and emotion recognition ability in children with autistic spectrum disorders and in psychiatric control children. *Journal of Child Psychology and Psychiatry and Allied Disciplines*, **40**(6), 869–81.

Bush, G., Luu, P., and Posner, M. I. (2000). Cognitive and emotional influences in anterior cingulate cortex. *Trends in Cognitive Sciences*, **4**, 215–22.

Calkins, S. D. (1994). Origins and outcomes of individual differences in emotion regulation. *Monographs of the Society for Research in Child Development*, **59**(2–3), 53–72, 250–83.

Calkins, S. D. and Fox, N. A. (1992). The relations among infant temperament, security of attachment, and behavioural inhibition at twenty-four months. *Child Development*, **63**, 1456–72.

Capps, L., Yirmiya, N., and Sigman, M. (1992). Understanding of simple and complex emotions in non-retarded children with autism. *Journal of Child Psychology and Psychiatry and Allied Disciplines*, **33**(7), 1169–82.

Capps, L., Kasari, C., Yirmiya, N., *et al.* (1993). Parental perception of emotional expressiveness in children with autism. *Journal of Consulting and Clinical Psychology*, **61**(3), 475–84.

Celani, G., Codispoti, O., and Giuberti, V. (2001). Capacita imitative ed espressivita emotiva facciale nelle persone con autismo [Imitation abilities and facial expressiveness of emotions in people with autism]. *Eta Evolutiva*, **65**, 46–58.

Cicchetti, D. and Tucker, D. (1994). Development and self-regulatory structures of the mind. *Development and Psychopathology*, **6**, 533–49.

Corona, R., Dissanayake, C., Arbelle, S., *et al.* (1998). Is affect aversive to young children with autism? Behavioural and cardiac responses to experimenter distress. *Child Development*, **69**, 1494–502.

Critchley, H. D., Daly, E. M., Bullmore, E. T., *et al.* (2000). The functional neuroanatomy of social behaviour: changes in cerebral blood flow when people with autistic disorder process facial expressions. *Brain*, **123**(11), 2203–12.

Damasio, A. R. and Tranel, D. (1992). Knowledge systems. *Current Opinion in Neurobiology*, **2**(2), 186–90.

Damasio, A. (2000). *A second chance for emotion*. In *Cognitive neuroscience of emotion* (ed. R. D. Lane and L. Nadel), pp. 12–23. New York, NY: Oxford University Press.

Denham, S. A., Blair, K. A., DeMulder, E., *et al.* (2003). Preschool emotional competence: Pathway to social competence? *Child Development*, **74**, 238–56.

Dyck, M. J., Ferguson, K., and Shochet, I. M. (2001). Do autism spectrum disorders differ from each other and from non-spectrum disorders on emotion recognition tests? *European Child and Adolescent Psychiatry*, **10**(2), 105–16.

Fein, D., Pennington, B., and Waterhouse, L. (1987). Implications of social deficits in autism for neurological dysfunction. In *Neurobiological issues in autism* (ed. E. Schopler and G. B. Mesibov), pp. 127–44. New York, NY: Plenum Press.

Fein, D., Lucci, D., Braverman, M., *et al.* (1992). Comprehension of affect in context in children with pervasive developmental disorders. *Journal of Child Psychology and Psychiatry and Allied Discipline*, **33**(7), 1157–67.

Field, T. (1994). The effects of mother's physical and emotional unavailability on emotion regulation. In *The development of emotion regulation: Biological and behavioural consideration* (ed. N. A. Fox), *Monographs of the Society for Research in Child Development*, **59**(2–3), 208–27.

Fotheringham, J. B. (1991). Autism and its primary psychosocial and neurological deficit. *Canadian Journal of Psychiatry*, **36**, 686–92.

Garcia-Villamisar, D. and Polaino-Lorente, A. (1999a). Atribucion causal de emociones. Un estudio diferencial entre autistas, deficientes mentales y poblacion general. [The attribution of causes of emotion: a differential study between people with autism, mentally handicapped and general population]. *Psiquis*, **20**(6), 23–33.

Garcia-Villamisar, D. and Polaino-Lorente, A. (1999b). Nominacion e identificacion de emociones: Un estudio comparativo entre autistas, deficientes mentales y poblacion general. [Nomination and identification of emotions: a comparative study between persons with autism, mental retardation and general population]. *Estudios de Psicologia*, **63–64**, 33–44.

Gibson, J. J. (1979). *The ecological approach to visual perception*. Boston, NH: Houghton-Mifflin.

Gillott, A., Furniss, F., and Walter, A. (2001). Anxiety in high-functioning children with autism. *Autism*, **5**(3), 277–86.

Glenn, S. and Cunningham, C. (2002). Self-regulation in children and young people with Down syndrome. In *Down syndrome across the life span* (ed. M. Cuskelly, A. Jobling, and S. Buckley), pp. 28–39. London, England: Whurr Publishers Ltd.

Grandin, T. (1995). How people with autism think. In *Learning and cognition in autism: current issues in autism* (ed. E. Schopler and G. B. Mesibov), pp. 137–56. New York, NY: Plenum Press.

Groden, J., Cautela, J., Prince, S., *et al.* (1994). The impact of stress and anxiety on individuals with autism and developmental disabilities. In *Behavioural issues in autism. Current issues in autism* (ed. E. Schopler and G. B. Mesibov), pp. 177–94. New York, NY: Plenum Press.

Grossman, J. B., Klin, A., Carter, A. S., *et al.* (2000). Verbal bias in recognition of facial emotions in children with Asperger syndrome. *Journal of Child Psychology and Psychiatry and Allied Disciplines*, **41**(3), 369–79.

Gunnar, M. R. and Barr, R. G. (1998). Stress, early brain development, and behaviour. *Infants and Young Children*, **11**, 1–14.

Hadwin, J., Baron-Cohen, S., Howlin, P., *et al.* (1996). Can we teach children with autism to understand emotions, belief, or pretence? *Development and Psychopathology*, **8**, 345–65.

Haviland, J. M., Walker-Andrews, A. S., Huffman, L. R., *et al.* (1996). Intermodal perception of emotional expressions by children with autism. *Journal of Developmental and Physical Disabilities*, **8**, 77–88.

Hobson, R. P. (1986a). The autistic child's appraisal of expressions of emotion. *Journal of Child Psychology and Psychiatry*, **27**, 321–42.

Hobson, R. P. (1986). The autistic child's appraisal of expressions of emotion: a further study. *Journal of Child Psychology and Psychiatry and Allied Disciplines*, **27**(5), 671–80.

Hobson, R. P. (1991a). Against the theory of 'theory of mind'. *British Journal of Developmental Psychology*, **9**(1), 33–51.

Hobson, R. P. (1991b). Methodological issues for experiments on autistic individuals' perception and understanding of emotion. *Journal of Child Psychology and Psychiatry and Allied Disciplines*, **32**(7), 1135–58.

Hobson, R. P. (1992). Social perception in high level autism. In *High functioning individuals with autism* (ed. E. Schopler and G. B. Mesibov), pp. 157–86. New York, NY: Plenum Press.

Hobson, R. P., Ouston, J., and Lee, A. (1989). Naming emotion in faces and voices: abilities and disabilities in autism and mental retardation. *British Journal of Developmental Psychology*, **7**(3), 237–50.

Howard, M. A., Cowell, P. E., Boucher, J., *et al.* (2000). Convergent neuroanatomical and behavioural evidence of an amygdala hypothesis of autism. *Neuroreport*, **11**(13), 2931–5.

Jones, R. S. P., Zahl, A., and Huws, J. C. (2001). First-hand accounts of emotional experiences in autism: a qualitative analysis. *Disability and Society*, **16**(3), 393–401.

Joseph, R. M. and Tager-Flusberg, H. (1997). An investigation of attention and affect in children with autism and Down syndrome. *Journal of Autism and Developmental Disorders*, **27**, 385–96.

Kagan, J. and Snidman, N. (1999). Early childhood predictors of adult anxiety disorders. *Biological Psychiatry*, **46**(11), 1536–41.

Kagan, J., Snidman, N., and Arcus, D. (1998). Childhood derivatives of high and low reactivity in infancy. *Child Development*, **69**(6), 1483–93.

Kamio, Y. (1998). Affective understanding in high-functioning autistic adolescents. *Japanese Journal of Child and Adolescent Psychiatry*, **39**(4), 340–51.

Kim, J. H. A., Szatmari, P., Bryson, S. E., *et al.* (2000). The prevalence of anxiety and mood problems among children with autism and Asperger syndrome. *Autism*, **4**(2), 117–32.

Kitlowski, K. M. (1995). Social perception: the ability to discriminate facial, vocal and cross-modal expressions of emotion in adults with autism. *Dissertation Abstracts International: Section B: the Sciences and Engineering*, **5**(11-B), 5096. Ann Arbor, MI: Univ Microfilms International.

Klin, A. S. (2000). Attributing social meaning to ambiguous visual stimuli in higher-functioning autism and Asperger syndrome: the Social Attribution Task. *Journal of Child Psychology and Psychiatry*, **41**, 831–46.

Klin, A., Jones, W., Schultz, R., *et al.* (2002). Visual fixation patterns during viewing of naturalistic social situations as predictors of social competence in individuals with autism. *Archives of General Psychiatry*, **59**(9), 809–16.

Lainhart, J. E. (1999). Psychiatric problems in individuals with autism, their parents and siblings. *International Review of Psychiatry*, **11**(4), 278–98.

Lainhart, J. E. and Folstein, S. E. (1994). Affective disorders in people with autism: a review of published cases. *Journal of Autism and Developmental Disorders*, **24**(5), 587–601.

Lengua, L. J., Sandler, I. N., West, S. G., *et al.* (1999). Emotionality and self-regulation, threat appraisal, and coping in children of divorce. *Development and Psychopathology*, **11**(1), 15–37.

Loveland, K. (1991). Social affordances and interaction: autism and the affordances of the human environment. *Ecological Psychology*, **3**, 99–119.

Loveland, K. A. (2001).Toward an ecological theory of Autism. In *The development of autism: Perspectives from theory and research* (ed. J. A. Burack, T. Charman, N. Yirmiya, and P. R. Zelazo) pp. 17–37. New Jersey: Erlbaum Press.

Loveland, K. and Tunali, B. (1991). Social scripts for conversational interactions in autism and Down syndrome. *Journal of Autism and Developmental Disorders*, **21**, 177–86.

Loveland, K., Tunali-Kotoski, B., Pearson, D., *et al.* (1994). Imitation and expression of facial affect in autism. *Development and Psychopathology*, **6**, 433–44.

Loveland, K., Tunali-Kotoski, B., Pearson, D., *et al.* (1995). Intermodal perception of affect by persons with Autism or Down syndrome. *Development and Psychopathology*, **7**, 409–18.

Loveland, K., Tunali-Kotoski, B., Chen, R., *et al.* (1997a). Affect recognition in autism: verbal and non-verbal information. *Development and Psychopathology*, **9**, 579–93.

Loveland, K. A., Tunali-Kotoski, B., Chen, Y. R., *et al.* (1997b). Emotion recognition in autism: Verbal and nonverbal information. *Development and Psychopathology*, **9**(3), 579–93.

Loveland, K. A., Nagy, E., Pearson, D. A., *et al.* (2001a). *Intermodal perception of emotion in autism.* Paper presented at the International Meeting for Autism Research, November, San Diego, CA.

Loveland, K., Bachevalier, J., Nemanic, S., *et al.* (2001b). *Prefrontal-limbic dysfunction and the development of autism.* Invited paper in a symposium on 'Neural bases of social behaviour: insights from autism', Meeting of the Society for Research in Child Development, April, Minneapolis, Minnesota.

Loveland, K., Pearson, D., Tunali-Kotoski, B., *et al.* (2001c). Judgments of social appropriateness by children and adolescents with autism. *Journal of Autism and Developmental Disorders*, **31**, 367–76.

Loveland, K., Pearson, D. A., Reddoch, S., *et al.* (2003). *Sources of anxiety in children and adolescents with autism.* Unpublished manuscript.

Macdonald, H., Rutter, M., Howlin, P., *et al.* (1989). Recognition and expression of emotional faces by autistic and normal adults. *Journal of Child Psychology and Psychiatry*, **30**, 865–77.

Manassis, K. and Bradley, S. (1994). The development of childhood anxiety disorders: toward an integrated model. *Journal of Applied Developmental Psychology*, **15**, 345–66.

Martin, A., Scahill, L., Klin, A., *et al.* (1999). Higher-functioning pervasive developmental disorders: rates and patterns of psychotropic drug use. *Journal of the American Academy of Child and Adolescent Psychiatry*, **38**(7), 923–31.

Mednolia, M. (2002). An index of self-regulation of emotion and the study of repression in social contexts that threaten or do not threaten self-concept. *Emotion*, **2**(3), 215–32.

Miller, D. C. and Byrnes, J. P. (2001). Adolescents' decision making in social situations: a self-regulation perspective. *Journal of Applied Developmental Psychology*, **22**(3), 237–56.

Minter, M. E., Hobson, R. P., and Pring, L. (1991). Recognition of vocally expressed emotion by congenitally blind children. *Journal of Visual Impairment and Blindness*, **85**(10), 411–15.

Moore, D. G., Hobson, R. P., and Lee, A. (1997). Components of person perception: An investigation with autistic, non-autistic retarded and typically developing children and adolescents. *British Journal of Developmental Psychology*, **15**, 401–23.

Ozonoff, S., Pennington, B. F., and Rogers, S. J. (1990). Are there emotion perception deficits in young autistic children? *Journal of Child Psychology and Psychiatry and Allied Disciplines*, **31(3)**, 343–61.

Pelphrey, K. A., Sasson, N.J, Reznick, J. S., *et al.* (2002). Visual scanning of faces in autism. *Journal of Autism and Developmental Disorders*, **32(4)**, 249–61.

Pennington, B. F. and Ozonoff, S. (1996). Executive functions and developmental psychopathology. *Journal of Child Psychology and Psychiatry*, **37(1)**, 51–87.

Pierce, K., Glad, K. S., and Schreibman, L. (1997). Social perception in children with autism: An attentional deficit? *Journal of Autism and Developmental Disorders*, **27**, 265–82.

Pierce, K., Muller, R.-A., Ambrose, J., *et al.* (2001). Face processing occurs outside the fusiform 'face area' in autism: evidence from functional MRI. *Brain*, **124(10)**, 2059–73.

Posner, M. I. and Rothbart, M. K. (2000). Developing mechanisms of self regulation. *Development and Psychopathology*, **12**, 427–41.

Quas, J. A., Murowchick, E., Bensadoun, J., *et al.* (2002). Predictors of children's cortisol activation during the transition to kindergarten. *Journal of Developmental and Behavioral Pediatrics*, **23(5)**, 304–13.

Reddy, V., Williams, E., and Vaughan, A. (2002). Sharing humour and laughter in autism and Down's syndrome. *British Journal of Psychology*, **93(2)**, 219–42.

Rieffe, C., Terwogt, M. M., and Stockmann, L. (2000). Understanding atypical emotions among children with autism. *Journal of Autism and Developmental Disorders*, **30(3)**, 195–203.

Rolls, E. T. (1990). A theory of emotion, and its application to understanding the neural basis of emotion. *Cognition and Emotion*, **4(3)**, 161–90.

Rolls, E. T., Hornak, J., Wade, D., *et al.* (1994). Emotion-related learning in patients with social and emotional changes associated with frontal lobe damage. *Journal of Neurology, Neurosurgery and Psychiatry*, **57(12)**, 1518–24.

Rosenblum, K. L., McDonough, S., Muzik, M., *et al.* (2002). Maternal representations of the infant: associations with infant response to the still face. *Child Development*, **73(4)**, 999–1015.

Saunders, R. C., Kolachana, B. S., Bachevalier, J., *et al.* (1998). Neonatal lesions of the medial temporal lobe disrupt prefrontal cortical regulation of striatal dopamine. *Nature*, **393**, 169–71.

Schore, A. N. (1994). *Affect regulation and the origin of the self: the neurobiology of emotional development*. Hillsdale, NJ: Lawrence Erlbaum.

Schore, A. N. (1996). The experience-dependent maturation of a regulatory system in the orbital prefrontal cortex and the origin of developmental psychopathology, *Development and Psychopathology*, **8**, 59–87.

Schore, A. N. (2000). Attachment and the regulation of the right brain. *Attachment and Human Development*, **2(1)**, 23–47.

Schultz, R. T., Gauthier, I., Klin, A., *et al.* (2000). Abnormal ventral temporal cortical activity during face discrimination among individuals with autism and Asperger syndrome. *Archives of General Psychiatry*, **57(4)**, 331–40.

Schultz, R. T., Romanski, L. M., and Tsatsanis, K. D. (2000). Neurofunctional models of autistic disorder and Asperger syndrome: clues from neuroimaging. In *Asperger syndrome* (ed. A. Klin and F. R. Volkmar), pp. 172–209. New York, NY: Guilford Press.

Serra, M., Minderaa, R. B., van Geert, P. L., *et al.* (1999). Social-cognitive abilities in children with lesser variants of autism: skill deficits or failure to apply skills? *European Child and Adolescent Psychiatry*, **8**, 301–11.

Sigman, M. D., Kasari, C., Kwon, J. H., *et al.* (1992). Responses to the negative emotions of others by autistic, mentally retarded, and normal children. *Child Development,* **63,** 796–807.

Stevens, J., Quittner, A. L., Zuckerman, J. B., *et al.* (2002). Behavioral inhibition, self-regulation of motivation, and working memory in children with attention deficit hyperactivity disorder. *Developmental Neuropsychology,* **21**(2), 117–40.

Stewart, S. L. and Rubin, K. D. (1995). The social problem-solving skills of anxious-withdrawn children. *Development and Psychopathology,* **7,** 323–36.

Swedo, S. E. and Rapoport, J. L. (1989). Phenomenology and differential diagnosis of obsessive-compulsive disorder in children and adolescents. In *Obsessive-Compulsive Disorder in children and adolescents* (ed. J. L. Rapoport), pp. 13–22. Washington, DC: American Psychiatric Press.

Tsai, L. Y. (1992). Diagnostic issues in high-functioning autism. In *High-functioning individuals with autism* (ed. E. Schopler and G. Mesibov), pp. 11–40. New York, NY: Plenum.

Walker-Andrews, A. S., Haviland, J. M., Huffman, L., *et al.* (1994). Brief report: preferential looking in intermodal preception by children with autism. *Journal of Autism and Developmental Disorders,* **24,** 99–107.

Weeks, S. and Hobson, R. P. (1987). The salience of facial expression for autistic children. *Journal of Child Psychology and Psychiatry,* **28,** 137–51.

Wehmeyer, M. L., Yeager, D., Bolding, N., *et al.* (2003). The effects of self-regulation strategies on goal attainment for students with developmental disabilities in general education classrooms. *Journal of Developmental and Physical Disabilities,* **15**(1), 79–91.

Yirmiya, N., Kasari, C., Sigman, M., *et al.* (1989). Facial expressions of affect in autistic, mentally retarded, and normal children. *Journal of Child Psychology and Psychiatry,* **30,** 725–36.

Yirmiya, N., Sigman, M., Kasari, C., *et al.* (1992). Empathy and cognition in high-functioning children with autism. *Child Development,* **63,** 150–60.

Chapter 15

Emotional regulation and affective disorders in children and adolescents with obsessive compulsive disorder

Martine Flament and David Cohen

Introduction

The clinical picture of obsessive compulsive disorder (OCD) is an ancient human experience, remarkably described in old writings as an existential struggle between 'Good and Bad' (Malleus Maleficarum, Kramer and Spzenger 1486), or as excessive 'Scrupple' (Taylor, 1660). Both the adult and child psychiatric literature contain early descriptions of typical cases of OCD with onset during childhood or adolescence. In his renowned 'Traité des maladies mentales', Esquirol (1838) reported the first case resembling current OCD, in a young woman whose obsessions and compulsions had started before 18 years of age. Forty years later, in a monograph entitled 'La folie du doute avec délire du toucher', Legrand du Saule (1875) first attempted to isolate what Janet and Freud later named Obsessional Neurosis, noting that the disorder often develops during adolescence and can remain hidden for years. At the beginning of the 20th century, Janet (1903) reported on a 5-year-old with classical obsessive compulsive (OC) symptoms, and Freud's famous patient, the Rat Man, described obsessional behaviours dating back from childhood (1906). Kanner, in 1957, noted the resemblance—and sometimes the association—between compulsive movements and tics, and Despert described, in 1955, the first large series of OCD children ($n = 68$), insisting on the children's perception of the abnormality and undesirability of their behaviours.

For years, OCD has been seen as a paradigm of a psychologically determined illness and psychological theories of OCD have encompassed psychoanalytic theories, as well as more general non-psychodynamic aetiological models, focusing alternatively on volitional, intellectual, and/or emotional impairment. Nevertheless, a variety of biological aetiologies have also been proposed for OCD since 1860 (for review, see Rapoport, 1989), and modern neurobiological theories have been based on a number of biochemical, neurological, autoimmune, and ethological models.

Clinical characteristics of OCD

OCD is defined by the presence of obsessions and/or compulsions. Obsessions are persistently recurring thoughts, impulses, or images that are experienced as intrusive, inappropriate, and distressing, and that are not simply excessive worries about realistic problems. Compulsions are repetitive behaviours or mental acts that a person feels driven to perform according to a rigidly applied rule, in order to reduce distress or to prevent some dreaded outcome. Both the DSM-IV (American Psychiatric Association, 1994) and the ICD-10 (World Health Organization, 1992) define OCD, regardless of age, by obsessions, and/or compulsions (criterion A), which are described, at some point during the course of the disorder, as excessive or unreasonable (criterion B), and are severe enough to cause marked distress or to interfere significantly with the person's normal routine, usual social activities, or relationships (criterion C). The specific content of the obsessions or compulsions cannot be restricted to another Axis I diagnosis, such as preoccupations about food resulting from an eating disorder, guilty thoughts from a major depressive disorder, or rituals resulting from hallucinations in schizophrenia (criterion D). The DSM-IV specifies that the disturbance is not due to the direct physiological effects of a substance or a general medical condition (criterion E). The ICD-10 allows for the subclassification of different forms with predominant obsessions, predominant compulsions, or mixed symptoms.

The clinical presentation of OCD during childhood and adolescence has been documented in various cultures, with clinical series reported from the US (Swedo *et al.*, 1989b), Japan (Honjo *et al.*, 1989), India (Khana and Srinath, 1989), Israel (Apter and Tyano, 1988), Denmark (Thomsen, 1991), and Spain (Toro *et al.*, 1992). In a group of 70 young patients examined at the National Institute of Mental Health (NIMH) in the US (Swedo *et al.*, 1989b), obsessions dealt primarily with fear of dirt or germs (40%), danger to self or a loved one (24%), symmetry (17%), or scrupulous religiosity (13%), and the major presenting rituals included, in order of decreasing frequency, washing rituals (85%), repeating (51%), checking (46%), touching (20%), counting (18%), ordering (17%), and hoarding (11%). Research suggests that there is an isomorphism between childhood and adult presentations of OCD. For comparison, we can refer to a population of 250 adult OCD patients from a specialty clinic in the US (Rasmussen and Eisen, 1992): the most common obsessions were fear of contamination (45%), pathological doubt (42%), somatic obsessions (36%), and the need for symmetry (31%), whereas the most frequent compulsions consisted of checking (63%), washing (50%), counting (36%), and the need to ask or confess (31%).

Typically, children and adolescents with OCD experience multiple obsessions and compulsions, whose content may change over time (Flament *et al.*, 1988; Swedo *et al.*, 1989b). Generally, compulsions are carried out to dispell anxiety and/or in response to an obsession (e.g. to ward off harm to someone). Some of the obsessions and rituals involve an internal sense that 'it does not feel right' until the thought or action is completed. Certain children with OCD may be unable to specify the dread event that the compulsive rituals are intended to prevent, beyond a vague premonition of something bad happening.

Simple compulsions, such as repetitive touching or symmetrical ordering, may even lack any discernable ideational component, and may be phenomenologically indistinguishable from complex tics (Cohen and Leckman, 1994). Children and adolescents with OCD may hide their symptoms, or will only allow them to appear at home or in the presence of close family members.

The age at onset of OCD appears bimodal (Rasmussen and Tsuang, 1986; Swedo *et al.*, 1989). Prepubertal onset is associated with a male preponderance and an increased risk for tic disorders, including Tourette's disorder (Swedo *et al.*, 1989; Riddle *et al.*, 1990). A second peak of onset is associated with puberty and the following years. Later in life, pregnancy and the immediate post-partum period is a time of increased risk, with reported rates among new mothers as high as 11% to 47% (Pauls *et al.*, 1991; Neziroglu *et al.*, 1992).

Epidemiology

Epidemiological studies on OCD in adolescents, using strict diagnostic criteria and structured clinical interviews, have been completed in several parts of the world (USA, Israel, New Zealand, Italy), with estimated prevalence ranging from 1 to 4%. In the first and largest study, conducted on 5596 US high school students (Flament *et al.*, 1988), the current prevalence of OCD, according to the DSM-III criteria, was estimated to 1% (± 0.5) and its lifetime prevalence to 1.9% (± 0.7). This study showed that the disorder was clearly under-diagnosed and under-treated in this age group: none of the adolescents identified with OCD had been previously diagnosed and only 20% had been treated in the past for co-morbid psychological problems. In a later study, in which 562 consecutive inductees into the Israeli Army aged 16 and 17 years were examined by Zohar *et al.* (1992), the current prevalence of OCD (using DSM-III-R criteria) was 3.6% (± 0.7); however, if the prevalence was estimated excluding those individuals with only obsessions, the point prevalence dropped to 1.8%. Two longitudinal studies followed cohorts of children in the community until they were 18 years of age. A US study found a lifetime prevalence for OCD of 2.1% (Reinherz *et al.*, 1993), and a study conducted in New Zealand had an overall 1-year prevalence of 4%, that decreased to 1.2% when subjects with only obsessions were excluded (Douglass *et al.*, 1995). Thus, it appears that OCD may be as frequent in adolescents as it is in adults (Robins *et al.*, 1984; Karno *et al.*, 1988; Weissman *et al.*, 1994). The first community study on OCD in children has been a nationwide survey of 5–15-year-olds in the UK; the weighted overall prevalence of OCD was 0.25%, with prevalence increasing exponentially as a function of increasing age (Heyman *et al.*, 2001). Of note, a study comparing prevalence of various mental disorders across ethnic groups in the US did not find any significant difference for the prevalence of OCD in children or adolescents (Costello *et al.*, 1996).

Comorbidity

OCD in children and adolescents is frequently associated with other symptoms, which have important implications in regard to clinical assessment, differential diagnosis and treatment planning. In both referred and community samples, the overall lifetime co-morbidity of OCD in children or adolescents is as high as 75% (Flament and Chabane, 2000).

Mood and anxiety disorders are the most common co-morbid conditions, with prevalence ranging across studies from 8 to 73% for mood disorders, and from 13 to 70% for anxiety disorders (Geller *et al.*, 1998). Among anxiety disorders, overanxious and separation anxiety disorders are the most frequent in children, and panic and generalized anxiety disorders the most frequent in adolescents. Typically, co-morbid anxiety disorders emerge prior to the diagnosis of OCD (Rasmussen and Eisen, 1992), while a major episode of depression follows the onset of OCD in at least half of child-referred children (Swedo *et al.*, 1989). The debilitating and seemingly uncontrollable nature of OCD symptoms has been considered depressogenic, while it has been suggested that co-morbidity between OCD and anxiety disorders may be due to shared genetic factors and pathological pathways of information processing. Family studies demonstrate elevated anxiety, but not depressive disorders in family members of OCD probands (Black *et al.*, 1992); levels of somatic arousal in individuals with OCD are comparable to those present in individuals with other anxiety disorders (Rachman and Hodgson, 1980).

Anorexia nervosa has been reported in 8% of OCD adolescents, when this disorder has been systematically assessed (Toro *et al.*, 1992). Conversely, OCD has been found in 3–66% of girls with anorexia nervosa, with the onset of OCD most often occurring before or at the onset of the eating disorder (Godart *et al.*, 2000). In a community study, bulimia nervosa was observed in 20% of adolescent OCD cases (Flament *et al.*, 1988).

Of particular importance in childhood onset OCD is the high rate of co-morbid tic disorders, including Tourette's disorder, which have been reported in 13–26% of referred OCD patients (Geller *et al.*, 1998), and in 25% of a community derived sample (Zohar *et al.*, 1992). In one study, nearly 60% of children and adolescents seeking treatment for OCD and followed over time proved to have a lifetime history of tics, that ranged across subjects from simple, mild, transient tics through Tourette's disorder (Leonard *et al.*, 1992). Similarly, about 50% of children and adolescents with Tourette's disorder develop some OCD symptoms or full-blown OCD by adulthood (Leckman, 1993). Elevated rates of OCD have been found in first degree relatives of probands with Tourette's disorder, suggesting a genetic relationship (Pauls *et al.*, 1991, 1995). While occurring less frequently in non referred subjects, a high rate of disruptive behaviour disorders—attention-deficit/hyperactivity disorder (ADHD) and oppositional defiant disorder—has been reported in subjects seen in childhood OCD clinics (Geller *et al.*, 1996). As for tic disorders, these co-morbid conditions appear in a chronological sequence, with ADHD or Tourette's disorder often identified years before the onset of OCD symptoms.

Etiopathogenesis

Psychological model of OCD

OCD involves various functions and dysfunctions of the mind and behaviour. OCD has been successively seen as:

- a disorder of intellect, with thoughts or doubts at or beyond the border of sanity;
- a disorder of volition, with distressing thoughts and actions against the person's wishes;
- a disorder of emotions, with fear, helplessness, and negative self-appraisal.

Accordingly, OCD has been classified among the psychoses, neurological disorders, or anxiety disorders. The view of OCD as primarily a disorder of the emotions, and its classification along with typical anxiety disorders, emerged during the early twentieth century, and was included in the major nosological systems (ICD, DSM).

In both the psychoanalytic and the cognitive behavioural models, the general assumption is that excessive anxiety is generated by a trauma, leading to conflicting cognitive-affective states. The OCD patient has experienced or is experiencing trauma, i.e. the feeling of being out of control over highly salient events, such as major illness or death (Freud, 1913; Rachman and Hodgson, 1980). In the absence of real control over such salient matters, the patient tries to avoid helplessness and anxiety by taking control over something actually within his/her power. Indeed, increased rates of OCD have been reported among high-combat-exposed Vietnam veterans (Pitman, 1993) and common stressful events typically exacerbate OCD symptoms in both children (Swedo *et al.*, 1989) and adults (Rasmussen and Tsuang, 1986). However, in most cases of OCD, there is no obvious trauma that might help explain the onset of the disorder. Anxiogenic experiences associated with OCD are likely to be in large part intrapsychic, i.e. reflect the individual's interpretation of otherwise ordinary events (Bolton, 1998).

For psychoanalysts, compulsive anxiety-reducing strategies draw on pre-rational, magical thinking (Freud, 1913). Freud's description of the Rat Man illustrates the central role of anal sadistic concerns with control, ambivalence, magical thinking, and the salience of defences of reaction formation, intellectualization, isolation, and undoing. Freud went on to formulate a theory of pregenital organization of the libido, determined by constitutional, rather than experiential factors, that is crucial to the development of obsessional neurosis. Anna Freud (1966) shared the view that 'obsessional outcomes are promoted by a constitutional increase in the intensity of the anal-sadistic tendencies . . . probably as the result of inheritance combined with parental handling'. However, despite the beautifully described dynamics of obsessional symptoms, most illustrative of unconscious processes, the psychoanalysts have also pointed out the extreme difficulty in treating severe OCD with classical analytic treatment.

Cognitive psychologists who subscribe to operant conditioning principles presume that the rate of OCD behavioural symptoms is maintained through reinforcement based on their symbolic power to reduce anxiety (Rachman and Hodgson, 1980). The view of OCD as a process that fundamentally involves anxiety reduction has been elaborated in various ways by cognitive psychologists as:

- an unrealistic threat appraisal, i.e. dysfunctional assumptions such as 'one should be perfect' or 'mistakes result in condemnation' or 'the self has power to prevent disasters' (McFall and Wollerstein, 1979);

- an inflated sense of responsability leading persons with OCD to misinterpret normal unwanted intrusive thoughts and to enter a vicious circle: intrusive thoughts→ feeling of responsibility and guilt→neutralizing the thoughts→recurrence (Salkovski, 1985);

- the thought-action fusion, that is the absence of clear distinction between having a negative thought, and carrying out the negative action itself (Rachman, 1993).

The 'Perceived impulsivity' model, proposed by Cottraux (1995), is an attempt to integrate the various modern psychological findings about OCD. Perceived impulsivity is considered to be an innate biological vulnerability. The subject believes he is unable to resist images, thoughts, and urges whose content involve common antisocial impulses that lead to negative self-appraisal. Interaction between social environment and impulsivity shapes responsibility-culpability schemes (ranging from normal altruistic beliefs to almost delusional beliefs regarding the impact of one's behaviour on others). Because of the thought-action fusion, the subject believes he is potentially dangerous to others. The struggle against cognitive intrusions encompasses the cognitive-behavioural system (rituals) intended to prevent the danger that the subject sees himself inflicting on others. Thus, the compulsions are the products of uncertainty about self-control, and have an altruistic function.

Developmental perspective

Obsessive and compulsive behaviour reflect a heterogeneous pattern of repetitive and intrusive thoughts and acts; both adaptive and maladaptive forms may be observed throughout development.

Obsessions, rituals and development

The frequency of repetitive behaviours in young children has been described by classical psychologists (Piaget, 1962; Gesell *et al.*, 1974) and psychoanalysts (Anna Freud, 1965). From a cognitive developmental perspective, repeating behaviours and activities, adhering to rules, and enacting rituals serve a critical role in establishing and maintaining new schemata, e.g. integrated perceptual, cognitive, and motor action patterns (Piaget, 1962). During the pre-school years, ritualistic behaviours appear to increase as children attempt to gain mastery regarding autonomy and/or self-control (Evans *et al.*, 1997; Zohar and Felz, 2001). These rituals may stress rules about daily life, help the child master anxiety, prevent a negative outcome paralleling magical thinking, and enhance the socializing process (Leonard *et al.*, 1990). Non-pathological compulsions also involve efforts to ensure security or hygiene (e.g. protective checking and cleaning) and, when used in moderation, are adaptative for basic survival needs. As children enter elementary school, they engage in complex rule-based games and rule-based superstitious behaviours (Carter, 1995). These superstitious beliefs are similar to adaptive behaviours, as they help master the anxiety associated with disturbing thoughts or impulses. Some reports have also illustrated that a variety of obsessional cognitions are endorsed by most healthy preadolescents and adolescents, but tend to diminish with age (Zohar and Bruno, 1997).

Figure 15.1 summarizes the developmental course and characteristics of normative versus pathological obsessive-compulsive behaviours and thoughts in children and youths. They mainly differ by their emotional context and by their use of adaptive versus maladaptive cognitive and behavioural strategies. Repetitive behaviours that are part of learning new skills will be accompanied by expressions of positive affect and interest. In contrast, perseverative behaviours in OCD are not goal-orientated, they are accompanied by a burdened, anxious affect and may further provoke frustration, as the child recurrently finds it impossible to arrive at a satisfactory closure (Pollock and Carter, 1999). Similarly, the distressing and lasting qualities of pathological obsessions might be related to distinct information-processing strategies used by individuals with OCD, who tend to assess intrusive thoughts as less controllable and more dangerous, experience a heightened feeling of responsibility, and resort to maladaptive coping strategies (e.g. self-punishment, worry). By contrast, healthy youths are more tolerant towards thought intrusion or they may use more developmentally appropriate strategies (e.g. reappraisal, distraction, social control; Wells and Davies, 1994; Amir *et al.*, 1997).

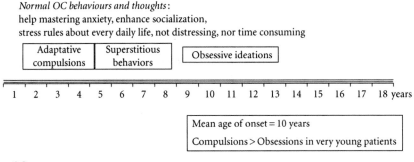

Fig. 15.1 Timing and characteristics of normal and pathological obsessive-compulsive (OC) behaviours and thoughts during childhood and adolescence.

Cognitive psychologists have illustrated the tendency of anxious individuals to preferentially process threat-relevant material. Variations in temperamental styles may be associated with the source and maintenance of obsessions and compulsions. In addition to individual differences, Pollock and Carter (1999) have suggested that certain developmental stages or transitions appear to confer a heightened risk, both for typically occurring obsessions and compulsions and disordered states. Developmental transitions that stress or imperil the child's sense of security, control, or mastery may elicit maladaptive coping strategies that include obsessional ideation and ritualistic behaviours. A 'successful' experience of 'control' during this time may involve repetitive, obsessional actions that increase in likelihood of occurrence and that eventually become organized into a disordered state (Pollock and Carter, 1999).

The family context and background

The familial nature of OCD has been observed since the 1930s, and both Freud and Janet believed that constitutional or genetic factors were important in the pathogenesis of the disorder. Twin studies have provided limited evidence for the role of genetic factors in the manifestations of OCD (Rasmussen and Tsuang, 1986), and several family studies have shown that the disorder is much more common among relatives of individuals with OCD than would be expected from estimated occurrence rates for the general population (Rasmussen, 1994). At the present time, however, it is not clear whether the inherited factors are specific for OCD, or whether OCD is part of a broader heritable anxiety spectrum (Pauls and Alsobrook, 1999).

Apart from chromosomal transmission, familial aggregation may reflect the fact that familial factors influence the development and maintenance of OCD, via socialization, interpersonal processes, and emotional regulation within the family group. Interaction with relatives influence both the emotional aura and the management of obsessions and compulsions in many youths (Lenane, 1989; Calvocoressi et al., 1995).

As young children depend on parents and care givers for interpreting social and emotional experiences, parental reactions, ideas, fears, and phantasms may contribute to the child's insecurity, and interpretation of intrusive and fearful ideations. Especially at times of developmental transitions, family members'cognitive and behavioural responses to the initial emergence of obsessional behaviours may influence the subsequent trajectory towards a disordered state, i.e. OCD. Parental psychopathology may also interfere with adaptive parenting through increased intrusiveness, expressed hostility and/or overprotection, as well as decreased emotional availability (Pollock and Carter, 1999). In a recent 2-year follow-up study, Black et al. (2003) demonstrated that children having a parent with OCD were more likely than control children to have social, emotional, and behavioural disorders, including OCD, separation anxiety, and overanxious disorder.

The attachment theory

Separation anxiety disorder is a frequent co-morbidity in OCD children. The inter-dependence and reciprocity of biological, emotional and social transmission in OCD is emphasized in the attachment-theory based model of emotional regulation. Preliminary results from several studies suggest that this model may be useful in understanding the origins of OCD. Manassis *et al.* (1995) examined the relationship between behavioural inhibition, insecure mother–child attachment and evidence of anxiety in the offspring of mothers with anxiety disorders. The study suggested an association between anxious mothers, inhibited temperament, attachment difficulties, and internalizing manifestations in offspring. Although a similar study in the field of OCD is still needed, Fonagy (1999) described the case of a severely disturbed adolescent with OCD using the attachment theory model of transgenerational trauma (the maternal grandmother was a holocaust survivor). He proposed that the transmission of specific traumatic ideas across generations may be mediated by a vulnerability established in the infant by frightened or frightening caregivers. Through the disorganized attachment organization of the self, the child was susceptible to the internalization of sets of trauma-related ideation from the attachment figure and, therefore, to the development of OC symptoms.

Biochemical model of OCD

Although a variety of biological etiologies have been proposed to explain OCD since 1860 (for review, see Rapoport, 1989), modern neurobiological theories of OCD emerged during the 1970s and 1980s, with the clinical studies showing that clomipramine and other serotonin reuptake inhibitors (SRIs), had a unique efficacy in treating the core symptoms of OCD. This inspired a 'serotonergic hypothesis' of the disorder (Insel *et al.*, 1990).

Several randomized, controlled clinical trials have been conducted in children and adolescents with OCD (for review see Flament and Cohen, 2000), all demonstrating the selective, and unique efficacy of several SRIs (i.e. clomipramine, fluoxetine, fluvoxamine, sertraline) in the short-term treatment of the disorder; in addition, a few open studies provide preliminary positive results for the efficacy of other specific serotonin reuptake inhibitors (SSRIs—i.e. citalopram, paroxetine). A summary of the design and results of existing studies is presented in Table 15.1. Overall, it appears that: (a) the anti-obsessional action of the SRIs is independent of the presence of depressive symptoms at baseline; (b) it is longer to appear than the antidepressant action; (c) the therapeutic response is gradual over a few weeks or a few months; (d) final response is most often incomplete, with a mean reduction from baseline on scales measuring intensity of OC symptoms between 20 and 50% across measures and across studies. Clinical evidence of serotonin dysfunction in OCD also comes from demonstration of the augmentation of clomipramine antiobsessional effect by other drugs with serotonergic activity (Walsh and

Table 15.1 Short-term Pharmacological Treatment Studies in Children and Adolescents with OCD

Study, Year	Subjects (age) Study duration	Drug (daily dose) Study design	Main results	% Improvement from baseline across OC symptom measures
Flament et al., 1985	19 (6–18 years) 5 weeks	Clomipramine (mean 141 mg) Crossover vs PBO	CMI > PBO at 3–5 weeks	22–44 %
Leonard et al., 1989	47 (7–19 years) 5 weeks	Clomipramine (mean 150 mg) Crossover vs desipramine	CMI > DES at 3–5 weeks	19–44 %
DeVeaugh-Geiss et al., 1992	60 (10–17 years) 8 weeks	Clomipramine (75–200 mg) Parallel vs PBO	CMI > PBO at 3–8 weeks	34–37 %
Riddle et al., 1992	14 (8–15 years) 8 weeks	Fluoxetine (20 mg) Crossover vs PBO	FLUO > PBO at 8 weeks	33–44 %
Apter et al., 1994	14 (13–18 years) 8 weeks	Fluvoxamine (100–300 mg) Open study	Improvement at 8 weeks	28%
Thomsen et al., 1997	23 (9–18 years) 10 weeks	Citalopram (mean 37 mg) Open study	Improvement at 10 weeks	20–29 %
March et al., 1998	187 (6–17 years) 12 weeks	Sertraline (mean 167 mg) Parallel vs PBO	SER > PBO at 3–12 weeks	21–28 %
Rosenberg et al., 1999	20 (8–17 years) 12 weeks	Paroxetine (mean 41 mg) Open study	Improvement at 4–12 weeks	28%
Riddle et al., 2001	120 (8–17 years) 10 weeks	Fluvoxamine (50–200 mg) Parallel vs PBO	FLUV > PBO at 1–10 weeks	21–25 %
Liebowitz et al., 2002	43 (8–17 years) 16 weeks	Fluoxetine (mean 64 mg) Parallel vs PBO	FLU > PBO at 16 weeks	42%

PBO = placebo; CMI = clomipramine; DES = desipramine; FLUO = fluoxetine; SER = sertraline; FLUV = fluvoxamine.

McDougle, 2001), the inefficacy of non-selective or norepinephrine selective uptake inhibitors (Leonard *et al.*, 1989), and relapse of OCD symptoms on discontinuation or desipramine substitution of clomipramine treatment (Leonard *et al.*, 1991).

Biochemical evidence of serotonin involvement in OCD first arose from the demonstration of a correlation between the antiobsessional effect of clomipramine and reduction of the cerebro-spinal fluid (CSF) concentration of the main metabolite of serotonin (5-hydroxyindolacetic acid, 5HIAA) in adult patients in one study (Thorèn *et al.*, 1980). Similarly, in a double-blind, placebo-controlled clomipramine treatment study involving 29 children and adolescents, clinical improvement of the OCD symptoms during clomipramine administration was strongly correlated with pre-treatment platelet serotonin concentrations, and with the decrease of platelet serotonin content during treatment (Flament *et al.*, 1987). In addition, there have been several reports of decreased density of the platelet serotonin transporter in children and adolescents with OCD compared to normals or to children with Tourette's disorder (Weizman *et al.*, 1992; Sallee *et al.*, 1996). In one study (Sallee *et al.*, 1996), the baseline binding capacity (B_{max}) of the ligand (^{3}H-paroxetine) was positively correlated with the clinical severity of OCD symptoms, only in patients who responded positively to pharmacological treatment. In another study, there was an increase in central serotonin turnover (higher concentrations of CSF 5HIAA) in children and adolescents with OCD compared to children and adolescents with disruptive behaviour disorders (Zahn *et al.*, 1992).

Several oral pharmacological challenge studies with the partial serotonin agonist methyl-chlorophenylpiperazine (m-CPP) resulted in the exacerbation of anxiety and OC symptoms in untreated OCD patients, suggesting hypersensitivity of at least some post-synaptic receptors; no behavioural effect of m-CPP was seen in patients treated for several months with clomipramine, possibly due to post-treatment down-regulation of the same receptors (Zohar and Insel, 1987; Hollander *et al.*, 1992). Of note, OCD patients are insensitive to noradrenergic or other provocative agents that exacerbate symptoms in non-OCD anxiety disorders (yohimbine, sodium lactate, caffeine).

However, although some evidence suggests that serotonin plays a prominent role in brain modulation of aggressive and impulsive behaviour (Insel and Winslow, 1992), the role of serotoninergic fibres in mediating specific behaviours remains speculative. In addition, the delayed and incomplete action of serotonergic drugs in OCD suggests that multiple factors may operate on other neurotransmitters as well. Both short term (Swedo *et al.*, 1992a) and long-term follow-up (Altemus *et al.*, 1992) studies have carefully examined CSF neurochemical changes during clomipramine treatment of patients with juvenile OCD. Changes were observed for many measures, including neuropeptides (corticotropin-releasing hormone, vasopressin, somatostatin, and oxytocin) and monoamine metabolites (5HIAA, homovanilic acid, 3-methoxy-4-hydroxyphenylglycol). Thus, despite numerous biochemical studies of OCD patients and controls, none has yet indicated a single biochemical abnormality as a primary aetiological mechanism in OCD.

Neurological model of OCD

It has been early reported that some OC symptoms could be associated with neurological disorders of motor control, including Tourette's Disorder, Huntington's disease, Parkinson's disease, as well as traumatic or infectious lesions of the basal ganglia (for review, see Rapoport, 1989). An increased incidence of motor tics and of choreiform movements have been reported in children and adolescents with OCD, and a significant proportion of children and adults with the disorder show impairment of visuo-motor integration, visual memory, and executive functioning (Behar *et al.*, 1984; Flament *et al.*, 1990; Hollander *et al.*, 1997).

Since Baxter *et al.*'s (1987) seminal study of OCD with positron emission tomography, neuroimaging techniques have been used extensively in OCD research. Despite some discrepant findings, most studies on brain morphology of adult patients reported the involvement of the caudate nuclei and/or the frontal lobes in OCD (for review, see Cottraux and Gérard, 1998). For example, a computerized tomography study by Luxemberg *et al.* (1988) found significantly smaller caudate volumes in young adult males with childhood onset OCD compared to controls. A magnetic resonance morphologic study showed that treatment-naive pediatric OCD patients had significantly larger anterior cingulate volumes than did controls (Rosenberg *et al.*, 1998).

Studies using single photon emission computed tomography, positron emission tomography (PET), and functional magnetic resonance imaging generally have identified abnormally high metabolic activity in the orbital cortex and the head of the striatal caudate nucleus in OCD subjects at rest, compared to various control populations (for review, see Baxter, 1998). Furthermore, the same two regions, as well as the thalamus to which each projects, have shown further increase in activity during OC symptom provocation. Several studies by Baxter and collaborators have also demonstrated significant correlations among PET measures obtained for the orbital cortex, the caudate and the thalamus in untreated OCD patients, but only in those who subsequently responded well to either drug or behavioural treatment (Baxter, 1998). Five of seven studies comparing brain functioning in OCD patients before and after successful pharmacological or psychological treatment found a reduction of the hypermetabolism in the frontal lobes and/or the caudate regions following the treatment (Saxena *et al.*, 1998). One of these studies was conducted pre- and post-pharmacological treatment in childhood-onset OCD patients at the NIMH (Swedo *et al.*, 1989c, 1992b).

The 'OCD neural system': orbito-frontal/cingulate cortex/basal ganglia circuitry

Thus, the findings from both morphological and functional brain imaging studies in OCD patients, suggest abnormality of a neural circuit involving the orbito-frontal cortex, the cingulate cortex and the basal ganglia. This circuit, known to play an important role in movement, is instrumental for a spectrum of behaviours, including planning of complex motor acts and routinized patterns of behaviours (Alexander *et al.*, 1990).

In primates, the frontal cortex and the basal ganglia function cooperatively in information processing. The frontal cortex acts when new rules need to be learned and older ones rejected; the basal ganglia potentiate previously learned rules based on the environment and context (Wise *et al.*, 1996). Serotonin is involved in the modulation of both the caudate nuclei (Insel, 1992) and the orbito-frontal cortex (el Mansari *et al.*, 1997). In his integrated 'perceived impulsivity' model, Cottraux (1995) speculates that orbito-frontal hyperactivity could be a state marker that reflects the obsessive struggle to control impulsivity (abnormal information processing resulting from a biological trait). The frontal lobes exert a modulating effect on initiation of motor activity by the basal ganglia. Failure of frontal lobe function would result in excessive and repetitive motor activity, stimulus-bound behaviours, and decreases in volitional and creative behaviours, all of which are found in OCD.

An alternative neurological model of OCD could suggest that the primary dysfunction has more to do with motor control than with information processing. A neurological deficit, either structural or functional (biochemical) or both, involving cortico-striatal-thalamo-cortical circuitry would trigger primary and meaningless compulsive behaviours. Obsessions would be mental versions of the rituals, *post hoc* rationalizations of compulsive behaviours (Rapoport and Wise, 1988; Insel, 1992; Rauch, 2000).

Drawing on computer programming terminology, and taking into account ethological research (see below), Baxter and his colleagues have termed 'macros' the complex sets of interrelated behaviours which entail the implicit learning of habits and cognitive/motor routines assembled from innate species-specific patterns. This process requires participation of the basal ganglia in conjunction with the ventral paralimbic prefrontal cortex and the thalamus, and Baxter (1998) proposed a model for brain mediation of OCD symptoms, summarized in Fig. 15.2. In this model, the neural activity from various cortical and limbic regions tends to course through the basal ganglia to the thalamus via two main pathways, separate but interacting in a multitude of ways: the lateral prefrontal association neocortex projects largely to the dorsolateral aspect of the head of the caudate nucleus and the globus pallidus externa (the 'indirect pathway', exercising a general moderating effect on the thalamus), while the orbital prefrontal paralimbic isocortex projects predominantly to the ventromedial regions of the same structures (the 'direct pathway', exercising a general disinhibiting effect on the thalamus). In well-functioning persons, the 'macros' having to do with threat response and impulses are mediated by the ventromedial system, while the more complex territorial dominance behaviours are mediated by the dorsolateral system, and the two counteracting pathways must be in proper dynamic balance to result in the appropriate expression or repression of specific behaviours. In OCD, there is an increased tone in the direct basal ganglia pathway, resulting in a disinhibited thalamus and the release of macros—or fragments of macros—in excess of actual environmental requirements. When major depression is superimposed, there is an additional decrease in dorsal tone through the striatum, resulting in a further relative increase drive

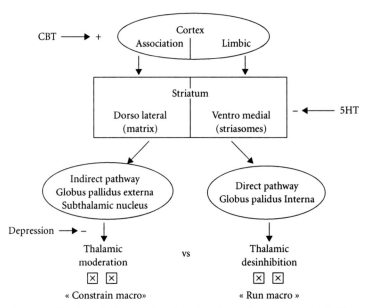

Fig. 15.2 Conceptualization of direct and indirect basal ganglia system striatal efferents as regards regulation of 'macros' in OCD. Negative effect of associated depression, as well as positive effect of serotoninergic (HT) agents and cognitive behavioural therapy (CBT) are indicated (modified from Baxter, 1998).

between the thalamus and the ventral paralimbic cortex, thus worsening OCD. Baxter and others suggest that some cognitive-behavioural therapies for OCD help by getting the patient to exercise dorsolateral routines, while the end result of SRI treatment might be a decreased tone in the ventral system relative to that in the dorsal system. The result of either treatment would then be to restore the balance.

An autoimmune model of OCD

In the 1990s, a finding of wide significance has been the demonstration of a strong association between acute onset OCD and Sydenham's chorea, and it has been suggested that Sydenham's chorea may serve as a medical model of pathogenesis for certain forms of OCD (Swedo *et al.*, 1994). Sydenham's chorea is a childhood movement disorder associated with rheumatic fever, which is thought to result from an antineuronal antibody-mediated response to group A beta-haemolytic streptococcus (GABHS), directed at portions of the basal ganglia in genetically vulnerable individuals. A first retrospective comparison of obsessionality in 23 Sydenham's chorea patients and 24 rheumatic fever patients without Sydenham's chorea showed significantly increased OC symptoms in the choreic patients, with three meeting full criteria for OCD (Swedo *et al.*, 1989a). In a second study of 11 children with Sydenham's chorea of recent onset, nine had acute onset of OCD symptoms that started shortly before the onset of the movement disorder, peaked as the chorea did, and waned over time, completely disappearing with cessation of the choreic movements; antibodies directed against human caudate tissue were present in the serum of 10 of the 11 patients (Swedo *et al.*, 1993). In Brazil, an investigation of children and adolescents who also had rheumatic fever with (*n* = 30) or without Sydenham's chorea (*n* = 20) found OC symptoms in 70% of subjects with chorea, and diagnosable OCD in 16.7%, while OC symptoms were absent in all patients without chorea (Asbahr *et al.*, 1998).

Even in the absence of the neurological symptoms of Sydenham's chorea, post-streptococcal cases of childhood onset OCD, tics and/or other neuropsychiatric syndromes have been described under the acronym of Pediatric Autoimmune Neuropsychiatric Disorders Associated with Streptococcal infections (PANDAS). Swedo *et al.* (1998) defined this novel group of patients using five diagnostic criteria: presence of OCD and/or tic disorder, prepubertal onset, episodic course of symptom severity, abrupt onset or dramatic exacerbations of symptoms associated with GABHS infections (as evidenced by positive throat culture and/or elevated anti-GABHS titres), and association with neurological abnormalities (motoric hyperactivity or adventitious movements, such as choreiform movements or tics).

An antigen labelled D8/17, on the surface of peripheral blood mononuclear cells, has been identified as a marker for the genetic tendency to generate abnormal antibodies to GABHS. Two independent groups of researchers (Murphy *et al.*, 1997 and Swedo *et al.*, 1997) found greater expression of the D8/17 antigen in the B-lymphocytes of patients with childhood-onset OCD (or Tourette's disorder) compared to healthy controls. Thus, the presence of the D8/17 antigen also may mark the susceptibility for OCD (Murphy *et al.*, 1997). Similar results have been reported in subjects with PANDAS (Swedo *et al.*, 1997).

Therapeutically, the finding of a probable autoimmune-caused OCD raises the clinical possibility that immunosuppressant treatments might be effective in treating or preventing some cases of OCD. This has been actually demonstrated in an experimental NIMH double-blind, placebo-controlled treatment study showing the efficacy of two immunomodulary treatments in subjects with PANDAS (Perlmutter *et al.*, 1999). However, the first double-blind attempt to demonstrate the efficacy of penicillin prophylaxis in preventing tic or OCD symptom exacerbation was negative, possibly due to failure to achieve an acceptable level of streptococcal protection in this study (Garvey *et al.*, 1999).

Ethological model of OCD
Culture, rituals and brain evolution

Freud (1924) provided interesting speculations on the similitude between OCD phenomena, children's games and religious rituals: 'It is easy to see the resemblance between the neurotic ceremonials of obsessions and compulsions, and the sacred acts of religious rituals'. More recently, Fiske and Haslam (1997) commented that 'the actions, thoughts, and concerns of meaningful, culturally legitimated religious rituals correspond, item for item, with the symptoms of OCD'.

Today, clinical and epidemiological studies conducted in highly diverse cultures (see above) confirm that OCD occurs in virtually all human groups: similar prevalence rates have been obtained across the world; symptoms are quasi-invariant in all cultures, and most often independent of individual life experiences; children have almost identical symptoms to those of adults. Thus, the clinical manifestations of OCD involve a limited number of integrated complex actions, affects, and ideas, e.g. fear of contamination, need for purification, prayer, scrupulous concerns, counting, and concerns with thresholds.

These findings have led Rapoport and others to propose an ethological model of OCD (Rapoport and Fiske, 1998), on the basis that OC symptoms are a relatively narrow group of rather complex behaviours and that the 'correct' behaviour is dependent on a context established by an earlier stimulus (e.g. when danger was present or when contamination was a real issue). Vertebrate ethologists have described 'fixed action patterns', which include complex social behaviours such as imprinting, combat, courtship, grooming, and feeding (Gould, 1982). The human central nervous system is known to contain highly conserved elements that have survived as messages across hundreds of millions of years. Studies of comparative ethology have shown that these highly conserved brain systems have evolved to establish selective advantages that work to ensure the functional integrity of sets of behavioural sequences and mental phenomena crucial for the species reproduction and survival (Eibl-Eibesfelt, 1971). Rapoport and Fiske (1998) speculated that direct, innate, neural control would be the most parsimonious explanation for the invariance of OC actions, affects, and ideas. In case of damage to selective areas of the brain, OC symptoms could emerge as an inappropriate recognition of a behavioural context that does not exist, causing intrusive behaviours that belong to a different context.

Preoccupations and behaviours associated with romantic and parental love: more about the phenomenology and origin of OCD

Winnicott (1969) had described, in young mothers, a withdrawn or dissociated mental state that he termed 'primary maternal preoccupation' and that, in the absence of pregnancy or a newborn, would resemble a mental illness of acute onset. Similarly, Leckman and Mayes (1999) have shown that many of the clinical manifestations of OCD resemble the behavioural patterns and mental states characteristic of both early parenthood and human courtship. These normal processes may be seen as altered mental and emotional states, with an acute onset, a typical course, and a waning phase of 'recovery', during which the extent of altered patterns of thought and behaviour tend to be minimized or no longer recalled. In the acute state, both conditions are characterized by a heightened sense of responsibility and vigilance towards the loved one's safety and well being. The preoccupation may focus on minute and relatively trivial aspects of the other or the environment. Intrusive worries about unexpected illness, imperfections, injuries, or, more generally, intrusive feelings of frightful calamity are common, as are excruciating doubts regarding one's own adequacy as a parent or a lover, including intrusive thoughts of the mother injuring her own child (Leckman and Mayes, 1999).

In the early phases of courtship and parental love, behavioural responses include altered repetitive behaviours, proximity seeking, separation distress, and excessive checking even at times when the subject knows the loved one is safe. Grooming and dressing behaviours are heightened, and actions might need to have a 'just right' character, exactly fitting the other's needs. These behavioural states are accompanied by reduced ability to attend to other potentially salient aspects of the environment (e.g. academic or work demands) and loss of interest in the outside world. There is an increased risk to develop mental disorders (e.g. post-partum OCD, postpartum depression).

Although all this is highly reminiscent of the symptoms of OCD, romantic love and early parental love are adaptive sets of human mental states and behaviours. It makes perfect evolutionary sense to have intrusive worrisome thoughts that focus one's attention on the beloved mate or offspring, and on potential environmental threat to their safety and survival. Leckman and Mayes (1999) provide interesting speculations on OCD based on human behaviours during developmental epochs, the functional neurobiology of the human brain, and evolutionarily conserved patterns of behaviours that are reflected in the genetic make-up of our species. Thus, the same conserved systems might be intimately involved in both adaptive sets of human behaviours and the vulnerability to certain forms of psychopathology, and OCD may occur when these systems are inappropriately activated or otherwise dysregulated. Such a view is consistent with previous neurobiochemical hypotheses since the monoamine systems are thought to constitute an endogenous 'value' system in the brain, that guides and reinforces vertebrates to 'know' what is important in the environment (Friston *et al.*, 1994). Pathways involving a variety of neuropeptides, such as central oxytocin and vasopressin, also appear to be involved in the initiation of conserved behaviours such as parental behaviours and pair bonding (Insel and Harbaugh, 1989; Carter *et al.*, 1997), and should be investigated further in OCD.

Animal models of OCD

Naturally occurring 'zoo behaviours' observed in certain breeds of animals may have particular relevance for OCD. For example, canine acral lick dermatitis involves 'compulsive' licking of a patch of skin on a paw or leg, leading initially to loss of fur, and ultimately to a chronic abrasion of the underlying skin. Goldberger and Rapoport (1991) first described the possible link between OCD and canine acral lick. This was followed by Rapoport *et al.* (1992) double-blind, crossover study demonstrating that 5 weeks of treatment with antiobsessional agents (clomipramine or SSRI) for 37 dogs afflicted with canine acral lick was significantly more effective than a nonspecific antidepressant treatment or a placebo! Similarly, Grindlinger and Ramsay (1991) proposed that compulsive feather picking in birds could be an avian analog to OCD and showed, in an open study, that the birds, like dogs, improved after treatment with clomipramine.

Conclusion and directions for future research

OCD is an ancient human experience, with specific, stable, severe emotional and cognitive disturbances, for which a variety of spiritual, psychological, neurobiological and ethological models have been successively proposed. Despite a relative diversity, the symptom 'pool' is remarkably finite, and very similar across ages, the life span, and cultures. Another unique feature of the disorder is the egodystonic quality of the symptoms, making individuals both the subjects and the observers of their own emotional states.

OCD has long been considered to be a model of psychologically determined illness. However, the last two decades of research have challenged our understanding of the disorder. Today, OCD might be the psychiatric syndrome for which scientists have the most specific and convincing information about the neural circuitry that mediates the abnormal behaviours, as well as evidence of naturally occurring medical models and animal models. Furthermore, the psychological and biological theories of OCD have evolved along with the demonstration of the specific efficacy of distinct psychological and pharmacological treatments, even though too many treatment resistant cases still challenge our understanding of the treatment processes. Figure 15.3 illustrates the proposed sites of action of current first-line treatments for OCD, the SRIs being likely to act on neurobiochemical and neurophysiological dysfunctions underlying the disorder, while cognitive and behavioural interventions address various distorsions of thought and behaviours, from magical thinking reminiscent of early childhood experiences to current overresponsability schemes and negative self-appraisal.

As is the case for all disorders of the mind and the brain, future research should aim at reconciling psychological and neurological approaches. The emotional states in untreated and treated patients, at different stages of their illness, should be examined using modern neuropsychological and neurophysiological tools, both when the subject is experiencing OCD symptoms, and during neutral affective states. This might bring better understanding of both normal and abnormal cognitive schemes in OCD subjects, as well as lead to better strategies for more effective psychological treatment. More research is needed on the links between emotional regulation and several neurotransmitter systems in both healthy subjects and OCD patients, to improve the efficacy of available pharmacological tools. Future studies should also examine whether there are distinct subtypes of OCD that could differ in clinical phenomenology, emotional reactivity, neurobiological concomitants, aetiology, responsiveness to psychological or pharmacological interventions, and long-term outcome. Early and chronic forms of OCD should be compared to each other

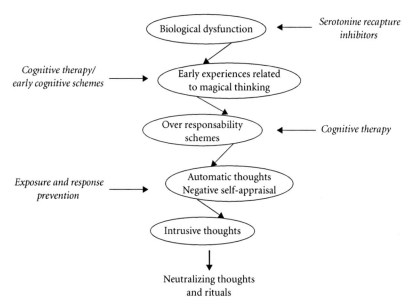

Fig. 15.3 Possible targets for psychological and drug treatments in obsessive compulsive disorder.

to distinguish between causative and adaptative mechanisms. The comparison should be made on both behavioural and emotional subjective states as well as on regional brain activity patterns. Especially in children and adolescents, the impact of the disorder on emotional and cognitive development should be studied prospectively.

In conclusion, OCD is a frequent and probably heterogeneous disorder in which emotional and cognitive disturbances are bound in complex ways to various neurological and biochemical dysfunctions. The disorder should be recognized, studied, and treated in its early stage, which most often occurs during childhood or adolescence. More research is needed into the intricacy of basic psychological and neurobiological mechanisms in order to improve our understanding and the long-term outcome of the disorder.

References

Alexander, G., Crutcher, M., and DeLong, M. (1990). Basal-ganglia thalamocortical circuits: parallel substrate for motor, oculomotor, 'prefrontal,' and 'limbic' functions. *Progress in Brain Research*, **85**, 119–45.

Altemus, M., Swedo, S.L., Leonard, H.L., *et al.* (1992). Changes in cerebrospinal fluid neurochemistry treatment of obsessive-compulsive disorder with clomipramine. *Archives of General Psychiatry*, **51**, 794–803.

American Psychiatric Association (1994). *Diagnostic and statistical manual of mental disorders*, 4th edn. Washington, DC, American Psychiatric Association.

Amir, N., Cashman, L., and Foa, E.B. (1997). Strategies of thought control in obsessive-compulsive disorder. *Behaviour Research & Therapy*, **35(8)**, 775–7.

Apter, A. and Tyano, S. (1988). Obsessive compulsive disorders in adolescence. *Journal of Adolescence*, 11, 183–94.

Asbahr F. R., Negrao A. B., Gentil V., *et al.* (1998). Obsessive-compulsive and related symptoms in children and adolescents with rheumatic fever with and without chorea: a prospective 6-month study. *American Journal of Psychiatry*, 155, 1122–24.

Baxter, L. R. (1998). Functional imaging of brain systems mediating obsessive-compulsive disorder. In *Neurobiology of Mental Illness* (ed. D. S. Charney, E. J. Nestler and B. S. Bunney), pp 534–47. Oxford: Oxford University Press.

Baxter, L., Mazziota, J., Guze, B., *et al.* (1987). Local cerebral glucose metabolic rates in obsessive-compulsive disorder. *Archives of General Psychiatry*, 44, 211–18.

Behar, D., Rapoport, J., Berg, C., *et al.* (1984). Computerized tomography and neuropsychological test measure in adolescents with obsessive-compulsive disorder. *American Journal of Psychiatry*, 141, 363–8.

Black, D., Gaffney, G., Schlosserr, S., *et al.* (2003). Children of parents with OCD: a 2-year follow-up study. *Acta Psychiatrica Scandinavica*, 107, 305–13.

Bolton, D. (1998). Obsessive compulsive disorder. In *Comprehensive clinical psychology*, Vol. 5, *Children and adolescents: clinical formulation and treatment* (ed. T. Ollendick), pp. 367–91. Elsevier Science.

Calvocoressi, L., Lewis, B., Harris, M., *et al.* (1995). Family accomodation in obsessive-compulsive disorder. *Amecian Journal of Psychiatry*, 152, 441–3.

Carter, C.S., Lederhendler, I., and Kirkpatrick, B. (1997). The integrative neurobiology of affiliation. *Annals of the New York Academy of Sciences*, 807, xiii–xviii.

Carter, A., Pauls, D., and Leckman, J. (1995). The development of obsessionality: continuities and discontinuities. In *Manual of developmental psychopathology* (ed. D. Cicchtti and D. Cohen), p. 609. New York, NY: John Wiley.

Cohen, D. and Leckman, J. (1994). Developmental psychopathology and neurobiology of Tourette's syndrome. *Journal of the American Academy of Child and Adolescent Psychiatry*, 33, 2–15.

Costello, E., Angold, A., Burns, B., *et al.* (1996). The great Smokey Montains study group. *Archives of General Psychiatry*, 53, 1129–36.

Cottraux, J. (1995). Behavioral and cognitive models of anxiety disorders. [French]. *Confrontations Psychiatriques*, No. 36, 231–60.

Cottraux, J. and Gérard, D. (1998). Neuroimaging and neuroanatomical issues in obsessive-cognitive disorder. In *Obsessive-compulsive disorder: theory, research, and treatment*. (ed. R. P. Swinson, M. M. Antony, S. Rachman), pp. 154–80. New York, NY: Guilford Press.

Despert, L. (1955). Differential diagnosis between obsessive-compulsive neurosis and schizophrenia in children. In *Psychopathology of childhood* (ed. P. H. Hoch and J. Zubin), pp. 240–53. New York, NY: Grune and Stratton.

DeVeaugh-Geiss, J., Moroz, G., Biederman, J., *et al.* (1992). Clomipramine hydrochloride in childhood and adolescent obsessive-compulsive disorder: a multicenter trial. *Journal of the American Academy of Child and Adolescent Psychiatry*, 31, 45–9.

Douglass, H.M., Moffitt, T.E., Reuven, D., *et al.* (1995). Obsessive-compulsive disorder in a birth cohort of 18-year-olds: Prevalence and predictors. *Journal of the American Academy of Child and Adolescent Psychiatry*, 31, 1057–61.

el Mansari, M. and Blier, P. (1997). In vivo electrophysiological characterization of 5-HT receptors in the guinea pig head of caudate nucleus and orbitofrontal cortex. *Neuropharmacology*, 36, 577–88.

Eibl-Eibesfeldt, I. (1971). Ethology of human greeting behavior: II. The greeting behavior and some other patterns of friendly contact by the Waika Indians (Yanoama). *Zeitschrift fur Tierpsychologie*, **29**(2), 196–213.

Esquirol, J. E. D. (1838). *Des maladies mentales*. Paris: JB Baillère.

Evans, D. W., Leckman, J. F., Carter, A., *et al*. (1997). Ritual, habits, and perfectionism: the prevalence and development of compulsive like behaviour in normal young children. *Child Development*, **68**, 58–68.

Flament, M., Chabane, N. (2000). Obsessive-compulsive disorder and tics in childhood and adolescence. *In The New Oxford Textbook of Psychiatry Volume 2* (ed. M. Gelder, J.J. Lopez-Ibor, N.C. Andreasen), Oxford University Press: New York, pp. 1771–81.

Flament, M. F. and Cohen, D. (2000). Childhood obsessive compulsive disorders. In *Obsessive-compulsive disorder: evidence and practice* (ed. M. Maj and N. Sartorius). Genève: Word Psychiatric Association.

Flament, M. F., Rapoport, J. L., Murphy, D. L., *et al*. (1987). Biochemical changes during clomipramine treatment of childhood obsessive compulsive disorder. *Archives of General Psychiatry*, **44**, 219–25.

Flament, M. F., Whitaker, A., Rapoport, J. L., *et al*. (1988). Obsessive compulsive disorder in adolescence: An epidemiological study. *Journal of the American Academy of Child and Adolescent Psychiatry*, **27**: 764–71.

Flament, M. F., Koby, E., Rapoport, J.L., *et al*. (1990). Childhood obsessive-compulsive disorder: A prospective follow-up study. *Journal of Child Psychology and Psychiatry*, **31**, 363–80.

Fiske, A. and Haslam, N. (1997). Is obsessive-compulsive disorder a pathology of the human disposition to perform socially meaningful rituals? Evidence of similar content. *Journal of Nervous and Mental Disease*, **185**(4), 211–22.

Fonagy, P. (1999). The transgenerational transmission of haulocost trauma. Lessons learned from the analysis of an adolescent with obsessive-compulsive disorder. *Attachments in Human Developments*, **1**, 92–114.

Freud, A. (1965). Some recent developments in child-analysis. *Psychotherapy & Psychosomatics*, **13**(1): 36–46.

Freud, A. (1966). Obsessional neurosis a summary of psychoanalytic views. *International Journal of Psycho-analysis*, **47**, 116–22.

Freud, S. (1913/1966). Totem and taboo. In *Standard edition of the complete psychological works of Sigmund Freud*, **13** (ed. J. Strachey), pp. 1–62. London: Hogarth Press.

Freud, S. (1924/1959). A short account of psychoanalysis. In *The complete psychological works of Sigmund Freud* (ed. J. Strachey). London: Hogarth Press.

Garvey, M. A., Perlmutter, S. J., Allen, A. J., *et al*. (1999). A pilot study of penicillin prophylaxis for neuropsychiatric exacerbations triggered by streptococcal infections. *Biological Psychiatry*, **45**, 1564–71.

Geller, D. A., Biederman, J., Griffin, S., *et al*. (1996). Comorbidity of obsessive-compulsive disorder with disruptive behavior disorders. *Journal of the American Academy of Child and Adolescent Psychiatry*, **35**, 1637–46.

Geller, D. A., Biederman, J., Jones, J., *et al*. (1998). Obsessive-compulsive disorder in children and adolescents: a review. *Harvard Review of Psychiatry*, **5**(5), 260–73.

Gesell, A., Ilg, F. L., and Ames, L. B. (1974). *Infant and Child in the Culture of Today: The Guidance of Development in Home and Nursery School*, p. 420.

Godart, N., Flament, M. F., Jeammet, P., *et al.* (2000). Eating disorders and anxiety disorders: comorbidity and chronology of appearance. *European Psychiatry*, in press.

Goldberger, E. and Rapoport, J. (1991). Canine acral lick dermititis: Response to the antiobsessional drug clomipramine. *J Am Animal Hosp Assoc*, **22**, 179–82.

Gould, J. (1982). *Ethology*. New York, NY: Norton.

Grindlinger, H. M. and Ramsay, E. D. (1991). Compulsive feather picking in birds. *Archives of General Psychiatry*, **48**(9), 857.

Heyman, I., Fombonne, E., Simmons, H., *et al.* (2001). Prevalence of obsessive-compulsive disorder in the British nationwide survey of child mental health. *British Journal of Psychiatry*, **179**, 324–9.

Hollander, E., Cohen, L., Richards, M., *et al.* (1997). A pilot study of the neuropsychology of obsessive-compulsive disorder and Parkinson's disease: basal ganglia disorders. *Journal of Neuropsychiatry and Clinical Neurosciences*, **5**, 104–7.

Hollander, E., DeCaria, C. M., Nitescu, A., *et al.* (1992). Serotonergic function in obsessive-compulsive disorder: behavioural and neuroendocrine responses to oral m-chlorophenylpiperazine and fenfluramine in patients and healthy volunteers. *Archives of General Psychiatry*, **49**, 21–8.

Honjo, S., Hirano, C., Murase, S., *et al.* (1989). Obsessive-compulsive symptoms in childhood and adolescence. *Acta Psychiatrica Scandinavica*, **80**, 83–91.

Insel, T. (1992). Toward a neuroanatomy of obsessive-compulsive disorder. *Archives of General Psychiatry*, **49**, 739–4480.

Insel, T. and Winslow, J. T. (1992). Neurobiology of obsessive compulsive disorder. *Psychiatric Clinics of North America*, **15**(4), 813–24.

Insel, T., Zohar, J., Benkelfat, C., *et al.* (1990). Serotonin in obsessions, compulsions, and the control of aggressive impulses. *Annals of the New York Academy of Sciences*, **600**, 574–85.

Janet, P. (1903). *Les obsessions et la psychasthénie*. Paris: Alcan.

Kanner, L. (1957). *Child psychiatry*. Springfield, IL: Thomas.

Karno, M., Golding, J. M., Sorenson, S. B., *et al.* (1988). The epidemiology of obsessive-compulsive disorder in five US communities. *Archives of General Psychiatry*, **45**, 1094–9.

Khanna S. and Srinath, S. (1989). Childhood obsessive compulsive disorder. I. Psychopathology. *Psychopathology*, **32**, 47–54.

Kramer, H. and Sprenger, J. (1486). *Malleus Maleficarum. (English Translation by M. Summers)*, Dover Publications, New York.

Leckman, J. F. and Mayes, L. C. (1999). Preoccupations and behaviors associated with romantic and parental love. Perspectives on the origin of obsessive-compulsive disorder. *Child & Adolescent Psychiatric Clinics of North America*, **8**(3), 635–65.

Leckman, J. F. (1993). Tourette's syndrome. In *Obsessive-Compulsive Related Disorders* (ed. E. Hollander), pp. 113–38.

Legrand du Saule, H. (1875). *La folie du doute avec délire du toucher*. Paris: A. Delahaye.

Lenane, M. (1989). Families in obsessive-compulsive disorder. In *Obsessive-compulsive disorder in children and adolescents* (ed. J. Rapoport), pp 237–49. Washington, DC: American Psychiatric Press.

Leonard, H. L., Goldberger, E. L., Rapoport, J. L., *et al.* (1990). Childhood rituals: normal development or obsessive-compulsive symptoms? *Journal of the American Academy Child and Adolescent Psychiatry*, **29**, 17–23.

Leonard, H., Lenane, M., Swedo, S., *et al.* (1992). Tics and Tourette's disorder: A 2- to 7-year follow-up of 54 obsessive-compulsive children. *American Journal of Psychiatry*, **149**, 1244–51.

Leonard, H. L., Swedo, S. E., Lenane, M. C., *et al.* (1991). A double-blind desipramine substitution during long-term clomipramine treatment in children and adolescents with obsessive-compulsive disorder. *Archives of General Psychiatry*, **48**, 922–7.

Leonard, H. L., Swedo, S. E., Rapoport, J. L., *et al.* (1989). Treatment of obsessive-compulsive disorder with clomipramine and desipramine in children and adolescents. *Archives of General Psychiatry*, **46**, 1088–92.

Liebowitz, M. R., Turner, S., Piacentini, J., *et al.* (2002). Fluoxetine in children and adolescents with OCD: a placebo-controlled trial. *Journal of the American Academy of Child and Adolescent Psychiatry*, **41**, 1431–8.

Luxemberg, J., Swedo, S., Flament, M., *et al.* (1988). Neuroanatomical abnormalities in obsessive-compulsive disorder detected with quantitative X-ray computed tomography. *American Journal of Psychiatry*, **145**, 1089–93.

Manassis, K., Bradley, S., Goldberg, S., *et al.* (1997). Behavioural inhibition, attachment and anxiety in children of mothers with anxiety disorders. *Canadian Journal of Psychiatry*, **42**, 87–92.

McFall, M. E. and Wollersheim, J. P. (1979). Obsessive-compulsive neurosis: a cognitive behavioural formulation and approach to treatment. *Cognitive Therapy and Research*, **3**, 333–48.

March, J. S., Biederman, J., Wolkow, R., *et al.* (1998). Sertraline in children and adolescents with obsessive-compulsive disorder: a multicenter randomized controlled trial. *Journal of the American Medical Association*, **280**, 1752–6.

Murphy, T., Goodman, W., Fudge, M., *et al.* (1997). B lymphocyte antigen D8/17: a peripheral marker for childhood onset obsessive-compulsive disorder and Tourette's syndrome? *American Journal of Psychiatry*, **154**, 402–7.

Neziroglu, F., Anemone, R., and Yaryura-Tobias, J. A. (1992). Onset of obsessive-compulsive disorder in pregnancy. *American Journal of Psychiatry*, **149(7)**, 947–50.

Pauls, D. L. and Alsobrook, J. P. (1999). The inheritance of obsessive-compulsive disorder. *Child and Adolescent Psychiatric Clinics of North America*, **8**, 481–96.

Pauls, D., Alsobrook, J., Goodman, W., *et al.* (1995). A family study of obsessive-compulsive disorder. *American Journal of Psychiatry*, **152**, 76–84.

Pauls, D. L., Raymond, C. L., Leckman, J. F., *et al.* (1991). A family study of Tourette's syndrome. *American Journal of Human Genetics*, **48**, 154–63.

Perlmutter, S. J., Leitman, S. F., Garvey, M. A., *et al.* (1999). Therapeutic plasma exchange and intravenous immunoglobulin for obsessive-compulsive disorders in childhood. *Lancet*, **354**, 1153–8.

Piaget, J. (1962). The relation of affectivity to intelligence in the mental development of the child. *Bulletin of the Menniger Clinic*, **26(3)**, 129–37.

Pitman, R. K. (1993). Posttraumatic obsessive compulsive disorder: a case study. *Comprehensive Psychiatry*, **34**, 102–7.

Pollock, R. and Carter, A. (1999). The familial and developmental context of obsessive-compulsive disorder. *Child and Adolescent Psychiatric Clinics of North America*, **8**, 461–79.

Rachman, S. (1993). Obsessions, responsibility, and guilt. *Behaviour Research and Therapy*, **31**, 149.

Rachman, S. and Hodgson, R. (1980). *Obsessions and compulsions*. Englewood Cliffs, NJ: Prentice Hall.

Rapoport, J. L. (1989). The neurobiology of obsessive compulsive disorder. *Journal of the American Medical Association*, **260**, 2888–90.

Rapoport, J. L. and Fiske, A. (1998). The new biology of obsessive compulsive disorder: implications for evolutionary psychology. *Perspectives in Biology and Medicine*, **41**, 159–75.

Rapoport, J. L., Ryland, D. H., and Kriete, M. (1992). Drug treatment of canine acral lick. *Archives of General Psychiatry*, **49**, 517–21.

Rapoport, J. L. and Wise, S. P. (1988). Obsessive-compulsive disorder: evidence for basal ganglia dysfunction. *Psychopharmacology Bulletin*, **24(3)**, 380–4.

Rasmussen, S. A. (1994). Genetic studies of obsessive compulsive disorder. In *Current insights in Obsessive Compulsive Disorder* (ed. E. Hollander, J. Zohar, D. Marazzati, and B. Olivier). New York: John Wiley and Sons.

Rasmussen, S. A. and Eisen, J. L. (1992). The epidemiology and differential diagnosis of obsessive compulsive disorder. *Journal of Clinical Psychiatry*, **53 (4 suppl)**, 4–10.

Rasmussen, S. A. and Tsuang, M. T. (1986). Clinical characteristics and family history in DSM-III obsessive-compulsive disorder. *American Journal of Psychiatry*, **143**, 317–22.

Rauch, S. L. (2000). Neuroimaging research and the neurobiology of OCD: where do we go from here? *Biological Psychiatry*, **47(3)**, 168–70.

Reinherz, H. Z., Giaconia, R. M., Lefkowitz, E. S., *et al.* (1993). Prevalence of psychiatric disorders in a community population of older adolescents. *Journal of the American Academy of Child and Adolescent Psychiatry*, **32**, 734–38.

Riddle, M. A., Scahill, L., King, R., *et al.* (1990). Obsessive compulsive disorder in children and adolescents: phenomenology and family history. *Journal of the American Academy of Child and Adolescent Psychiatry*, **29**, 766–72.

Riddle, M. A., Scahill, L., King, R. A., *et al.* (1992). Double-blind, crossover trial of fluoxetine and placebo in children and adolescents with obsessive-compulsive disorder. *Journal of the American Academy of Child and Adolescent Psychiatry*, **31**, 1062–9.

Riddle, M. A., Reeve, E. A., Yaryura-Tobias, J. A., *et al.* (2001). Fluvoxamine for children and adolescents with obsessive compulsive disorder: a randomized, controlled, multicenter trial. *Journal of the American Academy of Child and Adolescent Psychiatry*, **40**, 222–9.

Robins, L. N., Helzer, J. E., Weissman, M. M., *et al.* (1984). Lifetime prevalence of specific disorders in three sites. *Archives of General Psychiatry*, **41**, 949–58.

Rosenberg, D. R. and Keshavan, M. S. (1998). Toward a neurodevelopmental model of obsessive-compulsive disorder. *Biological Psychiatry*, **43**, 623–40.

Rosenberg, D. R., Stewart, C. M., Fitzgerald, K. D., *et al.* (1999). Paroxetine open-label treatment of pediatric outpatients with obsessive-compulsive disorder. *Journal of the American Academy of Child and Adolescent Psychiatry*, **38**, 1180–5.

Sallee, F. R., Richman, H., Beach, K., *et al.* (1996). Platelet serotonin transporter in children and adolescents with obsessive-compulsive disorder or Tourette's syndrome. *Journal of the American Academy of Child and Adolescent Psychiatry*, **35**, 1647–56.

Salkovski, P. (1985). Obsessional-compulsive problems: a cognitive-behavioural analysis. *Behaviour Research and Therapy*, **23**, 571.

Saxena, S., Brody, A. L., Schwartz, J. M., *et al.* (1998). Neuroimaging and frontal-subcortical circuitry in obsessive-compulsive disorder. *British Journal of Psychiatry*, **35**, 26–37.

Swedo, S. E. (1994). Sydenham's chorea: a model for childhood autoimmune neuropsychiatric disorders. *Journal of the American Medical Association*, **272**, 1788–91.

Swedo, S. E., Rapoport, J. L., Cheslow, D. L., *et al.* (1989a). High prevalence of obsessive-compulsive symptoms in patients with Sydenham's chorea. *American Journal of Psychiatry*, **146**, 246–9.

Swedo, S. E., Rapoport, J. L., Leonard, H., *et al.* (1989b). Obsessive-compulsive disorder in children and adolescents. Clinical phenomenology of 70 consecutive cases. *Archives of General Psychiatry*, **46**, 335–40.

Swedo, S., Shapiro, M., Grady, C., *et al.* (1989c). Cerebral glucose metabolism in childhood obsessive-compulsive disorder. *Archives of General Psychiatry*, **46**, 518–23.

Swedo, S. L., Leonard, H. L., Kruesi, M. J. P., *et al.* (1992a). Cerebrospinal fluid neurochemistry in children and adolescents with obsessive-compulsive disorder. *Archives of General Psychiatry*, **49**, 29–36.

Swedo, S., Pietrini, P., Leonard, H., *et al.* (1992b). Cerebral glucose metabolism in childhood obsessive-compulsive disorder: revisualization during pharmacotherapy. *Archives of General Psychiatry*, **49**, 690–4.

Swedo, S. E., Leonard, H., Shapiro, M. B., *et al.* (1993). Sydenham's chorea: physical and psychological symptoms of Saint Vitus dance. *Pediatrics*, **91**, 706–13.

Swedo, S., Leonard, H., Mittleman, B., *et al.* (1997). Identification of children with pediatric autoimmune neuropsychiatric disorders associated with streptococcal infections by a marker associated with rheumatic fever. *American Journal of Psychiatry*, **154**, 110–2.

Swedo, S., Leonard, H. L., Garvey, M., *et al.* (1998). Pediatric autoimmune neuropsychiatric disorders associated with streptococcal infections (PANDAS): clinical description of the first 50 cases. *American Journal of Psychiatry*, **155**, 264–71.

Taylor, J. (1660). *Ductor Dubitantium or the Rule of Conscience in all her Measures Serving as a Great Instrument for Determination of Cases of Conscience*, London.

Thomsen, P. H. (1991). Obsessive-compulsive symptoms in children and adolescents. A phenomenological analysis of 61 Danish cases. *Psychopathology*, **24**, 12–18.

Thomsen, P. H. (1997). Child and adolescent obssesive-compulsive disorder treated with citalopram: findings from an open trial of 23 cases. *Journal of Child and Adolescent Psychopharmacol*, **7**, 157–66.

Thoren, P., Asberg, M., Cronholm, B., *et al.* (1980). Clomipramine treatment of obsessive compulsive disorder. *Archives of General Psychiatry*, **37**, 1281–5.

Toro, J., Cervera, M., Osjeo, E., *et al.* (1992). Obsessive-compulsive disorder in childhood and adolescence: a clinical study. *Journal of Child Psychology and Psychiatry and Allied Disciplines*, **33**, 1025–37.

Walsh, K. H. and McDougle, C. J. (2001). Trichotillomania. Presentation, etiology, diagnosis and therapy. *Am J Clin Dermatol.*, **2**, 327–33.

Weissman, M. M., Bland, R. C., Canino, G. L., *et al.* (1994). The Cross National Epidemiology of obsessive-compulsive disorder. *Journal of Clinical Psychiatry*, **55**, 5–10.

Weizman, A., Mandel, A., Barber, Y., *et al.* (1992). Decreased platelet imipramine binding in Tourette syndrome children with obsessive-compulsive disorder. *Biological Psychiatry*, **31**, 705–11.

Wells, A. and Davies, M. I. (1994). The Thought Control Questionnaire: a measure of individual differences in the control of unwanted thoughts. *Behaviour Research & Therapy*, **32**(8), 871–8.

Winnicott, D. W. (1969). Human relations. *Physiotherapy*, **55**(6), 226–29.

Wise, S. P., Murray, E. A., and Gerefen, C. (1996). The frontal cortex-basal ganglia system in primates. *Critical Reviews in Neurobiology*, **10**, 317–56.

World Health Organization (1992). ICD-10 International Classification of Mental Disorders. Geneva: WHO.

Zahn, T. P., Kruesi, M. J. P., Swedo, S. E., *et al.* (1992). Autonomic activity in relation to cerebrospinal fluid neurochemistry in obsessive and disruptive children and adolescents. *Psychophysiology*, **33**, 731–9.

Zohar, A. H. and Bruno, R. (1997). Normative and pathological obsessive-compulsive behaviour and ideation in childhood: a question of timing. *Journal of Child Psychology and Psychiatry and Allied Disciples*, **38**, 993–9.

Zohar, A. H. and Felz, L. (2001). Ritualistic behaviour in young children. *Journal of Abnormal Child Psychology*, **29**, 121–8.

Zohar, A. H. and Insel, T. (1987). Obsessive-compulsive disorder: psychobiological approaches to diagnosis, treatment, and pathophysiology. *Biological Psychiatry*, **22**, 667–87.

Zohar, A. H., Ratzosin, G., Pauls, D. L., *et al.* (1992). An epidemiological study of obsessive-compulsive disorder and related disorders in Israeli adolescents. *Journal of American Academy of Child and Adolescent Psychiatry*, **31**, 1057–61.

Chapter 16

Loss of emotional fluency as a developmental phenotype: the example of anhedonia

Stéphanie Dubal and Roland Jouvent

ce n'est plus une douleur qui s'agite, qui se plaint, qui crie, qui
pleure, c'est une douleur qui se tait, qui n'a plus de larmes,
qui est impassible. Ce dont il se plaint le plus, c'est de ne plus
sentir. (E. Esquirol, *De la lypémanie ou mélancolie*, 1820)

Historically, *anhedonia* has been defined as the loss of the capacity to experience pleasure and has been considered a risk factor for psychopathology. In this chapter, we will consider anhedonia to be a loss of emotional fluency and will address the question: what are the cognitive developmental consequences of anhedonia?

Anhedonia: a clinical dimension

Symptoms of emotional deficit, referred to as negative symptoms, relate to the absence of a behaviour or function normally expected to be present. From affective blunting to analgesia, emotional deficit corresponds to a limitation of the emotional tone and to a lack of ability to react to external stimuli that normally provoke a wide range of emotional responses. Emotional dysfunction combines a loss of reactivity with a loss of feelings.

Emotional blunting affects positive as well as negative emotions. The concept of anhedonia related to the positive dimension of emotions was first introduced by Ribot in 1896 to describe the loss of capacity to experience pleasure. Kraepelin (1906) described anhedonia as a mild form of melancholia. Later anhedonia was distinguished from other negative symptoms in the category of endogenomorphic depression by Klein (1974) who developed an aetiological model of depression characterized by an enduring loss of capacity to anticipate and respond to pleasure. This long-standing anhedonia was thought to be generated by a dysfunction of the reward system. Anhedonic, or endogenomorphic, depression contrasts with reactive depressions that are induced principally by life event stressors.

In 1980, the *Diagnostic and statistical manual of mental disorders* (DSM III, APA, 1980) listed anhedonia as one of the three main symptoms in the diagnosis of a major depressive disorder. Several authors tried to isolate a subtype of anhedonic depression with the idea that anhedonia could refer to a stable personality trait (Fawcett *et al.*, 1983; Clark *et al.*, 1984). According to Clark, anhedonic depression characterizes 12–25 % of the depressed population (e.g. Hardy *et al.*, 1986; Young *et al.*, 1986). Conversely, others have argued that anhedonic depression is not a subtype of depression; instead, it is a depression of severe intensity (e.g. Zimmerman, 1986).

In the categorical approach, one seeks clinical signs that mark a rupture in normal functioning that allows one to identify the nosological entity, in this case anhedonia. However, researchers have failed to reach a consensus in their attempts to classify anhedonia as a particular depression subtype. Thus, the notion emerged that anhedonia is more properly considered as clinical dimension (Jouvent and Ammar, 1994) that corresponds to a psychopathological function without nosological specificity (Van Praag *et al.*, 1990). Those who focus on symptoms, rather than diagnostic categories, place the psychological symptoms of anhedonia on a continuum from normal functioning to pathological states. Even if critical criteria can be found to define the pathological state, the anhedonia model appears to be a better fit with the dimensional approach. Cassano *et al.* (1997) used the term 'spectrum' to characterize the continuum between core symptoms of each disorder and the associated prodromal, atypical, and subclinical psychopathological expression. The continuum includes both typical and atypical symptoms of the primary disorder, behavioural patterns, and other features related to the core symptoms that may either be prodromal or precursor states of a particular disorder and/or a personality trait.

The anhedonia personality trait

When anhedonia is studied as a symptom, research can be conducted on a 'normal' population that contains individuals who display anhedonia to varying degrees. An example of this approach is the study of college student populations by the Chapmans and their colleagues who developed scales to identify individuals at high risk for the development of psychosis (Chapman *et al.*, 1976). They used scales to measure traits that have been associated with psychosis proneness, including physical and social anhedonia. The anhedonia scales were developed following Meehl's descriptions of the schizotype as both lacking pleasure from social interaction and having weakened feelings of joy, affection, love, pride, and self-respect. Meehl (1962) reported that anhedonia was a quasi-pathognomonic sign of schizophrenia, one of the most consistent and dramatic behavioural signs of the disease. According to Meehl, what is phenomenologically a radical deficiency of pleasure may be roughly identified behaviourally with a quantitative deficit in the reinforcement circuit. Each of these—the inner and outer aspects of the organism's appetitive control system—reflect a quantitative deficit in the limbic 'positive' circuit control centre. Meehl suggested that the lack of pleasure in relationships with other people leads to social withdrawal, inappropriate behaviour, and even deviant logic reasoning. The anhedonia dimension actually parallels specific negative symptoms in psychopathological states, and relates to symptoms like social adjustment problems and attentional deficits. These symptoms are hypothesized to fall on a continuum from relative normality, to personality disorders, to fully pathological states.

Anhedonia measured by the Physical Anhedonia Scale (PAS) and Social Anhedonia Scale (SAS) is a lifelong personality defect in the ability to experience pleasure. Pleasure is characterized by a strong positive affect, a keen anticipation of the experience that evokes it, a satisfying recollection of the experience, and a willingness to expend effort to achieve the experience. Pleasures may be grouped into three categories: physical pleasure (e.g. pleasures of eating, touching, feeling, sex, temperature, movement, smell, and sound), interpersonal pleasure (e.g. being with people talking, exchanging expressions of feelings, doing things with them, competing, living, and interacting in multiple other ways), and intellectual pleasure including the pleasure of achievement.

The PAS is a self-report scale measuring pleasures of eating, touching, feeling, temperature, movement, smell and sound. Example items are: 'Beautiful scenery has been a great delight to me', or 'Trying new foods is something I have always enjoyed'. The SAS is also a self-report scale that measures interpersonal pleasures. Example items are: 'I have often felt uncomfortable when my friends touch me', 'I attach very little importance to having close friends'. Chapman defines anhedonic participants as those scoring two standard deviations or greater above the mean on either the PAS or SAS; those scoring at the mean or within 0.5 standard deviation below the mean are defined as normal controls.

Initial studies of anhedonia in children used the Chapman's physical anhedonia scale. In 1989, Kazdin developed a children's pleasure scale to assess anhedonia in children from 6 to 13 years of age. To fill in this scale, children have to decide whether doing a particular activity would make them feel very happy, happy, or if they wouldn't care. Example items are: 'You are lying in bed on a Saturday morning listening to your favourite songs', 'It is Christmas morning and as you open your gifts you discover that you got everything you hoped you would'. To test the construct validity study of the scale, Kazdin examined psychiatric inpatient children's reports of pleasurable experiences. Children high in anhedonia showed less active involvement in seeking rewards, were higher in their expectations of negative outcomes, and were more likely to attribute unrewarding outcomes to their own behaviour than to external causes.

The psychometric high risk approach

Using the above scales, investigators have examined test-score outliers whom they postulate to be at risk for developing schizophrenia. Disposition to schizophrenia is reflected in a continuum of personality and cognitive traits that may exist in psychiatrically healthy people, whereby some apparently well-adjusted persons will manifest mild versions of schizophrenic symptoms.

Investigation of individuals at elevated risk for psychopathology provides several unique opportunities. At-risk samples are generally not compromised by medication, gross impairment, or long-term consequences of severe disorder. Conversely, as pointed out by Holzman *et al.* (1995), the high-risk psychometric approach also has several weaknesses:

The scales screen for endorsement of only a subset of symptoms associated with schizotypy. They are not intended to identify all individuals with schizotypic characteristics. Nor do these scales claim to exclude individuals whose symptoms reflect conditions other than schizotypy. Therefore, the optimal expectation for this psychometric instrument is that it identifies a group of individuals, some of whom have circumscribed symptoms associated with schizotypic pathology.

Psychometrically at risk participants characteristics

Using the PAS, many studies examined anhedonic participants who were found to have clinical, cognitive, and psychophysiological abnormalities, promoting an interest in studying populations with an anhedonic personality trait. Non-psychotic students with high anhedonia scores were found to perform in the deviant direction displayed by schizophrenic patients.

Clinical studies showed that anhedonic college students had no more schizotypic personality disorders, and no difference in the number of psychotic symptoms or psychotic-like experiences, when compared with controls (Cadenhead *et al.*, 1996). Anhedonic participants are more socially isolated and withdrawn (Chapman *et al.*, 1978, 1980). The physical anhedonia scale will identify individuals at heightened risk for heterogeneous symptoms, mood disorders, substance-abuse disorders, eating disorders, but not specifically schizophrenia-spectrum disorders.

Participants scoring high on the Social Anhedonia Scale show schizoid withdrawal, that is, are socially anhedonic (Mishlove and Chapman, 1985). These participants are more deviant on social adjustment, schizotypal features, and psychotic-like experiences than are control participants. The pattern of social maladjustment refers to anhedonic participants being more reticent with their friends, engaging in fewer social interactions, having less interest in dating, experiencing more discomfort in social interactions. Although these results might be expected of either avoidant or schizoid individuals, the additional findings that the socially anhedonic participants do not report more hypersensitivity or loneliness than controls support the contention that a schizoid type of withdrawal is measured through the Social Anhedonia Scale (Mishlove and Chapman, 1985). Moreover, socially anhedonic participants report both that they enjoy the company of others less than most people do and that their lack of enjoyment was due to a diminished need for interpersonal contact. Kwapil (1998) also found that socially anhedonic participants experience more severe depressive symptoms than controls, but do not differ from controls on the severity of manic symptoms.

Unlike physically anhedonic participant, socially anhedonic participants exhibit more psychotic-like experiences than control participants. Examples of such experiences are feeling the presence of a person or a force not actually present, de-realization, feeling different from other people in a negative sense, time distortion, frequent déjà-vu experiences, and other unusual experiences. According to these findings, the socially anhedonic subgroup may be particularly psychosis prone, compared with the physically anhedonic group.

Follow-up studies

To answer the question of the predictive validity of diagnosed anhedonia, follow-up studies have been conducted to establish associations between early anhedonia and adult psychiatric outcomes. For example, Chapman *et al.* (1994) and Kwapil (1998) conducted a 10-year longitudinal study of young college students. Seventy participants scoring high on the physical anhedonia scale, 37 scoring high on the social anhedonia scale, and 153 control participants were included in the follow-up study. Participants were re-interviewed 10 years later. While physically anhedonic participants did not show a heightened incidence of clinical psychosis at the 10-year follow-up evaluation, results suggest a link between social anhedonia and later rates of psychotic-like experiences, schizotypal dimension scores, and poor overall social adjustment.

The general conclusion drawn from these studies is that the presence of social anhedonia predicts future illness, while physical anhedonia does not heighten the risk of developing a future psychopathology.

By contrast, the New York High Risk Project (NYHRP), a second follow-up study investigating predictive value of anhedonia diagnosis, reported a substantial case for the role of physical anhedonia in a person's vulnerability for schizophrenia (Cornblatt *et al.*, 1989, 1992, 1999; Erlenmeyer *et al.*, 1993, 2000; Freedman *et al.*, 1998). Three populations were followed for about 20 years in an attempt to define pre-clinical indicators that are related to later psychiatric outcomes. The children who were offspring of parents that had schizophrenia or affective disorders, or were psychiatrically normal were recruited and tested at 9 years of age. The children were assessed both for clinical outcomes and for attentional capacity. The combined assessment of emotional and attentional capacity made it possible to assess the interaction between anhedonia, and eventual cognitive and social outcomes. The attention index was measured by variants of the Continuous Performance Test, an Attention Span Task, and the digit span from the Wechsler. These tests provided indicators of sustained attention capacity, focused attention, and short-term memory. Anhedonia measures derived from Chapman's physical anhedonia scale and clinical interviews were used to check for the presence of psychosis, major affective disorders, and social isolation.

The findings on the physical anhedonia scale were consistent with the Chapman's earlier findings: participants at high genetic risk for schizophrenia or affective disorders who also had high anhedonia scores were more socially isolated and withdrawn. Furthermore, anhedonia in childhood and adolescence was related to social isolation in adulthood (Erlenmeyer *et al.*, 1993). In a follow-up of the NYHRP,

Freedman *et al.* (1998) confirmed that physical anhedonia in adolescence predicted poor social outcome in adulthood.

There also were new findings concerned by the relation between anhedonia and attention. Attentional dysfunction in childhood was related to anhedonia in adolescence in the participants at genetic risk for schizophrenia. The attentional deviance index was predictive of poor global adjustment at several points in adolescence in the participants at high risk for schizophrenia and predicted a social isolation in adulthood according to previous reports.

Both anhedonia and attention capacity indices are deviant in a larger percentage of children of schizophrenic parents than in the normal population. Meehl (1962) presumed that deficiencies in hedonic capacity and cognitive capacities were both heritable traits that potentiated the development of schizophrenia in individuals at genetic risk for the disorder. The NYHRP lead to the conclusion that relations between anhedonia in childhood and social withdrawal in adulthood are mediated through childhood attention disorders. The authors hypothesized that cognitive dysfunctions play key roles, along with anhedonia and social dysfunction, in predicting clinical decompensation. Participants at increased risk for schizophrenia have a greater likelihood for exhibiting attention deficits in childhood, which in turn lead to a lack of empathic behaviour and manifestations of suspiciousness and solitary behaviour in adulthood, independent of anhedonia. Poor attention in childhood may increase the risk for the development of later social dysfunctions including anhedonia. Chronic attention impairments are hypothesized to lead to inadequate processing of interpersonal cues and, thus, to increasing difficulties in social interactions during the course of development in some individuals with genetic susceptibility to schizophrenia. However, it may be the long-term response–either avoidance or perseverance in social situations–that shapes, in part, the expression of adulthood symptomatology. Anhedonia is postulated to interact at several levels: it would mediate long-term social development during adolescence, as well as various aspects of attention functioning in childhood. The hypothesized mechanism of vulnerability is the association between dysfunctional attention, anhedonia, and social withdrawal. This led us to explore attentional, cognitive, and social characteristics of young, anhedonic adults without diagnosed psychiatric illness.

Attention and anhedonia: experimental evidence in anhedonic young adults

Focused attention in anhedonia

Two main approaches have been used to study attention processing in anhedonic participants. One approach evaluates the resource allocation deficits that exist in anhedonic participants based on dual-task tests (Yee and Miller, 1994; Hazlett *et al.*, 1997) or Event-related Potential (ERP) studies (e.g. finding lower than normal P300 components in anhedonics; Simons, 1982; Josiassen *et al.*, 1985; Miller, 1986; Simons and Russo, 1987; Yee and Miller, 1994). Other studies involve more specific explorations of attentional visual processing. Anhedonic participants were found to have a number of difficulties maintaining conscious capacity-loading attention (Drewer and Shean, 1993) and switching their attention (Wilkins and Venables, 1992). Their performance on attention tasks suggest that they have an abnormal mode of attention control (Jutai, 1989) and reduced attention capacity (Simons and Russo, 1987). In the early stages of information processing, anhedonic participants exhibit normal performances both in a target detection paradigm (Silverstein *et al.*, 1992) and in the embedded figure test, a perceptual differentiation test (Shuldberg and London, 1989). This suggests that pre-attentive visual information processing is intact.

The findings are generally consistent with suggestion that perceptual organization processes are intact in anhedonics. Deficiencies appear when the task requires a higher level of attention, particularly when participants have to divide their attention. We investigated the ability of anhedonic participants to focus their attention (Dubal *et al.*, 2000).

Focused attention concerns the ability of participants to reject irrelevant or distracting messages, implying that participants process only one input at a time (a classic example involving the need to ignore irrelevant inputs is a cocktail party situation in which a guest tries to listen to one conversation and ignore all others). We measured focused attention abilities using the 'Eriksen response competition task' (Eriksen and Eriksen, 1974), which has been studied extensively (see Servan-Schreiber *et al.*, 1998). ERPs also were measured during the experiment to index neural resource allocation as reflected by the P300 amplitude. Eriksen's task consists of a centrally presented target letter flanked by noise letters. The participants are required to detect the target letter, and to ignore noise letters, which can be the same as the target letter (compatible condition) or different (incompatible condition), thereby causing interference. Anhedonics were predicted to have lower P300 wave amplitudes than controls. The identity of the noise letters surrounding the central target affect the task difficulty, producing larger interference in the incompatible than compatible condition.

First-year college students were selected based on their physical anhedonia scale scores. Anhedonic participants scored 2 standard deviations above the same-sex mean; control participants scored at the mean or within 0.5 standard deviations below the mean. Both groups were given tests of selective attention.

Although the performance of anhedonic participants was in the normal range, they had lower P300 amplitudes and slower reaction times (RTs) than control participants. Previous studies with the Eriksen task indicated that incompatible distractors should alter error rates, RTs and P300 latency. The incompatible condition should trigger the incorrect response, thereby slowing information processing (Eriksen and Eriksen, 1974). However incompatibility had less effect on error rates and RTs on our anhedonic sample than on controls.

Eriksen and Eriksen (1974) demonstrated that participants were unable to ignore irrelevant inputs, i.e. the noise letters; the explanation being that the processing of noise letters was automatic and therefore caused interference. When noise letters are incompatible, they trigger the incorrect response (i.e. HHNHH requires the H response, but not the N response). As shown by Eriksen and Eriksen, participants able to block out the distraction of the noise letters carried out controlled processing of these letters. In our experiment, anhedonic participants appeared to have treated noise letters in a more controlled way than did the controls, as shown by their slower RTs. The fact that anhedonic students showed slower RTs than controls, and the finding that RTs and that their performances were less affected in the incompatible condition suggest that anhedonic participants used a different response strategy. They may have developed a more conservative response strategy.

The P300 amplitude was diminished in anhedonic participants, particularly at the parieto-occipital sites. Posterior P300 has been considered to specify advanced cognitive factors and to partially reflect resource allocation to the task (Johnson, 1986). Evidence of low P300 has been observed in participants presenting physical anhedonia (Simons, 1982; Josiassen et al., 1985; Miller, 1986; Simons and Russo, 1987; Yee and Miller, 1994). In the literature, the P300 findings are inconsistent, perhaps due to the differential effort required by different task. No P300 reduction has been found in studies of tasks requiring minimal controlled processes (Ward et al., 1984; Yee et al., 1992; Giese-Davis et al., 1993). Miller et al. (1984) pointed out that task demand seems to determine the nature of observed electrocortical deficits: as the complexity of the task decreased, so did the difference between anhedonic and control participants. When participants process information in a more controlled way, i.e. a more complex way, fewer resources are available to allocate to the task. A lower P300 is thus consistent with a more conservative response strategy in anhedonics.

Our results confirm the presence of a low P300 and a resource allocation deficit in anhedonic participants. Anhedonic participants presented a number of attentional abnormalities that may represent discrete attention deficits, or may be the consequence of a global resource allocation deficit.

Automatic and controlled processes

Anhedonic participants tended to use more controlled processes than non anhedonic participants. The task was quite complex. We did not measure anhedonic participants' information processing strategies using a less complex task, e.g. a detection task. Therefore, we conducted a study to investigate automatic versus controlled processes in anhedonic participants (Dubal and Jouvent, 2003).

Automatic processes have the following characteristics: they might be accomplished in parallel, are not limited by short-term memory capacity, require little or no cognitive effort, require practice to develop, and are restricted to situations in which a given stimulus consistently involves the same response. In contrast, controlled process characteristics include being accomplished in sequence, restricted by the short-term memory capacity, effortful, improved by minimal practice, and typical of situations in which there is no consistent mapping between stimulus and response (Hasher and Zacks, 1979; Fisk and Schneider, 1981; Schneider *et al.*, 1984).

Theoretically, a simple detection task requires less attention than a task requiring both the detection and recognition of a stimulus. This latter task may require controlled processing while the former task should be automatic. In the present study, one task involved the detection of a stimulus, and the second task required more controlled processing, with both tasks being equal in the physical complexity. The added complexity introduced into the second task determined the supplementary effort needed to complete it: to maintain the same level of performance in the more complex task, participants would have to allocate more attention. ERPs were measured during the experiment to evaluate the P300 wave. The attention task had two conditions: the simple condition consisted of detecting a number and pressing a button as soon as a red square appeared. In the more complex condition, participants had to detect a number and then decide if it was a 3 multiple or not.

Although anhedonics performed within the normal range on both tasks, their P300 amplitude was lower than control participants in the effortful condition and no differences in ERPs were observed in the simple condition. Only control participants' P300 amplitude increased from the simple to the effortful condition.

Behavioural results validated the difference between the two tasks in terms of difficulty: error rates, as well as RTs were higher in the effortful condition than in the simple condition. This effect was found in both groups, showing that anhedonics, as well as controls, were sensitive to the effortful nature of the task. The normal behavioural performance in anhedonics confirmed previous findings.

Differences between groups were found at the electrophysiological level for the P300 amplitude. As shown in Fig. 16.1, the P300 amplitude was diminished in anhedonic participants, particularly at the parieto-occipital sites. As already mentioned, the posterior P300 has been considered as being specifically related to cognitive factors at a higher than basic level, and may partially reflect resource allocation to the task (Johnson, 1986).

The finding of a P300 reduction in anhedonic participants is not universal and we proposed that this may be due to the effort required by the task. In four studies using low-demand tasks, no P300 wave deficits in anhedonics were found. Simons (1982) used a simple tone habituation procedure; Ward (1984) used a simple tone counting task; Yee *et al.* (1992) used an auditory task with automatic elicitation of P300; and Giese-Davis *et al.* (1993) used a two tones discrimination task. All of these tasks could be executed automatically and necessitated fewer controlled processes than studies in which P300 reductions were found (e.g. Simons, 1982; Miller, 1986; Simons and Russo, 1987; Yee and Miller, 1994). Moreover, Simons's (1982) paradigm directly confirms the

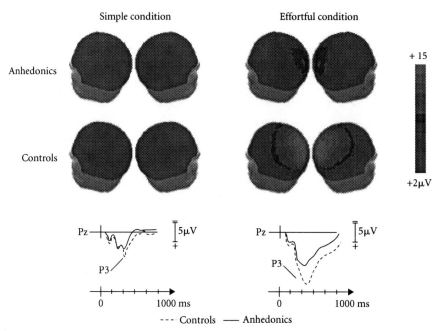

Fig. 16.1 Mean P300 voltage (μV) for simple condition (left) and effortful condition (right). For anhedonics (above), P300 voltage was mapped at the maximum peak amplitude, i.e. at 420 ms for the simple condition, and 450 ms in the effortful condition. For controls (below), P300 peaked at 420 and 460 ms in the simple and effortful condition, respectively.

hypothesis that these differences are due to the relatively amount of demand in each task. Participants were examined under both signal orientating and detection reaction time conditions. In the first phase of experiment, pure tones were presented to the participants without any response contingency. The second phase was a reaction time task in which different auditory warning stimuli were associated with subsequent visual stimuli that differed in hedonic content (nude or neutral slides). While the first phase didn't reveal any P300 differences, anhedonics produced markedly smaller P300 amplitudes than control participants in the second phase. As Simons proposed, these results suggest a resource deficit in the anhedonic group.

Similar findings were reported by Miller (1986). In this case, participants had to memorize three different tone pitches and to indicate which tone was presented. Miller also found a P300 decrement among anhedonic participants. Our results confirmed this hypothesis, by showing differential effects of task difficulty among groups: the smaller P300 for anhedonic participants was observed only in the effortful condition. By contrast, in the automatic task, the P300 was not smaller in the anhedonic group, relative to controls. Moreover, control participants' P300 increased from the simple to the difficult condition, which is typically observed in the P300 literature (Wickens *et al.*, 1983; Hoffman *et al.*, 1985; Kramer *et al.*, 1985; Strayer and Kramer, 1990).

The contrast between the similarity of the P300 in the two groups generated by the simple condition, and the smaller P300 in anhedonics, relative to controls, in the effortful condition confirms the proposition that anhedonia is related to difficulty in processing complex information. Electrophysiological correlates of anhedonic particip-ants' information processing deficits should be revealed when researchers employ effortful tasks.

Sustained attention

The studies carried out to date suggest that anhedonic participants have depleted processing resources, or difficulties mobilizing or allocating processing resources. The ability to sustain attention is likely to modulate performance in tasks for which anhe-donic participants have been reported to show deficits. As sustained attention is neces-sary for many of our cognitive tasks, we need to explore the ability of anhedonic groups to sustain attention before attributing the observed deficits to higher-order cognitive functions (Rueckert and Grafman, 1996). To meet this objective, we tested anhedonic participants using a time-on-task measure during the Eriksen task described above (Dubal and Jouvent, 2004). Sustained attention has not been studied previously in anhedonic participants, but anhedonics do perform normally on the continuous performance test (CPT; Simons and Russo, 1987). The CPT measures the ability to detect and to respond to specified stimulus changes occurring infrequently and at ran-dom intervals over a prolonged period of time, while simultaneously inhibiting responses to extraneous stimuli (Rosvold et al., 1956). The CPT is designed to measure vigilance (Nuechterlein, 1983); but if only the hit rate or sensitivity measure is con-sidered, this test does not measure sustained attention over time (Van den Bosh et al., 1996). Vigilance levels index the ability to discriminate a signal from noise throughout a vigilance period. Vigilance decrements refer to the decrease in vigilance levels over the course of the test; this process is more closely related to the concept of sustained attention, which implies sustained readiness to respond to task-relevant or signal stimuli over a period of time. If only overall detection rates are reported, with no analysis of trends over time on task, the results are more likely to reflect overall vigilance per-formance (Van den Bosh et al., 1996). As stressed by Nuechterlein et al. (1983b), the decrease in sensitivity over the vigilance period is an index of a deficit in sustaining attention.

Sustained attention involves the continuous maintenance over time of alertness and receptivity to a particular set of stimuli or stimulus changes (Parasuraman and Davies, 1984). Typically, it is assessed in tasks in which a target must be detected or discrimin-ated from non-targets (Warm, 1984) in a period lasting from minutes to an hour (Davies and Tune, 1969; Parasuraman, 1984). The vigilance decrement or decrement function, known as the time-on-task (TOT) effect, is the degree to which performance declines over time, and may be plotted for detection or response latency. Depending on the task, the TOT effect involves an increase in reaction times and in the proportion of targets missed, and there is often a similar increase in the number of false positive errors (Mackworth, 1948; Parasuraman and Davies, 1976; Rueckert and Levy, 1996). It depends on many factors, including task parameters (event rate, stimulus type) and extraneous environmental stimuli (e.g. noise, temperature; Ballard, 1996). For example, Deaton and Parasuraman (1993) reported a vigilance decrement in a sensory vigilance task, but found no such decrement in a cognitive task. However, when the event rate was increased, the decrease in hit rate was more pronounced in the cognitive than in the sensory task.

In the domain of schizophrenic disorders, very few studies have investigated the decrease in vigilance over time (Nuechterlein, 1983; Cornblatt *et al.*, 1989; Nestor *et al.*, 1990; Schmand *et al.*, 1994; Buchanan *et al.*, 1997; Mass *et al.*, 2000). However, the regulation of attention over time becomes important when the paradigms used involve central executive processes (Van den Bosh *et al.*, 1996). The dynamics of the response are not only important in sustained attention studies, but have also been observed in various cognitive tasks. Matthysse *et al.* (1999) proposed a model for these intermittent lapses, known as 'dialipsis' in the performance of schizophrenic patients. They observed that 'schizophrenic patients are impaired in many behaviours, but they do not show deficit functioning all the time'. Numerous examples of intra-participant variability, outliers, and shapes of distributions have emphasized the role of the dynamics of the response in cognitive studies. In the present study, sustained attention was determined by task-induced changes (in accuracy and RT) over the duration of the experiment. Participants completed six blocks of 100 hundred trials, with a 2-minute pause between each block. RTs were calculated each minute for each block, giving 5 measures for each block, across successive blocks.

As illustrated in Fig. 16.2, we found that anhedonic participants' reaction times increased with time on task, becoming longer from the first minute to the last minute

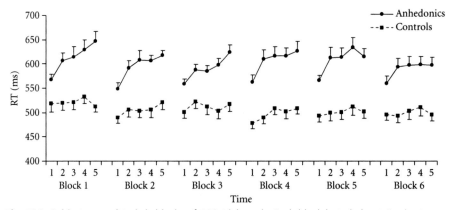

Fig. 16.2 Subjects completed six blocks of 100 trials each. Each block lasted about 5 minutes. Blocks are separated by a 2-minute pause. The whole task lasted about 40 minutes.

of each block. However, no change in accuracy was found. It appeared that anhedonic subjects displayed greater difficulty in maintaining rapidity over time, but did it without sacrificing accuracy. There was no effect of task repetition, as these effects did not vary between blocks.

RT can only be measured if the participant is paying sufficient attention to respond to the task. The proportion of targets missed may be a more sensitive measure of the ability to sustain attention under most conditions (Parasuraman, 1984). Therefore, our results may not reflect a pure sustained attention deficit. However, it should be borne in mind that our error rate was very low, and their participants may have been responding at the ceiling. Thus, before the hypothesis of a deficit in sustained attention is accepted, further tests are necessary with a more difficult task that would reduce performance from the ceiling.

How can a TOT effect on RT be related to cognitive processing of the task? According to Parasuraman, an increase in RT with time on task reflects a decrease in alertness (or arousal), whereas a decline in accuracy indicates a decline in vigilance (Parasuraman and Haxby, 1993). An increase in RT in the context of declining performance suggests a process involving fatigue or task disengagement. In contrast, an increase in RT with maintenance of the level of performance suggests an integrated process of behavioural adaptation.

The adaptive behaviour process hypothesis can be discussed in the light of incompatibility effects. Indeed, as expected, reaction times and error rates were affected by incompatibility, although this effect did not vary with time on task. Error rates were particularly strongly affected by incompatible conditions in the control group, similar to previous results obtained with the same procedure (Dubal *et al.*, 2000). We suggested that these results reflected the participants' use of a more conservative response strategy.

One possible way of accounting for vigilance decrements involves distinguishing between controlled and automatic processes (Baddeley *et al.*, 1999). As mentioned above, controlled strategies are very costly. If anhedonic participants use such strategies to approach this task, their attentional resources should be exhausted more rapidly than those of the controls; this should be reflected by an increase in response time with time on task. Our results for block repetitions are consistent with this hypothesis: the 2-minute pause between blocks allowed anhedonic participants to recover their baseline RTs at the beginning of each new block as shown in Fig. 16.2. However, RTs did not differ between blocks, suggesting that the TOT effect was not due to increasing fatigue.

Our results provide evidence of recovery during the final block. Such end spurts are found in previous studies on vigilance (Parasuraman, 1984; Ballard, 1996) and have been attributed to revival of the participant's attention in anticipation of the end of the test session (Baker and Ware, 1966). Indeed, although participants were not explicitly told when the task would end, there were inevitable subtle cues present that informed them of the approaching end of the testing session (e.g. the time arranged for a return visit).

One another important finding emerges from these data. The anhedonic group showed greater intra-participant RT variability, a common finding with attention and motor tasks in pathological populations. In particular, heterogeneity in the RTs of participants with schizophrenia is well known, and generally inter- and intra-participant variability in RTs is greater in pathological than control populations (Nuechterlein, 1977). As stated by Van den Bosh *et al.* (1996), this variability tends to be treated as 'noise', rather than as an interesting feature in its own right. Various attention and motor mechanisms may be involved, which are not specific for a particular diagnosis. For example, reaction time variability may be due to transient variations in the level of alertness.

The greater intra-participant variability in anhedonic participants may be the logical consequence of the TOT effect: as the RT of anhedonic participants increases within each block, one would expect a higher variability in response. Indeed, the increase in intra-participant variability shows that anhedonic participants had response times that were more variable between trials than those of the control participants. The response latency slopes suggest that this finding may reflect irregular performance (i.e. RT increases with TOT).

Alternatively, the greater intra-participant variability may reflect irregular performance throughout the task due to occasional distraction or intermittent lapses (Matthysse *et al.*, 1999). Hemsley (1987) described this cognitive deficit as a weakening of the influence of stored memories of the regularity of previous input on current perception. As a result, schizophrenic patients fail to use contextual information in cognitive processing (Van den Bosh *et al.*, 1996). Thus, the greater variability in the anhedonic group may be related to the TOT effect, constituting 'predictable variability', or it may correspond to an independent effect (i.e. 'unpredictable variability'), as modelled by Matthysse *et al.* (1999) in schizophrenic patients.

The classic disorders of attention that accompany anhedonia imply limitation of the ability to mobilize attentional processes, especially in high-demand situations. Our results are consistent with such a deficit in situations requiring effort, and tend to qualify the nature of the deficit. It may be that attentional resources, rather than being limited, are more rapidly exhausted. This hypothesis has already been put forward for psychotic patients (Schmand *et al.*, 1994).

Conclusion: the cognitive facets of anhedonia

Longitudinal studies of anhedonic children or young adults have emphasized the predominant role of anhedonia in the development of a psychosis-related disorder, *a fortiori* when anhedonia is coupled with attention deficits. Our work continues to explore the link between anhedonia and attention in young anhedonic adults in order to describe their particular attention profile. Non-clinical anhedonic participants do exhibit deviant attention characteristics compared with nonclinical controls. Their P300 response profile suggest a different neural resource allocation strategy operates when the task requires more effort, either in the quality of the attention processes or in the quantity of the control processes. The pattern of deviance reflects different strategies used to process information. Anhedonic participants achieve normal behavioural performance by resorting to task strategies that appear to be more conservative and less flexible than those used by typical populations.

Ahedonic participants exhibit emotional deficits as well as discrete cognitive dysfunctions. Nuechterlein (1991) proposed that anhedonic participants' loss of capacity to experience pleasure could originate in a resource allocation deficit. When confronted with pleasant stimuli, anhedonics would allocate fewer resources than controls in their responses. The consequence would be less emotional expressiveness and reactivity. According to this theory, both allocating resources and pleasure would be different aspects of the same process. Measuring attention allocation would then amount to measuring a different expression of the same anhedonia phenomena. In this framework, the attention dysfunction would constitute an indicator of risk in these participants, as well as the risk for the onset of illness. Anhedonia must then be viewed as a composite dimension, as a behavioural phenotype that expresses itself in both the emotional and cognitive domains. The vulnerability may be derived from the contact of anhedonia, in time, with cognitive, social, and environmental pressures.

In this chapter, we have illustrated the interest of an approach consisting in studying cognitive processing in relation to affect impairment. "*Emotional and motivational are unique experientially valenced state spaces that help organisms make cognitive choices*" (Panksepp, 2003). Panksepp's proposal relates to the fact that emotional states, mood, positive affect diffusely impact on diverse cognitive functions (e.g. Ashby, 1999). Several recent neuroimaging studies have led to the results that some cerebral networks involved in cognitive processes were found to be increased by emotional evoking qualities of the stimuli (e.g. Anderson and Phelps, 2001; Vuilleumier *et al.*, 2001; Gray, 2002; Perlstein *et al.*, 2003).

The study of the selectivity of emotional influence on cognitive processing is on process: Gray (2002) found that emotional states might selectively modulate components of cognitive control: mild anxiety enhances spatial Working memory and amusement enhances verbal memory. This does not only suggest that emotional states may have selective effects on cognition, this also states that these effects would act on cognitive control or executive function.

Within this theoretical context, our message was that studying emotional disorders may help exploring the effect of emotional processing on attention processing, and particularly the selective mechanism of attention, that is of major importance in making cognitive choices.

References

American Psychiatric Association (1980). *Diagnostic and statistical manual of mental disorders*, 3rd edn (DSM III). Washington, DC: American Psychiatric Association.

Anderson, A. K. and Phelps, E. A. (2001). Lesions of the human amygdala impair enhanced perception of emotionally salient events. *Nature*, **411**, 305–9.

Ashby, F. G., Isen, A. M., and Turken, A. U. (1999). A neuropsychological theory of positive affect and its influence on cognition. *Psychological Review*, **106**, 529–50.

Baddeley, A., Cocchini, G., Della Sala, S., *et al.* (1999). Working memory and vigilance: evidence from normal aging and Alzheimer's disease. *Brain Cognition*, **41**, 87–108.

Baker, R. A. and Ware, J. R. (1966). The relationship between vigilance and monotonous work. *Ergonomics*, **9**, 109–14.

Ballard, J. C. (1996). Computerized assessment of sustained attention: a review of factors affecting vigilance performance. *Journal of Clinical and Experimental Neuropsychology*, **18**, 843–63.

Buchanan, R. W., Strauss, M. E., Breier, A., *et al.* (1997). Attentional impairments in deficit and nondeficit forms of schizophrenia. *American Journal of Psychiatry*, **154**, 363–70.

Cadenhead, K., Kumar, C., and Braff, D. (1996). Clinical and experimental characteristics of 'hypothetically psychosis prone' college students. *Journal of Psychiatric Research*, **30**, 331–40.

Cassano, G. B., Michelini, S., Shear, M. K., *et al.* (1997). The panic-agoraphobic spectrum: a descriptive approach to the assessment and treatment of subtle symptoms. *American Journal of Psychiatry*, **154**, 27–38.

Chapman, L. J. and Chapman, J. P. (1978). *Revised physical anhedonia scale*. Unpublished scale.

Chapman, L. J. and Chapman, J. P. (1980). Scales for rating psychotic and psychotic-like experiences as continua. *Schizophrenia Bulletin*, **6**, 476–89.

Chapman, L. J., Chapman, J. P., and Raulin, M. L. (1976). Scales for physical and social anhedonia. *Journal of Abnormal Psychology*, **85**, 374–82.

Chapman, L. J., Chapman, J. P., Kwapil, T. R., *et al.* (1994). Putatively psychosis-prone participants 10 years later. *Journal of Abnormal Psychology*, **103**, 171–83.

Clark, D. C., Fawcett, J., Salazar-Grueso, E., *et al.* (1984). Seven-month clinical outcome of anhedonic and normally hedonic depressed inpatients. *American Journal of Psychiatry*, **141**, 1216–20.

Cornblatt, B. A., Lenzenweger, M. F., and Erlenmeyer-Kimling, L. (1989). The continuous performance test, identical pairs version: II. Contrasting attentional profiles in schizophrenic and depressed patients. *Psychiatry Research*, **29**, 65–85.

Cornblatt, B. A., Lenzenweger, M. F., Dworkin, R. H., *et al.* (1992). Childhood attentional dysfunctions predict social deficits in unaffected adults at risk for schizophrenia. *British Journal of Psychiatry*, **18**, 59–64.

Cornblatt, B. A., Obuchowski, M., Roberts, S., *et al.* (1999). Cognitive and behavioral precursors of schizophrenia. *Developmental Psychopathology*, **11**, 487–508.

Davies, D. R. and Tune, G. S. (1969). *Human vigilance performance*. New York, NY: Elsevier.

Drewer, H. B. and Shean, G. D. (1993). Reaction time crossover in schizotypal participants. *Journal of Nervous and Mental Disease*, **181**, 27–30.

Dubal, S. and Jouvent, R. (2003). *Attentional cost of emotional experience*. Unpublished manuscript.

Dubal, S. and Jouvent, R. (2004). Time-on-task effect in trait anhedonia. *European Psychiatry*, in press.

Dubal, S., Pierson, A., and Jouvent, R. (2000). Focused attention in anhedonia: a P3 study. *Psychophysiology*, **37**, 711–14.

Eriksen, C. W. and Eriksen, B. A. (1974). Effects of noise letters upon the identification of a target letter in a nonsearch task. *Perception and Psychophysics*, **16**, 143–9.

Erlenmeyer-Kimling, L., Cornblatt, B. A., Rock, D., *et al.* (1993). The New York High-Risk Project: anhedonia, attentional deviance, and psychopathology. *Schizophrenia Bulletin*, **19**, 141–53.

Erlenmeyer-Kimling, L., Rock, D., Roberts, S. A., *et al.* (2000). Attention, memory, and motor skills as childhood predictors of schizophrenia-related psychoses: the New York High-Risk Project. *American Journal of Psychiatry*, **157**, 1416–22.

Fawcett, J., Clark, D. C., Scheftner, W. A., et al. (1983). Assessing anhedonia in psychiatric patients. *Archives of General Psychiatry*, **40**, 79–84.

Fernandes, L. O. L. and Miller, G. A. (1995). Compromised performance and abnormal psychophysiology associated with the Wisconsin-Proneness Scales. In *The behavioral high-risk paradigm in psychopathology* (ed. G. A. Miller), pp. 47–87. New York, NY: Springer-Verlag.

Fisk, A. D. and Schneider, W. (1981). Control and automatic processing during tasks requiring sustained attention: a new approach to vigilance. *Human Factors*, **23**, 737–50.

Freedman, L. R., Rock, D., Roberts, S. A., et al. (1998). The New York High-Risk Project: attention, anhedonia and social outcome. *Schizophrenia Research*, **27**, 1–9.

Gray, J. R., Braver, T. S., and Raichle, M. E. (2002). Integration of emotion and cognition in the lateral prefrontal cortex. *Proceedings of the National Academy of Sciences*, **99**, 4115–20.

Giese-Davis, J. E., Miller, G. A., and Knight, R. A. (1993). Memory template comparison processes in anhedonia and dysthymia. *Psychophysiology*, **30**, 646–56.

Hardy, P., Jouvent, R., Lancrenon, S., et al. (1986). The Pleasure-Displeasure Scale. Use in the evaluation of depressive illness. *Encephale*, **12**, 149–54.

Hasher, L. and Zacks, R. T. (1979). Automatic and effortful processes in memory. *Journal of Experimental Psychology General*, **108**, 356–89.

Hazlett, E. A., Dawson, M. E., Filion, D. L., et al. (1997). Autonomic orienting and the allocation of processing resources in schizophrenia patients and putatively at-risk individuals. *Journal of Abnormal Psychology*, **106**, 171–81.

Hemsley, D. R. (1987). An experimental psychological model for schizophrenia. In *Search for the causes of schizophrenia* (ed. H. Häfner, W. F. Gattaz, and W. Janzarik), pp. 179–88. Berlin: Springer-Verlag.

Hoffman, J. E., Houck, M. R., MacMillan, F. W., et al. (1985). Event-related potentials elicited by automatic targets: a dual-task analysis. *Journal of Experimental Psychology: Human Perception and Performance*, **11**, 50–61.

Holzman, P. S., Coleman, M., Lenzenweger, M. F., et al. (1995). Working memory deficits, antisaccades, and thought disorders in relation to perceptual aberration. In *Schizotypal Personality* (ed. A. Raine, T. Lencz, and S. A. Mednick), pp. 353–81. Cambridge University Press.

Johnson, R. (1986). A triarchic model of P300 Amplitude. *Psychophysiology*, **23**, 367–84.

Josiassen, R., Shagass, C., Roemer, R., et al. (1985). Attention-related effects in somatosensory evoked potentials in college students at high risk for psychopathology. *Journal of Abnormal Psychology*, **94**, 507–18.

Jouvent, R. and Ammar, S. (1994). Modèles dimensionnels et psychobiologie. In *Traité de Psychopathologie* (ed. Widlöcher, D.), PUF, Paris.

Jutai, J. W. (1989). Spatial attention in hypothetically psychosis-prone college students. *Psychiatry Research*, **27**, 207–15.

Kazdin, A. E. (1989). Evaluation of the Pleasure Scale in the assessment of anhedonia in children. *Journal of American and Academic Child and Adolescent Psychiatry*, **28**, 364–72.

Klein, D. F. (1974). Endogenomorphic depression: a conceptual and terminological revision. *Archives of General Psychiatry*, **31**, 447–54.

Kraepelin, E. (1906). *Introduction à la Psychiatrie Clinique*. Paris: Navarin Ed.

Kramer, A. F., Wickens, C. D., and Donchin, E. (1985). Processing of stimulus properties: evidence for dual-task integrality. *Journal of Experimental Psychology: Human Perception and Performance*, **11**, 393–408.

Kwapil, T. R. (1998). Social anhedonia as a predictor of the development of schizophrenia-spectrum disorders. *Journal of Abnormal Psychology*, **107**, 558–65.

Mackworth, N. H. (1948). The Breakdown of vigilance during prolonged visual search. *Quarterly Journal of Experimental Psychology*, 1, 6–21.

Mass, R., Wolf, K., Wagner, M., *et al.* (2000). Differential sustained attention/vigilance changes over time in schizophrenics and controls during a degraded stimulus Continuous Performance Test. *European Archives of Psychiatry and Clinical Neurosciences*, 250, 24–30.

Matthysse, S., Levy, D. L., Wu, Y., *et al.* (1999). Intermittent degradation in performance in schizophrenia. *Schizophrenia Research*, 30, 131–46.

Meehl, P. E. (1962). Schizotaxia, schizotypy, schizophrenia. *American Pscyhologist*, 17, 827–38.

Miller, G. A. (1986). Information processing deficits in anhedonia and perceptual aberration: a Psychophysiological analysis. *Biological Psychiatry*, 21, 100–15.

Miller, G. A., Simons, R. F., and Lang, P. J. (1984). Electrocortical measures of information processing deficits in anhedonia. *Annals of the New York Academy of Sciences*, 425, 599–602.

Mishlove, M. and Chapman, L. J. (1985). Social anhedonia in the prediction of Psychosis proneness. *Journal of Abnormal Psychology*, 94, 394–6.

Nestor, P. G., Faux, S. F., McCarley, R. W., *et al.* (1990). Measurement of visual sustained attention in schizophrenia using signal detection analysis and a newly developed computerized CPT task. *Schizophrenia Research*, 3, 329–32.

Nuechterlein, K. H. (1977). Reaction time and attention in schizophrenia: a critical evaluation of the data and theories. *Schizophrenia Bulletin*, 3, 373–428.

Nuechterlein, K. H. (1983). Signal detection in vigilance tasks and behavioral attributes among offspring of schizophrenic mothers and among hyperactive children. *Journal of Abnormal Psychology*, 92, 4–28.

Nuechterlein, K. H. (1991). Methodological considerations in the search for indicators of vulnerability to severe psychopathology. In *Event-Related Brain Potentials: Basic issues and applications* (ed. J. W. Rohrbaugh, R. Parasuraman, and R. Johnson), pp. 364–73. Oxford: Oxford University Press.

Nuechterlein, K. H., Parasuraman, R., and Jiang, Q. (1983). Visual sustained attention: image degradation produces rapid sensitivity decrement over time. *Science*, 220, 327–9.

Panksepp, J. (2003). At the interface of the affective, behavioral, and cognitive neurosciences: decoding the emotional feelings of the brain. *Brain & Cognition*, 52, 4–14.

Parasuraman, R. (1984). Sustained attention in detection and discrimination. In *Varieties of attention* (ed. R. Parasuraman and D. R. Davies), pp. 243–89. New York, NY: Academic Press.

Parasuraman, R. and Davies, D. R. (1984). *Varieties of attention*. New York, NY: Academic Press.

Parasuraman, R. and Haxby, J. V. (1993). Attention and brain function in Alzheimer's disease. *Neuropsychology*, 7, 242–72.

Perlstein, W. M., Elbert, T., and Stenger, V. A. (2002). Dissociation in human prefrontal cortex of affective influences on working memory-related activity. *Proceedings of the National Academy of Sciences*, 99, 1736–41.

Ribot, T. (1896). *La psychologie des sentiments*. Alcan: Paris.

Rosvold, H. E., Mirsky, A. F., Sarason, I., *et al.* (1956). Continuous performance test of brain damage. *Journal of Consulting and Clinical Psychology*, 20, 343–50.

Rueckert, L. and Grafman, J. (1996). Sustained attention deficits in patients with right frontal lesions. *Neuropsychologia*, 34, 953–63.

Rueckert, L. and Levy, J. (1996). Further evidence that the callosum is involved in sustaining attention. *Neuropsychologia*, 34, 927–35.

Schmand, B., Kuipers, T., Van der Gaag, M., *et al.* (1994). Cognitive disorders and negative symptoms as correlates of motivational deficits in psychotic patients. *Psychological Medicine*, 24, 869–84.

Schneider, W., Dumais, S. T., and Shiffrin, R. M. (1984). Automatic and control processing and attention. In *Varieties of attention* (ed. R. Parasuraman and D. R. Davies), pp. 1–27. New York, NY: Academic Press.

Servan-Schreiber, D., Bruno, R. M., Carter, C. S., *et al.* (1998). Dopamine and the mechanisms of cognition: Part I. A neural network model predicting dopamine effects on selective attention. *Biological Psychiatry*, **15**, 713–22.

Shuldberg, D. and London, A. (1989). Psychological differentiation and schizotypal traits: Negative results with the Group Embedded Figures Test. *Perceptual and Motor Skills*, **68**, 1219–26.

Silverstein, S. M., Raulin, M. L., Pristach, E. A., *et al.* (1992). Perceptual organization and schizotypy. *Journal of Abnormal Psychology*, **101**, 265–70.

Simons, R. F. (1982). Physical Anhedonia and future psychopathology: an electrocortical continuity? *Psychophysiology*, **19**, 433–41.

Simons, R. F. and Russo, K. R. (1987). Event-related potentials and continuous performance in participants with physical anhedonia or perceptual aberrations. *Journal of Psychophysiology*, **2**, 27–37.

Strayer, D. L. and Kramer, A. F. (1990). Attentional requirements of automatic and controlled processing. *Journal of Experimental Psychology: Learning, Memory and Cognition*, **16**, 67–82.

Van den Bosch, R. J., Rombouts, R. P., and Van Asma, M. J. (1996). What determines continuous performance task performance? *Schizophrenia. Bulletin*, **22**, 643–51.

Van Praag, H. M., Asnis, G. M., and Kahn, R. S. (1990). Monoamines and abnormal behaviour: a multi-aminergic perspective. *British journal of Psychiatry*, **157**, 723–34.

Vuilleumier, P., Armony, J.L., Driver, J., *et al.* (2001). Effects of attention and emotion on face processing in the human brain: an event-related fMRI study. *Neuron*, **30**, 829–41.

Ward, P. B., Catts, S. V., Armstrong, M. S., *et al.* (1984). P300 and psychiatric vulnerability in university students. *Annals of the New York Academy of Sciences*, **425**, 645–52.

Warm, J. S. (1984). *Sustained Attention in Human Performance*. London: Wiley.

Wickens, C. D., Kramer, A. F., Vanasse, L., *et al.* (1983). The performance of concurrent tasks: A Psychophysiological analysis of the reciprocity if information processing resources. *Science*, **221**, 1080–2.

Wilkins, S. and Venables, P. H. (1992). Disorder of attention in individuals with schizotypal personality. *Schizophrenia Bulletin*, **18**, 717–23.

Yee, C. M. and Miller, G. A. (1994). A dual-task analysis of resource allocation in dysthymia and anhedonia. *Journal of abnormal Psychology*, **103**, 625–36.

Yee, C. M., Deldin, P. J., and Miller, G. A. (1992). Early processing stimulus in dysthymia and anhedonia. *Journal of abnormal Psychology*, **101**, 230–3.

Young, M. A., Scheftner, W. A., Klerman, G. L., *et al.* (1986). The endogenous sub-type of depression: a study of its internal construct validity. *British Journal of Psychiatry*, **148**, 257–67.

Zimmerman, M., Coryell, W., Pfohl, B., *et al.* (1986). The validity of four definitions of endogenous depression. II. Clinical, demographic, familial, and psychosocial correlates. *Archives of General Psychiatry*, **43**, 234–44.

Discussion

Emotion, body, and parent–infant interaction

George Downing

I have been asked to comment on the papers in this volume. It is a welcome task. Much in these stimulating papers broadens our picture of early development. My own professional activities are chiefly clinical, although I am engaged in research as well. I will therefore focus first upon theoretical issues and then go on to some implications for clinical intervention.

Beyond the face

When we think about emotion, should our focus be on the face or on the body as a whole? Research strategies limited to the face have had considerable success. However, we must be careful. It is in the nature of good research paradigms to be narrow. That is what gives manageable factors we can manipulate. Easy to forget, however, that this very narrowing of the field may cause us to marginalize phenomena that, in fact, are deserving of more attention.

So it has been, one could argue, concerning emotion and the body. I have elsewhere discussed this point extensively with respect to emotion theories centred upon adult affect (Downing, 2000). What is striking about the present papers is how they support a similar perspective upon infants and emotion. Affectively speaking, infants would seem to be full-body creatures from the start.

Here is an example. Oster[1] has written a wonderfully detailed article on Baby-FACS, her influential system for coding infant facial behaviour. [Baby-FACS is based upon Ekman and Friesen's FACS (Facial Action Coding System, Ekman and Friesen, 1978).] Among other issues, she discusses the widely asserted hypothesis that, during the first year, infants do not show fear or anger. Instead, it is claimed, they express only crying and/or undifferentiated distress.

Oster proposes that this claim is simply false. Once we look 'beyond the face', there are clear manifestations of fear and anger to be found (Wienberg and Tronick, 1994). In one study, 11-month-old infants were confronted by a growling toy gorilla head. They immediately made their bodies go still, while looking long and intently. Thus, they

---

[1] All specific references not otherwise indicated are to the articles in this volume.

organized their bodies as a whole differently, even though their faces showed only crying-distress. Observers, who were shown a videotape of this body reaction alone (the infants' faces were covered up on the videotape), immediately rated these infants as 'wary' or 'fearful'.

As part of the same design, at another point the infants had their wrists held in place by an experimenter. They responded to this restraint with evident body movements of angry struggle. Here again, to be seen on the face was only crying-distress. But the observers who judged by the body reaction alone, rated them as showing 'frustration'.

One is reminded here of Siegfried Frey's (e.g. 1999) seminal work coding the bodily affect displays of adults. Exploiting a sophisticated form of full-body coding, Frey demonstrates that affect signals in adult-with-adult interaction include far more than the face alone. Head tilts, torso shifts, shoulder movements and more, play an essential role. These other movements, even when fast in time (e.g. 0.1 second) and small in size, often influence and even change, the receiver's response and interpretative processing. Similar data, using a modified version of the same coding system, has been found by Heller (1997).

This is not to suggest that, face aside, how infants express affect is the same as how adults do. On the contrary, part of the strength of Oster's approach is its freedom from such a notion. Baby-FACS allows us to record simply which facial muscles move when and with what size of movement: nothing more and nothing less. No assumption about correspondences between infant and adult facial displays is necessary; this issue is left an empirical one. In contrast, for example, research paradigms using Izard's MAX (Maximally Discriminative Facial Movement Coding System; Izard, 1983; cf. Izard et al., 1995) usually revolve around asking the question: at what points in time do infant (facial) expressions look the same as adult (facial) expressions? Whereas Baby-FACS permits strategies which ask: in what ways are infant expressions like and in what ways unlike adult expressions?

In fact, what Oster has demonstrated is that infant expressions do not map neatly onto adult ones. Infant facial behaviour is a world in itself, a world we still know poorly. For example, the infant brow tends to be highly active. It takes on some configurations with expressions of interest, other configurations with distress, and unlike adults, still others in combination with smiles. Nose wrinkling and/or tongue protrusion also frequently go together with smiles, effects little seen in adult displays. The temporal sequencing of facial movements is often different as well. If we closely examine a video-tape of an infant who is displaying a 'cry face' for some seconds, we may discover a number of different muscle actions that come and go at different moments, with varying degrees of movement size. Much such behaviour appears relatively organized, if organized differently than the adult mode.

It also could be, as Oster remarks, that some functional purposes of early expressive behaviour are not quite the same as for adults. Precocious 'pouts', she suggests, perhaps serve at first as a means of regulating negative affect in general. The extended lips likely inhibit any further build-up of distress. Only at a later point in development, if this hypothesis is right, does pouting come to be coordinated more closely with sadness. Later still, it will take on additional signalling functions: as a result of contingent experience with adult reactions, the toddler will learn to use pouts as a 'warning'. As Oster herself stresses, however, what we most need is further mapping of these expressive displays themselves. We need more information about their muscular variants, their timing sequencings, and the like, independently of guesses about function.

Surely, the same is true once the full body is considered. We need expanded ways to record and quantify all forms of body expression, as well as designs which bring attention to the body as a whole. Oster's strong stance, that our investigations should be free from *a priori* assumptions that whatever fails to match adult expression is simple a 'precursor' of the latter, is exemplary.

Body micropractices

We might more generally think of an infant's early expressive maneuvers as body strategies, or, loosely following Bourdieu (1976)[2], as body micropractices (Downing, 2000). They are competencies of a kind, embodied skills. They are, what is sometimes called, procedural or implicit knowledge, a knowing-how as opposed to a knowing-that.

We are accustomed to thinking of embodied skills as activities like playing tennis or hammering a nail (Dreyfus, 1992). The term is more than apt for a lot of what a baby does, however. Many of the procedures he comes to implement are intricate, highly bodily, and goal-oriented.

Some early body micropractices first exist as wired-in anlage. Usually these are rudimentary versions, open to further development. They start out as almost reflexive in nature. In the beginning, their strategic element already may be important as, for example, with looking at the adult face, or it may be minimal. Gradually, the infant refines and alters the practice. Some such competencies eventually also become components of more complex body micropractices.

In developmental theory, it is more usual to think along such lines about pure motor skills, such as reaching and locomotion. However, if we accept that emotions (a) involve the whole body, and (b) have functions, then it makes a lot of sense to adopt an analogous point of view for understanding emotion.

More generally speaking, I am suggesting a wide concept of emotion (Downing, 2000). It can be seen as comprising:

- a neurophysiological and hormonal substrate;
- motor components ['action readiness', says Frijda (1986)];
- representational components (about which, more below).

---

[2] What Bourdieu (1976) called 'habitus' was meant to include procedural micro-behaviour. His interest of course was limited to older children and adults. He also emphasized only the cultural dimension of micro-behaviour.

Both Panksepp and Trevarthen here argue in a similar vein, as has Klaus Scherer (Scherer, 1999) elsewhere. Canamero and Gaussier too in their contribution have modeled a complex concept of emotion. In contrast, many (adult) emotion theories offer more reductive accounts, proposing that what emotion 'really is', is one of these dimensions alone, and at the most, two of them together. A more inclusive view, however, can avoid a number of theoretical impasses (Downing, 2000).

For one thing, this gives us a conceptual language which can easily handle both affect and the regulation of affect. Both aspects involve bodily skills and strategies, but as Oster remarks, there exist plenty of expressions (early pouts are one example) where we don't really know what is a prior-to-regulation motor tendency and what is regulation. Hence, the advantage of a terminology, which does not prejudge such issues. In a like vein, we can avoid too sharp a theoretical cleavage between the regulation of affect, and the regulation of interpersonal closeness and distance. A good many affective competencies have to do with both of these simultaneously, as has been widely remarked in developmental research.

Trevarthen, in his paper, emphasizes a similar point. Trevarthen claims that we introduce a misleading dichotomy when we separate infant affect from infant closeness-distance motoric regulation. He underlines, too, that this implies we must take account of full-body behaviour, such as rhythmic hand movements, as opposed to facial display alone. Other contributors here offer like suggestions, some more of which I will comment upon shortly. It is particularly apt that, in this collection, Tremblay *et al.* invoke the spirit of Henri Wallon (1942), who, as they remind us, long ago pleaded for an understanding of emotion based upon the full body.

Representations too

To call these 'body' micropractices or 'procedural' know-how does not preclude speaking about a cognitive or representational side. On the contrary, to acknowledge a representational dimension is necessary. Of course, we need to be careful about the term 'representation'. I am using it here in a broad sense, not in, for example, a Piagetian sense. Perception of one's surroundings is representational; it is how one portrays, consciously or unconsciously, the immediate spatial layout (Peacocke, 1992). Perception of one's body is representational. An animal's 'cognitive map', which guides his movement through the environment (e.g. a rat's memory of the route through a labyrinth), is representational. An infant's expectancies based upon contingent learning are representational. [For more extensive discussions see Dreske (1992), Peacocke (1992), Tye (1995), and Bermudez (1998, 2003).]

Meant in this sense, representational content can be either conceptual or non-conceptual (Peacocke, 1992; Tye, 1995; Bermudez, 2003). It can also be layered. I can represent the visual layout before me as including, over there to the right, a patch of orange with round contours. So far this is non-conceptual content. I can also represent that, over there, is an object and, in fact, an orange, and indeed the orange that I left on the kitchen counter last night.[3]

From this point of view what Piaget meant by 'representation', is more limited. This is to be expected given his Kantian background and given that his paradigm examples involved rather advanced mental capacities, such as deferred imitation or hidden object search.[4]

In a similar vein, when some proponents of dynamic system theory (henceforth DST) Thelen propose that we can explain much of development without invoking 'representations' (e.g. Thelen and Smith, 1994), it is to this Piagetian sense of the term that they are (rightly, I would suggest) reacting. DST explanations are often quite helpful for understanding the formation of body micropractices. However, once we move beyond the simplest motor acts, such as infant reaching or stepping, DST becomes more viable when linked with a broad sense of representation.[5]

From this standpoint affordances, too, in Gibson's sense, are representational. The infant represents a surface in front him not only as smooth and level, but also as affording crawling. To repeat, representational content, at this level, can be non-conceptual. Concepts need not be involved. Inferences need not be involved. Nevertheless, the representational content can do work, as when the infant's discrimination of the surface in front of him leads him actually to crawl forward.

As Soussignan and Schaal in their paper make clear, however, it would be a mistake to assume that early-appearing body strategies are necessarily coupled with some regular form of representational content. For some strategies, the link to specific contextual situations is formed only gradually, with a lot of hit-and-miss occurrences with respect to both sides of the equation. (Strategy occurs without eliciting situation. Situation occurs without strategy appearing.)

Most of Soussignan and Schaal's examples, from their own and others' research, are of taste and odor reactions. Some of the responses they measured are purely physiological, with (at least as far as they report) no motor aspects. However, some do involve muscle elements, such as a facial display of disgust or fuller breathing in reaction to a pleasurable stimulus. Soussignan and Schaal's helpful idea is that as infants assemble

---

[3] Thus, representations causally co-vary with objective factors in the world, under normal circumstances. Evolution has selected for that capacity. The orange both is portrayed by my representation and is (partially) causally responsible for my representation. When this brain-mind system does not function in the right way, then misrepresentation occurs (Dretske, 1992; Tye, 1995).

[4] Whereas with a concept of representation broadened to include non-conceptual content, room can also easily be made for what Piaget called sensory-motor schemas.

[5] Meltzoff and Moore (2001), in a interesting discussion, make a similar suggestion. From the point of view I am suggesting, however, their notion of representation, though wider than the classical Piagetian sense, is still too narrow, as it is limited to conceptual content.

their bodily skills, the tie between the skill and the infant's sense of what is 'out there', may also be a factor which evolves.

An example

Reddy gives us a nice example of an early body strategy. She challenges the notion that 'embarrassment' and 'shyness', can only be shown by those toddlers and older children who have already achieved mirror self-recognition. This familiar argument claims that, in order to feel and show embarrassment, I must be aware I have an 'outside', i.e. I must grasp that others can see me, just as I can see and recognize myself in the mirror.

Here, as so often, Reddy persuasively suggests, we have imposed too adult a mode of thinking onto infants. Perhaps an infant during the first half-year cannot quite conceive of 'what the other person sees', in our adult way of understanding this idea. For all that, starting with age 2 months they display a behaviour that looks remarkably close to what older children and adults perform when feeling embarrassed. While smiling, they look or turn away from contact. The adverting movement is brief. As the smile dies, or even before, they bring their gaze or head back, and appear ready to engage anew in an exchange. During this look away they may also narrow their eyelids. Frequently, too, they raise the arms into or towards the space just before their own faces. What is going on?

Reddy proposes that the typical timing of this occurrence casts light on its purpose. Usually, the event takes place right after there has been a pause in the interaction and just at the moment when the infant is returning to eye contact with the adult. The infant returns, but then looks or turns away, with the smile, ever so briefly. A reasonable hypothesis, Reddy suggests, is that the infant both wants the renewed exchange and yet also feels a risk of being too much stimulated, too quickly. With his smile, he indicates his positive readiness. With his glance or turn away he slows down the onset of his being activated.

So, here again is a body strategy implicating more than the face, and essentially so. Were we to code facial display alone, we would miss the phenomenon. The look/turn to the side modifies and qualifies the facial signal sent.

The bringing of the arms upwards is also an interesting part. Reddy offers an interpretation of this, which perhaps goes beyond what is necessary. She hypothesizes that the infant includes this piece of the total motor package in order to reduce how much the adult can see of the infant's face or body. A more parsimonious account is possible, however. Likely, by throwing up his arms the infant reduces what he sees: he can diminish the amount of 'big-person-thing-over-there' spatial presence in his own representational field. Initially, the body micropractice could be coupled with no more representational content than this. More complex representational layers, such as concepts about the other's experience and inferences drawn from that, could emerge in later developmental periods.

This evolution of representations, moreover, could go hand-in-hand with the child's increasing procedural sophistication in using 'coy' behaviour to control the other person.

Reddy aptly remarks that we can best think of a 'family' of affective behaviours and of corresponding (guessed at) subjective feelings. The 'embarrassment' behaviour of 2-month-olds is analogous to adult embarrassment behaviour. Yet there is no reason to think it has the same 'age-possible meanings', in Tronick's sense (see below).

Nor, clearly, does it yet have the range of body micropractice variations which may emerge later. For example, Marvin (Marvin and Britner, 1999) has shown how 2- and 3-year-olds use this and similar 'coy' behaviours to manipulate interaction with their caretakers. Some pre-school children make extensive use of such strategies. When you examine their micro-behaviour on a videotape, you find impressive procedural expertise. These being also predominantly children who have received a 'disorganized attachment' rating in the Ainsworth Strange Situation, we can guess that a felt need for protection is at play. In this case, not only has the behaviour become quite sophisticated; doubtlessly the accompanying representations are complex too.

Nevertheless, the age 2 months version clearly has its own procedural rightness. It is an organized strategy and seems to have a concrete function. If the later strategy grows out of it, this is an ontogeny unlike an oak growing from an acorn. What occurs later is an emergent process which is looser and more open-end.

Some different forms of body micropractice

One important distinction is between two general types of affective body micropractice. One type we might call self-directed, or individual-alone, or 'solo' strategies. These are self-regulatory and self-affecting. The second type we might call interpersonal body micropractices. These are capacities whose function influences the other and/or mutually to regulate shared affective states. Recently, Beebe (2003) has also spoken about the need to tease out this difference more carefully the concepts of 'self-regulation' and 'mutual regulation' are, too often, run together, she suggests.

That a strategy is self-directed, does not mean that the infant mobilizes it only when he is alone, naturally. It may well be used in interactional contexts. Self-touching can be seen in (for the infant) stressful interactional exchanges. Infants often do it during a Still Face episode, for example, but as far as we know, its purpose seems to be self-regulation only and not interpersonal regulation.[6]

Probably, some procedural skills first appear in solo versions, then later take on interpersonal aspects. Pouting, in Oster's account, is thought by her to follow this kind of developmental line. Other micropractices begin as interpersonal and only with time take on solo functions. It is widely believed (although, of course, it has yet to be proven) that the capacity for an infant to calm himself, is first built up through repeated interactional experiences of being calmed by a caretaker. In addition, there are capacities,

---

[6] Of course, caretakers might be responding to infant self-touching much more than we realize. If so, it might be playing more of an interactional regulatory role than has been thought (Beebe, personal communication).

such as greeting behaviour or Reddy's shyness behaviour, which are inherently interpersonal. They start out so and remain so, whatever their evolution.

Probably, many body micropractices are built up in an *ad hoc* manner, a process that is partly predictable and partly indeterminate. They are 'loosely assembled', as Tronick suggests. Much of an infant's earliest behaviour is quasi-random. Some spatial displacements of body parts occur by chance. Others, like slightly stretching a hand toward an adult face, are wired-in, but rather fragmentary. By responding to certain of these infant body events and not others, the caretaker operates in a selective fashion. Exactly to which events she responds, is open. How she responds is even more open. (The infant averts. Does the mother at once vocalize, or wait? Touch, or wait? 'Chase' the infant with her own head (i.e. reposition her face in front of his adverted face[7]), or wait? If she vocalizes, is her tone friendly or irritated?) Such acts will be a result of her own history, her own micropractice repertoire, her cultural background, and a certain element of chance and indeterminateness present on her side as well (Fogel, 1993).

Tronick gives several detailed accounts of such interactional processes. He shows how they take place with constraints, yet have fuzzy parameters. Mothers among the Gusii in Kenya, for example, select out and support in their infants some forms of greeting behaviour highly different from those reinforced in Western infants. Eventually, a slowed-down, more 'somber' moment of mutual looking becomes the typical embodied skill. This is an example of cultural influence. In a similar fashion, any mother and infant, in any culture, jointly create certain repetitive exchanges that, in part, are specific to their dyad. As a result, the infant's emerging body strategies will in part become unique to him.

Not all of the interpersonal procedural competencies that an infant develops have to do with just dyadic exchange. This point is brought out by Tremblay *et al.* They report on several interesting designs involving triadic interaction. They show that, by age 3 months, not only are infants highly sensitive to three-way exchange; they also employ bodily skills relevant to this context.

By age 11 months these strategies are considerably more evolved. For example, Tremblay and Nadel created one triadic setting composed of an experimenter and two infants, the infants being already familiar with each other. The adult would give his attention only to one infant at a time, shifting back and forth between the two. This 'exclusion design', as the authors call it, elicited rather elaborate body behaviour from the infants. When receiving the adult's attention, the infant would orientate his own body and attention towards the adult, but at the same time would gaze frequently at the other, excluded infant. When excluded, the infant would tend to amplify his own body signals by engaging in 'showing-off' behaviour, similar to that described by Reddy in her contribution here. These strategies included 'banging objects repetitively, jumping, making funny noises, and laughing noisily', behaviours directed toward the adult in a bid for her attention.

---

[7] Beebe and Stern (1977) called this pattern 'chase and dodge'.

It is instructive to see what tends to happen to microanalytic coding in designs exploring triadic, rather than dyadic interaction. Here, it becomes even more necessary that we observe more of the body than just facial display, and head and gaze orientation. In this widened interactional field, persons are pulled to organize their bodies in a greater variety of possible configurations. They twist and turn, lean one way or another. They may anchor the pelvis facing one person, while moving the head to face another. They may look at one person and speak to another. Tremblay *et al.* nicely explain how important it was to gather data at this level.

Fivaz-Depeursinge and Corboz-Warnery using their Lausanne Triadic Play paradigm with infant–mother–father groupings, have shown many other examples of triadic competencies that emerge during the first year. As for coding, with Fivaz-Depeursinge and Corboz-Warnery the story is the same. Their scales also reflect, rather extensively, body positionings and movements of this broader kind, in addition to facial display.[8]

Dyadic expansion

Tronick in this volume discusses 'dyadic expansion'. It is one of the fullest expositions he has given of this important concept. The notion is meant to be both descriptive of some interactional phenomena, and explanatory of some aspects of development.

Tronick's Still Face paradigm has generated so much research[9], and for so many years, that one central fact has become almost too familiar. Although scientists love the paradigm, infants just hate it. A mere 2 minutes of the mother going immobile is enough to produce dramatic infant protest and/or self-regulation attempts. Why should this be? Tronick suggests we should wonder anew. Clearly, something fundamental is at play. But what?

Descriptively speaking, dyadic expansion is a systemic phenomenon. It encompasses the action of the two persons who are in relation. When it occurs, their reciprocal acts display a visible coordination such that, first, certain elements in the action of each, match or complement the action of the other; and, secondly, the overall coherence of the system itself becomes greater than it was before. Often observable as well is an evident accompanying pleasure on both sides. At times, this pleasure appears intensely joyful.

More abstractly described, dyadic expansion seems a polar opposite to what takes place during a Still Face perturbation. Based on their behaviour, infants appear strongly

---

[8] Compare too, in attachment studies, the coding of the 'D' category (disorganized attachment) for the Ainsworth Strange Situation. Main and Solomon (1990) remark that they could never have discriminated this category without full-body coding. Compare as well Stern's (1995) influential concept of 'vitality affects', a core part of which includes full-body movement.

[9] For an interesting historical overview of Still Face research see Adamson and Frick (2003), as well as Tronick's, Muir's and Cohn's replies.

driven to seek dyadic expansion. In a like manner, they seem driven to avoid, and/or to defend themselves against, the kind of vacuum effected by a Still Face design.

Tronick's theoretical explanation of dyadic expansion is that it promotes far more than good feelings. It provides the infant with a matrix for learning. The infant's behaviour and presumably his subjective experience, can take on a complexity that otherwise would be a step 'beyond' his immediate capacities. Dyadic expansion stretches the infant. It teases out more skillfulness. It operates at his 'proximal edge', in Vygotsky's (1978) sense.

This may easily involve more of the body than just the face. One example given is of an infant reaching, and a caretaker moving in to help him complete the reach. Here the two bodies are achieving a moment of special coordination. This example shows as well that dyadic expansion may or may not include direct imitation. At times, the caretaker's coordinated response may be complementary, rather than imitative.

Of course, in many instances, imitation will play a central role. Usually, then, it is a matter of imitation *plus*. A lovely example is given by Kugiumutzakis *et al.*, a father was imitating the vowel sound 'aa' of his 3-month-old son. Then, to this baseline exchange, the father added a rhythmic movement of raising his head. The son immediately responded with a similar head movement and this matching head gesture continued on both sides for about 3 minutes, with evident intensified mutual pleasure. Here, we see two phases of imitative action. A beginning level of imitation has set the stage for a more creative level, one might say.

Doubtless, there are also many forms of lead-in to a potential dyadic expansion episode. These include how the mother positions the object which will be the target of joint attention, as well as how she uses her voice to reinforce the infant's looking. Joint attention is not yet dyadic expansion, but like some forms of imitation, clearly it can set the stage for it.

Dyadic expansion has a representational side too, we can assume. Tronick is cautious about this, however. He suggests the infant's 'meaning-making' is constrained by the many limitations of his discriminatory and other mental capacities. Only 'age-possible meanings' will be in play, on his side. Many (and at some ages perhaps all) of these meanings will be non-conceptual and closely linked to procedural skills. As Tronick remarks, the infant who can only hold an object with both hands, has one sense of that-graspable-thing-there; the infant capable of holding the object with one hand and exploring it with the other hand, has a slightly different sense. The represented affordance is not exactly the same.

Nor would it be the same again for a toddler, nor yet again for an older child. Tronick insists on this. It is not just that the toddler to a degree and the older child quite a bit, now have more concepts, and have language as well. Their body skills and body strategies are also not the same. As body micropractices evolve, what the world affords evolves alongside, the social world included. Older children, e.g. 42 months, also get upset in reaction to a Still Face, as Weinberg and Tronick have shown, but how they represent it is more complex, as their semantic behaviour during and after the Still Face demonstrates (Weinberg *et al.*, 2002).

Dyadic expansion can also have a negative side. The infant's need of it is so deep that he will go after it, systematically, even if the patterns he is joining are disadvantageous for him in the long run. Tronick describes how this occurs with a large subgroup of depressed mothers and their babies. What the infant buys into, are feelings of anger and/or depressive dampening. He becomes biased towards these affective 'centres of gravity', as Panksepp calls them. He builds up body strategies that, in part, reproduce and, in part, make more manageable the kinds of contingent exchange, which manifest such feelings. Given the pull of dyadic expansion, the infant has little alternative. Better to experience this kind of coherence than to experience no coherence at all.

This is a point full of clinical implications (see below). Tronick adds to it a second equally so. Not only does such an infant organize his body skills in this manner, he also tends to induce corresponding affective echos in another person who interacts with him. Research assistants interacting (blind to the infant's status) with babies of this category touched them less and maintained a greater physical distance to them, Tronick reports. The research assistants also described feeling a kind of atmospheric effect of 'stay away, don't connect', as if the infant were stimulating this reaction. Surely more is at play here than just 'temperament'.

We thus see how the body micropractices formed even by a young infant, already exert a strong constraining influence on interaction. Each person brings his own repertoire, but each has to shape what he does to fit the moves of the other.

Autism

What about the case of autism? Offhand, this would seem to be a counterexample to Tronick's claims about dyadic expansion. Notoriously, autistic children seem to display little drive towards micro-connection with others. Can that be explained?

There are rich insights concerning autism in both Loveland's and Tremblay *et al.*'s papers. Some of what they report is relevant to this question.

To start with, Loveland discusses the pervasive fearfulness of even high-functioning autistic children. They tend to react with fear to a much wider range of stimulii than other children. Some of what elicits fright are things and thing-related events, such as the noise of a particular machine. Especially, it is aspects of human interaction that upset them. From the point of view of non-autistic sensibility, these social elicitors may seem eccentric. Loveland gives the example of a 9-year-old boy who often flips into shrieks and tantrums when the experimenter asks questions that are too hard for him.

It is not just this wide range of threatening triggers that is a problem, however. There is also the matter of the fear reactions themselves. Autistic childen frequently react immediately with high intensities of negative emotion. Once so stimulated, they have a lot of difficulty regulating downwards. Their solo body affective strategies are little developed, in my language. Loveland adds the interesting idea that some of their more idiosyncratic behaviours, such as pacing, nail-biting, and hair-pulling, may actually be means they are using to limit fear reactions. Such actions may be self-directed body micropractices, so to speak. However idiosyncratic, they may, in fact, provide some help.

In addition, these children are extremely poor at bringing appropriate social reactions into play. Contrary to what is sometimes claimed, Loveland points out, for some autistic children, their capacity to recognize social signals and affective information in other persons may not be all that bad. Less good perhaps than is the case with IQ-equivalent normals, but this difference concerning emotion recognition is not always enormous. What is more difficult for them, however, is what to do with this information once they have it. Missing, in other words, are the appropriate interpersonal body micropractices. Loveland makes the persuasive point that this too contributes to their reluctance to engage themselves socially. Why join the dance if you have such trouble doing the steps.

If we add together these different factors and if we try to feel our way into the affective universe of autistic children, then a certain hypothesis begins to make a lot of sense. More exactly, the hypothesis begins to look perfectly possible. Perhaps autistic children do, indeed, have a drive for dyadic expansion and for micro-connection. However, perhaps this drive has been obscured by even stronger needs for protection and holding back. Now, does there exist any evidence that a hypothesis along these lines is not only possible, but also true?

Nadel and colleagues offer the beginnings of just such evidence. Their results are compelling. They used a paradigm with two separate Still Face episodes, as well as a short period of experimenter-to-child full-body imitation. The children were low-functioning, i.e. non-verbal, with a mean developmental age equivalent of 30 months.

Each child was brought alone into a room with a stranger. First, for the initial 3 minutes, the stranger maintained a Still Face. Every one of the children reacted by ignoring her. They seemed not in the least upset by her immobile behaviour. Nor did they seem interested. Secondly, for the next 3 minutes the stranger, moving now about the room in a dance-like fashion, closely imitated the full-body movements of the child. The children became attentive and appeared thoroughly to enjoy this. What was remarkable was the third 3 minutes. The stranger again went into a Still Face. This time, however, each child reacted immediately. Most of them came physically close to the stranger, vocalized, and smiled, and began touching her.

What seems clear is that these very special conditions allowed a strong underlying urge towards dyadic expansion to show itself. That the stranger herself did all the imitating and did it full-body to full-body, must have given the children a maximum experience of contingency, while making a minimum of demand upon their own capacities. All they had to do was 'let' themselves be mirrored and this they did willingly. Then, once the onset of the Still Face 2 episode came along, several things probably sharply lowered their usual fearfulness about contact. For one thing, they now had expectancies that an agreeable-feeling form of contingent exchange could continue. Secondly, a lot of positive affect was activated in them. Thirdly, the fact that the stranger was sitting in a Still Face, without speaking or moving, probably also made it easier for them to approach. As Loveland notes, autistic children generally seem somewhat less afraid of an adult who is stationary and vocally quiet.

So the summative effect of these combined conditions had a surprising consequence. In a dynamic system sense, the pull of an alternative attractor state was strengthened. Thanks, likely, to both the experience of contingency *and* the neutralizing of habitual fearfulness, these children exhibited a dramatic impulse to re-establish the contingent contact. If this is right, it would seem to constitute an additional strong confirmation of Tronick's claims about dyadic expansion. More research in this direction is certainly warrented.

Loveland raises a related issue. She remarks that therapeutic and educational programmes, which put their main emphasis upon teaching autistic children 'emotion recognition' may be off the mark. What is more needed are ways to help these children develop the response side, the ability to give back affective signals to the other. Plus, they need help building up new strategies to regulate negative emotion.

This seems to me on target. It is an idea which also receives support from some of Stanley Greenspan's treatment techniques with autistic children, and from the results he has obtained. Greenspan likewise emphasizes the active mobilization of emotional states which favoritize tiny new steps of learning and of social exchange (Greenspan and Weider, 1998; cf. Shanker, 2003). Similar too is the effective work of Maria Aarts (2002), who uses video-supported intervention with the families of autistic children.

Both our research designs and treatment strategies, comments Loveland, ought to put more focus upon 'the embeddedness of the person with autism within a social environment'.

Maternal depression

Maternal depression and its effects upon mother–infant relationships continue to be researched on many fronts (Reck *et al.*, in press). Tiffany Field brings together a helpful overview of her years of work in this area. The point she drives home most strongly is that the story begins long before the infant's birth. The mother's own high cortisol levels will lead to elevated cortisol levels in the fetus, for example. Such an infant, after birth, will not only respond to strong stress (e.g. an inoculation) with a (compared with control infants) higher cortisol level. The reaction will also last longer. This infant arrives in the world already somewhat in difficulty with respect to the learning of self-regulation.

Salisbury *et al.* add intriguing findings. Fetuses of depressed mothers were generally less (compared with controls) physically active. Presented with vibro-acoustic stimulation, they were also slower to react, measured by increase of heart rate. Once they did react, their heart rate increase was stronger, and remained higher for longer before returning to baseline. Salisbury and her colleagues interestingly speculate that this might be indexing not only regulatory problems, but also a slightly diminished capacity to respond to outside stimulii.

Nadel and colleagues found depressed mothers 'differed dramatically' in their affective body movements. They showed less expressive body displays. Perhaps more important, they provided significantly less body-to-body imitation of their infant's own movements and this with respect to various body parts. So, if we think about this in combination with Field's and Salisbury's findings, the vicious circle is apparent. Here is, in likelihood, an infant who has more than the usual need to build up self-directed body skills. He may also be an infant whose discrimination capacities are little reduced. Here, on the other side, is a parent who has difficulty sending clear, redundant, full-body signals. It may be a hard path for both of them.

Dubal and Jouvent's studies of anhedonia hint at another possible aspect. They found a number of positive correlations between lack of experienced pleasure and reduced attentional abilities. A depressed mother's incapacity for pleasure might then well go hand-in-hand with slightly diminished discrimination capacities, in the interaction, on her side as well.

Kugiumutzakis and his colleagues beautifully describe how neonate and infant imitation tends to be surrounded by pleasure. Both infant and adult often react with smiles, just before, during, and just after the imitative acts. They suggest that not only does imitation produce pleasure, but also that pleasure facilitates the occurrence of imitation. If this is true, it adds to our understanding of the vicious circle present in the case of depression. Less pleasure on both sides means less imitation likelihood. Less imitation likelihood means reduced opportunties for the infant to build up both self-directed and interpersonal body strategies (other than more defensive strategies, like withdrawl). Less such strategies on the infant's side makes him harder to reach in the ways that might give deeper satisfaction to the mother. Less pleasure on her side.

Clinical implications

How should we provide clinical help for parent–infant dyads who are in trouble and/or at risk? Much in these papers makes clear both the opportunity and the challenge.

The opportunity lies in a combination of the infant's discrimination skills and his behavioural plasticity. As for discrimination, one need only reread Muir *et al.*'s account of their many perturbation experiments to be awed by the infant's fine-tuned responsiveness to the procedural acts of an adult interactional partner.

This goes beyond the infant's sensitivity to contingency in general. While keeping the adult's behaviour contingent, we can manipulate the sound flow coming from the perceived partner; or the facial expression; or the gaze direction; or the presence or absence of accompanying touch. We can even reduce or alter any of these factors, in Muir's ingenious designs.

The result is that the infants quickly discriminate the manipulated aspect. They react, emotionally and behaviourally. Even effect size of their negative reactions can be altered by recombining manipulated stimulus factors. For example, if the adult continues touching during a Still Face or maintains a static smile, the infant may still be upset, but measurably less so. Moreover, as Kugiumutzakis and his colleagues' remind us in their review of their neonate imitation studies, some key elements of this interactional sensitivity are present already at birth.

As for behavioural plasticity, the degree of openness here is equally impressive. Even with chimp infants this is true, as is evident from Bard's descriptions of how chimp infants raised by human caretakers soon build up different interactional skills (well, 'skills' from a human standpoint!), such as more social smiles and vocalizations.

So, in clinical work with parent-infant relationships, how could these discrimination powers and this behavioural plasticity best be exploited? Unfortunately one is also confronted with the challenge. This concerns the reality that we are talking about a 'two-body psychology', as Nadel calls it (Nadel *et al.*, 2004). In other words, what clinically needs to change is not only systemic; it is procedural. Most of what occurs between parent and infant is body-with-body. It goes on in rapid, brief time-intervals. It lies for the most part outside the conscious awareness of the parent. Now, how are we going to help them change *that*?

One good answer is to use the medium of videotape. If videotape is so revelatory for research, why not put it to use clinically? Over the years, I have developed a methodology in this regard, called Video Microanalysis Therapy (VMT). Quite similar clinical procedures have been developed by Beebe (2003), Papousek (2000) and Marvin (Marvin *et al.*, in press), all of whom, of course, bring their research expertise to bear.

The governing idea is (Downing and Ziegenhain, 2001; Downing, 2003) is this. A therapeutic team or practitioner can make a short video of a parent and infant in interaction. Subsequently, the video can be informally analysed and, next, in a clinical session, brief portions of it can be shown to the parent.

What is seen can be discussed, reflected upon, and then used as a continuing point of reference for the rest of the session. The parent can better determine what she (or he or both parents together) wishes to have different in the relationship. She can explore what she might do differently on her side in the interactional exchange and she can generate concrete ideas about how to accomplish it. In other words, the emphasis, to the extent possible, is not upon instructional advice from the therapist.[10] It is upon a discovery process on the parent's side, one which activates insight and latent resources. Naturally, this need not exclude relevant information about infant development from the therapist.

Such a way to proceed provides the parent with a unique luxury. She can look at the interaction without, at that moment, being herself in the middle of it. She can discern

---

[10] Some approaches to video-supported intervention, such as the interesting work of Susan McDonough (2000), use a more didactic methodology.

aspects of the systemic exchange of which she had never before been fully conscious. Some events may even be watched in slow motion or frame-by-frame. All of this results in new representations of procedural doings, as well as a semantic vocabulary for them. If appropriate, reflections about her own childhood may be encouraged too.

Video is one key to this undertaking. There is a second. In the context of exploring how a parent proposes to change an interactional pattern, it can also be extremely useful to help her bring a focus to her own body. She can sense and make more explicit what she is doing on a procedural level, i.e. with her movements, face, gestures, posture, head and torso orientation, breathing, and the like. She can also track subjectively-experienced affects, finding out how they make themselves felt in her body and what she does motorically with them. This can set the stage for further discoveries, as the session continues, of what she might do differently on a body level. New procedural representations are also generated, in other words. The parent takes a small step towards reorganization of her (or his) own body competencies.

To intervene in this way, can be a rapid means of bringing about change in a parent–infant relationship. What makes it effective is the systemic dimension, naturally. Given the infant's sensitivity to everything the adult does, the altered procedural behaviours on the parent's side are likely to elicit new responses on his side. In turn, these fragments and beginnings of new infant behaviour can be further reacted to and supported by complementary acts from the parent. Other systemic cycles are brought into being.

Clinical work of this kind has many forms of application. It can be especially helpful for a compromised or otherwise less 'available' infant, for example. Such an infant's shifts will simply be smaller in size and will come more gradually. It is also useful not only for relationships affected by maternal depression, but for ones in which the parent has another kind of psychiatric disorder. For example, at Norbaden Psychiatric Hospital in Wiesloch, Germany, an in-patient psychiatric unit for mothers and their infants (i.e. mother and infant are hospitalized together) has been created with my help.[11] In collaboration with Ed Tronick and Antonella Brighi, we are conducting outcome studies for VMT treatment of schizophrenic, psychotic, and bipolar mothers, in addition to depression. Assessment includes blind coding of interaction videotapes before and after treatment. In a like vein, at the the University of Heidelberg, in a similair in-patient unit for mothers and their infants,[12] we are doing pilot studies of VMT treatment of traumatized mothers (here as well in collaboration with Ed Tronick). Results at both sites are looking highly favorable.

I have here focused on parent-infant psychotherapy, its closeness to infant research being obvious. There is plenty of food for thought in this book with respect to the therapy of older children and adults as well. Space being short, I can only hint at a few

---

[11] Under the direction of Dr Christiane Hornstein. Invaluable help and inspiration has also been provided by Dr. Mechthild Papousek.

[12] Under the direction of Dr Corinna Reck, and Dr. Thomas Fuchs.

[13] Under the direction of Dr Christiane Hornstein.

parallels. Lichtenberg's (1989) encompassing framework for understanding early affect and 'motivational areas' is close to the overall perspective of a number of these papers. The collective members of the Change Process Study Group (Stern *et al.*, 1998; cf. Stern, 2004) have extensively reflected upon the implications of such ideas for psychotherapy, and psychoanalytic explorations of transference and countertransference; as have, in a somewhat similar vein, Knoblauch (2000), and Beebe and Lachmann (2002). All have emphasized the usefulness, for adult treatment, of a better understanding of how early affect exchange really takes place, in its specifics. The better the psychotherapist's understanding of such processes, the more adept he will be at making sense of the patient's history, as well as seeing the parallels in transference and countertransference phenomena.

Harrison (Harrison and Tronick, 2004) has developed similar creative innovations with respect to the therapist–child relationship in child psychotherapy. Additionally, with respect to both adult and child psychotherapy, Worm (1998), Heisterkamp (2000), Moser (2001), Cornell (2002), Geissler (2002), myself (Downing, 2002), and others have discussed the usefulness of a focus upon the patient's subjective body experience, as a means of eliciting new body skills and strategies.

Future explorations

The more we know, the better focused our questions become. I want to point out one domain, however, where we know too little altogether. From a clinical standpoint, it is a major lack.

This is the area of physical contact and touch. Intuitively, it would seem that an infant's experiences of being touched, held, handled and carried, might be just as formative as his experiences of mutual gaze and acoustical reciprocity. Think how much of an infant's life takes place in this channel. Yet there have been few studies. It would be so fine to have more information. Darwin Muir (2002) in another context has eloquently made the same appeal.

Soussignan and Schaal cite Blass *et al.* (1984) concerning findings about touch and very precocious conditioning. A classical conditioning paradigm was used. Two-hour-old infants were stroked several times on their foreheads and then giving a tiny dose of sucrose. Increased sucking and head-turning soon became regular responses. Not only that: during extinction trials there was a rapid onset of negative behaviour, i.e. crying and distress facial displays. Now, this is interesting not only for what it indexes about precocious sensitivity to contingency in general. It also is suggestive about the power of touch itself. If an infant so quickly forms expectancies based upon touch, then what are the effects, positive or negative, of different caretakers' touching styles? Of their holding styles? Of their handling and carrying styles?

It seems safe to assume that some form of micro-exchange is taking place also on this level, with the two bodies making continual micro-adjustments one to another. How exactly does that work? What are the relevant time-intervals? How do the infant's responses alter the adult's responses and vice-versa? What is the range of possible reciprocal patterns at play here?

Field (2001) has written a lovely small book on touch. She is poetic and persuasive about the importance of physical exchange. It is striking at the same time how little empirical work she is able to cite.[14]

Of course, the problems of how to measure and quantify, in any fine-grained way, are formidable. Perhaps some good part of these questions will have to wait for new technological advances. Still, how adults touch infants in face-to-face settings is at least 'out there' enough, see-able and visible, to scale and record. ('Out there', as opposed to, for example, when the infant is held against the adult's body.) One could also think of other transactions which could be videotaped. In clinical work, I have seen a lot of videos of infants being given a bath, for example. This is a setting where a variety of touch and handling events are sufficiently readable that they could be tracked and evaluated.

Certainly the small amount of studies looking at touch in a face-to-face context demonstrate how fruitful such designs can be. Recall again Stack and Muir's study in which mothers lightly touched their infants during a 2-minute Still Face (Stack and Muir, 1992). Both Tronick and Field have looked at the touching (in face-to-face paradigms) of mothers with depression. Both demonstrated that a large subgroup touches quite a bit, but frequently with negative touch qualities, such as poking, pinching, and the like. Beebe and colleagues (2003) also has data indicating that negative qualities of maternal touch at infant age 4 months significantly predict insecure attachment (measured by the Ainsworth Strange Situation) at 12 months. These are tantalizing hints and more investigation using such types of design might be the right place to begin.

A related issue, probably even more difficult to tackle, concerns muscular tightening. Anyone who regularly handles infants and small children knows how they can stiffen up. They easily tense themselves in response to negative stimulation, perceived danger, losing their balance, and other stresses. Do some tightening-events become transformed into lasting chronic tensions? If so, which ones? When? Under what wider conditions? Are there particular patterns of precocious interaction that regularly are correlated with particular types of enduring muscular holding? One could think of many more such questions. Alan Fogel has also indicated how interesting it would be to have at least some beginning concrete information in this area.

So much for the future. Here, in the present, thanks to these rich contributions, we are already farther along the way towards a 'two-body psychology'.

References

Aarts, M. (2002). *The Marte Meo Program for Autism*. Harderwijk: Aarts Productions.

Adamson, L. and Frick, J. (2003). The still face: a history of a shared experimental paradigm. *Infancy*, 4(4), 452–74.

----

[14] As opposed to all the findings, many of them her own, which Field in another book (Field, 2000) is able to cite concerning the effects of massage.

Beebe, B. (2003). Brief mother-infant treatment: psychoanalytically informed video feeback. *Infant Mental Health Journal*, **24(1)**, 24–52.

Beebe, B. and Lachmann, F. (2002). *Infant Research and Adult Treatment: Co-contructing Interactions*. Hillsdale: Analytic Press.

Beebe, B., Jaffe, J., Chen, H.,*et al.* (2003). *Progress report to the National Institute of Mental Health*, November 1, 2003, Manuscript. New York, NY: New York State Psychiatric Institute.

Beebe, B. and Stern, D. (1977). Engagement-disengagement and early object experiences. In *Communicative Structures and Psychic Structures* (ed. N. Freedman and S. Grand). pp. 33–55. New York: Plenum Press.

Bermudez, J. (1998). *The paradox of self-consciousness*. Cambridge, MA: MIT Press.

Bermudez, J. (2003). *Thinking without words*. Oxford: Oxford University Press.

Bourdieu, P. (1976). *Outline of a theory of practice*. Cambridge: Cambridge University Press.

Camras, L. A., Meng, Z., Ujiie, T., *et al.* (2002). Observing emotion in infants: Facial expression, body behavior, and rater judgments of responses to an expectancy-violating event. *Emotion*, **2(2)**, 179–93.

Cornell, W. (2002). Body-centered psychotherapy. In *Comprehensive handbook of psychotherapy*, Vol. 3 (ed. R. Massey and S. Massey), pp. 587–613. New York: John Wiley and Sons.

Downing, G. (2000). Emotion theory reconsidered. In *Heidegger, Coping and Cognitive Science* (ed. J. Malpas and M. Wrathall), pp. 245–70. Cambridge, MA: MIT Press.

Downing, G. (2002). Zur Behandung von Essstörungen. *Psychoanalyse and Körper*, **1(1)**, pp. 9–36.

Downing, G. (2003). Video Microanalyse Therapie: Einige Grundlagen und Prinzipien. In *Wege zur Sicherheit: Bindungswissen in Diagnostik und Intervention* (ed. H. Scheuerer-English, G. J. Suess, and W-K. Pfeifer), pp. 51–68. Geissen: Psychosocial Verlag.

Downing, G. and Ziegenhain, U. (2001). Besonderheiten der Beratung und Therapie bei jugendlichen Müttern und ihren Säuglingen—die Bedeutung von Bindungstheorie und videogestützter Intervention. In *Bindungtheorie und Familiendynamik* (ed. G. J. Suess and W. Pfeifer), pp. 271–96. Giessen: Psychosozial.

Dretske, F. (1992). *Explaining behaviour: reasons in a world of causes*. Cambridge, MA: MIT Press.

Dreyfus, H. (1992). *What computers (still) can't do*. Cambridge, MA: MIT Press.

Ekman, P. and Friesen, W. V. (1978). *Facial Action Coding System*. Palo Alto, CA: Consulting Psychologists Press.

Field, T. (2000). *Touch therapy*. Edinburgh: Churchill Livingstone.

Field, T. (2001). *Touch*. Cambridge, MA: MIT Press.

Fivaz-Depeursinge, E. and Corboz-Warnery, A. (1999). *The primary triangle: a developmental systems view of mothers, fathers, and infants*. New York, NY: Basic.

Fogel, A. (1993). Two principles of communication: co-regulation and framing. In *New Perspectives in Early Communicative Development* (ed. J. Nadel and L. Camaioni), 9–21. London: Routledge.

Fogel, A. (2004). Remembering infancy: accessing our earliest experiences. In *Theories of Infant Development* (ed. G. Bremmer and A. Slater), pp. 204–30.

Frey, S. (1999). *Die Macht des Bildes: Der Einfluss der nonverbalen Kommunikation auf Kultur und Politik*. Bern: Hans Huber.

Frijda, N. (1986). *Emotion*. Cambridge: Cambridge University Press.

Geissler, P. (2002). Psychoanalyse und Körper: Überlegungen zum gegenwärtigen Stand analytisher Körperpsychotherapie. *Psychoanalyse and Körper*, **1(1)**, pp. 37–84.

Greenspan, S. and Wieder, S. (1998). *The child with special needs: encouraging intellectual and emotional growth*. Cambridge, MA: Perseus.

Harrison, A. and Tronick, E. (2004). Now we have a playground: emerging theories of therapeutic action. Manuscript in preparation.

Heller, M. (1997). Posture as an interface between biology and culture. In *Nonverbal communication: where nature meets culture* (ed. U. Segerstrale and P. Molnar), pp. 245–62. Mahwah, NJ: Lawrence Erlbaum.

Heisterkamp, G. (2000). Die leibliche Dimension in psychodynamischen Psychotherapien. In *Psychodynamische Psychotherapien: Lehrbuch der tienfenpsychologish orientierten Psychothapier* (ed. C. Reimer and U. Ruger), pp. 295–320. Berlin: Springer.

Izard, C. E. (1983). *The maximally discriminative vacial movement coding system.* (Rev. ed.). Newark, DE: Instructional Resources Center.

Izard, C. E., Fantauzzo, C.A., Castle, J.M., *et al.* (1995). The ontogeny and significance of infants' facial expressions in the first 9 months of life. *Developmental Psychology*, **31**, 997–1013.

Knoblauch, S. (2000). *The musical edge of therapeutic dialogue.* Hillsdale: Analytic Press.

Lichtenberg, J. (1989). *Psychoanalysis and Motivation.* Hillsdale: Analytic Press.

Main, M. and Solomon, J. (1990). Procedures for identifying infants as disorganized/disoriented during the Ainsworth Strange Situation. In *Attachment in the preschool years: theory, research, and intervention* (ed. M. Greenbrg, D. Cicchetti, and E. Cummings), pp. 161–83. Chicago: University of Chicago Press.

Marvin, R. and Britner, P. (1999). Normative development: the ontogeny of attachment. In *Handbook of attachment: theory, research, and clinical applications* (ed. J. Cassidy and P. Shaver), pp. 44–66. New York, NY: Guilford.

Marvin, R., Hoffman, K., and Powell, B. The Circle of Security Project: Attachment-Based intervention with caregiver-preschool child Dyads. *Attachment and Human Development* (in press).

McDonough, S. (2000). Interaction guidance: Understanding and treating early infant-caregiver relationship disturbances. In *Handbook of Infant Mental Health* (ed. C. Zeanah), pp. 485–92. New York: Guilford.

Meltzoff, A. and Moore, K. (2001). 'Discovery procedures' for people and things: the role of representations. In *Emerging cognitive abilities in early infancy* (ed. F. Larcerda, C. von Hofsten, and M. Heimann), pp. 212–39. Mahwah, NJ: Lawrence Erlbaum.

Moser, T. (2001). *Formen der analytischen Korperpsychotherapie.* Frankfurt a. M: Suhrkamp.

Muir, D. (2002). Adult communication with infants through touch: the forgotten sense. *Human Development*, **45**, 95–9.

Nadel, J., Revel, A., Andry, P., *et al.* (2004). Toward communication: First imitations in infants, low-functioning children with autism and robots. *Interaction Studies*, **5(1)**, 45–75.

Papousek, M. (2000). Einsatz von Video in der Eltern-Säuglings-Beratung und -Psychotherapie. *Praxis der Kinderpsychologie und Kinderspychiatrie*, **49**, 611–27.

Peacocke, C. (1992). *A study of concepts.* Cambridge, MA: MIT Press.

Reck, C., Hunt, A., Weiss, R., *et al.* (in press). Interactive regulation of affect in postpartum depressed mothers and their infants. *Psychopathogy.*

Scherer, K. (1999). "Appraisal Theory." In *The Handbook of Emotion and Cognition* (ed. T. Dalgeish and M. Power), Chichester NY: John Wiley and Sons.

Solomon, R. (2004). Emotion, thoughts, and feelings: Emotions as Engagements with the World. In *Thinking about Feeling: Contemporary Philosophers on Emotions* (ed. R. Solomon). Oxford: Oxford University Press.

Shanker, S. (2003). *Council on Human Development position paper.* Unpublished.

Stack, D. and Muir, D. (1992). Adult tactile stimulation during face-to-face interactions modeulates five-month-olds' affect and attention. *Child Development*, **63**, 1509–25.

Stern, D. (1995). *The Motherhood Constelltion: A Unified View of Parent-Infant Psychotherapy.* New York: Basic Books.

Stern, D. (2004). *The present moment in psychotherapy and everyday life.* New York, NY: Norton.

Stern, D. and Members of the Change Process Study Group (1998). The process of therapeutic change involving implicit knowledge: Some implications of developmental observations for adult psychotherapy. *Infant Mental Health Journal*, **19**(3), 300–8.

Thelen, E. and Smith, L. (1994). *A dynamic systems approach to the development of cognition and action.* Cambridge, MA: MIT Press.

Tronick, E. (2003). Thoughts on the Still Face: disconnection and dyadic expandion of consciousness. *Infancy*, **4**(4), 475–81.

Tye, M. (1995). *Ten problems of consciousness.* Cambridge, MA: MIT Press.

Vygotsky, L. (1978). *Mind in society: the development of higher psychological processes.* Cambridge, MA: Harvard University Press.

Wallon, H. (1942). *De l'acte à la pensée.* Paris: Flammarioxn.

Weinberg, M. K. and Tronick, E. (1994). Beyond the face: An empirical study of infant affective configurations of facial, vocal, gestural, and regulatory behaviors. *Child Development*, **65**, 1503–15.

Weinberg, M. K., Beeghly, M., and Olson, K. L. (2002). Preschoolers reactions to their still-faced mother. International Conference on Infant Studies, Toronto, Canada.

Worm, G. (1998). *Zum Umgang mit Ubertrangung in einer analytishen Korperpsychotherapie in der Praxis.* Stuttgart: Klett-Cott.

Index

Printed in the United Kingdom
by Lightning Source UK Ltd.
133031UK00001B/29/A